Ireland

by Robert Emmet Meagher

with Mark Meagher and
Elizabeth Neave

Macmillan • USA

ABOUT THE AUTHORS

Robert Emmet Meagher, a dual citizen of Ireland and the United States, is professor of humanities at Hampshire College in Amherst, Massachusetts. The author of more than a dozen books, plays, and translations, he has lived and worked in Ireland, twice holding visiting professorships at Trinity College Dublin.

Mark Meagher, an avid naturalist as well as a competitive cyclist and kayaker, has lived and studied in Ireland and is currently pursuing graduate studies in landscape architecture at the University of Pennsylvania.

Elizabeth Neave, after studying and teaching in Dublin, pursued her graduate studies in education at Smith College and currently teaches elementary school in the Connecticut public schools.

MACMILLAN TRAVEL

A Simon & Schuster Macmillan Company
1633 Broadway
New York, NY 10019

Find us online at **http://www.mgr.com/travel**
or on America Online at Keyword: **Frommer's**

ISBN 0-02-861577-8
ISSN 1080-9104

Editor: Matt Hannafin
Production Editor: Carol Sheehan
Design by Michele Laseau
Digital Cartograpy by Raffaele DeGennaro and Ortelius Design

SPECIAL SALES

Bulk purchases (10+ copies) of Frommer's and selected Macmillan travel guides are available to corporations, organizations, mail-order catalogs, institutions, and charities at special discounts, and can be customized to suit individual needs. For more information write to Special Sales, Macmillan General Reference, 1633 Broadway, New York, NY 10019.

Manufactured in the United States of America

Contents

List of Maps

This book is dedicated to Ireland's peacemakers, north and south.

ACKNOWLEDGMENTS

A book, like a barn, must be raised by many hands. In this case, the hands are too many to count or to name. Fortunately, the hospitality of the Irish is a legend that need not be retold in detail here. We have been welcomed, aided, and abetted every step of the way, and our deep thanks go out to everyone who helped us. A few special friends of this book, however, deserve special notice, so, to a book full of lists, we will add one more: Jack Broder, John and Jean Dillon, John and Lyndall Luce, Seona MacReamoinn, Emily and Nicholas Odlum, Susan Poole, and Mike Spring. Finally, special gratitude is due to Alice Fellows, whose clarity and support have been with this effort from the start, and to our editor, Matt Hannafin, whose wit and skill have made the process as rewarding as the product.

AN INVITATION TO THE READER

There are so many more of you than there are of us that this book can only be informed and enhanced when you share your experiences with us. We welcome your letters. Let us know when we've led you straight and when astray—and let us in on your secret finds, provided that you're willing to have them shared with other readers in future editions. Anticipating your letters, thanks in advance for your contributions. You can address your letters to:

Robert Emmet Meagher
Frommer's Ireland, 2nd Edition
Macmillan Travel
1633 Broadway
New York, NY 10019

AN ADDITIONAL NOTE

Please be advised that travel information is subject to change at any time—and this is especially true of prices. We therefore suggest that you write or call ahead for confirmation when making your travel plans. The authors, editors, and publisher cannot be held responsible for the experiences of readers while traveling. Your safety is important to us, however, so we encourage you to stay alert and be aware of your surroundings. Keep a close eye on cameras, purses, and wallets, all favorite targets of thieves and pickpockets.

WHAT THE SYMBOLS MEAN

✪ Frommer's Favorites

Hotels, restaurants, attractions, and entertainment you should not miss.

Ⓢ Super-Special Values

Hotels and restaurants that offer great value for your money.

The following abbreviations are used for credit cards:

AE	American Express	EU	Eurocard
CB	Carte Blanche	JCB	Japan Credit Bank
DC	Diners Club	MC	MasterCard
DISC	Discover	V	Visa
ER	enRoute		

The Best of Ireland

No one can put Ireland over a low flame and render its essence in a single sauce, or, the arguments of Guinness notwithstanding, set the country before you in a pint glass. Every person's favorite Ireland is bound to be different from all the others—you just can't please everybody.

But you can try, which is what we've done here. The best of anything can change, of course, and can even let you down on occasion, but the attractions listed in this chapter represent our own best effort to steer you right, to point out a few places where you're not likely to be disappointed.

1 The Best Picture-Postcard Small Towns

- **Dalkey** (Co. Dublin): This charming south-coast suburb of Dublin enjoys easy access to the city and freedom from its snarls and frenzy. It has a castle, an island, a mountaintop folly, a few parks, all in ample miniature. With all the fine and simple restaurants and pubs and shops anyone needs for a brief visit or a long stay, Dalkey is a tempting town to settle into. See Chapter 5.

- **Kilkenny** (Co. Kilkenny): Slightly larger than a small town but terribly picture-postcard nonetheless, Kilkenny may offer the best surviving Irish example of a medieval town. Its walls and splendidly restored castle, and the renowned design center housed in the castle stables, draw visitors from Ireland and abroad. Kilkenny, however, is no museum and is regarded by many as perhaps the most attractive large town in Ireland. See Chapter 7.

- **Kinsale** (Co. Cork): Kinsale's narrow streets all lead to the sea, dropping steeply from the hills that rim beautiful Kinsale Harbor. This is undoubtedly one of Ireland's most picturesque and picture-perfect towns, and the myriad visitors who crowd the streets every summer attest to the fact that the secret is out. The walk from Kinsale through Scilly to Charles Fort and Frower Point is breathtaking. Kinsale has the added benefit of possessing the greatest concentration of fine restaurants outside Dublin. See Chapter 9.

- **Westport** (Co. Mayo): It's never a surprise in Ireland when someone says Westport is his favorite town. It's small and bursting. Someday it might explode into a city, but for now Westport remains a hyperactive town that somehow manages to be as friendly and welcoming as a village. See Chapter 11.

2 The Best Natural Wonders

- **MacGillycuddy's Reeks** (Co. Kerry): One of several mountain ranges on the Iveragh Peninsula, MacGillycuddy's Reeks boasts the highest mountain in Ireland, Carrantuohill (3,404 feet). Whether gazed at from afar or explored up close on foot, the Reeks are among Ireland's greatest spectacles. See Chapter 10.
- **The Burren** (Co. Clare): The Burren—from the Irish *Boireann,* meaning "a rocky place"—is one of the strangest landscapes you're ever likely to see: a vast limestone grassland, spread with a quilt of wildflowers from as far afield as the Mediterranean, the Alps, and the Arctic. Its inhabitants include the pine marten and nearly every species of butterfly found in Ireland. See Chapter 11.
- **The Cliffs of Moher** (Co. Clare): Rising from Hag's Head to the south, these magnificent sea cliffs reach their full height of 760 feet just north of O'Brien's Tower. The views of the open sea, of the distant Aran Islands, and of the Twelve Bens of Connemara are spectacular. A walk south along the cliff edge at sunset makes a perfect end to any day. See Chapter 11.
- **Croagh Patrick** (Co. Mayo): Rising steeply 2,500 feet above the Mayo coast, Croagh Patrick is Ireland's holiest mountain, to which Patrick is said to have retreated in penance. The place is biblically imposing. Traditionally, it's climbed by barefoot pilgrims on the last Sunday of July, but in recent years hundreds of Nike-shod tourists have been making the ascent daily. The view from above can be breathtaking or nonexistent, as the summit is often wrapped in clouds, adding to its mystery. See Chapter 11.
- **The Twelve Bens** (Co. Galway): Amid Connemara's central mountains, bogs, and lakes rises a rugged range known as the Twelve Bens, crowning a landscape that is among the most spectacular in Ireland. Among the peaks themselves, some are bare and rocky, while others are clothed in peat. The loftiest of the Bens, Benbaun, reaches a height of 2,395 feet and is enclosed by the Connemara National Park. See Chapter 13.
- **Slieve League** (Co. Donegal): The Slieve League peninsula stretches for 30 miles into the Atlantic and is 12 miles across at its widest point. Its wonderfully pigmented cliffs are the highest sea cliffs in Europe, and can either be gazed at from Carrigan Head or walked along, if you dare. From below or from above, Slieve League serves up some of the most dazzling sights in Ireland. See Chapter 14.
- **The Slieve Bloom Mountains** (Co. Laois): Slieve Bloom, Ireland's largest and most unspoiled blanket bog, has been described as a "scenic bulge" rising gently above the midland's peat fields. Its beauty—comprised of gentle slopes, glens, rivers, waterfalls, and bog lands—is subtle rather than dramatic, but it is comparatively untouched and you can have it more or less to yourself, apart from its deer, foxes, badgers, and an occasional marten or otter. See Chapter 15.
- **The Giant's Causeway** (Co. Antrim): In case you lose your own count, there are roughly 40,000 tightly packed mostly hexagonal basalt columns comprising the giant Finn McCool's path from the Antrim headland into the sea toward the Scottish island of Staffa. This volcanic wonder, formed 60 million years ago, can either be marveled at from a distance or negotiated cautiously on foot. See Chapter 16.

3 The Best Castles

- **Cahir Castle** (Co. Tipperary): One of the largest of Ireland's medieval fortresses, this castle is in an extraordinary state of preservation. Tours explain some fascinating features of the castle's military architecture, then you're free to roam through a maze of tiny chambers, spiral staircases, and vertiginous battlements. See Chapter 7.

- **Kilkenny Castle** (Co. Kilkenny): Although parts of the castle date from the 13th century, the existing structure has the feel of an 18th-century palace. There have been many modifications since medieval times, including the addition of beautiful landscaping on the grounds around the castle. See Chapter 7.

- **Blarney Castle** (Co. Cork): Despite the mobs of tourists who besiege the castle daily, this majestic tower house is worth a visit. While you're there check out the Badger Cave and dungeons at the tower's base, as well as the serpentine paths that wind through the castle gardens, set in a picturesque rocky glen. Need we mention the Stone? You sidle in under the upper wall with your head hanging over a 10-story drop. You kiss it. It's a thing people do. See Chapter 8.

- **Charles Fort** (Co. Cork): Located on a promontory in stunning Kinsale Harbor, the fort's massive walls enclose a complex array of buildings in varying states of repair. At the entrance you're handed a map and then left on your own to explore, discover, and almost certainly get lost in the maze of courtyards, passages, walls, and barracks. See Chapter 9.

- **Bunratty Castle** (Co. Clare): The castle has been restored and filled with a curious assortment of medieval furnishings, giving the modern-day visitor a glimpse into the life of its past inhabitants. This is the first stop for many arrivals from Shannon, so expect crowds. See Chapter 11.

- **Carrickfergus Castle** (Co. Antrim): This fortress on the bank of Belfast Lough is the best preserved Norman castle in Ireland, and consists of an imposing tower house and high wall punctuated by corner towers. See Chapter 16.

- **Dunluce Castle** (Co. Antrim): The castle ruins surmount a razor-sharp promontory jutting into the sea. This was no doubt a highly defensible setting, and the castle wasn't abandoned until a large section collapsed and fell into the breakers one day in 1639. See Chapter 16.

4 The Best of Ancient Ireland

- **Newgrange** (Co. Meath): Poised atop a low hill north of the River Boyne, Newgrange is the centerpiece of a dramatic megalithic cemetery dating from more than 5,000 years ago. This massive, heart-shaped mound and passage tomb was constructed, it seems, as a communal vault to house the cremated remains of the dead. The tomb's passage is so perfectly aligned with the equinoctial sunrise that the central chamber, deep within the mound, is marvelously illuminated at each year's winter solstice. See Chapter 6.

- **Tara** (Co. Meath): Of ritual significance from the Stone Age to the Christian period, Tara has seen it all and kept it all a secret. This was the traditional center and seat of Ireland's high kings, who could look out from here and survey their realm. Although it's only 512 feet above sea level, from the Tara hill you can see each of Ireland's four Celtic provinces on a clear day. The site is mostly unexcavated and tells its story in whispers. It's a place to be walked slowly, with an imagination steeped in Ireland's past. See Chapter 6.

- **Lough Gur** (Co. Limerick): This lakefront site will convince you that the Neolithic farmers of Ireland had an estimable sense of real estate. Inhabited for more than 4,000 years, this ancient farming settlement offers a number of prehistoric remains, the most impressive of which is the largest surviving stone circle in Ireland, comprised of 113 stones. See Chapter 11.
- **Dún Aengus** (Co. Galway): No one knows who built this massive stone fort, or when. The eminent archaeologist George Petrie called Dún Aengus "the most magnificent barbaric monument in Europe." Facing the sea, where its three stone rings meet steep 200-foot cliffs, Dún Aengus stands guard today as ever over the southern coast of the island of Inishmore, the largest of the Arans. See Chapter 12.
- **Carrowmore and Carrowkeel** (Co. Sligo): These two megalithic cities of the dead, Europe's largest, on the Coolera Peninsula may have once contained well over 200 passage tombs. The two together, the one in the valley and the other atop a nearby mountain, convey an unequaled sense of the scale and wonder of the ancient megalithic peoples' reverence for the dead. Carrowmore is well presented and interpreted, while Carrowkeel is left to itself and to those who seek it out. See Chapter 14.

5 Remnants of the Golden Age: The Best Early Christian Ruins

- **Glendalough** (Co. Wicklow): Nestled in "the glen of the two lakes," this important monastic settlement was founded in the 6th century by St. Kevin, a man looking for tranquil seclusion. Its setting is disarmingly scenic, exactly the opposite of the harsh environment you'd expect ascetic medieval monks would've sought out. Although quite remote, Glendalough suffered numerous assaults from the Vikings and the English and eventually dwindled into insignificance. Today its picturesque ruins collude with the countryside to create one of the most lovely spots in Ireland. See Chapter 6.
- **The Rock of Cashel** (Co. Tipperary): In name and appearance "the Rock" suggests a citadel, a place more familiar with power than prayer. In fact, Cashel (or *Caiseal*) means "fortress," and so it was. The rock itself is a huge outcropping— or rather *up*cropping—of limestone topped with some of the most spectacular ruins in Ireland, including what was formerly the country's finest Romanesque chapel. This was the seat of clerics and kings, a center to rival Tara. Now, however, the two sites vie only for tourists. See Chapter 7.
- **Jerpoint Abbey** (Co. Kilkenny): Jerpoint is perhaps the finest representative of the many Cistercian abbeys whose ruins dot the Irish landscape. What draws visitors to Jerpoint are its splendid cloister, the most richly carved in Ireland, and its impressive tomb sculptures. The abbey's tower is the tallest of its kind in Ireland. See Chapter 7.
- **Skellig Michael** (Co. Kerry): Eight miles offshore of the Iveragh Peninsula and rising sharply 714 feet out of the Atlantic is a stunning crag of rock dedicated to the Archangel Michael. In flight from the world, early Irish monks in pursuit of "white martyrdom" chose this spot to build their austere hermitage. Today, the journey to Skellig, across choppy seas, and the arduous climb to its summit are challenging and unforgettable. See Chapter 10.

- **Inishmurray** (Co. Sligo): This uninhabited island nearly 4 miles off the Sligo coast is home to a most striking monastic complex, surrounded by what appear to be the walls of an even more ancient stone fort. Despite its remoteness, this outpost of peace-seeking monks was sought out for destruction by the Vikings in 802. Today its circular ruins and the surrounding sea present a stunning sight, well worth the effort required to reach the shores of Inishmurray. See Chapter 14.
- **Clonmacnois** (Co. Offaly): This was once one of Ireland's most important religious, artistic, and literary centers, a place of pilgrimage and high culture. Founded in the mid–5th century at the axis of the Shannon River and the medieval east-west thoroughfare known as the Eiscir Riada, Clonmacnois thrived for centuries until its prime riverfront location nearly proved its undoing. In the 830s, Vikings sailed up the Shannon from Limerick and brought a havoc that returned many times in the ensuing centuries. Even in ruins, Clonmacnois remains today a place of peculiar beauty and serenity. See Chapter 15.

6 The Best Literary Spots

- **Glasnevin Cemetery** (Co. Dublin): Besides being the setting for part of the sixth episode of *Ulysses*, this is the resting place of Joyce's parents and several other members of his family. The English-born poet Gerard Manley Hopkins is buried here, in the Jesuit plot. Maud Gonne, the Irish nationalist and longtime Dublin resident who is said to have inspired Yeats's play *Cathleen ní Houlihan* is buried in the Republican plot. See Chapter 5.
- **Newman House** (Co. Dublin): Cardinal John Henry Newman was the first rector of the Catholic University in Dublin, housed in two buildings on St. Stephen's Green in the center of the city's south side, and worked in this capacity from 1852 to his retirement in 1859. The Catholic University later became University College Dublin, and it is to this institution that Gerard Manley Hopkins was sent in 1884, as a professor of Greek; after five years of teaching here, Hopkins died at the age of 44. James Joyce studied here from 1899 to 1902. See Chapter 5.
- **North Dublin:** The streets north of the Liffey are home to many of the characters in James Joyce's stories and novels; this is a part of Dublin in which Joyce himself lived and for which he had a special affinity. Much has changed since Joyce's time, and Bloom's house at 7 Eccles St. has been replaced by a new wing of the Mater Private Hospital, but there are still many mementos of the city as it was in 1904. Tours of the area begin from the James Joyce Center. See Chapter 5.
- **St. Patrick's Cathedral** (Co. Dublin): Jonathan Swift was born in Dublin in 1667, and entered Trinity College in his 15th year. He later became dean of St. Patrick's Cathedral, and is buried alongside Hester Johnson (Stella) in the cathedral's south aisle. See Chapter 5.
- **The Aran Islands:** John Millington Synge set his play *Riders to the Sea* on Inishmaan, and wrote an account of life on the islands, titled simply *The Aran Islands*. Native islander Liam O'Flaherty, known for his novel *Famine*, is from the island of Inishmore. See Chapters 12 and 13.
- **County Sligo:** It seems at times that every hill, house, and lake in the county is signposted in recognition of some relation to the poet W. B. Yeats, whose writing was informed by the landscape, mythology, and people of this region. Many of the natural and historic monuments of Sligo appear in Yeats's poetry, including Lough Gill, Glencar Lake, Benbulben Mountain, and Maeve's tomb atop Knocknarea Mountain. There are also several museums housing first editions, photographs, and other memorabilia, and of course Yeats's grave in Drumcliff. See Chapter 14.

7 The Best Gardens

- **Powerscourt Gardens** (Co. Wicklow): One of the most grandiose of Irish gardens, set amid the natural splendor of the northern Wicklow Hills. Only 12 miles from Dublin, the gardens and nearby waterfall make a great day's outing, and a welcome respite from the noise and congestion of the city. See Chapter 6.

- **Japanese Gardens** (Co. Kildare): On the grounds of the National Stud, this is considered to be the only authentic Japanese garden in Ireland, and one of the finest in Europe. The structure and symbolism of the garden were planned by a Japanese specialist, and most of the plants and even the stones were imported from Japan. See Chapter 6.

- **Creagh Gardens** (Co. Cork): Meandering paths lead the visitor past a sequence of exquisite vistas, with many hidden corners to explore. The garden is situated on a beautiful estuary. See Chapter 9.

- **Ilnacullin** (Co. Cork): A ferry conveys visitors from a lovely, rhododendron-rimmed bay in the town of Glengarriff to Garinish Island, the unlikely site of a fine Italianate garden. The formal garden, with the Casita at its center, is linked to a "wild garden" that showcases a collection of rhododendrons, azaleas, and rare trees. See Chapter 9.

- **Glenveagh** (Co. Donegal): The gardens and castle are situated in a barren and beautiful valley high in the hills of Donegal, along the banks of Lough Veagh. There is a statuary garden, a walled garden, and a rhododendron-lined path that leads to a stunning vista overlooking castle and lake. See Chapter 14.

- **Mount Stewart Gardens** (Co. Down): Built upon an elaborate plan, Mount Stewart contains within it several small gardens of distinctive character. The Ards Peninsula provides a climate conducive to the cultivation of numerous subtropical species. A touch of whimsy is reflected in the statuary, topiary, and planting designs. See Chapter 16.

8 The Best Attractions for the Whole Family

- **The Ark: A Cultural Centre for Children** (Co. Dublin): A unique chance for kids to have a hands-on learning experience of art, music, and theater in workshop sessions with artists. There are also excellent theater productions for families. See Chapter 5.

- **Dublin's Viking Adventure** (Co. Dublin): This is a fun learning experience where kids can travel back in time and be part of Viking life with "real Vikings" working and interacting in a model Norse town. It's set on the actual site where the Vikings made their home in Dublin. See Chapter 5.

- **Dublin Zoo in the Phoenix Park** (Co. Dublin): Kids love this 30-acre zoo with its array of creatures, animal-petting corner, and train ride. The surrounding park has room to run, picnic, and explore for hours (or days!). See Chapter 5.

- **The Irish National Heritage Park** (Co. Wexford): Nearly 9,000 years of Irish history come alive here in ways that will fascinate visitors of every age. The whole family will be captivated by the story of ancient Ireland, from its first inhabitants to its Norman conquerors. See Chapter 7.

- **Muckross House, Garden, and Traditional Farms** (Killarney, Co. Kerry): This stunning Victorian mansion with its exquisite gardens is also home to skilled artisans at their work. Nearby are a series of reconstructed traditional farms, complete with animals and docents, providing a gateway to rural Ireland as it was for centuries. See Chapter 10.

Tips for Kids from a Kid: Ireland

I like living in Ireland because there are lots of places to go, things to do. First I'd like to recommend two restaurants in Dublin that I've been to and I really liked. Their names are Strike 4 and Pasta Presto (see "Dining," Chapter 5). Strike 4 is in the Virgin Cinema in Parnell Street. In Strike 4 you get burgers, nuggets, and criss-cross chips. Pasta Presto is in Ballsbridge and they specialize in pasta and pizza. I like them both because of the friendly service and nice food.

Now I would like to tell you about a tour called "The Bord na Mona Bog Tour" (see "Attractions," Middle Shannon section, Chapter 15). You sit in a train and as you go round the bog, the guide tells you about the bog. At one point the train stops and you can get off and dig turf. I like it because it tells you interesting facts about the bog. The Bog Tour is in County Offaly.

Another place in Kildare is called the Japanese Gardens (see "Attractions," Chapter 6). At the start they give you a map and you can go into tunnels, up stairs, and there are lots of places to go and hide. After the gardens there is a walk through the Irish National Stud. When you are walking there are horses with nameplates. One of them is called "Approach the Bench"!

There is an adventure center in Lucan named Fort Lucan. It is a great place for parties or as a day trip. In Fort Lucan there are slides, bridges, tunnels, ladders, poles, and there is even a small go-cart ring with go-carts.

Out in Westport, County Mayo, there are two beaches called Old Head and Bertra. Old Head has a nature walk through the woods and up onto a cliff. Bertra is a 4-mile beach up and back. At the end is a river where you see lots of different sea birds and sometimes a lone seal.

I hope that you have enjoyed my short guide to my favorite places in Ireland.

—Emily Odlum, age eight, Dublin

- **Bunratty Castle and Folk Park** (Co. Clare): Kids are enthralled by this great restored medieval castle and recreated 19th-century village complete with school and loaded with active craftspeople. See Chapter 11.
- **Marble Arch Caves** (Marlebank, Co. Fermanagh): Adventurous families are guided by boat through well-lit underground waterways to explore caves and view amazing stone formations. See Chapter 16.

9 Greens Amid the Green: The Best Golf

- **Portmarnock Golf Club** (Co. Dublin): These links are located on a peninsula 10 miles north of Dublin, where the rapidly changing winds add to the challenges. It was founded in 1894, and is thought by some to offer Ireland's most difficult golf. See Chapter 5.
- **Ballybunion Golf Club** (Co. Kerry): This seaside club offers two 18-hole courses, with the Old Course often ranked among the world's finest. See Chapter 10.
- **Waterville Golf Links** (Co. Kerry): This course, situated on a treeless plain overlooking the Atlantic breakers, is one of Ireland's most stunningly scenic golf venues. See Chapter 10.
- **County Sligo Golf Club** (Co. Sligo): Also known as "Rosses Point," the championship course lies between the sea and a ridge of majestically imposing hills. See Chapter 14.

- **Royal County Down** (Co. Down): One of the treasures of Northern Ireland, this club was referred to as one of the world's best little-known courses by *Golf Magazine* in 1993. See Chapter 16.

10 The Best Active Vacations

- **Sailing Ireland's West Coast:** Spectacular coastal scenery, interesting harbor towns, and an abundance of islands make the West Coast a delight for cruising sailors. Yacht charter is available in Kilrush, Co. Clare. See Chapter 4.
- **Horseback Riding in the Galty Mountains:** The gentle contours of Tipperary's Galtees offer the perfect scenic backdrop for trail riding. You'll be provided with all you need for a horse-riding holiday at Bansha House, a commodious B&B with an excellent equestrian program. See Chapter 7.
- **Sea Kayaking in West Cork:** The many bays, headlands, and islands of this wild, rocky coast provide innumerable opportunities for kayak exploration. A great base is Maria's Schoolhouse, where you'll find comfortable and friendly accommodations and an outstanding sea kayaking program run by Jim Kennedy. See Chapter 9.
- **Bicycling in the Southwest:** The peninsulas and islands of Cork and Kerry are perfect for cycling, with light traffic and an abundance of beautiful places to visit. Roycroft's Stores in Skibbereen, Co. Cork, rent bikes that are a notch above the usual rental equipment. See Chapters 9 and 10.
- **Walking the Donegal Coast:** The cliff-rimmed headlands of Donegal are the most spectacular in Ireland, and the best way to explore them is on foot. Among the finest walks are Slieve League, Glen Head, and Horn Head. See Chapter 14.

11 The Best Bird-Watching

- **Great Saltee** (Co. Wexford): A barren and seemingly lifeless rock during much of the year, this island becomes an avian paradise during the summer months, when it is filled to overflow capacity with nesting seabirds. See Chapter 7.
- **North Slob** (Co. Wexford): The north side of Wexford Harbor is the site of the Wexford Wildfowl Reserve, home to thousands of geese from October to April each year. There's an interpretive center that's open year-round and has exhibits about the geese, other avian visitors to the Slob, and nearby areas of ornithological interest. See Chapter 7.
- **Loop Head** (Co. Clare): Remote Loop Head and the nearby Bridges of Ross are known as a great sea-watching site from late summer to early fall. See Chapter 11.
- **Cape Clear** (Co. Cork): There is a bird observatory and resident warden on this island at the southernmost extremity of Ireland, where many important discoveries regarding patterns of migration have been made. Boat tours for birders are available from North Harbor. See Chapter 9.
- **Shannon Callows** (Co. Galway, Tipperary, and Offaly): The low-lying meadows along the Shannon and Little Brosna River flood in the winter, creating a massive temporary lake that is the wintering grounds for many species of wildfowl. In the summer, the meadows are home to one of the few remaining corncrake populations in Ireland. See Chapter 4.

12 The Best Luxury Accommodations

- **Shelbourne Hotel** (Co. Dublin): The Shelbourne, built in 1824 on the north side of Stephen's Green, may just be the most distinguished visitor's address in Dublin.

In 1921 the Irish Constitution was drafted here in room 112, and the guests' register is a partial who's who of the past century and a half. The Shelbourne epitomizes old Dublin charm and elegance. See Chapter 5.

- **Marlfield House** (Co. Wexford): This grand 1820 house, situated amidst mature gardens and woods, is one of Ireland's most elegant and comfortable guest mansions. Equally renowned is the cuisine, served either in its dining room or in the conservatory. Amenities abound. See Chapter 7.

- **Scilly House Inn** (Co. Cork): For those with simpler but rigorous taste, Scilly House is a prize waiting to be found. With disarming charm and splendid views of the sea, this Kinsale country house is just what many discerning travelers have been looking for. As a bonus, it is said to be happily haunted. See Chapter 9.

- **Ashford Castle** (Co. Mayo): *Accommodation* is, of course, an understatement for the degree of luxury and elegance you'll find at this castle on the north shore of Lough Corrib. Its magnificent grounds comprise 350 acres of park and woods and include a golf course, and its two restaurants, the Connaught Room and the George V Room, will likely leave you unmotivated to search elsewhere. See Chapter 11.

- **Delphi Lodge** (Co. Galway): This was once the country hideaway for the Marquis of Sligo, and now it can be yours, too. Inside, the emphasis is on clean, bright simplicity in perfect taste, while outside the grounds and environs are among the most beautiful in Ireland. Tranquility, comfort, and fishing are the operative words here. You will want to stay longer than you'd planned, and, by renting one of the cottages for a week or more, you can make this indulgence more affordable. See Chapter 13.

13 The Best Moderately Priced Accommodations

- **Foxmount Farm** (Co. Waterford): The Kents are tremendous hosts, and their elegant 18th-century home is a perfect place to base yourself for exploring the southeast. Kids will enjoy the family farm, and there's a great pub just down the lane. See Chapter 7.

- **Maria's Schoolhouse** (Co. Cork): This stone schoolhouse was built in 1883, and has been creatively restored as a hostel and guest house. Breakfast and dinner are served in the lofty dining room, and a small kitchen is available for those who prefer to do their own cooking. The place has the added attraction of being the base for an excellent sea-kayaking program. See Chapter 9.

- **Bruckless House** (Co. Donegal): This mid–18th-century farmhouse, restored with impeccable taste, has many charms, including award-winning gardens and a stable of Connemara ponies. Spacious, welcoming, and comfortable, Bruckless House feels like home (or better) after a very short time. See Chapter 14.

- **Glencarne House** (Co. Leitrim): This attentively restored late-Georgian house on a 100-acre working farm offers a rare quality of hospitality and charm to midland lake region visitors. Lovely, spacious rooms, chiropractic beds, gracious hosts, and award-winning breakfasts are yours for surprisingly affordable rates. Dinners here are the high point, so there's no need to venture out once you've settled in. See Chapter 15.

- **Ross Castle** (Co. Cavan): A tower room in a centrally heated haunted castle— with the longest bathtub I've ever seen—awaits you at Ross Castle, and it won't take too big a bite out of your wallet, either. This may not be elegance, but it is unquestionably memorable. Ross Castle and nearby Ross House are warm, comfortable, and great places to relax beside Lough Sheelin, a noteworthy source of trout and pike. See Chapter 15.

14   The Best Restaurants

- **Patrick Guilbaud** (Co. Dublin): The only thing modest and unassuming about this exquisite Dublin home of French nouvelle cuisine is its location. The head chef, Guillaume Le Brun, combines the finest of Irish ingredients and French artistry to create consistently lauded specialties of the house, such as wild Irish salmon, Connemara lobster, and fillet of lamb. See Chapter 5.
- **Arbutus Lodge** (Co. Cork): Formerly the home of the lord mayor, Arbutus Lodge House is king of the hill in more ways than one in Cork, with commanding views of the River Lee and the surrounding hills. The restaurant, however, is what puts it on the map of Ireland. The chef's eight-course tasting menu and a fine wine from the lodge's extensive list will leave a lasting impression. See Chapter 8.
- **Ballymaloe House** (Co. Cork): Ballymaloe, which includes its school, restaurant, and gardens, has become synonymous with Irish cooking raised to the highest level. Committed to the adage that well begun is half done, Ballymaloe focuses on the finest and freshest local ingredients, requiring only art and not alchemy to produce what is arguably the finest Irish fare on the island. See Chapter 9.
- **Lettercollum House** (Co. Cork): The emphasis here is on fresh, local, and organic ingredients; a walled garden provides the vegetables, and pigs are raised on the premises. With these fine materials, chef Con McLoughlin concocts dishes of pure delight, simple yet surprising. There is always a vegetarian entrée. See Chapter 9.
- **Moran's Oyster Cottage** (Co. Galway): A short drive from Galway center, this seafood mecca is worth a drive from Dublin. For six generations, the Morans have focused on what they know and do best; the same menu—seafood and nothing but—all day every day brings the point home. You may not find better oysters and wild salmon anywhere, and surely not at this price. See Chapter 12.
- **Cromleach Lodge** (Co. Sligo): In this lovely country house with panoramic views of Lough Arrow and environs, Christy and Moira Tighe have created a culinary destination with few peers. The menu, Irish in focus, changes daily and never fails to delight. The eight-course gourmet menu is the ultimate indulgence. See Chapter 14.

15   The Best Pubs

- **The Abbey Tavern** (Co. Dublin): A short outing from Dublin center, the Abbey Tavern is the perfect place to recover and refuel after exploring Howth Head, Ireland's Eye, and the attractive fishing and yachting village of Howth on the northern tip of Dublin Bay. The Abbey is known far and wide for its ballads as well as its brew. See Chapter 5.
- **The Brazen Head** (Co. Dublin): Nearly qualifying as one of Ireland's ancient sites, the Brazen Head, commissioned by Charles II, is more than 300 years old, and its stout is as fresh as it comes. Among its illustrious alumni are Wolfe Tone, Daniel O'Connell, and Robert Emmet, who planned the Dublin rising of 1803 under the Head's low timbers. In fact, he was hanged not far from here when everything went wrong. See Chapter 5.
- **An Bodhran** (Co. Cork): A hangout for UCC (University College Cork) students serious about their traditional music and stout, An Bodhran has a lot of old-style character, which has only been enhanced by recent renovations. See Chapter 8.
- **The Blue Haven** (Co. Cork): Everything the Blue Haven offers is first rate: food, drink, lodging, and a cozy bar with an open fire. This particular haven is also

in the center of one of Ireland's most appealing seaside towns. You'll soon measure everyone else's traditional Irish lamb stew by what you found here. See Chapter 9.

- **Gus O'Connor's** (Co. Clare): Doolin, a dot of a town on the Clare coast, is a hot spot for traditional Irish music, and Gus O'Connor's has been at the center of the action here for more than 150 years. Great music and distinguished seafood make this otherwise ordinary spot worth a major detour. See Chapter 11.

- **Moran's Oyster Cottage** (Co. Galway): Famed for its seafood, this centuries-old thatched-cottage pub on the weir also draws a perfect pint. This may well be the oyster capitol of Ireland. It's 12 miles out of Galway and well worth the drive, or the walk, for that matter. See Chapter 12.

- **Smugglers Creek** (Co. Donegal): This place would be worth a stop if only for its spectacular cliff-top views of Donegal Bay. Stone walls, beamed ceilings, open fires, excellent fare, and the brew that's true are among the charms proprietor Conor Britton has on tap. See Chapter 14.

- **Crown Liquor Saloon** (Co. Antrim): This National Trust pub, across from the Grand Opera House in Belfast, is a Victorian gem. Your mouth will drop open at its antique publican splendor even before you lift your first pint. See Chapter 16.

2 Getting to Know Ireland

"The modern American tourist," wrote historian Daniel J. Boorstin, "has come to expect both more strangeness and more familiarity than the world naturally offers." That said, Ireland continues to offer more than its share of both.

When I first traveled to Ireland more than 20 years ago, I was not expecting a foreign country. Born and raised in an Irish-American enclave in Chicago, I was taught by Irish nuns, and baptized and chastised by Irish priests. I went off to Ireland anticipating pretty much what I had known as a child, only with more green. I imagined that I had already had "the Irish experience" in Chicago, over the counter, as it were, and that now, in the motherland, I would have the same experience in prescription strength. It turned out I was wrong about that.

At first glance, Ireland presents a familiar face to its American visitors. The language is the same, only "hillier," the faces are familiar, the food recognizable, the stout legendary. Many visitors, notably Irish Americans, experience their arrival in Ireland as a kind of homecoming. It takes a while for this experience to wear off. When it does, the other face of Ireland shows itself, and this is when the country becomes truly exciting.

Ireland is a place of profound contradiction and complexity. For one thing, it is at the same time both ancient and adolescent. It's as young as it is old.

Ireland's age is obvious to anyone with a car. Within a half day's drive of downtown Dublin lie Neolithic tombs, Bronze Age forts, early Christian monastic sites, Viking walls, Norman castles, Georgian estates—enough antiquity to make your head spin, all in open sight, each bit as commonplace as a Wal-Mart in the United States. The Irish past doesn't exist just in books; it's in the backyard. A shovel, digging for peat or potatoes, may well strike a 5,000-year-old grave. Thousands of unexcavated ancient sites litter the countryside. Any visitor to Ireland who ventures beyond its shops and pubs will soon be struck by how the country reeks of age.

What is less obvious is how new Ireland is, as a nation. The Republic of Ireland, with its own constitution and currency, is less than 50 years old. Mary Robinson, the current president of Ireland, is only the seventh person to hold that office. In political age, Ireland, for all its antiquity, is a mere adolescent. Like any adolescent, it's doing many things for the first time; and at least a few of its contradictions make sense when this fact is kept in mind. Compounding Ireland's youth as a nation is the youth of its people. Roughly half of Ireland's population is under 25, while a quarter is under 15. This means that, in many homes, those who once fought for Irish independence and those who have never known anything else live under the same roof. In these same homes, the gap between generations is often seismic. It is indeed ironic that in a country where what happened a thousand years ago reads like yesterday's news, it is common to feel old and outnumbered at 30.

The quality that defines a people derives not from what they wear or eat or drive but from what they have been through, and the Irish people have been through a lot. Ireland's past has been remarkably tumultuous, provoking a tradition of courage, humor, and creativity. Change is nothing new to the island, yet the rate and scale of the changes occurring in Ireland today are without precedent. Recalling again my first trip to Ireland—with my family, to settle there for a while—I was in Dun Laoghaire, just off the boat from Wales. I had been trying to place a call to the realtor who had the keys to our home, but one pay phone after another had failed to work. As I held a fourth dead handset to my ear, I heard someone calling out to me. It was an Irish motorist, a stranger to me, who had noticed my plight, pulled over to the curb, and rolled down his window. "You're in Ireland now," he pointed out to me, "where you'll sooner see the statues movin' than a phone that works." That was Ireland 20 years ago, more boastful of its magic than its machines. In Ireland today, you have to look harder for the magic than for a phone that works, but both are still there.

1 The Lay of the Land

The island of Ireland lies well over 2,000 miles due east of Newfoundland and, on a clear day, can be glimpsed from the northern Welsh coast. The capital city of the Republic shares nearly the same latitude as Edmonton, Alberta, and Bremen, Germany, but distinguishes itself from these by its palm trees and bougainvillea. It's the Gulf Stream that's responsible for Ireland's mild disposition, originating in the Caribbean and sending its warm currents and tropical sea life northward to Ireland's grateful shores. On occasion, as part of the bargain, it sends a hurricane, as in 1987, when tropical storm Charlie tore into the east coast of Ireland and brought Caribbean havoc to the resort town of Bray. We were living at the time in Killiney, on the coast just north of Bray. Our house leaked like a ship going down, and, with each blast, we expected to see the prow of a ship come smashing through our bedroom window. The Irish Sea has a notorious temper—something worth remembering when planning to cross it—but needs inspiration from the tropics to throw a truly dangerous fit.

With a land mass of approximately 32,600 square miles, Ireland is roughly the same size as the state of Maine, though shaped somewhat differently. In rounded figures, it is at most 300 miles north to south, and 170 miles east to west. No point in Ireland is farther than 70 miles from one of its encircling waters: the Atlantic Ocean, the Irish Sea, and the St. George and North channels. What may seem strange is that in the past the Irish rarely saw their offshore waters as a resource. Traditionally, the Irish disliked fish and avoided learning to swim. The sea was to be feared. It was perilous to cross and, worse, its waves brought invaders, one after another.

The topography of Ireland is unusual. Instead of its shores sloping to the sea and its interior rising to mountain peaks, the reverse is the case. Shaped like a saucer, Ireland's twisted, 2,000-mile coastline is, with a few notable exceptions, a breachless bulwark of mountains, cliffs, and highlands, while its interior is generally flat, a broad limestone plain comprised of fertile farmland and raised bogs, graced with the occasional lake and wetland. Some would say that Ireland has only hills, as its highest peak, Carantuohill in Co. Kerry, reaches to only about 3,400 feet. All would agree that Ireland has few crags. Most of its heights, whether mountains or hills, were rounded off and smoothed into graceful slopes tens of thousands of years ago by receding glaciers. Ireland's longest and greatest river is the Shannon, flowing 230 miles south and west across the midlands from its source in the Cuileagh Mountains of Co. Cavan to its estuary in Co. Limerick. The island's largest lake, Lough Neagh, occupies 153 square miles of counties Antrim and Armagh in the north.

One of the least densely populated countries of Europe (third behind Finland and Sweden), Ireland is commonly described as unspoiled, even "untouched." Not so. Lovely as it is, the Irish landscape is no wilderness and is certainly not "untouched." For example, only about 1% of Ireland's hardwood forests have survived 6,000 years of deforestation. In fact, Ireland, once a rich source of timber for the British fleet, has imported virtually all of its wood for more than 200 years. The recent planting of pine forests around the island is only another, though more positive, instance of human intervention.

On the bright side, the predominance of small-scale mixed agriculture has long contributed to the preservation of an unusually wide range of flora and fauna in the Irish countryside, with the notable and famous exception of snakes and other reptiles. As it happens, Mother Nature, not St. Patrick, deserves credit for Ireland's "snakelessness"—all she gave to the island, herpetologically speaking, is one sole, lonely type of common lizard, currently featured on a 32p postage stamp.

In recent years, Ireland has gone increasingly "green" in its policies, one of which has been to create a number of national parks for the sake of both enjoying and protecting the island's natural beauty. Four are already open to the public: Connemara National Park in Co. Galway, Glenveagh National Park in Co. Donegal, Killarney National Park in Co. Kerry, and Wicklow Mountains National Park in Co. Wicklow. Others are being planned and developed, including the future Burren National Park in Co. Clare.

2 The Regions in Brief

Ireland is a land divided many different ways, all of which are significant in finding your way through its history, along its roads, and amid its people.

The first and most recent division is between "the South" (the Republic of Ireland, Eire, or simply, the "Free State") and "the North" (Northern Ireland, commonly and confusingly referred to as "Ulster"). The South is a sovereign, independent nation comprised of 26 counties, while the North, with six counties, remains part of Great Britain. The line partitioning the land and people of Ireland into two distinct political entities was drawn in the Anglo-Irish Treaty of 1921 and remains a matter of bitter dispute. In simplest practical terms, for the tourist, this line between north and south represents a national border, with all of the attending formalities. Still very much alive on the maps and in the minds of the Irish, however, is another, much older, Gaelic set of divisions corresponding to the four points of the compass. In this early scheme of things Ulster is north, Leinster is east, Munster is south, and Connaught is west, while the traditional center of Ireland is the hill of Uisneach in Co. Westmeath.

Next, there are the counties, in terms of which the Irish and their visitors mostly orient themselves. These are the "states" of Ireland, from which individuals and families hail and in terms of which mail is routed. They are signposts one needs to know. Each of the counties has its boasts and its reputation. One county is frequently the butt of another's jokes, and they all find themselves annually pitted against one another in fierce athletic contests as they pursue the national titles in Gaelic football

What's in a Name?

Article 4 of the Irish Constitution indicates two official names for the Republic: *Éire* for use in all Irish-language documents and *Ireland* for use in all English-language documents.

The name *Éire* is very old and of uncertain origin. The Old Irish form, *Ériu*, occurs in the earliest Irish literary text, the *Book of Invasions*, as one of the three sovereign goddesses of Ireland, who at first opposed the invading Gaels or Celts. Much earlier still, in Egypt, when Ptolemy of Alexandria drew his map of the island in the 2nd century A.D., he called it *Iouernia*, which may be traced to the earlier form *Ierne* (clearly related to *Ériu* and *Éire*).

Julius Caesar, who was familiar with but no friend of the Celts, wrote of Ireland as *Hibernia*, which could be translated "land of winter." Neither Caesar nor any future Roman general made a point of getting there.

The English name "Ireland" is an Irish-Germanic hybrid: *Éire-land.*

and hurling. The island's 32 counties, grouped under the four traditional provinces of Ireland cited above, are as follows:

> *In Ulster to the North:* Cavan, Donegal, and Monaghan in the Republic; and Antrim, Armagh, Derry, Down, Fermanagh, and Tyrone in Northern Ireland.

> *In Munster to the South:* Clare, Cork, Kerry, Limerick, Tipperary, and Waterford.

> *In Leinster to the East:* Dublin, Carlow, Kildare, Kilkenny, Laois, Longford, Louth, Meath, Offaly, Westmeath, Wexford, and Wicklow.

> *In Connaught to the West:* Sligo, Mayo, Galway, Roscommon, and Leitrim.

Lastly, in more immediately practical terms for the tourist, Ireland may be divided into regions: the southeast, the southwest, the west, the northwest, the midlands, and Northern Ireland. These, together with several specific cities and their environs—Dublin, Cork, and Galway—comprise the principal areas of interest for Ireland's visitors and serve to structure the information in this guide.

DUBLIN & ENVIRONS   Dublin is "ground zero" for the profound, high-speed changes transforming Ireland into a prosperous, venturesome European country. What was old and venerable in the city remains so, though it now shares space with an all-out 20- and 30-something Irish renaissance. There's something here for everyone. Within an hour or slightly more north and south of Dublin—either by car or by public transport—lie a handful of engaging coastal towns, the barren beauty of the Dublin Mountains, some of the most important prehistoric and early Christian ruins of Europe, Kildare thoroughbred country, the beaches and lush gardens of Co. Wicklow, and the new Wicklow Mountains National Park.

THE SOUTHEAST   Boasting the best (read: warmest and least wet) weather in Ireland, the southeast coast is, on most days, one alternative to a pub for getting out of the rain. Besides its weather, the southeast offers sandy beaches, Waterford's city walls and crystal works, Kilkenny and Cahir castles, the Rock of Cashel, the Irish National Heritage Park at Ferrycarig, and Ireland's largest bird sanctuary on the Saltee Islands.

CORK & ENVIRONS   Cork, Ireland's second city in size, is Dublin's rival in sport and stout but little else. All the same, Cork provides a congenial gateway to the south and west of Ireland, which many consider Ireland's Oz, the ultimate destination.

Ireland

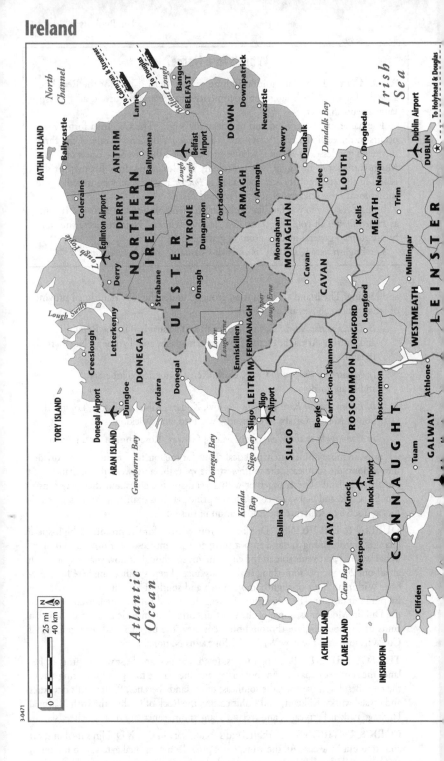

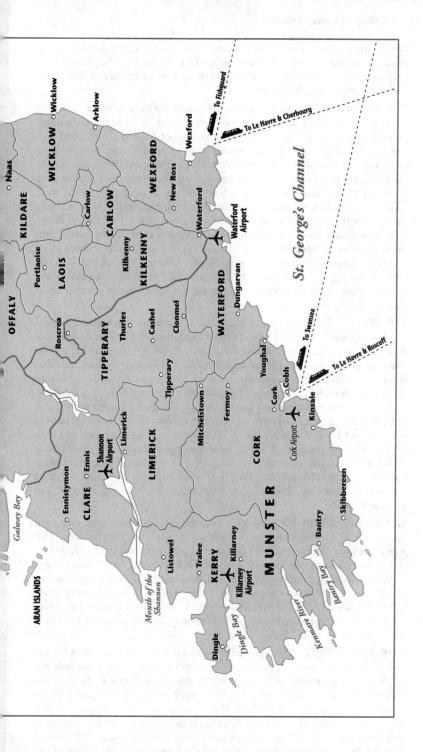

Within arm's reach of Cork is the truly impressive Blarney Castle with its less impressive stone, the culinary and scenic delights of Kinsale, the Drombeg Stone Circle, Sherkin and Clear Islands, Mizen Head, and the spectacular expanses of West Cork, one of my very favorite landscapes.

THE SOUTHWEST   The mountains and seascapes of the southwest, the wettest corner of Ireland, make the same point as Seattle: There are more important things in life than staying dry. The once-remote splendors of Co. Kerry are no longer a secret, so at least during high season visitors must be prepared to share the view. Some highlights of this region are the Dingle Peninsula, the Skellig and the Blaskett Islands, Staigue Fort, Tralee and its annual international and folk festivals, and dazzling views of sea, shore, and mountains—a new one, it seems, at every bend in the road. Killarney is a world destination not for itself but for what lies nearby: its famed lakes, mountain peaks (the tallest in Ireland) and the ever-present sea. The "Ring of Kerry" is less glamorously known as N70 and N71, a 110-mile circuit of the Iveragh Peninsula. Next to the Book of Kells, it's the most visited attraction in Ireland, which is both a recommendation and a warning. Nearby, Killarney National Park—25,000 acres of mountains, woodlands, waterfalls, and wildlife—provides a carless and dramatic haven from tour buses and from the din and clatter of massed camera shutters clicking away.

THE WEST   The west of Ireland, once a land of last resort, today offers a first and hardly disappointing taste of Ireland's beauty and diversity for those who fly into Shannon Airport. Co. Clare's natural offerings, the 700-foot Cliffs of Moher and the limestone grasslands of the Burren, are unforgettable. Counties Limerick and Clare also contain a number of historic sites, from the Stone Age center at Lough Gur to an array of impressive castles, including Knappogue, Bunratty, King John's, Ashrod, and (actually just over the county line in Galway) Dunguaire. Farther to the north of Galway lies Co. Mayo, whose most charming artificial effort may be the town of Westport on Clew Bay. Nearby, though 2,500 feet up, stands Croagh Patrick, a place of pilgrimage for centuries. Another, more recent pilgrimage site is the shrine of Knock with its massive basilica. Also nearby, off the Connemara and southern Mayo coasts, are a string of islands including Inishbofin, Inishturk, and Clare, which are well worth the crossing. Achill Island, Ireland's largest, is a favored vacation spot and is accessible by car.

GALWAY & ENVIRONS   Galway, on the threshold of Connemara, one of the more desolate inhabitable landscapes in the world, is like an exile's last fling. That is, it defies what lies just around the corner. It's a prospering port and university city, sought out by foreign tourists and Irish youth. There's nothing sleepy about Galway.

Just beyond the city stretches Connemara, boasting (besides the greatest number of rocks you'll ever see in one place) the Twelve Bens, Kylemore Abbey, a nearly 4,000-acre national park, and its charming "capital," the town of Clifden. Meanwhile, offshore, lie the legendary Aran Islands—Inishmore, Inishmaan, and Inisheer—further studies in irresistible desolation.

THE NORTHWEST   One becomes convinced that bleak is beautiful in Ireland, and the northwest surely matches the rest of Ireland in beauty. This is especially true of Donegal, with its 200 miles of drenched, jagged coastline that, for the cold-blooded, offers some of the finest surfing in the world. Inland, the Deeryveagh Mountains and Glenveagh National Park offer as much wilderness as can be found anywhere in Ireland. Co. Sligo, for its part, contains the greatest concentration of megalithic sites in Ireland: the stone circles, passage tombs, dolmens, and cairns of, most notably, Carrowmore, Knocknarea, and Carrowkeel. Also among Sligo's time-

❷ Did You Know?

- Four signers of the American Declaration of Independence were born in Ireland, and another nine claimed Irish ancestry.
- 40 million current U.S. citizens trace their roots, at least in part, to Ireland.
- Lights or will-o'-the-wisps on the bog land in the dead of night have long been a source of terror and legend. One such legend tells of a shoemaker who murdered a child and was condemned to walk the bogs by night, carrying a lamp. He was known as Jack O'Lantern.
- A piece of turf, a sprig of shamrock, and a chip from the family hearthstone: These were the common mementos carried by Irish exiles to their new homes abroad.
- Rumor has it that local boys pee on the Blarney Stone at night.
- Turf ash was traditionally placed on the threshold of the family cottage to protect an unattended infant from abduction by the faeries.

less monuments is the poetry of Yeats, who might be called the poet laureate of Sligo. Nearby Leitrim's unspoiled lakes are a favorite retreat, particularly for people carrying fishing poles.

THE MIDLANDS   The thought of midlands, *any* midlands, is likely to bring yawns, until you get there. The lush center of Ireland, bisected by the mighty but lazy Shannon, is no exception. This is a land of pastures, rivers, lakes, woods, and gentle mountain slopes, an antidote to the barren beauty of Connemara and a retreat, in high season, from the throngs of tourists who crowd the coasts. The midlands have no cities, and their towns are not their attractions; it's the shores and waters of the Shannon and Lough Derg and of their many lesser cousins that provide much of the lure. Outdoor activities—cycling, boating, fishing, trekking, hunting—are at the heart of the matter here, as well as visits to some remarkable sites, such as Birr Castle and its splendid gardens, and Clonmacnois, now the stunning ruins of a famous Irish monastic center.

NORTHERN IRELAND   Across the border, in a corner of both Ireland and the United Kingdom, Northern Ireland's six counties are well worth an excursion or a stay. The stunning Antrim coast (particularly between Ballycastle and Cushendum), the 37,000 black basalt columns of the Giant's Causeway, and the luring nine Glens of Antrim are perhaps the greatest draw for sightseers. Written in a minor key is the loveliness of the Fermanagh Lake District to the south, while Co. Down with its Mourne Mountains marks the sunniest and driest spot in the North. The city walls of Derry, Carrickfergus Castle, Belfast's "Golden Mile," and Navan Fort (or Emain Macha, the royal center of Ulster for 800 years), are only some of the sites and sights, ancient and current, which the North has to offer.

3 Ireland Today

The Irish landscape remains breathtaking, its natural beauty intact, its rivers and lakes more or less pollution-free, and its people disarmingly gracious. These are the essential components of Irish tourism, according to a recent (1995) document issued by Ireland's Department of Foreign Affairs. They bring 3.6 million visitors to Ireland each year, an ever-growing number that already exceeds Ireland's decreasing population. Irish hospitality is legendary, and deservedly so.

Impressions

There are no overall certitudes in Ireland any more. There's a lot of diversity of thinking, a lot of uncertainty, a lot of trying to assimilate other cultures. It's a time when we need to take stock, to look into our hearts, and find a sense of Irishness, to find pride in ourselves that will make us sure of what we are.

—Mary Robinson, President of Ireland,
from her 1990 presidential campaign

Included in that hospitality, however, can be a misleading sense of tranquility, continuity, and cohesion. Like an overgrown family, Ireland is mostly inclined to keep its turmoil to itself and to offer its guests the vacation of their lives, which is what its guests are mostly looking for.

What is easy for any visitor to miss or to underestimate is the depth and pace of the change occurring in Ireland today. Ireland has long been a land of profound conflicts, and never more so than at the present. To mention one, *Irish* and *Roman Catholic* are assumed by many to be synonymous. The truth is that they have never meant the same thing, nor made lasting peace with each other. The Roman Catholicism preached by Patrick was transformed as fast as it was embraced by the Celts of Ireland. The Vatican, like the British royalty, found the Irish to be unruly and bent on taking their own road, regardless. For all their faith and devotion, Irish Catholics have never finally decided whether to trust or mistrust their hierarchy, appointed from Rome. Recent public scandals in the Church, followed not by candor but by cover-up, have only served to widen ancient misgivings. The 1996 referendum to permit legal divorce—as well as the decriminalizing of homosexuality and the passing of the abortion information law—all urged and supported by Ireland's first female president, Mary Robinson, point to an Ireland where the iron grip of Rome is being pried away a finger at a time.

The Ireland of today, which may present such a traditional face to the tourist, is increasingly defined and determined by its youth, whose sheer numbers and unconventional ways are creating a generation gap of seismic proportions. For one thing, they aren't marrying and they aren't having children with anything approximating the regularity of their parents. In 1993, the Irish birth rate fell, for the first time in recorded history, below the minimum population replacement rate of 2.1 children per woman of child-bearing age, and it continues to fall even further. This is not to say that the Irish are endangered. What are endangered, however, are the stereotypes visitors may have of them.

While Ireland today is increasingly prosperous, European, and committed to pluralistic human values, it is at the same time determined to preserve its rich legacy and distinct character. While Irish-speaking and -reading citizens represent a minority of the population, Irish writers, especially poets, continue to create new work, and an Irish-language television channel is scheduled to begin broadcasting this year.

Finally, it may be said with some confidence that the will for peace in and with the North has never been more widely or deeply shared on both sides of the border. Factions on both sides, however, continue to defy the will of the people, common sense, and common decency. The IRA's recent resumption of violence after the paramilitary cease-fires of 1994, and the disturbances of July 1996, have broken the optimism of the past two years and pushed the North to the brink again. Even so, peace may well break out one day soon. In this and in so many other ways, Ireland and the Irish remain unpredictable.

4 History 101

The Irish past, like that of every other people, may be divided into two parts: prehistory and history. This is a distinction *we* make, looking back at them. History here means written history: texts, not stories; words, not pictures. *Prehistoric* has a hunched-over, savage ring to it, but that's our problem. People who didn't write about themselves were still people, and they might have had better things to do.

So how do we know about the prehistoric past? Except for some monuments still staring us in the face, prehistoric Ireland has to be dug up like a grave rather than opened up like a book. Indeed, Ireland has richly rewarded the archaeologist's shovel, and the farmer's plow, for that matter, as a great many of Ireland's treasures have been unearthed by chance in the course of other chores. To be found underfoot or under bog are the remains of houses, forts, tombs, tools, weapons, ornaments—all the whatnots of earlier lives—offering wordless clues to the past. They say that ancient stones speak. Actually, they mumble at best. It's up to archaeologists and prehistorians, using both science and intuition, very much like the common sleuth, to turn those mumblings into a confession.

The first Irish antiquaries, the earliest writings of the Irish about their own past, characterize that past as a series of "invasions" beginning before the deluge and continuing into the present. That too, from a later vantage point, is mostly how modern historians tell the story of the Irish past, which I'll retell briefly here.

IRISH PREHISTORY

THE FIRST SETTLERS   At the end of its last ice age, around the year 8000 B.C., Ireland warmed up to agreeable, even attractive, temperatures, so we can with some degree of confidence place the date for the first human habitation of the island somewhere between the late 8000s and the early 6000s B.C. Regardless of where in that span the date actually fell, Ireland seems to have been among the last lands in Europe to have felt the human footprint.

Ireland's first colonizers, Mesolithic Homo sapiens, walked, waded, or floated—depending on the status of the early land bridges—across the narrow strait from Britain in search of flint and, of course, food. They found both and stayed on, more or less uneventfully (from our perspective, at least), for a good 4,000 to 5,000 years. Their contribution to the

Dateline

- **8000 B.C.** Earliest human immigration to Ireland.
- **3500 B.C.** Farmers and megalithic builders reach Ireland.
- **2000 B.C.** First metalworkers come to Ireland.
- **700 B.C.** Celtic settlement of Ireland begins.
- **A.D. 432** Traditional date for Patrick's return to Ireland.
- **500–800** Ireland's "Golden Age."
- **795** First Viking invasion.
- **841** The Norse build a sea fort on the River Liffey.
- **853** Danes take possession of the Norse settlement.
- **988** Dublin officially recognized as an Irish city.
- **1014** Battle of Clontarf. Brian Boru defeats the Vikings.
- **1167–69** Norman invasion of Ireland.
- **1171** Henry II visits Ireland and claims feudal lordship.
- **1204** Dublin Castle becomes base of British power.
- **1297** First parliamentary sessions in Dublin.
- **1541** Henry III proclaims himself king of Ireland.
- **1534–52** Henry VIII begins suppression of Catholic Church in Ireland.
- **1558–1603** Reign of Elizabeth I. Elizabeth conducts several Irish wars, initiates the "plantation" of Munster, divides Ireland in counties, and in 1591 founds Trinity College, Dublin.
- **1601** Mountjoy defeats combined Spanish and Irish forces at Kinsale.
- **1603** The Articles of Confederation introduced and the "plantation" of Ulster commences.

continues

- **1607** The flight of the Irish earls, marking the demise of the old Gaelic order.
- **1641** Irish Catholic revolt in Ulster led by Sir Phelim O'Neill ends in defeat.
- **1649** Oliver Cromwell invades and begins the reconquest of Ireland.
- **1690** The forces of James II, a Catholic, are defeated at the Battle of the Boyne, assuring British control of Ireland.
- **1691** Patrick Sarsfield surrenders Limerick. He and some 14,000 Irish troops, the "Wild Geese," flee to the Continent.
- **1704** Enactment of first Penal Laws. Apartheid comes to Ireland.
- **1778** The Penal Laws are progressively repealed.
- **1782** The Irish Parliament is granted independence.
- **1791** Wolfe Tone founds the Society of the United Irishmen.
- **1796–97** Wolfe Tone launches an invasion from France, fails, is taken captive, and commits suicide.
- **1798** "The Year of the French." A French invasion force is defeated at Killala Bay. General Humbert surrenders to Cornwallis.
- **1800** The Irish Parliament is induced to dissolve itself.
- **1803** In Dublin, Robert Emmet leads a rising of less than 100 men and is hung.
- **1829** Daniel O'Connell secures passage of the Catholic Emancipation Act.
- **1841** Daniel O'Connell is named lord mayor of Dublin.
- **1845–48** The Great Famine. Two million Irish either die or emigrate.
- **1848** The revolt of the Young Irelanders ends in failure.

continues

future of Ireland may seem minimal, but most beginnings are. And they did, after all, begin the gene pool.

THE NEOLITHIC AGE   The next momentous prehistoric event was the arrival of Neolithic farmers and herders, sometime around 3500 B.C. The Neolithic "revolution" was the first of many to come to Ireland a bit late, at least 5,000 years after its inception in the ancient near east. The domestication of the human species—settled life, agriculture, animal husbandry—brought with it a radically increased population, enhanced skills, stability, and all the implications of leisure. Unlike Ireland's Mesolithic hunters, who barely left a trace, this second wave of colonizers began at once to transform the island. They came with stone axes fabricated in factories and widely traded, which could fell a good-sized elm in less than an hour. The hardwood forests of Ireland, slashed and burned one hour at a time, began to recede to make room for tilled fields and pastureland. Villages sprang up, like those discovered and reconstructed at Lough Gur, Co. Limerick. Larger, more permanent homes, planked with split-oak, appeared roughly at this time.

Far more startling, however, is the appearance of massive megalithic monuments including court cairns, dolmens, passage tombs, and wedge tombs, only a small percentage of which have been excavated. All the same, more than 1,000 megalithic monuments have been unearthed in Ireland, mumbling symphonically about beliefs, cults, and aspirations as profound as any we might imagine. A visit to Newgrange and Knowth in the Boyne Valley and to Carrowmore in Co. Sligo (once possibly the largest megalithic cemetery in Western Europe until the grave robbers arrived in the last century) will both dazzle and deepen anyone's understanding of the human past. It certainly did this for the later Celtic inhabitants of the island, who wondered and told stories about the tremendous stones and mounds raised by what, they assumed, must have been giants—their ancestors, whom they imagined to inhabit them still. They called them the people of the *sí,* who eventually became the *Tuatha Dé Danann,* and then the faeries, the once great and now little people, living a quite magical life mostly underground in the thousands of *raths,* or earthwork structures, coursing the island like giant mole works.

In the ensuing millennia of the prehistoric period, these first farmers were followed by others, skilled in prospecting and metallurgy. Bronze implements and ornaments, and some jewelry wrought in gold, were now added to the pots and woven fabrics already being produced on the island. A still later wave of farmers and craftsmen moved their settlements from the edges of lakes to the center, where they constructed artificial islands surrounded by palisades. An example of these curious creations, called *crannógs,* has been reconstructed at the Craggaunowen Project, Co. Clare. A visit there—as well as to Lough Gur in Co. Limerick and to the Irish National Heritage Park at Ferrycarrig, Co. Wexford—would reward anyone interested in learning more about life in prehistoric Ireland. While the Bronze Age Irish, like the Stone Age Irish who preceded them, left no written records behind, they did bequeath to their dead and so to us works of exquisite beauty, examples of which may be seen in the National Museum in Dublin.

THE CELTS   The first "invasion" of Ireland that can be traced with historical confidence is that of the Celts, cousins of the *Celtae* who sacked Rome and the *Keltoi* who did the same to Delphi. Indeed, Irish history, before the modern period, may be sketched in terms of four invasions: those of the Celts, the Vikings, the Normans, and the English. Each left their indelible imprint on the landscape and the psyche of the island. Ireland and the Irish people today are the heirs, culturally and genetically, of their prehistoric and historic invaders.

Of all of Ireland's uninvited guests, the Celts made the greatest impact. They came in waves, the first as early as perhaps the 6th century B.C. and continuing until the end of the millennium. In time, they controlled the island and absorbed into their culture everyone they found there. Their ways and their genes were, in a word, dominant. They brought iron weapons, war chariots, codes of combat and honor, cults and contests, poetic and artistic genius, music and mania, all of which took root and flourished in Irish soil as if they were native plants. The Celts, however, were dismally disorganized in comparison with the kingdoms and empires of Europe. They divided the island among themselves into as many as 150 tribes, or *tuatha,* grouped under alliances with allegiance to one of five provincial kings. The provinces of Munster, Leinster, Ulster, and Connaught date from this period. They fought among themselves, fiercely, over cattle (their "currency" and standard of wealth), land, and women. None among them ever achieved high kingship of the island, though not for lack of trying.

- **1858** The Irish Republican Brotherhood, a secret society known as the Fenians, is founded in New York.
- **1867** A Fenian uprising is easily crushed.
- **1879** Michael Davitt founds the National Land League to support the claims of tenant farmers.
- **1879–82** The "land war" forces the enactment of reform. The tenant system unravels and land returns to those who work it.
- **1884** Gaelic Athletic Association is formed to preserve native sports.
- **1893** The Gaelic League is founded to revive the Irish language.
- **1886 and 1894** Bills for Home Rule are defeated in Parliament.
- **1904** Establishment of the Abbey Theatre.
- **1905–08** Founding of Sinn Féin, "we ourselves," with close links to the Irish Republican Brotherhood.
- **1912** Third Home Rule bill passes in the House of Commons and is defeated by the House of Lords.
- **1913** Founding of the Irish Citizens Army.
- **1916** Patrick Pearse and James Connolly lead an armed uprising on Easter Monday to proclaim the Irish Republic. Defeat is followed by the execution of 15 leaders of the revolt.
- **1918** Sinn Féin wins a landslide election victory against the Irish Parliamentary Party.
- **1919** Sinn Féin, led by Eamon de Valera, constitutes itself as the first Irish Dáil and declares independence.
- **1919–21** The Irish War of Independence.

continues

Michael Collins commands the Irish forces.

- **1921** Anglo-Irish Treaty. Ireland is partitioned. Twenty-six counties form the Free State. William Cosgrave becomes the first President. His party, Cumann na nGaedheal, later becomes Fine Gael.
- **1922** The Free State adopts its first constitution.
- **1922–23** The Irish civil war, between the government of the Free State and those who opposed the treaty. Michael Collins is assassinated.
- **1932** Eamon de Valera leads Fianna Fáil to victory and becomes head of government.
- **1932–38** Economic war with Britain brings great hardship.
- **1937** Ireland's 26 counties adopt a new constitution, abandoning membership in British Commonwealth.
- **1938** Douglas Hyde inaugurated as Eire's first president.
- **1939** Dublin is bombed by Germany at start of World War II, but Ireland remains neutral.
- **1948** The Republic of Ireland Act. Ireland severs its last constitutional links with Britain.
- **1955** Ireland is admitted into the United Nations.
- **1959** Eamon de Valera becomes president of Ireland.
- **1963** U.S. Pres. John F. Kennedy visits Dublin.
- **1969** Violence breaks out in Northern Ireland. British troops are called in.
- **1972** In Derry, a peaceful rally turns into "Bloody Sunday." The Northern Irish Parliament is dissolved and the North is ruled directly from Britain.
- **1973** Ireland joins the European Community.

continues

One of the most impressive monuments from the time of the warring Celtic chiefs is the stone fortress of Dún Aengus on the Aran Islands.

IRISH HISTORY

THE COMING OF CHRISTIANITY   The Celtic powers-that-be neither warmly welcomed nor violently resisted the Christians who, beginning in the 5th century A.D., came ashore and walked the island with a new message. Although threatened to the core, the Celtic kings and bards settled for a bloodless rivalry and made no Christian martyrs.

Not the first but eventually the most famous of these Christian newcomers was Patrick, a young Roman citizen torn from his British homeland in a Celtic raid and brought to Ireland as a slave. In time, he escaped slavery but not Ireland, to which he felt himself called. Ordained a priest and consecrated a bishop, Patrick made his own raid on Ireland and took its people by storm. He abhorred slavery, which he had known firsthand, and he preached it off the island. Within 30 years, the Christian church, like a young forest, was well rooted and spreading in every direction. By the time of his death, around A.D. 461, the Roman empire was in near collapse while Ireland was on the brink of its golden age.

The full truth of Ireland's conversion to Christianity, however, was that it was mutual. The church of Patrick was, like the man who brought it, Roman, something Ireland never was and never would be. Roman Catholicism didn't "take" in Ireland. Instead, it "went native" and became uniquely Celtic. Patrick's eminent successors, Columcille, Bridgit, and Columbanus, were Irish in a way that Patrick could never be and so was their church. Although orthodox on most points of doctrine, the Irish church was Celtic in structure, tribal and unruly by Roman standards. To Ireland, an island without towns or cities, the Roman system of dioceses and archdioceses was beside the point. Instead, the Irish built monasteries with extended monastic families, each more or less autonomous and regional. The pope, like an Irish high king, was essentially a peer. He had to defend his title with every challenge, like a prizefighter. Besides, the pope reigned in "a place out of mind," a place currently in a shambles.

IRELAND OF THE SAINTED MISSIONARIES   Meanwhile, Ireland flourished for several centuries as a land of saints and scholars. Its monasteries were centers of learning and culture—some of the few left in post-Roman Europe—where literacy

itself was effectively kept alive through the volumi-
nous and imaginative work of scholars and scribes.
Moreover, some of these monasteries, Bridgit's own,
for instance, were models of sexual equality,
populated by both men and women and sometimes
presided over by a woman, a high abbess, who
was likely to have a handful of bishops under her
jurisdiction.

Not only were monks and scholars drawn to
Ireland in great numbers, but they were sent out
in great numbers as well, to Britain and the Continent, bearing with them all the otherwise forgotten
knowledge of Europe. As historian Thomas Cahill
wrote in his *How the Irish Saved Civilization,* "Wherever they went the Irish brought with them their
books, many unseen in Europe for centuries and tied
to their waists as signs of triumph, just as Irish heroes had once tied to their waists their enemies'
heads." The influence of these monks cannot be
underestimated. They went everywhere; it's likely
that some of them even reached North America.
And they worked with a fervor, so much so that
more than half the biblical commentaries written between 650 and 850 were penned by Irishmen.

The prime legacy of these monks lies in knowledge perpetuated, but like their megalithic ancestors,
they too left some enduring monuments to their
profound spirituality. With any imagination, visits
to the early monastic sites of Glendalough in Co.
Wicklow, Clonmacnois in Co. Offaly, and Skellig
Michael off the Kerry coast, together with a stop at
Trinity College Dublin to see the Book of Kells, will
help bring to life Ireland's lost age of splendor.

- **1986** Ireland signs the Anglo-Irish Agreement.
- **1990** Ireland elects Mary Robinson to be its first woman president.
- **1992** Ireland approves the European Union.
- **1993** The Joint Declaration on Northern Ireland establishes the principles and framework for a peaceful, democratic resolution of issues regarding the political status of the North.
- **1994** The IRA announces a cease-fire, and the Protestant paramilitaries follow suit. Commencement of peace talks.
- **1995** The British and Irish governments issue "A New Framework for Agreement," and U.S. Pres. Clinton makes a historic visit to Ireland, speaking to large crowds in Belfast and Derry. Received with great enthusiasm in the Republic, he is made a "freeman" of the City of Dublin.
- **1996** The IRA resumes its campaign of violence. New disturbances in the North. The cease-fire is over and the peace process in tatters.

THE VIKING INVASIONS The monastic city-states of early medieval Ireland
died no natural death. After several centuries of dazzling peace, the sea brought new
invaders, this time the Vikings, seagoing berserkers from Scandinavia, who, in as-
saulting Ireland's monasteries, went straight for the jugular of Irish civilization. Regardless of their Celtic blood, the monks were not warriors, and the round towers to
which they retreated were neither high enough nor strong enough to protect them
and their treasures from the Scandinavian pirates, who knew a soft touch when they
saw one and just kept coming, from around the year 800 into the 10th century. The
Vikings knew how to pillage and they knew how to plunder, but, thankfully, they
didn't know how to read. Thus they didn't much bother with the books they came
across, allowing the monks some means besides their memories of preserving their
knowledge and of passing their history down to us.

For better or worse, the Vikings did more than hit and run. They settled as well,
securing every major harbor on Ireland's east coast with a fortified town. These were
the first towns in Ireland: Dublin, Cork, Waterford, and the river city of Limerick.
Eventually, the Irish, disinclined to unite, did so anyway. This led to decisive Viking
defeats by the armies of Brian Boru in 999 and 1014. When the Vikings left,
however, they left their towns behind, forever altering the Irish way of life. The legacy

Impressions

The great Gaels of Ireland
Are the men that God made mad,
For all their wars are merry,
And all their songs are sad.

—G. K. Chesterton, "The Ballad of the White Horse," 1911

of the Vikings in Ireland is complex, and a visit to Dublin's Wood Quay and the city walls of Waterford may put those interested on the scent.

With the Vikings gone, Ireland enjoyed something of a renaissance in the 11th and 12th centuries. Meanwhile, its towns grew, its regional kings made their bids for high kingship, and its church came under concerted pressure to conform with the Vatican. All of these, in fact, played their part in ripening Ireland for its next invasion. Prosperous and factionalized, Ireland made attractive prey, and it was tragically an Irish king who opened the door to the predator. Diarmait Mac Murchada, King of Leinster, whose ambition was to be king of all of Ireland, decided he needed outside help and called on a Welsh Norman, Richard de Clare, better known as Strongbow. Strongbow and his army, in turn, acted on behalf of Henry II of England, who had taken the pious and political precaution of securing a papal blessing for the invasion of Catholic Ireland. The accommodating pope was Adrian IV, who must have envisioned not only a more papal Ireland but also a more British one. After all, he was the first and only Britain ever to ascend to the papacy.

THE NORMAN INVASION   In successive expeditions from 1167–1169, the Normans crossed the Irish Sea with crushing force. When you see the massive Norman fortifications at Trim, you'll realize the clout the Normans brought with them. Two years later, in 1171, Henry II of England made a royal visit to what was now one of his domains. Across the next century, the Norman invaders settled in, consolidated their power, developed Irish towns and cities, and grew terribly fond of the island, becoming as Irish as the Irish themselves.

In 1314, Scotland's Robert the Bruce defeated the English at Bannockburn and set out to fulfill his dream of a united Celtic kingdom. He installed his brother Edward on the Irish throne, but the constant state of war took a heavy toll and within two years famine and economic disorder had eroded any public support Edward might have enjoyed. By the time he was defeated and killed at Dundalk in 1317, few were prepared to mourn him. Over the next two centuries, attempts to rid Ireland of its Norman overlords were laudable but fell short. Independent Gaelic lords in the north and west continued to maintain their territories, and by the close of the 15th century, British control of the island was effectively limited to the Pale, a walled and fortified cordon around what might have been called "greater Dublin." The Normans themselves became more and more Irish and less and less British in their loyalties. Ireland was becoming British in name only.

ENGLISH POWER & THE FLIGHT OF THE EARLS   In the 16th century, under the Tudors, the brutal reconquest of Ireland was set in motion. In mid-century, Henry VIII proclaimed himself king of Ireland, something his predecessors had never done, but it wasn't until late in the century that the claim was backed up by force, now under the banner of Elizabeth I, Henry's daughter, who declared that all Gaelic lords in Ireland must surrender their lands to her, with the altruistic pronouncement that she would immediately regrant them—a proposition that was met with no great joy, to say the least. The Irish, under Ulster's Hugh O'Neill and Red

Hugh O'Donnell, struck out, defeating the earl of Essex, whom Elizabeth had personally sent to subdue them. In 1600, a massive force commanded by Lord Mountjoy landed and set about subduing the country, and by 1603 O'Neill was left with few allies and no option but surrender, which he did on March 23, the day before Elizabeth died. Had he waited, who knows how history would have differed. As it was, O'Neill had his lands returned, but constant harassment by the English prompted him, along with many of Irelands other Gaelic lords, to sail for the continent on September 14, 1607, abandoning their lands and their aspirations.

THE COMING OF CROMWELL   By the 1640s, Ireland was effectively an English plantation. Family estates had been seized and foreign (Scottish) labor brought in to work them. The persecution of Catholics, begun with Henry VIII's split from Rome, barred them from practicing their faith. Resentment led in 1641 to uprisings in Ulster and Leinster, and by early 1642 most of Ireland was again controlled by the Irish, but any hope of extending their victories was destroyed by internal disunion and by the eventual decision to support the Royalist side in the English civil war. In 1648, English King Charles I was beheaded, and the following year the Royalist forces in Ireland were defeated at Rathmines. The stage was set for disaster.

In 1649, Oliver Cromwell arrived in Dublin as commander in chief and lord lieutenant of Ireland, and set about destroying all opposition. One of the most brutal and effective butchers any empire has ever enlisted, Cromwell simply devastated Ireland, which still bears the scars of his savagery. To this day, some Irish spit when they say his name. Cromwell left no doubt who was in charge. His campaign lasted only seven months, but his brutal and bloodthirsty methods broke the back of all resistance. In his siege of the town of Drogheda alone, 3,552 Irish were killed, while Cromwell lost only 64 men. After subduing all but Galway and Waterford, Cromwell left Ireland and its administration in the care of his lieutenants and returned to England, but his stamp would linger for centuries, and the memory of it still burns.

The Irish were offered a choice after the massacres: Anyone suspected of resisting the English forces could leave the country, give up their lands and resettle in Connaught or Co. Clare, or die. With this expropriation, the English gained control over most of the country's arable land, and cemented English power.

After the restoration of the British monarchy in 1660, and especially after the succession to the throne of the Catholic King James II in 1685, Irish Catholics began to sense hope in the air. By 1688, Protestant power in the country was seriously diminished, but the seizure of the English throne by William of Orange in November of that year reversed the trend. James fled to France to regroup, then sailed to Ireland to launch his counterattack. He struck first at Londonderry, to which he laid siege for 15 weeks before being defeated by William's forces at the Battle of the Boyne, a battle that effectively ended James's cause and the last Irish hope of freedom in Ireland. Soon after, the Treaty of Limerick sealed the defeat, and many Irish patriots sailed for America to fight the British empire in a war that could be won.

THE PENAL LAWS   After the defeat of James, the boot of English power sat heavier than ever on Ireland's neck. Protestant lords were granted total political power and control of the land, and laws were enacted to effectively impoverish the Catholic population. Catholics could not purchase land; Catholic landholdings were split up unless the family that held them converted; Catholic schools and priests were banned; Catholics were barred from professions or commissions in the army and were forced to pay a tax to the Anglican church. The laws had an unintended consequence, though: As happens whenever unjust laws are inflicted on a people, they institutionalized civil disobedience and inspired creative sedition.

Meanwhile, the new British lords and landlords of Ireland settled in, sunk their own roots, planted crops, made laws, and sowed their own seed. Inevitably, over time, the "Angles" became the Anglo-Irish. Hyphenated or not, they were Irish, and their loyalties were increasingly unpredictable. Colonialism only works effectively for one generation, after all—the very next generation is native to the new country, not the old. As this process played out in Ireland, history settled into one of its periodic states of inactivity, and little of note transpired. Prosperity remained on the Protestant side of the fence, and deprivation on the Catholic side. The Penal Laws continued to be in effect for a century, with the first of them being relaxed in 1770 and the bulk of them being repealed with England's 1783 acknowledgment of the Irish Parliament's right, along with the king, to determine the laws by which Ireland should be governed.

WOLFE TONE, THE UNITED IRISHMEN & THE 1798 REBELLION

England's difficulty is Ireland's opportunity, or so the saying goes, so when war broke out between the British and French in the 1790s, the United Irishmen—a nonviolent society formed to lobby for admission of Catholic and landless Irishmen to the Irish parliament—went underground to try and persuade the French to intervene on Ireland's behalf against the British. Their emissary in this venture was a Dublin lawyer named Wolfe Tone. In 1796, Tone sailed with a French invasion force bound for Ireland, but was turned back by storms.

Come 1798, Ireland was embroiled in insurrection. Wexford and Ulster teetered, with the United Irishmen proving to have united not enough of their countrymen to mount a credible, sustainable campaign. The nadir of the rebellion came when Wolfe Tone, having raised another French invasion force, sailed into Lough Swilley in Donegal and was promptly captured by the British. At his trial, wearing a French uniform, Tone requested that he be shot. When the request was refused, he slit his own throat. The rebellion was over. In the space of three weeks more than 30,000 Irish had been killed. In the aftermath of "The Year of the French," as it came to be known, the British induced the Irish parliament to dissolve itself, and Ireland reverted to strict British rule.

DANIEL O'CONNELL

In 1828, a Catholic lawyer named Daniel O'Connell, who had earlier formed the Catholic Association to represent the interests of tenant farmers, was elected to the British parliament to represent Ireland. Public opinion was so solidly behind him that he was able to persuade the duke of Wellington, Britain's prime minister at the time, that the only way to avoid an Irish civil war was to force the Catholic Emancipation Act through parliament. Once this was secured, O'Connell accepted the position as Ireland's MP (Member of Parliament). For 12 years he served in this post, winning concessions and fighting against unpopular leftovers of the Penal Laws. In 1841 he left parliament and was elected lord mayor of Dublin, and from here began his push for repeal of the Irish/British union imposed after the 1798 rebellion. Toward this end, he organized enormous meetings that often reached the hundreds of thousands, but succeeded in provoking an unresponsive conservative government to such an extent that it eventually arrested O'Connell on charges of seditious conspiracy. The charges were dropped, but the incident—coupled with dissension among the Irish, criticism by a group known as the Young Irelanders, and distress from the incipient famine—led to the breaking of his power base. "The Liberator," as he had been known, faded, his health failed, and he eventually died on a trip to Rome. The Young Irelanders, led by "Meagher of the Sword," went on to stage a pathetic revolt in 1848, which was easily put down by the English authorities.

THE GREAT HUNGER   As the efforts of Ireland's hoped-for liberators failed, the Irish were faced with something they could barely imagine: a worse state of affairs.

In the years 1845–48, famine struck. The majority of Ireland owned by the Irish was harsh, difficult land, unsuitable for most farming, and for this reason the Irish had come to depend on the potato, one of the hardiest of crops, as the staple of their diet. When blight struck, they were left with nothing to keep body and soul together.

It has often been said that colonialism can only succeed when it's paired with genocide, and in the "Great Hunger," as it's called, this collusion nearly came to pass. Whether the famine was an act of God, the British, or bad farming practices on the part of the Irish peasantry remains unresolved, yet the fact stands that it claimed a million Irish lives and dispatched another million to the sea on death-ships, most pointed toward the United States. Those who remained faced only continued hardship, and in the years ahead emigration reached flood level. Within a century the population of Ireland was less than half of what it had been in 1841.

THE STRUGGLE FOR HOME RULE   Fewer Irish did not mean more manageable Irish, however. On multiple fronts, violent and non-violent, the Irish people kept up the pressure on Britain, and some partial concessions were won, but gratitude was minimal, all the same. The return of selected stolen goods appears generous only to thieves. What the Irish wanted back was Ireland, intact: land, religion, language, and law. In the 1870s and 1880s, Ireland's Member of Parliament, Charles Stewart Parnell, was able to unite various factions of Irish nationalists, including the Fenian Brotherhood in America and the Land League, to fight for home rule. In a tumultuous decade of legislation, he came close, but revelations about his long affair with Kitty O'Shea, wife of a former follower, brought about his downfall, and brought an end to the legislative quest for home rule.

THE EASTER REBELLION & THE WAR OF INDEPENDENCE   Coming close may count for something in horseshoes or high tuba notes, but not in revolution, and near-misses on the negotiated front opened the way to violence. The 1912 defeat of the third Home Rule Bill in the House of Lords, after it had passed in the House of Commons, was followed in 1913 by the founding of the Irish Citizens Army and the Irish Volunteers. Revolution was imminent. The motive had been there for centuries, the ability was in development, and the opportunity was around the corner. In 1916, the Irish would celebrate Easter, the feast of the Resurrection, in unique fashion.

On Easter Monday, 1916, the Irish tricolor flag was raised over the General Post Office in the heart of Dublin. Inside were 1,500 fighters, led by the Gaelic League's Patrick Pearse and Socialist leader James Connolly. From here, Pearse read the newly written Proclamation of the Irish Republic, and from here his men fought off the British for six days before being captured. Pearse, Connolly, and twelve other leaders were imprisoned, secretly tried, and speedily executed.

In looking back over Irish history for those turning points that cumulatively led to the violence of 1916, the War of Independence, and the Irish Civil War, William Butler Yeats wrote of four bells that tolled for Ireland, one at each of its irreversibly decisive moments: the Flight of the Earls, the Battle of the Boyne, the spread of French revolutionary ideas under the United Irishmen, and the fall of Parnell. However it is that we trace the path to violence, the 1916 rising, compounded by the savage stupidity of the British response, all but guaranteed that Ireland's future would be decided by the gun. Like the religious faith they had strained for centuries to preserve, the Irish faith in revolution was seeded and nourished by the blood of martyrs, martyrs the British had been fools enough to provide.

1916

From the Proclamation of the Irish Republic, issued April 24, 1916, the day the Dublin Rising began:

Irishmen and Irishwomen: In the name of God and of the dead generations from which she receives her old tradition of nationhood, Ireland, through us, summons her children to her flag and strikes for her freedom.

Having organized and trained her manhood through her secret revolutionary organization, the Irish Republican Brotherhood, and through her open military organizations, the Irish Volunteers and the Irish Citizen Army, having patiently perfected her discipline, having resolutely waited for the right moment to reveal itself, she now seizes that moment, and, supported by her exiled children in America and by gallant allies in Europe, but relying in the first on her own strength, she strikes in full confidence of victory.

We declare the right of the people of Ireland to the ownership of Ireland, and to the unfettered control of Irish destinies, to be sovereign and indefeasible. The long usurpation of that right by a foreign people and government has not extinguished the right, nor can it ever be extinguished except by the destruction of the Irish people . . .

The Irish republic is entitled to, and hereby claims, the allegiance of every Irishman and Irishwoman. The republic guarantees religious and civil liberty, equal rights and equal opportunities to all its citizens, and declares its resolve to pursue the happiness and prosperity of the whole nation and of all its parts, cherishing all the children of the nation equally, and oblivious of the differences carefully fostered by an alien government, which have divided a minority from the majority in the past . . .

The last straw for the British was the landslide victory of Sinn Féin in the general election of 1918 and Sinn Féin's subsequent proclamation of the first Dáil, or independent parliament. The declaration of independence issued two years earlier from the General Post Office now seemed a good deal more real. When the British attempted to smash the new parliament, the result was the War of Independence, in which the Irish forces, led by Michael Collins, eventually forced the British to the negotiating table.

The Anglo-Irish Treaty of 1921 gave independence to only 26 of 32 Irish counties. The fate of the remaining six counties in Ulster was yet to be decided. Meanwhile, they would remain within the United Kingdom. Some of the Irish, weary of war, accepted compromise as close enough to victory and embraced the Free State of Ireland. Others, led by Eamon de Valera, shouted betrayal and declared the Free State their latest enemy. The ensuing civil war claimed many casualties, including Michael Collins and Cathal Brugha, two of the revolution's shining heroes.

Victory, if civil wars have winners, went to de Valera and those who opposed the treaty. They did not overturn it, though, and their successors have yet to do so. Instead, they reformed the government and led the new Free State of Ireland out of the ravages of war and into the rigors of peace. The Free State, in passing the Republic of Ireland Act in 1948, severed its last constitutional ties to Britain and only 25 years later joined the European Community, pursuing its ties to Europe where the Irish people had for centuries looked for friendship and support.

Ireland was the first colony acquired by the British empire and nearly the last to be relinquished, but regrettably, this story still has no proper ending. The "troubles" spawned by the partitioning of Ireland in 1921 live on, a wound so far refusing to

Hatred answering hatred, death answering to death through the generations like clerks at the mass.

—Lady Gregory (1852–1932)

be healed. There remain two Irelands, fewer than there have been in the past and yet, for some, still one too many.

5 Some Movers & Shapers of Ireland's 20th Century

SAMUEL BECKETT (1906–89)   Playwright and novelist, Beckett is one of four Irish winners of the Nobel Prize for Literature (1969). A native of Dublin, he taught French at Trinity College, Dublin. In 1938, he moved to France, where he served as a secretary to James Joyce, became involved with the French Resistance, worked with the Irish Red Cross, and wrote. His most performed drama, *Waiting for Godot* (1952), remains one of the definitive plays of the 20th century. Beckett's brilliance was minimalist in style, paring words and gesture to the bone, creating more with less.

BRENDAN BEHAN (1923–64)   Playwright, travel writer, journalist, IRA activist, and raconteur, Behan is remembered for his boisterous ways as well as for his writings. His best works include his autobiography, *Borstal Boy* (1958), and the plays *The Quare Fellow* (1954) and *The Hostage* (1958), first written in Irish. The streets of his native Dublin are the setting for many of his works.

CHRISTY BROWN (1932–81)   Novelist and poet, this Dubliner was born with severe physical disabilities and was educated at home by his mother, who taught him to write with his left foot. His autobiography, *My Left Foot* (1954), was adapted into the Oscar-winning film of the same name. His other works include *Down All the Days* (1970) and *Wild Grow the Lillies* (1976).

MICHAEL COLLINS (1890–1922)   Michael Collins was born and raised in West Cork, the son of a farmer, and at age 15 emigrated to London, where he joined Sinn Féin, the Irish Republican Brotherhood, and in 1914 the Irish Volunteers. Two years later, he returned to Ireland to avoid British conscription. Within several months, at age 26, Collins found himself in the General Post Office fighting a losing revolution, and subsequently returned to Britain in irons. Before the year was out, however, he was back in Dublin, on the supreme council of the IRB. In the war for independence, Collins was the legendary commander-in-chief of the IRA, everywhere and nowhere, striking and eluding the British as if he were a phantom. Having brought the British to the negotiating table, he accepted the division of Ireland with great reluctance, hoping to avoid further bloodshed and judging it to be the best deal the Irish would get. He knew and said, at the same time, that the treaty would prove to be his death warrant. He was right. On August 22, five days before he would have turned 31, he was ambushed and assassinated. In 1996, his story, with Liam Neeson in the title role, was put on film by director Neil Jordan.

JAMES CONNOLLY (1868–1913)   Born of poor Irish Catholic parents in Edinburgh, Connolly worked from age 11 and at 14 falsified his age to enlist in the British army. After being posted in Dublin, he deserted, returned to Scotland, and eventually made his way back to Ireland where he founded the Irish Socialist Republican Party. Unable to support a family in Dublin, Connolly emigrated to America, where he was active in the launching of the I.W.W. (Industrial Workers of the World) and himself founded the Irish Socialist Federation in New York City. Several years later, however, he was back in and at it in Ireland, closing the port of Dublin to bring about the release of James "Big Jim" Larkin (see below). In 1916, Connolly was appointed commandant-general of the Dublin forces and led the assault on the General Post Office. Wounded and unable to stand for his own execution, he was strapped to a chair when brought before the Kilmainham firing squad.

EAMON DE VALERA (1882–1975)   This Irish nationalist politician was born in New York of an Irish mother and Spanish father. When his father died in 1885, de Valera was sent by his mother back to Ireland, where he was raised by his grandmother in Co. Limerick. He joined the Irish Volunteers in 1913 and commanded the Boland's Mills garrison in the 1916 Easter Rising, for which he received the death sentence, eventually commuted on account of his American citizenship. After fiercely opposing the Anglo-Irish Treaty and serving with the IRA in the Irish civil war, de Valera formed Fianna Fáil and went on to become the first president of Dail Eireann, the Irish Parliament, and the first Taoiseach (prime minister). From 1959 to 1973, he served as president of the Republic.

OLIVER ST. JOHN GOGARTY (1878–1957)   Poet, wit, surgeon, senator, and athlete, Gogarty served as a model for the Buck Mulligan character in *Ulysses,* written by his friend James Joyce. His own writings include *As I Was Going Down Sackville Street* (1937), *Tumbling in the Hay* (1939), and *I Follow Saint Patrick* (1939). He was born in Dublin but spent most of his life in Connemara.

MAUD GONNE (1865–1953)   Born in England and educated on the French Riviera, Gonne spent several years in Ireland when her father, a colonel in the British army, was posted to Dublin Castle. Moved by the Irish cause, she pledged herself to the Irish struggle. Although she turned down a proposal of marriage from W. B. Yeats, Gonne founded with him the Association Irlandaise in Paris and later played the title role in his momentous production of *Cathleen ní Houlihan.* She was a member of the secret Irish Republican Brotherhood and later founded two organizations: Inghinidhe na hÉireann (Daughters of Ireland) and the Women's Prisoner's Defense League. Imprisoned in 1923, she was released after beginning a hunger strike. Maud Gonne has been called Ireland's Joan of Arc.

SEAMUS HEANEY (b. 1938)   Born and educated in Derry, this celebrated contemporary poet has been called Ireland's Robert Frost and, perhaps more appropriately, a latter-day Yeats. Heaney's poems about his homeland in the North of Ireland can be found in his collections *North* (1975), *Field Work* (1979), *Station Island* (1984), and *Seeing Things* (1991). In 1995 he was awarded the Nobel Prize in Literature, the fourth Irishman to be so honored.

EVIE HONE (1894–1955)   One of Dublin's great 20th-century artists, Hone specialized in stained-glass work. Her windows are featured in many churches and public buildings in Dublin, including the National and Hugh Lane Galleries, and as far away as Eton College in England.

NATHANIEL HONE (1831–1917)   An engineer who turned to art, Hone is one of the foremost and most prolific Irish painters of the 19th century. Principally a landscape and seascape artist, this Dubliner painted in a muted color range, and his works are considered a precursor to Impressionism. A large collection of his works is found at the National Gallery.

JAMES JOYCE (1882–1941)   Born in Dublin, Joyce left the city at age 22 and spent most of his life abroad. Even so, he used Dublin as the setting for all of his writings, including his masterwork, *Ulysses* (1922). Joyce's other writings include *Portrait of the Artist as a Young Man* (1916), *Dubliners* (1914), and *Finnegan's Wake* (1938). Although his imaginative stream-of-consciousness works were banned in Ireland when they were first published (for indecency), he eventually was recognized as a great 20th-century novelist by his own people.

JAMES LARKIN (1876–1947)   James Larkin, born into an impoverished Irish emigrant family in Liverpool, spent his first eight years with his grandparents in Co. Down. At the age of nine he returned to Liverpool and went to work. Larkin, a dockworker, eventually rose to foreman, but lost his job and became a union organizer after he supported his fellow workers in a strike. He thereafter became notorious for his militancy and eloquence. In Dublin in 1909, "Big Jim" founded the Irish Transport and General Workers' Union and served as its general secretary. In and out of prison in Ireland, he sailed to America to raise money for the struggle and wound up spending nearly three years in Sing Sing, having been convicted of "criminal anarchy." Returning to Ireland, he founded the Irish Workers' League, became a Dublin city councilor, and served in the Dáil (parliament) from 1937 to 1938 and again from 1943 to 1944.

HUGH LEONARD (b. 1926)   Born John Keyes Byrne, this master playwright is one of the most successful of Dublin's contemporary writers. *Da* (1975) dramatizes his relationship with his maddeningly selfless foster father, and *A Life* (1981) reflects his own experience in Dublin.

CONSTANCE MARKIEVICZ (1868–1927)   Born in London but raised at Lissadell, Co. Sligo, she studied in Paris and married Count Casimir Dunin-Markievicz, who returned with her to live in Ireland. Inspired by the cause of Irish freedom, she joined the Irish Citizen Army, participated in the 1916 Rising, and was president of Cumann na mBan, the women's auxiliary force of the Irish Volunteers. She later became the first woman elected to the parliament in Westminster but chose to serve instead in the first Irish Dáil and became Ireland's first minister for labor.

SEAN O'CASEY (1880–1964)   Born into poverty as John Casey in Dublin, this Abbey Theatre playwright based three of his greatest works on his early life in Dublin tenements: *The Shadow of a Gunman* (1923), *Juno and the Paycock* (1924), and *The Plough and the Stars* (1926).

FRANK O'CONNOR (1882–1941)   Michael O'Donovan's mother, to whom he was greatly devoted, was an O'Connor, and as a writer he took her name. His father was a laborer and had served as a bandsman in the British Army. In his teens, he worked as a railway clerk and volunteered for the IRA. Later, in the civil war, he fought against the treaty and was imprisoned at age 20. After his release from prison, he became a librarian and began to publish the stories that would soon make him famous. In 1935 he directed the Abbey Theatre, a position he resigned several years later. Throughout his life, O'Connor's voice and pen gave expression to a balance of wit, poignancy, integrity, and severe criticism, which made him both a delight and a challenge to his readers.

PATRICK PEARSE (1879–1916)   Trained as a lawyer in Dublin, Pearse was an educator and poet who worked, fought, and died in the cause of Irish freedom. As commander-in-chief of the Irish Republican Brotherhood and the Irish Volunteers, he led the 1916 Easter Rising, proclaimed the birth of the Irish Republic, and accepted unconditional surrender five days later. He was executed by firing squad in Kilmainham Jail. His poems such as "The Rebel" and "The Mother," found together in *Collected Works* (1917), have brought him further acclaim in recent years.

AUGUSTA PERSSE / LADY GREGORY (1852–1932)   Born in Co. Galway, she married Sir William Gregory of Coole Park. Influenced by a childhood familiarity with Irish folklore, she developed an interest in literature and a friendship with W. B. Yeats; together, they founded the Abbey Theatre. She wrote more than 30 plays, including *Spreading the News* (1904) and *Goal Gate* (1906) and made Coole Park the headquarters of the Irish Literary Revival.

GEORGE BERNARD SHAW (1856–1950)   Author of *Man and Superman* (1903), *Major Barbara* (1905), *Pygmalion* (1912), *Candida* (1903), and *St. Joan* (1923), Shaw won the Nobel Prize for Literature in 1926. Although he left school at age 15, Shaw spent a great deal of time at the National Gallery in Dublin and later credited the institution with providing the best part of his early education (and he bequeathed one third of his royalties to the gallery). His birthplace, at 33 Synge St., is a museum in his honor.

JOHN MILLINGTON SYNGE (1871–1909)   Noted Abbey Theatre playwright and one of the founders of the Irish Literary Revival, Synge was born in Dublin but is best remembered for plays that reflect rural life in western Ireland, including *The Shadow of the Glen* (1903), *Riders to the Sea* (1904), and *Playboy of the Western World* (1907).

JACK BUTLER YEATS (1871–1957)   Like his older brother the poet, Jack Yeats's imagination was profoundly influenced by the west of Ireland, specifically Sligo, where he spent much of his childhood. After studying art in London and settling in Devon, Yeats returned to Ireland in 1910 and, after illustrating works at the heart of the Irish Literary Revival, began to establish his own international repute as a painter in oils. Yeats wrote a number of books, including memoirs, novels, and plays, although these garnered less recognition than his drawings and paintings.

WILLIAM BUTLER YEATS (1865–1939)   Poet and dramatist, Yeats was also a founding member of the Abbey Theatre. His poems and plays, which deal with mystic and Celtic legendary themes, won him a Nobel Prize for Literature in 1923. Yeats served in the Irish Senate but rejected a knighthood in 1915. He was born in Dublin and summered in the West, particularly in Sligo, where he is buried.

6 Language

Ireland has two official languages, Irish and English. Today, English is the first and most commonly spoken language for the vast majority of the Irish people, although Irish instruction is compulsory in the public schools. In fact, every public school teacher must pass a proficiency examination in Irish in order to be certified. All Irish citizens are entitled by law to conduct any official business with the state in the Irish language: legal proceedings, university interviews, and the filing of taxes, for example. According to a 1991 census, the population of the *Gaeltacht,* comprising those scattered regions of the country where Irish is the first and, in some cases, only language spoken, was nearly 80,000. Irish speakers, however, are not confined to the *Gaeltacht.* Dublin, for instance, has a significant number of Irish-speaking individuals and families.

Irish, a Celtic language, belongs to the same Indo-European family as most European tongues. Modern Irish descends from Old Irish, the language of Ireland's Golden Age and the earliest variant of the Celtic languages. While the Irish-speaking population of Ireland was reckoned at four million in 1835, it stands now at only a quarter of that figure. Even so, poets and playwrights continue to write in Ireland's mother tongue, and Irish programming holds its own on television and radio.

This [Ireland] has never been a rich or powerful country, and, yet, since earliest times, its influence on the world has been rich and powerful . . . and no larger nation has ever provided the world with more literary or artistic geniuses.
—John F. Kennedy, addressing the Irish Parliament, June 1963

7 The Arts

VISUAL ARTS

Three-dimensional, geometric figures etched into prehistoric granite slabs and burial tombs in the Irish countryside are the earliest specimens of Irish art. The 6th century saw delicate enamel work and manuscript illumination produced at monasteries. The Tara Brooch, the Ardagh Chalice, the Cross of Cong, and the recently restored Derrynaflan chalice and paten are just some of the early Irish artistic gems displayed in the National Museum.

Without question, the Book of Kells, on view at Trinity College Dublin, is Ireland's greatest treasure. Dating from the late 8th or early 9th century, the Book of Kells predates the monastery of Kells in Co. Meath, where it was found, and may have been produced on the island of Iona.

The decorative arts flourished in Ireland in the 17th and 18th centuries. Exquisite silverware, plasterwork, cut glass, hand-carved furniture, and tapestries were created and filled the great Georgian and Palladian-style homes built for the gentry who settled in Ireland from Great Britain.

The lush Irish countryside, with its varied colors and ever-changing skies, lends itself wonderfully to landscape painting. Among Ireland's great artists of this genre were James Arthur O'Connor and Paul Henry, the latter of whom studied at Whistler's studio in Paris before settling down to paint in Connemara. Contemporary artists Brian Bourke and Camille Souter take a post-modern approach to landscapes. Patrick Hickey and Pauline Bewick are acclaimed for their distinctive graphic arts. North and South, Ireland boasts more than 100 art galleries. In Dublin, no less than 50 galleries are found, and it seems more spring up each day. The relatively new Irish Museum of Modern Art (IMMA) also showcases contemporary creativity.

ARCHITECTURE

The fortification walls surviving at least in part around many Irish towns and cities can be credited to the Normans, who also built great churches and cathedrals but are best remembered for their castles. Many Norman castles are still occupied today, while others recline, moss-covered, more or less as ruins, some with rectangular keeps, lichened towers, and time-worn turrets making mute gestures into the empty air above.

The British left their own unique architectural legacy, from the Georgian avenues, squares, and public buildings of Dublin, Limerick, and Armagh to the sprawling "big houses" of the countryside. Built by the Anglo-Irish aristocracy and absentee landlords, these manor homes date from the 17th and 18th centuries and reflect a spirit of "spare no expense." More than 40 of these great houses, originally occupied by the rich and powerful, are now open to the public as museums. Others have been converted into hotels.

Also dotting the rural landscape are simple whitewashed, thatched-roof stone cottages, traditionally the homes of farming people, though many of these have traded in their cottages for modern bungalows and two-story stucco homes.

Modern Irish architecture tends toward glass-and-concrete construction, but many newer buildings are designed to blend harmoniously with nearby Georgian, Edwardian, and Victorian landmarks.

CRAFTS

One of the most famous of Irish crafts is the thick bainin sweater, which is made of oiled wool and was first hand knit on the Aran Islands to protect the local fishermen against the elements and, forgive the ghoulishness, to identify them through their distinctive individual weave patterns if they drowned at sea. These oatmeal-colored garments are still knit in cottages on the islands and in homes all over the west of Ireland.

With all the sheep that graze on the Irish hillsides, it's not surprising that wool is a source for another major craft: hand-weaving. Weaving is done in homes and local factories, the latter of which are usually open to visitors, particularly in areas like Donegal and Connemara. Ireland's oldest hand-weaving mill, dating from 1723, is found in a cluster of stone buildings at Avoca in Co. Wicklow. With mauve, heather, and teal tones, the Avoca tweeds reflect the colors of the local landscape; these tweeds are fashioned into capes, coats, ponchos, suits, jackets, bedspreads, and rugs.

Waterford is one of Ireland's most famous craft trademarks. At the Waterford Crystal Factory, every step of the creative process can be viewed, from glass-blowing and shaping to hand-cutting and engraving to polishing and packaging. More than 3,000 visitors pass through the factory each workday. Other glass-making centers that welcome the public are located in Dublin, Tipperary, Galway, Cavan, Sligo, Killarney, Kinsale, Wexford, Cork, Belfast, and Tyrone.

Pottery and porcelain making is done in all parts of the Emerald Isle. Some of the leading names include Royal Tara China (Galway), Donegal Parian China (Ballyshannon), and the most famous of all, Belleek (Fermanagh).

Other Irish crafts include basketry, heraldry, batik, patchwork, wood carving, doll making, enamel painting, lace making, pewter casting, candle making, gold and silver jewelry design, printmaking, stained glass, and beaten copper art. Shopping for these crafts often provides an opportunity to talk with the artisans and to watch them practice their trades.

MUSIC

Music seems to inhabit Ireland and follow the Irish wherever they go. It is as commonplace as conversation. Many traditional Irish instruments—the flute and bodhran come to mind—are easily made from what lies ready to hand, nearly as available as the human voice. From these the Irish have created a tradition that continues to delight and to captivate musicians and listeners worldwide.

Many Irish Americans may think they know a thing or two about Irish music, but often the songs that are close to their hearts and that they'll belt out at family gatherings—songs like "Mother Macree" and "When Irish Eyes Are Smiling"—are not, in fact, authentically Irish. They belong to the Irish American tradition, expressing the sentiments and sensibilities of those for whom Ireland is a matter of reminiscence or reverie rather than daily lived experience.

The authentic music of Ireland is of a slightly different sort. Modern scholarship continues to plumb the past of this music, and recent speculation has proposed that Celtic music may be ancient. In fact, the music's timbral and tonal qualities point to a meeting at some point in the distant past between the people who would become the Celts and the people who would become the Asians. This would explain the uncanny results obtained when The Chieftains, Ireland's preeminent traditional

Impressions

No harp hath the sound so long and so melting as the Irish harp.

—Francis Bacon

ensemble, performed with a traditional Chinese ensemble in 1985 (documented on Shanachie Records's *The Chieftains in China*). In terms of history, music in Ireland, as in most of Europe, can trace its beginnings to the bards of medieval times, who traveled the countryside singing songs, usually to the accompaniment of a harp. In Ireland, the harp was the principal musical instrument in historical times and was adopted, in the 17th century, as the central figure in Ireland's coat of arms. In fact, the harp remains the chief symbol or emblem of the Irish Republic. Although the songs of the bards were seldom written down, the works of one such poet, harpist, and composer, Turlough O'Carolan, have survived and provide the basis for many modern-day airs.

First used almost 300 years ago, the uilleann (pronounced *ill*-un) pipes are often referred to as the Irish organ. This popular form of bagpipe is pumped with the elbow and produces a softer, more resonant sound that its Scottish counterpart. Other instruments used to produce the distinctive sounds of Irish music are the concertina (a smaller version of the accordion), fiddle, flute, tin whistle, and bodhran (pronounced *bour*-awn), a hand-held drum that is played with a distinctive technique and can best be described as a large, jingleless tambourine. The Irish have also been known to improvise with anything from a washboard to a set of spoons. In recent years, groups like The Chieftains and individual performers such as James Galway from Belfast and Phil Coulter from Derry have done much to popularize authentic Irish music throughout the world. Others, like Shaun Davey, Mícheál Ó Súilleabháin, and Vincent Wallace have experimented with Irish music in a larger, orchestral setting.

At any time, one of the best places to hear good Irish music is, of course, a pub. No matter when you visit, scheduled and spontaneous music sessions are on tap. Irish music is also featured at festivals, hotel cabarets, summer shows, and at venues dedicated to traditional entertainment, such as the National Folk Theatre of Ireland in Tralee, An Taibhdhearc in Galway, the Bru Boru Center at Cashel, Culturlann na hÉreann near Dublin, Cois na hAbhna in Ennis, and the Shannon Traditional Evening at the Bunratty Folk Park.

On the contemporary music scene, the Irish continue to make an audible contribution. The members of U2, musician and concert organizer Bob Geldof, Sinead O'Connor, and Mary Black call Dublin home. Van Morrison hails from Belfast. Other Irish musicians and groups—like Enya, Chris de Burgh, Clannad, the Cranberries, the Saw Doctors, the Pogues, and Dervish—are household names well beyond the Liffey and the Irish Sea. Ireland is to bands what Findhorn is to squash, so there's always a chance that the street musician you hear on Grafton Street or the noname group you stumble across in a Dublin club may be on the cover of *Time* within the year.

8 Keeping Body & Soul Together: Irish Food & Drink

NOT JUST BOILED POTATOES ANYMORE

In the last 25 years, Irish cuisine has undergone a major makeover. Previously, Ireland enjoyed a singular reputation for overcooked meats, waterlogged vegetables, piles of potatoes, and cream-on-cream desserts. Recently, however, healthful preparation and appealing presentation of fresh natural ingredients have become the norm, or at least the measure of success.

The transformation of Irish cuisine did not have to start from scratch. The raw materials had always been there—beef and lamb nurtured on Irish pastures, an abundance of freshwater fish and ocean seafood, a bounty of agrarian produce, and dairy goods straight from the local creamery. It seems that travel inspired Irish chefs to take the next step. Abroad, they learned the arts of French nouvelle cuisine and California au courant. At the same time, visitors came to Ireland in greater numbers and requested crisper, more recognizable vegetables and a wider selection of seafood. In kitchens from Dublin to Donegal, the "new Irish cuisine" now reigns. To prove it, Irish chefs regularly bring home dozens of gold medals from the International Food Olympics.

A note of caution: Although a new standard has been set for Irish cooking, it is still quite common to find vegetables boiled into oblivion, and the once rampant white sauce is far from endangered or extinct.

MEALS & DINING CUSTOMS   Mealtimes in Ireland are similar to those in the United States, with most hotels and restaurants offering breakfast from 6 or 7am to around 10am, lunch from noon to 2 or 3pm, and dinner from 6 or 7pm to 10 or 11pm.

Breakfast in Ireland can be continental (juice, rolls or toast, coffee or tea) or "full Irish" (juice, fruits, yogurt, cereal, eggs, bacon, sausage, brown bread, toast or scones, coffee or tea, and sometimes fish). If you choose the full breakfast, you'll probably be content with a snack for lunch.

In many rural parts of Ireland, the agrarian tradition of a big dinner at midday still holds, with a light supper, or high tea, at night. In the cities, lunch can be a light or full meal, and the evening dinner is usually the main family meal of the day. The upper-priced restaurants prefer to sell set lunches, usually three or four courses, but most others offer snacks, sandwiches, salads, or a variety of hot and cold entrées.

Most restaurants have fixed-price three- or four-course dinner menus, known locally as table d'hôte, and an à la carte menu for picking and choosing. The fixed-price menus usually offer the best value, unless, of course, you want to skip an appetizer and dessert and just have a salad/soup and a main course.

To all of this, add morning coffee, usually around 11am, and afternoon tea around 3 or 4pm. The latter can be as simple as a cup of tea on the run or as formal as a sit-down gathering at a fine hotel with a brewed pot of tea, finger sandwiches, pastries, and other sweets arrayed on a silver tray and accompanied by piano or harp music. After a proper afternoon tea, some visitors have been known to skip dinner.

THE CUISINE   The star of most menus is seafood, formerly considered penitential fare. In particular, it's hard to equal wild Irish salmon, caught daily from local rivers. Served steamed or broiled with a wedge of lemon, it's pink, delicate, and sweet. As an appetizer—or starter, as the Irish say—think Irish salmon, slowly oak-smoked and thinly sliced with capers and lemon. Most visitors become so addicted to it that they take home at least a side of smoked salmon, vacuum-packaged for travel. Another good prospect is the Dublin Bay prawn, one of Ireland's most popular seafoods. It's a more tender version of a shrimp but a cousin to the Norway lobster in flavor. Plump and succulent, prawns are equally tempting served either hot with melted butter or cold with a light cocktail sauce. Want more? There's Galway Bay oysters, Kinsale and Wexford mussels, Kerry scallops, Dingle Bay lobster, and Donegal crab. Dig in.

And lest you think the Irish have gone Inuit (Eskimo), there's the traditional land-based fare. Irish beef, for instance, has always been a favorite with the natives as well as with visitors, and it's exported all over the world. These days you'll not only get your choice of steaks, but you can also order fillet of beef en croûte, stir-fry beef, beef stuffed with oysters, beef flambèed in Irish whiskey, or beef sautèed in Guinness. And then there's lamb, lean racks and legs of which are the pride of Irish chefs. Ever wonder about all those sheep roaming the countryside? Not all of them are there to be made into sweaters.

As part of the standard, traditional Irish breakfast, you'll almost certainly be served a hefty portion of pork, whether it's the famous Limerick ham, zesty homemade sausages, or thick country bacon, which is one of the great pleasures of life (assuming you're not vegetarian).

Traditional roast chicken will usually be the tasty free-range variety, accompanied by lean Irish bacon or ham and an herby bread stuffing. Breast of chicken wrapped around local mushrooms or smoked salmon mousse are also popular choices.

One of Ireland's most humble foods is also one of its greatest culinary treasures: brown bread. Made of stone-ground whole meal flour, buttermilk, and other "secret" ingredients, Irish brown bread is served on the tables of every restaurant in the country. Brown bread, be it light or dark, firm or crumbly, sweet or nutty, is always delicious, especially when the crust is crispy. Shedding all restraint, add a little rich creamery butter or homemade raspberry jam.

Some traditional dishes adapted to the new lighter cuisine might include boxty (a potato pancake filled with meats, vegetables, or fish), crubeens (pig's feet), colcannon (potatoes mashed with scallions and cabbage), coddle (boiled bacon, sausages, onions, and potatoes), boiled bacon and cabbage (a precursor to the Irish American St. Patrick's Day favorite, corned beef and cabbage), and, above all, the classic Irish lamb stew.

Irish desserts (sometimes called sweets) range from cakes (often called gâteaux), pies, and American-style cheesecakes to a seasonal array of fruit salads or simple dishes of fresh strawberries. With a little effort, you can still find some of the rich traditional dishes such as trifle, a fruit salad combined with custard and sherry-soaked cake and topped with a roof of rich double cream, and plum pudding, a whiskey-based soft fruitcake usually reserved for Christmas and special occasions. Other native desserts include barm brack, a light and yeasty fruitcake, and raisin-filled soda cake.

Irish farmhouse cheeses offer a piquant alternative to rich and sweet confections. More than 60 cheeses are now produced throughout the land, and many restaurants pride themselves on the quantity and quality of their all-domestic cheese boards.

THE BLACKNESS OF THE ALE & OTHER STORIES OF IRISH DRINK

With apologies to every nationality in the world (the opinions expressed do not reflect the views of the author, Macmillan Publishing, etc., etc.), there's an old, old ditty that goes like this:

> The Dutchman for a drinker
> The Dane for golden locks
> The Irishman for uisce beatha
> The Frenchman for you-know-what.

Crude, yes, but it makes a good introduction to the story, which goes that Irish monks concocted the first brew of whiskey for medicinal purposes in the 6th century. These same inventive monks carried the recipe on a mission to Scotland. They called their brew uisce beatha (pronounced ish-ka ba-ha) which in Irish means "the water of life"; shortly afterward, it was Anglicized to whiskey. In 1608, a license to distill alcohol was granted to Old Bushmills; it remains the world's oldest distillery still in operation, and invites visitors.

Irish whiskey differs from Scotch or English whiskey in the method of distillation. While the Scottish/English mode requires the use of smoke-dried malted barley, the Irish use a combination of local malt and unmalted barley, which is allowed to dry naturally without the aid of heat and smoke. The result gives Irish whiskey a clear, smooth, and smokeless taste. Among the leading brands of Irish whiskey are the afore-mentioned Bushmills, John Jameson, Powers, Paddy's, Tullamore Dew, Murphy, and Dunphy.

The Irish like to drink their whiskey "neat," which means without ice, water, or other mixers. Whiskey is also the sine qua non for Irish Coffee, an after-dinner drink made by adding some to a goblet of hot coffee mixed with sugar, and then topping it off with a dollop of fresh cream.

In recent years, Irish Coffee has met competition from sweet Irish whiskey–based drinks like Bailey's Irish Cream and Irish Mist. These after-dinner libations have, in turn, inspired desserts like Irish Mist soufflè and Bailey's Irish ice cream.

And then there's Guinness. A black, yeasty ale with a thick, foamy head, it's the most widely consumed national drink, the undisputed king of the pubs, and one of the world's great beers. Brewed in Dublin since Arthur Guinness first established the drink in 1759, it depends for full effect on being trucked fresh from the brewery at St. James's Gate straight to the nation's pubs. Even then, the quality of the draft you'll be served depends on the artfulness of its server. It requires a deftness of hand, a sure command of timing, and a little bit of magic to pour the perfect pint, and once you've sipped a few, you'll begin to appreciate the difference. Once sold under the slogan "Guinness Is Good for You," the stuff is still almost considered a healthful drink, a meal in a glass. Mother's milk, as it were. The Guinness Company also produces a light lager beer called Harp and a nonalcoholic beer known as Kaliber. Other Irish beers include Smithwicks, brewed in Kilkenny, and Beamish and Murphys, produced in Cork.

Tap water in Ireland is both pure and plentiful. Sparkling Irish bottled waters, such as Ballygowan, Glenpatrick, and Tipperary, are readily available, rivaling Perrier and other international brands. Not surprisingly, Irish tea holds its own. Barry's Tea is produced in Cork. For coffee drinkers, Bewley's is the name to remember.

9 Irish Hospitality

Every guide to Ireland has a section on "the people" in which the Irish are consis-tently and concisely canonized. You would think it was compulsory. In fact, the Irish people are at least as complex as any other. Yes, Ireland has its share of saints and scholars, but they remain the exception. Then why do visitors return home so charmed? No two ways about it: It's precisely because of these complex people. Ireland without the Irish would be like Elvis's guitar without Elvis. Ireland would just sit there without the Irish to play it.

We may assume that at home, with his family, Elvis was not greeted by screams as he entered the kitchen in the morning. Similarly, visitors rave about the Irish more than the Irish rave about themselves. So what is there to rave about? I think a story may do this job better than anything else.

Six or seven years ago, when a friend from Boston—we'll call him Dan Smith—stopped by our home south of Dublin, he told us how he had been traveling around Ireland for a week, after taking a ferry to Rosslare. It was his first time in the coun-try. On his first day he tried to place a collect call to his sister in Detroit from a pay phone. There was no answer. He explained to the operator that he would be making his way west to Ballycullane, where he had booked a B&B, and would try later from there.

Impressions

In Ireland the inevitable never happens, and the unexpected constantly occurs.
—Sir John Pentland Mahaffy (1839–1919)

That same evening, Dan found his way to a pub in Ballycullane, after checking into his B&B. While he was still on his first pint, the phone rang and the bartender answered it. A moment later he held up the phone and shouted "Is there a Dan Smith here?" Dan called out and went over to the phone.

"Mr. Smith," said the operator, "I have your sister in Detroit on the line for you." "My sister?" muttered a confused Dan. "Yes, your sister in Detroit, who you were trying to ring at noontime." "But how did you . . ." started Dan, before being cut off. "Now you said you would be in Ballycullane," interrupted the operator, "and Ballycullane has only two pubs. And I'm just after trying the other one. This is long distance, Mr. Smith, would you be wanting to talk with your sister, then?"

What is most startling about this story is how commonplace it is. It's just the kind of story visitors to Ireland come back with.

10   Recommended Books, Periodicals & Films

BOOKS

Published in 1984, *The Course of Irish History* remains an excellent, accessible introduction to the full sweep of Irish history and prehistory, written by a collection of Irish scholars and edited by T. W. Moody and F. X. Martin, of Trinity College Dublin and University College Dublin, respectively (Cork: Mercier, 1987). Another Irish scholar, Peter Harbison, has produced a number of fine books on Ireland's history, art, and architecture, any of which, read in advance, would enhance your visit to Ireland. I single out his most recent, written with Jacqueline O'Brien: *Ancient Ireland* (London: Weidenfeld and Nicolson, 1996), a coffee-table book with dazzling photographs of ancient sites and generous, illuminating text. Next, a recent best-seller, Thomas Cahill's *How the Irish Saved Civilization* (New York: Doubleday, 1995), presents a compelling and extremely readable glimpse into Ireland's golden age.

With the framework of Irish history in place, you may want to read some of Ireland's oldest texts, in translation. Thomas Kinsella's translation of *The Tain* (New York: Oxford University Press, 1970) provides a stunning version of this epic, Ireland's *Iliad,* which recounts the invasion of Ulster and the feats of Cúchulainn, a Bronze Age superhero. John J. O'Meara's translation of *The Voyage of St. Brendan,* (Humanities Press), and Tim Severin's *The Brendan Voyage* (New York: McGraw Hill, 1978) make a fascinating double-feature for anyone intrigued by the claim that Irish monks discovered America in the 6th century. Next, Seamus Heaney's version of the medieval *Buile Suibhne* (Sweeney Astray) retells the adventures of Sweeney, a king gone mad in battle, cursed by a saint, and turned poet (New York: Noonday, 1995). Finally, Marie Heaney, wife of the Nobel laureate, has provided a marvellous compendium of Irish stories, from the oldest myths to the lives of the Irish saints, in *Over Nine Waves: A Book of Irish Legends* (Boston: Faber and Faber, 1994).

Let's face it. Celts are really "in" at the moment, and so it may be helpful to recommend several titles for Celts or Celt wannabes eager to explore their roots. Peter Beresford Ellis, made an official Cornish bard in 1987, has written two books of special interest: *The Celtic Empire: The First Millennium of Celtic History* (Durham, N.C.: Carolina Academic Press, 1990) and *The Druids* (Grand Rapids, Mich.: Eerdmans, 1994). Two other related and intriguing books are Nigel Pennick's *Celtic*

Sacred Landscapes (New York: Thames and Hudson, 1996) and Miranda Green's *Celtic Goddesses: Warriors, Virgins and Mothers* (New York: George Braziller, 1996).

Finally, there's about a zillion books by and about Irish immigration, but a recent standout is New York educator and author Frank McCourt's best-selling memoir *Angela's Ashes,* which recounts the author's boyhood in Co. Limerick and eventual emigration as a young man (New York: Simon and Schuster, 1996).

For general information about Ireland, one volume, available from the Irish Department of Foreign Affairs, is near indispensable. Its understated title, *Facts About Ireland,* might well be altered to read *Everything You Ever Wanted to Know About Ireland But Didn't Know Who to Ask.* Copies may be requested from your nearest Irish consulate.

PERIODICALS

For the most up-to-date news on Ireland, consider a subscription to any of these periodicals, all published in Dublin:

- *ie Ireland* on the Net is Ireland's first guide to the Internet and interactive media, published bimonthly by Ryan Media and offering the latest on Ireland's life on the Web. Its newsstand price is £1.95 ($3.10) per issue, but its online edition can be found at **http://www.iol.ie/.ie**.
- *Inside Ireland* is a quarterly newsletter packed with the latest details on life in Dublin and happenings all over Ireland. It also provides an information service, genealogical advice, regular updates on buying property and/or retiring in Ireland, shopping news, and coupons that entitle subscribers to discounts at hotels and restaurants. It's the next best thing to having your own correspondent in Dublin, for just $40 a year or $3 for a sample copy. Contact *Inside Ireland,* Rookwood, Stocking Lane, Ballyboden, Dublin 16, Ireland (☎ **01/493-1906**).
- *Ireland of the Welcomes* is a full-color bimonthly magazine published by the Irish Tourist Board, but it's not just another tourism promotion publication. It is a finely written, well-researched periodical that spotlights ongoing events and celebrations, new attractions, unique driving routes, legends and lore, flora and fauna, traditions and the arts, noteworthy trends, and interesting personalities. If you're planning a trip, it offers regular sections on where to stay and shopping. $21 a year. Contact *Ireland of the Welcomes,* P.O. Box 84, Limerick, Ireland.

FILMS

Throughout film history, Ireland and the Irish have been a focal movie subject, and everyone has his or her favorites: *The Quiet Man,* various Bing Crosby films, Barry Fitzgerald as the Irish curmudgeon or the Irish drunk. What many of these films have partly created and unquestionably preserved is an impression of Irish life that may be endearing at a distance but is demeaning at close range. Sentimentality, superstition, and stout form the core of that impression. Malarkey, in a word. As an antidote, I would suggest a handful of films that are more fair to the facts in their depiction of contemporary Irish life. They describe the Ireland visitors are more likely to encounter on the ground: Noel Pierson and Jim Sheridan's *My Left Foot;* Alan Parker's *The Commitments; A Man of No Importance,* starring Albert Finney; and *In the Name of the Father,* filmed partly in Dublin's Kilmainham Jail. Two additional films for the whole family, deeply magical without bursting into sentimentality, are *Into the West* and *The Secret of Roan Innish.* Lastly, for a highly affecting look at the War of Independence and the civil war, check Neil Jordan's *Michael Collins.*

Planning a Trip to Ireland

It may be well to begin with a caution, offered in this case by John Steinbeck in *Travels With Charley:* "A journey is like a marriage. The certain way to be wrong is to think you control it." Fair enough. A trip too tightly packed and planned, with no room for the spontaneous and unexpected, is often not worth the effort. And yet, when we are so poorly prepared that surprise runs riot, we may wish we'd stayed home. In travel as in Buddhism, the middle ground is to be recommended. Lay down your plans like pavement, and then romp on the grass at will. Our aim in this chapter is to help you prepare the way.

1 Visitor Information & Entry Requirements

SOURCES OF INFORMATION

To get your planning underway, contact the following offices of the Irish Tourist Board and/or the Northern Ireland Tourist Board. They're anxious to answer your questions, and they've got bags of genuinely helpful information, mostly free of charge. After you've perused the brochures, take a quick surf through the Net if you're online, to scoop up even more information.

In the United States
- **Irish Tourist Board,** 345 Park Ave., New York, NY 10154 (☎ **800/223-6470** from the U.S., or 212/418-0800; fax 212/371-9052).
- **Northern Ireland Tourist Board,** 551 Fifth Ave., Ste. 701, New York, NY 10176 (☎ **800/326-0036** from the U.S., or 212/922-0101; fax 212/922-0099).

In Canada
- **Irish Tourist Board,** 160 Bloor St. E., Ste. 1150, Toronto, Ontario M4W 1B9 (☎ **416/929-2777;** fax 416/929-6783).
- **Northern Ireland Tourist Board,** 111 Avenue Rd., Ste. 450, Toronto, Ontario M5R 3J8 (☎ **416/925-6368;** fax 416/961-2175). Internet: http://interknowledge.com/northern-ireland

In the United Kingdom

- **Irish Tourist Board / Bord Failte,** 150 New Bond St., London W1Y OAQ (☎ **171/493-3201;** fax 171/493-9065).
- **Northern Ireland Tourist Board / All Ireland Desk,** British Travel Centre, 12 Lower Regent St., Picadilly Circus, London SW1 4PQ (☎ **0800/282662**).

In Australia

- **Irish Tourist Board,** 36 Carrington St., 5th Level, Sydney, NSW 2000 (☎ **02/ 9299-6177;** fax 02/9299-6323).

In Ireland

- **Irish Tourist Board / Bord Failte,** Baggot Street Bridge, Dublin 2 (☎ **01/ 676-5871;** fax 01/676-4764).
- **Northern Ireland Tourist Board,** 16 Nassau St., Dublin 2 (☎ **1/850/230230** reduced toll [in Ireland], or 01/679-1977).

In Northern Ireland

- **Irish Tourist Board,** 53 Castle St., Belfast BT1 1GH (☎ **1232/327-888;** fax 1232/240-201).
- **Northern Ireland Tourist Board,** 59 North St., Belfast BT1 1NB (☎ **01232/ 246-609;** fax 01232/240-960).

INTERNET SITES

Ireland is far more Net-savvy than you might suspect. The principal Irish server is **ireland on-line.** One useful directory of sites that would be of general interest to visitors to Ireland is **http://www.paddynet.com**, which offers a comprehensive list of Irish Web sites, various information on all things Irish, and the opportunity to send PaddNet postcards to your friends. Fun!

Like the cells in our bodies or the hairstyles on supermodels, it is the nature of the Net to undergo constant change and proliferation, so don't curse us too loudly if the specific listings below have changed by the time they reach you. The point we're trying to make here is that there is a mother lode of information about Ireland on the Net, and that these are some good places to position your shovel as you start digging:

- **Best of Ireland**
  http://www.iol.ie/~discover/welcome.htm
- **The Eirepages**
  http://ezinfo.ucs.indiana.edu/~kerfishe/home.html
- **Every Celtic Thing on the Web (Irish)**
  http://www.mi.net/users/ang/angiris.html
- **Ireland: The Internet Connection**
  http://itdsrv1.ul.ie/information/ireland.html
- **Irish Interests Links Page**
  http://www.indigo.ie/poreilly/ireland.html
- **Irish Web Server Map**
  http://slarti.ucd.ie/maps/ireland.html
- **IRLnet**
  http://wombatix.physics.ucg.ie/cgi-bib/irlnet-dir

In addition to these general listings, a number of cities, provinces, and regions have sites of their own on the Net, providing up-to-date local information. The URL or

Internet address is the same for all of these, except for the last name of the city or area in question. For example, the city.net URL for Dublin is:

http://www.city.net/countries/ireland/dublin/

For Cork, replace /*dublin*/ with /*cork*/, and so on. At the time of writing, 18 cities and counties have sites posted. All of the major universities in Ireland also have their own sites.

ENTRY REQUIREMENTS

DOCUMENTS   For citizens of the United States, Canada, Australia, and New Zealand entering the Republic of Ireland for a stay of up to three months, no visas are necessary but a valid passport is required.

Citizens of the United Kingdom, when traveling on flights originating in Britain, do not need to show documentation to enter Ireland. Nationals of the United Kingdom and Colonies not born in Great Britain or Northern Ireland must have a valid passport or national identity document.

For entry into Northern Ireland, the same conditions apply.

CUSTOMS   Since the European Union's (EU) introduction of a single market on January 1, 1993, goods brought into Ireland and Northern Ireland fall into two categories: (1) goods bought duty-paid and value-added-tax (VAT)-paid in other EU countries; and (2) goods bought under duty-free and VAT-free allowances at duty-free shops.

Regarding the first category, provided that the goods are for personal use, there is no further duty or VAT to be paid. The limits for goods in this category are as follows: 800 cigarettes, 10 liters of spirits, 45 liters of wine, and 55 liters of beer. This category normally applies to Irish citizens, visitors from Britain, and travelers from other EU countries.

Regarding the second category, which pertains primarily to overseas visitors such as U.S. and Canadian citizens, the following duty-free and VAT-free items may be brought into the country for personal use: 200 cigarettes, one liter of liquor, two liters of wine, and other goods (including beer) not exceeding the value of £34 ($42.70) per adult. There are no restrictions on bringing currency into Ireland.

The Irish and Northern Irish customs systems operate on a Green-, Red-, and Blue-Channel format. The first two choices are for passengers coming from the United States and non-EU countries. The Green Channel is for anyone not exceeding the duty-free allowances, while the Red Channel is for anyone with extra goods to declare. If you are like most visitors, bringing in only your own clothes and personal effects, choose the Green Channel. The Blue Channel, the latest addition to the system, is exclusively for use by passengers entering Ireland from another EU country.

In addition to your luggage, you may bring in sports equipment for your own recreational use or electronic equipment for your own business or professional use while in Ireland. Prohibited goods include firearms, ammunition, and explosives; narcotics; meat, poultry, plants, and their by-products; and domestic animals from outside the United Kingdom.

Impressions

Journeys, like artists, are born not made. A thousand differing circumstances contribute to them, few of them willed or determined by the will—whatever we may think.
—Lawrence Durrell (1914–91)

2 Money

CASH/CURRENCY   Until the adoption, possibly in the year 2000, of a single EU currency (the EURO), the 26 counties of the Republic of Ireland continue to have an independent currency system, the basic unit of which is the Irish pound £ or punt. Inside Ireland, it is mostly referred to as "the pound," as distinct from the British pound, known as "the pound sterling." The Irish and British pounds trade independently on the currency market and fluctuate more or less freely with respect to each other and to the dollar. Until quite recently, the British pound dominated the Irish pound. The traditional and assumed subservence of the Irish pound, however, appears to be a thing of the past, as the Irish pound has lately taken the lead. I recall that, when I first traveled to Ireland, the punt and the dollar were at parity. Or am I dreaming that?

Remember that the six counties of Northern Ireland, as part of Great Britain, use the British pound, not the Irish. The Irish pound is not accepted as legal tender in the North.

Both the Irish and the British pounds are generically symbolized by a £ sign. The Irish pound is, however, officially designated by the £ sign preceded by IR: IR£. Each unit of paper currency is called a note. The pound notes, which are printed in denominations of £5, £10, £20, £50, and £100, come in different sizes and colors (the larger the size, the greater the value). There are still some £1 notes in circulation, although these are being phased out in favor of the £1 coin. (The old £1 note is a work of art, so try to find one before they disappear.) Since 1971, the Irish monetary system has been on the decimal system; so, for instance, every pound is divided into 100 pence ("p"); coins come in denominations of £1, 50p, 20p, 10p, 5p, and 1p.

The British currency used in Northern Ireland, identified by engravings of British royalty, follows pretty much the same pattern as that of the Republic, with notes in denominations of £5, £10, £20, £50, and £100. Coins are issued to the value of £1, 50p, 20p, 10p, 5p, 2p, and 1p.

Note: The value of both the Irish and the British pound fluctuates daily, so it is best to begin checking the exchange rates well in advance of your visit so as to gain a sense of their recent range. It's always a gamble when and where to convert and how much. Shop around and avoid exchanging in airports and train stations. Banks are best, and on any given day one bank will be offering a better rate than another. Since any purchase on a U.S. credit card offers an exchange rate far more favorable than

Irish Punt & U.S. Dollar Equivalents

At the time of writing, one punt costs $1.60 and the pound sterling stands at $1.55, which are the figures used to calculate all dollar costs in this book. The dollar is considered weak at the moment. May you fare better!

IR£	U.S.$	U.S.$	IR£
0.50	0.80	0.50	0.31
1.00	1.60	1.00	0.62
5.00	8.00	5.00	3.12
10.00	16.00	10.00	6.25
50.00	80.00	50.00	31.25
100.00	160.00	100.00	62.50

Northern Irish / British Pound & U.S. Dollar Equivalents

£	U.S.$	U.S.$	£
0.50	0.78	0.50	0.32
1.00	1.55	1.00	0.64
5.00	7.75	5.00	3.22
10.00	15.50	10.00	6.45
50.00	77.50	50.00	32.25
100.00	155.00	100.00	64.50

anything an individual is likely to negotiate, I make a point of converting as little currency as possible and using my credit card to the max. Whatever you do, don't convert small amounts daily, as if you were shopping for bread. The fees alone will impoverish you. Rates of exchange are, of course, available daily in most newspapers, and on the Net you can consult **http://vacation-inc.com/exchange_rates.html**, or, if you want your math done for you, check out the GNN/Klobas Currency Converter at **http://www.macgrawnet.com/currenc.htm**.

TRAVELER'S CHECKS   Traveler's checks are readily accepted in the Republic of Ireland and Northern Ireland, and they bring a better exchange rate than does cash. In general, banks provide the best exchange rates, followed by bureaux de change. Most banks and exchange bureaus post their daily exchange rates up front, so you can window-shop for the best rate.

   Hotels, restaurants, and stores also accept traveler's checks, though often at a less than favorable rate. *Note:* Personal checks, even when presented with your passport, are not usually accepted by banks or places of business, unless you are a member of the Eurocheque scheme or have made prior arrangements in advance.

CREDIT CARDS   Leading international credit cards such as American Express, Carte Blanche, Diners Club, MasterCard (also known as Access or Eurocard), and Visa (also known as Visa/Barclay) are readily acceptable throughout all 32 counties. Most establishments display the symbols or logos of the credit cards they accept on their windows or shop fronts.

3 When to Go

CLIMATE

You have to be part psychic to even begin making bets on Irish weather, but don't bet too heavily. The only thing consistent about Irish weather is its changeability; often, the best of times and the worst of times may be only hours, or sometimes even minutes, apart.

   With that disclaimer solidly in place, it's safe to offer a few useful observations. If you think east equals dry and west equals wet, you'll be right except when you're wrong, which will be less than half the time. More specifically, the driest and sunniest parts of Ireland are the northeast and the southeast, which is not to say that they are reliably either dry or sunny.

   Irish thermometers, gratefully, are a lot less busy than their barometers. That's to say that the temperatures in Ireland are mild and fluctuate within what any New Englander would call "spring." The generally coldest months, January and February, bring frosts but seldom snow, and the warmest months, July and August, rarely become hot. Remember, in Ireland anything over 70° is "hot" and 32° is considered

What Things Cost in Dublin	U.S. $
Taxi from the airport to the city center (£13)	20.80
Express bus from airport to city center (£2.50)	4.00
Bus minimum fare (55p)	.88
Local telephone call (20p)	.32
Double room at the Shelbourne Hotel (deluxe) (£159)	254.00
Double room at Temple Bar Hotel (moderate) (£95)	152.00
Double room at Jurys Christchurch (inexpensive) (£49)	78.40
Double room at Avalon House (budget) (£26)	41.60
Lunch for one at Il Primo (moderate) (£7.50)	12.00
Lunch for one at Juice (inexpensive) (£4.95)	7.92
Lunch for one at Bewley's (budget) (£3.50)	5.60
Dinner for one, without wine, at The Commons (deluxe) (£32)	51.20
Dinner for one at Roly's Bistro (moderate) (£21)	33.60
Dinner for one at Chez Jules (inexpensive) (£8.90)	14.24
Pint of Guinness (£2.10)	3.36
Shot of Irish whiskey (£1.85)	2.96
Glass of wine (£3)	4.80
Coca-Cola in a cafe (80p)	1.28
Cup of coffee (80p)	1.28
Admission to see the Book of Kells at Trinity College (£3.50)	5.60
Admission to the National Museum	Free
Movie ticket (£4.75)	7.60
Ticket to the Abbey Theatre (£10)	16.00

freezing. Both are unusual. For a complete guide to Irish weather on the Net, including year-round averages and daily updates, consult **http://www.iol.ie/~discover/ meteo1.htm**.

When packing, "layers" is the word to remember, anytime of year. And don't forget wool—the Irish attraction to it is no accident. One further tip: The Irish are becoming more and more casual in their dress, so you can think Oregon rather than Manhattan.

In sum, the weather is neither the reason for coming to Ireland nor a reason for staying away, unless you're looking for the beaches of Mexico or Greece, which remain in Mexico and Greece.

Average Monthly Temperatures in Dublin

	Jan	Feb	Mar	Apr	May	June	July	Aug	Sept	Oct	Nov	Dec
Temp (°F)	36–46	37–48	37–49	38–52	42–57	46–62	51–66	50–65	48–62	44–56	39–49	38–47
Temp (°C)	2–8	3–9	3–9	3–11	6–14	8–17	11–19	10–18	9–17	7–13	4–9	3–8

HOLIDAYS

The Republic observes the following national holidays: New Year's Day (January 1); St. Patrick's Day (March 17); Good Friday (mostly observed, though not statutory); Easter Monday; May Day (first Monday in May); first Monday in June and August

What Things Cost in Galway	U.S. $
Bus flat-rate fare (65p)	1.04
Local telephone call (20p)	.32
Double room at the Glenlo Abbey (deluxe) (£159)	254.40
Double room at Ardilaun House Hotel (moderate) (£70)	112.00
Double room at Jury's Inn (inexpensive) (£42)	67.20
Lunch for one at the Grapevine (moderate) (£7)	11.20
Lunch for one at Conlon and Sons (inexpensive) (£3.95)	6.32
Lunch for one at Bewley's (budget) (£3.50)	5.60
Dinner for one, without wine, at de Burgos (deluxe) (£26)	41.60
Dinner for one at Bridge Mills (moderate) (£20)	32.00
Dinner for one at Conlon and Sons (inexpensive) (£16)	$25.60
Pint of Guinness (£1.65)	2.64
Shot of Irish whiskey (£2.05)	3.08
Glass of wine (£2.50)	4.00
Coca-Cola in a cafe (65p)	1.04
Cup of coffee (60p)	.92
Admission to the Dun Guaire Castle (£2.50)	4.00
Admission to Galway Museum (£1)	1.60
Cruise on Lough Corrib (£5)	8.00
Round-trip boat to Aran Islands (£16)	25.60
Ticket to the Druid Theatre (£8)	12.08

(Summer Bank Holidays); last Monday in October (Autumn Bank Holiday); Christmas (December 25); and St. Stephen's Day (December 26).

In the North, the schedule of holidays is the same as in the Republic, with several exceptions: the North's Bank Holidays fall on the last Monday of May and August; the Battle of the Boyne is celebrated on Orangeman's Day (July 12); and Boxing Day (December 26), not St. Stephen's Day, follows Christmas.

The only Irish holiday that's likely to attract tourists to Ireland is St. Patrick's Day, which in Ireland is traditionally a religious and family day. The massive parade and adjunct delirium associated with March 17 in Boston, New York, and Chicago is a recent import to Ireland—an accommodation on Ireland's part to an idea hatched abroad. The tail wags the dog: Dublin's St. Patrick's Day parade is an imitation of those in the United States, not the original thing. Although the Irish participation in and taste for the event are growing, many of the bands and marchers, and a great many of the crowd, are visitors, creating what they came over to watch. For some, this is the day of all days to be in Dublin; and who's to say it's not? I'd recommend another day, though. Any other day.

IRELAND CALENDAR OF EVENTS

This sampling of events is drawn from 1996 schedules. Be sure to consult the corresponding calendars available from the tourist boards of Ireland and of Northern Ireland for the year in which you plan to travel.

What Things Cost in Belfast	U.S. $
Taxi from the airport to the city center (£15)	23.25
Express bus from the airport to the city center (£3.70)	5.73
Bus minimum fare (90p)	1.39
City sightseeing tour (£7.50)	11.62
Local telephone call (10p)	.16
Double room at the Culloden (deluxe) (£150)	232.50
Double room at Dukes (moderate) (£95)	147.25
Double room at Ash Rowan (inexpensive) (£60)	93.00
Lunch for one at Saints and Scholars (moderate) (£8)	12.40
Lunch for one at Skandia (inexpensive) (£6)	9.30
Dinner for one, without wine, at Roscoff (deluxe) (£28.95)	44.87
Dinner for one, without wine, at Nick's Warehouse (moderate) (£24)	37.20
Dinner for one, without wine, at Harvey's (inexpensive) (£16)	24.80
Bottle of beer (£1.90)	2.94
Shot of Bushmills whiskey (£2)	3.10
Glass of wine (£1.80)	2.79
Cup of coffee (80p)	1.24
Admission to Ulster Museum	Free
Movie ticket (£3.80)	5.89
Ticket to Grand Opera House (£12)	18.60

January

- **From Here to the White House.** A major exhibition tracing the Irish roots of 15 U.S. presidents, from Andrew Jackson to Bill Clinton. **Where:** Ulster-American Folk Park, Omagh. **When:** January 2 to June 30.
- **Coca-Cola International Cross-Country.** International Amateur Athletics Federation world competition. **Where:** Mallusk, Belfast. **When:** January 6.

February

- **Éigese na Brídeoige / Biddy Festival.** A bilingual festival celebrating spring, the feast of St. Brigid, and the local culture of south Kerry. **Where:** Waterville, Ballinskelligs, Co. Kerry. **When:** February 2 to 4. **How:** Contact Pádraig de Buis, Cliff Road, Waterville, Co. Kerry (☎ **066/74123;** fax 066/74503).
- **Cavan International Song Festival.** An international competition for original (popular) songs. **Where:** Hotel Kilmore, Cavan, Co. Cavan. **When:** February 3.

March

- **Belfast Musical Festival.** Held every year since 1911, this is a youth competition in speech, music, and drama categories. **Where:** Balmoral, Belfast. **When:** March 4 to 15.
- **St. Patrick's Day.** Parades and other festivities in celebration of Ireland's patron saint. **Where:** All over Ireland. **When:** March 17.
- **North-West Storytelling Festival.** Captivating tales performed by a dozen of the Northwest's most celebrated storytellers. **Where:** Derry. **When:** March 28 to 31.

- **West Cork Drama Festival.** An annual event showcasing the finest amateur drama groups. **Where:** Rossmore, Clonakilty, Co. Cork. **When:** March 7 to 17. **How:** Contact Mr. Gerard Finn, Rossmore, Clonakilty, Co. Cork (☎ **066/74123;** fax 023/38681 or 023/38607).
- **Limerick International Church Music Choral Festival.** A competitive festival that attracts choirs and choral groups from throughout Ireland and the world. **Where:** St. Mary's Cathedral, Limerick. **When:** March 22 to 24. **How:** Contact Fergus Quinlivan (☎ **061/41799** or 061/22194).

April

- **Tour of the North.** An international cycling race starting from Bangor and finishing in Ballymena. **When:** April 5 to 8.
- **Samhlaíocht / Kerry Arts '96.** A spring festival of music, drama, dance, film, literature, craft, and visual art. **Where:** Siamsa Tíre Theatre and Arts Centre, Tralee, Co. Kerry. **When:** April 6 to 9. **How:** Contact Maggie Fitsimmons, director (☎ **066/29934;** fax 066/27276).
- **Féile Pan-Cheilteach / Pan-Celtic Festival.** Heading into its 26th year, this Pan-Celtic festival includes competitions in traditional music, song, and dance. **Where:** Tralee, Co. Kerry. **When:** April 9 to 14. **How:** Contact Kaye O'Keefe, chairperson, Cnoc Mhuire, Oakpark, Tralee, Co. Kerry (☎ **066/26027**).
- **Punchestown Irish National Hunt Festival Race Meeting. Where:** Naas, Co. Kildare. **When:** April 22 to 24. **How:** Contact Charles Murless, manager, Punchestown Racecourse, Naas, Co. Kildare (☎ **045/897704;** fax 045/897319).
- **City of Belfast Spring Flower Festival.** Floral show, with trade stands, crafts, and bands. **Where:** Maysfield, Belfast. **When:** April 27 to 29.

May

- **Cork International Choral Festival.** Ireland's premier choral event featuring competitive and noncompetitive performances by adult choirs of international standing, as well as performances by Irish and foreign dance groups. **Where:** Multiple venues in Cork. **When:** May 2 to 5. **How:** Contact Sheila Kelleher, administrator, P.O. Box 68, Cork (☎ **021/308308;** fax 021/308309).
- **Wicklow Mountains May Walking Festival.** Choice of organized walks, roughly either 9 or 16 miles, including an ascent of Lugnaquillia. **Where:** West Co. Wicklow. **When:** May 4 and 5. **How:** Contact Wicklow County Tourism, Kilmantin Hill, Wicklow (☎ **0404/66058;** fax 0404/66057).
- **Belfast Marathon and Fun Runs.** An epic race of 4,500 runners through the city. **Where:** Start and finish at Masfield, Belfast. **When:** May 6. **How:** Contact the Northern Ireland Tourist Board for further details.
- **Belfast Civic Festival.** Floats, bands, concerts, exhibitions, and guided tours mark this two-week celebration. **When:** May 11-25. **How:** Contact the Northern Ireland Tourist Board for further details.
- **County Wicklow Gardens Festival.** Heritage properties and gardens, as well as many private properties, open their gates to visitors on selected dates. **Where:** Throughout Co. Wicklow and surrounding areas. **When:** May 17 to June 23. **How:** Contact Wicklow County Tourism, Kilmantin Hill, Wicklow (☎ **0404/66058;** fax 0404/66057).

June

- **Strawberry Fair.** A feast of luscious and ripe Wexford-grown strawberries is the focus at this event, which also includes kite flying, craft exhibitions, pub talent, photo and art exhibitions, sports, and open-air entertainment. **Where:**

Enniscorthy, Co. Wexford. **When:** June 2 to July 7. **How:** For details, contact Margot Hogan, Riverdale, Parklands, Enniscorthy, Co. Wexford (☎ **054/34623**).

- **Edenderry Three-Day Canal Angling Festival.** A festival organized by the Edenderry Coarse Angling Club to promote angling in the area. Tourists are welcome to take part, provided they book in advance. **Where:** Canals around Edenderry, Co. Offaly. **When:** June 3, 5, 7. **How:** Contact Mr. Paddy Joe Foy, chairman, or Mrs. Frankie Staunton, secretary (☎ **098/26206** or 098/25626).

- **AIB Music Festival in Great Irish Houses.** A series of classical music concerts in great houses throughout Ireland. **When:** June 5 to 16. **How:** Contact Crawford Tipping, Blackrock Post Office, Co. Dublin (☎ **01/278-1528;** fax 01/2781529).

- **Fleadh Amhrán agus Rince.** A festival in celebration of traditional Irish song and dance. **Where:** Ballyclare, Co. Antrim. **When:** June 14 to 16.

- **Siamsa / Galway Folk Festival.** Celebration of Irish music, singing, and dance. **Where:** Taibhdhearc Theatre, Middle Street, Galway. **When:** June 25 to August 31. **How:** Contact Cepta Byrne, director, 18 Wood Lands Green, Renmore, Co. Galway (☎ **091/755479** or 091/562024; fax 091/563195).

- **Feis na nGleann.** A festival of traditional Irish music, dance, poetry, crafts, and sports. A chance to see a number of traditional Gaelic games. **Where:** Glenariff, Co. Antrim. **When:** June 29 and 30.

- ✪ **Irish Open Golf Championship.** This is Ireland's premier international golf event, televised to over 90 countries and featuring the world's top players. **Where:** St. Margaret's Golf Club, Dublin. **When:** Last weekend of June. **How:** For details, contact the Irish Tourist Board.

July

- ✪ **Budweiser Irish Derby.** One of the richest races in Europe and widely accepted as the definitive European middle-distance classic, this race is Ireland's version of the Kentucky Derby or Royal Ascot. It's a fashionable gathering of racing fans from all over Ireland and abroad. The Curragh Racecourse has recently added a new betting hall, bars, and a food hall. **Where:** The Curragh, Co. Kildare. **When:** Last Sunday in June or first weekend of July. **How:** For full information, contact the Curragh Racecourse Office, the Curragh, Co. Kildare (☎ **045/441205;** fax 054/441442). **Note:** An Irish Racing Calendar for each calendar year is also available from the Irish Tourist Board.

- **Festival of West Cork.** A week of daytime and evening entertainment, including brass band competitions, poetry readings, parades, pub singing finals, art shows, and other events. **Where:** Clonakilty, Co. Cork. **When:** July 5 to 14. **How:** Contact Christy Hinchy, Gullane, Clonakilty, Co. Cork (☎ **023/33532**).

- **Battle of the Boyne Commemoration.** This annual event, sometimes called Orangeman's Day, recalls the historic battle between two 17th-century kings and is a national day of parades and celebration all over Northern Ireland. **Where:** Belfast and 18 other centers. **When:** July 12. **How:** Contact the Northern Ireland Tourist Board.

- **Ballina Salmon Festival.** A celebration in honor of Ireland's salmon, providing a week of free family entertainment, including various children's events. **Where:** Ballina, Co. Mayo. **When:** July 12–21. **How:** Contact Des Clarke, PRO, c/o Moy Valley Resources, Cathedral Road, Ballina, Co. Mayo (☎ **096/70905**).

- **Lughnasa Fair.** A spectacular revival set in a 12th-century Norman castle. Costumed magicians, entertainment, and crafts. **Where:** Carrickfergus Castle, Co. Antrim. **When:** July 27.

✪ **Galway Arts Festival and Races.** A two-week feast in the streets of Galway, featuring international theater, big-top concerts, literary evenings, street shows, arts, parades, music, and more, followed by five days of racing and more merriment, music, and song. **Where:** Galway City and Racecourse. **When:** July 17 to 28. **How:** Contact Galway Arts Festival Office, P.O. Box 123, Galway (☎ **091/ 561516**).

August

• **International Maiden of the Mournes Festival.** With the Mountains of Mourne as its setting, this festival includes concerts, music, dance, cabaret, banquets, and the crowning of the Maiden of the Mournes. **Where:** Warrenpoint, Co. Down. **When:** August 3 to 11.

✪ **Letterkenny International Folk Festival.** For several decades, this event has drawn people to north Donegal for the music of top Irish and international artists, plus ceilis (evenings of Irish music and dance), workshops, and more. **Where:** Letterkenny, Co. Donegal. **When:** August 12 to 18. **How:** Contact Pat Gallagher, Letterkenny Festival Office, Letterkenny, Co. Donegal (☎ **074/27856;** fax 074/ 27016).

✪ **Yeats International Summer School.** For more than 35 years, this has set the standard for Ireland's many summer schools. Designed for literary enthusiasts and followers of Yeats, it offers lectures, seminars, poetry, reading, tours, music, and more. **Where:** Yeats Memorial Bldg., Hawk's Well Theatre, Sligo. **When:** August 3 to 17. **How:** Contact Maura McTighe, president, Yeats Memorial Bldg., Hyde Bridge, Sligo (☎ **071/42693;** fax 071/42780).

• **Puck Fair.** Each year the residents of this tiny Ring of Kerry town carry on an ancient tradition by capturing a wild goat and enthroning it as "king" over two days of unrestricted merrymaking. **Where:** Killorglin, Co. Kerry. **When:** August 10 to 12. **How:** Contact Geraldine O'Sullivan (☎ **066/61595;** fax 066/61654).

✪ **Rose of Tralee Festival.** A carnival-like atmosphere prevails at this five-day event, with a full program of concerts, street entertainment, horse races, and a beauty/ talent pageant leading up to the selection of the "Rose of Tralee." **Where:** Tralee, Co. Kerry. **When:** August 23 to 29. **How:** Contact Eileen Kenny or Eleanor Carrick, Rose of Tralee Festival Office, Ashe Memorial Hall, Denny Street, Tralee, Co. Kerry (☎ **066/21322** or 066/23227; fax 066/22654), or E-mail Liam Looney at **llooney@staffmail.rtc-tralee.ie**.

✪ **Kilkenny Arts Week.** This one-week festival features a broad spectrum of the arts, from classical and traditional music to plays, one-person shows, readings, films, poetry, and visual arts exhibitions. **Where:** Kilkenny. **When:** August 17 to 25. **How:** Contact Sighle Tóibin, Kilkenny Arts Week, Rothe House, Parliament Street, Kilkenny (☎ **056/63663;** fax 056/51704).

• **Fleadh Cheoil.** This is Ireland's major summer festival of traditional music, with competitions to select the all-Ireland champions in all categories of instruments and singing. **Where:** The venue changes each year. **When:** Last weekend of August.

• **Oul' Lammas Fair.** Chartered in 1606, this is Ireland's oldest traditional fair. **Where:** Ballycastle, Co. Antrim. **When:** Last weekend of August.

September

✪ **Galway International Oyster Festival.** First held in 1954, this event attracts oyster aficionados from all over the globe. Highlights include the World Oyster-Opening Championship, golf tournament, yacht race, art exhibition, gala banquet, traditional music and song, and lots of oyster eating. **Where:** Galway and environs. **When:** September 2 to 29. **How:** Contact The Secretary, Galway Oyster Festival Aras Failte, Galway (☎ **091/527282** or 091/522066; fax 091/527282).

- **Causeway Coast International Triathlon.** Swimming, cycling, and running for a total of 32 miles. **Where:** Portrush, Co. Antrim. **When:** September 7. **How:** Contact the Northern Ireland Tourist Board.

- **Irish Bird-Watching and Wildlife Fair.** Marks the arrival in Ireland of huge flocks of swans and other birds. **Where:** Lough Neagh Discovery Centre, Co. Armagh. **When:** September 14 and 15. **How:** Contact the Northern Ireland Tourist Board.

- **Waterford International Festival of Light Opera.** For nearly 40 years, this has been a major gathering for amateur music societies from all over Ireland and Britain. **Where:** Theatre Royal, Waterford. **When:** September 21 to October 6. **How:** Contact Seán Dower, general secretary (☎ **051/75437**).

October

- **Twentieth International Gourmet Festival.** Participants feast on the best cuisine of the many restaurants in the gourmet capitol of Ireland. Entertainment provided by the Kinsale Good Food Circle. **Where:** Kinsale, Co. Cork. **When:** October 3 to 6. **How:** Contact Peter Barry, c/o Kinsale Chamber of Tourism, Kinsale, Co. Cork (☎ **021/774026**).

- ✪ **Wexford International Festival Opera.** For more than 40 years this event has been highly acclaimed for its productions of 18th- and 19th-century operatic masterpieces plus classical music concerts, recitals, and more. **Where:** Wexford. **When:** October 17 to November 3. **How:** Contact the Box Office, Theatre Royal, High Street, Wexford (☎ **053/22144;** fax 053/47438).

November

- ✪ **Belfast Festival at Queens.** Ulster's best-known arts festival, this annual 19-day event attracts a huge following to enjoy drama, opera, music, and film events in and around Queens University. **Where:** Queens University, Belfast. **When:** November 4 to 23. **How:** For details, contact the Northern Ireland Tourist Board.

- **West Cork One-Act Drama Festival.** Amateur drama groups produce a festival of one-act plays. **Where:** Rossmore, Clonakilty, Co. Cork. **When:** November 15 to 17. **How:** Contact The Secretary (☎ **023/38681**).

December

- **Enniscorthy Cultural and Street Festival.** A seasonal weekend of carol singing, street pageantry, busking competition, and street entertainment. **Where:** Enniscorthy, Co. Wexford. **When:** December 7 to 10. **How:** Contact Richard Barry, secretary, 58 Weafer St., Enniscorthy, Co. Wexford (☎ **054/35893;** fax 054/88822).

- **Cinemagic International Film Festival for Young People.** Ten-day festival of short and feature-length films for children and teenagers. **Where:** Various venues throughout the North. **When:** Early December. **How:** For details, contact the Northern Ireland Tourist Board.

DUBLIN CALENDAR OF EVENTS

January

- **Rugby International, Ireland v. Scotland. Where:** Landsdowne Road, Ballsbridge. **When:** January 20. **How:** Contact Irish Rugby Football Union, 62 Lansdowne Rd., Dublin 4 (☎ **01/668-4601;** fax 01/660-5640).

March

⚫ **Dublin Film Festival.** More than 100 films are featured, with screenings of the best of Irish and world cinema, plus seminars and lectures on filmmaking. **Where:** Irish Film Centre and at various movie houses. **When:** March 5 to 14. **How:** For schedules and ticket information, contact the Irish Film Centre, 6 Eustace St., Dublin 2 (☎ **01/679-2937**).

• **St. Patrick's Day Parade.** Ireland's biggest parade, with marching bands, drill teams, floats, and delegations from around the world. **Where:** O'Connell Street, Dublin. **When:** March 17. **How:** Contact the Irish Tourist Board.

April

⚫ **Feis Ceoil.** In spite of its Gaelic name, this 11-day springtime event is not a traditional music gathering. It is a mostly classical competitive music festival that covers all instruments including voice. There are more than 150 categories featuring orchestral and choral events, with duets, trios, and ensembles of all sizes. **Where:** RDS, Ballsbridge. **When:** Between mid-March and mid-April (dates change annually). **How:** For full information, contact Feis Ceoil Office, 37 Molesworth St., Dublin 2 (☎ **01/676-7365**).

• **Howth Jazz Festival.** The attractive fishing port of Howth, 10 miles north of Dublin, hosts three days of nonstop jazz in a variety of local venues. **When:** April 6 to 8. **How:** Contact Declan Hanratty, 3 Sutton Downs, Dublin 13 (☎ **01/ 835-4777**).

May

• **Irish Garden Festival.** A focal event for the avid home gardener as well as for landscape professionals. **Where:** Royal Hospital, Kilmainham. **When:** May 30 to June 3. **How:** Contact Liam Plunkett, festival director, SDL Ltd., 18 Main St., Rathfarnham, Dublin 14 (☎ **01/490-0600;** fax 01/490-8934).

June

⚫ **Bloomsday.** Dublin's unique day of festivity commemorates 24 hours in the life of Leopold Bloom, the central character of James Joyce's *Ulysses.* Every aspect of the city, including the menus at restaurants and pubs, seeks to duplicate the aromas, sights, sounds, and tastes of Dublin on June 16, 1904. Special ceremonies are held at the James Joyce Tower and Museum, and there are guided walks of Joycean sights. **Where:** The streets of Dublin and various venues. **When:** June 16. **How:** Contact the James Joyce Cultural Centre, 35 North Great George's St., Dublin 1 (☎01/873-1984).

• **Co-operation North Maracycle Event.** Several thousand cyclists race between the cities of Dublin and Belfast, each making a 206-mile round-trip. **Where and When:** Starting in Dublin on June 21, and in Belfast on June 22. **How:** Contact Alison McCrum, organizer, 37 Upper Fitzwilliam St., Dublin 2 (☎ **01/661-0588** or 01/676-3608; fax 01/661-8456).

⚫ **AIB Music Festival in Great Irish Houses.** This is a continuous ten-day festival of classical music performed by leading Irish and international artists in some of the Dublin area's great Georgian buildings and mansions. **Where:** Various venues throughout Dublin and neighboring Counties Wicklow and Kildare. **When:** June 5 to 16. **How:** Contact Crawford Tipping, Blackrock Post Office, Main Street, Blackrock, Co. Dublin (☎ **01/278-1528;** fax 01/278-1529).

July

• **Temple Bar Blues Festival.** Dublin's "West Bank" plays host to bands from England, Ireland, and the United States, offering more than 200 hours of blues performances, films, and workshops, including a free open-air concert at College

Green and a "blues trail" of free live blues in 18 different pubs. **Where:** Streets and pubs, Temple Bar area. **When:** July 19 to 21. **How:** Contact Una Carmody, events manager, Temple Bar Properties, Ltd., 18 Eustace St., Dublin 2 (☎ **01/677-2255;** fax 01/677-2525).

- **Dun Laoghaire Festival.** A weeklong celebration in the seafront suburb of Dun Laoghaire, 7 miles south of Dublin, with arts and crafts, concerts, band recitals, sports events, and talent competitions. **When:** Mid-July.

- **Summer Schools.** Study sessions meeting in Dublin include the Irish Theatre Summer School in conjunction with the Gaiety School of Acting at Trinity College, the James Joyce Summer School at Newman House, and the International Summer Schools in Irish Studies at Trinity College and the National University of Ireland. **When:** July and August. **How:** Contact the Irish Tourist Board.

August

✪ **Kerrygold Dublin Horse Show.** This is the principal sporting and social event on the Irish national calendar, attracting visitors from all parts of the world. More than 2,000 horses, the cream of Irish bloodstock, are entered for this show, with dressage, jumping competitions each day, and more. Highlights include a fashionable ladies day (don't forget your hat!), formal hunt balls each evening, and the awarding of the Aga Khan Trophy and the Nation's Cup by the president of Ireland. **Where:** RDS Showgrounds, Ballsbridge. **When:** August 7 to 11. **How:** Contact Niamh Kelly, RDS, Merrion Road, Ballsbridge, Dublin 4 (☎ **01/668-0866;** fax 01/660-4014).

- **Summer Music Festival.** St. Stephen's Green is the setting for this series of free lunchtime band concerts of popular and Irish traditional music, as well as afternoon open-air performances of Shakespearean plays, sponsored by the Office of Public Works. **When:** Last two weeks of August.

September

✪ **All-Ireland Hurling and Football Finals.** Tickets must be obtained months in advance for these two national amateur sporting events, the equivalent of Super Bowls for Irish national sports. **Where:** Croke Park. **When:** First and second weekends in September. **How:** Contact the Irish Tourist Board.

- **Irish Antique Dealers' Fair.** Annual show sponsored jointly by the RDS and the Irish Antique Dealers' Association. **Where:** RDS Showgrounds, Ballsbridge. **When:** September 28 to 30. **How:** Contact George Stacpoole, Irish Antique Dealers' Association, Adare, Co. Limerick (☎ **061/396409;** fax 061/396733).

October

✪ **Dublin Theatre Festival.** A world-class theater festival showcasing new plays by Irish authors and presenting a range of productions from abroad. **Where:** Theaters throughout Dublin. **When:** October 17 to 19. **How:** Contact Tony O Dálaigh, director, 47 Nassau St., Dublin 2 (☎ **01/677-8439;** fax 01/679-7709).

✪ **Golden Pages Dublin Marathon.** More than 3,000 runners from both sides of the Atlantic and the Irish Sea participate in this popular run through the streets of Dublin City. **Where:** Dublin city center. **When:** Last Monday in October. **How:** For entry forms and information, contact the Dublin Marathon Office, 2 Clare St., Dublin 2 (☎ **01/676-4647;** fax 01/6761383).

November/December

- **Dublin Grand Opera.** This is the second half of Dublin's twice-yearly operatic fling, with great works presented by the Dublin Grand Opera Society at the Gaiety Theatre. **When:** Early December.

- **Christmas Horse Racing Festival.** Three days of winter racing for thoroughbreds. **Where:** Leopardstown Racetrack. **When:** December 26 to 29.

4 From Cottages to Castles: Putting a Roof Over Your Head

In Ireland, a man's (or woman's) home is often quite literally a castle, and some of these castles are homes away from home for visitors. Ireland, in fact, offers a remarkable array of roofs, some quite affordable and others quite outrageously lavish. The point is that there is something in Ireland for everyone, from families on a budget to lovers on the splurge of a lifetime. There are a number of different types of lodging, and short of joining up with a Tinkers' caravan nearly all of them are presented here. These generic possibilities may be sketched out as follows:

BED-AND-BREAKFAST HOMES   Throughout Ireland, in the cities and in the sticks, private homes are often open to lodgers, by the night or longer. A warm bed and a solid, hot breakfast can be expected, and other meals are negotiable. Although B&Bs are regulated and inspected by the department of tourism (look for the Shamrock seal of approval), they are all different, as are your hosts. The Irish Tourist Board, for a small fee, will send a 400-page detailed listing of the approved B&Bs, complete with color photos of each. Or, better yet, you can follow our recommendations. Needless to say, you receive the personal touch when you stay in someone's home, and more often than not this is a real bonus. For those on a budget, this choice is hard to beat. Make your reservation at least 24 hours in advance (48 in high season); your room will ordinarily be held until 6pm. The cost for a room with private bath is roughly $22 to $32 per person, per night. *Note:* Most B&Bs do not accept credit cards.

HOTELS & GUEST HOUSES   *Be Our Guest,* a full guide to the hotels and inns of Ireland, is distributed by the Irish Hotel Federation and is available from the Irish Tourist Board. Hotels and guest houses, depending on their size and scope, offer a good deal more than a bed for the night and a breakfast to get you underway—everything from night clubs to golf courses. Some were castles in a former life, others have been elegant hotels from birth, and many are nondescript. All hotels and guest houses are inspected and rated by the Board of Tourism either of the Republic or of the North. In the Republic, hotels may aspire to five stars, while guest houses can reach no higher than four. In the North, hotels receive one to four stars, while guest houses are either grade A or grade B. The least expensive options may cost no more than a home-style bed-and-breakfast, and the most expensive can be 10 times that.

FARMHOUSE ACCOMMODATIONS   The vast majority of Irish farms, 170,000 in all, are relatively small and remain family owned and operated. In recent years, many of these farms have opened their doors to visitors and provide an attractive alternative to hotels, guest houses, and more standard bed-and-breakfast homes, particularly for families. The Irish Farm Holidays Association produces an annual book of listings of farmhouse accommodations throughout the country. It is available from the Irish Tourist Board. The **Irish Organic Farmers and Growers Association** also provides on request a brochure listing their members who offer accommodations (contact IOGFGA, 56 Blessington St., Dublin 7; ☎ **01/ 830-7996**). In the North, the Northern Ireland Farm and Country Holidays Association offers a similar book, available from the Northern Ireland Tourist Board.

Farm holidays can take various forms, from one-night-at-a-time bed-and-breakfasts to extended self-catering rentals. Many of the farmhouse accommodations, in addition to breakfast, offer high tea and/or a full dinner. Some of these farms are everything you could dream of—full working family farms in untouched, often spectacular surroundings— while others stretch the meaning of *farm* to include country houses with a garden and a dog nearby, or guest houses that are more "lodging with greenery" than "farm with lodging."

One of the newest developments on the Irish tourism scene is Irish Country Holidays, a program that invites visitors to share everyday life with the Irish in communities that are usually off the tourist track. Visitors are put up in homes, farms, self-catering cottages, or hotels, and they're given the opportunity to take part in turf-cutting, bread-baking, cheese-making, butter-churning, salmon-smoking, wood-turning, and pottery-making. Leisure activities such as fishing, canoeing, rock climbing, hill walking, cycling, and horse riding are also part of the holiday. At night there's traditional Irish music, song, dance, and amateur drama productions. Each holiday package is custom-planned. For more information, contact Dervla O'Neill, **Irish Country Holidays,** 5 Lord Edward Court, Bride Street, Dublin 8 (☎ **01/676-5790;** fax 01/676-5793).

THE HIDDEN IRELAND   The Hidden Ireland offers still another alternative to hotels, guest houses, and B&Bs. This is an organization of homeowners whose homes, often some of Ireland's oldest and grandest, are of particular architectural merit and character—in other words, the houses you drive past and wonder how you could talk your way into, just to have a look around. The good news and the bad news about The Hidden Ireland is that there are *people* living in these houses, people who take visitors into their family, eat their meals with them, and share the evening with them. This can mean "big house, close quarters," or it can mean something delightfully unforgettable, depending upon the personalities involved, both yours and theirs.

SELF-CATERING   If you want to stay awhile and establish a base of your own, then you may wish to consider renting an Irish cottage. The minimum rental period is usually one week. For families or small groups this is definitely the least costly way to go. In high season, in both the Republic and the North, a cottage sleeping seven may cost anywhere from $200 to $500 per week. This guide does not list self-catering accommodations. If you wish to pursue this option, I would recommend requesting specific information from **Irish Cottage Holiday Homes,** Central Reservations Office, 3 Whitefriars, Aungier Street, Dublin 2 (☎ **01/475-1932;** fax 01/ 475-5321), Limerick, Co. Limerick (☎ **061/411109;** fax 061/314-821). For cottages in the North, contact Susie Orr, **Rural Cottage Holidays, Ltd.,** St. Anne's Court, 59 North St., Belfast BT1 1NB (☎ **01232-231221;** fax 01232-240960).

RATES   All room charges quoted include 12.5% government tax (VAT) in the Republic of Ireland and 17.5% VAT in Northern Ireland, but do not include service charges, which are usually between 10% and 15%, with the majority adding 12.5%. Most hotels and guest houses will automatically add the service charge onto your final bill, although in recent years many family-run or limited-service places have begun the practice of not charging for service, leaving it as an option for the guest. Home-style B&Bs do not ordinarily charge for service.

We have classified "places to stay" into categories of price. The price levels as specified below and followed throughout this guide indicate the cost of a double room for two per night, including tax but not service charges.

Very Expensive	£150 and up ($240 and up)
Expensive	£120–£150 ($192–$240)
Moderate	£60–£120 ($96–$192)
Inexpensive	£30–£60 ($48–$96)

Ordinarily, the Irish cite the per-person price of a double room, a policy not followed in this guide, which for the sake of uniform comparison assumes double occupancy. Most accommodations will make adjustments for children.

If you have a talent for it, room prices in hotels—especially privately owned hotels in off-season—can be negotiated downward. I have it on the best of authorities (the experienced manager of a revered old hotel) that a polite entry into such negotiations would be to ask, "Is that your best rate?" or "Can you do a little bit better?"

A note on terminology: The Irish use the phrase "en suite" to indicate a room with private bath. A "double" has a double bed, while a "twin" has two twin beds.

RESERVATIONS   Many hotels can be booked through toll-free 800 numbers in the United States. For those properties that do not have a U.S. reservation number, the fastest way to reserve is by telephone or fax. Fax is preferable since you then have a printed confirmation. You can then follow up by sending a deposit check (usually the equivalent of one night's room rate) or by giving your credit card number.

If you arrive in Ireland without a reservation, the staff members at the various tourist offices throughout the Republic and Northern Ireland will gladly find you a room via a computerized reservation service known as Gulliver. You can also call the Gulliver line directly yourself by dialing **1/800/600-800.** This is a nationwide and cross-border "freephone" facility for credit-card bookings.

QUALITY & VALUE   Despite the various systems of approval, regulation, and rating, guest accommodations in Ireland are quite uneven in quality and cost. A budget hostel may be cleaner and more accommodating than a guest house or hotel and be only a third as costly. Tourism in Ireland is a boom industry and there is a general rush to be a part of it. Understandably and regrettably, the gatekeepers are not as rigorous as their reputation; so it is always well to consult a fellow traveler or a reliable guide book in booking your lodgings. Which, of course, is what you're doing.

If possible, it is always advisable to ask to see your room before committing yourself to a stay. In any given lodging, the size and quality of the rooms can vary considerably, often without any corresponding variation in cost. This is particularly true of single rooms, which even in a semiluxurious hotel can approach boarding-house standards. Don't be discouraged by this, but be alert so you're not disappointed.

TIPS ON ACCOMMODATIONS   Many older hotels and guest houses consider the lobby level as the ground floor (not the first floor); the first floor is the next floor up, or what Americans would call the second floor. So, if your room is on the first floor, that means it is one flight up, not on ground level.

Elevators, readily available in hotels but not so plentiful in guest houses, are called lifts. Remember to press "G" for the main floor or lobby, not "1."

Concierges or hall porters, as they are sometimes called, arrange all types of services, from taking luggage or delivering packages to your room to obtaining theater tickets, booking a rental or chauffeur-driven car, selling postage stamps and mailing letters/cards, dispensing tourist literature, or reserving taxis. Many of Dublin's concierges consider their craft a real art form and are members of the prestigious international organization known as Les Clefs d'Or, so you may have to prepare yourself to be pampered!

5 Health & Insurance

HEALTH   As a general rule, there are no health documents required to enter Ireland or Northern Ireland from the United States, Canada, the United Kingdom, Australia, New Zealand, or most other countries. If in the last 14 days a traveler has visited areas where a contagious disease is prevalent, however, proof of immunization for such disease may be required.

If you have a condition that may require emergency care but may not be readily recognizable, you may consider joining the **Medic Alert Foundation,** P.O. Box 1009, Turlock, CA 95381 (☎ **800/432-5378**), which provides ID tags, cards, and hotline access. If you are diabetic, you can call the **American Diabetes Association,** 1660 Duke St., Alexandria, VA 22314 (☎ **800/232-3472**), for a copy of *Travel and Diabetes.*

If you require the services of a physician, dentist, or other health professional during your stay in Ireland, your accommodations host may be in the best position to recommend someone local. Otherwise, you can call the **Irish Medical Association,** 10 Fitzwilliam Place, Dublin (☎ **01/676-7273**), for a referral.

INSURANCE   When planning a trip, it is wise to consider insurance coverage for the various risk aspects of travel: health and accident, cancellation or disruption of services, and lost or stolen luggage. Travel insurance makes especially good sense when purchasing nonrefundable airline tickets.

Before buying any new coverage, check your own insurance policies (automobile, medical, and homeowner) to ascertain if they cover the elements of travel abroad. Also check the membership contracts of automobile and travel clubs, and the benefits extended by credit card companies.

If you decide you need further coverage, consult your travel agent or tour planner. In many cases, tour operators provide insurance as part of a package or offer optional coverage for a small additional fee. Alternatively, you may wish to contact one of the following companies, specializing in short-term policies for travelers:

- **Access America,** 6600 West Broad St., Richmond, VA 23230 (☎ **800/284-8300**).
- **Insure America / Travel Guard International,** 1145 Clark St., Stevens Point, WI 54481 (☎ **800/826-1300** or 715/345-0505).
- **Tele-Trip Company,** at Mutual of Omaha Plaza, Omaha, NE 68175 (☎ **800/228-9792**).
- **Travel Insurance International,** Travelers Insurance Co., P.O. Box 280568, Hartford, CT 06128-0568 (☎ **800/243-3174;** fax 860/528-8005).

6   Tips for Travelers with Special Needs

FOR TRAVELERS WITH DISABILITIES

For the last 30 years, the **National Rehabilitation Board of Ireland,** The Square Shopping Center, Dublin 24 (☎ **01/462-0444**), has encouraged facilities to accommodate the disabled. Consequently, some hotels and public buildings now have ramps or graded entrances, and rooms specially fitted for wheelchair access.

Unfortunately, many of the older hotels, guest houses, and landmark buildings still have steep steps both outside and within. For a list of the properties that cater to the needs of the disabled, contact the National Rehabilitation Board in advance.

The **Irish Wheelchair Association,** 24 Blackheath Drive, Clontarf, Dublin 3 (☎ **01/833-8241**), loans free wheelchairs for travelers in Ireland. A donation is appreciated. Branch offices are located at Parnell Street, Kilkenny (☎ **056/62775**); White Street, Cork (☎ **021/966544**); Henry Street, Limerick (☎ **061/313691**); and Dominick Street, Galway (☎ **091/565598**).

For advice on travel to Northern Ireland, contact **Disability Action,** 2 Annandale Ave., Belfast (☎ **01232/491011**).

Grimes Travel, 54 Mamaroneck Ave., White Plains, NY 10601 (☎ **914/ 937-9767**), offers tours to Ireland specifically for the disabled.

FOR SENIOR CITIZENS

Seniors, known in Ireland and Northern Ireland as OAPs (old age pensioners), enjoy a variety of discounts and privileges. Native OAPs ride the public transport system free of charge, but this privilege does not extend to tourists. Visiting seniors can avail themselves of other discounts, particularly on admission to attractions and theaters. Always ask about a senior discount if special rates are not posted; the discount is usually 10%.

The Irish Tourist Board publishes a list of reduced rate hotel packages for seniors, **Golden Holidays / For the Over 55s.** These packages are usually available in the months of March to June, and September to November.

Some tour operators in the United States, such as **CIE Tours** (☎ **800/ CIE-TOUR** or 201/292-3438), which operates in Ireland and Northern Ireland, give senior citizens over age 55 cash discounts on selected departures of regular tour programs throughout the year. In addition, the following U.S. firms operate tours to Ireland specifically geared to seniors: **SAGA Tours,** 222 Berkeley St., Boston, MA 02116 (☎ **800/343-0273** or 617/262-2262); and **Elder Hostel,** 75 Federal St., Boston, MA 02110 (☎ **617/426-7788**), offering a range of educational travel programs for seniors. Call the number above for a free Elder Hostel international catalogue.

FOR STUDENTS, TEACHERS & YOUTH

With almost half of its population under age 25, Ireland is well geared to students, whether you're planning to study there or are just passing through.

The country has a distinguished and vital academic tradition. Dublin alone is home to three universities—Trinity College Dublin, University College Dublin, and Dublin University—and to many other fine schools and institutes of higher learning. Campuses of the National University of Ireland are located in Cork, Limerick, Galway, and Maynooth. In Northern Ireland, the leading universities are Queen's University in Belfast and Ulster University, with branches in Belfast, Coleraine, and Derry.

Two excellent sourcebooks will help you to explore the opportunities for study in Ireland: *The Transitions Abroad Alternative Travel Directory,* an annual guide to living, learning, and working overseas, and *Work, Study, Travel Abroad: The Whole World Handbook,* compiled by CIEE, The Council on International Educational Exchange. Both are available in bookstores.

Ireland in general is extremely student-friendly. Most attractions have a reduced student-rate admission charge, obtainable on the presentation of a valid student ID card, and a range of travel discounts are available to students, teachers (at any grade level, kindergarten through university), and youth (anyone under 25). For further information on international student/teacher/youth identity cards and fares, call the national office of **Council Travel** at **800/2-COUNCIL,** where they can make your reservations or refer you to the Council Travel office nearest you. Council Travel operates 43 offices in the United States and works through a network of world affiliates. (Even if you're not eligible for any of Council's student/teacher/youth discounts, they offer full travel services, with the advantage of a growing network of local offices and overseas affiliates.)

In Canada, CIEE's counterpart is **Travel CUTS,** 187 College St., Toronto, Ontario M5T1P7 (☎ **416/979-2406;** fax 416/979-8167).

In Ireland, Council Travel's affiliate is **USIT,** the **Irish Student Travel Service,** 19 Aston Quay, Dublin 2 (☎ **01/677-8117**). In Northern Ireland, contact USIT in the Sountain Centre, College Street, Belfast BT1-6ET (☎ **1232/324073**), or at Queens University Travel, Student Union Bldg., University Road, Belfast BT7-1PE (☎ **1232/241-830**). In the United States, USIT is located at 895 Amsterdam Ave., New York, NY 10025 (☎ **212/663-5435**). (For the hopelessly curious among you, USIT is the acronym for the organization's original name, "Union of Students of Ireland Travel," but as the man told me when I asked, "It doesn't stand for anything anymore. It's just USIT.")

U.S. firms offering educational programs to Ireland include: **Academic Travel Abroad,** 3210 Grace St. NW, Washington, DC 20007 (☎ **800/556-7896** or 202/785-9000); **Cultural Heritage Alliance,** 107-115 S. Second St., Philadelphia, PA 19106 (☎ **800/323-4466** or 215/923-7060); and **Irish American Cultural Institute,** 1 Lackawanna Place, Morristown, NJ 07960 (☎ **800/232-3746** or 612/962-6040).

FOR FAMILIES

Roughly 27% of the Irish population is under 15 years of age, so it's no wonder that Ireland is so youth and family oriented. A love of children (*lots* of them) is one of the hallmarks of the Irish-Catholic tradition, and of the country in general, so you'll always find people quick to be helpful and to suggest places to go and things to do with children.

Instead of hotels or B&Bs, families might well consider a farm stay or a vacation rental home, where children are likely to have the opportunity to meet and to make friends with local children. The information provided above regarding farmhouse accommodations and self-catering will be helpful in pursuing such options.

En route, if given 24-hour advance notice, airlines will arrange for a special child menu, and will warm any baby food you bring with you. On arrival, car-rental companies will have children's car seats on hand, provided a request has been made ahead of time. Throughout the island, entrance fees and tickets on public transportation are often reduced by at least half for children, and inclusive family rates for parents with more than two children may be available. Aside from all too familiar fast-food fare, many hotels and restaurants offer children's menus. Baby-sitting is provided in some hotels, guest houses, and B&Bs, and can be arranged in others. See the "Fast Facts" feature for each major city for listings of pharmacies and other crucial health information.

For accommodations, meals , and attractions, be sure to read the "Family-Friendly" and "Especially for Kids" features throughout this guide.

Other Helpful Resources

Travel With Your Children (TWYCH), 45 W. 18th St., 7th Floor, New York, NY 10011 (☎ **212/206-0688**) can send you an information packet of its publications, such as *Family Travel Times,* and a sample issue for $2.

Wilderness Press, 2440 Bancroft Way, Berkeley, CA 94704 (☎ **800/443-7227**) offers *Sharing Nature with Children* and *Backpacking with Babies and Small Children.*

Mason-Grant Publications, P.O. Box 6547, Portsmouth, NH 03802 (☎ **603/436-1608**) offers *Take Your Kids to Europe* by Cynthia W. Harriman, a guide to budget family travel.

FOR GAY & LESBIAN TRAVELERS

Gay Ireland has rapidly come out of the closet since homosexuality became legal in the North in 1982 and in the Republic in July 1993. Though the gay and lesbian community has received increasing support over the last several years, much of Ireland on the whole continues to discourage its gay population. In cities such as Dublin, Cork, and Galway, gay and lesbian visitors will find more formal support and an open, if small, gay community. In Dublin, the July 1996 weeklong celebration of gay and lesbian Ireland, called PRIDE, happily went without a hitch and the city enjoys an increasingly lively lesbian and gay scene.

Two essential publications for the gay or lesbian visitor to Ireland are the *Gay Community News* and *In Dublin* magazine.

Gay Community News is a free newspaper of comprehensive Irish gay-related information published the last Friday of each month. You can pick up a copy in Dublin at the Temple Bar Information Centre at 18 Eustace St. or at the **National Lesbian and Gay Federation (NLGF),** Hirschfeld Centre, 10 Fownes St. (☎ **01/ 671-0939**), where it is published and where you can obtain advice on gay-related legal issues. Please note that the NLGF will soon be changing its location, but they are hoping to keep their current phone number. The *Gay Community News* is also distributed by Books Upstairs at 36 College Green across from Trinity College; Waterstone's on Dawson Street, also near Trinity; The Well Fed Cafe on Crow Street in Temple Bar; The George on South Greater Street George's Street off Dame Street; and other progressive haunts.

In Dublin, which comes out twice a month and is for sale at news agents and bookstores throughout the city, has a page of gay events, current club information, AIDS and health information resources, accommodation options, and helpful organizations.

The following organizations and help lines are staffed by knowledgeable and friendly people:

National Lesbian and Gay Federation (NLGF), Hirschfeld Centre, 10 Fownes St. (☎ **01/671-0939**), Monday to Friday noon to 5:30pm.

Gay Switchboard Dublin at Carmichael House, North Brunswick Street, Dublin 7 (☎ **01/872–1055**), Sunday to Friday 8 to 10pm and Saturday 3:30 to 6pm.

Lesbian Line (☎ **01/661-3777**), Thursday 7 to 9pm, operated by Gay Switchboard Dublin.

Lesbian Line Dublin (☎ **01/872-9911**), Thursday 7 to 9pm.

LOT (Lesbians Organizing Together), the central umbrella group of the lesbian community, 5 Capel St. (☎ **01/872-7770**). (LOT also sponsors LEA / Lesbian Education Awareness, telephone and fax 01/872-0460 or E-mail: leanow@indigo.ie. Further information and newsletter on the World Wide Web: http://qrd.tcp.com/ qrd/www/world/europe/ireland/leanow.html.

Outhouse, a new gay and lesbian organization currently at P.O. Box 4767, Dublin 2, and hoping to establish a comprehensive community and resource center this year.

AIDS Helpline Dublin (☎ **01/872-4277**), Monday to Friday, 7 to 9pm and Saturday 3 to 5pm, offering assistance with HIV/AIDS prevention, testing, and treatment.

Gay and Lesbian travelers seeking further information on travel abroad may wish to join the **International Gay Travel Association (IGTA),** P.O. Box 4974, Key West, FL 33041 (☎ **800/448-8550** or 305/292-0217), and consult the following resources: *Ferrari's Places for Men, Ferrari's Places for Women,* and *Inn Places: US and Worldwide Gay Accommodations,* all three published by Ferrari Publications, P.O. Box 37887, Phoenix, AZ 85069; and *Women Going Places,* Inland Book Company, P.O. Box 12061, East Haven, CT 06512. Also, Council Travel (☎ **800/2-COUNCIL** for an office near you) can provide a free pamphlet—*AIDS and International Travel—*

that includes information on hotlines, HIV testing, blood transfusions, and traveling with AIDS overseas.

7 Getting There

BY PLANE

About half of all visitors from North America arrive in Ireland via direct transatlantic flights to Dublin Airport, Shannon Airport, or Belfast Airport. (Since March 27, 1994, transatlantic flights to the Republic are no longer required to stop in Shannon.) The other half fly first into Britain or Continental Europe and then "backtrack" into Ireland by air or sea. In Ireland, there are seven smaller regional airports, each of which receives some EC international traffic: Cork, Donegal, Galway, Kerry, Knock, Sligo, and Waterford. As services and schedules are always subject to change, be sure to consult your preferred airline or travel agent as soon as you begin to sketch your itinerary. The routes and carriers listed below are provided to suggest the range of possibilities for air travel to Ireland.

FROM THE U.S.

The Irish national "air fleet" or **Aer Lingus** (☎ **800/223-6537**) is the leader in providing transatlantic flights to Ireland. Aer Lingus offers scheduled flights from Boston, Chicago, Las Vegas, and New York to Dublin and Shannon International Airports, with connecting flights to Belfast and Ireland's regional airports. A new fleet of wide-body Airbus 330 aircraft was introduced in summer 1994, and on March 14, 1996, Aer Lingus announced a new corporate identity and "a major period of customer-led product and service changes." Connections are available from more than 100 U.S. cities via American, TWA, or USAir.

Note: Aer Lingus offers educational discounts to full-time students, which can be booked through CIEE / Council Travel, listed above, and an attractively priced Eurosaver Green Pass for those who wish to combine an Aer Lingus round-trip transatlantic flight to Ireland with a side trip to Britain or the Continent, or a domestic flight within Ireland, including the North.

Scheduled daily flights are offered by **Delta Airlines** (☎ **800/241-4141**) from Atlanta to both Dublin and Shannon, with feed-in connections from Delta's network of gateways throughout the United States. Delta also has a co-share arrangement with Aer Lingus, which allows Delta to offer daily service to Shannon and every-other-day service to Dublin from New York / JFK, at very competitive prices.

In addition, scheduled service to Belfast, Dublin, and Shannon is provided by **American Trans Air** (☎ **800/225-2995**); and limited (mostly weekend) service to Shannon is offered by **Aeroflot** (☎ **800/995-5555**) from Chicago, Washington, D.C., and Miami.

There is no disputing that Aer Lingus offers a taste of Ireland prior to arrival, but no matter who carries you there, Ireland is only hours off, and so it makes sense to shop around for a flight that best suits your schedule and budget.

BACKTRACKING TO IRELAND

Many travelers opt to fly to Britain and backtrack into Dublin (see "From Britain," below). Carriers serving Britain from the United States include **Air India** (☎ 800/442-4455); **American Airlines** (☎ 800/433-7300); **British Airways** (☎ 800/247-9297); **Continental Airlines** (☎ 800/231-0856); **El Al** (☎ 800/223-6700); **Kuwait Airways** (☎ 800/458-9248); **Northwest Airlines** (☎ 800/447-4747); **TWA** (☎ 800/892-4141); **United** (☎ 800/241-6522); **USAir** (☎ 800/428-4322); and **Virgin Atlantic Airways** (☎ 800/862-8621).

From Britain

Air service from Britain into Dublin is operated by **Aer Lingus** (☎ 800/223-6537 from the U.S., or 081/899-4747 in Britain) from Birmingham, Bristol, East Midlands, Edinburgh, Glasgow, Leeds/Bradford, London/Heathrow, Manchester, and Newcastle; **British Midland** (☎ 800/788-0555 from the U.S., or 1345/554554 in Britain) from London/Heathrow; **Brymon Airways** (☎ 0752/705151 in Britain) from Plymouth; **Manx Airlines** (☎ 0624/824313 in Britain) from Blackpool, Cardiff, Guernsey, Isle of Man, Jersey, and Liverpool; **Ryanair** (☎ 800/365-5563 from the U.S., or 171/435-7101 in Britain) from Birmingham, Liverpool, and London/Stansted; **SAS** from Manchester (☎ 800/221-2350 from the U.S., or 161/499-1441 in Britain).

Air service from Britain to Shannon is operated by **Aer Lingus** from London/Heathrow. Service to Cork is provided by **British Airways Express** (☎ 800/247-9297 from the U.S., or 081/897-4000 in Britain) from Birmingham, Bristol, Manchester, and Plymouth; **Orient Air** (☎ 0452/855565 in Britain) from Coventry; **Air Southwest** (☎ 0392/446447 in Britain) from Cornwall; and **Ryanair** from London/Stansted.

Air service into Belfast International Airport is provided by **AirUK** (☎ 0279/680146 in Britain) from Leeds/Bradford; **Brymon Airways** from Birmingham; **Britannia Airways** (☎ 061/489-2084 in Britain) from London/Luton; and **British Midland** from East Midlands and Jersey. In addition, there is service into Belfast City Airport via **Gill Air** (☎ 091/286-9665) from Aberdeen and Newcastle-upon-Tyne; **Jersey European** (☎ 0232/460630 in Britain) from Blackpool, Bristol, Guernsey, Isle of Man, Jersey, Teeside, London/Gatwick, Leeds/Bradford, Exeter, and Birmingham; **Loganair** from Edinburgh, Glasgow, Manchester, Jersey, Channel Islands, and Blackpool; **Manx Airlines** from Isle of Man, Aberdeen, London/Luton, Cardiff, and Liverpool; and **Yorkshire European** (☎ 0345/626217) from Southampton.

There is also regular service into Ireland's regional airports such as Waterford via Manx Airlines from London/Stansted and Orient Air from Gloucester; Knock via Logan Air from Glasgow and Manchester, and Ryanair from London/Stansted and Liverpool; Donegal's Carrickfinn Airport via Loganair from Glasgow; and Derry's Eglinton Airport via Loganair from Glasgow and Manchester.

From the Continent

Major air connections into Dublin from the continent include service from Brussels via **Aer Lingus** and **Sabena** (☎ 800/952-2000); Copenhagen via **Aer Lingus** and **SAS**; Paris via **Aer Lingus** and **Air France**; Munich via **Ryanair** and **Lufthansa** (☎ 800/645-3880); Rome via **Aer Lingus** and **Alitalia**; Amsterdam via **Aer Lingus**; Lisbon and Faro via **TAP Air Portugal** (☎ 800/221-7370); and Zurich via **Aer Lingus.**

Service to Shannon includes **Aer Lingus** from Dusseldorf, Paris, and Zurich; and **Aeroflot** from Moscow and St. Petersburg. Flights into Cork are operated by **Aer Lingus** from Amsterdam, Paris, and Rennes; **Brit Air** (☎ 098/621022 from France) from Brest and Nantes; and **KLM** from Amsterdam.

Service into Belfast International includes **KLM CityHopper** from Amsterdam.

Best-Value Airfares

The expression "You get what you pay for, and you pay for what you get" has dubious relevance to airfares. We all know that the fellow in the seat next to us, the silent fellow with the grin, may be paying a lot less than we are. Budget fares are not always loudly hawked. Like newts, they sometimes hide under rocks. A little looking around can uncover them.

Avoiding high season, the defining dates of which vary somewhat, is the first and most effective step anyone can take in reducing the cost of travel, lodging, car rental, and so on. The next step is to plan far enough ahead to be able to meet advance-purchase restrictions, which mostly vary from a week to a month. That brings you to a fork in the road: between scheduled service and charters. On any given day, charters are likely to be less costly. They also offer fewer frills, and their tickets are ordinarily nonrefundable. Among airlines offering scheduled service, there is no predicting who will be making the best offer on any one day in any one year.

CHARTERS

FROM THE U.S.   The largest and most reliable charter program to Ireland is operated by **Sceptre Charters,** 101-13 101st Ave., Ozone Park, NY 11416 (☎ **718/ 738-9400,** or outside New York State 800/221-0924). Using American Trans Air, Sceptre offers charter seats from New York to Dublin or Shannon priced from $399 to $579 round-trip, as well as air/car/hotel packages. This operator also flies to Shannon from Boston, Philadelphia, Chicago, and Los Angeles.

FROM CANADA   Several companies in Canada operate charter flights from Toronto to Ireland, including **Adventure Tours** (☎ Canada **800/268-7063** or 416/ 967-1112); **Air Canada Vacations** (☎ Canada **800/263-0882** or 416/615-8000); **Air Transat Holidays** (☎ Canada **800/268-8805** or 416/485-3377); and **Regent Holidays** (☎ Canada **800/387-4860** or 416/673-3343).

BY FERRY

If you're traveling to Ireland from Britain or the Continent, especially if you're behind the wheel of a car, ferries can get you there. The Irish Sea has a reputation, however, so it's always a good idea to consider an over-the-counter pill or patch to guard against seasickness.

Several car/passenger ferries offer reasonably comfortable furnishings, cabin berths (for the longer crossings), restaurants, duty-free shopping, and lounges.

Prices fluctuate seasonally and further depend on your route, time of travel, and whether you are on foot or in a car. It's best to check with your travel agent for up-to-date details.

FROM BRITAIN

Irish Ferries (☎ **201/768-1187** from the U.S.) operates from Holyhead, Wales, to Dublin and from Pembroke, Wales, to Rosslare, Co. Wexford. **Stena Line** (☎ **800/ 677-8585** from the U.S.) sails from Holyhead to Dun Laoghaire, 8 miles south of Dublin; from Fishguard, Wales, to Rosslare; and from Stranraer, Scotland, to Belfast, Northern Ireland. **Swansea/Cork Ferries** (☎ **1792/456116** in Britain) links Swansea, Wales, to Cork. **P&O European Ferries** (☎ **201/768-1187** from the U.S. and Canada) operates from Cairnryan, Scotland, to Larne, Northern Ireland. **Isle of Man Steam Packet Company** (☎ **0624/661661** in Britain) connects Douglas, Isle of Man, to Dublin and Belfast. **Seacat Scotland Ltd.** (☎ **800/677-8585** from the U.S.) operates ferries from Stranraer, Scotland, to Belfast.

FROM CONTINENTAL EUROPE

Irish Ferries sails from Le Havre and Cherbourg, France, to Rosslare and Cork. **Brittany Ferries** (☎ **021/277801** in Cork) connects Roscoff and St. Malo, France, to Cork.

Note: Because the Irish Ferries company is a member of the Eurail system, you can travel free on the ferries between Rosslare and LeHavre if you hold a valid Eurailpass.

BY BUS FROM BRITAIN

Bus service links Dublin with London and other major cities in Britain using the B&I or Stena ferry trips as part of the bus ride. Operated jointly by Ireland's Bus Eireann and Britain's National Express and known as **Supabus,** these routes operate daily. One-way fares between Dublin and London start at £16 ($26); round-trip fares start at £30 ($48), making this connection a true bargain. From Dublin, this same express coach service from London extends to a number of Irish cities. For full details on the Supabus routes, contact **CIE Tours International** in the United States (☎ 800/243-7687).

PACKAGE TOURS

This guide is not really directed toward those who have decided on a prepackaged group tour of Ireland. Not all package tours, however, are group tours. Many package tours are designed for individuals or couples traveling together. Such packages may include airfare, car rental, and hotel accommodations or just a hotel room plus sightseeing, all for a price lower than the sum of its parts.

It's wise to prepay for a vacation package in U.S. dollars soon after you make reservations, as many tour operators guarantee no increase in the land costs of a tour package as soon as the deposit is paid. So, even if the dollar weakens, your price is locked in at the original rate.

The leading firms offering package tours of Ireland and Northern Ireland include the following:

- **Aer Lingus "Discover Ireland" Vacations** (☎ 800/223-6537) offers an array of options, including Dublin City packages, golf tours, cycling holidays, and self-drive vacations designed for individual travelers.
- **CIE Tours International** (☎ 800/CIE-TOUR), Ireland's national tour company, was established more than 60 years ago and is the leader in escorted vacations to Ireland. It offers Dublin City–based packages, self-drive vacations, and Ireland/Britain combination trips. CIE also offers rail/bus touring arrangements within Ireland for individuals and for groups.
- **Grimes Travel** (☎ 800/937-9767) offers various travel packages year-round and is best known for its travel arrangements coinciding with the annual Dublin Marathon in October. Other tour operators include: **Brendan Tours** (☎ 800/421-8446); **Brian Moore International Tours** (☎ 800/982-2299); **Lismore Tours** (☎ 800/547-6673); **Lynott Tours** (☎ 800/221-2474); and **Owenoak-Castle Tours** (☎ 800/426-4498).

8 Getting Around

BY PLANE

Since Ireland is such a small country, it's unlikely that you'll be flying from place to place. If you do require an air transfer, however, **Aer Lingus** (☎ 01/844-4777) operates daily scheduled flights linking Dublin with Cork, Galway, Kerry, Knock, Shannon, and Sligo.

BY TRAIN

Iarnrod Eireann / Irish Rail, Travel Centre, 35 Lower Abbey St., Dublin 1 (☎ 01/836-6222), operates a network of train services throughout Ireland. With the exception of flying, train travel is the fastest way to get around the country. Most lines radiate from Dublin to other principal cities and towns. From Dublin, the journey time to Cork is 3 hours; to Belfast, 2 hours; to Galway, 3 hours; to Limerick, $2^1/4$ hours; to Killarney, 4 hours; to Sligo, $3^1/4$ hours; and to Waterford, $2^3/4$ hours. Outside of regular business hours, call Monday to Friday, 5:30 to 10pm (☎ 01/836-5420); Saturday, 7:30am to 10pm (☎ 01/836-5421); and Sunday, 5 to 10pm (☎ 01/836-5421).

In addition to the Irish Rail service between Dublin and Belfast, **Northern Ireland Railways,** Central Station, East Bridge Street, Belfast (☎ **01232/899411**), runs trains from Belfast's new Great Victoria Street Station to Derry, Coleraine, Bangor, and Newry.

BY BUS

Bus Eireann, with its hub at Busaras / Central Bus Station, Dublin 1 (☎ **01/836-6111**), operates an extensive system of express bus service on routes such as Dublin to Donegal ($4^1/4$ hours), Killarney to Limerick ($2^1/4$ hours), Limerick to Galway (2 hours), and Limerick to Cork (2 hours), as well as local service to nearly every town in Ireland.

For bus travel within Northern Ireland, contact **Ulsterbus,** Europa Buscentre, 10 Glengall St., Belfast (☎ **01232/333000**).

RAIL/BUS TRAVEL PASSES

For extensive travel by public transport, you can save money by purchasing a rail/bus pass or a rail-only pass. The options include:

* **Brit/Ireland Pass:** For all standard-class rail travel throughout Great Britain and Ireland, including a round-trip ferry crossing via Stena Line. Valid for one month, it costs $299 for 5 days of travel or $429 for 10 days of travel. Must be purchased before departure for Ireland or Britain. Available from **Britrail Travel International,** 1500 Broadway, New York, NY 10036 (☎ **800/677-8585** or 212/575-2667) or from **CIE Tours International,** 100 Hanover Ave., Cedar Knolls, NJ 07927-0501 (☎ **800/243-7687** or 201/292-3438 from the U.S.; ☎ 800/387-2667 in Canada).

* **Emerald Card:** This pass is good for rail and bus services throughout Ireland and Northern Ireland, and is priced at £180 ($288) for 15 days, and £105 ($168) for 8 days. It's available from **Iarnrod Eireann / Irish Rail,** Travel Centre, 35 Lower Abbey St., Dublin 1 (☎ **01/836-6222**), and **Busaras / Central Bus Station,** Dublin 1 (☎ **01/836-6111**), as well as all major bus and train stations.

* **Eurail Pass:** For unlimited rail travel in 17 European countries. It is not valid, however, in Britain or Northern Ireland. In the Republic, the Eurail Pass is good for all rail travel, Expressway coaches, and the Irish Continental Lines ferries between France and Ireland. This pass must be purchased 21 days before departure for Ireland by a non–European Union resident. For further details or for purchase, call **Rail Pass Express** (☎ **800/722-7151**). Also available from Council Travel and other travel agents.

* **Freedom of Northern Ireland:** Seven days unlimited travel on bus and train in the North for £30 ($46.50). It's available from **Northern Ireland Railways,** Central Station, East Bridge Street, Belfast (☎ **01232/899411**) and **Ulsterbus,** Europa Buscentre, 10 Glengall St., Belfast (☎ **01232/333000**), as well as all major bus and train stations in Northern Ireland.

* **Irish Explorer:** For use in the Republic of Ireland, this pass gives 8-day combined rail and bus services for £90 ($144), or rail only for £75 ($120). It's available from **Iarnrod Fireann / Irish Rail,** Travel Centre, 35 Lower Abbey St.,

North Channel

Atlantic Ocean

Portrush
Ballycastle
Coleraine
Larne Harbour
Derry
Ballymoney
Larne
Whitehead
Antrim
Carrickfergus
Belfast York Road
Bangor
Lurgan
BELFAST CENTRAL
Portadown
Lisburn
Enniskillen

Ballina
Sligo
Colloney
Boyle
Carrick-on-Shannon
Foxford
MANULLA JUNCTION
Dromod
Castlebar
Ballyhaunis
Westport
Longford
Claremorris
Castlerea
Roscommon
Woodlawn
Mostrim
Tuam
Athenry
Athlone
Galway
Ballinasloe
Clara
Attymon
Tullamore
PORTARLINGTON
Roscrea
Portlaoise
Cloughjordan
Nenagh
Temple-more
BALLYBROPHY
Birdhill
Kilkenny
Limerick
Castle-connell
Thurles
Thomastown
LIMERICK JUNCTION
Clonmel
Campile
Tipperary
Cahir
Carrick-oh-Suir
Tralee
Charleville
Farranfore
Rathmore
MALLOW
WATERFORD
Ballycullane
Killarney
Banteer
Millstreet
Fota
Cork
Cobh
Wellington Bridge
Bridgetown

Newry
Dundalk
Irish Sea
Drogheda
Mosney
Balbriggan
Skerries
Mullingar
Enfield
Malahide
Dublin Connolly
Maynooth
Dublin Pearse
Kildare
Dublin Heuston
Dun Laoghaire
Newbridge
Bray
Greystones
Athy
Rathdrum
Carlow
Wicklow
Muine Bheag
Arklow
Gorey
Enniscorthy
Wexford
Rosslare Strand
Rosslare Harbour

Mouth of the Shannon
Listowel
Ennistymon
Ennis
ARAN ISLANDS

St. George's Channel

0   25 mi
     40 km

N

3-0473

Dublin 1 (☎ 01/836-6222), and **Busaras / Central Bus Station,** Dublin 1 (☎ 01/836-6111), as well as all major bus and train stations.

- **Irish Rambler:** For use in the Republic of Ireland, this pass gives services for 3 days at £28 ($44.80), 8 days at £68 ($105.40), and 15 days at £98 ($156.80). It's available from **Busaras / Central Bus Station,** Dublin 1 (☎ 01/836-6111), and all other major bus stations.
- **Irish Rover:** For use both in the Republic of Ireland and in the North, this pass entitles you to 5 days of rail travel for £75 ($120). It's available from **Iarnrod Eireann / Irish Rail,** Travel Centre, 35 Lower Abbey St., Dublin 1 (☎ 01/ 836-6222), and all major train stations.
- **Rail Runabout**: For 7 days of unlimited rail travel in the North only. Available at most railway stations in Northern Ireland.

Note: Three-day passes are good for any 3 days in an 8-day period; 5-day passes are good for any 5 days in a 15-day period; 8-day passes for any 8 days in a 15-day period; and 15-day passes for any 15 days in a 30-day period. The Emerald Card, the Irish Explorer, and the Irish Rover passes can be purchased in Ireland at most mainline rail stations and Bus Eireann ticket offices or, in the United States, from **CIE Tours International,** 100 Hanover Ave., Cedar Knolls, NJ 07927-0501 (☎ 800/243-7687).

BY CAR

Although Ireland offers an extensive network of public transportation, the advantages of having your own car for your travels are obvious. The disadvantages begin with the cost of rental and continue with each refueling. In high season, weekly rental rates on a compact vehicle begin around $240 (if you've shopped around) and ascend steeply from there—but it's at the pump that you're likely to go into shock. Irish gas prices can easily be triple what you pay in the United States. The sole consolation here is that Ireland is comparatively small, and so distances are comparatively short. Another fact of life on the road in Ireland is that space is limited. Irish roads and high-ways are surprisingly narrow, made to order for what many Americans would regard as miniature cars, just the kind you'll wish you had rented once you're underway. So think small when you pick out your rental car. The choice is yours: between room in the car and room on the road.

Unless your stay in Ireland extends beyond six months, your own valid U.S. or Canadian driver's license (provided you've had it for at least six months) is all you need to drive in Ireland. Rules and restrictions for car rental vary slightly and correspond roughly to those in the United States. This was not, however, always the case. When I first rented a car in Ireland, nearly 20 years ago, one of the questions on the rental agreement read as follows: "Have you ever been in jail or worked in the theater?" As it happened, I had worked in the theater. In fact, I was working with a Dublin theater at that very time. What happened next? When I explained that I was a playwright and not an actor, I was given the keys.

Car-rental rates as quoted by many companies do not include the inevitable 12.5% government tax (VAT); nor do they include CDW (collision damage waiver) or insurance against theft of the rental vehicle. If you have a credit card that provides free collision protection on rental cars and/or theft protection, be sure to call your card's customer service line to make certain that there are no silent, invisible restrictions on that coverage. Best to tell them exactly where you are going, for how long, and let them assure you that all is well. One common hitch is that the complimentary CDW may be invalid beyond 30 consecutive days, which means that you must return the

Irish Bus Routes

car within thirty days and then take out a second rental to extend the coverage beyond the 30-day limit.

If you are renting a car in the Republic and taking it into the North (or vice-versa), be sure to ask the car rental firm if the rental insurance they provide covers cross-border transport. If not, you may be required to purchase extra insurance. If you rent a car in the Republic, it is best to return it to the Republic, and if you rent it in the North, return it in the North (some firms will charge extra for cross-border drop-offs).

DRIVING LAWS & TIPS

A common concern for would-be motorists from abroad is the fact that the Irish, in both the North and South, drive on the left. The thought of this whitens some knuckles even before they touch the wheel. In my own experience and from what I know more widely, it really isn't a matter for dread. The sight of oncoming vehicles in one's accustomed lane is instantly instructive, even persuasive. "Roundabouts" admittedly take a little getting used to. Just remember to yield to vehicles on the right. If you're going to slip up and forget momentarily where you belong, it's more likely to happen after you return home, when you're guard is down and before you realize you've formed a strange habit overseas. Seriously, be careful in the first days and weeks after you return home, especially when making sharp left turns.

There are no major highways to speak of in the Republic (extended, limited access, divided highways), only national (N), regional (R), and rural or unclassified roads. N50 and higher are primary roads, with numbers lower than 50 indicating secondary roads. Regional roads are usually given a name and not a number. In the North, there are two Major Motorways (M), equivalent to interstates, as well as a network of lesser A- and B-level roads. Speed limits are posted. In general, the limit for urban areas is 48kmph (30 m.p.h.), for open but non-divided highways 97kmph (60 m.p.h.), and for divided highways and Major Motorways 113 kmph (70 m.p.h.).

The enforcement of speed limits is said to be spotty, but Irish roads have some built-in enforcers. They are often slick, with many bends and rises, any one of which can present a sheep or other four-legged pedestrian on very short notice. The low density of traffic on Ireland's roads can promote the deadly fantasy that you have the road to yourself. Don't wait to be contradicted.

Both the North and the South have appropriately severe laws on the books against drunk driving, and they will gladly throw them at you. Irish hospitality has its limits. Both also enforce the mandatory use of seat belts in the front seat, and the North extends that to rear-seated passengers. Additionally, it is against the law in the Republic for any child under 12 to sit in the front seat.

It would be unfair to rate Irish drivers as a group, and yet some description may be helpful. They are not as homicidal as the French, nor as skilled as the Italians. They do have a wild streak, however, and they are far more experienced on rough, winding, narrow lanes than are most Americans. Best to avoid any contests. Bostonians, on the other hand, will be in their element.

CAR RENTALS

Major international car-rental firms are represented at airports and cities throughout Ireland and Northern Ireland, including **Alamo** (☎ 800/522-9696 from the U.S.); **Auto-Europe** (☎ 800/223-5555 from the U.S.); **Avis** (☎ 800/331-1084 from the U.S.); **Budget** (☎ 800/284-2354 from the U.S.); **EuroDollar** (☎ 800/472-3325 from the U.S.); **Hertz** (☎ 800/654-3001 from the U.S.); **National/Europcar** (☎ 800/227-3876 from the U.S.); **Payless** (☎ 800/524-0555 from the U.S.); and **Thrifty** (☎ 800/367-2277 from the U.S.).

Now I'm not trying to tell you what to do, but I would definitely urge you to make any car-rental arrangements long in advance of departure. Leaving such arrangements to the last minute—or worse, leaving them until your arrival in Ireland—can mean that you will wind up either walking or wishing your were. Ireland is a small country, and in high season it can completely run out of rental cars—but before it does, it will run out of *affordable* rental cars. Discounts are common in the off-season, of course, but it's also possible to negotiate a decent deal for July and August, if you put in enough time and effort. In my experience, Budget stands out as consistently competitive and unusually accommodating to the plans and needs of individual travelers. If you plan to rent or lease a car in Britain or Europe and then bring it by ferry to Ireland (which will entail a modest additional surcharge), I would recommend a long-term rental or lease from **Europe by Car** (☎ **800/223-1516**), a company whose rates and service are hard to beat on the Continent.

In addition, there are a variety of Irish-based companies, with desks at the major airports and/or full-service offices in city or town locations. The leader among the Irish-based firms is **Dan Dooley Rent-a-Car** (☎ **800/331-9301** from the U.S.).

DRIVING SERVICES

There is still another way of getting around Ireland by car. If cost is no concern, or if you can't shake the fear of the left lane, you may want to consider being chauffeured in style. The fleets of such services usually begin at ground level with a basic Mercedes and stretch from there. If you're interested, contact **Carey Limousine International** at **800/336-4646,** or in Ireland c/o **Murray's Chauffeur Drive Service** (☎ **01/ 660-1660**). Also in Ireland, and Bord Fáilte approved, is **Emerald Chauffeur Service,** with a toll-free Irish number: **1800/513514.** A representative one-day bottom line for two people driving 100 miles in and around Dublin in a Mercedes might be around $600.

PARKING

When arriving in cities, be sure to observe local rules, including where to park. Some small cities and most towns have free street parking, but larger cities confine parking to metered spaces or parking garages and lots. "Disk-parking" is also in effect in many places, requiring you to purchase a paper disk and display it for the time you are parked in a certain area. Disks usually cost from 20p to 40p (32¢ to 64¢) per hour of use, and they're sold in most shops, hotels, and tourist offices. Some towns also follow the "pay and display" system, which is very similar to the disk system: You buy a parking voucher (again, usually from 20p to 40p per hour) from a machine at the site and display the voucher for the time you are parked.

In Belfast and other large cities in the North, certain security measures are in place. Signs stating "Control Zone" indicate that no vehicle can be left unattended there at any time. This means that if you are a single traveler, you cannot park and leave your car; if you are a traveling twosome, one person must remain in the car while it is parked. Also, unlocked cars anywhere in the North are subject to a fine, for security reasons.

BY FERRY

Since the coast of Ireland is not so razor-straight as, say, the borders of Kansas, there are a number of passenger/car ferries that cut across the wider gaps, shaving hours off your point-to-point driving times. These routes operate between Tarbert, Co. Kerry, and Killimer, Co. Clare; Passage East, Co. Waterford, and Ballyhack, Co. Wexford; and Glenbrook, east of Cork City, and Carrigaloe, outside of Cobh. Full details on these routes are in the County Clare, Southeast, and Cork City chapters.

Additionally, since Ireland includes a number of must-see islands, getting around can and ought to mean getting on a boat now and then. Some boats, including all major ferries, are licensed and offer regular scheduled service. Sometimes, however, it's a matter of staring out across a body of water to where you want to be and asking someone with a boat to take you there. Both work. To supplement the generous boat listings in this guide, you may want to request a copy of Information Sheet 50C—"Island Boat / Air Services"—from the Irish Tourist Board.

9 Suggested Itineraries

To make the rounds of Ireland, North and South, you'll need at least two or, better, three weeks. With even a week, however, you can convince yourself and others you've been there.

Here are a few recommended itineraries, with the number of days suggested for each city or touring center indicated in parentheses. Each tour starts or finishes near Shannon or Dublin, the two main arrival/departure points. You can ask your travel agent to design a trip based on your interests or on the amount of time you can spend.

One Week—Southern Coast   Shannon area (1), Kerry (2), Cork (2), Wexford (1), Dublin (1).

One Week—Main Highlights   Shannon area (1), Kerry (1), Cork (1), Waterford (1), Dublin (2), Galway (1).

One Week—East Coast   Dublin (3), Dundalk (1), Kilkenny (1), Waterford (1), Wexford (1).

One Week—West Coast   Kerry (2), Galway and Connemara (2), Sligo (2), Shannon area (1).

One Week—The Northwest   Shannon area (1), Sligo (2), Donegal (3), Shannon (1).

One Week—The North   Newcastle (1), Belfast (2), Antrim Coast (2), Derry (1), Enniskillen (1).

Two Weeks—The Coastal Circuit   Shannon (1); Kerry (2); Cork (1), Dublin (2), Belfast (2), Sligo (1), Donegal (2), Galway, Mayo, and Connemara (2), Shannon (1).

Three Weeks—The Complete Tour   Shannon (1), Kerry (2), Cork (1), Kilkenny (1), Waterford or Wexford (1), Dublin (3), Belfast (2), Portrush (1), Derry or Enniskillen (2), Sligo (1), Donegal (2), Mayo (1), Galway and Connemara (2), Shannon (1).

All of the above itineraries describe circles, which are not for everyone. When time is scarce, some people, like me, prefer to settle into one place for a week and to reach out and down from there. This is the "hub" plan, surely a viable alternative to the seven-day dash. If it's your first time in Ireland, Dublin or Galway would make great hubs. Whether you decide to tour or to stay put may depend on whether you're primarily in search of sights or stories. You'll see more sights moving around, but you'll likely hear more stories if you stay around for them.

10 Tips on Restaurants & Pubs

RESTAURANTS
Ireland has an admirable range of restaurants in all price categories. The settings range from old-world hotel dining rooms, country mansions, and castles to skylit terraces,

shopfront bistros, riverside cottages, thatched-roof pubs, and converted chapels. Best of all, the food is fresh, varied, and delicious (see "Keeping Body & Soul Together: Irish Food & Drink," in Chapter 2). Before you hasten to book a table, here are a few things you should know.

RESERVATIONS   Except for self-service eateries, informal cafes, and some popular seafood spots, most all restaurants encourage reservations. The more expensive restaurants absolutely require reservations, since there is little turnover—once a table is booked, it is yours for the whole lunch period or for the evening until closing. Friday and Saturday nights (and Sunday lunch) seatings are often booked out a week or more in advance at some places, so have a few choices in mind if you are booking at the last minute.

Here's a tip for Americans who don't mind dining early. If you stop into or phone a restaurant and find that it is booked out from 8 or 8:30pm onward, ask if you can dine early (at 6:30 or 7pm), with a promise to leave by 8pm, and you will sometimes get a table. A few restaurants are even experimenting with early bird menus at reduced prices to attract people for early evening seating. Irish restaurateurs are just beginning to learn that it is doubly profitable to have more than one seating a night.

TABLE D'HÔTE OR À LA CARTE   In most restaurants, two menus are offered: table d'hôte, a fixed-price three- or four-course lunch or dinner, with a variety of choices; and à la carte, a menu offering a wide choice of appetizers (starters), soups, main courses, salads or vegetables, and desserts (sweets), each individually priced.

With the former, you pay the set price whether you take each course or not, but, if you do take each course, the total price offers very good value. With the latter, you choose what you want and pay accordingly. If you are just a salad-and-entrée person, then à la carte will probably work out to be less expensive; but if you want all the courses and the trimmings, then stick with the table d'hôte.

In the better restaurants, the table d'hôte menu is pushed at lunch time, particularly for the business clientele. In the evening, both menus are readily available. In the less expensive restaurants, coffee shops, and cafes, you can usually order à la carte at any time, whether it be a soup and sandwich for lunch or steak and salad at night.

Here's a tip for those on a budget: If you want to try a top-rated restaurant but can't afford or accept the dinner prices, then have your main meal there in the middle of the day by trying the table d'hôte set lunch menu. You'll experience the same great cuisine at half the price of a nighttime meal.

PRICES   Meal prices at restaurants include 12.5% VAT in the Republic of Ireland and a 17.5% VAT in Northern Ireland, but service charge is extra. In more than half of all restaurants, a set service charge is added automatically to your bill—this can range from 10% to 15%. In the remaining restaurants, it is now the custom not to add any service charge, leaving the amount of the tip up to you. Needless to say, this diversity of policy can be confusing for a visitor, but each restaurant normally prints its policy on the menu. If it is not clear, ask.

When no service charge is added, then you should tip as you normally would in the United States, up to 15% depending on the quality of the service. If 10% to 12.5% has already been added to your bill, then you should leave an appropriate amount that will total 15% if service has been satisfactory.

We have classified the restaurants described in this book into categories of price. The price levels are based on what it costs for a complete dinner (or lunch, if dinner is not served) for one person including tax and tip, but not wine or alcoholic beverages.

Very Expensive	£35 ($56.00) and up
Expensive	£25–£35 ($40.00–$56.00)
Moderate	£10–£25 ($16.00–$40.00)
Inexpensive	£5–£10 ($8.00–$16.00)
Budget	Under £5 ($8.00)

MONEY-SAVING TIP   Some restaurants, in all categories of price, offer a fixed-price three-course tourist menu during certain hours and days. These menus offer limited choices, but are usually lower in price than the restaurant's regular table d'hôte menu. Look for a tourist menu with a green Irish chef symbol in the window, listing the choices and the hours when the prices are in effect.

SOME DINING TIPS   If you are fond of a cocktail or beer before or during your meal, be sure to check in advance if a restaurant has a full license—some restaurants are only licensed to sell wine.

Don't be surprised if you are not ushered to your table as soon as you arrive at a restaurant. This is not a delaying tactic—many of the better dining rooms carry on the old custom of seating you in a lounge or bar area while you sip an aperitif and peruse the menu. Your waiter then comes to discuss the choices and to take your order. You are not called to the table until the first course is about to be served.

PUBS

The mainstay of Irish social life, both by night and by day, is unquestionably the pub. With more than 10,000 specimens presenting themselves throughout the island, there are pubs in every city, town, and hamlet, on every street and at every turn.

The origin of pubs reaches back several centuries to a time when, for lack of trendy coffee bars or health clubs, neighbors would gather in a kitchen to talk and maybe sample some home brew. As a certain spot grew popular, word spread and people would come from all directions, always assured of a warm welcome. Such places gradually became known as public houses—pubs, for short. In time, the name of the person who tended a public house was mounted over the doorway, and hence many pubs still bear a family or proprietor's name, such as Davy Byrnes, Doheny and Nesbitt, or W. Ryan. Many, in fact, have been in the same family for generations, and though they might've added televisions, pool tables, and dartboards to their decor, their primary purpose is still to be a stage for conversation and a warm spot to down a pint or pack in an inexpensive lunch of "pub grub."

PUB HOURS   In the Republic of Ireland, hours May through September are from 10:30am to 11:30pm Monday through Saturday, closing a half-hour earlier during the rest of the year. On Sunday, bars are open from 12:30pm to 2pm and from 4pm to 11pm all year.

In the North, pubs are open year-round from 11:30am to 11pm Monday through Saturday, and from 12:30pm to 2pm and 7pm to 10pm on Sunday.

DRINK PRICES   Charges are more or less standardized throughout Ireland, with hotel bar prices sometimes being slightly higher than the norm. A pint of draft beer or stout averages £2 ($3.20), a bottle of beer £1.90 ($3.04), a short of whiskey (a shot and then some) around £1.85 ($2.96), and a glass of wine approximately £2.50 ($4).

11 Tips on Attractions & Shopping

ATTRACTION DISCOUNTS   Sightseeing on a budget? Ireland offers several ways to cut costs and stretch a dollar (or a pound). Here are a few ways to save on admission charges at major attractions.

A **Heritage Card** entitles you to unlimited admission into the more than 50 attractions all over Ireland operated by the Office of Public Works. These include castles, stately homes, historic monuments, national parks, and more. The card, which costs £15 ($24) adults, £10 ($16) seniors, and £6 ($9.60) children/students, is available from participating attractions or from **Visitor Services,** Office of Public Works, 51 St. Stephen's Green, Dublin 2 (☎ **01/661-3111,** ext. 2386).

Heritage Island VIP Discount Entry Card entitles you to discounted admissions at more than 60 attractions in the Republic of Ireland and Northern Ireland. These sites range from castles, stately homes, and heritage centers to caves, planetariums, forts, national parks, museums, and abbeys. The card comes with a guide to the attractions, on sale for £3 ($4.50) at tourist offices and shops, or from **Heritage Island,** 37 Main St., Donnybrook, Dublin 4 (fax **01/260-0058**). It is also available in the United States in advance of your trip by sending $10 to Heritage Island, 795 Franklin Ave., Franklin Lakes, NJ 07417.

The **Passport to Ireland,** a guide to 100 major Irish attractions, North and South—museums, zoos, castles, historical parks, and more—also contains discount vouchers to each listed site, usually in the form of one free admission when one adult ticket is purchased at full price. The current cost of the Passport booklet is $11.95 ($16.95 in Canada). If you're traveling with anyone who likes the same things you do, it won't be long before you recoup the cost of this booklet. To order a copy call **800/229-5305** from the U.S. or **800/268-4395** in Canada.

Detailed information about **National Trust** attractions in Northern Ireland is available from the Northern Ireland Tourist Board.

VAT TAX REFUNDS   When shopping in the Republic of Ireland and Northern Ireland, bear in mind that the price of most goods, excluding books and children's clothing/footwear, already includes valued added tax (VAT), a government tax of 17.36%. VAT is a hidden tax—it is already included on the price tags and in prices quoted to you.

Fortunately, as a visitor, you can avoid paying this tax, *if* you follow a few simple procedures. (*Note:* EU residents are not entitled to a VAT refund on goods purchased.)

The easiest way to make a VAT-free purchase is to arrange for a store to ship the goods directly abroad to your home; such a shipment is not liable for VAT. However, you do have to pay for shipping, so you may not save that much in the end.

If you wish to take your goods with you, then you must pay the full amount for each item, including all VAT charges. However, you can have that tax refunded to you in a number of ways. Here are the main choices:

For a **Store Refund,** obtain at the time of purchase a full receipt showing name, address, and VAT paid (cash register tally slips are not accepted by Customs). A passport and other forms of identification (driver's license) may be required. When departing Ireland, go to the Customs Office at the airport or ferry port to have your receipts stamped and goods inspected. Stamped receipts should then be sent to the store of purchase, which will then issue a VAT refund check to you by mail to your home address. Most stores will deduct a small handling fee for this service.

Europe Tax-Free Shopping (ETS) is a private company offering you a cash refund on purchases made at shops displaying an ETS sticker anywhere in Ireland or throughout the European Union. Refunds can be collected in the currency of your choice as you depart from Dublin or Shannon Airport. The nominal fee for this service is calculated on the amount of money you spend in each store. The ETS booths are open at Dublin Airport from 6am to 5:30pm year-round, and at

Shannon Airport from 7am to 6pm from the end of April to the end of October, and 9:30am to 5:30pm from the end of October to the end of April.

To obtain a refund, you must do the following:

1. Make purchases from stores displaying an ETS sticker, and be sure to obtain an ETS voucher from these participating shops each time you make a purchase.
2. Fill out each form with your name, address, passport number, and other required details.
3. When departing Ireland, have any vouchers with a value of over £200 ($320) stamped and validated by a customs official.
4. You can then go to the ETS booth at Dublin Airport (Departures Hall) or Shannon Airport (in the Arrivals Hall), turn in your stamped ETS forms, and receive cash payments in U.S. or Canadian dollars, British pounds sterling, or Irish punts, whichever you prefer.

If you are departing from Ireland via a ferry port, or if you don't have time to get to the ETS booth before you leave, you can mail your stamped receipts to the **ETS Headquarters at Spiddal Industrial Estate,** Spiddal, County Galway (☎ **091/ 83258;** fax 091/83043). Your refund, issued as a check, will be mailed to your home within 21 days. You can also request to have your value-added tax refund applied to your credit card account.

TaxBack is a private company offering VAT refunds after you leave Ireland by charging a flat fee averaging 2% of the gross price of goods purchased. On departure from Ireland, go to the TaxBack service desk at Shannon or Dublin Airport and turn in your receipts. Any receipts over £200 ($320) in value must first be stamped by a customs official. If time is short, you can return home, have your receipts stamped by a notary public, and then mail them to TaxBack, P.O. Box 132 CK, 125 Patrick St., Cork City, Co. Cork (☎ **021/277010**). If you charged your purchases on a credit card, TaxBack will arrange a credit to your account in the amount of the VAT refund; if you paid cash, then you will receive a check in U.S. dollars sent to your home with the refund.

12 Tracing Your Irish Roots

Whether your name is Kelly or Klein, you may have some ancestral ties with Ireland—about 40 million Americans do. If you are planning to visit Ireland to trace your roots, you'll enjoy the greatest success if you do some planning in advance. The more information you can gather about your family before your visit, the easier it will be to find your ancestral home or even a distant cousin once you arrive.

When in Ireland, you can do the research and footwork yourself or you can use the services of a commercial agency. One of the best firms to contact is **Hibernian Research Co.,** P.O. Box 3097, Dublin 6 (☎ **01/496-6522;** fax 01/497-3011). These researchers, all trained by the Chief Herald of Ireland, have a combined total of over 100 years professional experience in working on all aspects of family histories. Among the cases that Hibernian Research has handled in the past were U.S. President Ronald Reagan, Canadian Prime Minister Brian Mulrooney, and Ireland's own President Mary Robinson. If your ancestors were from the North, a similar service is operated by the **Irish Heritage Association,** A. 215–217, Portview, 310 Newtownards Rd., Belfast BT4 1HE (☎ **1232/455325**). Minimum search fees average £50 ($80).

If you prefer to do the digging yourself, be advised that Dublin City is the location for all of the Republic of Ireland's centralized genealogical records, and

Belfast is the place to go for Ulster ancestral hunts. Here are the major sources of information:

The Genealogical Office, 2 Kildare St., Dublin (☎ **01/661-8811**), incorporates the office of the Chief Herald and operates a specialist consultation service on how to trace your ancestry. Minimum personal consultation fee (approximately one hour) is £25 ($40); postal consultation is £30 ($48).

The National Library, Kildare Street, Dublin 2 (☎ **01/661-9911**). The resources include an extensive collection of pre-1880 Catholic records of baptisms, births, and marriages, plus other genealogical material, including trade directories, journals of historical and archaeological societies, local histories, and most newspapers. In addition, the library has a comprehensive indexing system that will enable you to identify the material you need to consult.

Office of the Registrar General, Joyce House, 8/11 Lombard St. East, Dublin 2 (☎ **01/671-1000**). The General Register Office is the central repository for records relating to births, deaths, and marriages in the Republic (Catholic marriages from January 1, 1864; all other marriages from April 1, 1845). This office does not engage in genealogical research. Full birth, death, or marriage certificates each cost £5.50 ($8.80). General searches cost £12 ($19.20). The office is open weekdays from 9:30am to 12:30pm and 2:15 to 4:30pm.

The National Archives, Bishop Street, Dublin 8 (☎ **01/478-3711**). Previously known as the Public Record Office, this facility was severely damaged by a fire in the early 1920s and many valuable source documents predating that event were lost. However, numerous records rich in genealogical interest are still available here. These include Griffith's Primary Valuation of Ireland, 1848–63, which records the names of all those owning or occupying land or property in Ireland at the time; the complete national census of 1901 to 1911; and tithe listings, indexes to wills, administrations, licenses, and marriage bonds. In addition, there is also an ever-expanding collection of Church of Ireland Parish Registers on microfilm, partial surviving census returns for the 19th century, rebellion reports and records relating to the period of the 1798 rebellion, crime and convict records, and details of those sentenced to transportation to Australia.

Registry of Deeds, Henrietta Street, Dublin 1 (☎ **01/670-7500**). Its records date from 1708 and relate to all the usual transactions affecting property, notably leases, mortgages, and settlements, and some wills. A fee of £2 ($3.20) per day is charged, which includes instruction on how to handle the indexes.

Public Record Office of Northern Ireland, 66 Balmoral Ave., Belfast BT9 6NY (☎ **01232/251318**). This office has the surviving official records of Northern Ireland, including tithe and valuation records from the 1820s and 1830s, copy wills from 1858 for Ulster, the records of many landed estates in Ulster, and copies of most pre-1900 registers of baptisms, marriages, and burial papers for all denominations in Ulster.

If you know the county or town that your ancestors came from, then you can also consult the various local genealogical centers, parish records, and libraries throughout Ireland and Northern Ireland.

FAST FACTS: Ireland

American Express   The Dublin office of **American Express International** is a full-service travel agency also offering currency exchange, traveler's checks, and (for members) mail-holding. It is located at 116 Grafton St., Dublin 2

(☎ **01/677-2874**), and can refer you to American Express representatives in Cork, Galway, and Limerick.

In the North, the American Express representative is **Hamilton Travel,** 10 College St., Belfast BY1 6BT (☎ **01232/322455**).

Baby-sitters   With advance notice, most hotels and guest houses will arrange for baby-sitting.

Business Hours   As a rule, banks are open for service throughout all of Ireland from 10am to 12:30pm and 1:30 to 3pm, Monday through Friday, with one late-closing day (Thursdays in Dublin), when they close at 5pm. In larger cities, some banks now remain open through the lunch hour as well. Airport banks are open 7:30am to 11pm every day of the year, with the exception of Christmas.

Most business offices are open from 9am to 5pm, Monday through Friday. Stores and shops are open from 9am to 5:30pm Monday through Saturday. In cities such as Dublin, Belfast, Cork, and Galway, stores remain open until 8pm or 9pm on Thursday or Friday, and, in some country towns, there is an early closing day when shops close at 1pm. Some tourist-oriented shops also open on Sunday from 11am or noon until 5pm or later. For exact shopping hours, see each individual chapter.

Camera & Film   One-hour photo-developing services can be found in major cities. Film for color prints and slides is readily available at camera shops and pharmacies.

Climate   See "When to Go," earlier in this chapter.

Currency   See "Money," earlier in this chapter.

Currency Exchange   A currency exchange service in Ireland is signposted as a Bureau de Change. There are bureaux de change at all banks and at many post office branches. In addition, many hotels and travel agencies offer currency exchange services, although the best rate of exchange is usually given at banks.

Customs   See "Visitor Information & Entry Requirements," earlier in this chapter.

Dentists   For listings, look under "Dental Surgeons" in the Golden Pages (yellow pages) of the Irish telephone book or in the Yellow Pages of the Northern Ireland telephone book.

Doctors   In an emergency, most hotels and guest houses will contact a house doctor for you. You can also consult the Golden Pages of the Irish telephone book or the Yellow Pages of the Northern Ireland telephone book under "Doctors—Medical." In the Republic you can call the **Irish Medical Association,** 10 Fitzwilliam Place, Dublin (☎ **01/676-7273**), for a referral.

Documents Required   See "Visitor Information & Entry Requirements," earlier in this chapter.

Driving Rules   See "Getting Around," earlier in this chapter.

Drugs & Firearms   The laws against the importation of illegal drugs and firearms are quite severe in the North and the South and will be enforced. Consult the nearest Irish or Northern Ireland consulate before presuming to bring any firearm into Ireland.

Drugstores   Drugstores are usually called chemist shops or pharmacies. Look under "Chemists—Pharmaceutical" in the Golden Pages of the Irish telephone book or "Chemists—Dispensing" in the Yellow Pages of the Northern Ireland telephone book.

Electricity   The standard electrical current is 220 volts AC in the Republic of Ireland and 240 volts in Northern Ireland. Most hotels have 110-volt shaver points for use in bathrooms, but other 110-volt equipment (such as hair dryers) will not work without a transformer and a plug adapter. Computers and sensitive electronic equipment may require more than the standard over-the-counter voltage converter. Some laptops and powerbooks, on the other hand, have built-in converters. Consult the manufacturer of your computer for specifics. In any event, you will always need a plug adapter.

Embassies/Consulates   The **American Embassy** is located at 42 Elgin Rd., Ballsbridge, Dublin 4 (☎ **01/668-8777**); the **Canadian Embassy** at 65/68 St. Stephen's Green, Dublin 2 (☎ **01/678-1988**); the **British Embassy** at 33 Merrion Rd., Dublin 4 (☎ **01/669-5211**); and the **Australian Embassy** at Fitzwilton House, Wilton Terrace, Dublin 2 (☎ **01/676-1517**). In addition, there is an **American Consulate** at 14 Queen St., Belfast BT1 6EQ (☎ **0232/328239**).

Emergencies   For police, fire, or other emergencies, dial **999.**

Etiquette   The Irish still observe a range of traditional courtesies, such as males holding doors for females and the young and strong giving up a seat on a bus for senior citizens and pregnant women. Contrary to their media image, the Irish are generally neither loud nor assertive in public. If you prefer not to be spotted as a tourist, mind your decibels and your stride. Even when we whisper, it's our gait that gives us away. Try not looking at your fellow pedestrians as members of the other team, "tacklers" as it were, and you'll suddenly blend in.

   The one concept we need to remember at all times is that we are the strangers, the outsiders, when we travel abroad. In an embarrassing moment, when what's going on makes no sense, chances are the joke is on us. We can react in two ways: belligerently or with humor. Try the latter.

   One deep breach in hospitality that many travelers from the United States will note is the obliviousness and insensitivity of many Irish smokers to the discomfort they bring to nonsmokers. Smokers still pretty much have the wheel in Ireland. For some pubs I'd recommend gas masks, were it practicable.

Fare Terminology   Transport fares—air, ferry, train—are either "single" (one-way) or "return" (round-trip).

Hairdressers/Barbers   Consult the Golden Pages or Yellow Pages under "Hairdressers—Ladies" and "Hairdressers—Men."

Hospitals   See listings in individual chapters.

Language   See the "Language" section in Chapter 2.

Laundry/Dry Cleaning   Most hotels provide same-day or next-day laundry and/or dry-cleaning services. If you wish to make your own arrangements, look under "Dry Cleaners" in the Golden Pages or Yellow Pages of the telephone book.

Liquor Laws   Individuals must be age 18 or over to be served alcoholic beverages in Ireland. For pub hours, see "Tips on Restaurants & Pubs," earlier in this chapter. Restaurants with liquor licenses are permitted to serve alcohol during the hours meals are served. Hotels and guest houses with licenses can serve during normal hours to the general public; overnight guests, referred to as residents, can be served after closing hours. Alcoholic beverages by the bottle can be purchased at liquor stores, pubs displaying "off-license" signs, and at some supermarkets.

   Ireland has very strict laws and penalties regarding driving while intoxicated.

Mail   In Ireland, mailboxes are painted green with the word *Post* on top. In Northern Ireland, they are painted red with a royal coat of arms symbol. From the

Republic, an airmail letter to the United States or Canada, not exceeding 20 grams, costs 52p (83¢), while a postcard costs 38p (60¢). Pre-stamped aerogrammes or air-letters are 45p (72¢) individually and £2.20 ($3.53) for five. From Northern Ireland to the United States or Canada, airmail letters cost 39p (60¢) and postcards 34p (53¢). Delivery takes about five days to a week.

The best way to receive mail while in Ireland is to have it sent care of your hotel or guest house. Otherwise, you can have mail sent to the GPO (general post office). This service is called *Poste Restante*. To use it, mail should be addressed to your name, in care of the post office in the city where you will be staying. Poste Restante mail is ordinarily held for a maximum of one month. If unclaimed during that period, it is returned to the sender. There is no charge for this service. Mail can be picked up at the Dublin GPO Monday to Saturday 10:30am to 8pm and Sunday 9am to 8pm. Generally, other GPOs are open weekdays 9am to 5:30pm.

Newspapers/Magazines   The national daily newspapers in the Republic of Ireland are the *Irish Times, Irish Independent, The Examiner, The Herald, Cork Examiner,* and *Evening Echo.* The national Sunday editions are the *Sunday Independent, Sunday Press, Sunday Tribune, Sunday World,* and the Irish-language *Anola.* Prime dailies in the North are the *Belfast Newsletter* and the *Belfast Telegraph.* For useful and up-to-date listing of events throughout Ireland, *The Event Guide* is published biweekly and is available free of cost practically wherever you look for it.

Police   In the Republic of Ireland, a law enforcement officer is called a **Garda,** a member of the *Garda Siochana* (guardian of the peace); in the plural, it's *Gardai* (pronounced *gar*-dee) or simply "the Guards." Dial **999** to reach the Gardai in an emergency. Except for special detachments, Irish police are unarmed and wear dark blue uniforms. In Northern Ireland, the police can also be reached by dialing **999.**

Radio/TV   In the Republic of Ireland, RTÉ (Radio Telefís Éireann) is the national broadcasting authority with two nationwide TV channels, RTÉ 1 and Network 2; a new Irish language channel, Teilifís na Gaeilge; and three nationwide VHF radio networks, Radio 1, 2FM, and Radió na Gaeltachta (in both Irish and English). Additionally, FM3 offers classical music programming. Other, smaller local stations, like Cork Local Radio, serve specific regions. In North America, RTÉ radio is available via the Galaxy 5 satellite and on the World Wide Web at: http://town.hall.org/radio/wrn.html.

RTÉ, jointly with Telecom Éireann, owns and operates Cablelink Ltd., providing a range of cable and satellite channels from Britain and further abroad.

In the North, there is Ulster Television, BBC-TV (British Broadcasting Corporation), and ITN-TV (Independent), plus BBC Radio 1, 2, and 3. Satellite programs via CNN, SKY News, and other international operators are also received.

Rest Rooms   Public rest rooms are usually simply called toilets, or are marked with international symbols. In the Republic of Ireland, some of the older ones still carry the Gaelic words *Fir* (Men) and *Mna* (Women). The newest and best-kept rest rooms are found at shopping complexes and at multistory car parks—some cost 10p (16¢) to enter. Free use of rest rooms is available to customers of sightseeing attractions, museums, hotels, restaurants, pubs, shops, theaters, and department stores. Gas stations normally do not have public toilets.

Safety   The Republic of Ireland has enjoyed a traditionally low crime rate, particularly when it comes to violent crimes. Those days are not over, but they do regrettably seem to be passing. By U.S. standards, Ireland is still very safe, but not so safe as to warrant carelessness. Travelers should take normal precautions to protect their belongings from theft and themselves from harm.

In recent years, the larger cities have been prey to pickpockets, purse snatchers, car thieves, and drug traffickers. To alert visitors to potential dangers, the Garda Siochana publishes a small leaflet, *A Short Guide to Tourist Security,* available at tourist offices and other public places. The booklet advises you not to carry large amounts of money or important documents like your passport or airline tickets when strolling around (leave them in a safety deposit box at your hotel). Do not leave cars unlocked or cameras, binoculars, or other expensive equipment unattended. Be alert and aware of your surroundings, and do not wander in lonely areas alone at night.

In the north of Ireland, safety is a somewhat greater concern because of the political unrest that has prevailed there for the past 30 years. Before traveling to Northern Ireland, visitors are advised to contact the U.S. State Department and the Northern Ireland Tourist Board to obtain the latest safety recommendations. The **U.S. Department of State 24-hour hotline** provides travel warnings and security recommendations, as well as emergency assistance. Call **202/647-5225.**

Taxes As in many European countries, sales tax is called VAT (value-added tax) and is often included in the price quoted to you. In the Republic, VAT rates vary—for hotels, restaurants, and car rentals, it is 12.5%; for souvenir and gifts, it is 17.36%. In Northern Ireland, the VAT is 17.5% across the board. VAT charged on services such as hotel stays, meals, car rentals, and entertainment cannot be refunded to visitors, but the VAT charged on products such as souvenirs is refundable. For full details on VAT refunds for purchases, see "VAT Tax Refunds," earlier in this chapter.

Telephone In the Republic, the telephone system is known as Telecom Éireann; in Northern Ireland, it's British Telecom.

To telephone Ireland, dial the international access code (**011** from the United States), then the country code—**353** for the Republic, **44** for the North—and finally the number, remembering to omit the initial 0, which is only for use *within* Ireland. Thus, to call the Co. Kerry number 066/00000 from the United States, you'd dial 011/353-66/00000. For direct-dial calls *to* the United States, dial the international access code (**00** from Ireland), then the country code (**1**), followed by area code and number. To place a collect call to the United States from Ireland, dial **1-800/550-000** for USA Direct service.

Phone numbers in Ireland are currently in flux, as digits are added to accommodate expanded service. Every effort has been made to assure that the numbers in this guide are accurate at the time of writing. If you have difficulty reaching a party, the Irish toll-free number for directory assistance is **1190.** From the States the (toll) number to call is **00353-91-770220.**

Local calls from a phone booth cost 20p (32¢) within the Republic of Ireland, and 10p (16¢) in the North. The most efficient way to make calls from public phones is to use a Callcard in the Republic and a Phonecard in the North. Both are prepaid computerized cards that insert into the phone in lieu of coins. They can be purchased in a range of denominations at phone company offices, post offices, and many retail outlets (such as newsstands).

If you happen to confront one of the old pay phones in the Republic (you'll know it by its two buttons: A and B), this is how you make it work. Insert 20p (32¢), dial the number, and, as soon as your party answers, push button A. (The person on the other end cannot hear you until you do so.) If there is no answer, push button B for coin return.

Time Ireland follows Greenwich mean time (one hour earlier than central European time) from November through March, and British standard time (the same as central European time) from April through October. This means that Ireland is five time zones earlier than the eastern United States (that is, when it's noon in New York, it's 5pm in Ireland).

Ireland's latitude makes for longer days and shorter nights in the summer, and the reverse in the winter. In June, there is bright sun until 11pm, while in December it is truly dark at 4pm.

Tipping   Most hotels and guest houses add a service charge to the bill, usually 12.5% to 15%, although some smaller places add only 10% or nothing at all. Always check to see what amount, if any, has been added to your bill. If it is 12.5% to 15%, and you feel this is sufficient, then there is no need for further gratuities. However, if a lesser amount has been added or if staff members have provided exceptional service, then it is appropriate to give additional cash gratuities. For porters or bellmen, tip 50p (80¢) to £1 ($1.60) per piece of luggage. For taxi drivers, hairdressers, and other providers of service, tip as you would at home, an average of 10% to 15%.

For restaurants, the policy is usually printed on the menu—either a gratuity of 10% to 15% is added to your bill or, in some cases, no service charge is added, leaving it up to you. Always ask if you are in doubt. As a rule, bar staff do not expect a tip, except when table service is provided.

Water   Tap water throughout the island of Ireland is safe to drink. If you prefer bottled water, it is readily available at all hotels, guest houses, restaurants, and pubs.

Yellow Pages   The classified section of telephone books in the Republic of Ireland is called the Golden Pages. In the North, it's the Yellow Pages.

Ireland Outdoors   4

When you think of Ireland, you may think "green" but you almost certainly don't think "wilderness." After all, it's a relatively small island, and the country's prefamine population used every square foot they could find to eke a living out of what is often not the most forgiving land.

As a result, you'll find signs of human habitation almost everywhere you go, from the most verdant field to the most inaccessible, craggy and forbidding plot. Stone walls, sometimes hundreds of years old and constructed without benefit of mortar, crisscross the countryside, while ancient dolmens rise atop remote hills and pub-and-post-office towns hide around the next bend in the road.

This said, it's also true that there are places where you can walk for days and not see another living soul, where at night the silence and seclusion make you forget the 20th century and your hectic workaday life entirely. Beauty, history, and an almost tangible connection to the past infuse the whole of the Irish landscape. In this chapter we investigate some of the best ways of getting out there and connecting with it.

1 Bicycling

Bicycling is surely the best way to see the Irish landscape in its many forms, from barren bogland to crashing surf and inland lakes. The distances are quite manageable, and with a week or two on the bike you can travel through several of the regions described in this guide or explore one in greater detail. Accommodation in the form of hostels, B&Bs, and hotels is abundantly available for touring cyclists who don't want to deal with the extra weight of a tent and sleeping bag. For those on more conventional (read motorized) tours, day trips on the bike can be a great way to stretch your legs after spending too much time in the car, and rentals are available in most towns that cater in any way to tourists.

Roads in Ireland are categorized as either M (Motorway), N (National), or R (Regional), with some still bearing the older T (Trunk) and L (Link) designations. For reasons of scenery as well as safety, you'll probably want to avoid the busier roads; the "R" and "L" roads are always suitable for cycling, and the "N" roads as well in outlying areas where there isn't too much traffic. The disadvantage of the smallest roads in remote areas is that they are rarely signposted, so

---

A Few Helpful Addresses

The following organizations provide useful resources, including maps and accommodations information, of use to anyone investigating Ireland's outdoors.

An Oige (Irish Youth Hostel Association), 61 Mountjoy St., Dublin (☎ **01/8304555;** fax 01/6715270).

Association for Adventure Sports and Mountaineering Council of Ireland, House of Sport, Longmile Road, Dublin 12 (☎ **01/4509845;** fax 01/4502805).

YHANI (Northern Ireland's Youth Hostels Association), 56 Bradbury Place, Belfast, BT7 1RU (☎ **01232/324733**).

---

you will want a good map and compass to be sure of your way. In some areas of the west and northwest, *only* the "N" roads are consistently signposted.

Anyone planning a bicycle tour will want to bring his or her own bicycle—the ones available for rental are with few exceptions impossibly heavy and fitted with unreliable components. If you must rent a bike, there are a few small items you'll want to bring. Helmets are only sporadically available, and your chances of finding one that fits are poor, so bring one if you care about your head. The panniers (saddlebags) offered for rental are often unbelievably flimsy, and may begin to fall apart shortly after departure, so bring your own unless you want to leave a trail of your stuff as you go. If you have cycling shoes and good pedals, you can easily attach them to the rental bike; this will make your trip immeasurably more enjoyable. With advance notice most rental shops can outfit a bike with such handy extras as toe clips, bar ends, and water bottle cages; an advance booking will also improve your chances of reserving the right size bike. Many rental outfits can also arrange a one-way rental over a short distance (up to 100 miles or so), and the national companies such as Irish Cycle Hire or Raleigh Rent-A-Bike are set up for one-way rentals throughout the country.

Anyone cycling in Ireland should be prepared for two inevitable obstacles to forward progress: wind and hills. Outside of the midlands there are hills just about anywhere you go in Ireland, and those on the back roads can have outrageously steep grades: Road engineering is rather primitive and instead of using switchbacks on a steep slope a road will often climb by the most direct route. The prevailing winds on Ireland's west coast blow from south to north, so by traveling in the same direction you can save yourself a lot of effort over the course of a long tour.

The coastal roads of the southwest, west, and northwest have long been favored by cyclists. The quiet roads and rugged scenery of the Beara Peninsula (see Chapter 9) make it perfect for a cycling tour, along with the nearby Dingle Peninsula (see Chapter 10); the spectacular Iveragh Peninsula (also Chapter 10) is okay for cycling if you don't mind dodging tour buses on the renowned "Ring of Kerry" road. Donegal is one of the hilliest regions, and rewards the energetic cyclist with some of the most spectacular coastal and mountain scenery in Ireland.

Also ideal for cycling are Ireland's many islands: you can bring your bike on all the passenger ferries, often for no extra charge, and discover roads with little or no traffic. Some of the best islands with accommodations are Cape Clear, Co. Cork (see Chapter 9); Great Blasket Island, Co. Kerry (see Chapter 10); and the Aran Islands, Co. Galway (see Chapter 12).

If you want your cycling trip to Ireland to be orchestrated and outfitted by affable experts on the ground, you may wish to consult or sign on with **Irish Cycling Safaris,** run by Eamon Ryan and family, who offer trips to practically every part of

Ireland suitable for two wheels. They're found at 7 Dartry Park, Dublin 6 (☎ **01/ 260-0749;** fax 01/706-1168).

BICYCLING RESOURCES

There are several rental agencies with depots nationwide that permit one way rental, including **Irish Cycle Hire,** Mayoralty Street, Drogheda, Co. Louth (☎ **041/41067;** fax 041/35369), which will rent you a bike for £6 ($9.60) per day or £30 ($48) per week. Other agencies include **Rent A Bike,** at 58 Lower Gardiner St., Dublin 1 (☎ **01/8744247;** fax 01/8364763), and **Raleigh Ireland,** Raleigh House, Kylemore Road, Dublin 10 (☎ **01/6261333).**

2 Walking

In recent years, much work has been done to promote walking in Ireland, a notable example being the creation of a network of long-distance trails. The first of these to open was the **Wicklow Way,** which begins just outside Dublin and proceeds through rugged hills and serene pastures on its 82-mile course. Others include the **South Leinster Way,** the **Beara Way** (see Chapter 9), the **Kerry Way** (see Chapter 10), and the **Dingle Way** (see Chapter 10). Most trails are routed so that meals and accommodations—whether in B&Bs, hostels, or hotels—are never more than one day's walk away.

The long-distance routes are the best-marked trails in Ireland, although the standards for signposting will seem surprisingly inadequate to those familiar with similar trails in America. It is generally assumed in Ireland that walkers will possess a map and compass, and know how to use them. Markers are frequently miles apart, and often seem to be lacking at crucial crossroads. Since visibility is rarely impeded by trees on Irish hillsides, the way between two peaks is usually indicated by a post or cairn on the summit of each peak, with the expectation that the walker will find his or her own way in between. A compass becomes absolutely crucial when a fog blows in, as all landmarks quickly disappear. Be warned: This can happen quite unexpectedly.

The walks listed in this guide are on clearly marked trails whenever possible, and if sections are without markings this is indicated. We can't provide you with *all* the information you'll need for the walks, of course, so you should consult the appropriate sources before setting out. There are guides with maps published for most of the long-distance trails in Ireland, available from bookstores, shops, and tourist offices in the local area. For those wishing to plan ahead, many of the relevant guides can be obtained from **An Oige,** the Irish Youth Hostel Association, 61 Mountjoy St., Dublin (☎ **01/8304555;** fax 01/6715270). Ordnance Survey maps are available in several scales, of which the most helpful to the walker is the 1:50,000 or 1.25 inches to 1 mile scale; this series is currently available for all of Northern Ireland and a limited number of locations in the Republic. The half-inch-to-one-mile series covers the whole country in 25 maps, and local maps are available in most shops; these indicate roads, major trails, and historic monuments in some detail, and although they are on too small a scale for walkers they are all that is available in many areas. For a helpful guide covering the whole country, pick up a copy of *Best Irish Walks* edited by Joss Lynam, Passport Books, 1995; or *Irish Long Distance Walks: A Guide to the Waymarked Trails* by Michael Fewer, Gill and Macmillan, 1993.

For inland hill walking try the Wicklow Hills (see Chapter 6), the Blackstairs Mountains (see Chapter 7), the Galty Mountains (see Chapter 7), or Glenveagh National Park (see Chapter 14). For coastal walks, the best-known kind in this island country, try the Beara Peninsula (see Chapter 9), the Iveragh Peninsula (see

Chapter 10), the Dingle Peninsula (see Chapter 10), the Maumturks in Connemara (see Chapter 13), and the Donegal coast (see Chapter 14).

WALKING RESOURCES

The Ballyknocken House B&B, Ashford, Co. Wicklow (☎ **0404/44614;** fax 0404/ 44627) offers two- to seven-day walking tours of the Wicklow Mountains for individuals or groups. The tours include lodging, meals (breakfast, picnic lunch, and dinner), and transport to and from the trail heads. Rates are £210 ($336) per person for one week; and £130 ($208) per person for three days. Both assume double occupancy. The owner of Ballyknock House, Mary Byrne, is quite knowledgeable about the Wicklow trails, and will assist all her guests in choosing a route suitable to their interests and fitness.

The Northern Ireland Tourist Board's official Web site has a walking and hiking page listing self-guided tours, 14 short hikes along the Ulster Way, and names and addresses of organizations offering guided walks throughout the North (**http://new.interknowledge.com/northern-ireland/**).

Western Heritage, 34 Carragh Hill, Knocknacarra, Galway, Co. Galway (☎/fax **091/521699**), offers a number of field trips and guided walks in the west of Ireland, including a Burren hill walk in Co. Clare and an exploration of ancient sites on Inishmore in the Aran Islands. Free pick-up is provided to and from Galway City accommodations. Bookings are available through the Galway Tourist Office, Victoria Place, off Eyre Square, Galway (☎ 091-563081).

3 Bird-Watching

Due to its small size, Ireland cannot offer a tremendous diversity of habitats to its avian inhabitants, and partially for this reason has only two-thirds as many recorded nesting species as Great Britain. Nevertheless, the country has remained a place of great interest to birders primarily because of its position on the migration routes of many passerines and seabirds, which find the isle a convenient stopping point on their Atlantic journeys. Most of the important seabird nesting colonies are on the west coast, the westernmost promontory of Europe; exceptions to this rule are Lambey Island, near Dublin, and Great Saltee in Co. Wexford. Sandy beaches and tidal flats on the east and west coasts are nesting grounds for large populations of winter waders and smaller, isolated tern colonies.

The lakes and wetlands of Ireland serve as a wintering ground for great numbers of wildfowl. Every year as many as 10,000 Greenland white-fronted geese winter on the north shores of Wexford Harbor, making this a mecca for birders. In the winter, flooded fields, or "callows," provide habitat for wigeons, whooping swans, and plover; the callows of the Shannon and the Blackwater are especially popular with birders.

Until recently, rural Ireland was home to large numbers of a small bird known as the corncrake (*Crex crex*), whose unusual cry during breeding season was a common feature of the Irish early summer night. Sadly, the introduction of heavy machinery for cutting silage has destroyed the protective high-grass environment in which the mother corncrake lays her eggs and subsequently raises her chicks. (The period for cutting silage coincides with the corncrake breeding period.) There are now only a few areas where the corncrake still breeds in Ireland, one of these being the Shannon Callows, where their cry can often be heard after night's quiet replaces the noises of the day.

One of the best resources for obtaining information about birding in Ireland is the **Wexford Wildfowl Reserve,** North Slob, Wexford (☎ **053/23129;** fax 053/24785;

E-mail cjwilson@iol.ie), which has a visitor center with information on local bird-watching sites and a full-time warden, Chris Wilson, who can direct you to other places corresponding to your particular areas of interest. Clive Hutchinson's book *Where to Watch Birds in Ireland* (Gill and Macmillan, 1994) will be a great help in choosing sites to visit. You can also obtain information from the **Irish Wildbird Conservancy,** Ruttledge House, 8 Longford Place, Monkstown, Co. Dublin (☎ 01/2804322), an organization devoted to bird conservation in the Republic of Ireland. An equivalent organization in Northern Ireland is the **Royal Society for the Protection of Birds,** Belvoir Park Forest, Belfast BT8 4QT (☎ 0232-491547).

Some of Ireland's best bird-watching sites are Great Saltee in early summer (see Chapter 7), the Wexford Slobs from October to April (see Chapter 7), Cape Clear Island in the summer and fall (see Chapter 9), the Skellig Islands during the summer (see Chapter 10), and Loop Head in the summer and fall (see Chapter 11).

BIRD-WATCHING RESOURCES

Weekend courses in ornithology are offered at the **Altamont Gardens,** Tullow, Co. Wicklow (☎ 0503/59128). See Chapter 6 for more information.

The Irish Bird-Watching Home Page (http://www.geocities.com/RainForest/2801/) lists and links you to information on birding events, sites, and news.

4 Golf

With nearly 300 championship courses and myriad others of lesser repute, Ireland has devoted a greater percentage of her soil to the game of golf than has any other country in the world. The Irish landscape and climate, like that of Scotland, seem almost to have been custom-designed to provide some of the fairest fairways, the greenest greens, and the most dramatic traps you'll ever encounter. And, in Ireland, there is never a shortage of 19th holes. In short, Ireland is for the golfer a place of pilgrimage.

GOLF RESOURCES

Golfing Ireland, 18 Parnell Sq., Dublin 1 (☎ 01/872-6711; fax 01/872-6632; E-mail golf@iol.ie), will book your tee times and arrange your itinerary for 28 clubs located throughout Ireland. **Jerry Quinlan's Celtic Golf,** P.O. Box 417, Cape May, NJ 08204-0417 (☎ 800/535-6148 or 609/884-8090; fax 609/884-8682), offers package tours of the championship courses and an Irish Open tour. Prices range from $1,595 to $1,795. **Golf International,** 275 Madison Ave., New York, NY 10016 (☎ 800/833-1389 or 212/986-9176; fax 212/986-3720), offers tours ranging from $1,575 to $3,695. **Owenoak International,** One Norwalk West, 40 Richards Ave., Norwalk, CT 06854 (☎ 800/426-4498), offers a variety of tours, including competition in handicap tournaments. Prices are $775 to $1,770 off-season and $895 to $1,960 full-season.

5 Horseback Riding

Ireland is a horse-loving country, and there are few areas where you cannot find a stable offering trail rides and instruction. The **Association of Irish Riding Establishments (AIRE)** is the regulatory body that accredits riding stables, assuring adequate safety standards and instructor competence. Riding prices range from £7 ($11.20) to £20 ($32) per hour, but you can expect to pay £10 ($16) on average. Listings of accredited stables throughout the country can be obtained from the Irish Tourist Board.

Outdoor Equipment Retailers

You forgot the dehydrated pineapple and the camp stove, didn't you? Now what are you going to do? Don't sweat it; Ireland has a number of outlets for outdoor gear. Here's a few of them:

Everything Outdoors, 18 Michael St., Waterford (☎ **051/50228**).

Great Outdoors, Chatham Street, Dublin 2 (☎ **01/6794293**).

The Mountain Man, Strand Street, Dingle, Co. Kerry (☎ **066/51868**).

Out & About, 21 Market St., Sligo (☎ **071/44550**).

Outside World, 7 Parnell Place, Cork (☎ **021/278833**).

Radar Stores, 7 Fox's Bow, Limerick (☎ **061/417262**).

River Deep Mountain High, Unit 10, The Cornstore, Middle Street, Galway (☎ **091/563938**).

A great variety of riding options can be found to suit different interests and levels of experience. Pony trekking caters primarily to beginners, and usually no experience is needed for these equine excursions into the countryside. Trail riding over longer distances requires the ability to trot for extended periods of time, and can be quite exhausting for the novice. Riding establishments also commonly offer such advanced options as jumping and dressage, and some have enclosed arenas, an attractive option on rainy days. There are a number of establishments that have accommodations on site, and offer packages that include meals, lodging, and riding. Post-to-post trail riding allows a rider to stay at different lodgings each night, riding on trails all day. Not all stables are able to accommodate young children, although some make a point of being open to riders of all ages.

The Irish National Stud and **The Curragh** in Co. Kildare are the center of a region famous for horse racing, and there are many fine stables nearby (see Chapter 6). The Wicklow Hills (see Chapter 6) have a number of fine riding establishments, as do counties Wexford (see Chapter 7) and Tipperary (see Chapter 7).

6 Hunting

In Ireland, the term *hunting* refers to the venerable tradition of the fox hunt, which has become increasingly controversial in recent years but nevertheless takes place throughout the country during the winter months. Advanced equestrian skills are required of participants, as the hunt involves chases at high speed through fields, jumping fences and hedgerows. It is becoming increasingly difficult to gain direct admission to the hunt, so your best option is to go through one of the many riding stables that provide horses for foreigners wishing to join in. They will need to check out your riding ability in advance, so it is recommended that you arrive at least one day before the hunt begins. The fee for a day's hunting averages £50 ($80), not including the hire of a horse.

7 Fishing

With a coastline of more than 3,472 miles, a plethora of lakes and ponds, and countless creeks, rills, streams, and rivers, Ireland offers an abundance of prime fish habitat, and the sport of catching those fish—referred to by the Irish as angling—

Angling for Trout & Salmon

The poet Yeats imagined his ideal fisherman "climbing up to a place / where stone is dark under froth," and vividly pictured "the down-turn of his wrist / when the flies drop in the stream." Anglers visiting Ireland may readily enjoy such an experience, for no license is needed to take brown trout, and many a small stream or mountain tarn offers free fishing. Check with the local tourist office or tackle dealer before venturing forth. The trout will not be large, but will make a sweet dish for your supper. You will be well advised to bring rod, reel, and waders with you, since hire of basic equipment is not a normal feature of the Irish angling scene. Suitable flies can always be bought locally.

If your quest is for larger brown trout, you should head for the bigger lakes where the underlying rock is limestone rather than granite. Oughterard in Co. Galway, Ballinrobe in Co. Mayo, and Pontoon in Co. Mayo are good centers for Lough Carrib, Lough Mask, and Lough Conn, respectively. No permit is required, but the hire of boat and experienced boatman is essential. May and June are the best months, and this would be true also of the great midland lakes that can easily be reached from Mullingar in Co. Westmeath. The lakes round Ennis in Co. Clare fish well in March or April. Excellent brown trout fishing may also be had in the rivers of Co. Cork and Co. Tipperary, but here you will usually have to apply to the local angling club for a visitor's ticket.

Many of the rivers and lakes of Ireland hold good stocks of salmon and sea trout. Sea trout run from late June through July and August. There are two main salmon runs, the spring run of older and bigger fish and the "grilse" run in June and July. Opening and closing dates vary from river to river, but most waters are open from March through September.

A license (obtained locally) is required, and advanced booking is a virtual necessity for the more famous locations like the Salmon Weir pool in Galway city or the Ridge pool in Ballina. Serious anglers will reserve accommodations by the week in centers like Waterville in Co. Kerry, or Newport in Co. Mayo. But if you are touring by car it is always worth inquiring locally as day tickets are often to be had from hotels or angling clubs.

Two excellent books by Peter O'Reilly, *Trout and Salmon Rivers of Ireland* (3rd edition, 1995), and *Trout and Salmon Loughs of Ireland* (1987) give full and systematic coverage of the waters available.

—J. V. Luce, Royal Irish Academy and Trinity College, Dublin.

Dr. Luce, an avid world-traveled angler, learned the art from his father, A. A. Luce, former chaplain and professor of philosophy at Trinity and author of a noted book on Irish angling.

has a venerable tradition. Many festivals and competitions are held during the summer to celebrate the many forms of this sport.

The seasons are as follows: salmon, January 1 to September 30; brown trout, February 15 to October 12; sea trout, June 1 to September 30; and course fishing and sea angling, January to December. A license is required for salmon and sea trout angling; the cost is £3 ($4.80) for one day, £10 ($16) for 21 days, and £25 ($40) annually. For all private salmon and sea trout fisheries a permit is required in addition to the license; prices are £15 to £100 ($24 to $160) per rod per day. A helpful brochure titled *Angling in Ireland*, which details what fish can be caught where, is available from the **Central Fisheries Board,** Balnagowan House, Mobhi Boreen, Glasnevin, Dublin 9 (☎ **01/837-9206**). Another helpful resource, *The Angler's Guide,* is published by the Irish Tourist Board. Permits, licenses, and specific information can be obtained from local outfitters or the Central Fisheries Board.

In Northern Ireland, you will have to obtain a rod license from the **Fisheries Conservancy Board,** 1 Mahon Rd., Portadown, Craigavon, Co. Armagh (☎ **01762-334666**). A permit may be required in addition; information can be obtained from local outfitters or the **Department of Agriculture, Fisheries Division,** Stormont, Belfast BT4 3PW (☎ **01232-63939**).

Some hotels possess exclusive access to lakes and ponds, and provide boats, angling gear, and ghillies (fishing guides) for hire by their patrons. Examples include Newport House and Enniscoe House, both in Mayo (see Chapter 11), Adare Manor in Limerick (see Chapter 11), Gurthalougha House on the shore of Lough Derg in Tipperary (see Chapter 15), and Delphi Lodge in Co. Galway (see Chapter 13).

Most of Ireland's angling festivals and competitions take place between March and September; for dates and locations contact the Irish Tourist Board. Advance notice must be given for participation in most of the competitions. Among the festivals are Killybegs International Fishing Festival and the Baltimore Angling Festival in July, and the Cobh Sea Angling Festival in September.

In the Northwest, Killybegs (see Chapter 14) is a center for sea angling, while in the West, Loughs Corrib, Conn, and Mask (see Chapters 11 and 13) offer much to entice the freshwater angler. The Killarney area (see Chapter 10) is a popular angling destination, as is the Blackwater River near Cork (see Chapter 9), and Kinsale (see Chapter 9) for sea angling. Also, be sure to consider the Shannon River and its lakes, especially Lough Derg (see Chapter 15).

8 Kayaking

Known as canoeing in Ireland, this sport enjoys considerable popularity. The season for white water is the winter, when frequent rains fill the rivers sufficiently for good paddling. By early summer most white-water streams are reduced to a trickle, with one exception being the Liffey, which is dam-controlled and has some minor rapids upstream from Dublin that are sometimes passable during the summer months.

Sea kayaking is much better suited to the Irish landscape and climate, as it can be done year-round and permits access to one of the isle's greatest treasures: its remote sea coast.

In a sea kayak, the myriad wonders of the Irish coast can be investigated at close hand. You'll find caves and tiny inlets, out-of-the-way cliffs and reefs inhabited by abundant sea birds, colorful crustaceans, seals, and the occasional dolphin. Many islands are within easy reach of the mainland, and with experience and good conditions a sea kayaker can reach any of Ireland's innumerable island outposts.

There are a number of adventure centers that offer kayaking lessons, and a few schools devoted to kayaking. Some of these will rent equipment as long as you can demonstrate adequate proficiency; call ahead to make arrangements if this is what you plan to do. For those new to the sport or unfamiliar with the Irish coast, a guided excursion is the best option.

The deeply indented coast of West Cork (see Chapter 9) and Kerry (see Chapter 10) is a sea kayaker's paradise, with clear water, cliffs rising to dizzying heights, and rocky shorelines so full of caves in some places that they seem hollow. The West of Ireland (see Chapter 11) offers many tiny islands and remote spots to explore.

KAYAKING RESOURCES

Jim Kennedy, a former world champion in kayak marathon racing, offers instruction and guided excursions along the spectacularly beautiful West Cork coast. He is based at **Maria's Schoolhouse,** Union Hall, Co. Cork (☎ **028/33002**) (see Chapter 9). Kayaking vacations are also available at **Delphi Adventure Holidays,** Leenane, Co. Galway (☎ **095/42307;** fax 095/42303) (see Chapter 13); **Tiglin Adventure Center,** Ashford, Co. Wicklow (☎ **0404/40169;** fax 0404/40701) (see Chapter 6); and **Brookhill House,** Courtmacsherry, Co. Cork (☎ **023/46177**) (see Chapter 9).

9 Sailing

Whether cruising from port to port or dinghy sailing on the lakes, there are many regions of Ireland that can best be experienced from the water. The elaborately indented coastline offers a plethora of safe havens for overnight stops (there are more than 140 between Cork Harbor and the Dingle Peninsula alone). This region of West Cork and Kerry is the most popular coastline for cruising, and there are several companies offering yacht charters.

The sailing schools of Ireland hold courses for sailors at all levels of experience, and sometimes offer day sailing as well. Ireland also has more than 120 yacht and sailing clubs along the coast and lakes. The best sources for information are the Irish Tourist Board; the **Irish Sailing Association,** 3 Park Rd., Dun Laoghaire, Co. Dublin (☎ **01/2800239;** fax 01/2807558); and the **Irish Cruising Club,** 8 Heidelberg, Ardilea, Dublin 14 (☎ **01/2884733**). The *Irish Cruising Club Sailing Directions* is a publication that gives information on harbors, port facilities, tides, and other topics of interest; it can be obtained in bookshops or through Mrs. B. Fox-Mills, "The Tansey," Baily, Co. Dublin (☎ **01/322823**).

Some of the harbors in the Southwest that are most popular with sailors include Cork, Kinsale, Glandore, Baltimore, and Bantry. On the West Coast, Killary Harbour, Westport, and Sligo have sailing clubs and are located in areas of great beauty. There is also a number of sailing clubs and yacht charter companies in the Dublin area.

SAILING RESOURCES

The Glenans Sailing School, 28 Merrion Sq., Dublin 2 (☎ **01/6611481;** fax 01/6764249) (see Chapter 9) has two locations in West Cork and one in Mayo, and offers classes at all levels; day sailing is available during the summer at the Baltimore location. Yacht charter is available from **Sail Ireland Charters,** Trident Hotel Marina, Kinsale, Co. Cork (☎ **021/772927;** fax 021/774170) (see Chapter 9); **Shannon Sailing LTD,** Callista, Dromineer, Nenagh, Co. Tipperary (☎ **067/24295;** fax 067/33488); and **Atlantic Adventures,** Frances Street, Kilrush, Co. Clare (☎ **065/52133;** fax 065/51720).

10 Diving

With visibility averaging 49 feet and occasionally reaching 98 feet, and numerous wrecks to explore, the west coast of Ireland possesses great appeal for divers.

The Irish dive season generally starts in March and ends sometime in October, though of course these dates are entirely dependent on your comfort zone. Outside of these months, weather and ocean conditions may make jumping into the sea unappealing for some. The PADI open water diver certification is the minimum requirement for all dives; introductory dives for novices are also offered at most schools.

The rocky coast of West Cork and Kerry is great for diving, with centers in Baltimore (see Chapter 9) and Dingle (see Chapter 10). On the west coast there are many great locations, one of which is the deep and sheltered Killary Harbor (see Chapter 13). Northern Ireland offers many interesting dives, with over 400 named wrecks located off the coast, many in the Irish Sea and in Belfast Lough.

DIVING RESOURCES

The **Irish Underwater Council** (CFT, or Comhairle Fo-Thuinn), 78A Patrick St., Dun Laoghaire, Co. Dublin (☎ **01/2844601;** fax 01/2844602; Web site **http://www.indigo.ie/scuba-irl/**) is an association of more than 70 Irish diving clubs, operating under the aegis of the CMAS (Confederation Mondiale des Activites Subaquatiques), the world federation for diving. Their Web site lists information on diving, dive centers, and dive hotels (no pun intended) throughout the Republic, and they publish the *CFT Guide to Dive Sites* and other information on exploring the Emerald Isle's emerald waters.

The **UK Diving** Web site (**http://www.cru.uea.ac.uk/ukdiving/**) features information on diving in the North, including a wreck database you can access either through a conventional listing or by pinpointing on a map. Wrecks are marked as red dots, which can be clicked on to find more information.

11 Windsurfing

Windsurfing has become a popular sport in Ireland, and there are some spots that are host to vast flotillas of colorful sails and wetsuited windsurfers when the conditions are good. Some of the best locations, though, are in remote areas of the west coast, and these are rarely crowded. Windsurfing schools with board hire can be found in most regions of the country, with the greatest concentration on the southeast and southwest coast.

In Dublin, the most popular spot is Dollymount Beach; Salthill, behind Dun Laoghaire Harbour, is another good choice. In the southeast, try Brittas Bay (Co. Wicklow), Cahore (Co. Wexford), and Rosslare (Co. Wexford); Dunmore East (Co. Waterford), Dungarvan (Co. Waterford), and Cobh (Co. Cork) are good in the south. The most challenging waves and winds are to be found in the west: Brandon Bay on the Dingle Peninsula, Roundstone in Galway, Achill Island in Mayo, and Magheroarty and Rossnowlagh in Donegal.

WINDSURFING RESOURCES

Learn to windsurf at the **Oysterhaven Windsurfing Centre,** Oysterhaven, Kinsale, Co. Cork (☎ **021/770738;** fax 021/770776); **The Surf Dock Centre,** Grand Canal Dock, Ringsend, Dublin 4 (☎ **01/6683945;** fax 01/6681215); and **Glenans Irish Sailing Club,** 28 Merrion Square, Dublin 2 (☎ **01/6611481;** fax 01/6764249), which has three centers in Ireland. Equipment rental and lessons are available at the **Courtmacsherry Leisure Center,** Courtmacsherry, Co. Cork (☎ **023/46177**).

Dublin 5

Dublin, like most ancient cities, lies sprawled along a river. In fact, three visible and three underground rivers converge and flow into the Irish Sea here, on the shore of Dublin Bay. The greatest of these, or perhaps just the least lazy, is the Liffey, which has divided Dublin into north and south for more than 1,000 years, much as tracks divide the core of a railroad town. Not as romantic as the Seine or as mighty as the Mississippi, the Liffey is just there, old and polluted, with walls to sit on or lean against when your legs give out. Still, it is and always has been at the center of things, and it does make for a pretty picture on a good day.

While the river may not be a swift and rushing torrent, the city around it is a different story. Motion is always experienced and measured with reference to fixed points, so it may not be apparent to first-time visitors that Dublin is moving *fast*. Ask anyone who has watched the city since the sixties and they will be at a loss to describe the Dublin that was. Like a child running so fast that the only way to stay up is to keep going, Dublin is on its way at last. Once the second city of the British empire, it's again full of aspiration and ideas and attitude. In one generation it has leapt from town to metropolis and left a lot of people behind. That's the way it is with change. Fortunately, the woman at the helm, if there is a helm, Irish Pres. Mary Robinson, possesses a strong, rooted vision of an Ireland in touch with its past and open to its future, a generous, inclusive Ireland.

The phrase "seedy elegance" was used long ago to depict Dublin's visual charm, and, to a degree, it still serves that purpose. The Georgian splendor of the 18th century can still be stumbled upon, surrounded by decay or dazzling development. The Liffey, however, continues to divide the town as it once divided Viking from Celt and Norman from Norse. The "new Dublin" is mostly south of the Liffey. A walk from the top of Grafton Street down O'Connell and into north Dublin is a walk through time and, simultaneously, a glimpse of some of the pieces that must eventually be put together.

The tourist precinct of Dublin, as in most cities, is a small, well-defined compound comprising a large part of Dublin 2 and a smaller fraction of Dublin 1 (we'll talk about postal codes a couple of pages on): Grafton Street, St. Stephen's Green, and Temple Bar are the operative terms, and they are well worth the effort to see. That said, a visit to Dublin confined to these areas is not a visit to Dublin, the Dublin that kicked some of the greatest writers in the English language into song. Explore, get a haircut (in a barber shop, not a salon), get lost and ask directions, and you may uncover a time capsule from the Dublin of a century ago—or was it only a generation?

Honesty, they say, is the best policy. The truth is that Dublin is not, by world standards or even Irish standards, a beautiful city. The old Dublin is like an old fishing hat or a pair of shoes worn into familiarity: of no appeal to anyone else but something you wouldn't trade for your life. It simply fits some people's heads, and by virtue of that fact they prefer it to Paris, Rome, or London. The new Dublin is too new to know. It's a happening, not a place. It is yet to be defined. So far it's extremely young, costly, fast-paced, and cosmopolitan, and on all of those counts is a creature quite new to Ireland. Old and new, Dublin is not stopping for anything or anyone and is, for reasons widely felt yet rarely explained (who has time?), the place to be.

1 Orientation

Dublin is 138 miles NE of Shannon Airport, 160 miles NE of Cork, 104 miles S of Belfast, 192 miles NE of Killarney, 136 miles E of Galway, 147 miles SE of Derry, 88 miles N of Wexford.

ARRIVING

BY PLANE   Regularly scheduled flights into Dublin International Airport are operated from Chicago, Boston, and New York by **Aer Lingus,** Ireland's national airline, and from Atlanta and New York by Delta Airlines. Charters also operate from a number of U.S. and Canadian cities. Alternatively, you can fly from the United States to London or other European cities and backtrack into Dublin Airport. (See "Getting There" in Chapter 3).

Dublin International Airport (☎ 01/704-4222) is located 7 miles north of the city center. **Dublin Bus** (☎ 01/873-4222) provides express coach service from the airport into the city's central bus station, Busaras, Store Street. Service runs daily, 7:30am until 7:45pm (8:30pm Sundays), with departures every 20 to 30 minutes. One-way fare is £2.50 ($4) adults and £1.25 ($2) for children under age 12. These services are expanded during high season, and a local city bus (no. 41) is also available to the city center for £1.10 ($1.80).

For speed and ease, a taxi is the best way to get directly to your hotel or guest house. Depending on your destination, fares average between £10 ($16) and £13 ($20.80). Taxis are lined up at a first-come, first-served taxi stand outside of the arrivals terminal.

Major international and local car-rental companies operate desks at Dublin Airport (for a list of companies, see "Getting Around Dublin," below).

BY FERRY   Passenger/car ferries from Britain arrive at the **Dublin Ferryport** (☎ 01/874-3293), on the eastern end of the North Docks, and at the **Dun Laoghaire Ferryport.** Call **01/661-0511** for Irish ferries bookings and information. There is bus and taxi service from both ports.

BY TRAIN   Irish Rail (☎ 01/836-6222) operates daily train service into Dublin from Belfast in Northern Ireland and all major cities in the Irish Republic, including Cork, Galway, Limerick, Killarney, Sligo, Wexford, and Waterford. Trains from the south, west, and southwest arrive at **Heuston Station,** Kingsbridge, off St. John's Road; from the north and northwest at **Connolly Station,** Amiens Street; and from the southeast at **Pearse Station,** Westland Row, Tara Street.

BY BUS **Bus Eireann** (☎ **01/836-6111**) operates daily express coach and local bus services from all major cities and towns in Ireland into Dublin's central bus station, Busaras, Store Street.

BY CAR If you are arriving by car from other parts of Ireland or via car ferry from Britain, all main roads lead into the heart of Dublin and are well signposted to An Lar (City Centre). To bypass the city center, the East Link (toll bridge 55p; 50¢) and West Link are signposted, and the M50 circuits the city on three sides.

VISITOR INFORMATION

Dublin Tourism operates five year-round walk-in visitor centers in greater Dublin. The principal center is at **St. Andrew's Church,** Suffolk Street, Dublin 2 (☎ 01/ 605-7700), open Monday to Saturday from 9am to 8:30pm, Sunday 11am to 5:30pm. The other four centers are at the **Arrivals Hall of Dublin Airport** (☎ 01/ 844-5387) open daily 8am to 10:30pm; the new **ferry terminal, Dun Laoghaire** (☎ 01/284-6361) open Monday to Saturday 10am to 9pm; **Baggot Street Bridge,** Dublin 2 (☎ 01/284-4768) open Monday to Friday 9:15am to 5:15pm; and **The Square,** Tallaght, Dublin 24 (☎ 01/462-0671) open Monday to Saturday 9:30am to 5pm (closed noon to 12:30pm). In addition, there is an independent information center for the **Temple Bar area** at 18 Eustace St., Temple Bar, Dublin 2 (☎ 01/ 671-5717) open year-round Monday to Friday 9am to 6pm, and June to August Saturday 11am to 4pm, Sunday noon to 4pm.

CITY LAYOUT

Compared with other European capitals, Dublin is a relatively small metropolis and easily traversed. The city center, identified in Irish on bus destination signs as "An Lar," is bisected by the River Liffey flowing west to east into Dublin Bay and is ringed by canals, the north half by the Royal Canal and the south half by the Grand Canal.

To the north of the Royal Canal are the northside suburbs such as Drumcondra, Glasnevin, Howth, Clontarf, and Malahide; to the south of the Grand Canal are the southside suburbs of Ballsbridge, Blackrock, Dun Laoghaire, Dalkey, Killiney, Rathgar, Rathmines, and other residential areas.

MAIN ARTERIES, STREETS & SQUARES The focal point of Dublin is the River Liffey, with no fewer than 14 bridges connecting its north and south banks. On the north side of the river, the main thoroughfare is O'Connell Street, a wide, two-way avenue that starts at the riverside quays and runs northward to Parnell Square. Enhanced by statues, trees, and a modern fountain, O'Connell Street of earlier days was the lifeblood of the city, and it is still important today although neither as fashionable nor as safe as it used to be.

On the south side of the Liffey, Grafton Street is Dublin's main upscale shopping street and has clearly bent over backward in recent years to attract and please tourists. Narrow and restricted to pedestrians, Grafton Street sits at the center of Dublin's commercial district, surrounded by smaller and larger streets where a variety of shops, restaurants, and hotels are situated. At the south end of Grafton Street is St. Stephen's Green, a lovely park and urban oasis ringed by rows of historic Georgian townhouses, fine hotels, and restaurants.

Nassau Street, which starts at the north end of Grafton Street and rims the south side of Trinity College, is noted not only for its fine shops but because it leads to Merrion Square, another fashionable Georgian park noted for the historic brick-front townhouses that surround it. Merrion Square is also adjacent to Leinster House, the Irish House of Parliament, the National Gallery, and the National Museum.

Dublin Orientation

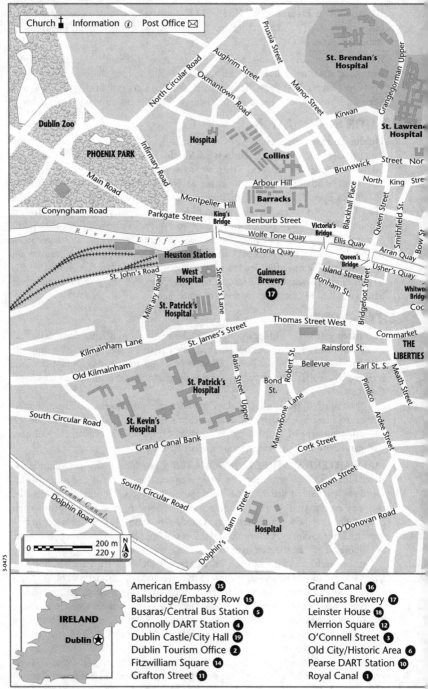

Church ✝   Information ⓘ   Post Office ✉

American Embassy 🔟⑮
Ballsbridge/Embassy Row ⑮
Busaras/Central Bus Station ❺
Connolly DART Station ❹
Dublin Castle/City Hall ⑲
Dublin Tourism Office ❷
Fitzwilliam Square ⑭
Grafton Street ⑪

Grand Canal ⑯
Guinness Brewery ⑰
Leinster House ⑱
Merrion Square ⑫
O'Connell Street ❸
Old City/Historic Area ❻
Pearse DART Station 🔟
Royal Canal ❶

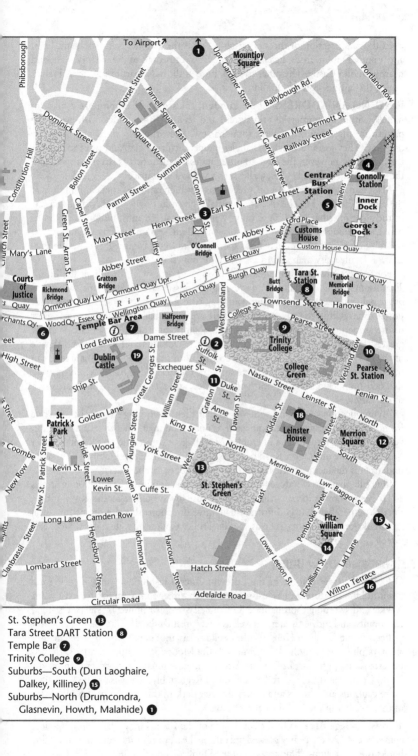

St. Stephen's Green ⓭
Tara Street DART Station ⓼
Temple Bar ⓻
Trinity College ⓽
Suburbs—South (Dun Laoghaire,
 Dalkey, Killiney) ⓯
Suburbs—North (Drumcondra,
 Glasnevin, Howth, Malahide) ❶

In the older section of the city, High Street is the gateway to much of medieval and Viking Dublin, from the city's two medieval cathedrals to the old city walls, and nearby Dublin Castle. The other street of note in the older part of the city is Francis Street, the antique row of Dublin.

FINDING AN ADDRESS   Like London, the streets of Dublin are a maze of names, without a numerical grid system and seemingly assembled with no logical pattern in mind. Some are wide, some narrow, a few run two ways, and many are one-way. They form rectangles, triangles, perpendicular angles, and run parallel. For the most part, however, the larger thoroughfares are identified as streets or roads and the smaller ones are called lanes, alleys, rows, closes, and places.

Most names are posted not on street signs but high on the corners of buildings at the end of each street. The names are usually given in English and Irish, but a few of the older ones have Irish signs only. Within each street, most buildings are numbered, but numbers are often not displayed and are seldom used by the locals. "At the top of Grafton Street" may be as specific an address as you will get. Best to purchase a detailed city map and to ask freely for directions.

For starters, always ask if an address is on the north or south side of the Liffey. That'll put you in the ballpark, narrowing the possibilities 50% in one swipe. Another helpful strategy for finding your way is to acclimate yourself to the various postal zones within the city. Although there are more than 24 different zones, most of the attractions—hotels, restaurants, pubs, shops, and other activities that are of greatest interest to visitors—lie within six zones: Dublin 1 and 9 on the north side of the city, and Dublin 2, 4, 6, and 8 on the south side of the city. There is a map of Dublin's postal zones in the front section of all telephone books. Keep in mind that odd-numbered zones are north of the Liffey, and even-numbered zones are south of the Liffey.

A complication to finding your way is that there is nothing to prevent one zone from having a street with the same name as one found in another zone. For instance, you'll find a Pembroke Lane in Dublin 2, off Baggot Street, and you'll find another Pembroke Lane off Raglan Road near the American Embassy in Dublin 4. This only underscores the fact that attention to the postal zones can be crucial.

One rule that you can depend on for further direction is the designation of streets as Upper or Lower. Streets that are Lower are always closer to the River Liffey. Finally, remember that Dubliners usually give directions that are defined by local landmarks or major sights, such as "beside Trinity College" or "just off St. Stephen's Green."

NEIGHBORHOODS IN BRIEF

O'Connell Street (North of the Liffey)   Once a fashionable and historic focal point in Dublin, this area has lost much of its charm and importance in recent years. A wide and sweeping thoroughfare, O'Connell Street is rimmed by shops, fast-food restaurants, and movie theaters, as well as a few great landmarks like the General Post Office and the Gresham Hotel. Within walking distance of O'Connell Street are four theaters plus the Catholic Pro-Cathedral, the Moore Street open markets, the all-pedestrian shopping area of Henry Street, the new Financial Services Centre, the ILAC Centre, and the Central Bus Station. Regrettably, it is wise to be somewhat more cautious after hours and especially after dark in this section of the city. Most of this area lies in the Dublin 1 postal code.

Trinity College Area   On the south side of the River Liffey, the Trinity College complex is a 42-acre center of academia in the heart of the city, surrounded by fine bookstores and shops. This area lies in the Dublin 2 postal code.

Temple Bar   Wedged between Trinity College and the Old City, this section has recently been spruced up and made the scene of massive development as the cultural and entertainment hub of Dublin. As Dublin's self-proclaimed Left Bank, Temple Bar is the place to see and to be seen. It offers a vibrant array of unique shops, art galleries, recording studios, theaters, trendy restaurants, and atmospheric pubs. Largely the preserve of the young, it is easy to feel over the hill here if you're past 25. This area lies in the Dublin 2 postal code.

Old City / Historic Area   Dating from Viking and medieval times, this cobble-stoned enclave includes Dublin Castle, the remnants of the city's original walls, and the city's two main cathedrals, Christ Church and St. Patrick's. The adjacent Liberties section, just west of High Street, takes its name from the fact that the people who lived here long ago were exempt from the local jurisdiction within the city walls. Although it prospered in its early days, the Liberties fell on hard times in the 17th and 18th centuries and is only now feeling a touch of urban renewal. Highlights here range from the Guinness Brewery and Royal Hospital to the original Cornmarket area. Most of this area lies in the Dublin 8 zone.

St. Stephen's Green / Grafton Street Area   A focal point for visitors to Dublin, this district is home to some of the city's finest hotels, restaurants, and shops. There are some residential townhouses near the Green, but this area is primarily a business neighborhood. It is part of the Dublin 2 zone.

Fitzwilliam & Merrion Square   These two little square parks are surrounded by fashionable brick-faced Georgian townhouses, each with its own distinctive and colorful doorway. Some of Dublin's most famous citizens once resided here, although today many of the houses have been turned into offices for doctors, lawyers, and other professionals. This area is part of the Dublin 2 zone.

Ballsbridge / Embassy Row   Situated south of the Grand Canal, this is Dublin's most prestigious suburb, yet it is within walking distance of downtown. Although primarily a residential area, it is also the home of some of the city's leading hotels, restaurants, and embassies, including that of the United States. This area is part of the Dublin 4 zone.

2 Getting Around Dublin

BY BUS   Dublin Bus operates a fleet of green double-decker buses, high-frequency single-deck buses, and minibuses throughout the city and its suburbs. Most buses originate on or near O'Connell Street, Abbey Street, and Eden Quay on the north side; and from Aston Quay, College Street, or Fleet Street on the south side. Bus stops are located every two or three blocks. Destinations and bus numbers are posted above the front windows; buses destined for the city center are marked with the Gaelic words "An Lar."

Bus service runs daily throughout the city, starting at 6am (10am on Sunday), with the last bus at 11:30pm, excluding Thursday, Friday, and Saturday nights, when there is a Nitelink service from city center to the suburbs running from midnight to 3am. Frequency ranges from every 10 to 15 minutes for most runs; schedules are posted on revolving notice boards at each bus stop.

Fares are calculated on distances traveled; minimum fare is 55p (90¢); maximum fare is £1.25 ($2). Nitelink fare is a flat £2.50 ($4). Buy your tickets from the driver as you enter the bus; exact change is welcomed but not required. Notes of £5 or higher, however, may not be accepted. One-day and four-day passes are available at reduced rates: one-day bus-only for £3.30 ($5.28) and four-day bus and city rail for £10 ($16), restricted to travel after 9:45am.

For more information, contact **Dublin Bus,** 59 Upper O'Connell St., Dublin 1 (☎ **01/873-4222**).

BY DART   Dublin's electric rapid transit system, known as **DART (Dublin Area Rapid Transit),** links several city-center stations at Tara Street, Pearse Street, and Connolly Street with suburbs and seaside communities as far as Howth to the north and Bray to the south.

The DART is in operation from 7am to midnight, Monday through Saturday, and from 9:30am to 11pm on Sunday, and is admirably punctual. Schedules are available at all stations during operating hours, but, depending on the time of day and the particular station, you can generally expect that the time between trains will be 10 to 20 minutes. Minimum single-journey fare is 80p ($1.28). An individual one-day RAMBLER ticket for unlimited DART travel is available for £3.20 ($5.15), and a family ticket (any two adults with up to two children) for £5 ($8). A four-day bus and rail **Dublin Explorer** pass costs £10 ($16). Longer weekly and monthly commuter passes require ID cards and are not geared for tourists. For further information, contact **DART,** Pearse Station Street, Dublin 2 (☎ **01/703-3504**).

BY TAXI   Dublin taxis do not cruise the streets looking for fares; instead, they line up at *ranks*. Ranks are located outside all of the leading hotels, at bus and train stations, and on prime thoroughfares such as Upper O'Connell Street, College Green, and the north side of St. Stephen's Green. You can also phone for a taxi. Some of the companies that operate a 24-hour radio-call service are **All Fives Taxi** (☎ 01/455-5555 and 01/455-7777); **Access Taxis** (☎ 01/668-3333); **Blue Cabs** (☎ 01/676-1111); and **Co-op Taxis** (☎ 01/676-6666).

Rates are fixed by law and posted in each taxi. Minimum fare for one passenger within the city is £1.80 ($2.90) for any distance not exceeding 1 mile or nine minutes; after that, it's £1.20 ($1.95) for each mile. The per-journey additional charge for each extra passenger and for each suitcase is 40p (65¢). The extra charge for hiring a taxi before 8am or after 8pm and all day Sunday is also 40p (65¢).

BY CAR   Unless you are going to be doing a lot of driving from Dublin to neighboring counties, it is not logistically or economically advisable to rent a car. In fact, getting around the city center and its environs is much easier without a car.

If you must drive in Dublin, remember to keep to the *left-hand side of the road* and not drive in bus lanes. The speed limit within the city is 30 mph and seat belts must be worn at all times by driver and passengers.

Rentals   Most major international **car-rental firms** are represented in Dublin, as are many Irish-based companies, with desks at the airport and/or full-service offices downtown. The rates vary greatly according to company, season, type of car, and duration of rental. In high season, the average weekly cost of a car, from subcompact standard to full-size automatic, ranges from £225 all the way up to £700 ($360 to $1,120), which makes this a prime moment to remind you of the advantage of making car-rental arrangements well in advance from the States or your point of origin.

International firms represented in Dublin include: **Avis/Johnson and Perrott,** 1 Hanover St. E., Dublin 1 (☎ 01/605-7500) and Dublin Airport (☎ 01/605-7500); **Budget,** at Dublin Airport (☎ 01/844-5919); **Hertz,** 149 Upper Leeson St., Dublin 4 (☎ 01/660-2255) and at Dublin Airport (☎ 01/844-5488); **Murray's Europcar,** Baggot Street Bridge, Dublin 4 (☎ 01/668-1777) and at Dublin Airport (☎ 01/844-4179); and **Thrifty,** at Dublin Airport (☎ 01/844-4199).

The leader among the Irish-based firms is **Dan Dooley Rent-a-Car,** 42/43 Westland Row, Dublin 2 (☎ 01/677-2723) and at Dublin Airport (☎ 01/844-5156).

Dublin Area Rapid Transit (DART) Routes

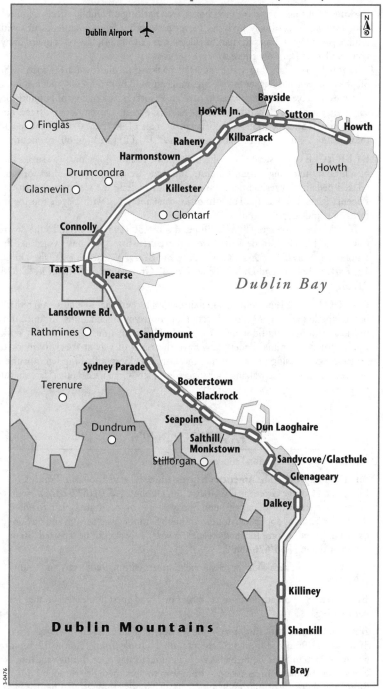

Dublin Airport

Finglas

Drumcondra

Glasnevin

Howth Jn.   Bayside   Sutton   Howth

Raheny   Kilbarrack

Harmonstown   Howth

Killester

Clontarf

Connolly

Tara St.   Pearse

Lansdowne Rd.   *Dublin Bay*

Rathmines

Sandymount

Sydney Parade

Terenure   Booterstown   Blackrock

Dundrum   Seapoint   Dun Laoghaire

Salthill/
Monkstown   Sandycove/Glasthule

Stillorgan   Glenageary

Dalkey

Killiney

Dublin Mountains   Shankill

Bray

3-0476

Parking During normal business hours, **free parking** on Dublin streets is limited, and is marked accordingly by signs. Never park in bus lanes or along a curb with double yellow lines. Fines for parking illegally are £15 ($24); if a car is towed away, it costs £100 ($160) to retrieve it.

Normally you can find some **metered parking** in midtown areas such as St. Stephen's Green and Baggot Street; rates range upward from 50p (80¢) per half hour. The most reliable and safest places to park are at surface parking lots or in multistory car parks in central locations such as Kildare Street, Lower Abbey Street, and Marlborough Street. Parking lots charge on average £1.40 ($2.25) per hour and £13 ($20.80) for 24 hours. Night rates vary from £1 ($1.60) to £3 ($4.80) per hour.

BY BICYCLE The steady flow of Dublin traffic rushing down one-way streets may be a little intimidating for most cyclists, but there are many opportunities for more relaxed pedaling in residential areas and suburbs, along the seafront, and around Phoenix Park. The Dublin Tourism office can supply you with bicycle touring information and suggested routes.

Bicycle-rental averages £8 ($12.80) per day or £30 ($48) per week. In the downtown area, bicycles can be rented from the **Bike Store,** 58 Lower Gardiner St., Dublin 1 (☎ **01/872-5931**); **C. Harding for Bikes,** 30 Bachelor's Walk, Dublin 1 (☎ **01/8732455**); and **Dublin Bike Hire,** 27 Gr. Georges St., Dublin 1 (☎ **878-8473**).

ON FOOT Small and compact, Dublin is ideal for walking, so long as you remember to look left and right (in the direction opposite your inclinations) for oncoming traffic and to obey traffic signals. Each traffic light has timed "walk / don't walk" signals for pedestrians. Pedestrians have the right of way at specially marked, zebra-striped crossings; as a warning, there are usually two flashing lights at these intersections. For some walking tour suggestions, see "Organized Tours," later in this chapter.

FAST FACTS: Dublin

Airport See "Orientation" above, in this chapter.

American Express The **American Express office** is located opposite Trinity College, just off College Green, at 116 Grafton St., Dublin 2 (☎ **01/677-2874**). Hours for most services are Monday through Friday 9am to 5pm, Saturday 9am to noon; the foreign exchange operates Monday through Saturday 9am to 5pm and on Sunday from 11am to 4pm. In an emergency, traveler's checks can be reported lost or stolen by dialing **800/626-0000.**

Area Code The area code for telephone numbers within Dublin city and county is **01.**

Baby-sitters With advance notice, most hotels and guest houses will arrange for baby-sitting.

Business Hours Banks are open Monday through Wednesday and on Friday from 10am to 12:30pm and from 1:30 to 3pm, on Thursday from 10am to 12:30pm and from 1:30 to 5pm. Some banks are beginning to stay open through the lunch hour. Most business offices are open from 9am to 5pm, Monday through Friday. Stores and shops are open from 9am to 5:30pm Monday through Wednesday and Friday to Saturday, and from 9am to 8pm on Thursday. Some bookshops and tourist-oriented stores also open on Sunday from 11am or noon until 4 or 5pm.

During the peak season (May through September), many gift and souvenir shops post Sunday hours.

Car Rentals   See "Getting Around Dublin," above.

Currency Exchange   A currency exchange service in Ireland is signposted as a Bureau de Change. There are bureaux de change at all banks and at many branches of the Irish Post Office system, known as An Post. A bureau de change operates daily during flight arrival and departure times at Dublin Airport; a foreign currency note-exchanger machine is also available on a 24-hour basis in the main Arrivals Hall. In addition, many hotels and travel agencies offer exchange bureau services, although the best rate of exchange is usually given at banks.

Dentist   For dental emergencies, contact the **Eastern Health Board Headquarters,** Dr. Steevens Hospital, Dublin 8 (☎ **01/679-0700**). See also "Dental Surgeons" in the Golden Pages (yellow pages) of the telephone book.

Doctor   In an emergency, most hotels and guest houses will contact a house doctor for you. You can also call either the **Eastern Health Board Headquarters,** Dr. Steevens Hospital, Dublin 8 (☎ **01/679-0700**), or the **Irish Medical Organization,** 10 Fitzwilliam Place, Dublin 2 (☎ **01/676-7273**), 9:15am to 5:15pm. See also "Doctors—Medical" in the Golden Pages of the telephone book.

Drugstores   Centrally located drugstores, known locally as pharmacies or chemist shops, include **Hamilton Long and Co.,** 5 Lower O'Connell St., Dublin 1 (☎ **01/874-8456**) and **Smith's Pharmacy,** 50 Grafton St., Dublin 2 (☎ **01/677-9288**). A late-night drugstore is **Crowley's Pharmacy,** Kilbarrack Road, Dublin 5 (☎ **01/832-5332**).

Embassies/Consulates   The **American Embassy** is located at 42 Elgin Rd., Ballsbridge, Dublin 4 (☎ **01/668-8777**); **Canadian Embassy,** 65/68 St. Stephen's Green, Dublin 2 (☎ **01/478/1988**); **British Embassy,** 29 Merrion Rd., Dublin 4 (☎ **01/205-3700**); **Australian Embassy,** Fitzwilton House, Wilton Terrace, Dublin 2 (☎ **01/676-1517**).

Emergencies   For police, fire, or other emergencies, dial **999.**

Eyeglasses   For one-hour service on glasses or contact lenses, try **Specsavers,** Unit 9, GPO Arcade, Henry Street, Dublin 1 (☎ **01/872-8155**) or look in the Golden Pages of the telephone book under "Opticians—Ophthalmic."

Gay & Lesbian Resources   **Gay Switchboard Dublin,** Carmichael House, No. Brunswick St., Dublin 7, (☎ **01/872-1055**); **LOT / Lesbians Organizing Together,** 5 Capel St., Dublin 1 (☎ **01/872-7770**).

Hairdressers/Barbers   The leading hairstyling names for women and men are **Peter Mark** and **John Adam.** Peter Mark has more than two dozen locations throughout Dublin and its suburbs, including 74 Grafton St., Dublin 2 (☎ **01/671-4399**), and 11A Upper O'Connell St., Dublin 1 (☎ **01/874-5589**). John Adam has shops at 13A Merrion Row, Dublin 2 (☎ **01/661-0354**) and 112A Baggot St., Dublin 2 (☎ **01/661-1952**). Also consult the Golden Pages under "Hairdressers."

Hospitals   For emergency care, two of the most modern health care facilities are **St. Vincent's Hospital,** Elm Park, Dublin 4 (☎ **01/269-4533**), on the south side of the city, and **Beaumont Hospital,** Beaumont, Dublin 9 (☎ **01/837-7755**) on the north side.

Hotlines   In Ireland, hotlines are called helplines. For **emergencies, police, or fire,** dial 999; **Rape Crisis Centre** (☎ **01/661-4911**) and FreeFone

(800/778-888); **Samaritans** (☎ 01/872-7700); **Alcoholics Anonymous** (☎ 01/453-8998 and after hours 01/679-5967); and **Narcotics Anonymous** (☎ 01/830-0944).

Information   For information on finding a telephone number, dial **1190.** For visitor information, see "Tourist Information" under "Orientation," above.

Laundry / Dry Cleaning   Most hotels provide same-day or next-day laundry and/or dry-cleaning services. If you wish to make your own arrangements, two centrally located choices are **Craft Cleaners,** 12 Upper Baggot St., Dublin 2 (☎ 01/668-8198), and **Grafton Cleaners,** 32 S. William St., Dublin 2 (☎ 01/679-4309). More are listed under "Dry Cleaners" in the Golden Pages of the telephone book.

Libraries   For research materials and periodicals, try the **National Library of Ireland,** Kildare Street, Dublin 2 (☎ 01/661-8811), or **Dublin's Central Library,** ILAC Centre, Henry Street, Dublin 1 (☎ 01/873-4333).

Lost Property   Most hotels have a lost-property service, usually under the aegis of the housekeeping department. For items lost in public places, contact the **Dublin Garda Siochana (Police) Headquarters,** Harcourt Square, Dublin 2 (☎ 475-5555).

Newspapers/Magazines   The three morning Irish dailies are the *Irish Times* (except Sunday), *Irish Independent,* and *The Examiner.* In the afternoon, one tabloid, *The Herald,* hits the stands. There are also two weeklies, *The Sunday World* and *The Sunday Tribune.* Papers from other European cities can be purchased at **Eason and Son,** 40 Lower O'Connell St., Dublin 1 (☎ 01/873-3811). The leading magazine for upcoming events and happenings is *In Dublin,* published every two weeks (£1.50 at newsagents; $2.40). *The Event Guide,* also published biweekly, contains a useful and up-to-date listing of events throughout Ireland, with a focus on Dublin, and is available free of cost practically wherever you look for it.

Photographic Needs   For photographic equipment, supplies, and repairs, visit **Camera Exchange,** 63 S. Great George's St., Dublin 2 (☎ 01/478-4125), or **City Cameras,** 23A Dawson St., Dublin 2 (☎ 01/676-2891). For fast developing, try the **Camera Centre,** 56 Grafton St., Dublin 2 (☎ 01/677-5594), or **One Hour Photo,** 5 St. Stephen's Green, Dublin 2 (☎ 01/671-8578), 110 Grafton St., Dublin 2 (☎ 01/677-4472), and at the ILAC Centre, Henry Street, Dublin 1 (☎ 01/872-8824).

Police   Dial **999** in an emergency. The metropolitan headquarters for the **Dublin Garda Siochana (Police)** is at Harcourt Square, Dublin 2 (☎ 01/475-5555).

Post Office   The **General Post Office (GPO)** is located on O'Connell Street, Dublin 1 (☎ 01/705-7000). Hours are Monday through Saturday 8am to 8pm, Sunday and holidays 10:30am to 6:30pm. Branch offices, identified by the sign "Oifig An Post / Post Office," are open Monday through Saturday only, 9am to 6pm.

Radio/TV   **RTÉ (Radio Telefis Éireann)** is the national broadcasting authority and controls two TV channels—RTÉ 1 and Network 2—and three radio stations—RTE 1, 2FM, and Radió na Gaeltachta (all Irish-language programming). Besides RTE programming, there are other privately owned local stations including Anna Livia Radio on 103.8 FM and Classic Hits Radio and Ireland Radio News on 98 FM. In addition, television programs from Britain's BBC-TV (British Broadcasting Corporation) and ITN-TV (Independent) can be picked up by most receivers in the Dublin area. BBC Radio 1, 2, and 3 can also be heard. Satellite programs, via CNN, SKY News, and other international operators are also fed into the Dublin area.

Shoe Repairs   Two reliable shops in midcity are **O'Connell's Shoe Repair,** 3 Upper Baggot St., Dublin 2 (☎ **01/667-2020**), and **Rapid Shoe Repair,** Sackville Place, off Lower O'Connell Street, Dublin 1 (no phone).

Weather   Phone **1550/123-854.**

Yellow Pages   The classified section of the Dublin telephone book is called the Golden Pages.

3 Accommodations

From legendary old-world landmarks to sleek glass-and-concrete high-rises, Dublin offers a great diversity of places to stay. It may not be the cheapest city to visit, but even travelers on a budget should be able to find comfortable and attractive accommodation.

As in the rest of Ireland, Dublin's hotels and guest houses are inspected, registered, and graded by the Irish Tourist Board (Bord Failte). In 1994, the board introduced a new grading system that ranks them with one to five stars, consistent with other European countries and international standards. Five hotels in Dublin currently merit the five-star rating: Berkeley Court, Conrad, Jurys, Shelbourne, and Westbury.

In general, rates for Dublin hotels do not vary greatly with the seasons, as they do in the Irish countryside. Some hotels charge slightly higher prices during special events, such as the Dublin Horse Show. For the best deals, try to reserve a room in Dublin over a weekend, and ask if there is a reduction or a weekend package in effect. Some Dublin hotels cut their rates by as much as 50% on Friday and Saturday nights, when business traffic is low.

HISTORIC OLD CITY & TEMPLE BAR / TRINITY COLLEGE AREA
VERY EXPENSIVE

Clarence
6/8 Wellington Quay, Dublin 2. ☎ **01/677-6178.** Fax 01/677-7487. 50 rms. TV TEL. £154–£194 ($246.40–$310.40) double. Includes full Irish breakfast and service charge. AE, DC, MC, V. Bus: 51B, 51C, 68, 69, 79.

Situated between the south bank of the Liffey and Temple Bar, this Regency-style hotel belongs to an investment group that includes the rock band U2. Built in 1852, the Clarence was totally refurbished in 1995 to offer larger rooms and suites upgraded to deluxe standards. The rooms are elegant and contemporary, and the hotel offers a bar and noted restaurant.

EXPENSIVE

Blooms
Anglesea St., Dublin 2. ☎ **800/44-UTELL** from the U.S., or 01/671-5622. Fax 01/671-5997. 86 rms. TV TEL. £138.74 ($222) double. Includes full Irish breakfast and service charge. AE, DC, MC, V. DART to Tara St. Station. Bus: 21A, 46A, 46B, 51B, 51C, 68, 69, 86.

Lovers of Irish literature will feel at home at Blooms. Named after Leopold Bloom, a character in James Joyce's *Ulysses,* this hotel is in the heart of Dublin, near Trinity College and on the edge of the Temple Bar district. The bedrooms are modern and functional, with useful extras like garment presses and hair dryers. Concierge, 24-hour room service, and valet/laundry service are available, and the hotel has an enclosed private parking lot.

Dublin Accommodations

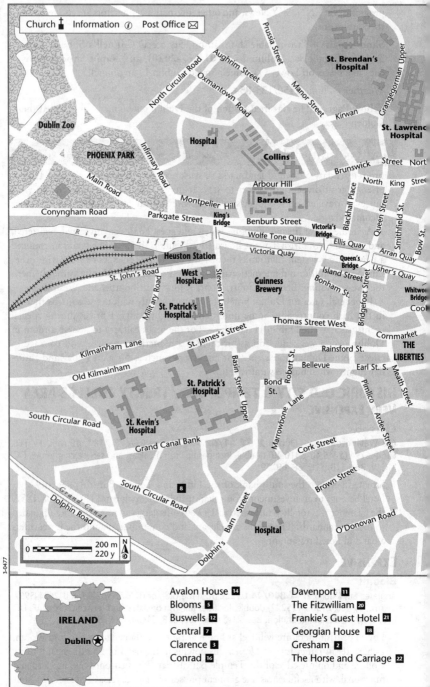

Church ✝ Information ⓘ Post Office ✉

Prussia Street

St. Brendan's Hospital

Grangegorman Upper

Aughrim Street

North Circular Road

Oxmantown Road

Manor Street

Kirwan

St. Lawrenc Hospital

Dublin Zoo

PHOENIX PARK

Infirmary Road

Hospital

Collins

Brunswick

Street   Nort

North   King   Stree

Main Road

Montpelier Hill

Arbour Hill

Barracks

Blackhall Place

Queen Street

Smithfield St.

Bow St.

Conyngham Road

Parkgate Street

King's Bridge

Benburb Street

Victoria's Bridge

Wolfe Tone Quay

Ellis Quay

Arran Quay

River Liffey

Heuston Station

Victoria Quay

Queen's Bridge

Usher's Quay

St. John's Road

West Hospital

Steven's Lane

Guinness Brewery

Island Street

Bonham St.

Bridgefoot Street

Whitwor Bridge

Military Road

St. Patrick's Hospital

Thomas Street West

Cool

Cornmarket

THE LIBERTIES

Kilmainham Lane

St. James's Street

Rainsford St.

Old Kilmainham

Basin Street Upper

Bellevue

Earl St. S.

Meath Street

Robert St.

Pimlico

South Circular Road

St. Patrick's Hospital

Bond St.

Ardee Street

St. Kevin's Hospital

Marrowbone Lane

Grand Canal Bank

Cork Street

South Circular Road

Barn Street

Brown Street

Grand Canal

Dolphin Road

8

Hospital

O'Donovan Road

Dolphin's

0 — 200 m / 220 y

N

3-0477

IRELAND

Dublin ★

Avalon House 14	Davenport 11
Blooms 5	The Fitzwilliam 20
Buswells 12	Frankie's Guest Hotel 21
Central 7	Georgian House 18
Clarence 3	Gresham 2
Conrad 16	The Horse and Carriage 22

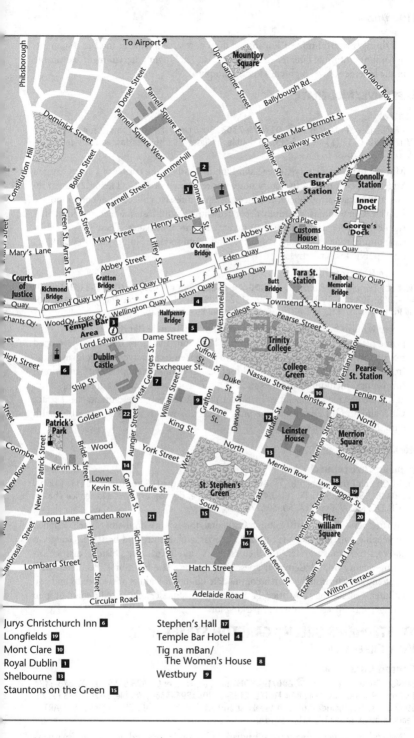

Jurys Christchurch Inn 6
Longfields 19
Mont Clare 10
Royal Dublin 1
Shelbourne 13
Stauntons on the Green 15

Stephen's Hall 17
Temple Bar Hotel 4
Tig na mBan/
   The Women's House 8
Westbury 9

Dining/Entertainment: For formal dining, reserve a table at the Bia restaurant, or for more informal fare, try the Anglesea Bar. Late-night entertainment is available in the basement-level nightclub known simply as M.

EXPENSIVE/MODERATE

Central

1–5 Exchequer St., Dublin 2. ☎ **01/679-7303.** Fax 01/679-7303. 70 rms, 2 suites. MINIBAR TV TEL. £92–£152 ($147.20–$243.20) double. Includes full Irish breakfast and service charge. AE, DC, MC, V. Bus: 22A.

Midway between Trinity College and Dublin Castle at the corner of Great George's Street, this century-old five-story hotel was renovated in 1991. The public areas retain a Victorian atmosphere, enhanced by an impressive collection of contemporary Irish art. Guest rooms, cheerfully decorated with colorful Irish-made furnishings, offer such extras as a garment press, hair dryer, and tea/coffeemaker. There's a Victorian-style dining room, two bars, concierge, and room service. No on-premises parking, but a public lot is nearby.

Temple Bar Hotel

Fleet St., Temple Bar, Dublin 2. ☎ **800/44-UTELL** from the U.S., or 01/677-3333. Fax 01/677-3088. 108 rms. TV TEL. £95–£130 ($152–$208) double. No service charge. Rates include full Irish breakfast. MC, V. DART to Tara St. Station. Bus: 78A or 78B.

If you want to be in the heart of the action in the Temple Bar district, then this is a prime place to stay. Opened in summer 1993, this five-story hotel was developed from a row of town houses and great care was taken to preserve the Georgian brick-front facade with Victorian mansard roof. Guest rooms are modern with traditional furnishings, including amenities such as a garment press, towel warmer, hair dryer, and tea/coffeemaker. Facilities include a skylit garden-style restaurant, the Terrace Cafe, and an Old Dublin–theme pub, Buskers, as well as access to a nearby health club. Fee-parking on street.

INEXPENSIVE

⑤ Jurys Christchurch Inn

Christ Church Place, Dublin 8. ☎ **800/44-UTELL** from the U.S., or 01/475-0111. Fax 01/475-0488. 183 rms. A/C TV TEL. £49 ($78.40) single, double, or triple. No service charge. AE, CB, DC, MC, V. Bus: 21A, 50, 50A, 78, 78A, 78B.

Situated across from Christ Church Cathedral, this is a new four-story hotel, designed in keeping with the area's Georgian/Victorian architecture and heritage. Geared to the cost-conscious traveler, it is the first of its kind for the city's historic district, offering quality hotel lodgings at guest house prices. The bedrooms, decorated with contemporary furnishings, can accommodate up to three adults or two adults and two children—all for the same price. Facilities include a moderately priced restaurant, pub lounge, and adjacent multistory parking lot.

ST. STEPHEN'S GREEN / GRAFTON STREET AREA
VERY EXPENSIVE

Conrad International

Earlsfort Terrace, Dublin 2. ☎ **800/HILTONS** from the U.S., or 01/676-5555. Fax 01/676-5424. 188 rms, 9 suites. A/C MINIBAR TV TEL. £185–£240 ($296–$384) double; £420–£583 ($672–$932.80) suites. Includes full Irish breakfast and service charge. AE, CB, DC, MC, V. DART to Pearse Station. Bus: 11A, 11B, 13, 14A.

A member of the international subsidiary of Hilton Hotels and one of the city's newest deluxe hotels, this seven-story red-brick high-rise is situated opposite the National

Concert Hall and across from the southeast corner of St. Stephen's Green. The spacious public areas are rich in marble, brass, contemporary art, and lots of leafy plants. Each guest room is outfitted with contemporary furnishings, blond woods, and pastel tones, with extras such as electronic safety lock, minibar, writing desk, bathrobes, and three telephone lines.

Dining/Entertainment: Choices include The Alexandra, a clubby room known for a range of gourmet Continental and Irish fare; Plurabelle, a brasserie-style restaurant; The Lobby Lounge, for traditional afternoon tea or drinks with piano background music; and Alfie Byrne's, a pub named for a former lord mayor of Dublin and serving light lunches.

Services: 24-hour room service, concierge, valet, shoe-shine, express checkout.

Facilities: Foreign currency exchange, car parking garage, hairdressing salon.

✪ Shelbourne

27 St. Stephen's Green, Dublin 2. ☎ **800/225-5843** from the U.S., or 01/676-6471. Fax 01/661-6006. 164 rms. MINIBAR TV TEL. £159–£182 ($254.40–$291.20) double. Service charge 15%. AE, CB, DC, MC, V. DART to Pearse Station. Bus: 10, 11A, 11B, 13, 20B.

With a fanciful red-brick and white-trimmed facade enhanced by wrought-iron railings and window boxes brimming with flowers, this grand six-story hostelry stands out on the north side of St. Stephen's Green. Built in 1824, it has played a significant role in Irish history (the new nation's constitution was signed in Room 112 in 1921) and it has often been host to international leaders, stars of stage and screen, and literary giants. The public areas, replete with glowing fireplaces, Waterford chandeliers, and original art, are popular rendezvous spots for Dubliners. The guest rooms vary in size, but all offer up-to-date comforts and are furnished with antique and period pieces. The front units overlook the bucolic setting of St. Stephen's Green. In 1996, nearly $2.5 million was spent refurbishing the Shelbourne's bedrooms and meeting rooms.

Dining/Entertainment: The Dining Room offers Irish/Continental cuisine, while the Horseshoe Bar or Shelbourne Bar are both ideal for a convivial drink. The Lord Mayor's Lounge is favored by the locals for a proper afternoon tea.

Services: 24-hour room service, concierge, baby-sitting, safe deposit boxes.

Facilities: Foreign currency exchange, private enclosed parking lot, beauty salon, boutiques, access to nearby health club.

Westbury

Grafton St., Dublin 2. ☎ **800/44-UTELL** from the U.S., or 01/679-1122. Fax 01/679-7078. 200 rms, 6 suites. AC TV TEL. £206.25–£221.30 ($330–$354.15) double; £275–£414 ($440–$662.40) suites; £450 ($720) presidential suite. Includes full Irish breakfast and service charge. AE, CB, DC, MC, V. DART to Tara St. or Pearse Station. Bus: 10, 11A, 11B, 13, 20B.

A tasteful hybrid of modern and traditional design, this relatively new midtown hotel blends a sleekly styled contemporary facade with a serene interior of soft pastel tones and antique furnishings. It sits in the heart of the city's fashionable shopping district and near all the major sights. The guest rooms, many with half-canopy or four-poster beds, are furnished with dark woods, brass trim, and floral designer fabrics. Many of the suites have Jacuzzis.

Dining/Entertainment: Choices include The Russell Room, a French/Irish restaurant; The Sandbank, a nautical-style pub serving fresh seafood; Charlie's Coffee Shop for a quick meal; and the Terrace Bar and Lounge, a favorite venue for afternoon tea or a drink, with live piano music.

Services: 24-hour room service, concierge, express checkout.

Facilities: Hairdressing salon, 20-shop arcade, underground parking, fitness room, access to Riverview Health and Fitness Club.

EXPENSIVE

Buswells

25 Molesworth St., Dublin 2. ☎ **800/473-9527** from the U.S., or 01/676-4013. Fax 01/676-2090. 72 rms. TV TEL. £140 ($235.20) double. Includes full breakfast. No service charge. AE, CB, DC, MC, V. DART to Pearse Station. Bus: 10, 11A, 11B, 13, 20B.

Situated on a street that's oddly quiet considering it's only two blocks from Trinity College and opposite the National Museum, Library, and Art Gallery, and Leinster House, this vintage four-story hotel has long been a meeting point for artists, poets, scholars, and politicians. Originally two Georgian town houses (dating from 1736), it was launched as a hotel in 1928. After having been managed by three generations of the Duff family, Buswells was purchased by the Sean Quinn Hotel group in 1996. The public rooms have period furniture, intricate plasterwork, Wedgwood flourishes, old prints, and memorabilia. Extensive refurbishment throughout the hotel is underway and should be completed by the time this guide reaches print. The Georgian decor and character will be preserved. Facilities include an à la carte restaurant, carvery, two bars, concierge, and room service.

Stephen's Hall

14–17 Lower Leeson St., Earlsfort Terrace, Dublin 2. ☎ **800/223-6510** from the U.S., or 01/661-0585. Fax 01/661-0606. 37 suites. TV TEL. £140 ($224) double for one-bedroom suite; £180 ($288) double for two-bedroom suite; £210 ($336) for penthouse/town house suite. No service charge. AE, CB, DC, MC, V. DART to Pearse Station. Bus: 14A, 11A, 11B, 13, 46A, 46B, 86.

With a gracious Georgian exterior and entranceway, this is Dublin's first all-suite hotel, situated on the southeast corner of St. Stephen's Green. It's ideal for visitors who plan an extended stay or who want to entertain and/or do their own cooking. All of the suites were redecorated in March/April 1996. Each contains a hallway, sitting room, dining area, kitchen, bathroom, and one or two bedrooms. The luxury penthouse suites, on the upper floors, offer views of the city, while the ground-level town house suites have private entrances. Free underground parking.

Services: Concierge, twice-daily maid service, baby-sitting, safe deposit boxes, and valet parking.

Facilities: Bistro and bar, underground parking, access to nearby health club.

EXPENSIVE/MODERATE

Georgian House

20 Lower Baggot St., Dublin 2. ☎ **01/661-8832.** Fax 01/661-8834. 33 rms. TV TEL. £78–£140 ($124.80–$224) double. Service charge 10%. Rates include full breakfast. AE, DC, MC, V. DART to Pearse Station. Bus: 10.

Located less than two blocks from St. Stephen's Green, this four-story, 200-year-old brick town house sits in the heart of Georgian Dublin, within walking distance of most major attractions. Bedrooms are smallish, but offer all the essentials and a colorful decor with pine furniture. As at most small hotels in landmark buildings, there is no elevator, but there is an enclosed parking lot at the rear, a restaurant specializing in seafood, The Ante Room, in the basement, and a lively in-house pub, Maguire's.

MODERATE

⑤ Stauntons on the Green

83 St. Stephen's Green, Dublin 2. ☎ **01/478-2300.** Fax 01/478-2263. 32 rms. TV TEL. £81–£92 ($129.60–$147.20) double. Includes full breakfast. No service charge. AE, DC, MC, V. DART to Pearse Station. Bus: 14A or 62.

Opened in 1993, this beautifully restored guest house occupies a four-story Georgian town house on the south side of St. Stephen's Green, next door to the Irish Department of Foreign Affairs. As befits a landmark building, there is no elevator, but there are rooms on the ground level. The guest rooms are decorated in traditional style, enhanced by tall windows and high ceilings; front rooms overlook the Green and rooms at the back have views of the adjacent Iveagh Gardens. Public areas include a breakfast room and a parlor with open fireplace. Valet parking £5 ($8) per day.

INEXPENSIVE

Avalon House

55 Aungier St., Dublin 2. ☎ **01/475-0001.** Fax 01/475-0303. 42 rms (10 with shower), 3 dorms. £28 ($44.80) double. No service charge. AE, MC, V. Bus: 16, 16A, 19, 22.

With a four-story red sandstone facade, this strikingly ornate Victorian building was erected in 1879 as a medical school, later used for commercial offices, and then completely gutted and transformed into a custom-built hostel in 1992. Great care was taken to preserve original turf fireplaces, some of the more artistic wallpaper, and the wide windows, while at the same time installing the most modern equipment for showers, toilets, and other guest facilities. Geared for students and budget-conscious travelers, it is situated less than two blocks from St. Stephen's Green. Facilities include a coffee shop, study/reading room, currency exchange bureau, TV lounge room, international pay phones, lockers, luggage storage, self-catering kitchen, and guest laundry.

Frankie's Guest Hotel

8 Camden Place (off of Harcourt St.), Dublin 2. ☎ **01/478-3087.** 12 rms (9 with shower). TV. £44–£55 ($70.40–$88) double. Rates include breakfast. AE, EU, MC, V. Safe backstreet parking. Bus: 62.

Frankie has been running this very pleasant guest hotel for eight years, adding to the lovely walkway and roof garden and maintaining the smallish but fresh, simple white rooms to a high standard. Set in a quiet back street, the house has a Mediterranean feel, welcoming mature gay, lesbian, and straight visitors alike. There is a double bedroom downstairs that can accommodate a traveler with disabilities. It is an easy walk to St. Stephen's Green and Grafton Street and you can make coffee or tea in your room to renew yourself. I recommend that you book well in advance, especially over a weekend.

The Horse and Carriage Guest Hotel

15 Aungier St., Dublin 2 (Aungier continues So. Great George's St.). ☎ **01/478-3537.** Fax 01/478-4010. E-mail: liamtony@indigo.ie. 9 rms with shared baths. TV. £30–£50 ($48–$80). All rates include breakfast and unlimited use of the attached Incognito Sauna Club facilities. AE, EU, MC, V. Pay parking lot nearby. Bus: 14, 14A, 47, 47A.

Set in the heart of busy Dublin center, this three-year-old hotel, warmly welcoming people of all ages and orientations (and both genders), has predominantly gay male visitors. The Incognito Sauna Club is part of the hotel complex and the atmosphere is very casual and bustling. Most rooms have king-size beds—a rarity in Ireland—and the shared bathrooms are very clean and private. The three highest priced rooms, the "carriage rooms," are more spacious and quieter than the others, which face a busy street. Heavily flowered wallpaper makes the rooms feel small and a bit dark, but all the accommodations are comfortable. The hotel has won awards for its remodeled turn-of-the-century facade. Hosts Liam Ledwidge and Tony Keogan are very helpful and well informed on Dublin life.

Tig na mBan / The Women's House

24 Church Ave. South, Rialto, Dublin 8 (in Dolphin's Barn area off Reuben Ave., between St. Anthony's Rd. and Haroldville Ave.). ☎ **01/473-1781.** 4 rms with shared baths. £28 ($54.80) double. No credit cards. On-street parking. Bus: 19A, 19.

A 10-minute bus ride south of Dublin center will bring you to the welcoming and cozy Women's House, which offers women travelers a wide range of options: single, up to four women sharing, standard B&B, and self-catering, all with optional evening meal. Every room has tea/coffee-making facilities. The knowledgeable owners will help you plan your stay in Dublin and give you the latest on women's and gay events. I recommend that you book in advance as this is a popular spot.

FITZWILLIAM SQUARE / MERRION SQUARE AREA
VERY EXPENSIVE / EXPENSIVE

Davenport Hotel

Merrion Sq., Dublin 2. ☎ **800/44-UTELL** from the U.S., or 01/661-6800. Fax 01/661-5663. 116 rms. A/C TV TEL. £180–£220 ($288–$352) double. Includes full Irish breakfast and service charge. AE, DC, MC, V. DART to Pearse Station. Bus: 5, 7A, 8, 62.

Opened as a hotel in 1993, this building incorporates the neoclassical facade of Merrion Hall, an 1863 church. Inside there is an impressive domed entranceway with a six-story atrium lobby of marble flooring and plaster moldings, encircled by classic Georgian windows and pillars. The guest rooms, in a newly built section, have traditional furnishings, orthopedic beds, textured wall coverings, quilted floral bedspreads and matching drapes, and brass accouterments. There are three telephone lines in each room plus a computer data line, work desk, personal safe, garment press, tea/coffee welcome tray, mirrored closet, and hair dryer. It is a sister hotel to the Mont Clare, which is across the street, and shares valet car parking arrangements.

Dining/Entertainment: The Georgian-theme restaurant, Lanyon's, is named after a leading Irish architect of the 19th century. The clubby President's Bar, decorated with framed pictures of world leaders, past and present, serves drinks as well as morning coffee and afternoon tea.

Services: Room service, concierge, valet laundry.

Mont Clare Hotel

Merrion Sq., Clare St., Dublin 2. ☎ **800/44-UTELL** from the U.S., or 01/661-6799. Fax 01/661-5663. 74 rms. AC MINIBAR TV TEL. £100–£190 ($160–$304) double. Includes full Irish breakfast and service charge. AE, DC, MC, V. DART to Pearse Station. Bus: 5, 7A, 8, 62.

Overlooking the northwest corner of Merrion Square, this vintage six-story brick-faced hotel was thoroughly restored and refurbished in recent years. It has a typically Georgian facade, matched tastefully inside by period furnishings of dark woods and polished brass. The guest rooms, decked out in contemporary style, offer every up-to-date amenity including hair dryer, tea/coffeemaker, and garment press.

Dining/Entertainment: The main restaurant, Goldsmith's (named for Oliver Goldsmith, one of Ireland's great writers), has a literary theme. There is also a traditional lounge bar.

Services: 24-hour room service, concierge.

Facilities: Foreign currency exchange, private valet parking lot.

MODERATE

Longfields

9/10 Lower Fitzwilliam St., Dublin 2. ☎ **800/223-1588** from the U.S., or 01/676-1367. Fax 01/676-1542. 26 rms. MINIBAR TV TEL. £88–£112 ($140.80–$179.20) double. No service charge. Rates include full breakfast. AE, DC, MC, V. DART to Pearse Station. Bus: 10.

Created from two 18th-century Georgian town houses, this smart little hotel is named after Richard Longfield, also known as Viscount Longueville, who originally owned this site and was a member of the Irish Parliament two centuries ago. Totally restored and refurbished several years ago, it combines Georgian decor and reproduction period furnishings of dark woods and brass trim. Bedrooms offer extras such as clock radios and hair dryers. Facilities include a restaurant with bar, room service, and foreign currency exchange, but no parking lot.

MODERATE/INEXPENSIVE

The Fitzwilliam

41 Upper Fitzwilliam St., Dublin 2. ☎ **01/662-5155.** Fax 01/676-7488. 12 rms. TV TEL. £49–£70 ($78.40–$112) double. Service charge 10%. Rates include full breakfast. AE, DC, MC, V. DART to Pearse Station. Bus: 10.

Named for the wide thoroughfare it overlooks, this cozy guest house is a restored and refurbished 18th-century Georgian home. The entrance parlor has a homey atmosphere, with a marble fireplace and antique furnishings, while the bedrooms are outfitted with contemporary amenities including hair dryers and clock radios. Facilities include a French restaurant. Free overnight parking.

BALLSBRIDGE / EMBASSY ROW AREA
VERY EXPENSIVE

✪ Berkeley Court

Lansdowne Rd., Ballsbridge, Dublin 4. ☎ **800/42-DOYLE,** 800/223-6800, 800/44-UTELL from the U.S., or 01/660-1711. Fax 01/661-7238. 187 rms, 30 suites. TV TEL. £159–£175 ($254.40–$280) double; £250–£450 ($400–$720) suite; £1,600 ($2,560) penthouse suite. Service charge 15%. AE, CB, DC, MC, V. DART to Lansdowne Rd. Bus: 5, 7A, 8, 46, 63, 84.

The flagship of the Irish-owned Doyle Hotel group and the first Irish member of Leading Hotels of the World, the Berkeley Court (pronounced *bar*-kley) is nestled in a residential area near the American Embassy on well-tended grounds that were once part of the Botanic Gardens of University College. A favorite haunt of diplomats and international business leaders, the hotel is known for its posh lobby decorated with fine antiques, original paintings, mirrored columns, and Irish-made carpets and furnishings. The guest rooms, which aim to convey an air of elegance, have designer fabrics, semicanopy beds, dark woods, and bathrooms fitted with marble accouterments.

Dining/Entertainment: Choices include the formal Berkeley Room for gourmet dining; the skylit Conservatory for casual meals; the Royal Court, a Gothic-style bar for drinks; and the Court Lounge, a proper setting for afternoon tea or a relaxing drink.

Services: 24-hour room service, concierge, laundry service, express checkout.

Facilities: Foreign currency exchange, shopping boutiques, health club, Jacuzzis in suites, free valet parking.

Burlington

Upper Leeson St., Dublin 4. ☎ **800/42-DOYLE** from the U.S., or 01/660-5222. Fax 01/660-3172. 477 rms. TV TEL. £165.45–£174 ($264.75–$278.40) double. Includes full Irish breakfast and service charge. AE, CB, DC, MC, V. Bus: 10 or 18.

A favorite headquarters for conventions, meetings, conferences, and group tours, this is the largest hotel in Ireland, situated a block south of the Grand Canal in a fashionable residential section within walking distance of St. Stephen's Green. It's a modern, crisply furnished seven-story property that is constantly being refurbished. The bedrooms are outfitted with brass-bound oak furniture and designer fabrics. The interconnecting units are ideal for families.

Dining/Entertainment: Choices include the Sussex, a large formal dining room; a buffet restaurant; and a coffee shop for light meals. For a real Old Dublin pub atmosphere, try Buck Mulligans, which serves a carvery-style lunch (read: *lots of meat*) and light evening meals as well as drinks. Annabel's is the basement-level nightclub. From May to early October, the main ballroom offers Doyle's Irish Cabaret, a three-hour cabaret dinner show.

Services: 24-hour room service, concierge, valet/laundry service.

Facilities: Foreign currency exchange, underground and outdoor parking, gift shops, newsstand, hairdressing salons.

○ Hibernian Hotel

Eastmoreland Place, Ballsbridge, Dublin 4. ☎ **800/525-4800** from the U.S., or 01/668-7666. Fax 01/660-2655. 41 rms. TV TEL. £150 ($240) double; £180 ($288) junior suite. No service charge. Rates include full Irish breakfast. AE, CB, DC, MC, V. Bus: 10.

Although it bears a similar name, this is not a reincarnation of the legendary Royal Hibernian Hotel that was ensconced on Dawson Street until the early 1980s. Instead, this handsome red-brick four-story Victorian building was originally part of Baggot Street Hospital. After a complete restoration, it was modeled into a hotel in 1993, and offers its guests up-to-date comforts with the charm of a country inn. In 1995, it became a member of the "Small Luxury Hotels of the World," and in 1996 it added 12 new rooms, including eight junior suites, a boardroom, and a sun lounge. The public areas are filled with antiques, graceful pillars, and floral arrangements. The top floor sports a beautifully restored dome-shaped skylight. The bedrooms, of varying size and layout, are individually decorated with dark woods, floral fabrics, and specially commissioned paintings of Dublin and wildlife scenes. In-room conveniences include a full-length mirror, garment press, hair dryer, and tea/coffeemaker. Unlike some converted 19th-century buildings, it has an elevator. Private parking lot at no extra charge.

Dining/Entertainment: On the lobby level, a cozy, parlorlike guests' bar and a conservatory-style restaurant with a Georgian decor.

Services: Room service, concierge, 24-hour butler, turn-down service, valet laundry.

○ Jurys Hotel and Towers

Pembroke Rd., Ballsbridge, Dublin 4. ☎ **800/843-3311** from the U.S., or 01/660-5000. Fax 01/660-5540. 390 rms. TV TEL. Main hotel £142 ($227.20) double; Towers wing (with continental breakfast) £191 ($305.60) double. Service charge 12.5%. AE, DC, MC, V. DART to Lansdowne Rd. Station. Bus: 6, 7, 8, 18, 45, 46, 84.

Setting a progressive tone in a city steeped in tradition, this unique hotel welcomes guests to a skylit, three-story atrium lobby with a marble and teak decor. Situated on its own grounds opposite the American Embassy, this sprawling property is actually two interconnected hotels in one: a modern, eight-story high-rise and a new 100-unit tower with its own check-in desk, separate elevators, and private entrance, as well as full access to all of the main hotel's amenities. The guest rooms in the main wing, recently refurbished, have dark wood furnishings, brass trim, and designer fabrics. The Towers section, a first for the Irish capital, is an exclusive wing of oversized concierge-style rooms with bay windows. Each unit has computer-card key access, stocked minibar, three telephone lines, well-lit work area with desk, reclining chair, tile and marble bathroom, walk-in closet, and either a king- or queen-size bed. Decor varies,

Ballsbridge / Embassy Row Area Accommodations

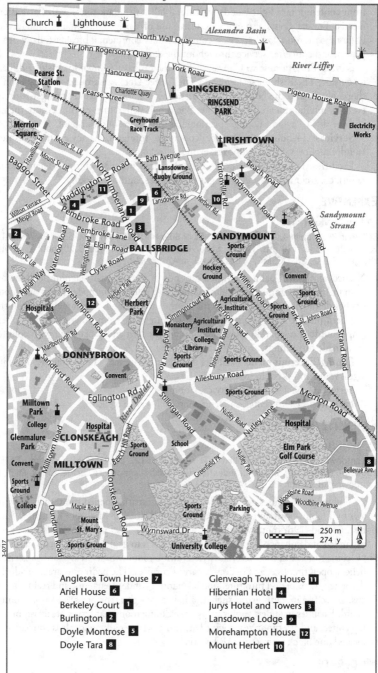

Anglesea Town House **7**
Ariel House **6**
Berkeley Court **1**
Burlington **2**
Doyle Montrose **5**
Doyle Tara **8**

Glenveagh Town House **11**
Hibernian Hotel **4**
Jurys Hotel and Towers **3**
Lansdowne Lodge **9**
Morehampton House **12**
Mount Herbert **10**

from contemporary light woods with floral fabrics to dark tones with Far Eastern motifs. Towers guests also enjoy exclusive use of a private hospitality lounge with library, board room, and access to complimentary continental breakfast, daily newspapers, and coffee/tea service throughout the day.

Dining/Entertainment: Choices include the Embassy Garden for Irish/Continental cuisine; The Kish for seafood; and The Coffee Dock, an around-the-clock coffee shop. This is also the home of Jurys Irish Cabaret Show, Ireland's longest-running evening entertainment; The Dubliner Bar, a pub with a turn-of-the century theme; and the skylit Pavilion Lounge, overlooking the indoor/outdoor pool.

Services: 24-hour room service, concierge, foreign currency exchange, valet/laundry service, safe deposit boxes, express checkout.

Facilities: Heated indoor/outdoor pool, therapeutic hot whirlpool, hairdressing salons, craft/clothes shop, Aer Lingus ticket office, outdoor parking.

EXPENSIVE

✪ Doyle Montrose

Stillorgan Rd., Dublin 4. ☎ **800/42-DOYLE** or 800/44-UTELL from the U.S., or 01/269-3311. Fax 01/269-3376. 179 rms. TV TEL. £126.90–£133.70 ($203.10–$213.90) double. Service charge 15%. AE, CB, DC, MC, V. Bus: 10, 46, 46A, 46B, 63.

Nestled on its own palm tree–lined grounds in a residential neighborhood, across from the Belfield campus of Dublin's University College, this modern four-story hotel sits beside the main road (N11) to the southeast of Ireland. The largest hotel on the southern outskirts of the city, it is a 10-minute drive from downtown, and offers ample outdoor car parking. Guest rooms are modern and functional, with colorful Irish-made furnishings.

Dining/Entertainment: Facilities include a restaurant, The Belfield Room, plus a grill room and skylit lounge bar.

Services: Concierge, room service, laundry service.

Facilities: Health center, souvenir shop, full-service bank.

EXPENSIVE/MODERATE

✪ Ariel House

52 Lansdowne Rd., Ballsbridge, Dublin 4. ☎ **01/668-5512.** Fax 01/668-5845. 28 rms. TV TEL. £50–£150 ($80–$240) double. Includes full Irish breakfast and service charge. MC, V. DART to Lansdowne Rd. Station. Bus: 5, 7A, 8, 46, 63, 84.

As Dublin guest houses go, this one is the benchmark, opened more than 25 years ago by Dublin-born and San Francisco–trained hotelier Michael O'Brien. With a historic mid–19th century mansion as its core, this bastion of hospitality has been expanded and enhanced continually over the years to its present capacity. Guests are welcome to relax in the Victorian-style drawing room with its Waterford glass chandeliers, open fireplace, and delicately carved cornices. The bedrooms are individually decorated, with period furniture, fine oil paintings and watercolors, and real Irish linens, as well as modern extras such as a hair dryer, garment press, and iron/ironing board. Facilities include a conservatory-style dining room that serves breakfast, morning coffee, and afternoon tea; a wine bar; and a private parking lot. It is conveniently located one block from the DART station.

MODERATE

Anglesea Town House

63 Anglesea Rd., Ballsbridge, Dublin 4. ☎ **01/668-3877.** Fax 01/668-3461. 7 rms. TV TEL. £90–£100 ($144–$160) double. No service charge. Rates include full breakfast. AE, MC, V. DART to Lansdowne Rd. Station. Bus: 46, 63, 84.

In case you want to see the world.

At American Express, we're here to make your journey a smooth one. So we have over 1,700 travel service locations in over 120 countries ready to help. What else would you expect from the world's largest travel agency?

do more.

AMERICAN EXPRESS

Travel

http://www.americanexpress.com/travel

In case you want to be welcomed there.

We're here to see that you're always welcomed at establishments everywhere. That's why millions of people carry the American Express® Card – for peace of mind, confidence, and security, around the world or just around the corner.

do more

In case you're
running low.

We're here to help with more than 118,000 Express Cash

locations around the world. In order to enroll, just call

American Express before you start your vacation.

do more

**Express
Cash**

And just in case.

We're here with American Express® Travelers Cheques
and Cheques *for Two.*® They're the safest way to carry
money on your vacation and the surest way to get a
refund, practically anywhere, anytime.

Another way we help you...

do more

AMERICAN
EXPRESS

**Travelers
Cheques**

A true bed-and-breakfast experience is the best way to describe this 1903 Edwardian-style guest house. Located in the Ballsbridge section of the city, close to the Royal Dublin Showgrounds and the American Embassy, it is furnished with comfort in mind—rocking chairs, settees, a sundeck, and lots of flowering plants, as well as all modern conveniences in every guest room. You can count on a warm welcome from hostess Helen Kirrane, and a homemade breakfast worth getting up for.

✪ Doyle Tara

Merrion Rd., Dublin 4. ☎ **800/42-DOYLE** from the U.S., or 01/269-4666. Fax 01/269-1027. 100 rms. TV TEL. £94–£115 ($150.40–$184) double. Service charge 15%. AE, DC, MC, V. DART to Booterstown Station. Bus: 5, 7, 7A, 8.

Positioned along the coast road between downtown Dublin and the ferryport of Dun Laoghaire, just 10 minutes from the city center in a residential area, this modern seven-story hotel offers wide-windowed views of Dublin Bay. It's an ideal place for car renters, as there is ample parking space. For those who prefer to use public transport, it's within easy walking distance of major bus routes and a DART station. Guest rooms, with every modern convenience, have attractive Irish-made furnishings. Concierge, room service, and laundry service are available, and there are a foreign currency exchange and a souvenir shop on the premises. For dining, there's a conservatory-style restaurant and a Joycean lounge bar.

Lansdowne Lodge

4 Lansdowne Terrace, Shelbourne Rd., Ballsbridge, Dublin 4. ☎ **01/660-5755** or 01/660-5578. Fax 01/660-5662. 12 rms. TV TEL. £66–£85 ($105.60–$136) double. 10% service charge. Rates include full breakfast. MC, V. DART to Lansdowne Rd. Station. Bus: 5, 7, 7A, 8, 45.

With a lovely two-story brick town house facade, this guest house enjoys a very convenient location, between Lansdowne and Haddington Roads, and within a block of the DART station and major bus routes. Owner Finbarr Smyth offers a variety of individually styled bedrooms with armchairs and homey furnishings, including decorative bed coverings and framed paintings. Some rooms are on the ground floor. Full renovation of bedrooms should be completed by the time you read this. The grounds include a garden and private parking lot.

Mount Herbert

Herbert Rd., Ballsbridge, Dublin 4. ☎ **01/668-4321.** Fax 01/660-7077. 145 rms. TV TEL. £63–£79 ($100.80–$126.40) double. No service charge. AE, DC, MC, V. DART to Lansdowne Rd. Station. Bus: 2, 3, 5, 7, 7A, 8, 18, 45.

Although technically classified as a guest house, this much-expanded three-story property is more like a small hotel. Originally the family home of Lord Robinson, it is a gracious residence set in its own grounds and gardens in a residential neighborhood near the DART station and major bus routes. Operated by the Loughran family, it offers bedrooms of various vintages and sizes, but all have standard amenities including a garment press. Guest facilities include a restaurant, wine bar, sauna, indoor solarium, gift shop, and guest parking lot.

MODERATE/INEXPENSIVE

Glenveagh Town House

31 Northumberland Rd., Ballsbridge, Dublin 4. ☎ **01/668-4612.** Fax 01/668-4559. 11 rms. TV TEL. £50–£81 ($80–$130) double. No service charge. Rates include full breakfast. MC, V. DART to Lansdowne Rd. Station. Bus: 5, 6, 6A, 7A, 8, 18, 45.

Fashioned into a guest house by the Cunningham family, this converted three-story Georgian residence is situated south of the Grand Canal on a quiet, tree-lined street. It offers a homey atmosphere with a glowing fireplace in the sitting room, high ceilings, and tall windows bedecked with floral drapery. Guest rooms are decorated with light woods, lots of frilly pastel fabrics, and all the modern conveniences. There is a private parking lot, free of charge.

INEXPENSIVE

Morehampton House

78 Morehampton Rd., Donnybrook, Dublin 4. ☎ **01/668-8866.** Fax 01/668-8794. 85 beds (no private baths). £30 ($48) double in twin-bed rooms. MC, V. Bus: 10, 46A, 46B.

In a residential area south of the city center and within a 15-minute walk from St. Stephen's Green, this four-story Victorian house has been recently converted into a hostel. Designed for the budget-minded traveler, it offers a choice of twin rooms and dorm-style accommodations. Facilities include a 24-hour reception desk, TV room, common room, self-catering kitchen, car and bike parking, and lovely gardens outside.

O'CONNELL STREET AREA
VERY EXPENSIVE

Gresham

23 Upper O'Connell St., Dublin 1. ☎ **800/44-UTELL** from the U.S., or 01/874-6881. Fax 01/878-7175. 202 rms, 6 suites. TV TEL. £158–£225 ($252.80–$360) double. Includes full Irish breakfast and service charge. AE, CB, DC, MC, V. DART to Connolly Station. Bus: 40A, 40B, 40C, 51A.

Centrally located on the city's main business thoroughfare, this Regency-style hotel is one of Ireland's oldest (1817) and best-known lodging establishments. Although much of the tourist trade in Dublin has shifted south of the River Liffey in recent years, the Gresham is still synonymous with stylish Irish hospitality and provides easy access to the Abbey and Gate Theatres and other northside attractions. The lobby and public areas are a panorama of marble floors, molded plasterwork, and crystal chandeliers. With high ceilings and individual decor, guest rooms vary in size and style, with heavy emphasis on deep blue and pink tones, soft lighting, tile bathrooms, and period furniture, including padded headboards and armoires. One-of-a-kind luxury terrace suites grace the upper front floors.

Dining/Entertainment: Choices include the bilevel Aberdeen Restaurant for formal meals and Toddy's, a trendy pub/lounge offering light meals all day. Another bar, Magnums, attracts a late-night crowd.

Services: Concierge, 24-hour room service, valet laundry service.

Facilities: Private parking garage, ice machines, foreign currency exchange.

MODERATE

Royal Dublin

40 Upper O'Connell St., Dublin 1. ☎ **800/528-1234** from the U.S., or 01/873-3666. Fax 01/873-3120. 120 rms. TV TEL. £94–£114 ($117–$177) double. Includes full Irish breakfast and service charge. AE, DC, MC, V. DART to Connolly Station. Bus: 36A, 40A, 40B, 40C, 51A.

Romantically floodlit at night, this modern five-story hotel is positioned near Parnell Square at the north end of Dublin's main thoroughfare, within walking distance of all the main theaters and northside attractions. It combines a contemporary skylit lobby full of art deco overtones with adjacent lounge areas that were part of an original building dating from 1752. These Georgian-theme rooms are rich in high molded ceilings, ornate cornices, crystal chandeliers, gilt-edged mirrors, and open fireplaces. The bedrooms are strictly modern with light woods, pastel fabrics, and three-sided full-length windows that extend over the busy street below. Corridors are extremely well lit, with individual lights at each doorway. Concierge, 24-hour room service, and laundry service are available, and there's a currency exchange bureau, underground car park, and car-rental desk in the hotel. Dining choices include the Cafe Royale Brasserie for full meals; Raffles Bar, a clubby, skylit room with portraits of Irish literary greats, for snacks or drinks; and the Georgian Lounge for morning coffee or afternoon tea beside the open fireplace.

4 Dining

You're here. You're famished. Where do you go? A formal, old-world hotel dining room? Or perhaps a casual bistro or wine bar? Ethnic cuisine, maybe? Dublin has the goods, across a wide range of price categories. Expect, however, generally higher prices than you'd pay for comparable fare in a comparable U.S. city. (Hey, Dublin's hip—you always have to pay for hip.) As befits a European capital, there's plenty of continental cuisine, with a particular leaning toward French and Italian influences, plus a fine selection of international eateries, with menus from Scandinavia, Russia, the Mediterranean, China, and even exotic fare from someplace called California.

HISTORIC OLD CITY / LIBERTIES AREA

EXPENSIVE

Lord Edward

23 Christ Church Place, Dublin 8. ☎ **01/454-2420.** Reservations required. Main courses £12.95–£17.95 ($20.70–$28.70). AE, DC, MC, V. Mon–Fri noon–2:45pm and 5–10:45pm, Sat 5–10:45pm. Bus: 21A, 50, 50A, 78, 78A, 78B. SEAFOOD.

Established in 1890 and situated in the heart of the Old City opposite Christ Church Cathedral, this cozy upstairs dining room claims to be Dublin's oldest seafood restaurant. A dozen different preparations of sole, including au gratin and Veronique, are served; there are seven variations of prawns, from thermidor to Provençal; fresh lobster is prepared au naturel or in sauces; and there's fresh fish from salmon and sea trout to plaice and turbot—grilled, fried, meunière, or poached. Vegetarian dishes are also available. At lunchtime, light snacks and simpler fare are served in the bar.

EXPENSIVE/MODERATE

Old Dublin

90/91 Francis St., Dublin 8. ☎ **01/454-2028** or 01/454-2346. Reservations recommended. Fixed-price menu £12.50 ($18.75); 3-course dinners £19–£25 ($27.50–$37.50). AE, DC, MC, V. Mon–Fri 12:30–2:30pm and 6–11pm, Sat 6–11pm. Bus: 21A, 78A, 78B. SCANDINAVIAN/RUSSIAN.

Located in the heart of Dublin's antique row, this shopfront restaurant is also on the edge of the city's medieval quarter, once settled by Vikings. It's not surprising, therefore, that many recipes featured here reflect this background, with a long list of imaginative Scandinavian and Russian dishes. Among the best entrées are novgorod, a rare beef thinly sliced and served on sauerkraut with fried barley, mushrooms, garlic butter, sour cream, and caviar; salmon kulebjaka, a pastry filled with salmon, dill herbs, rice, egg, mushrooms, and onion; black sole Metsa, filled with mussels and served with prawn butter and white wine; and a varied selection of vegetarian dishes.

INEXPENSIVE

Leo Burdock's

2 Werburgh St., Dublin 8. ☎ **01/454-0306.** Reservations not necessary. £2.50–£3.50 ($4–$5.60). No credit cards. Mon–Fri 12:30–11pm, Sat 2–11pm. Bus: 21A, 50, 50A, 78, 78A, 78B. FISH AND CHIPS / FAST FOOD.

Dublin Dining

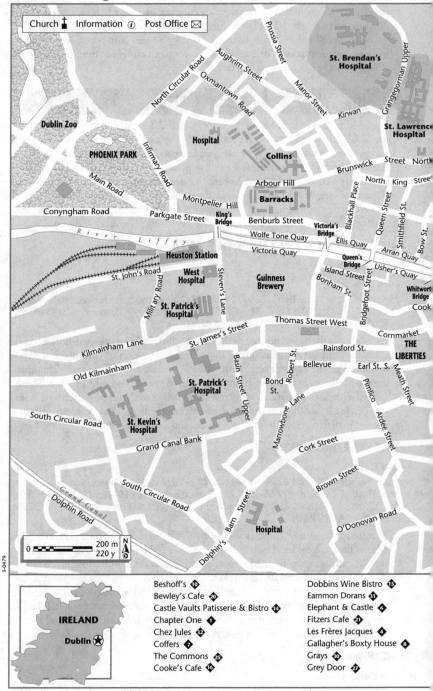

Church ✝   Information ⓘ   Post Office ✉

Prussia Street
Aughrim Street
Oxmantown Road
North Circular Road
Manor Street
St. Brendan's Hospital
Grangegorman Upper
Kirwan
St. Lawrence Hospital
Dublin Zoo
Hospital
Collins
Brunswick Street North
PHOENIX PARK
Infirmary Road
Arbour Hill
Barracks
North King Street
Blackhall Place
Queen Street
Smithfield St.
Bow St.
Main Road
Montpelier Hill
Conyngham Road
Parkgate Street
King's Bridge
Benburb Street
Victoria's Bridge
Ellis Quay
Arran Quay
River Liffey
Wolfe Tone Quay
Victoria Quay
Queen's Bridge
Usher's Quay
Heuston Station
West Hospital
Steven's Lane
Guinness Brewery
Island Street
Bonham St.
Bridgefoot Street
Whitworth Bridge
St. John's Road
Military Road
St. Patrick's Hospital
Cook
Thomas Street West
Cornmarket
THE LIBERTIES
Kilmainham Lane
St. James's Street
Rainsford St.
Old Kilmainham
Basin Street Upper
Bellevue
Robert St.
Earl St. S.
Pimlico
Meath Street
St. Patrick's Hospital
Bond St.
Marrowbone Lane
Ardee Street
South Circular Road
St. Kevin's Hospital
Cork Street
Grand Canal Bank
Brown Street
Grand Canal
Dolphin Road
South Circular Road
Barn Street
Dolphin's Barn Street
Hospital
O'Donovan Road

0 ——— 200 m / 220 y   N

3-0479

IRELAND

Dublin ★

Beshoff's ⑩	Dobbins Wine Bistro ⑮
Bewley's Cafe ㉙	Eammon Dorans ㉛
Castle Vaults Patisserie & Bistro ⑭	Elephant & Castle ⑥
Chapter One ❶	Fitzers Cafe ㉑
Chez Jules ㊷	Les Frères Jacques ❹
Coffers ❼	Gallagher's Boxty House ❽
The Commons ㉕	Grays ㉚
Cooke's Cafe ⑯	Grey Door ㉗

122

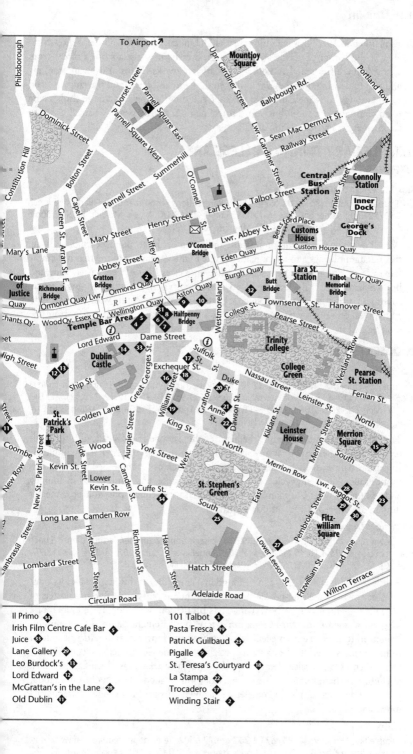

Il Primo 🔶34
Irish Film Centre Cafe Bar 🔶5
Juice 🔶13
Lane Gallery 🔶29
Leo Burdock's 🔶18
Lord Edward 🔶12
McGrattan's in the Lane 🔶28
Old Dublin 🔶11

101 Talbot 🔶3
Pasta Fresca 🔶19
Patrick Guilbaud 🔶23
Pigalle 🔶9
St. Teresa's Courtyard 🔶16
La Stampa 🔶22
Trocadero 🔶17
Winding Stair 🔶2

Established in 1913, this is a quintessential Dublin take-out fish-and-chips shop. Situated at the corner of Castle and Werburgh Streets, it is just a stone's throw from Christ Church Cathedral and other Old City landmarks. Types of fish vary from ray and cod to whiting, but they are always fresh, light, and flaky, and the chips are said to be among the crispest in town, whether you order a single or a large chip. There is no seating at the shop, but you can recline on a nearby bench or stroll down to the park at St. Patrick's Cathedral.

TEMPLE BAR / TRINITY COLLEGE AREA
EXPENSIVE

Les Frères Jacques

74 Dame St., Dublin 2. ☎ **01/679-4555**. Reservations recommended. Fixed-price lunch £13.50 ($21.60); dinner entrées £16–£20 ($25.60–$32). AE, DC, MC, V. Mon–Fri 12:30–2:30pm and 7–10:30pm, Sat 7–11pm. Bus: 50, 50A, 54, 56, 77. FRENCH.

Well situated between Crampton Court and Sycamore Street opposite Dublin Castle, this restaurant brings a touch of haute cuisine to the lower edge of the trendy Temple Bar district. The menu offers such creative entrées as fillet of beef in red wine and bone marrow sauce; duck supreme on a sweet corn pancake in tangy ginger sauce; rosette of spring lamb in meat juice sabayon and tomato coulis with crispy potato straws; veal on rainbow pasta with garlic and basil sauce; and grilled lobster from the tank flamed in whiskey.

MODERATE

Coffers

6 Cope St., Dublin 2. ☎ **01/671-5740**. Reservations recommended. Lunch main courses £7.50–£8.50 ($12–$13.60); dinner main courses £11.95–£14.95 ($19.12–$23.92). AE, DC, MC, V. Mon–Fri 12:15–2:30pm and 6–11pm, Sat 6–11pm. DART to Tara St. Station. Bus: 21A, 46A, 46B, 51B, 51C, 68, 69, 86. CONTINENTAL/IRISH.

This little restaurant, tucked in the heart of the Temple Bar district off Crown Alley, offers a homey fireside atmosphere and down-to-earth prices. The menu blends European flair with Irish ingredients, in dishes such as Coquille St-Jacques in vermouth sauce, duck in peach cream and Madeira sauce, and lamb chops in a honey and rosemary sauce. On many evenings, special three-course pre- and post-theater dinners are offered at very affordable prices.

Eammon Dorans

3A Crown Alley, Dublin 2. ☎ **01/679-9114**. Reservations recommended for dinner. Lunch main courses £4.95–£10.95 ($7.90–$17.50); dinner main courses £7.95–£15.15 ($12.70–$24.80). AE, DC, MC, V. Daily 11am–2:30am. IRISH/AMERICAN.

A little bit of New York City can be found in Temple Bar at this huge two-story pub/restaurant with a melting-pot decor—original murals of Temple Bar and posters of U.S. cities—and serving a New York–style brunch on weekends. It's a branch of a long-established midtown Manhattan eatery, both branches named for Eammon Doran, an Irish-born entrepreneur who flies back and forth across the Atlantic to tend to his business interests. Restaurant specialties include Gaelic steak, shepherd's pie, fish and chips, and braised lamb stew. Universal favorites—roast duck flambée, rack of lamb, and chateaubriand—are offered along with a good selection of fresh seafood, pastas, sandwiches, salads, and omelets. The downstairs level is a venue for traditional music and plays.

Pigalle

14 Temple Bar, Dublin 2. ☎ **01/671-9262** or 679-6602. Reservations required on weekends. Fixed-price lunch £12 ($19.20); fixed-price dinner £20.50 ($32.80). Service charge 12.5%.

DC, MC, V. Mon–Fri 12:30–2:30pm and 7–10:45pm, Sat 7–10:45pm. DART to Tara St. Station. Bus: 21A, 46A, 46B, 51B, 51C, 68, 69, 86. FRENCH.

Overlooking Merchant's Arch and Crown Alley in the heart of Temple Bar, this upstairs restaurant attracted a loyal following long before the surrounding neighborhood was a hot spot. The decor is simple bistro style, with white walls, crisp linens, and plant-filled window ledges. The menu, which changes daily, is table d'hôte, with up to six courses on weekends. Entrées often include dishes such as fillet of beef with green peppercorn sauce; rack of lamb with fresh rosemary sauce; breast of duck with blueberry sauce, and wild salmon with capers, tomato, and shallots. The skills and service of the staff make it a true culinary outpost of France wedged in the midst of Dublin's own Left Bank.

MODERATE/INEXPENSIVE

Chez Jules

16a D'Olier St., Dublin 2 (across from the north wall of Trinity College). ☎ **01/677-0499.** Reservations recommended. Main courses £5.75–9.95 ($9.20–15.90); fixed-price lunch £4.90 ($7.85); fixed-price 3-course dinner £8.90 ($14.25). No service charge. EU, MC, V. Mon–Sat noon–3pm and 6–11pm, Sun 12:30–4pm and 5–10pm. DART to Tara St. Station. Bus: 5, 7A, 8, 15A, 15B, 15C, 46, 55, 62, 63, 83, 84. FRENCH COUNTRY.

One of Dublin's newest ventures, Chez Jules fills a niche: relaxed French dining at pub-grub prices. Except for the checkered tablecloths, this is a dining hall, with long tables, benches, bright lights, and bustle. The staff is especially warm and friendly. Some of the dishes, like the au gratin potatoes, are delivered in their skillet. The menu is modest, augmented by daily specials on the chalkboard. This is solid, tasty French country fare, most affordable and satisfying. The vin de pays house wines at £7.50 ($12) a bottle are very drinkable and a real bargain.

Elephant & Castle

18 Temple Bar, Dublin 2. ☎ **01/679-3121.** Reservations not necessary. Lunch main courses £5.50–£8.95 ($8.80–$14.30); dinner main courses £6.50–£12.50 ($10.40–$20). AE, DC, MC, V. Sun–Thurs 11:30am–11:30pm, Fri–Sat 11:30am–midnight. DART to Tara St. Station. Bus: 21A, 46A, 46B, 51B, 51C, 68, 69, 86. CALIFORNIAN/INTERNATIONAL.

Located in the heart of the Temple Bar district, this is an informal and fun restaurant, a favorite with kids, with simple pinewood tables and benches and a decor blending modern art with statues of elephants and cartoon figures. The menu is eclectic, made up of exotic salads and multi-ingredient omelets as well as sesame chicken with spinach and cucumber; fettuccine with shrimp, sun-dried tomatoes, and saffron; linguine with goat cheese, tomato, broccoli, and thyme; and a house-special Elephant Burger with curried sour cream, bacon, scallions, cheddar, and tomato.

INEXPENSIVE

Beshoff's

14 Westmoreland St., Dublin 2. ☎ **01/677-8026.** Reservations not necessary. All items £1.90–£4.50 ($3.05–$7.20). No credit cards. Sun–Thurs 11:30am–11pm, Fri–Sat 11:30am–3am. DART to Tara St. Station. Bus: 7A, 8, 15A, 15B, 15C, 46, 55, 62, 63, 83, 84. SEAFOOD/FISH AND CHIPS.

Little wonder that the Beshoff name is synonymous with fresh fish in Dublin—Ivan Beshoff settled here in 1913 from Odessa, Russia, and started a fish business that developed into this top-notch fish-and-chips eatery, reminiscent of an Edwardian oyster bar. The atmosphere is informal and the self-service menu is simple: crisp chips (french fries) are served with a choice of fresh fish, from the original recipe of cod to classier variations using salmon, shark, prawns, and other local sea fare—some days as many as 20 different varieties. The potatoes are grown on a 300-acre farm in

Tipperary and freshly cut each day. A second shop is located at 5/6 Upper O'Connell St. in the International Food Court (☎ **01/872-4400**).

Castle Vaults Patisserie and Bistro

Dublin Castle, Palace St. (off Dame St.), Dublin 2. ☎ **01/677-0678** or 01/679-3713. Reservations not necessary. £1.50–£5.95 ($2.40–$9.50) for most items. No credit cards. Mon–Fri 8am–5pm, Sat–Sun 11:30am–5pm. Bus: 50, 50A, 54, 56A, or 77. INTERNATIONAL/ SELF-SERVICE.

With stone walls, paned windows, and colorful medieval banners, the old vaults of Dublin Castle serve as the setting for this bustling indoor-outdoor cafe. The menu focuses on pastries, snacks, or light lunch items such as homemade soups, pâtés, quiche, lasagna, sausage rolls, stuffed baked potatoes, salads, and sandwiches.

Gallagher's Boxty House

20–21 Temple Bar, Dublin 2. ☎ **01/677-2762.** Reservations recommended. Lunch main courses £2.95–£4.50 ($4.70–$7.20); dinner main courses £5.95–£9.95 ($9.50–$15.90). MC, V. Daily noon–11:30pm. DART to Tara St. Station. Bus: 21A, 46A, 46B, 51B, 51C, 68, 69, 86. TRADITIONAL IRISH.

Although native Irish cooking is sometimes hard to find in Dublin restaurants, here is one spot that keeps traditions alive, with a particular emphasis on Irish stew, bacon and cabbage, and a dish called "boxty." Boxty is an Irish potato pancake grilled and rolled with various fillings such as beef, lamb, chicken, fish, or combinations like bacon and cabbage. Besides all types of boxty, salmon, and steaks, there are hearty sandwiches served on open wedges of brown bread at lunchtime.

✪ Irish Film Centre Cafe Bar

6 Eustace St., Temple Bar, Dublin 2. ☎ **01/677-8788** or 01/677-8099. Reservations not necessary. Lunch and dinner prices range from £2–£6 ($3.20–$9.60). MC, V. Daily noon–3pm and 5:30–9pm. Bus: 21A, 78A, 78B. IRISH/INTERNATIONAL.

One of the most popular drinking spots in Temple Bar, the Cafe Bar features an excellent menu that changes daily. A vegetarian / Middle Eastern menu is available for both lunch and dinner. Weekend entertainments include music and comedy.

Juice

Castle House, South Great George's St., Dublin 2. ☎ **01/473-7856.** Reservations recommended Fri–Sat. Main courses £4.95–£7.25 ($7.90–$11.15); early bird fixed-price dinner Mon–Thurs 6:30–7pm £6.95 ($11.12). Service charge 10%. EU, MC, V. Sun–Thurs 11am–10pm, Fri–Sat 11am–midnight, Fri–Sat late-night light menu midnight–4am. Bus: 50, 50A, 54, 56, 77. VEGETARIAN.

Juice tempts carnivorous, vegan, macrobiotic, celiac, and yeast-free diners alike, using organic produce to create delicious dressings and entrées among its largely conventional but very well-prepared offerings. The avocado fillet of blue cheese and broccoli wrapped in filo was superb, and I highly recommend the spinach and ricotta cheese cannelloni. The latter is included in the early bird dinner—a great deal. Coffees, fresh-squeezed juices, organic wines, and late weekend hours add to the lure of this modern, casual eatery frequented by mature diners who know their food.

ST. STEPHEN'S GREEN/GRAFTON STREET AREA

VERY EXPENSIVE/EXPENSIVE

✪ The Commons

85–86 St. Stephen's Green, Dublin 2. ☎ **01/475-2597** or 01/478-0530. Reservations required. Fixed-price lunch £18 ($28.80); fixed-price dinner £32 or £42 ($51.20 or $67.20). AE, DC, MC, V. Mon–Fri 12:30–2:15pm and 7–10pm, Sat 7–10pm. DART to Pearse Station. Bus: 11, 13, 10 or 46A. MODERN EUROPEAN.

Nestled on the south side of St. Stephen's Green, this Michelin-starred restaurant occupies the basement level of Newman House, the historic seat of Ireland's major university, comprised of two elegant town houses dating back to 1740. The interior of the dining rooms is a blend of Georgian architecture, cloister-style arches, and original contemporary artworks with Joycean influences. For an aperitif in fine weather, there is a lovely stone courtyard terrace surrounded by a "secret garden" of lush plants and trees. The inventive menu changes daily, but you'll often see dishes such as confit of duck leg on a beetroot boxty, grilled shark with peppered carrot, and loin of rabbit with a stuffing of marinated prune.

EXPENSIVE/MODERATE

✪ Cooke's Cafe

14 S. William St., Dublin 2. ☎ 01/679-0536. Reservations required. Lunch main courses £9.75–£16 ($15.60–$25.60), dinner main courses £11.95–£16.95 ($19.10–$27.10). AE, DC, MC, V. Mon–Fri 10am–midnight, Sat–Sun noon–3pm and 6–midnight. DART to Tara St. Station. Bus: 16A, 19A, 22A, 55, 83. CALIFORNIAN/MEDITERRANEAN.

Named for owner/chef Johnny Cooke, this shopfront restaurant is such a favorite with Dublin's fashionable set that reservations often have to be made weeks in advance. It is located opposite the Powerscourt Townhouse Centre, two blocks from Grafton Street. The decor is dominated by an open kitchen and art murals on the walls; there is also seating outdoors on antique tables and chairs originally from Brighton Pier. Specialties include grilled duck with pancetta, marsala balsamic sauce, and wilted endive; angel hair pasta with clams, cockles, chili, and tomato; sautéed brill and Dover sole with capers and croutons; and baked grouper with a ragout of mussels, clams, artichokes, and tomatoes.

La Stampa

35 Dawson St., Dublin 2. ☎ 01/677-8611. Reservations recommended. Fixed-price lunch £12.50 ($20); dinner main courses £9.95–£16.95 ($15.90–$27.10). AE, DC, MC, V. Mon–Thurs noon–2:30pm and 6–11:30pm, Fri–Sat noon–2:30pm and 6–midnight, Sun 12:30–2:30pm and 6–11:30pm. DART to Pearse Station. Bus: 10, 11A, 11B, 13, 20B. FRENCH/INTERNATIONAL.

A half block from St. Stephen's Green and opposite the Lord Mayor's Mansion House, this trendy Renaissance-style restaurant is always busy and sometimes noisy, frequented by a clientele of politicians, senior government officials, models, and entertainers. It features a long and spacious dining room with a glass-domed ceiling, tall pillars, and mirrors that make it seem even larger. In spite of its Italian name, the food is international, with an emphasis on French. House specialties are lobster ravioli, fillet of cod on puree of potatoes rimmed with green beans and bacon, saddle of lamb stuffed with wild mushrooms and spinach, and grilled red mullet with a confit of fennel. The fish soup is not to be missed as a starter.

MODERATE

Il Primo

16 Montague St., Dublin 2 (off Harcourt St., 50 yards down from St. Stephen's Green). ☎ 01/478-3373. Reservations required on weekends. Main courses £7.90–£14.90 ($12.65–$23.85); lunch menu £1.50–£8.90 ($2.40–$14.25). No service charge. All credit cards accepted. Mon–Sat 12–3pm and 6–11pm. MODERN ITALIAN.

Word of mouth is what brought me to Il Primo—little else would have, so obscurely is it tucked away off Harcourt Street. From the street all you see are several tables, a bar, an assembly of wooden stools, and a staircase, which happens to lead to some of the most distinguished, innovative Italian cuisine you'll ever meet up with outside of Rome or Tuscany. Awaken your palate with a glass of sparkling Venetian prosecco;

open with a plate of Parma ham, avocado, and balsamic vinaigrette; and then go for broke with the ravioli Il Primo, an open handkerchief of pasta over chicken, Parma ham, and mushrooms in a light tarragon cream sauce. The proprietor, Dieter Bergman, will assist gladly in selecting appropriate wines, all of which he personally chooses and imports from Tuscany. Wines are by the milliliter, not the bottle. Open any bottle and you pay for only what you drink. Il Primo is full of surprises.

Trocadero

3 St. Andrew St., Dublin 2. ☎ **01/677-5545.** Reservations recommended. Main courses £7.95–£12.95 ($12.70–$20.70). AE, DC, MC, V. Mon–Sat 6pm–12:15am, Sun 6–11:15pm. DART to Tara St. Station. Bus: 16A, 19A, 22A, 55, 83. INTERNATIONAL.

In many ways the Troc is the Sardi's of Dublin, and has been for almost 20 years. Located close to the Andrews Lane and other theaters, it is a favorite gathering spot for theatergoers, performers, and press—not least because it serves food after the theaters let out. Pre- and post-theater specials are offered, and as might be expected, the decor is theatrical, with subdued lighting, banquette seating and close-knit tables, and photos of entertainers on the walls. Steaks are a specialty, but the menu also offers rack of lamb, daily fish specials, pastas, and traditional dishes such as Irish stew or corned beef and cabbage with parsley sauce.

MODERATE/INEXPENSIVE

✪ Fitzers Cafe

51 Dawson St., Dublin 2. ☎ **01/677-1155.** Reservations recommended. Lunch main courses £5.95–£9.95 ($9.50–$15.90); dinner main courses £6.95–£12.95 ($11.10–$20.70). AE, DC, MC, V. Daily 9am–11:30pm. DART to Pearse Station. Bus: 10, 11A, 11B, 13, 20B. INTERNATIONAL.

Wedged in the middle of a busy shopping street, this bright and airy Irish-style bistro has a multiwindowed shopfront facade and a modern Irish decor of light woods inside. The food, excellent and reasonably priced, is contemporary and quickly served, with choices ranging from chicken breast with hot chili cream sauce or brochette of lamb tandoori with mild curry sauce to gratin of smoked cod. Fitzers has two other Dublin locations, one just a few blocks away at the National Gallery, Merrion Square West (☎ **01/668-6481**), and the other, in Ballsbridge, at 24 Upper Baggot St. (☎ **01/660-0644**).

INEXPENSIVE

✪ Bewley's Cafe

78/79 Grafton St., Dublin 2. ☎ **01/677-6761.** Reservations not required. All items £1.65–£5 ($2.65–$8). AE, DC, MC, V. Mon–Wed 7:30am–1am, Thurs–Sat 8am–2am, Sun 9:30am–10pm. DART to Pearse Station. Bus: 15A, 15B, 15C, 46, 55, 63, 83. IRISH.

Bewley's, a three-story landmark founded in 1840 by a Quaker named Joshua Bewley, is part of the Dublin experience. With a traditional decor of high ceilings, stained-glass windows, and dark woods, this busy coffee shop/restaurant serves breakfast and light meals, but is best known for its dozens of freshly brewed coffees and teas, accompanied by home-baked scones, pastries, or sticky buns. There are several branches throughout Dublin, including 11/12 Westmoreland St. (☎ **01/677-6761**) and 13 S. Great George's St. (☎ **01/679-2078**).

Pasta Fresca

3/4 Chatham St., Dublin 2. ☎ **01/679-2402.** Reservations suggested. Entrées £6.95–£11.95 ($11.10–$19.10). MC, V. Mon–Sat 11:30am–11:30pm, Sun 11:30am–6pm. Bus: 10, 11A, 11B, 13, 20B. ITALIAN.

Situated just a block from Grafton Street and St. Stephen's Green and around the corner from the Gaiety Theatre, this trattoria is popular with shoppers and for pre- and post-theater dinners. The menu features a variety of pastas, from fettuccine or tagliatelle to lasagna, spaghetti, and ravioli, as well as veal and steak dishes.

⑤ St. Teresa's Courtyard

Clarendon St., Dublin 2. ☎ 01/671-8466. Reservations not required. All items £1–£2.50 ($1.60–$4). No credit cards. Mon–Sat 10:30am–4pm. DART to Tara St. Station. Bus: 16, 16A, 19, 19A, 22A, 55, 83. IRISH / SELF-SERVICE.

Situated in the cobbled courtyard of early 19th-century St. Teresa's Church, this serene little dining room is one of a handful of new eateries inconspicuously springing up in historic or ecclesiastical surroundings. With high ceilings and an old-world decor, it's a welcome contrast to the bustle of Grafton Street a block away or Powerscourt Townhouse Centre across the street. The menu changes daily but usually includes homemade soups, sandwiches, salads, quiches, lasagnas, sausage rolls, hot scones, and other baked goods.

FITZWILLIAM SQUARE / MERRION SQUARE AREA
VERY EXPENSIVE

✪ Patrick Guilbaud

46 James Place (off Lower Baggot St.), Dublin 2. ☎ 01/676-4192. Reservations required. Fixed-price lunch £17 ($27.20); main courses £17–£21 ($27.20–$33.60). AE, DC, MC, V. Tues–Sat 12:30–2pm and 7:30–10:15pm. DART to Pearse Station. Bus: 10. FRENCH NOUVELLE.

Tucked in a lane behind a Bank of Ireland building, this modern skylit restaurant could be easily overlooked except for its glowing Michelin-star reputation for fine food and artful service. The menu features such dishes as casserole of black sole and prawns, steamed salmon with orange and grapefruit sauce, fillet of spring lamb with parsley sauce and herb salad, roast duck with honey, and breast of guinea fowl with Madeira sauce and potato crust.

EXPENSIVE

✪ Dobbins Wine Bistro

15 Stephen's Lane (off Upper Mount St.), Dublin 2. ☎ 01/676-4679 or 01/676-4670. Reservations recommended. Fixed-price lunch £14.95 ($23.92); dinner main courses £12.95–£19.95 ($20.70–$31.90). AE, DC, MC, V. Mon–Fri 12:30–3pm; Tues–Sat 8pm–midnight. DART to Pearse Station. Bus: 5, 7A, 8, 46, 84. IRISH/CONTINENTAL.

Almost hidden in a lane between Upper and Lower Mount Streets a block east of Merrion Square, this friendly enclave is a haven for inventive cuisine. The menu changes often, but usually includes such items as duckling with orange and port sauce; steamed paupiette of black sole with salmon, crab, and prawn filling; panfried veal kidneys in pastry; and fillet of beef topped with crispy herb bread crumbs with a shallot and Madeira sauce. You'll have a choice of sitting in the bistro, with checkered tablecloths and sawdust on the floor, or in the tropical patio, with an all-weather sliding glass roof.

Grey Door

23 Upper Pembroke St., Dublin 2. ☎ 01/676-3286. Reservations required. Fixed-price lunch £15 ($24); dinner entrées £13–£21 ($20.80–$33.60). AE, DC, MC, V. Mon–Fri 12:30–2:30pm and 7–11pm, Sat 7–11pm. Bus: 46A, 46B, 86. RUSSIAN/SCANDINAVIAN.

In a fine old Georgian town house with a gray front door, this place is known for its Northern and Eastern European delicacies. Specialties include seafood Zakuski in puff pastry; Kotlety Kiev, a variation of chicken Kiev stuffed with vodka butter; Galupsti Maskova (minced lamb wrapped in cabbage); and Scandinavian seafood combinations. Pier 32, the Grey Door's basement-level restaurant, has a more informal setting; it's like a country inn, complete with traditional music on many nights.

Fresh seafood at modest prices is the emphasis here. The Grey Door and Pier 32 are located less than a block southwest of Fitzwilliam Square near the junction of Leeson Street.

MODERATE

⑤ The Lane Gallery

55 Pembroke Lane (off Pembroke St.), Dublin 2. ☎ **01/661-1829.** Reservations recommended. Fixed-price lunch £5.95 ($9.50); dinner main courses £9.95–£13.50 ($15.90–$21.60). MC, V. Mon 12:30–2:30pm, Tues–Fri 12:30–2:30pm and 7:30–11pm, Sat 7:30–11pm. DART to Pearse Station. Bus: 10. FRENCH.

An ever-changing display of paintings and works by local artists is the focal point of this restaurant, tucked in a lane between Baggot Street and Fitzwilliam Square, near the Focus Theatre. The decor complements the art with skylight or candlelight, whitewashed brick walls, and pastel linens. The menu is equally artistic, with choices such as rack of lamb with tomato coulis and mint jus, prawns in chive and ginger sauce, salmon on a bed of leeks with spinach butter sauce, and roast brace of quail with white and black pudding and whiskey sauce. There is live piano music most evenings from 9pm. The lunch and dinner specials offer great value.

McGrattan's in the Lane

76 Fitzwilliam Lane, Dublin 2. ☎ **01/661-8808.** Reservations recommended. Lunch main courses £5–£9 ($8–$14.40); dinner main courses £11.95–£14.95 ($19.10–$23.90). AE, MC, V. Sun–Fri noon–3pm and 6–11pm, Sat 6–11pm. IRISH/FRENCH.

Out of view from the general flow of traffic, this restaurant is in a lane between Baggot Street and Merrion Square. There is a lovely Georgian doorway at the entrance, and inside the decor ranges from a homey fireside lounge with oldies background music to a bright skylit and plant-filled dining room. The creative menu includes main dishes such as breast of chicken Fitzwilliam stuffed with cheddar cheese in pastry, half of roast pheasant with wild mushrooms and red wine sauce, paupiette of salmon stuffed with scallop mousse and wrapped in a pancake of puff pastry, and charcoal-grilled steaks.

INEXPENSIVE

Grays

109D Lower Baggot St., Dublin 2. ☎ **01/676-0676.** Reservations not required. All items £2–£5.95 ($3.20–$9.50). MC, V. Mon–Fri 7:30am–4pm. DART to Pearse Station. Bus: 10. INTERNATIONAL/SELF-SERVICE.

A popular self-service eatery, this cozy old place has a decor that is eclectic, with choir benches, caned chairs, and lots of hanging plants. Seating is offered on ground and upstairs levels, including an outdoor courtyard for dining in fine weather. The menu choices concentrate on sandwiches and salads made to order, as well as pastas, quiches, curries, and casseroles.

BALLSBRIDGE / EMBASSY ROW AREA
VERY EXPENSIVE

✪ Le Coq Hardi

35 Pembroke Rd., Ballsbridge, Dublin 4. ☎ **01/668-9070.** Reservations required. Fixed-price lunch £18 ($22.45) for full menu, £10 ($16) for one course and coffee; dinner main courses £16–£25 ($25.60–$37.50). AE, CB, MC, V. Mon–Fri 12:30–2:30pm and 7–10:45pm, Sat 7–10:45pm. DART to Lansdowne Rd. Station. Bus: 18, 46, 63, 84. FRENCH.

Ballsbridge / Embassy Row Area Dining

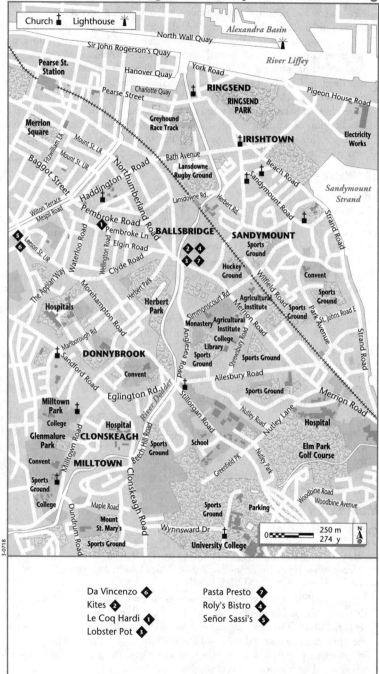

Church ✝ Lighthouse ⚲

Alexandra Basin
North Wall Quay
Sir John Rogerson's Quay
River Liffey
Hanover Quay
York Road
Pearse St. Station
Pigeon House Road
Charlotte Quay
Pearse Street
RINGSEND
Merrion Square
RINGSEND PARK
Greyhound Race Track
Electricity Works
Mount St. LR
Mount St. UR
✝IRISHTOWN
Baggot Street
Bath Avenue
Beach Road
Fitzwilliam La
Lansdowne Rugby Ground
Sandymount Road
Sandymount Strand
Wilton Terrace
Mespil Road
Lansdowne Rd.
Herbert Rd.
Haddington Road
Northumberland Road
Pembroke Road
Strand Road
Leeson St. UR
Pembroke Ln
BALLSBRIDGE
SANDYMOUNT
Sports Ground
Wellington Road
Elgin Road
Convent
Sports Ground
The Appian Way
Waterloo Road
Clyde Road
Hockey Ground
Wilfield Road
Herbert Park
Park Avenue
St. Johns Road E
Hospitals
Morehampton Road
Herbert Park
Simmonscourt Rd.
Agricultural Institute
Sports Ground
Marlborough Rd
Monastery
Agricultural Institute
Merrion Road
Anglesea Road
Shrewsbury Road
Strand Road
DONNYBROOK
College Library
Sports Ground
Sports Ground
Sandford Road
Convent
Ailesbury Road
Eglington Rd.
Sports Ground
Merrion Road
Milltown Park
River Dodder
Stillorgan Road
Nutley Road
Hospital
College
Hospital
Nutley Lane
Glenmalure Park
CLONSKEAGH
Sports Ground
School
Nutley Park
Elm Park Golf Course
Convent
MILLTOWN
Milltown Road
Beech Hill Road
Greenfield Pk
Sports Ground
College
Clonskeagh Road
Woodbine Road
Maple Road
Dundrum Road
Mount St. Mary's
Sports Ground
Parking
Woodbine Avenue
Sports Ground
Wynnsward Dr
UNIVERSITY COLLEGE

0   250 m
      274 y
N

3-0718

Da Vincenzo **6**   Pasta Presto **7**
Kites **2**   Roly's Bistro **4**
Le Coq Hardi **1**   Señor Sassi's **5**
Lobster Pot **3**

131

Newly decorated in radiant autumn colors and offering a new cocktail bar, this may be the only place in Dublin where Rolls-Royces vie nightly for parking. Located on the corner of Wellington Road in a Georgian town-house setting close to the American Embassy and leading hotels such as Jurys and the Berkeley Court, this plush 50-seat restaurant has no trouble drawing a well-heeled local and international business clientele. Chef John Howard has garnered many an award by offering such specialties as Dover sole stuffed with prawns, darne of Irish wild salmon on fresh spinach leaves, fillet of hake roasted on green cabbage and bacon with Pernod butter sauce, fillet of prime beef flamed in Irish whiskey, and warm terrine of Clonakilty black and white pudding with confits of apple. The 700-bin wine cellar boasts a complete collection of Château Mouton Rothschild, dating from 1945 to the present.

EXPENSIVE

Kites
17 Ballsbridge Terrace, Ballsbridge, Dublin 4. ☎ **01/660-7415.** Reservations recommended. Lunch main courses £6.50–£13 ($7.80–$20.80); dinner main courses £8.50–£17 ($13.60–$27.20). AE, DC, MC, V. Mon–Fri 12:30–2pm and 6:30–11:30pm. DART to Lansdowne Rd. Station. Bus: 5, 7, 7A, 8, 46, 63, 84. CHINESE.

Handily located between the American Embassy and the Royal Dublin Society Showgrounds, this Oriental-theme restaurant is housed in a Georgian town house just off Pembroke Road and diagonally across the street from Jurys Hotel. The menu features the usual chow mein, curries, and sweet-and-sour dishes, as well as a host of creative entrées such as king prawns with Chinese leaves in oyster sauce, stuffed crab claws, Singapore fried noodles, and bird's nests of fried potatoes.

Lobster Pot
9 Ballsbridge Terrace, Ballsbridge, Dublin 4. ☎ **01/668-0025.** Reservations required. Lunch main courses £9–£14 ($14.40–$22.40); dinner main courses £10.95–£17.95 ($17.50–$28.70). AE, DC, MC, V. Mon–Fri 12:30–2:30pm and 6:30–10:30pm, Sat 6:30–10:30pm. DART to Landsdowne Rd. Station. Bus: 5, 7, 7A, 8, 46, 63, 84. SEAFOOD.

Positioned between the American Embassy and the Royal Dublin Society Showgrounds, almost opposite Jurys Hotel, this upstairs restaurant is known for its lobster dishes, as you might guess from its name. Other entrées on the menu range from prawns mornay, monkfish thermidor, and sole on the bone and coquilles St. Jacques to tableside preparations of steak Diane, prawns sautéed in garlic butter, pepper steak, and steak tartare.

MODERATE

○ Roly's Bistro
7 Ballsbridge Terrace, Dublin 4. ☎ **01/668-2611.** Reservations required. Fixed-price lunch £9.50 ($14.25); dinner main courses £7.50–£12.95 ($12–$20.70). AE, DC, MC, V. Mon–Sat noon–3pm and 6–10pm, Sun noon–3pm and 6–9:30pm. DART to Lansdowne Rd. Station. Bus: 6, 7, 8, 18, 45, 46, 84. IRISH/INTERNATIONAL.

Opened in 1992, this two-story shopfront restaurant quickly skyrocketed to success, thanks to a magical blend of people and place—genial and astute host Roly Saul, master chef Colin O'Daly, a young and enthusiastic wait staff, a trendy location between the American Embassy and the Royal Dublin Society—and, above all, excellent and imaginatively prepared food at mostly moderate prices. The main dining rooms, with a bright and airy decor and lots of windows, can be noisy when the house is full, but the nonsmoking section has a quiet enclave of booths laid out in an Orient Express style for those who prefer a quiet tête-à-tête. The bistro serves such entrées as new season lamb pie, fillet of prime Irish beef, panfried ray wing, and medallions of monkfish.

Señor Sassi's

146 Upper Leeson St., Dublin 4. ☎ **01/668-4544.** Reservations recommended. Lunch main courses £4.95–£8.50 ($7.90–$13.60); dinner main courses £9.75–£14.95 ($15.60–$23.90). AE, DC, MC, V. Mon 6–11:30pm, Tues–Wed noon–2:30pm and 6–11:30pm, Thurs–Fri noon–2:30pm and 6:30–midnight, Sat 6:30–midnight, Sun noon–4pm and 5:30–10:30pm. Bus: 10, 11A, 11B, 13, 46A, 46B. MEDITERRANEAN.

New and innovative, this restaurant blends the simple and spicy flavors of Spain, Italy, southern France, and the Middle East in its busy shopfront location at the juncture of Sussex and Mespil Roads, within a block of the Burlington Hotel. The contemporary and casual setting includes slate floors, marble-topped tables, and walls painted a sunny shade of yellow; seating is also available in a conservatory extension overlooking a courtyard garden. The menu includes items such as Moroccan-style couscous, tagliatelle, prawns sautéed in rum with creole sauce, charcoal steaks, tortilla Español (traditional omelet with potato and onions), and all-vegetarian dishes and warm salads. Be sure to try the olive bread, unusual for Dublin.

INEXPENSIVE

Da Vincenzo

133 Upper Leeson St., Dublin 4. ☎ **01/660-9906.** Reservations recommended. Fixed-price lunch £6.95 ($11.10); dinner main courses £6.50–£12.25 ($10.40–$19.60). AE, MC, V. Mon–Fri 12:30pm–midnight, Sat 1pm–midnight, Sun 1–10pm. Bus: 10, 11A, 11B, 46A, 46B. ITALIAN.

Occupying a shopfront location within a block of the Hotel Burlington, this informal and friendly owner-run bistro offers ground level and upstairs seating amid a casual decor of glowing brick fireplaces, pine walls, vases and wreaths of dried flowers, modern art posters, blue and white pottery, and a busy open kitchen. Pizza with a light pita-style dough, cooked in a wood-burning oven, is a specialty here. Other entrées range from pastas such as tagliatelle, lasagna, cannelloni, spaghetti, and fettucine to veal and beef dishes, including an organically produced fillet steak.

✪ Pasta Presto

16 Merrion Rd., Ballsbridge, Dublin 4. ☎ **01/668-1052.** Reservations recommended Fri–Sun evenings. Main courses £5.50–£10.95 ($8.80–$17.50). EU, MC, V. Daily 7:30am–11:30pm. DART to Booterstown Station. Bus: 5, 7, 7A, 8. CONTEMPORARY ITALIAN.

Whether you're in a hurry or plan to drop anchor, Pasta Presto won't let you down. Quality and good value are the bywords of this newcomer to Dublin dining. Its clean, bright, Mediterranean decor is all about light in the daytime and soft hues when the lights go down. Pasta Presto starts with the freshest ingredients, including their own homemade pasta, and finishes strong with excellent coffee and extraordinary tiramisu. Kids rave about Pasta Presto and appreciate the extent to which their culinary dictates are accommodated. And you're never too old for that! This is an excellent choice for first-rate fare on a midrange budget.

O'CONNELL STREET AREA
EXPENSIVE/MODERATE

✪ Chapter One

18/19 Parnell Sq. N., Dublin 1. ☎ **01/873-2266** or 01/873-2281. Reservations recommended. Fixed-price lunch £10 ($16); dinner main courses £9.50–£14 ($15.20–$22.40). AE, MC, V. Tues–Fri noon–2:30pm and 6–11pm, Sat–Sun 6–11pm. DART to Connolly Station. Bus: 10, 11, 11A, 11B, 12, 13, 14, 16, 16A, 19, 19A, 22, 22A, 36. IRISH.

A literary theme prevails at this restaurant, housed in the basement of the Dublin Writers Museum, just north of Parnell Square and the Garden of Remembrance. The layout is spread over three rooms and alcoves, all accentuated by stained-glass windows, paintings, sculptures, and literary memorabilia. The catering staff, affiliated with the Old Dublin Restaurant, has added a few Scandinavian influences. Main courses include fillet of salmon on a bed of avocado with smoked tomato vinaigrette; black sole with citrus fruit and dill cucumber cream sauce; pot-roasted breast of chicken with onions, sage, garlic, and pea pods; and roast half-duck with apricot sauce.

MODERATE

⑤ 101 Talbot

101 Talbot St., Dublin 1. ☎ **01/874-5011.** Reservations recommended. Lunch main courses £3.25–£5.50 ($5.20–$8.80); dinner main courses £7.90–£9.90 ($12.65–$15.85). AE, DC, MC, V. Mon 10am–3pm; Tues–Sat 10am–11pm. DART to Connolly Station. Bus: 27A, 31A, 311B, 32A, 32B, 42B, 42C, 43, 44A. INTERNATIONAL/VEGETARIAN.

Opened in 1991, this second-floor shopfront restaurant features light and healthy foods, with a strong emphasis on vegetarian dishes, including choices for vegans. The setting is bright and casual, with contemporary Irish art on display, big windows, yellow rag-rolled walls, ash-topped tables, and newspapers to read. Entrées include jambalaya of lamb, smoked sausage, and black-eyed peas; vegetable satay with rice; and tandoori chicken with mango. The lunch menu changes daily, and the dinner menu weekly. Espresso and cappuccino are always available for sipping, and there is a full bar. It's located at Talbot Lane near Marlborough Street, convenient to the Abbey Theatre.

INEXPENSIVE

The Winding Stair

40 Lower Ormond Quay, Dublin 1. ☎ **01/873-3292.** Reservations not necessary. All items £1–£4.50 ($1.60–$7.20). MC, V. Mon–Wed and Fri–Sat 10am–6pm, Thurs 10am–2pm, Sun 1–5pm. Bus: 70 or 80. IRISH/SELF-SERVICE.

Retreat from the bustle of the north side's busy quays at this cafe/bookshop and join some customers in examining old books while others indulge in a light meal. There are three floors, each chock-full of used books (from novels, plays, and poetry to history, art, music, and sports), and all connected by a winding 18th-century staircase. A cage-style lift serves those who prefer not to climb the stairs. Tall and wide windows provide expansive views of the Halfpenny Bridge and River Liffey. The food is simple and healthy—sandwiches made with additive-free meats or fruits (such as banana and honey), organic salads, homemade soups, and natural juices.

DINING BETWEEN HOURS & OUT OF DOORS

AFTERNOON TEA   As in Britain, afternoon tea is a time-revered tradition in Ireland, especially in the grand hotels of Dublin. Afternoon tea in its fullest form is a sit-down event and a relaxing experience, not just a quick hot beverage taken on the run.

Properly presented, afternoon tea is also almost a complete meal, including a pot of freshly brewed tea accompanied by finger sandwiches, pastries, hot scones, cream-filled cakes, and other sweets arrayed on a silver tray. To enhance the ambience, there is usually live background music, provided by a pianist or harpist. Best of all, this sumptuous midafternoon pick-me-up is priced to please, averaging £6 to £8 ($9.60 to $12.80) per person, even in the lobby lounges of the city's best hotels.

Afternoon tea hours are usually 3 to 4:30pm. Among the hotels offering this repast are the Berkeley Court, Conrad, Davenport, Gresham, Royal Dublin,

Shelbourne, and Westbury (see "Accommodations," above, for full address and phone numbers of each).

LATE NIGHT / 24-HOUR   There is really only one restaurant in Dublin that approaches the 24-hour category: the **Coffee Dock at Jurys Hotel,** Ballsbridge, Dublin 4 (☎ **01/660-5000**). It is open Monday to Saturday from 6am to 4:30am and Sunday 6am to 10:45pm. **Bewley's,** at 78/79 Grafton St., Dublin 2 (☎ **01/ 677-6761**), is open Monday through Wednesday until 1am, Thursday through Saturday until 2am, and Sunday until 10pm.

PICNIC FARE   The many parks of Dublin offer sylvan and relaxed settings for a picnic lunch. Most of the parks have plentiful benches or you can pick a grassy patch and spread open a blanket. In particular, try **St. Stephen's Green** at lunchtime (in the summer there are open-air band concerts), **Phoenix Park,** and **Merrion Square.** You can also take a ride on the DART to the suburbs of **Dun Laoghaire** (to the south) or **Howth** (to the north) and set up a picnic along a bay-front pier or promenade.

In recent years, Dublin has fostered some fine delicatessens and gourmet food shops, ideal for picnic fare. For the best selection of good picnic fixings, we recommend two: **Gallic Kitchen,** 49 Francis St., Dublin 8 (☎ **01/454-4912**), for gourmet prepared food to go, from salmon en croûte to pastries filled with meats or vegetables, pâtés, quiches, sausage rolls, and homemade pies, breads, and cakes; and **Magills Delicatessen,** 14 Clarendon St., Dublin 2 (☎ **01/671-3830**), for Asian and continental delicacies, meats, cheeses, spices, and salads.

5 Attractions

Dublin is a city of many moods and landscapes. There are medieval churches and imposing castles, graceful Georgian squares and lantern-lit lanes, broad boulevards and crowded bridges, picturesque parks and pedestrian walkways, intriguing museums and markets, gardens and galleries, and—if you have any energy left after all that—an electric night scene. Enjoy!

SUGGESTED ITINERARIES

If You Have 1 Day

Start at the beginning, Dublin's medieval quarter, the area around Christ Church and St. Patrick's Cathedrals. Tour these great churches and then walk the cobblestone streets and inspect the nearby old city walls at High Street. From Old Dublin, take a turn eastward and see Dublin Castle and then Trinity College with the famous Book of Kells. Cross over the River Liffey to O'Connell Street, Dublin's main thoroughfare. Walk up this wide street, passing the landmark General Post Office (GPO), to Parnell Square and the picturesque Garden of Remembrance. If time permits, visit the Dublin Writers Museum, then hop on a double-decker bus heading to the south bank of the Liffey for a relaxing stroll amid the flora of St. Stephen's Green. Cap the day with a show at the Abbey Theatre and maybe a drink or two at a nearby pub.

If You Have 2 Days

Day 1   Spend Day 1 as above.
Day 2   In the morning, take a Dublin Bus city sightseeing tour to give you an overview of the city. You'll see all of the local downtown landmarks, plus the major buildings along the River Liffey and some of the leading sites on the edge of the city, such

Dublin Attractions

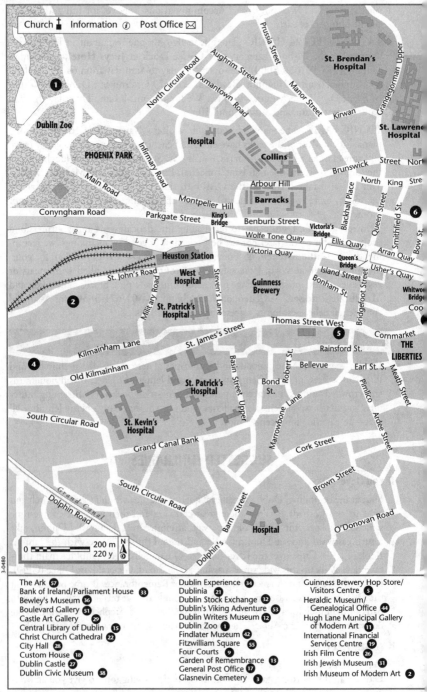

Church ✝ Information ⓘ Post Office ✉

Dublin Zoo

PHOENIX PARK

North Circular Road

Aughrim Street

Oxmantown Road

Prussia Street

Manor Street

St. Brendan's Hospital

Grangegorman Upper

Kirwan

St. Lawrence Hospital

Infirmary Road

Hospital

Collins

Brunswick

Street

Nor

North King Stre

Main Road

Arbour Hill

Blackhall Place

Queen Street

Smithfield St.

Montpelier Hill

Barracks

6

Conyngham Road

Parkgate Street

King's Bridge

Benburb Street

Victoria's Bridge

Bow St.

River Liffey

Wolfe Tone Quay

Ellis Quay

Arran Quay

Victoria Quay

Queen's Bridge

Usher's Quay

Heuston Station

St. John's Road

West Hospital

Island Street

Whitwo Bridge

St. Patrick's Hospital

Steven's Lane

Guinness Brewery

Bonham St.

Bridgefoot Street

Coo

Military Road

Thomas Street West

5

Cornmarket

THE LIBERTIES

Kilmainham Lane

St. James's Street

Rainsford St.

Old Kilmainham

Basin Street Upper

Bellevue

Robert St.

Earl St. S.

Pimlico

Meath Street

St. Patrick's Hospital

Bond St.

Marrowbone Lane

Ardee Street

South Circular Road

St. Kevin's Hospital

Grand Canal Bank

Cork Street

Brown Street

South Circular Road

Grand Canal

Dolphin Road

Barn Street

Dolphin's

Hospital

O'Donovan Road

0   200 m   220 y   N

3-0480

The Ark 57
Bank of Ireland/Parliament House 33
Bewley's Museum 36
Boulevard Gallery 51
Castle Art Gallery 29
Central Library of Dublin 15
Christ Church Cathedral 22
City Hall 28
Custom House 18
Dublin Castle 27
Dublin Civic Museum 38

Dublin Experience 34
Dublinia 21
Dublin Stock Exchange 32
Dublin's Viking Adventure 53
Dublin Writers Museum 12
Dublin Zoo 1
Findlater Museum 42
Fitzwilliam Square 55
Four Courts 9
Garden of Remembrance 13
General Post Office 17
Glasnevin Cemetery 3

Guinness Brewery Hop Store/
  Visitors Centre 5
Heraldic Museum/
  Genealogical Office 44
Hugh Lane Municipal Gallery
  of Modern Art 11
International Financial
  Services Centre 19
Irish Film Centre 26
Irish Jewish Museum 31
Irish Museum of Modern Art 2

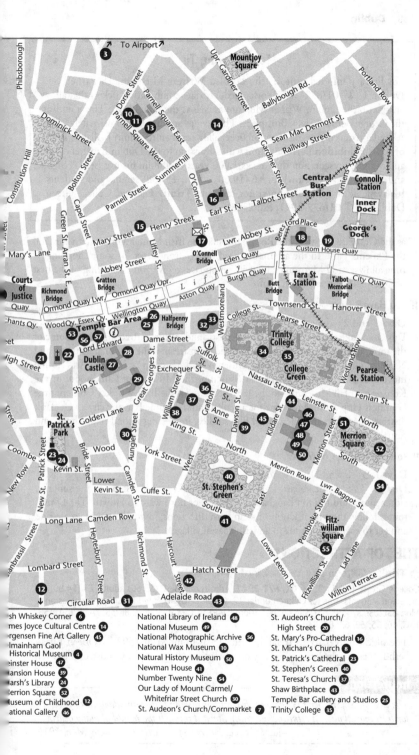

To Airport ↗

Mountjoy Square

Phibsborough

3

Upr. Gardiner Street

Ballybough Rd.

Portland Row

Dorset Street

Parnell Square East

10

11

13

14

Parnell Square West

Sean Mac Dermott St.

Lwr. Gardiner Street

Railway Street

Amiens Street

Central Bus Station

Connolly Station

Dominick Street

Bolton Street

Summerhill

O'Connell

16

Earl St. N.

Talbot Street

Beresford Place

Inner Dock

George's Dock

Constitution Hill

Green St. Arran St. E.

Capel Street

Parnell Street

Mary Street

Henry Street

15

17

Lwr. Abbey St.

18

19

Custom House Quay

Mary's Lane

Liffey St.

Abbey Street

O'Connell Bridge

Eden Quay

Tara St. Station

City Quay

Courts of Justice

Richmond Bridge

Gratton Bridge

Ormond Quay Upr.

Burgh Quay

Butt Bridge

Talbot Memorial Bridge

Quay

Ormond Quay Lwr.

River Liffey

Townsend St.

Hanover Street

hants Qy.

WoodQy. Essex Qy.

Wellington Quay

Aston Quay

Westmoreland

College St.

Pearse Street

erchants Qy.

53

56 57

Temple Bar Area

26

25

Halfpenny Bridge

33

32

College St.

Trinity College

34

Pearse St. Station

Dame Street

i

Suffolk St.

35

College Green

21

22

Lord Edward

28

Exchequer St.

Nassau Street

Fenian St.

Westland Row

High Street

Dublin Castle

27

29

Great Georges St.

William Street

36

Duke St.

Dawson St.

44

Leinster St.

46

51

Merrion Square

Ship St.

37

38

Grafton St.

Anne St.

45

Kildare St.

47

48

52

St. Patrick's Park

Golden Lane

King St.

39

49

Merrion Street

Coombe

23

24

Kevin St.

Bride Street

30

York Street

West

North

50

54

New Row

New St.

Patrick Street

Aungier Street

Wood

North

Merrion Row

South

Lower Kevin St.

Camden St.

40

St. Stephen's Green

East

Long Lane

Camden Row

Cuffe St.

South

Lwr. Baggot St.

Richmond St.

Heytesbury

41

Newman House

Pembroke Street

Fitz-william Square

55

Lad Lane

Lombard Street

Harcourt

Lower Leeson St.

Fitzwilliam St.

brassil Street

12

↓

Circular Road

31

42

Hatch Street

Adelaide Road

43

Wilton Terrace

sh Whiskey Corner 6

mes Joyce Cultural Centre 14

ergensen Fine Art Gallery 45

lmainham Gaol Historical Museum 4

einster House 47

ansion House 39

arsh's Library 24

errion Square 52

useum of Childhood 12

ational Gallery 46

National Library of Ireland 48

National Museum 49

National Photographic Archive 56

National Wax Museum 10

Natural History Museum 50

Newman House 41

Number Twenty Nine 54

Our Lady of Mount Carmel/ Whitefriar Street Church 30

St. Audoen's Church/Cornmarket 7

St. Audoen's Church/ High Street 20

St. Mary's Pro-Cathedral 16

St. Michan's Church 8

St. Patrick's Cathedral 23

St. Stephen's Green 40

St. Teresa's Church 37

Shaw Birthplace 43

Temple Bar Gallery and Studios 25

Trinity College 35

137

Money-Saving Tip

For literary-minded visitors, the **Dublin Writers Museum,** 18 Parnell Sq., Dublin 1 (☎ **01/872-2077**), offers reduced-rate combination tickets that allow entry into the Dublin Writers Museum as well as the James Joyce Tower and/or the George Bernard Shaw Birthplace. The savings amount to approximately 25%. A similar reduced-rate combination ticket allows entry into Trinity College's **Book of Kells Exhibition** in conjunction with admission to the Dublin Experience, an audio-visual presentation that tracks 1,000 years of Dublin history (see "A Sight and Sound Show," below) for £6 ($9.60) adults, £5 ($8) seniors and students. It's available at the bookshop/visitor center at **Trinity College,** College Green, Dublin 2 (☎ **01/677-2941,** ext. 2308).

as the Guinness Brewery, the Royal Hospital, the Irish Museum of Modern Art, and the Phoenix Park. In the afternoon, head for Grafton Street for some shopping. If time allows, stroll Merrion or Fitzwilliam Square to give you a sampling of the best of Dublin's Georgian architecture.

If You Have 3 Days

Days 1 and 2   Spend Days 1 and 2 as above.

Day 3   Make this a day for Dublin's artistic and cultural attractions. Visit some of the top museums and art galleries, from the mainstream—the National Museum and National Gallery, Natural History Museum, and Museum of Modern Art—to the more specialized—the Irish Jewish Museum, the Museum of Childhood, or the Kilmainham Jail Museum—to the *very* specialized—the Irish Whiskey Corner or the Guinness Hop Store. Save time for a walk around Temple Bar, the city's Left Bank district, lined with art galleries and film studios, interesting second-hand shops, and casual eateries.

If You Have 4 Days or More

Days 1–3   Spend Days 1 through 3 as above.

Day 4   Take a ride aboard DART, Dublin's rapid transit system, to the suburbs, either southward to Dun Laoghaire or Dalkey, or northward to Howth. The DART routes follow the rim of Dublin Bay in both directions, so you'll enjoy a scenic ride and get to spend some time in an Irish coastal village.

THE TOP ATTRACTIONS

✪ Trinity College and the Book of Kells

College Green, Dublin 2. ☎ **01/677-2941.** Admission £3.50 ($5.60) adults, £3 ($4.80) seniors and students, free for children under 12. Credit cards accepted for shop purchases only. Mon–Sat 9:30am–5:00pm, Sun noon–4:30pm. DART to Tara St. Station. Bus: 5, 7A, 8, 15A, 15B, 15C, 46, 55, 62, 63, 83, 84.

The oldest university in Ireland, Trinity was founded in 1592 by Queen Elizabeth I. It sits in the heart of the city on a beautiful 40-acre site just south of the River

Impressions

The trees in St. Stephen's Green were fragrant of rain and the rainsodden earth gave forth its mortal odor, a faint incense rising upward through the mould of many hearts.
— James Joyce, *Portrait of an Artist as a Young Man,* 1916

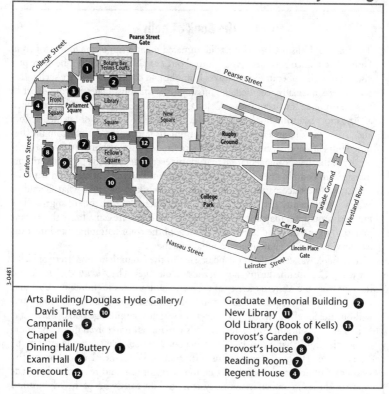

Arts Building/Douglas Hyde Gallery/
Davis Theatre **10**
Campanile **5**
Chapel **3**
Dining Hall/Buttery **1**
Exam Hall **6**
Forecourt **12**

Graduate Memorial Building **2**
New Library **11**
Old Library (Book of Kells) **13**
Provost's Garden **9**
Provost's House **8**
Reading Room **7**
Regent House **4**

Liffey, with cobbled squares, gardens, a picturesque quadrangle, and buildings dating from the 17th to the 20th centuries. The college is home to the Book of Kells, an 8th-century version of the four Gospels with elaborate scripting and illumination. One page per day is turned for public viewing. This famous treasure and other early Christian manuscripts are on permanent public view in the Colonnades, an exhibition area located on the ground floor of the Old Library. The complete Trinity College Library contains more than three million volumes. If you want a look at the place before you go, rent the 1983 Michael Caine film *Educating Rita,* in which Trinity stood in for a British university.

National Gallery

Merrion Sq. West, Dublin 2. ☎ **01/661-5133.** Free admission. Mon–Wed and Fri–Sat 10am–6pm, Thurs 10am–8:30pm, Sun 2–5pm. Guided tours, Sat at 3pm and Sun at 2:30, 3:15, and 4pm. DART to Pearse Station. Bus: 5, 7, 7A, 8, 10, 44, 47, 48A, 62.

Established by an act of Parliament in 1854, this gallery first opened its doors in 1864, with just over 100 paintings. Today the collection is considered one of Europe's finest, with more than 2,400 paintings; 15,200 drawings, watercolors, and miniatures; 3,000 prints; and 300 pieces of sculpture, vestments, and objets d'art. Every major European school of painting is represented, as is an extensive grouping of Irish work.

✪ National Museum

Kildare St. and Merrion St., Dublin 2. ☎ **01/677-7444.** Free admission. Tues–Sat 10am–5pm, Sun 2–5pm. DART to Pearse Station. Bus: 7, 7A, 8, 10, 11, 13.

The Book of Kells

The Book of Kells is a large-format illuminated manuscript of the four Gospels in Latin, dated on comparative grounds to about A.D. 800. One cannot be more precise about its date because some leaves from the end of the book, where such information was normally recorded, are missing. It is the most majestic work of art to survive from the early centuries of Celtic Christianity, and has often been described as "the most beautiful book in the world." Produced by a team of talented scribes and artists working in a monastic scriptorium, its fascination derives from the dignified but elusive character of its main motifs and the astonishing variety and complexity of the linear ornamentation that adorns every one of its 680 pages. Its creators managed to combine new artistic influences from Eastern Christendom with the traditional interlace patterning of Celtic metalwork to produce what Gerald of Wales, a 13th-century chronicler, called "the work not of men, but of angels." The message sometimes may not be easy to read, but everyone can admire the elegant precision of the standard script, the subtlety of the color harmonies, and the exuberant vitality of the human and animal ornament.

The Book was certainly in the possession of the Columban monastery of Kells, a town in Co. Meath, during most of the Middle Ages. The *Annals of Ulster* record its theft from the western sacristy of the stone-built monastic church in 1007, and relate that it was recovered two to three months later from "under the sod," and without the jewel-encrusted silver shrine in which such prestige books were kept. Whether it was originally created in Kells remains an unresolved question. Some authorities think that it may have been begun, if not completed, in the great monastery founded by St. Columba himself (in about 561) on the island of Iona off the west coast of Scotland. Iona had a famous scriptorium, and remained the headquarters of the Columban monastic system until the early years of the 9th century. It then became an untenable location because of repeated Viking raids, and in 807 a remnant of the monastic community retreated to the Irish mainland to build a new headquarters at Kells. It has been suggested that the great Gospel book that we call "of Kells" may have been started in Iona, possibly to mark the bicentenary of St. Columba's death in 797, and later transferred to Kells for completion. But it is also possible to argue that the work was entirely done in Kells, and that its object was to equip the monastery with a great new book to stand on the high altar of the new foundation.

In the medieval period the Book was (wrongly) regarded as the work of St. Columba himself, and was known as the "great Gospel book of Colum Cille" (Colum of the Churches). The designation "Book of Kells" seems to have originated with the famous biblical scholar James Ussher, who made a study of its original Latin text in the 1620s. There is a large selection of illustrative materials relating to the Book of Kells in the gift shop located in the Colonnades of the Old Library in Trinity College.

—J. V. Luce, Trinity College and the Royal Irish Academy

Opened in 1890, this museum is a reflection of Ireland's heritage from 2000 B.C. to the present. It is the home of many of the country's greatest historical finds, including "The Treasury" exhibit, which toured the United States and Europe in the 1970s with the Ardagh Chalice, Tara Brooch, and Cross of Cong. Other highlights range from the artifacts from the Wood Quay excavations of the Old Dublin Settlements to "Or," an extensive exhibition of Irish Bronze Age gold ornaments dating from

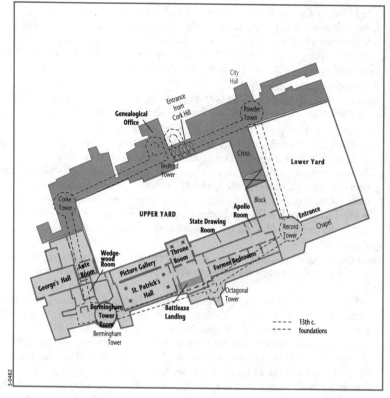

2200 to 700 B.C. Facilities include a shop and cafe. A new branch of the National Museum is scheduled to open in March 1997 at the Collins Barracks, adjacent to Heuston Station.

✪ Irish Film Centre

6 Eustace St., Dublin 2. ☎ **01/679-5744**; cinema box office 01/679-3477. Free admission to Institute; £2.50–£4 ($4–$6.40) for cinemas; £2 ($3.20) adults, £1.50 ($2.40) seniors and students for *Flashback*. Institute Mon–Sat 10am–11:30pm, Sun 11am–11:30pm; cinemas daily 2–11:30pm; cinema box office daily 2–9pm; *Flashback* on Wed–Sun at noon. Bus: 21A, 78A, 78B.

Opened in 1991, this institute has fast become a focal point in Dublin's artsy Temple Bar district. The Centre houses two cinemas, the Irish Film Archive, a library, a bookshop and bar, and eight film-related organizations. The Wednesday to Sunday noontime screenings of *Flashback*, a history of Irish film since 1896, followed by a lunch in the bar, make a perfect midday outing.

✪ Dublin Castle

Palace St. (off Dame St.), Dublin 2. ☎ **01/679-3713.** Admission £2 ($3.20) adults, £1 ($1.60) seniors, students, and children under 12. Mon–Fri 10am–12:15pm and 2–5pm, Sat–Sun 2–5pm. Guided tours are conducted every 20–25 minutes. Bus: 54, 50, 50A, 56A, 77.

Built between 1208 and 1220, this complex represents some of the oldest surviving architecture in the city, and was the center of British power in Ireland for more than seven centuries until it was taken over by the new Irish government in 1922. Highlights include the 13th-century Record Tower; the State Apartments, once the residence of English viceroys; and the Chapel Royal, a 19th-century Gothic building with particularly fine plaster decoration and carved oak gallery fronts and fittings. The newest developments are the Undercroft, an excavated site on the grounds where an early Viking fortress stood, and the Treasury, built between 1712 and 1715 and believed to be the oldest surviving office building in Ireland.

✪ Christ Church Cathedral

Christ Church Place, Dublin 8. ☎ **01/677-8099.** Admission: suggested donation £1 ($1.60) adults. Daily 10am–5pm (except Dec 26). Bus: 21A, 50, 50A, 78, 78A, 78B.

Standing on high ground in the oldest part of the city, this cathedral is one of Dublin's finest historic buildings. It dates from 1038 when Sitric, Danish king of Dublin, built the first wooden Christ Church here. In 1171, the original simple foundation was extended into a cruciform and rebuilt in stone by Strongbow. The present structure, though, dates mainly from 1871 to 1878, when a huge restoration was undertaken. Highlights of the interior include magnificent stonework and graceful pointed arches, with delicately chiseled supporting columns. It is the mother church for the diocese of Dublin and Glendalough of the Church of Ireland.

✪ Dublinia

Christ Church Place (at High St.), Dublin 8. ☎ **01/679-4611.** Admission £4 ($6.40) adults, £3 ($4.80) seniors, students, and children, £10 ($16) family. Daily 10am–5pm. Bus: 21A, 50, 50A, 78, 78A, 78B.

What was Dublin like in medieval times? Here is a historically accurate presentation of the Old City from 1170 to 1540, re-created through a series of theme exhibits, spectacles, and experiences. Highlights include an illuminated Medieval Maze complete with visual effects, background sounds, and aromas that lead you on a journey through time from the first arrival of the Anglo-Normans in 1170 to the closure of the monasteries in the 1530s. The next segment depicts everyday life in medieval Dublin with a diorama, as well as a prototype of a 13th-century quay along the banks of the Liffey. The finale takes you to The Great Hall for a 360° wrap-up portrait of medieval Dublin via a 12-minute cyclorama-style audiovisual.

✪ St. Patrick's Cathedral

Patrick's Close, Patrick St., Dublin 8. ☎ **01/475-4817.** Admission £1.20 ($1.90) adults and 50p (80¢) students and children under 12. April–Oct, Mon–Fri 9am–6pm, Sat 9am–5pm, Sun 10am–4:30pm; Nov–Mar, Mon–Fri 9am–6pm, Sat 9am–4pm, Sun 10:30am–4:30pm. Bus: 50, 50A, 54, 54A, 56A.

It is said that St. Patrick baptized converts on this site and consequently a church has stood here since A.D. 450, making it the oldest Christian site in Dublin. The present cathedral dates from 1190, but because of a fire and a rebuilding in the 14th century, not much remains from the cathedral's foundation days. It is mainly early English in style, with a square medieval tower that houses the largest ringing peal bells in Ireland, an 18th-century spire, and a 300-foot-long interior, making it the longest church in the country. St. Patrick's is closely associated with Jonathan Swift, who was dean here from 1713 to 1745 and whose tomb lies in the south aisle. Others who are memorialized within the cathedral include Turlough O'Carolan, a blind harpist and composer and the last of the great Irish bards; Michael William Balfe, the composer; and Douglas Hyde, the first president of Ireland. St. Patrick's is the national cathedral of the Church of Ireland.

✪ Dublin Writers Museum

18/19 Parnell Sq. N., Dublin 1. ☎ **01/872-2077.** Admission £2.75 ($4.40) adults, £2.35 ($3.75) seniors and students, £1.15 ($1.85) children under 12, £7.50 ($12) families. Mon–Sat 10am–5pm, Sun and public holidays 11:30am–7pm; June, July, Aug late opening Mon–Fri

10am–7pm. DART to Connolly Station. Bus: 10, 11, 11A, 11B, 12, 13, 14, 16, 16A, 19, 19A, 22, 22A, 36.

Housed in a stunning 18th-century Georgian mansion with splendid plasterwork and stained glass, the museum is itself an impressive reminder of the grandeur of the Irish literary tradition. Yeats, Joyce, Beckett, Shaw, Wilde, Swift, and Sheridan are among those whose lives and works are celebrated here. One of the museum's rooms is devoted to children's literature.

✪ The Phoenix Park
Parkgate St., Dublin 7. ☎ **01/677-0095.** Free admission. Daily 24 hours. Bus: 10, 25, 26.

This is Dublin's playground, the largest enclosed urban park in Europe, opened in 1747, with a circumference of 7 miles and a total area of 1,760 acres. Situated 2 miles west of the city center, it is traversed by a network of roads and quiet pedestrian walkways, and informally landscaped with ornamental gardens, nature trails, and broad expanses of grassland separated by avenues of trees, including oak, beech, pine, chestnut, and lime. The homes of the Irish president and the U.S. ambassador are on its grounds. Livestock graze peacefully on pasturelands, deer roam the forested areas, and horses romp on polo fields.

MORE ATTRACTIONS
ART GALLERIES

Boulevard Gallery
Merrion Sq. West, Dublin 2. Free admission. May–Sept, Sat–Sun 10:30am–6pm. DART to Pearse Station. Bus: 5, 7A, 8, 46, 62.

The fence around Merrion Square doubles as a display railing on summer weekends in an outdoor display of local art similar to those you'll find in New York's Greenwich Village or Paris's Montmartre. Permits are given to local artists only to sell their own work, so this is a chance to meet an artist as well as to browse or buy.

Hugh Lane Municipal Gallery of Modern Art
Parnell Sq., Dublin 1. ☎ **01/874-1903.** Free admission; donations accepted. Tues–Fri 9:30am–6pm, Sat 9:30am–5pm, Sun 11am–5pm. DART to Connolly Station. Bus: 10, 11, 11A, 11B, 12, 13, 14, 16, 16A, 19, 19A, 22, 22A, 36.

Housed in a finely restored 18th-century building known as Charlemont House, this gallery is situated next to the Dublin Writers Museum. It is named after Hugh Lane, an Irish art connoisseur who was killed in the sinking of the *Lusitania* in 1915 and who willed his collection (including works by Courbet, Manet, Monet, and Corot) to be shared between the government of Ireland and the National Gallery of London. With the Lane collection as its nucleus, this gallery also contains paintings from the Impressionist and post-Impressionist traditions, sculptures by Rodin, stained glass, and works by modern Irish artists.

Irish Museum of Modern Art (IMMA)
Military Rd., Kilmainham. ☎ **01/671-8666.** Free admission. Tues–Sat 10am–5:30pm, Sun noon–5:30pm. Bus: 78A, 79, 90.

Housed in the splendidly restored 17th-century edifice known as the Royal Hospital, IMMA is a showcase of Irish and international art from the latter half of the 20th century. The buildings and grounds also provide a venue for theatrical and musical events, overlapping the visual and performing arts.

Temple Bar Gallery and Studios
5–9 Temple Bar, Dublin 2. ☎ **01/671-0073.** Free admission. Mon–Sat 10am–6pm, Sun 2–6pm. Bus: 21A, 46A, 46B, 51B, 51C, 68, 69, 86.

Founded in 1983 in the heart of Dublin's "Left Bank," this is one of the largest studio/gallery complexes in Europe. More than 30 Irish artists work here at a variety of contemporary visual arts, among them sculpture, painting, printing, and photography. Only the gallery section is open to the public, but, with advance notice, appointments can be made to view individual artists at work.

BREWERIES/DISTILLERIES

✪ Guinness Brewery Hop Store / Visitor Centre

Crane St. (off Thomas St.), Dublin 8. ☎ **01/453-6700**, ext. 5155. Admission £2 ($3.20) adults, £1.50 ($2.40) seniors and students, 50p (80¢) children under 12. Mon–Fri 10am–4pm. Bus: 21A, 78, 78A.

Founded in 1759, the Guinness Brewery is one of the world's largest breweries, producing the distinctive dark beer called stout, famous for its thick, creamy head. Although tours of the brewery itself are no longer allowed, visitors are welcome to explore the adjacent Guinness Hop Store, a converted 19th-century four-story building. It houses the World of Guinness Exhibition, an audiovisual presentation showing how the stout is made, plus a museum and a bar where visitors can sample a glass or two of the famous brew. The two top floors of the building also serve as a venue for a variety of art exhibits.

Irish Whiskey Corner

Irish Distillers, Bow St., Dublin 7. ☎ **01/872-5566**. Admission £3 ($4.80). May–Oct, tours Mon–Fri at 11am, 2:30pm, and 3:30pm, Sat at 2:30 and 3:30pm, Sun at 3:30pm. Nov–Apr, tour Mon–Fri at 3:30pm. Bus: 34, 70, 80.

This museum illustrates the history of Irish whiskey, known as *uisce beatha* (the water of life) in Irish. Housed in a former distillery warehouse, it presents a short introductory audiovisual presentation, an exhibition area, and a whiskey-making demonstration. At the end of the tour, whiskey can be sampled at an in-house pub.

PLACES OF BUSINESS

✪ Bank of Ireland / Parliament House

2 College Green, Dublin 2. ☎ **01/661-5933**, ext. 2265. Free admission. Mon–Wed and Fri 10am–4pm, Thurs 10am–5pm; guided 45-minute tours of the House of Lords chamber Tues at 10:30am, 11:30am, and 1:45pm (except holidays). DART to Tara St. Station. Bus: 15A, 15B, 15C, 21A, 46, 46A, 46B, 46C, 51B, 51C, 55, 63, 68, 69, 86, 78A, 78B, 83.

Although now a busy bank, this building was erected in 1729 to house the Irish Parliament, but it became superfluous when the British and Irish Parliaments were merged in London. In fact, the Irish Parliament voted itself out of existence, the only recorded parliament in history to do so. Highlights include the windowless front portico, built to avoid distractions from the outside when Parliament was in session; and the unique House of Lords chamber, famed for its Irish oak woodwork, 18th-century tapestries, golden mace, and sparkling Irish crystal chandelier of 1,233 pieces, dating from 1765.

✪ General Post Office (GPO)

O'Connell St., Dublin 1. ☎ **01/872-8888**. Free admission. Mon–Sat 8am–8pm, Sun 10:30am–6:30pm. DART to Connolly Station. Bus: 25, 26, 34, 37, 38A, 39A, 39B, 66A, 67A.

With a 200-foot-long, 56-foot-high facade of Ionic columns and pilasters in the Greco-Roman style, this is more than a post office; it is the symbol of Irish freedom. Built between 1815 and 1818, it was the main stronghold of the Irish Volunteers in 1916. Set afire, the building was gutted and abandoned after the surrender and execution of many of the Irish rebel leaders. It reopened as a post office in 1929 after the formation of the Irish Free State. In memory of the building's dramatic role in Irish history, there is today an impressive bronze statue of Cuchulainn, the legendary Irish hero, on display. Look closely at the pillars outside—you can still see bullet holes from the siege.

CATHEDRALS & CHURCHES

Our Lady of Mount Carmel / Whitefriar Street Carmelite Church

57 Aungier St., Dublin 2. ☎ **01/475-8821.** Free admission. Mon and Wed–Fri 8am–6:30pm, Tues 8am–9:30pm, Sat 8am–7pm, Sun 8am–7:30pm. Bus: 16, 16A, 19, 19A, 22, 22A, 55, 83.

One of the city's largest churches, it was built between 1825 and 1827 on the site of a pre-Reformation Carmelite priory (1539) and an earlier Carmelite abbey (13th century). It has since been extended, with a new entrance from Aungier Street. This is a favorite place of pilgrimage on February 14th, because the body of St. Valentine is enshrined here, presented to the church by Pope Gregory XVI in 1836. The other highlight is the 15th-century black oak Madonna, Our Lady of Dublin.

St. Audeon's Church

Cornmarket (off High St.), Dublin 8. ☎ **01/677-8714.** Free admission. Fri–Wed 11:30am–1:30pm. Bus: 21A, 78A, 78B.

Situated next to the only remaining gate of the Old City walls (1214), this church is said to be the only surviving medieval parish in Dublin. Although it is partly in ruins, significant parts have survived, including the west doorway, which dates from 1190, and the nave from the 13th century. In addition, the 17th-century bell tower houses three bells cast in 1423, making them the oldest in Ireland. It's a Church of Ireland property, but nearby is another St. Audeon's Church, this one Catholic and dating from 1846. It was here that Father Flash Kavanagh used to say the world's fastest mass so that his congregation could be out in time for the football matches.

St. Mary's Pro-Cathedral

Cathedral and Marlborough sts., Dublin 1. ☎ **01/874-5441.** Free admission. Mon–Fri 8am–6pm, Sat 8am–9pm, Sun 8am–8pm. DART to Connolly Station. Bus: 28, 29A, 30, 31A, 31B, 32A, 32B, 44A.

Since Dublin's two main cathedrals (Christ Church and St. Patrick's) belong to the Protestant Church of Ireland, St. Mary's is the closest the Catholics get to having a cathedral of their own. Tucked into a corner of a rather unimpressive back street, it is situated in the heart of the city's north side and is considered the main Catholic parish church of the city center. Built between 1815 and 1825, it is of the Greek Revival Doric style, providing a distinct contrast to the Gothic Revival look of most other churches of the period. The exterior portico is modeled on the Temple of Theseus in Athens, with six Doric columns, while the Renaissance-style interior is patterned after the Church of St. Philip de Reule of Paris. The church is noted for its Palestrina Choir, which sings every Sunday at 11am.

✪ St. Michan's Church

Church St., Dublin 8. ☎ **01/872-4154.** Admission £1.50 ($2.40), £1 ($1.60) seniors and students, 50p (80¢) children under 12. Mon–Fri 10am–12:45pm and 2–5pm, Sat 10am–12:45pm. Bus: 34, 70, 80.

Built on the site of an early Danish chapel (1095), this 17th-century edifice claims to be the only parish church on the north side of the Liffey surviving from a Viking foundation. Now under the Church of Ireland banner, it has some very fine interior woodwork and an organ (dated 1724) on which Handel is said to have played his *Messiah*. The most unique (and, let it be noted, macabre) feature of this church, however, is the underground burial vault. Because of the dry atmosphere, bodies have lain for centuries without showing signs of decomposition.

St. Teresa's Church

Clarendon St., Dublin 2. ☎ **01/671-8466.** Free admission; donations welcome. Daily 8am–8pm or longer. Bus: 16, 16A, 19, 19A, 22, 22A, 55, 83.

With its foundation stone laid in 1793, the church was opened in 1810 by the Discalced Carmelite Fathers, to be continuously enlarged until its present form was reached in 1876. This was the first post–Penal Law church to be legally and openly erected in Dublin, following the Catholic Relief Act of 1793. Among the artistic highlights are John Hogan's *Dead Christ,* a sculpture displayed beneath the altar, and Phyllis Burke's seven beautiful stained-glass windows.

WHERE THE BODIES ARE BURIED

Glasnevin Cemetery

Finglas Rd., Dublin 11. ☎ **01/830-1133.** Free admission. Daily 8am–4pm. Bus: 19, 19A, 40, 40A, 40B, 40C.

Situated north of the city center, this is the Irish National Cemetery, founded in 1832 and covering more than 124 acres. The majority of people buried here are ordinary citizens, but there are also many famous names to be found on the headstones, from former Irish presidents such as Eamon de Valera and Sean T. O'Kelly to other political heroes such as Michael Collins, Daniel O'Connell, Roger Casement, and Charles Stewart Parnell. Literary figures also have their place here, including poet Gerard Manley Hopkins and writers Christy Brown and Brendan Behan. Though open to all, this is primarily a Catholic burial ground, with more than the usual share of Celtic crosses. A heritage map, on sale in most bookshops, serves as a guide to who's buried where, or you can take one of the guided tours offered by members of the National Graves Association on Sundays, June through August, at 11:50am. For more information, call 01/832-1312 or 01/842-3787.

HISTORIC BUILDINGS

Custom House

Custom House Quay, Dublin 1. ☎ **01/874-2961.** Not open to the public, but worth looking at the exterior. Bus: 27A, 27B, 53A.

Sitting prominently on the Liffey's north bank is the Custom House, one of Dublin's finest Georgian buildings. Designed by James Gandon and completed in 1791, it is beautifully proportioned, with a long classical facade of graceful pavilions, arcades, columns, a central dome topped by a 16-foot statue of Commerce, and 14 keystones over the doors and windows, known as the Riverine Heads because they represent the Atlantic Ocean and the 13 principal rivers of Ireland. Although burned to a shell in 1921, the building has been masterfully restored and its bright Portland stone recently cleaned.

✪ Four Courts

Inns Quay, Dublin 8. ☎ **01/872-5555.** Free admission. Mon–Fri 11am–1pm, 2–4pm. Bus: 34, 70, 80.

The home of the Irish law courts since 1796, this fine 18th-century building overlooks the north bank of the River Liffey on the west side of Dublin. With a sprawling 440-foot facade, it was designed by James Gandon and is distinguished by its graceful Corinthian columns, massive dome (64 feet in diameter), and exterior statues of Justice, Mercy, Wisdom, and Moses (sculpted by Edward Smyth). The building was severely burned during the Irish Civil War of 1922, but has been artfully restored. The public is admitted only when court is in session, so it is best to phone in advance.

Political Parties

There are six political parties represented in the Irish Dáil, or Parliament.

Fianna Fáil was founded in 1926 by Eamon de Valera. Its central commitments are to the unity and independence of the Republic, the preservation of Irish traditions and language, and the general welfare of the Irish people. Throughout the brief history of the Republic, it has consistently held the largest number of parliamentary seats.

Fine Gael was formed in 1933 by the merging of Cumann na nGaedheal with a number of other, smaller parties. The current leader of Fine Gael is John Bruton, the Irish An Taoiseach (prime minister). A central aim of the party is to promote a broader, more inclusive, pluralism in Irish political life. It has supported reconciliation with Northern Ireland and the creation of a united Europe.

Labour, founded in 1912, is a member of the Party of European Socialists. The oldest political party in Ireland, Labour pursues policies that reach toward greater democracy and equality. In 1990, Mary Robinson, nominated by the Labour Party, was elected president. Two years later, in the general election of 1992, Labour had its highest showing ever, winning 19.3% of the vote and 33 seats.

The **Democratic Left,** founded in 1992, is organized both in the Republic and in the North. Its aims include a pluralist, socialist society in Ireland; gender equality; Irish neutrality; cooperative, global security; and the protection of the environment. While the Democratic Left supports the European Union, it opposes any European ambition to become a military superpower.

The **Progressive Democrats** were founded in 1985 in the mold of other European liberal parties, committed to government-fostered economic growth and to further integration among the member states of the European Union.

The **Green Party** was founded in 1982 and sent its first member to parliament in 1989. Since that time, its influence and success have grown measurably. Its motto, "Think Globally, Act Locally," is a familiar one. The Irish Green Party is in close league with the Green movement throughout Europe and focuses on environmental and other social issues that bear on achieving a just society and a sustainable world.

Leinster House

Kildare St. and Merrion Sq., Dublin 2. ☎ **01/678-9911.** Free admission. Oct–May, Tues–Thurs; hours vary. DART to Pearse Station. Bus: 5, 7A, 8.

Dating from 1745 and originally known as Kildare House, this building was once considered the largest Georgian house in Dublin, because of its 11-bay, 140-foot facade. With an impressive central pediment and Corinthian columns, it is also said to have been the model for Irish-born architect James Hoban's design for the White House in Washington, D.C. It was sold in 1815 to the Royal Dublin Society, which developed it as a cultural center, with the National Museum, Library, and Gallery all surrounding it. In 1924, however, it took on a new role when it was acquired by the Irish Free State government as a parliament house. Since then, it has been the meeting place for the Dáil Eireann (Irish House of Representatives) and Seanad Eireann (Irish Senate), which together constitute the Oireachtas (National Parliament). Tickets for admission when the Dáil is in session must be arranged by writing in advance, or by contacting a member of Parliament directly.

Mansion House

Dawson St., Dublin 2. ☎ **01/676-1845.** Not open to the public, but worth looking at the exterior. DART to Pearse Station. Bus: 10, 11A, 11B, 13, 20B.

Built by Joshua Dawson, this Queen Anne–style building has been the official residence of Dublin's lord mayors since 1715. It was here that the first Dáil Eireann assembled, in 1919, to adopt Ireland's Declaration of Independence and ratify the Proclamation of the Irish Republic by the insurgents of 1916.

✪ Newman House

85–86 St. Stephen's Green, Dublin 2. ☎ **01/706-7422** or 01/475-7255. Guided tours £2 ($3.20) adults, £1 ($1.60) seniors, students, and children under 12. June, July, and Sept Tues–Fri noon–5pm, Sat 2–5pm, Sun 11am–2pm; otherwise, by appointment only. Bus: 14, 14A, 15A, 15B.

Situated in the heart of Dublin on the south side of St. Stephen's Green, this is the historic seat of the Catholic University of Ireland. Named for Cardinal John Henry Newman, the 19th-century writer and theologian and first rector of the university, it is comprised of two of the finest Georgian town houses in Dublin, dating from 1740 and decorated with outstanding Palladian and Rococo plasterwork, marble tiled floors, and wainscot paneling. No. 85 has been magnificently restored to its original splendor.

LIBRARIES

✪ Chester Beatty Library and Gallery of Oriental Art

20 Shrewsbury Rd., Ballsbridge, Dublin 4. ☎ **01/269-2386.** Free admission. Tues–Fri 10am–5pm and Sat 2–5pm; free guided tours on Wed and Sat at 2:30pm. DART to Sandymount Station. Bus: 5, 7A, 8, 10, 46, 46A, 46B.

Bequeathed to the Irish nation in 1956 by Sir Alfred Chester Beatty, this collection contains approximately 22,000 manuscripts, rare books, miniature paintings, and objects from Western, Middle Eastern, and Far Eastern cultures. The library is planning to move to Dublin Castle sometime in 1997.

Marsh's Library

St. Patrick's Close, Upper Kevin St., Dublin 8. ☎ **01/454-3511.** Free admission, but a donation of £1 ($1.50) expected. Mon and Wed–Fri 10am–12:45pm and 2–5pm, Sat 10:30am–12:45pm. Bus: 50, 50A, 54, 54A, 56A.

This is Ireland's oldest public library, founded in 1701 by Narcissus Marsh, Archbishop of Dublin. It is a repository of more than 25,000 scholarly volumes, chiefly on theology, medicine, ancient history, maps, Hebrew, Syriac, Greek, Latin, and French literature.

National Library of Ireland

Kildare St., Dublin 2. ☎ **01/661-8811.** Free admission. Jan–Oct and Dec, Mon 10am–9pm, Tues–Wed 2–9pm, Thurs–Fri 10am–5pm, Sat 10am–1pm. Closed Nov for inventory. DART to Pearse Station. Bus: 10, 11A, 11B, 13, 20B.

For visitors who come to Ireland to research their roots, this library is often the first point of reference, with thousands of volumes and records yielding ancestral information. Opened at this location in 1890, this is the principal library of Irish studies, and is particularly noted for its collection of first editions and the works of Irish authors. It also has an unrivaled collection of maps of Ireland.

National Photographic Archive

Meeting House Sq., Temple Bar, Dublin 2. ☎ **01/661-8811.** Free admission. Mon–Sat 11am–6pm. DART to Tara St. Station. Bus: 21A, 46A, 46B, 51B, 51C, 68, 69, 86.

The newest member of the Temple Bar cultural complex, the National Photographic Archive will house the extensive photo collection of the National Library and serve as its photo exhibition space. The full collection should be in place by March 1997, while the exhibition space is already in full swing, currently presenting "Fadographs of a Yestern Scene" celebrating Dublin, photography, and the literature of James Joyce. This is a striking contemporary building sure to offer exciting programs in the years ahead.

MORE MUSEUMS

Dublin Civic Museum

58 S. William St., Dublin 2. ☎ **01/679-4260.** Free admission. Tues–Sat 10am–6pm, Sun 11am–2pm. Bus: 10, 11, 13.

Located in the old City Assembly House next to the Powerscourt Townhouse Centre, this museum focuses on the history of the Dublin area from medieval to modern times. In addition to old street signs, maps, and prints, you can see Viking artifacts, wooden water mains, coal covers, and even the head from the statue of Lord Nelson, which stood in O'Connell Street until it was blown up in 1965.

Irish Jewish Museum

3–4 Walworth Rd. (off Victoria St.), South Circular Rd., Dublin 8. ☎ **01/497-4252.** Free admission; donations welcome. Oct–Apr, Sun 10:30am–2:30pm; May–Sept, Tues, Thurs, Sun 11am–3pm. Bus: 15A, 15B, 47, 47B.

Housed in a former synagogue, this is a museum of Irish/Jewish documents, photographs, and memorabilia, tracing the history of the Jews in Ireland over the last 500 years.

Natural History Museum

Merrion St., Dublin 2. ☎ **01/677-7444.** Free admission. Tues–Sat 10am–5pm, Sun 2–5pm. Bus: 7, 7A, 8.

A division of the National Museum of Ireland, the recently renovated Natural History Museum is considered one of the finest traditional museums in the world. In addition to presenting the zoological history of Ireland, there are examples of major animal groups from around the world, including many rare or extinct groups. The Blaschka glass models of marine animals are quite famous.

Number Twenty Nine

29 Lower Fitzwilliam St., Dublin 2. ☎ **01/702-6165.** Admission £2 ($3.20) adults, £1 ($1.60) seniors and students, children under 16 free. Tues–Sat 10am–5pm, Sun 2–5pm. Closed two weeks before Christmas. DART to Pearse Station. Bus: 6, 7, 8, 10, 45.

Situated in the heart of one of Dublin's fashionable Georgian streets, this is a unique museum. The restored four-story town house is designed to reflect the lifestyle of a Dublin middle-class family during the period from 1790 to 1820. The exhibition ranges from artifacts and artworks of the time to carpets, curtains, decorations, plasterwork, and bell pulls. The nursery includes dolls and toys of the era.

A SIGHT & SOUND SHOW

Dublin Experience

Trinity College, Davis Theatre, Dublin 2. ☎ **01/677-2941.** Admission £3 ($4.80) adults, £2.50 ($4) seniors and students, £1.50 ($2.40) children under 12, £6 ($9.60) family. May 20–Sept 29, hourly showings 10am–5pm. DART to Tara St. Station. Bus: 5, 7A, 8, 15A, 15B, 15C, 46, 55, 62, 63, 83, 84.

An ideal orientation for first-time visitors to the Irish capital, this 45-minute multi-media sight-and-sound show traces the history of Dublin from the earliest times to the present. It is presented in the Davis Theater of Trinity College, on Nassau Street.

ESPECIALLY FOR KIDS

✪ The Ark: A Cultural Centre for Children

Eustace St., Temple Bar, Dublin 2. ☎ **01/670-7788.** Fax 01/670-7758. Prices from 50p–£5 (80¢–$8) depending on activity or event. Daily 10–4pm. Closed mid–Aug to mid–Sept. DART to Tara St. Station. Bus: 51, 51B, 37, 39.

The Ark is a unique new cultural center for children in the Temple Bar area of Dublin, where children are taught with respect and sensitivity by experienced professionals. The handsomely renovated building has three modern main floors housing a wonderful semicircular theater that can open out onto Meeting House Square, a gallery, and a workshop for hands-on learning sessions. This exciting center offers organized minicourse experiences (one to two hours long) designed around particular themes in music, visual arts, and theater. In their debut year, The Ark offered numerous activities in photography, the concept of an Ark and animal-making, music and instrument-making, and the art of architecture. The workshops, performances, tours, and artist/musician-in-residence program are geared toward specific age groups and the associated activities are kept small, so it is important to check the current themes and schedule of events and book accordingly. The Ark enjoys huge popularity with children, families, and teachers.

Dublin's Viking Adventure

Temple Bar, Dublin 2 (entrance from Essex St.). ☎ **01/605-7777.** Fax 01/679-6033. Admission £4.50 ($7.20) adults, £2.75 ($4.40) children, £12.50 ($20) family. Mon and Thurs–Sat 10am–4:30pm, Sun 11:30am–5:30pm. DART to Tara St. Station. Bus: 51, 51B, 37, 39.

This popular new attraction brings adults and children on an imaginative journey through time to an era when Dublin was a bustling Norse town. A lively, authentic atmosphere is created by the "Vikings" who populate the village in their period houses and detailed costumes. The Viking townspeople engage in the activities of daily life in the Wood Quay area along the Liffey, while their visitors watch and interact with them. The "Viking Feast" is a further opportunity to experience living history at the berserk price of £33.50 ($53.60) per person—even for Viking-wannabe children. Feasts are at 7:30pm daily except Tuesdays. Call the number above for reservations.

✪ Dublin Zoo

The Phoenix Park, Dublin 8. ☎ **01/677-1425.** Admission £5.50 ($8.80) adults, £4 ($6.40) seniors and students, £3 ($4.80) children under 12. Summer, Mon–Sat 9:30am–6pm, Sun 10:30am–6pm; winter, Mon–Fri 9:30am–4pm, Sat 9:30am–5pm, Sun 10:30am–5pm. Bus: 10, 25, 26.

Established in 1830, this is the third oldest zoo in the world (after London and Paris), nestled in the midst of the city's largest playground, the Phoenix Park, about 2 miles west of the city center. This 30-acre zoo provides a naturally landscaped habitat for more than 235 species of wild animals and tropical birds. Highlights for youngsters include the Children's Pets' Corner and a train ride around the zoo. Other facilities include a restaurant, coffee shop, and gift shop. The zoo is currently undergoing a $24 million redevelopment. In the works are a new free-flight aviary, monkey world, additions to the Arctic exhibition, and more, all planned for opening in May 1997.

Lambert Puppet Theatre and Museum

5 Clifden Lane, Monkstown, Co. Dublin. ☎ **01/280-0974.** No box office; book by phone daily. Admission £4 ($6.40). Shows Sat–Sun 3:30pm. DART to Salthill Station. Bus: 7, 7A, or 8.

Tips for Kids from a Kid: Dublin

Cinemas   There are a lot of cinemas in Dublin. The biggest ones are Tallaght, which has 12 screens and is in Tallaght Shopping Centre, and Coolock, which has 10 screens and is on the Malahide Road. The newest cinema is Virgin Cinema in Parnell Street. It has 9 screens. In Virgin Cinemas there are some shops: There is Flix, which is a cafe; Strike 4, which is a restaurant; and Century City, which has virtual reality, Internet, and video games. Other good cinemas are the Ormonde in Stillorgan and the Stella in Rathmines.

Sweets   We have a lot of different sweets in Dublin. My favorite bars are Twix, Moro, Time Out, and Twirl. The biggest chocolate factory in Dublin is Cadburys. There are a lot of chocolate bars in the shops. There are also a lot of ice creams in Dublin. The best ones are Magnum, Chunky, Super Split, and Tangle Twister. We also have cones. There are three different types of cones: small, plain, and 99. There is a huge variety of sweets in Dublin. In some places they even have a sweet stall! My favorite sweets are Werther's Originals and Polos.

Restaurants   The restaurants in Dublin are very nice and child friendly. If you want fast-food or take-out I would go to McDonalds, Burger King, or Fortes. McDonalds and Burger King both have burgers, chips, and soft drinks. Fortes offers other things like chicken, southern fried chicken, steak, and pizza. They are all around the City Centre. If you don't want fast-food, though, I would go to somewhere like Strike 4 or Pasta Presto. Strike 4 is in Parnell Street and has a special children's menu and there are lots of American baseball gear everywhere. Pasta Presto is in Ballsbridge and it does pasta and pizza. In Pasta Presto they give you free breadsticks.

Adventure Centers   There are quite a few adventure centers around Dublin. If you want a place with slides, ball ponds, etc., I would go to Wally Wabbits, Bambams, or Fun Factory. Wally Wabbits is in Dundrum and is suitable for up to eight-year-olds. Bambams is in Stillorgan Bowl. It is very good and there is a little cinema there. The Fun Factory is the biggest one. It has a freefall and a bouncing castle and much more. It is in Dun Laoghaire. If you want guns, though, I would go to Quazar in Tallaght. You each get a toy gun and you are split into two teams. Then you go around and try to take over the opponent's station.

—Nicholas Odlum, age nine, Dublin

Founded by master ventriloquist Eugene Lambert, this 300-seat suburban theater presents puppet shows designed to delight audiences who are both young and young at heart. During intermission, you can also browse in the on-premises puppet museum.

Museum of Childhood

The Palms, 20 Palmerston Park, Rathmines, Dublin 6. ☎ **01/497-3223.** Admission £1 ($1.60) adults, 75p ($1.20) children under age 12. July–Aug, Wed and Sun 2–5:30pm; Sept and Nov–June, Sun 2–5:30pm. Bus: 13 or 14.

Part of a large suburban house on the south side of Dublin, this museum specializes in dolls and doll houses of all nations, from 1730 to 1940. Among the unique items on display are doll houses that belonged to the Empress Elizabeth of Austria and Daphne du Maurier. In addition, there are antique toys, rocking horses, and doll carriages.

National Wax Museum

Granby Row (at Upper Dorset St., off Parnell Sq.), Dublin 1. ☎ **01/872-6340**. Admission £3.50 ($5.60) adults, £2 ($3.20) children under age 12. Mon–Sat 10am–5:30pm, Sun 1–5:30pm. Bus: 11, 13, 16, 22, 22A.

For an overall life-size view of Irish history and culture, this museum presents wax figures of Irish people of historical, political, literary, theatrical, and sporting fame. In addition, there is a wide range of tableaux featuring everything from the Last Supper, Pope John Paul II, and various world leaders to music stars like U2, Michael Jackson, and Elvis Presley. For younger children, Children's World depicts characters from fairy tales such as *Jack and the Beanstalk*, *Sleeping Beauty*, and *Snow White*.

A SIGHT FOR THE GENEALOGY MINDED

✪ Heraldic Museum / Genealogical Office

2 Kildare St., Dublin 2. ☎ **01/661-8811**. Free admission. Mon–Wed 10am–8:30pm, Thurs–Fri 10am–4:30pm, Sat 10am–12:30pm. DART to Pearse Station. Bus: 5, 7A, 8, 9, 10, 14, 15.

The only one of its kind in the world, this museum focuses on the uses of heraldry. Exhibits include shields, banners, coins, paintings, porcelain, and stamps depicting coats of arms. The office of Ireland's chief herald also offers a consultation service on the premises, for a fee of £20 ($32), so this is the ideal place to start researching your own roots.

SIGHTS FOR THE LITERARY MINDED

James Joyce Cultural Centre

35 N. Great George's St., Dublin 1. ☎ **01/878-8547**. Admission £2.50 ($4) adult, £1.75 ($2.80) student, 70p ($1.12) child, £6 ($9.60) family; admission and walking tour: £5.50 ($8.80) adult, £3.75 ($6) student, £2.50 ($4) child, £8 ($12.80) family. Summer, Mon–Sat 9:30am–5pm, Sun 12:30–5pm; winter, Tues–Sat 10am–4:30pm, Sun 12:00–4:30pm, closed Mon. DART to Connolly Station. Bus: 1, 40A, 40B, 40C.

Located near Parnell Square and the Dublin Writers Museum, this newly restored Georgian town house, built in 1784, gives literary enthusiasts one more reason to visit Dublin's north side. Aiming to impart an increased understanding of the life and works of James Joyce, it contains various exhibits plus a Joycean archive, reference library, and workshop. In addition, there are talks and audiovisual presentations daily, and Ken Monaghan, Joyce's nephew, conducts tours of the house and, occasionally, walking tours through the neighborhood streets of "Joyce Country" in Dublin's north inner city (tours by special arrangement only). Planned additions to the center, likely to be completed by 1997, are a coffee shop and a "Ulysses Experience."

Shaw Birthplace

33 Synge St., Dublin 2. ☎ **01/475-0854**. Admission £3.20 ($5.10) adults, £1.80 ($2.90) seniors, students, and children under 18, £1.10 ($1.75) children ages 3–11, £6.50 ($10.40) family. Combination ticket with the Dublin Writers Museum available at reduced rate. May–Oct, Mon–Sat 10am–1pm and 2–6pm, Sun 11:30am–1pm and 2–6pm. Bus: 16, 16A, 19, 19A, 22, 22A, 155.

Situated off S. Circular Road, this simple two-story terraced house, built in 1838, was the birthplace in 1856 of George Bernard Shaw, one of Dublin's three winners of the Nobel Prize for Literature. Recently restored, it has been furnished in Victorian style to re-create the atmosphere of Shaw's early days. Rooms on view are the kitchen, maid's room, nursery, drawing room, and a couple of bedrooms, including young Bernard's.

6 Organized Tours

BUS TOURS

Dublin Bus
59 Upper O'Connell St., Dublin 1. ☎ **01/703-3028** or 01/873-4222.

This company operates several different tours. Seats can be booked in advance at the Dublin Bus office or at the Dublin Bus ticket desk, Dublin Tourism, Suffolk Street. All tours depart from the Dublin Bus office, but free pick-up from many Dublin hotels is available for morning tours. Tours include a nearly three-hour **Grand Dublin Tour** via double-decker bus, with either an open-air or glass-enclosed upper level. It's a great vantage point for picture-taking. The cost is £8 ($12.80) adults, £4 ($6.40) children under 16, and £20 ($32) for a family of four. It operates year-round at 10:15am and 2:15pm.

For more flexible touring, there is a **Dublin City Tour,** a continuous guided bus service connecting 10 major points of interest including museums, art galleries, churches and cathedrals, libraries, and historic sites. For the flat fare of £5 ($9)—£2 ($3.20) children under 16, £12 ($19.20) for a family of four—you can ride the bus for a full day, getting off and on as often as you wish. It operates from mid-April through September daily from 9:30am–4:30pm.

Gray Line Tours—Ireland
3 Clanwilliam Terrace, Grand Canal Quay, Dublin 2. ☎ **01/661-9666.**

A branch of the world's largest sightseeing organization, this company offers a range of full-day and half-day sightseeing tours of Dublin City from May through October, with a more limited service, subject to demand, in April and November to December.

The selection of tours includes a two-hour **morning tour,** providing an overview of the city's historical sights and attractions; a three-hour **afternoon city tour** including admission to the Book of Kells exhibit at Trinity College, the State Apartments of Dublin Castle, and St. Patrick's Cathedral; and a **full-day tour** combining the morning and afternoon tours described above to create a seven-hour exploration of Dublin's highlights. Prices range from £8 to £20 ($12.80 to $32) per person.

WALKING TOURS

Small and compact, Dublin lends itself to walking tours. You can grab a map and a pith helmet and set off on your own, of course, but if you want some guidance, some historical background, and some assurance that you haven't just walked past something important, you might want to consider one of the following self-guided or escorted group tours.

SELF-GUIDED WALKING TOURS

TOURIST TRAILS The **Dublin Tourism Office,** St. Andrew's Church, Suffolk St., Dublin 2 (☎ **01/605-7700**), has pioneered in the development of self-guided walking tours around Dublin. To date, there are four different tourist trails that have been mapped out and signposted throughout the city: Old City, Georgian Heritage, Cultural Heritage, and Rock 'n' Stroll / Music Theme. For each trail, the tourist office has produced a handy booklet that maps out the route and provides a commentary about each place along the trail.

Escorted Group Walking Tours

Discover Dublin Tours

20 Lower Stephen St., Dublin 2. ☎ **01/478-0191.** Tickets £5 ($8) per person. Year-round daily by reservation.

Walks with a literary or music theme are the specialty of this company, whose tours include a two-hour literary/historical tour during which the costumed guides recite works from Dublin's literary greats while walking you through the city's famous landmarks and a two-hour musical pub crawl that focuses on Irish music, from traditional to rock. Departures from various venues; reservations required.

Dublin Footsteps

Glendenning House, Wicklow St., Dublin 2. ☎ **01/845-0772.** Tickets £4 ($6.40) per person. June–Sept, daily starting at 10:30am, but hours vary depending on tour; call in advance for schedule.

This company offers a variety of themed two-hour tours including a Medieval Walk, Literary Walk, 18th-Century / Georgian Walk, and City Centre Walk.

Dublin Literary Pub Crawl

☎ **01/454-0228.** Tickets £6 ($9.60) per person. Year-round Sun at noon; May and Sept daily 7:30pm; June–Aug daily at 3pm and 7:30pm; Oct–April Sat–Sun at 7:30pm.

Walking in the footsteps of Joyce, Behan, Beckett, Shaw, Kavanagh, and other Irish literary greats, this guided tour rambles from pub to pub, with appropriate commentary between stops. The tour assembles on Duke Street, and it can be booked in advance at the Dublin Tourism Office (St. Andrew's Church, Suffolk Street, Dublin 2; ☎ 01/605-7700; see "Visitor Information" at the beginning of this chapter for other offices).

Historical Walking Tours of Dublin

Leaving from Trinity College. ☎ **01/845-0241.** Tickets £5 ($8) adults, £4 ($6.40) seniors and students. June–Sept, Mon–Sat 11am, noon, and 3pm, Sun 11am, noon, 2pm, 3pm; Oct–May, Sat–Sun noon.

This basic two-hour sightseeing walk takes in Dublin's historic landmarks, from medieval walls and Viking remains around Wood Quay to Christ Church, Dublin Castle, City Hall, and Trinity College. All guides are history graduates of Trinity College and participants are encouraged to ask questions. Tours assemble at the front gate of Trinity College; no reservations are needed.

James Joyce's Dublin Walking Tours

James Joyce Cultural Centre, 35 N. Great George's St., Dublin 1. ☎ **01/878-8547.** Tickets include admission to the James Joyce Cultural Centre: £5.50 ($8.80) adults, £3.75 ($6) students, £2.50 ($4) children, £8 ($12.80) families. Summer, Mon–Sat 9:30am–5pm, Sun 12:30–5pm; winter, Tues–Sat 10am–4:30pm, Sun noon–4:30pm, closed Mon. Advance booking is essential.

Joyce fans, take note: You can walk in the footsteps of the great novelist with Joyce's nephew, Ken Monaghan, the Centre's curator, as your guide. Monaghan (on request only) conducts walking tours of approximately one-hour's duration through the streets of Dublin's north inner city. Tours depart from the James Joyce Cultural Centre. When Mr. Monaghan is not available, tours are conducted by other members of the center's staff.

Old Dublin Walking Tours

90 Meath St., Dublin 8. ☎ **01/453-2407** or 01/453-3423. Tickets £4 ($6) per person. Year-round Sun at 2pm and by appointment.

This company offers guided walks in and around Old Dublin amid the city's medieval and Viking remains. Conducted by native Dubliners, these two-hour tours give visitors the opportunity to soak up the atmosphere and meet the people of the area. Tours assemble at the main gate of Christ Church Cathedral.

Traditional Music Pub Crawl

To explore and sample the Dublin traditional music scene, meet at the Oliver St. John Gogarty pub/restaurant, at the corner of Fleet Street and Anglesea Street, Temple Bar, at 7:30pm, Saturday to Thursday, from May to October; £5 ($8) per person.

Trinity College Walking Tours

Tour Guides Ireland, 12 Parliament St., Dublin 2. ☎ **01/679-4291,** ext. 2308. Tickets £4.50 ($7.20) adults; £3.50 ($5.60) seniors. May–Oct, Mon–Sat 9:30am–4:30pm, Sun noon–4pm.

These are walking tours around Trinity College, including admission to the Colonnades to see the Book of Kells. Tours depart every 15 minutes from Front Square of Trinity College. Reservations aren't necessary, but are appreciated.

BICYCLE TOURS

City Cycle Tours

1A Temple Lane, Dublin 2. ☎ **01/671-5610.** Tickets £10 ($16) per person. Mon–Sat 10:30am and 2:30pm, Sun 1:30pm.

Pedal your way around Dublin on a three-hour narrated bicycle tour of Temple Bar and the surrounding area. The route covers more than a dozen sightseeing landmarks and includes guided tours of the Royal Hospital, Kilmainham Gaol, and the National Gallery. Tours depart from 1A Temple Lane; reservations are not necessary but participants are asked to arrive at least 20 minutes before a tour departure. Bicycles and helmets are provided as part of the tour price.

HORSE-DRAWN CARRIAGE TOURS

Dublin Horse-Drawn Carriage Tours

St. Stephen's Green, Dublin 2. ☎ **01/453-8888** or 01/821-6463. Tickets £5 to £30 ($8–$48) for 2 to 5 passengers, depending on the duration of ride. April–Oct, daily and nightly, depending on weather.

Tour Dublin in style via a handsomely outfitted horse-drawn carriage whose driver comments on the sights as you travel around the streets and squares of the city. To arrange a ride, consult with one of the drivers stationed with carriages at the Grafton Street side of St. Stephen's Green. Rides range from a short swing around the Green to an extensive half-hour Georgian tour or an hour-long Old City tour. Rides are available on a first-come basis, but can also be booked by phone in advance.

7 The Great Outdoors

BEACHES   The following beaches on the outskirts of Dublin offer safe swimming and sandy strands and can all be reached via city buses heading northward: **Dollymount,** 3.5 miles away; **Sutton,** 7 miles away; **Howth,** 9 miles away; and **Portmarnock** and **Malahide,** each 10 miles away. In addition, the southern suburb of **Dun Laoghaire,** 7 miles away, offers a beach (at Sandycove) and a long bay-front promenade ideal for strolling in the sea air. For more details, inquire at the Dublin Tourism Office.

BIRD-WATCHING   The estuaries, salt marshes, sand flats, and islands in the vicinity of Dublin Bay provide varied habitat for a diversity of bird species. **Rockabill Island,** off the coast at Skerries, is home to an important colony of roseate terns; there is no public access to the island, but the birds can be seen from shore. **Rogerstown**

and Malahide Estuaries, on the north side of Dublin, are wintering grounds for large numbers of Brent geese, ducks, and waders. **The North Bull** is a spit of sand just north of Dublin Harbor, with salt marsh and extensive intertidal flats on the side facing the mainland; 198 species in all have been recorded here. **Sandymount Stand** on Dublin's south side has a vast intertidal zone; around dusk in July and August you can often see large numbers of terns here, including visiting roseate terns from Rockabill Island.

GOLF   Dublin's courses welcome visitors on weekdays, but starting time on weekends can be difficult to arrange. The following four are among the leading 18-hole courses in the Dublin area.

The **Elm Park Golf Club,** Nutley Lane, Dublin 4 (☎ 01/269-3438), is located on the south side of Dublin. This inland par-69 course is very popular with visitors because it is located within 3.5 miles of the city center and close to the Jurys, Berkeley Court, and Burlington hotels. Greens fees are £30 ($48) on weekdays and £35 ($56) on weekends.

The ✪ **Portmarnock Golf Club,** Portmarnock, Co. Dublin (☎ 01/846-2968), is located 10 miles from the city center on Dublin's north side, on a spit of land between the Irish Sea and a tidal inlet. First opened in 1894, this par-72 championship links has been the scene of leading tournaments during the years—from the Dunlop Masters (1959, 1965), Canada Cup (1960), Alcan (1970), and St. Andrews Trophy (1968), to many an Irish Open. Many experts consider this course as the benchmark of Irish golf. Greens fees are £40 ($64) on weekdays, £50 ($80) on weekends.

The ✪ **Royal Dublin Golf Club,** Bull Island, Dollymount, Dublin 3 (☎ 01/833-6346), is often compared to St. Andrews in layout. This century-old par-73 championship seaside links is situated on an island in Dublin Bay, 3.5 miles north of the city center. Like Portmarnock, it has been rated among the top courses of the world and has also hosted several Irish Open tournaments. The home base of Ireland's legendary champion Christy O'Connor Sr., the Royal Dublin is well known for its fine bunkers, close lies, and subtle trappings. Greens fees are £35 ($56) on weekdays, £45 ($72) on weekends.

St. Margaret's Golf Club, Skephubble, St. Margaret's, Co. Dublin (☎ 01/864-0400), one of Dublin's newest championship golf venues, is a par-72 parkland course located 3 miles west of Dublin Airport. In 1995, St. Margaret's was host to the Irish Open. Greens fees are £40 ($37.50) seven days a week.

HORSEBACK RIDING   For equestrian enthusiasts of whatever experience level, Dublin offers almost a dozen riding stables within easy reach. Prices average about £10 ($16) an hour, with or without instruction. Many stables offer guided trail-riding as well as courses in show-jumping, dressage, prehunting, eventing, and cross-country riding. Among the riding centers nearest to downtown are **Calliaghstown Riding Centre,** Calliaghstown, Rathcoole, Co. Dublin (☎ 01/458-9236); **Carrickmines Equestrian Centre,** Glenamuck Road, Foxrock, Dublin 18 (☎ 01/295-5990); **Spruce Lodge Equestrian Centre,** Kilternan, Co. Dublin (☎ 01/295-2109); and **Malahide Riding School,** Ivy Grangge, Malahide, Co. Dublin (☎ 01/846-3622).

WALKING   The walk from Bray to Greystones along the rocky promontory of **Bray Head** is a great excursion, with beautiful views back toward Killiney Bay, Dalkey Island, and Howth. Bray, the southern terminus of the DART line, is readily accessible from Dublin. Follow the beachside promenade south through town; at the outskirts of town the promenade turns left and up, beginning the ascent of Bray

Head. Shortly after the beginning of this ascent a trail branches to the left—this is the cliffside walk, which continues another 3 ¹/₂ miles along the coast to Greystones. From the center of Greystones there is a train that will take you back to Bray. This is an easy walk, about two hours one-way.

Dalkey Hill and **Killiney Hill** drop steeply into the sea, and command great views of Killiney Bay, Bray Head, and Sugarloaf Mountain. To get there, go south on Dalkey Avenue from the center of Dalkey (say, in front of the post office), a short distance from the Dalkey DART station. About .6 miles from the post office you'll pass a road ascending through fields on your left—this is the entrance to the Dalkey Hill Park. From the parking lot, climb a series of steps to the top of Dalkey Hill; from here you can see the expanse of the Bay, the Wicklow Hills in the distance, and the obelisk topping nearby Killiney Hill. If you continue on to the obelisk, there is a trail leading from there down on the seaward side to Vico Road, itself a lovely place for a seaside walk. It's about ¹/₂ mile from the parking lot to Killiney Hill.

WINDSURFING   Instruction and equipment rental are available at **The Surf Dock Centre,** Grand Canal Dock, Ringsend, Dublin 4 (☎ **01/6683945,** fax 01/ 6681215).

8 Spectator Sports

GAELIC SPORTS   If your schedule permits, don't miss attending one of Ireland's national games, **Gaelic football,** which vaguely resembles soccer but allows use of the hands in punching the ball, and **hurling,** a game in which 30 men wielding heavy sticks rush around thrashing at a hard leather ball called a *sliotar*. These two amateur sports are played every weekend throughout the summer at various local fields, culminating in September with the **All-Ireland Finals,** an Irish version of the Super Bowl. For schedules and admission charges, phone the **Gaelic Athletic Association,** Croke Park, Jones Road, Dublin 3 (☎ **01/836-3222**).

GREYHOUND RACING   Watching these lean and swift canines is one of the leading spectator sports in the Dublin area. Racing is held throughout the year at **Shelbourne Park Stadium,** Bridge Town Road, Dublin 4 (☎ **01/668-3502**), and **Harold's Cross Stadium,** 151 Harold's Cross Rd., Dublin 6 (☎ **01/497-1081**). For a complete schedule and details, contact **Bord na gCon** (The Greyhound Board), Shelbourne Park, Bridge Town Road, Dublin 4 (☎ **01/668-3502**).

HORSE RACING   Dublin's racing fans gather at **Leopardstown Race Course,** off the Stillorgan road (N11), Foxrock, Dublin 18 (☎ **01/289-3607**). Located 6 miles south of the city center, this is a modern facility with all-weather glass-enclosed spectator stands. Races are scheduled throughout the year, two or three times a month, on weekdays or weekends.

POLO   With the Dublin Mountains as a backdrop, polo is played from May to mid-September on the green fields of the Phoenix Park, on Dublin's west side. Matches take place on Wednesday evenings and on Saturday and Sunday afternoons. Any of these games can be attended free of charge. For full details, contact the **All Ireland Polo Club,** the Phoenix Park, Dublin 8 (☎ **01/677-6248**), or check the sports pages of the newspapers.

9 Shopping

Known the world over for its handmade products and fine craftsmanship, Ireland offers many unique shopping opportunities, and Dublin, as Ireland's commercial center, is a one-stop source for the country's best wares.

Grafton Street is Dublin's miniature answer to New York's Fifth Avenue, with a parade of fine boutiques, fashionable department stores, and specialty shops. Restricted to pedestrians, Grafton Street often attracts street performers and sidewalk artists, giving it a festive atmosphere. The smaller streets radiating out from Grafton—Duke, Dawson, Nassau, and Wicklow streets—are also lined with fine small book, handcraft, and souvenir shops.

Nearby is **Temple Bar,** the hub of Dublin's Left Bank artsy district and the setting for art and music shops, secondhand clothing stores, and a host of other increasingly fine and interesting boutiques.

On the north side of the Liffey, the **O'Connell Street** area is the main inner-city shopping nucleus, along with its nearby offshoots—Abbey Street for crafts, Moore Street for its open-air market, and Henry Street, a pedestrian-only strip of department stores and indoor malls.

In general, Dublin shops are open from 9 or 9:30am to 5:30 or 6pm, Monday through Saturday, with late hours on Thursday until 8pm. There are exceptions, however, particularly in the tourist season (May through September or October), when many shops also have Sunday hours, usually midmorning through 4pm or 5pm. Throughout the year, many bookshops are also open on Sundays.

Major department stores include **Arnotts,** 12 Henry St., Dublin 1, and 112 Grafton St., Dublin 2 (☎ **01/872-1111**); **Brown Thomas,** 15–20 Grafton St., Dublin 2 (☎ **01/679-5666**); **Clerys,** Lower O'Connell Street, Dublin 1 (☎ **01/878-6000**); and **Marks and Spencer,** 28 Grafton St., Dublin 2 (☎ **01/679-7855**) and 24 Mary St., Dublin 1 (☎ **01/872-8833**).

Dublin also has several clusters of shops in the format of **multistory malls** or ground-level arcades, ideal for indoor shopping on rainy days. These include the **ILAC Centre,** Henry Street, Dublin 1; **Royal Hibernian Way,** 49/50 Dawson St., Dublin 2; and **St. Stephen's Green Shopping Complex,** St. Stephen's Green, Dublin 2.

SHOPPING A TO Z
ART

Combridge Fine Arts
24 Suffolk St., Dublin 2. ☎ **01/677-4652.** DART to Pearse Station. Bus: 15A, 15B, 15C, 55, 83.

In business more than 100 years, this shop features works by modern Irish artists as well as quality reproductions of classic Irish art.

The Davis Gallery
11 Capel St., Dublin 1. ☎ **01/872-6969.** Bus: 34, 70, 80.

Located one block north of the Liffey, this shop offers a wide selection of Irish watercolors and oil paintings, with emphasis on Dublin scenes as well as wildlife and flora.

M. Kennedy and Sons Ltd.
12 Harcourt St., Dublin 2. ☎ **01/475-1749.** Bus: 62.

If you are looking for a souvenir reflecting Irish art, try this interesting shop, established more than 100 years ago. It's a treasure trove of books on Irish artists and works, and also stocks a lovely selection of fine-arts greeting and postal cards and bookmarks. There are all types of artists' supplies as well, and an excellent art gallery on the upstairs level.

BOOKS

✪ Eason and Son Ltd.

40–42 Lower O'Connell St., Dublin 1. ☎ **01/873-3811.** DART to Connolly Station. Bus: 25, 34, 37, 38A, 39A, 39B, 66A, 67A.

For more than a century, Eason's has been synonymous with books at this central location and at its many branches throughout Ireland. This branch offers a comprehensive selection of books and maps about Dublin and Ireland.

Fred Hanna Booksellers Ltd.

27–29 Nassau St., Dublin 2. ☎ **01/677-1255.** DART to Pearse Station. Bus: 5, 7A, 8, 62.

Located across from Trinity College, this is a fine, serious bookshop for academic texts, as well as new, used, and antiquarian volumes on all topics.

✪ Greenes Bookshop Ltd.

16 Clare St., Dublin 2. ☎ **01/676-2554.** DART to Pearse Station. Bus: 5, 7A, 8, 62.

Established in 1843 and close to Trinity College, this is one of Dublin's treasures for bibliophiles. It's chock full of new and secondhand books on every topic from religion to the modern novel.

✪ Hodges Figgis

56/58 Dawson St., Dublin 2. ☎ **01/677-4754.** DART to Pearse Station. Bus: 10, 11A, 11B, 13, 20B.

This three-story landmark store has great charm and browse appeal. Although all topics are covered, there are particularly good sections on Irish literature, Celtic studies, folklore, and maps of Ireland. A new addition is the Hodges Figgis Cafe on the first floor, seating 60 and serving wine and light meals.

Waterstone's

7 Dawson St., Dublin 2. ☎ **01/679-1415.** DART to Pearse Station. Bus: 10, 11A, 11B, 13, 20B.

Less than a block south of Trinity College, this literary emporium has extensive sections on Irish interests, as well as crime, gay literature, health, New Age, sport, women's studies, and wine.

CHINA & CRYSTAL

China Showrooms

32/33 Abbey St., Dublin 1. ☎ **01/878-6211.** DART to Connolly Station. Bus: 27B, 53A.

Established in 1939, this shop is a one-stop source for fine china such as Belleek, Aynsley, Royal Doulton, and Rosenthal; hand-cut crystal from Waterford, Tipperary, and Tyrone; and handmade Irish pottery.

✪ Dublin Crystal Glass Company

Brookfield Terrace, Carysfort Ave., Blackrock, Co. Dublin. ☎ **01/288-7932.** DART to Blackrock Station. Bus: 114.

This is Dublin's own distinctive hand-cut crystal business, founded in 1764 and revived in 1968. Visitors are welcome to browse in the factory shop and see the glass being made and engraved.

CRAFT COMPLEXES

✪ Design Yard

12 E. Essex St., Dublin 2. ☎ **01/677-8453.** DART to Tara St. Station. Bus: 21A, 46A, 46B, 51B, 51C, 68, 69, 86.

The first thing you'll notice about Design Yard is its own design: a Victorian warehouse gorgeously converted into a chic contemporary applied-arts center, whose commissioned set of four wrought-iron gates are abstracts of the city plans of Dublin, Madrid, New York, and Vienna. This is a nonprofit gallery for the finest contemporary Irish and European jewelry, furniture, ceramics, glass, lighting, and textiles. All exhibited pieces are for sale. Whether you see it as a shop or a museum, Design Yard is a sight worth seeking out. Open Monday through Saturday from 10:30am to 5:30pm.

✪ Powerscourt Townhouse Centre

59 S. William St., Dublin 2. ☎ **01/679-4144.** Bus: 10, 11A, 11B, 13, 16A, 19A, 20B, 22A, 55, 83.

Housed in a restored 1774 town house, this four-story complex consists of a central skylit courtyard and more than 60 boutiques, craft shops, art galleries, snackeries, wine bars, and restaurants. The wares include all kinds of crafts, antiques, paintings, prints, ceramics, leather work, jewelry, clothing, hand-dipped chocolates, and farmhouse cheeses.

Tower Design Centre

Pearse St. (off Grand Canal Quay), Dublin 2. ☎ **01/677-5655.** DART to Pearse Station. Bus: 2 or 3.

Located along the banks of the Grand Canal, this 1862 sugar refinery was beautifully restored in 1983 and developed into a nest of craft workshops. Watch the artisans at work and then purchase a special souvenir, from fine-art greeting cards and hand-marbled stationery to pewter, ceramics, pottery, knitwear, hand-painted silks, copper-plate etchings, all-wool wall hangings, silver and gold Celtic jewelry, and heraldic gifts. Full restaurant and limited free parking available.

FASHIONS FOR WOMEN

✪ Cleo

18 Kildare St., Dublin 2. ☎ **01/676-1421.** DART to Pearse Station. Bus: 10, 11A, 11B, 13, 20B.

For more than 50 years, the Joyce family has been creating designer ready-to-wear clothing in a rainbow of vibrant tweed colors—elegant ponchos, capes, peasant skirts, coat-sweaters, decorative crios belts, and brimmed hats.

Pat Crowley

3 Molesworth Place, Dublin 2. ☎ **01/661-5580.** DART to Pearse Station. Bus: 10, 11A, 11B, 13, 20B.

The emphasis is on individuality with this designer, known for her exclusive line of tweeds and couture evening wear.

Sybil Connolly

71 Merrion Sq., Dublin 2. ☎ **01/676-7281.** DART to Pearse Station. Bus: 5, 7A, 8.

Irish high fashion is synonymous with this world-renowned made-to-measure designer. Evening wear and Irish linen creations are a specialty.

FASHIONS FOR MEN

F.X. Kelly

48 Grafton St., Dublin 2. ☎ **01/777-8211.** DART to Pearse Station. Bus: 10, 11A, 11B, 13, 20B.

A long-established men's ready-to-wear shop, this place blends old-fashioned charm with modern design. It offers a handsome selection of styles, with emphasis on conventional clothing as well as items like creased linen suits, painted ties, and designer sportswear.

◑ **Kevin and Howlin**

31 Nassau St., Dublin 2. ☎ **01/677-0257.** DART to Pearse Station. Bus: 5, 7A, 8, 15A, 15B, 46, 55, 62, 63, 83, 84.

Located opposite Trinity College, this shop has specialized in men's tweed garments for more than 50 years. The selection includes Donegal tweed suits, overcoats, and jackets. In addition, there is a wide selection of scarves, vests, Patch caps, and Gatsby, Sherlock Holmes, and Paddy hats.

○ **Louis Copeland and Sons**

39–41 Capel St., Dublin 1. ☎ **01/872-1600.** Bus: 34, 70, 80.

With a distinctive old-world shopfront, this store stands out on the north side of the River Liffey. It is known for high quality work in made-to-measure and ready-to-wear men's suits, coats, and shirts. Other branches are located at 30 Pembroke St., Dublin 2 (☎ **01/661-0110**) and at 18 Wicklow St., Dublin 2 (☎ **01/677-7038**).

GIFTS & KNICKKNACKS

Fergus O'Farrell Workshop

62 Dawson St., Dublin 2. ☎ **01/454-2624.** DART to Pearse Station. Bus: 10, 11A, 11B, 13, 20B.

Irish design from the 5th to 15th centuries has been the inspiration for much of the craft work at this unique shop. These conversation-piece souvenirs range from Book of Kells art and bog-oak figurines to hand-carved fish boards and beaten copper wall hangings, as well as Irish road signs, handmade dolls and animals, and more.

House of Ireland

37–38 Nassau St., Dublin 2. ☎ **01/671-4543.** DART to Pearse Station. Bus: 5, 7A, 15A, 15B, 46, 55, 62, 63, 83, 84.

Located opposite Trinity College, this shop is a happy blend of European and Irish products, from Waterford and Belleek to Wedgwood and Lladro, as well as tweeds, linens, knitwear, Celtic jewelry, mohair capes, shawls, kilts, blankets, and dolls.

○ The Irish Times Collection

10–16 D'Olier St., Dublin 2. ☎ **01/671-8446.** DART to Tara St. Station. Bus: 14A or 54A.

The general services department of *The Irish Times* operates this shop, which features Irish-made crafts, many of which are commissioned by the newspaper for special offers to its readers. Items include jewelry and watches; bog oak; silver, pewter, and bronze sculptures; and books on Ireland and Dublin written exclusively for the *Times.*

The Kilkenny Shop

6–10 Nassau St., Dublin 2. ☎ **01/677-7066.** DART to Pearse Station. Bus: 5, 7A, 15A, 15B, 46, 55, 62, 63, 83, 84.

A sister operation of the Blarney Woollen Mills, this modern multilevel shop is a showplace for original Irish designs and quality products including pottery, glass, candles, woollens, pipes, knitwear, jewelry, books, and prints. There is a pleasant cafe on the premises, ideal for coffee and pastries or a light lunch.

Weir and Sons

96–99 Grafton St., Dublin 2. ☎ **01/677-9678.** DART to Pearse Station. Bus: 10, 11A, 11B, 13, 20B.

Established in 1869, this is the granddaddy of Dublin's fine jewelry shops, selling new and antique jewelry as well as silver, china, and glass items. A second branch is at the Ilac Centre, Henry Street (☎ **01/872-9588**).

HERALDRY

Heraldic Artists

3 Nassau St., Dublin 2. ☎ **01/679-7020.** Fax 01/679-4717. DART to Pearse Station. Bus: 5, 7A, 8, 15A, 15B, 46, 55, 62, 63, 83, 84.

For more than 20 years, this shop has been known for helping visitors locate their family roots. In addition to tracing surnames, it also sells all of the usual heraldic items, from family crest parchments, scrolls, and mahogany wall plaques to books on researching ancestry.

House of Names

26 Nassau St., Dublin 2. ☎ **01/679-7287.** DART to Pearse Station. Bus: 5, 7A, 8, 15A, 15B, 46, 55, 62, 63, 83, 84.

As its name implies, this company offers a wide selection of Irish, British, and European family names affixed along with their attendant crests and mottoes to plaques, shields, parchments, jewelry, glassware, and sweaters.

KNITWEAR

Blarney Woollen Mills

21–23 Nassau St., Dublin 2. ☎ **01/671-0068.** DART to Pearse Station. Bus: 5, 7A, 8, 15A, 15B, 46, 55, 62, 63, 83, 84.

A branch of the highly successful Cork-based enterprise of the same name, this shop is ideally located opposite the south side of Trinity College. Known for its competitive prices, it stocks a wide range of woollen knitwear made at the home base in Blarney, as well as crystal, china, pottery, and souvenirs.

Dublin Woollen Mills

41–42 Lower Ormond Quay, Dublin 1. ☎ **01/677-0301.** Bus: 70 or 80.

Situated on the north side of the River Liffey next to the Halfpenny Bridge, since 1888 this shop has been a leading source of Aran hand-knit sweaters, vests, hats, jackets, and scarves, as well as lambswool sweaters, kilts, ponchos, and tweeds at competitive prices.

✪ Monaghan's

15/17 Grafton Arcade, Grafton St., Dublin 2. ☎ **01/677-0823.** DART to Pearse Station. Bus: 10, 11A, 11B, 13, 20B.

Established in 1960 and operated by two generations of the Monaghan family, this store is a prime source of cashmere sweaters for men and women, with the best selection of colors, sizes, and styles anywhere in Ireland. Other items stocked include traditional Aran knits, lambswool, crochet, and Shetland wool products. Also located at 4/5 Royal Hibernian Way, off Dawson Street (☎ **01/679-4451**).

MARKETS

Moore Street Market

Moore St., Dublin 1. No phone. DART to Connolly Station. Bus: 25, 34, 37, 38A, 66A, 67A.

For a flashback of what life was like for fishmonger Molly Malone, don't miss this Dublin enclave, full of streetside barrow vendors plus plenty of local color and chatter. It's the principal open-air fruit, flower, fish, and vegetable market of the city.

✪ Mother Red Caps Market

Back Lane (off High St.), Dublin 8. ☎ **01/854-4655.** Bus: 21A, 78A, 78B.

Located in the heart of Old Dublin, this enclosed market is one of Dublin's best. The various stalls offer everything: antiques, used books and coins, silver, handcrafts,

Impressions

Dublin is a state of mind as much as a city.

—Tom McDonagh (b. 1934), *My Green Age*

leather products, knitwear, music tapes, furniture, and even a fortune teller! It's worth a trip here just to sample the wares at the Ryefield Foods stall (farm-made cheeses, baked goods, marmalades, and jams).

SHEEPSKINS & LEATHERS

Sheepskin Shops
20 Wicklow St., Dublin 2. ☎ **01/671-9585.** DART to Pearse Station. Bus: 5, 7A, 8, 15A, 46, 55, 62, 63, 83, 84.

As its name indicates, this is a good place to find sheepskin jackets, hats, and moccasins, as well as suede coats and lambskin wear.

UMBRELLAS & WALKING STICKS

H. Johnston
11 Wicklow St., Dublin 2. ☎ **01/677-1249.** DART to Pearse Station. Bus: 5, 7A, 8, 15A, 46, 55, 62, 63, 83, 84.

Just in case it rains, which it will, this centrally located shop is a good source for durable umbrellas. And if you're looking for an Irish blackthorn stick, otherwise known as a shillelagh, this spot has been specializing in them for more than 110 years. Hang one on your wall and tell the grandkids you used to chase around the old country with it.

10 Dublin After Dark

As a matter of fact, in high season Dublin's nightlife takes place mostly in daylight. Situated roughly 53° north of the equator, Dublin is becoming really dark in June only as the pubs are closing. Night, then, is really as much a state of mind as anything else.

One general fact to keep in mind concerning Dublin's night life is that there are very few fixed points. Apart from a handful of established institutions, venues come and go, change character, open their doors to ballet one night and cabaret the next. *In Dublin* provides the most thorough and up-to-date listings of what's on and can be found on most every magazine stand; along with a detailed street map to the city, this handy-dandy biweekly should be a first purchase on entry. If that's not soon enough, it's online at **http://www.indublin.ie/**.

THE PUB SCENE

The mainstay of Dublin social life, both by night and by day, is unquestionably the pub. More than 1,000 specimens are spread throughout the city; there are pubs on every street, at every turn. In *Ulysses,* James Joyce referred to the puzzle of trying to cross Dublin without passing by a pub; his characters quickly abandoned the quest as fruitless, preferring instead to sample a few pubs in their path. Needless to say, most visitors should follow in their footsteps and drop in on a few pubs.

You will need no assistance finding a pub in Dublin, but here are a few suggestions for finding some of the city's most distinctive.

PUBS FOR CONVERSATION & ATMOSPHERE

✪ Brazen Head
20 Lower Bridge St., Dublin 8. ☎ **01/679-5186.**

This brass-filled and lantern-lit pub claims to be the city's oldest, and it might very well be, considering that it was licensed in 1661 and occupies the site of an even earlier tavern dating from 1198. Nestled on the south bank of the River Liffey, it is at the end of a cobblestone courtyard and was once the meeting place of Irish freedom fighters such as Robert Emmet and Wolfe Tone. A full à la carte menu is now offered.

Davy Byrnes
21 Duke St., Dublin 2. ☎ **01/677-5217.**

Referred to as a "moral pub" by James Joyce in *Ulysses,* this imbibers' landmark has drawn poets, writers, and lovers of literature ever since. Located just off Grafton Street, it dates from 1873, when Davy Byrnes first opened the doors. He presided here for more than 50 years and visitors today can still see his likeness on one of the turn-of-the-century murals hanging over the bar.

Doheny and Nesbitt
5 Lower Baggot St., Dublin 2. ☎ **01/676-2945.**

The locals call this Victorian-style pub simply "Nesbitt's." The place houses two fine old snugs, small rooms with trap doors where women were served a drink in days of old.

Flannery's
48 Temple Bar, Dublin 2. ☎ **01/677-3807.**

Nestled in the heart of the Temple Bar district on the corner of Temple Lane, this small three-room pub was established in 1840. The decor is a homey mix of crackling fireplaces, globe ceiling lights, old pictures on the walls, and shelves filled with local memorabilia.

✪ Keating's Bar and Restaurant
14 Mary St., Dublin 1. ☎ **01/873-1567.**

Situated north of the Liffey at the corner of Jervis Street, this bilevel pub is known for its old-world decor, with its marble-top bar and spiral staircase leading to its upstairs loft, and its pub food is excellent. The only drawback to the place is that it's in an area where you might want to be a little extra alert.

The Long Hall
51 S. Great George's St., Dublin 2. ☎ **01/475-1590.**

Tucked into a busy commercial street, this is one of the city's most photographed pubs, with a beautiful Victorian decor of filigree-edged mirrors, polished dark woods, and traditional snugs. The hand-carved bar is said to be the longest counter in the city.

Neary's
1 Chatham St., Dublin 2. ☎ **01/677-8596.**

Adjacent to the back door of the Gaiety Theatre, this celebrated enclave is a favorite with stage folk and theatergoers. Trademarks here are the pink-and-gray marble bar and the brass hands that support the globe lanterns adorning the entrance.

Palace Bar
21 Fleet St., Dublin 2. ☎ **01/677-9290.**

This old charmer is decorated with local memorabilia, cartoons, and paintings that tell the story of Dublin through the years.

✪ Stag's Head

1 Dame Court, off Dame St. (look for the stag sign inlaid into the sidewalk), Dublin 2. ☎ **01/ 679-3701.**

Mounted stags' heads and eight stag-theme stained glass windows dominate the decor, and there are also wrought iron chandeliers, polished Aberdeen granite, old barrels, skylights, and ceiling-high mirrors. This place is a classic.

✪ W. Ryan

28 Parkgate St., Dublin 7. ☎ **01/677-6097.**

Three generations of the Ryan family have contributed to the success of this public house, located on the north side of the Liffey near the Phoenix Park. Some of Dublin's best traditional pub features are a part of the scene here, including a metal ceiling, a domed skylight, beveled mirrors, etched glass, brass lamp holders, a mahogany bar, and four old-style snugs.

PUBS WITH TRADITIONAL & FOLK MUSIC

✪ Kitty O'Shea's

23–25 Upper Grand Canal St., Dublin 4. ☎ **01/660-9965.** No cover.

Situated just south of the Grand Canal, this popular pub is named after the sweetheart of 19th-century Irish statesman Charles Stewart Parnell. The decor reflects the Parnell era, with ornate oak paneling, stained-glass windows, old political posters, cozy alcoves, and brass railings. Traditional Irish music is on tap every night.

Mother Redcaps Tavern

Back Lane, Dublin 8. ☎ **01/453-8306.** No cover except for concerts £5–£6 ($8–$9.60).

A former shoe factory wedged in the heart of the Liberties section of the city, this large two-story pub exudes an Old Dublin atmosphere, with eclectic mahogany and stripped pine furnishings, antiques and curios on the shelves, and walls lined with old paintings and newspaper clippings dating from the 19th century. On Sundays, there is usually a midday session of traditional Irish music, with everyone invited to bring an instrument and join in. On many nights, there is also traditional music on an informal basis or in a concert setting upstairs.

O'Donoghue's

15 Merrion Row, Dublin 2. ☎ **01/661-4303.** No cover for music.

Tucked between St. Stephen's Green and Merrion Street, this smoke-filled enclave is widely heralded as the granddaddy of traditional music pubs. A spontaneous session is likely to erupt at almost any time of the day or night.

Oliver St. John Gogarty

57/58 Fleet St., Dublin 2. ☎ **01/671-1822.** No cover for music.

Situated in the heart of Temple Bar and named for one of Ireland's literary greats, this pub has an inviting old-world atmosphere, with shelves of empty bottles, stacks of dusty books, a horseshoe-shaped bar, and old barrels for seats. There are traditional music sessions on Saturday from 3:30 to 7pm, Sunday from 12:30 to 3pm, and every night from 9 to 11pm.

Sean O'Casey

105 Marlborough St., Dublin 1. ☎ **01/874-8675.** £1 ($1.50) music charge.

Located a block from the Abbey Theatre and named for one of Ireland's great playwrights, this Tudor-style pub is appropriately decorated with playbills and posters. There is traditional music or Irish ballads on most nights from 9pm on.

LATE-NIGHT PUBS

If you're going strong when the pubs shut down (11pm in winter and 11:30pm in summer), you may want to crawl to a "late night pub"—a pub with a loophole allowing it to remain open after hours. Late-nighters for the 18 to 25 set include **Hogans,** 35 So. Great George's St., Dublin 2 (☎ 01/677-5904), and **The Mean Fiddler** (see below). After-hours pubs that host the young and hip but are still congenial for those over 25 include **Whelans,** 25 Wexford St., Dublin 2 (☎ 01/478-0766), and **Bleeding Horse,** 24–25 Camden St., Dublin 2 (☎ 01/475-2705). For the over-30 late crowd, these will fill the bill and the glass: **Break for the Border,** Lower Steven's St., Dublin 2 (☎ 01/478-0300); **Bad Bob's Backstage Bar,** East Essex Street, Dublin 2 (☎ 01/677-5482); **Major Tom's,** So. King Street, Dublin 2 (☎ 01/478-3266); and **Sinnotts,** So. King Street, Dublin 2 (☎ 01/478-4698).

THE CLUB & MUSIC SCENE

The club and music scene in Dublin is confoundingly complex and changeable. Jazz, blues, folk, country, traditional, rock, comedy and so on move from venue to venue, night by night. The same club may be a gay fetish scene one night and a traditional music hot spot the next, so you have to stay on your toes to find what you want. The first rule is to get the very latest listings and see what's on and where. Keeping all this in mind, a few low-risk generalizations might prove helpful to give you a sense of what to expect.

One fact unlikely to change is that the night scene in Dublin is definitively young, with a retirement age of about 25. The only exception is some hotel venues that are either outside the city center or very costly, or both. If you're over 25, your club choices are limited, unless you happen to be a recognizable celebrity. In fact, even if you are or can pass for under 25, you may find yourself excluded unless you can present just the right image—a composite of outfit, hair, attitude, and natural endowment. Many of the most sizzling spots in Dublin (we'll call them *trendy* from here on) have a "strict" or "unfriendly" door policy, admitting only those who look and feel right for the scene within. The sought-after "look" might be unkindly described as "geek-chic" or, more neutrally, "retro." An advance outing to **Sé Sí** (pronounced *shay shee*), 11 Upper Fownes St., Dublin 2 (☎ 01/677-4779), for a consultation and a costume should enhance your odds for admission.

Most trendy clubs have DJs and live music, and the genre of current choice is something called "rave," which I won't try to put into words. Another occasional ingredient of the trendy club scene in Dublin is "E" or "Ecstasy," the drug of choice among even the youngest club-goers. Clubbers on "E" don't drink anything but water, which they must consume in great quantities. Though it may seem commonplace in this milieu, Ecstasy is both illegal and potentially lethal, and definitely not a wise vacation experience.

Cover charges tend to fluctuate not only from place to place but from night to night and from person to person (some people can't buy their way in, while others glide in gratis). Average cover charges range from nominal to £8 ($12.80)

HIPPER THAN THOU

If you think you might pass muster, the most established cutting-edge clubs (with reputedly strict door policies) are the following:

The Kitchen

6/8 Wellington Quay, Dublin 2. ☎ 01/677-6178. Wed–Sun 11pm–2am.

Housed in the basement of the Clarence Hotel in the heart of the Temple Bar district, this is one of Dublin's hottest, hippest nightclubs, partly owned by the rock group U2.

Lillie's Bordello

45 Nassau St., Dublin 2. ☎ **01/679-9204.** Daily 10pm–1pm or later.

A private three-story nightclub with two bars open to members and nonmembers seven nights a week. The place has a stylish and self-consciously decadent ambience, with a mix of music seven days a week.

POD

Harcourt St., Dublin 2. ☎ **01/478-0166.** Wed–Sun 11pm–3am or later.

POD, by the way, stands for "Place of Dance." Operated by John Reynolds (nephew of the former prime minister of Ireland, Albert Reynolds) the POD, a "European nightclub of the year," has also won a European design award for its colorful Barcelona-inspired decor and is as loud as it is dazzling to behold.

Rí-Rá

1 Exchequer St., Dublin 2. ☎ **01/677-4835.** Nightly 11:30pm–4am or later. Cover £4–£5 ($6–$7.50).

Though trendy, Rí-Rá has a more friendly door policy than most of its competition, so this may be the place to try first.

System

21 South Anne St., Dublin 2. ☎ **01/677-4402.** Most nights 11pm–3am or later.

If you can crash this door, you're in the scene, on the pulse, and soon to be deaf.

KINDER & GENTLER CLUBS

Another set of established clubs, while they attract young singles and couples, have friendly door policies and are places where people of most any age and ilk are likely to feel comfortable. These include:

Annabel's

Burlington Hotel, Leeson St. Upper, Dublin 4. ☎ **01/660-5222.** Tues–Sat 10pm–2am. Cover £7 ($11.20).

Located in the Burlington Hotel just south of the Lower Leeson Street nightclub strip, this club is one of the longest lasting in town. It welcomes a mix of tourists and locals of all ages to a disco party atmosphere.

Club M

Anglesea St., Dublin 2. ☎ **01/671-5622.** Tues–Sun 10pm–2am. Cover £4–£8 ($6.40–$12.80).

Housed in the basement of Blooms Hotel in the trendy Temple Bar district and close to Trinity College, this club boasts Ireland's largest laser lighting system and offers either DJ-driven dance or live music, for the over-23 age bracket.

YET MORE CLUBS

Other comparable clubs in the city center are **Buck Whaley's,** Leeson Street Lower, Dublin 2 (☎ **01/676-1755**); **Court,** Harcourt Hotel, Harcourt Street, Dublin 2 (☎ **01/478-3677**); and **Rumours,** Gresham Hotel, O'Connell Street, Dublin 1 (☎ **01/874-1635**).

For live music, there are several top choices. On a given night, you can find most anything one place or another—jazz, blues, rock, traditional Irish, country, or folk. Rock was dominant in the '80s when Dublin spawned new bands weekly, each aspiring to be the next U2, but it is no longer in the front seat. Instead, there's a real mix, so again, check the listings. The principal ongoing live music venues include **Whelans,** 25 Wexford St., Dublin 2 (☎ **01/478-0766**); **Eamon Doran's** (mostly an under-25 crowd), 3A Crown Alley, Temple Bar, Dublin 2 (☎ **01/679-9114**);the **Mean Fiddler,** 26 Wexford St., Dublin 2 (☎ **01/475-8555**); and a real favorite, **"Midnight at the Olympia,"** 74 Dame St., Dublin 2 (☎ **01/677-7744**).

COMEDY CLUBS

The Irish comedy circuit is relatively new and quite popular. The timing, wit, and twist of mind required for comedy seems to me so native to the Irish that I find it difficult to draw a sharp line between those who practice comedy as a living and those who practice it as a way of life. You'll find both in the flourishing Dublin comedy clubs. Here are some of our favorites.

Comedy Improv / Comedy Cellar

International Bar, 23 Wicklow St., Dublin 2. ☎ **01/677-9250.** Comedy Improv, Mondays 9–11pm; Comedy Cellar, Wednesdays 9–11pm. Admission £3.50 ($5.60).

A very small, packed venue, full of enthusiastic exchange.

Corduroy Comedy Club

Attic / White Horse Inn, 1 George's Quay, Dublin 2. ☎ **01/679-3068.** Thursdays 8pm. £4 ($6.40).

A foal in the comedy circuit, only a couple of months old at this writing and not yet on its feet.

Stirfry

City Arts Centre, 23 Moss St. at City Quay, Dublin 2. ☎ **01/677-0643.** Fridays from 11:30pm. £5 ($8).

Stirfry is the current prime-time king of the Irish comedy circuit, attracting the most popular stand-ups on the Irish scene—the O'Seinfelds, as it were. Each Stirfry menu includes the comic du jour, a singer, and a performance artist.

DINNER SHOWS & TRADITIONAL IRISH ENTERTAINMENT

Most of these shows are aimed at tourists, although they are attended and enjoyed by locals as well.

✪ Abbey Tavern

Abbey Rd., Howth, Co. Dublin. ☎ **01/839-0307.** Box office, Mon–Sat 9am–5pm; dinner/show daily Mar–Oct and Mon–Sat Nov–Feb; dinner 7pm, show 9pm. Tickets for dinner/entertainment £23–£28 ($36.80–$44.80); entertainment only £3 ($4.80).

A complete four-course meal, accompanied by Irish ballad music, with its blend of fiddles, pipes, tin whistles, and "bones," is on tap at this authentic old-world tavern.

The Castle Inn

5–7 Lord Edward St., Dublin 8. ☎ **01/475-1122.** May–Sept, pre-show dinner 7:30pm, show at 8:45pm. Tickets for show only, £7 ($11.20); show with Irish stew, £12 ($19.20); show with four-course dinner £21 ($33.60).

Situated between Dublin Castle and Christ Church Cathedral, this recently rejuvenated bilevel pub exudes an "old city" atmosphere, with stone walls, flagstone steps, knightly suits of armor, big stone fireplaces, beamed ceilings, and lots of early Dublin memorabilia. It is also the setting for an Irish Ceili and Banquet featuring Irish traditional musicians and set dancers.

✪ Culturlann Na hEireann

32 Belgrave Sq., Monkstown, Co. Dublin. ☎ **01/280-0295.** Year-round ceili dances, Fri 9:30pm–12:30am; informal music sessions, Fri–Sat 9:30–11:30pm; June–Sept, traditional

music stage show, Sat–Thurs 9–10:30pm. Tickets for Ceilis, £4 ($6.40); informal music sessions, £1.50 ($2.40); stage shows, £5 ($8).

This is the home of Comhaltas Ceoltoiri Eireann, an Irish cultural organization that has been the prime mover in encouraging a renewed appreciation of and interest in Irish traditional music. The year-round entertainment programs include old-fashioned ceili dances on Fridays and informal music sessions on Fridays and Saturdays. In the summer months, an authentic fully costumed show featuring traditional music, song, and dance is staged. No reservations are necessary for any of the events.

Doyle's Irish Cabaret

Upper Leeson St., Dublin 4. ☎ **01/660-5222**, ext. 1162. May–Oct, Mon–Sat dinner 7pm, show 8pm. Tickets for dinner/show £30.90 ($49.45); show with two drinks £19.50 ($31.10).

Staged in the ballroom of the Hotel Burlington, this colorful dinner/show features some of Ireland's top performers in a program of Irish music, dancing, ballad singing, and storytelling.

✪ Jury's Irish Cabaret

Pembroke Rd., Ballsbridge, Dublin 4. ☎ **01/660-5000.** May–Oct, Tues–Sun dinner 7:15pm, show 8pm. Tickets for dinner/show £33.90 ($54.25); show with two drinks £22 ($35.20). AE, DC, MC, V.

As Ireland's longest-running show (more than 30 years), this production offers a unique mix of traditional Irish and international music, rousing ballads and Broadway classics, toe-tapping set dancing and graceful ballet, humorous monologues and telling recitations, plus audience participation. Free parking.

THE GAY & LESBIAN SCENE

New gay and lesbian bars, clubs, and venues appear monthly, it seems, and many clubs and organizations, such as the Irish Film Centre, have special gay events or evenings once a week to once a month, so it's best to check the *Gay Community News* and *In Dublin* for the latest listings. (See "For Gay & Lesbian Travelers" in Chapter 3 for details on where to pick up these publications.) Cover charges range from £2 to £8 ($3.20 to $12.80) depending on the club or venue, with discounts for students and seniors. The social scene ranges from quiet pub conversation and dancing to fetish nights and hilarious contests. Folks on the help lines through **LOT (Lesbians Organizing Together;** ☎ **01/872-7770)** and **Gay Switchboard Dublin** (☎ 01/872–1055) are also extremely helpful in directing you to activities of particular interest. (See page 63 for their hours of operation.) All that said, here are some well established and new bars and clubs I can suggest:

Club Curve

78 Lower Camden St. / Pleasants St., Dublin 2. No phone. £2 ($3.20) cover. Saturdays 8–12pm. Bus: 26.

On the corner, upstairs over Devitts Pub (☎ 01/475-3414), is a casual new Saturday night club for women only. Women of all ages meet to lift a glass and mingle with couples and friends.

The George Bar and Bistro

South Great George's St., Dublin 2. ☎ **01/478–2983.** DART to Tara St. Station Bus: 22A.

The George was the first gay bar established in Dublin and now houses two bars—one quiet and the other trendy, with dance music nightly—and an after-hours nightclub called The Block upstairs, with full bar from 11pm to 2:30am, Wednesday to Saturday, with a cover charge of £3 ($4.80) before 11pm and £5 ($8) after. It is a comfortable mixed-age venue with something for everyone.

Out on the Liffey

27 Upper Ormond Quay, Dublin 1. ☎ **01/872–2480.** DART to Tara St. Station and walk up the Liffey; cross at Parliament Bridge. Bus: 34, 70, 80.

A 1996 addition to the gay and lesbian scene, this relaxed and friendly pub caters to a balance of men and women and serves up pub food with good conversation until closing time at 11:30pm.

Stonewallz

The Barracks, Griffith College, South Circular Rd., Dublin 8. £3 ($4.80) cover. Saturdays 9pm–2am . Bus: 19, 22.

Music from the '60s to the '90s keeps feet moving at this women-only late-night venue. Pool tables are available, plus a video screen for when your feet get tired.

THE PERFORMING ARTS
THEATER

Dublin has a venerable and vital theatrical tradition, in which imagination and talent have always outstripped funding. Production budgets and ticket prices are modest, even miniscule, compared with those in New York or any major U.S. city, but apart from a few theaters offering a more or less uninterrupted flow of productions, most theaters mount shows only as they find the funds and opportunity to do so. That said, there are a few venerable (or at least well-established) theaters offering serious drama that we can pretty much count on to be around when we need them.

✪ Abbey Theatre

Lower Abbey St., Dublin 1. ☎ **01/878-7222.** Box office, Mon–Sat 10:30am–7pm; shows Mon–Sat 8pm. Tickets £8–£14 ($12.80–$22.40) with Mon–Thurs reductions for students.

For more than 90 years, the Abbey has been the national theater of Ireland. The original theater, destroyed by fire in 1951, was replaced in 1966 by the current quite functional though uninspired 600-seat house. The Abbey's artistic reputation within Ireland has risen and fallen many times and is at present reasonably strong.

Andrews Lane Theatre

12/16 Andrews Lane, Dublin 2. ☎ **01/679-5720.** Box office, Mon–Sat 10:30am–7pm; shows, Mon–Sat 8pm in theater and 8:15pm in studio. Tickets £6–£12 ($9.60–$19.20).

This relatively new venue has an ascending reputation for fine theater. It consists of a 220-seat main theater wherein is presented contemporary work from home and abroad, and a 76-seat studio geared for experimental productions.

The Gate

1 Cavendish Row, Dublin 1. ☎ **01/874-4368.** Box office, Mon–Sat 10am–7pm; shows, Mon–Sat 8pm. Tickets £10–£12 ($16–$19.20).

Situated just north of O'Connell Street off Parnell Square, this recently restored 370-seat theater was founded in 1928 by Hilton Edwards and Michael MacLiammoir to provide a showing for a broad range of plays. This policy prevails today, with a program that includes a blend of modern works and the classics. Although less well known by visitors, the Gate is easily as distinguished as the Abbey.

Peacock

Lower Abbey St., Dublin 1. ☎ **01/878-7222.** Box office, Mon–Sat 10:30am–7pm; shows, Mon–Sat at 8pm. Tickets £8–£10 ($12.80–$16).

In the same building as the Abbey, this small, 150-seat theater features contemporary plays and experimental works, including poetry readings and one-person shows, as well as plays in the Irish language.

Other theatrical venues presenting fewer though on occasion quite impressive productions, as well as music and dance performances, include the **City Arts Centre,** 23 Moss St. at City Quay, Dublin 2 (☎ **01/677-0643**); the **Focus Theatre,** 6 Pembroke Place, off Pembroke Street, Dublin 2 (☎ **01/676-3071**); the **Gaiety Theatre,** S. King Street, Dublin 2 (☎ **01/677-1717**); the **Olympia,** 72 Dame St., Dublin 2 ☎ **01/677-7744**); the **Players,** Trinity College, Dublin 2 (☎ **01/677-3370,** ext. 1239); and the **Tivoli,** Francis Street, opposite Iveagh Market, Dublin 8 (☎ **01/544-4472**). **The Project Arts Centre,** 39 E. Essex St., Temple Bar, one of Dublin's most inventive and distinguished venues, is currently planning a major renovation that may close their doors for up to two years.

CONCERTS

Music and dance concerts are likely to occur in a range of Dublin venues—theaters, churches, clubs, museums, sports stadiums, castles, parks, and universities—all of which can be found in the local listings. The three institutions listed below, however, stand out as venues where most world-class performances take place. Advance bookings for most large concerts may be made through **HMV,** Henry Street, Dublin 1 (☎ **01/873-2899**) and 65 Grafton St., Dublin 2 (☎ **01/679-5344**), or at one of the many **Golden Discs** outlets (☎ **01/677-1025**).

National Concert Hall

Earlsfort Terrace, Dublin 2. ☎ **01/671-1533.** Box office, Mon–Sat 11am–7pm and Sun (if concert scheduled) from 7pm. Performances at lunchtime (1:05pm) and 8pm. Tickets £3–£20 ($4.80–$32). All major credit cards accepted.

This magnificent 1,200-seat hall is home to the National Symphony Orchestra and Concert Orchestra and host to an array of international orchestras and performing artists. In addition to classical music, there are evenings of Gilbert and Sullivan, opera, jazz, and recitals. Recently, the foyer and Carolan room have been completely renovated. Parking on street.

The Point Depot

East Link Bridge, North Wall Quay, Dublin 1. ☎ **01/836-3633.** Box office, Mon–Sat 10am–6pm; matinees at 2:30pm and evening shows at 8pm. Tickets £10–£50 ($16–$80).

With a seating capacity of 3,000, this is Ireland's newest large theater and concert venue, attracting top Broadway-caliber shows and international stars.

Royal Dublin Society (RDS)

Merrion Rd., Ballsbridge, Dublin 2. ☎ **01/668-0645.** Box office hours vary according to events; shows at 8pm. Tickets £10–£30 ($16–$48).

Although best known as the venue for the Dublin Horse Show, this huge show-jumping arena is also the setting for major music concerts, with seating/standing room for over 6,000 people.

11 Side Trips from Dublin

Fanning out a little over 12 miles in each direction, Dublin's southern and northern suburbs offer a variety of interesting sights and experiences, all easy to reach via public transportation or rental car.

DUBLIN'S SOUTHERN SUBURBS

Stretching southward from Ballsbridge, Dublin's prime southern suburbs, such as Dun Laoghaire, Dalkey, and Killiney, are on the edge of Dublin Bay. They offer lovely seaside views and walks. There is also a long promenade and a bucolic park at Dun Laoghaire.

Thanks to DART service, these towns are very accessible from downtown Dublin. They are mostly residential areas, so there is a good selection of restaurants, and there are fine places to stay. A hillside overlooking Dublin Bay outside the village of Killiney is the setting for the Dublin area's only authentic deluxe castle hotel, Fitzpatrick Castle (see "Accommodations," below).

For visitors to Ireland who travel by ferry from Holyhead, Wales, the first glimpse of Ireland they see is the port of Dun Laoghaire. Many people decide to stay and base themselves here, commuting into downtown Dublin each day. As a base it is less expensive than Dalkey, but less attractive, too.

ATTRACTIONS

The Joyce Tower

Sandycove, Co. Dublin ☎ **01/280-9265.** Admission £2 ($3.20) adults, £1.60 ($2.55) seniors, students, and children, £6 ($9.60) family. Apr–Oct Mon–Sat 10am–1pm and 2–5pm, Sun 2–6pm. DART to Sandycove Station. Bus: 8.

Sitting on the edge of Dublin Bay about 6 miles south of the city center, this 40-foot granite monument is one of a series of martello towers built in 1804 to withstand a threatened invasion by Napoleon. The tower's great claim to fame is that it was inhabited in 1904 by James Joyce, as the guest of Oliver Gogarty, who had rented the tower from the Army for an annual fee of £8. Joyce, in turn, made the tower the setting for the first chapter of *Ulysses,* and it has been known as Joyce's Tower ever since. Its collection of Joycean memorabilia includes letters, documents, first and rare editions, personal possessions, and photographs.

The Ferryman

Coliemore Rd. (at stone wharf, adjacent to Dalkey Island Hotel). ☎ **01/298-2834.** Island ferry round-trip £3 ($4.80) adults, £2 ($3.20) children; rowboat rental £5 ($8)/hr. Jun–Aug, weather permitting.

Young Aidan Fennel heads the third generation of Fennels to ferry visitors to nearby Dalkey Island, whose only current inhabitants are a small herd of wild Irish goats and the occasional seal. Aidan is a boatbuilder and his brightly painted fleet are mostly from his hand. The island, settled about 6000 B.C., offers three modest ruins: a church over 1,000 years old, ramparts dating from the 15th century, and a martello tower constructed in 1804 to make Napolean think twice. Now the island is little more than a lovely picnic spot. And if you want to build up an appetite and delight your children or sweetheart, row out there under your own power in one of Aidan's handmades.

ACCOMMODATIONS

Expensive

✪ Fitzpatrick's Castle

Killiney Hill Rd., Killiney, Co. Dublin. ☎ **01/284-0700.** Fax 01/285-0207. 88 rms. TV TEL. £95–£160.60 ($152–$256.95) double. Includes full Irish breakfast and service charge. AE, CB, DC, MC, V. DART to Dalkey Station. Bus: 59.

With a fanciful Victorian facade of turrets, towers, and battlements, this restored 1741 gem is an ideal choice for those who want to live like royalty. A 15-minute drive from the center of the city, it is situated between the villages of Dalkey and Killiney, on nine acres of gardens and hilltop grounds with romantic vistas of Dublin Bay. Two generations of the Fitzpatrick family pamper guests with 20th-century comforts in a regal setting of medieval suits of armor, Louis XIV–style furnishings, Irish antiques, original oil paintings, and specially woven shamrock-pattern green carpets. Most of

Side Trips from Dublin

Bernageragh Bay

Balbriggan ⑦

ST. PATRICK'S ISLAND

R127

Skerries

SHENICK'S ISLAND

N1

R127

R128

R108

R126

LAMBAY ISLAND

⑧ Donabate

Swords ⑨
R106

Malahide

Irish Sea

⑩ ⑪

R122

R106

N1

Dublin Airport ✈
⑥

M1

Portmarnock

R104

R107

IRELAND'S EYE

Sutton

Howth ⑫ ⑬ ⑭

N2 ④ ③

⑮ △ Ben of Howth

② R103 ⑤

R105

① ● Clontarf

NORTH BULL ISLAND

N3

N4 ● **DUBLIN**

Dublin Bay

Liffey

N7

R119

Royal Canal

⑱

N11

⑯ ⬦⑰

R117

Dun Laoghaire

R112

⑲ ⑳ ㉗ ㉘ ㉖

Sandycove

Dalkey

㉕ **DALKEY ISLAND**

Dalkey Hill △
Killiney Hill △

㉑ ㉒

R113

㉓

Killiney

To Shankill ↓

㉔

0 ▬▬▬ 4 km
2.5 mi

N ▲

3-0075

ATTRACTIONS
Ardgillan Castle ⑦
Casino at Marino ⑤
Ferryman ㉕
Fry Model Railway ⑩
Howth Castle Gardens ⑮
Joyce Tower ⑳
Malahide Castle ⑪
National Botanic Gardens ②
Newbridge
   House & Park ⑧

ACCOMMODATIONS
Abrae Court Guest House ⑱
The Court ㉔
Doyle Skylon ①
Egan's House ④
Fitzpatrick's Castle ㉓
Forte Posthouse ⑥
Forte Travelodge ⑨
Iona Guest House ③
Royal Marine ⑯
Tudor House ㉖

DINING
Abbey Tavern ⑫
Dee Gee's Wine
   & Steak Bar ⑬
De Selby's ⑰
Guinea Pig ㉑
Kellerman's ㉘
King Sitric ⑭
La Romana ㉒
P.D.'s Woodhouse ㉗
South Bank ⑲

the guest rooms have four-poster or canopy beds, and many have balconies with sweeping views of Dublin and the surrounding countryside. In spite of its size and exacting standards, the castle never fails to exude a friendly, family run atmosphere.

Dining/Entertainment: Choices include a Victorian-style French/Irish restaurant known as Truffles; the Castle Grill for informal meals; the Cocktail Bar for a relaxing drink in a posh setting; and The Dungeon for a pub/nightclub atmosphere.

Services: 24-hour room service, concierge, laundry service, courtesy minibus service to downtown and to the airport.

Facilities: Indoor swimming pool, gym, saunas, squash and tennis courts; hairdressing salon; guest privileges at nearby 18-hole golf course; extensive outdoor parking.

Royal Marine

Marine Rd., Dun Laoghaire, Co. Dublin. ☎ **800/44-UTELL** from the U.S., or 01/280-1911. Fax 01/280-1089. 104 rms. TV TEL. £110–£160 ($176–$256) single or double. Service charge 15%. AE, DC, MC, V. DART to Dun Laoghaire Station. Bus: 7, 7A, 8.

A tradition along the seafront since 1865, this four- and five-story landmark sits on a hill overlooking the harbor, seven miles south of Dublin City. It's a good place to stay for ready access to the ferry that travels across the Irish Sea to and from Wales. Basically a Georgian building with a wing of modern bedrooms, the Royal Marine has public areas that have been beautifully restored and recently refurbished, with original molded ceilings and elaborate cornices, crystal chandeliers, marble-mantled fireplaces, and antique furnishings. The guest rooms, many of which offer wide-windowed views of the bay, carry through the Georgian theme, with dark woods, traditional floral fabrics, and four-poster or canopy beds. Some of the newer rooms have light woods and pastel tones. All units have up-to-date facilities, including hair dryers and garment presses.

Dining/Entertainment: There is a dining room with a panoramic view of the bay and a lounge bar.

Services: 24-hour room service, concierge, laundry service.

Facilities: Garden, ample outdoor parking.

Moderate

Abrae Court Guest House

9 Zion Rd., Rathgar, Dublin 6. ☎ **01/492-2242.** 18 rms, shower only. TV TEL. £55 ($88) double; £10 ($16) children ages 5–10; children under 5 free. Includes full Irish breakfast. No service charge. EU, MC, V. Open year-round. Free locked parking lot. Bus: 15, 15A, 15B.

This attractive, comfortable guest house, brightly decked with fresh flowers and set in an established residential neighborhood 15 minutes by bus southwest of Dublin center, is a good spot for families and couples wanting both access to and relief from the rush of the inner city. Every room, though not spacious, is so light as to open out rather than close in on its occupants. Orthopedic mattresses and tea/coffee-making facilities are standard. Proprietor Neville Keegan, on request, will gladly prepare evening meals (accommodating children's tastes and portions), arrange for baby-sitting, and provide laundry services. Bushy Park, one of Dublin's most spacious and lovely, is a 15-minute walk away. A health club and tennis courts are nearby.

The Court

Killiney Bay Rd., Killiney, Co. Dublin. ☎ **800/221-2222** or 01/285-1622. Fax 01/285-2085. 86 rms. TV TEL. £72–£130 ($115.20–$208) double. Includes full Irish breakfast and service charge. AE, DC, MC, V. DART to Killiney Station. Bus: 59.

Situated on four acres of gardens and lawns overlooking Dublin Bay, this three-story, multigabled Victorian-style hotel offers a relaxing country inn atmosphere, yet it is within 20 minutes (12 miles) of downtown Dublin. Best of all, guests who stay here don't even have to rent a car, because a DART station is adjacent to the grounds. The bedrooms, most of which have lovely views of the bay, are decorated with Victorian flair, full of scalloped headboards, tasseled lampshades, Queen Anne–style tables and chairs, gilt-framed paintings, brass lamps, quilted fabrics, and floor-to-ceiling drapery. Concierge, room service, and laundry service are available, and there's ample outdoor parking. Dining choices include a Victorian-theme restaurant with bay views, a coffee shop, and a conservatory-style lounge bar.

Tudor House

Dalkey, Co. Dublin (off of Castle St. between the church and Archbolds Castle). ☎ **01/ 285-1528.** Fax 01/284-8133. 6 rms, shower only. TV TEL. £56 ($89.60) double. EU, MC, V. 7-minute walk from DART; 1.75 miles from Dun Laoghaire ferry port.

This handsome Gothic Revival Victorian Manor House, built in 1848, has been lovingly restored to its original elegance by Katie and Peter Haydon. Set back from the town center, nestled behind a church, Tudor House rises to give all the guest rooms a pleasing view of Dublin Bay over the roof and treetops of Dalkey. The decor throughout the house is tasteful and serene, enhanced by antiques and fresh flowers. The blue Wedgwood Room is particularly spacious and offers a firm double bed beneath a glittering chandelier, while down the hall the cozy corner room is bright and comfortable with twin beds. The nearby DART commuter rail cannot be seen but may be heard by a light sleeper. Business and touring guests alike appreciate the splendid breakfast and helpful attention of the knowledgeable hosts. The Haydons can arrange for baby-sitting, laundry, dry-cleaning, fax, and Internet services.

DINING

Expensive

Guinea Pig

17 Railway Rd., Dalkey, Co. Dublin. ☎ **01/285-9055.** Reservations required. Main courses £11–£21 ($17.60–$33.60). 5-course fixed-price meal £21.95 ($35.10). Special value menu, Sun–Fri 6–9pm, Sat 6–8pm, £10.95 ($17.50). AE, DC, MC, V. Mon–Sat 5:30–11:30pm, Sun 5 –9:30pm. DART to Dalkey Station. Bus: 8. SEAFOOD/FRENCH.

Emphasizing whatever is freshest and in season, the menu often includes a signature dish called symphony de la mer (a potpourri of fish and crustaceans), fillets of lemon sole with cockle and mussel sauce, roast stuffed pork with a burgundy sauce, and rack of lamb. The culinary domain of chef/owner Mervyn Stewart, a former mayor of Dalkey, it is decorated in a stylish Irish country motif with Victorian touches.

Moderate

✪ P.D.'s Woodhouse

1 Coliemore Rd. (Dalkey center, several blocks from DART station). ☎ **01/284-9339.** Reservations recommended. Main courses £6.95–£14.95 ($12.65–$23.85); lunch menu £4.95–£8.95 ($2.40–$14.25). Service charge 10%. AE, MC, V. Tues–Sat noon–2:30pm and 6–11pm (two sittings, 7 and 9:30pm). IRISH/MEDITERRANEAN.

This restaurant is brought to you by Hurricane Charlie, the worst tropical storm to hit Ireland in recent memory. The first and only oakwood barbecue bistro in Ireland, P.D.'s Woodhouse depends daily on the oaks ripped up by Charlie seven years ago and stored now in Wicklow. Like Charlie, this bistro's wild Irish salmon in caper and herb butter is devastating, as is the white sole. But whatever you do, don't launch any meal here without trying the Halumi cheese kebabs—conversation-stopping grilled Greek goat cheese. The nut kebabs, on the other hand, one of several vegetarian entrées, are unnecessarily austere. The early bird menu—served from 6 to 7pm for

£9.95 ($15.90)—is modest, limited fare: burgers, chicken, ribs, and catch of the day, grilled to satisfy discerning budget hunger.

✪ South Bank

1 Martello Terrace (at Islington Ave.), Dun Laoghaire, Co. Dublin. ☎ **01/280-8788.** Reservations recommended. Fixed-price lunch £10.95 ($17.50); dinner main courses £11–£14 ($17.60–$22.40). MC, V. Tues–Sat 6–10:30pm, Sun 12:30–3pm. DART to Sandycove Station. Bus: 8. IRISH/CONTINENTAL.

On the seafront across from the waterside promenade, this cozy, 50-seat, candlelit restaurant is one of the few Dublin eateries that offers glimpses of the sea. A relaxing atmosphere pervades as chamber music plays in the background. The eclectic menu changes often, but usually includes such dishes as maple chicken with grapefruit and watercress; breast of turkey with bourbon and peaches; pork steak with cider, nutmeg, and apple; roast duck with Cointreau and kumquat sauce; and fresh salmon in a dill-and-light-lemon sauce.

Moderate/Inexpensive

⑤ DeSelby's

17/18 Patrick St., Dun Laoghaire. ☎ **01/284-1761** or 01/284-1762. Reservations recommended. Lunch main courses £4.25–£5.95 ($6.80–$9.50); dinner main courses £5.75–£11.75 ($9.20–$18.80). AE, CB, DC, MC, V. Mon–Sat 5:30–11pm, Sun noon–10pm. DART to Dun Laoghaire Station. Bus: 7, 7A, 8, 46A. INTERNATIONAL.

Named after a self-styled Dun Laoghaire philosopher in a Flann O'Brien book, this restaurant is in the center of the town, just off George's Street. DeSelby's now has a totally new look, with partially restored brick walls and fresh decor to accompany their new menu, which features more fresh fish entrées. There's also a new outdoor eating area. The menu includes traditional Irish stew, Dublin Bay scampi, salmon en croûte, roast rack of lamb, and burgers. It's a busy spot, especially on weekends, patronized by those enjoying a day's outing at the seaport.

La Romana

Castle St., Dalkey, Co. Dublin. ☎ **01/285-4569.** Reservations required for dinner. Dinner main courses £4.95–£10.95 ($7.90–$17.50); bar menu £2–£7.95 ($3.20–12.70). MC, V. Mon–Sat 5:30–11:30pm, Sun 12:30–10pm; bar food daily noon–6pm. DART to Dalkey Station. Bus: 8. ITALIAN.

Housed in the front section of the historic Queens Pub in the center of town, this informal trattoria has its own open kitchen—a contrast to the usual pub grub. The menu concentrates on pastas and pizzas, but also lists chicken breast stuffed with cream cheese and chives and pork escalope in Italian sherry with cream and mushroom sauce. In addition, there are daily specials and an interesting selection of antipasti.

Inexpensive

Kellermans

4 St. Mary's Terrace, Dalkey. ☎ **01/285-7201.** Reservations recommended Fri–Sun. Most items under £8 ($12.80). AE, MC, V. May–Aug, Mon–Wed noon–10pm, Thurs noon–11pm, Sun 1–10pm; Sept–April Tues–Thurs 6–10pm, Fri–Sun 6–11pm. PIZZA/INTERNATIONAL.

Kellermans offers generous portions at affordable prices from its menu of pizza and daily blackboard specials such as fresh Dalkey fish pie, hot thai curry, and barbecue chicken. The food is simple and fresh and is complemented by the offerings of Kellermans' wine bar. Children are made especially welcome among the wooden tables and booths lined with red cafe chairs. The young, friendly staff keeps the atmosphere casual and cozy. This is a pleasant spot for a family to have an early dinner after a day on Dalkey Island or for a couple to enjoy a glass of wine after a walk around town.

PUBS

P. McCormack and Sons
67 Lower Mounttown Rd. (off York Rd.), Dun Laoghaire. ☎ 01/280-5519.

If you rent a car and head toward the city's southern seaside suburbs, this is a great pub to stop for refreshment. Park in McCormack's lot and step into the atmosphere of your choice. The main section has an old-world feeling, with globe lamps, stained-glass windows, books and jugs on the shelves, and lots of nooks and crannies for a quiet drink. For a change of pace, there is a skylit and plant-filled conservatory area where classical music fills the air, and outdoors you'll find a festive courtyard beer garden. The pub grub here is top notch, with a varied buffet table of lunchtime salads and meats.

The Purty Kitchen
Old Dunleary Rd., Dun Laoghaire, Co. Dublin. ☎ 01/284-3576. No cover charge for traditional music; £4–£5 ($6.40–$8) for blues and rock in The Loft.

Housed in a building that dates from 1728, this old pub has a homey atmosphere with open brick fireplaces, cozy alcoves, a large fish mural, and pub poster art on the walls. There's often free Irish traditional music in the main bar area (the schedule varies, so call ahead), and also blues and rock music upstairs in The Loft Wednesday to Saturday from 9pm and dance music with a DJ on Sundays from 9pm.

The Queen's Pub
12/13 Castle St., Dalkey, Co. Dublin. ☎ 01/285-4569.

If you venture south of the city, this is a good pub to know, in a delightful seaside suburb that's studded with palm trees, of all things. Situated on the main street, the Queen's Pub has a decidedly 18th-century atmosphere, with dark-wood beams and pillars; oak and pine furnishings; floors of polished tile, rough timber, and coarse flag; and a collection of memorabilia such as copper jugs and urns, lanterns, and nautical bric-a-brac, all scattered amid nooks and alcoves and on fireplace mantles. In warm weather, seating is outside on an umbrella-shaded patio.

DUBLIN'S NORTHERN SUBURBS

ATTRACTIONS

Dublin's northern suburbs are best known as the home of Dublin International Airport, but there's also a delightful assortment of castles, historic buildings, and gardens to draw visitors. In addition, the residential suburbs of Drumcondra and Glasnevin offer many good lodgings en route to and from the airport.

Further north, the picturesque suburb of Howth is synonymous with panoramic views of Dublin Bay, beautiful hillside gardens, and many fine seafood restaurants. Best of all, it is easily reached via DART.

Casino at Marino
Malahide Rd., Marino, Dublin 3. ☎ 01/833-1618. Admission £2 ($3.20) adults, £1 ($1.60) seniors, students and children. Mid-June to mid-Sept, daily 10am–6:30pm. Bus: 20A, 20B, 27, 27A, 32A, 42, 42B.

Standing on a gentle rise 3 miles north of the city center, this 18th-century building is considered to be one of the finest garden temples in Europe. Designed in the Franco-Roman style of neoclassicism by Scottish architect Sir William Chambers, it was constructed in the garden of Lord Charlemont's house by the English sculptor Simon Vierpyl. Work commenced in 1762 and was completed 15 years later. It is particularly noteworthy for its elaborate stone carvings and compact structure, which make it appear to be a single story from the outside, when it is actually two stories tall.

✪ Malahide Castle

Malahide, Co. Dublin. ☎ **01/845-2337.** Admission £2.85 ($4.55) adults, £2.30 ($3.70) seniors and students, £1.50 ($2.40) children under 12, £7.75 ($12.40) family ticket; gardens free. Combination tickets available with Fry Model Railway and Newbridge House. Apr–Oct, Mon–Fri 10am–5pm, Sat 11am–6pm, Sun 11:30am–6pm; Nov–March, Mon–Fri 10am–5pm, Sat–Sun 2–5pm; gardens May–Sept daily, 2–5pm. Closed for tours 12:45–2pm (restaurant remains open). Bus: 42.

Situated about 8 miles north of Dublin, Malahide is one of Ireland's most historic castles, founded in the 12th century by Richard Talbot and occupied by his descendants until 1973. Fully restored, the interior of the building is the setting for a comprehensive collection of Irish furniture, dating from the 17th through the 19th centuries, and the walls are lined with one-of-a-kind Irish historical portraits and tableaux on loan from the National Gallery. The furnishings and art reflect life in and near the house over the past eight centuries.

After touring the house, you can explore the 250-acre estate, which includes 20 acres of prized gardens with more than 5,000 species of plants and flowers. The Malahide grounds also contain the Fry Model Railway Museum (see below).

✪ Newbridge House and Park

Donabate, Co. Dublin. ☎ **01/843-6534.** Admission £2.50 ($4) adults, £2 ($3.20) seniors and students, £1.50 ($2.40) children. Apr–Oct, Tues–Fri 10am–1pm and 2–5pm, Sat 11am–1pm and 2–6pm, Sun 2–6pm; Nov–March, Sat–Sun 2–5pm. Bus: 33B.

Situated 12 miles north of Dublin, this country mansion dates from 1740 and was once the home of Dr. Charles Cobbe, an Archbishop of Dublin. Occupied by the Cobbe family until 1984, the house is a showcase of family memorabilia such as hand-carved furniture, portraits, daybooks, and dolls, as well as a museum of objects collected on world travels. The Great Drawing Room, in its original state, is reputed to be one of the finest Georgian interiors in Ireland. The house sits on 350 acres, laid out with picnic areas and walking trails. The grounds also include a 20-acre working Victorian farm, stocked with farmyard animals.

National Botanic Gardens

Botanic Rd., Glasnevin, Dublin 9. ☎ **01/837-7596.** Free admission. May–Sept, Mon–Sat 10am–6pm, Sun 11am–6pm; Oct–Apr, Mon–Sat 10am–4:30pm, Sun 11am–4:30pm. Bus: 13, 19, 34, 34A.

Established by the Royal Dublin Society in 1795 on a rolling 50-acre expanse of land north of the city center, this is Dublin's horticultural showcase. The attractions include more than 20,000 different plants and cultivars, a Great Yew Walk, a bog garden, water garden, rose garden, and an herb garden. There are also a variety of Victorian-style glass houses filled with tropical plants and exotic species.

The Fry Model Railway Museum

Malahide, Co. Dublin. ☎ **01/845-2758.** Admission £2.50 ($4) adults, £2 ($3.20) seniors and students, £1.25 ($2) children. Mon–Thurs 10am–1pm and 2–6pm; Fri, June–Aug 10am–5pm; Sat, Sept–May 10am–1pm and 2–6pm, June–Aug 2–5pm; Sun, Oct–Mar 2–5pm, Apr–Sept 2–6pm. Bus: 42.

Housed on the grounds of Malahide Castle, this is an exhibit of rare handmade models of more than 300 Irish trains, from the introduction of rail to the present. The trains were built in the 1920s and 1930s by Cyril Fry, a railway engineer and draftsman. The complex includes items of Irish railway history dating from 1834, and models of stations, bridges, trams, buses, barges, boats, the River Liffey, and the Hill of Howth.

Howth Castle Gardens

Howth, Co. Dublin. ☎ **01/832-2624.** Free admission. Daily 8am–sunset. DART to Howth Station. Bus: 31

Set on a steep slope about 8 miles north of downtown, this 30-acre garden was first planted in 1875 and is best known for its 2,000 varieties of rhododendron. Peak bloom time is in May and June. *Note:* The castle on the grounds is not open to the public.

Ardgillan Castle and Park

Balbriggan, Co. Dublin. ☎ **01/849-2212.** Admission to House, £2.50 ($4) adults, £1.50 ($2.40) seniors and students. House, Apr–Sept Tues–Sun 11am–6pm; Oct–Dec and Feb–Mar Wed and Sun 11am–4:30pm. Closed Jan. Free parking year-round daily 10am–dusk. Bus: 33.

Located between Balbriggan and Skerries, north of Malahide, this recently restored 18th-century castellated country house sits right on the Irish coastline. The house, home of the Taylour family until 1962, was built in 1738, and has some fine period furnishings and antiques. But the real draw here is the setting, right on the edge of the Irish Sea, with miles of walking paths and coastal views as well as a rose garden and herb garden.

ACCOMMODATIONS

Expensive

Doyle Skylon

Upper Drumcondra Rd., Dublin 9. ☎ **800/42-DOYLE**, 800/44-UTELL from the U.S., or 01/837-9121. Fax 01/837-2778. 92 rms. TV TEL. £126.90–£133.70 ($203.10–$213.90) double. Includes full Irish breakfast and service charge. AE, CB, DC, MC, V. Bus: 3, 11, 16, 41, 41A, 41B.

With a modern five-story facade of glass and concrete, this hotel stands out on the city's north side, situated midway between downtown and the airport. Set on its own grounds in a residential neighborhood next to a college, it is just 10 minutes from the heart of the city via several major bus routes that stop outside the door. The guest rooms have all the latest amenities, with colorful Irish-made furnishings.

Dining/Entertainment: For full-service dining, it's The Rendezvous Room, a modern, plant-filled restaurant with an Irish/Continental menu. For drinks, try the Joycean pub.

Services: Concierge, room service, laundry service.

Facilities: Gift shop, ample outdoor parking.

Moderate

Forte Posthouse

Airport Rd., Dublin Airport, Co. Dublin. ☎ **800/225-5843** from U.S., or 01/844-4211. Fax 01/842-6002. 195 rms. TV TEL. £79–£99 (126.40–$158.40) double. Service charge 15%. AE, DC, MC, V. Bus: 41, 41C; Express Airport Coach.

This is the only lodging on the grounds of the airport, situated 7 miles north of city center. With a modern three-story brick facade, it has a sunken skylit lobby with a central courtyard surrounded by guest rooms. The bedrooms are contemporary and functional, with windows looking out into the courtyard or toward distant mountain vistas. Each unit is equipped with standard furnishings plus full-length mirror, hair dryer, tea/coffee-making facilities, and garment press. Concierge, 24-hour room service, valet laundry service, and courtesy coach between hotel and airport are available. There's a gift shop on the premises, and parking outdoors. Dining choices include the Garden Room restaurant for Irish cuisine and Sampans for Chinese food (dinner only). The Bodhrán Bar is a traditional Irish bar with live music on weekends.

Inexpensive

Egan's House

7/9 Iona Park, Glasnevin, Dublin 9. ☎ **01/830-3611.** Fax 01/830-3312. 23 rms. TV TEL. £55–£64.90 ($88–$103.85) double. Includes full Irish breakfast and service charge. MC, V. Bus: 3, 11, 13, 13A, 19, 19A, 16, 41, 41A, 41B.

Located on the north side of the city between Botanic and Lower Drumcondra Roads, this two-story red-brick Victorian guest house is in the center of a pleasant residential neighborhood, within walking distance of the Botanic Gardens. Operated by John and Betty Egan, it offers bedrooms in a variety of sizes and styles, including ground-floor rooms, with such conveniences as hair dryers and tea/coffee-makers. The comfortable public rooms have an assortment of traditional dark woods, brass fixtures, and antiques. Car parking is provided for guests.

Forte Travelodge

Pinnock Hill, Swords, Co. Dublin. ☎ **800/CALL-THF** from the U.S., or 1800/709709. 40 rms. TV. £66 ($105.60) double. Includes full Irish breakfast. No service charge. AE, MC, V. Bus: 41, 43.

Located about 8 miles north of downtown and 1.5 miles north of Dublin airport on the main N1 Dublin–Belfast road, this new two-story motel offers large no-frills accommodations at reasonable prices. The guest rooms, each with double bed, sofa bed, and private bath/shower, are basic and can sleep up to four people. The red-brick exterior blends nicely with the Irish countryside and the interior is clean and modern. Public areas are limited to a modest reception area, public pay phone, and adjacent budget-priced Little Chef chain restaurant and lounge.

Iona Guest House

5 Iona Park, Glasnevin, Dublin 9. ☎ **01/830-6217.** Fax 01/830-6732. 11 rms. TV TEL. £50–£60 ($80–$96) double. No service charge. Rates include full breakfast. MC, V. Closed Dec–Jan. Bus: 3, 11, 13, 13A, 19, 19A, 16, 41, 41A, 41B.

A sitting room with a glowing open fireplace, chiming clocks, brass fixtures, and dark wood furnishings sets a tone of welcome for guests to this two-story red-brick Victorian home. Built around the turn of the century and operated as a guest house since 1963 by John and Karen Shouldice, it is located in a residential neighborhood midway between Lower Drumcondra and Botanic Roads, within walking distance of the Botanic Gardens. The guest rooms offer modern hotel-style appointments and contemporary Irish-made furnishings. Facilities include a lounge, small patio, and outdoor parking for guests.

DINING

Very Expensive / Expensive

✪ King Sitric

East Pier, Howth, Co. Dublin. ☎ **01/832-5235.** Reservations required. Lunch main courses £6–£16 ($9.60–$25.60); dinner main courses £13–£23 ($20.80–$36.80). AE, DC, MC, V. Mon–Fri 12:30–3pm and 6:30–11pm. DART to Howth Station. Bus: 31. SEAFOOD.

Situated on the bay 9 miles north of Dublin, this long-established restaurant is housed in a 150-year-old former harbormaster's building. On a fine summer's evening, it is well worth a trip out here to savor the finest of local fish and crustaceans, prepared and presented in a creative way. Entrées include fillet of sole with lobster mousse, fillet of brill Deauvillaise (in a cream and wine sauce), grilled monkfish on a bed of egg-plant topped with tomato coulis, and Howth fish ragout, a signature combination of the best of the day's catch.

Expensive/Moderate

✪ Abbey Tavern

Abbey St., Howth, Co. Dublin. ☎ **01/839-0307.** Reservations recommended. Main courses £11–£20 ($17.60–$32). MC, V. Mon–Sat 7–11pm. DART to Howth Station. Bus: 31. SEAFOOD/INTERNATIONAL.

Well known for its nightly traditional music ballad sessions, this old-world 16th-century tavern also has a full-service restaurant upstairs. Although the menu changes by season, entrées often include such dishes as scallops Ty Ar Mor (with mushrooms, prawns, and cream sauce), crepes fruit de mer, poached salmon, duck with orange and Curaçao sauce, and veal à la crème. After a meal, diners are welcome to descend to the lower level and join the audience for some lively Irish music.

Moderate/Inexpensive

Dee Gee's Wine and Steak Bar

Harbour Rd., Howth, Co. Dublin. ☎ **01/839-2641.** Reservations recommended on weekends. Lunch main courses £2.50–£5 ($4–$8); dinner main courses £6–£10 ($9.60–$16). MC, V. Daily 12:30–2pm and 6–10pm. DART to Howth Station. Bus: 31. IRISH.

If you plan a day's outing at Howth, don't miss this place. Located opposite the local DART station and overlooking Dublin Bay across from the harbor, this infor-mal seaside spot is ideal for a cup of coffee, a snack, or a full meal. A self-service snackery by day and a more formal table-service restaurant at night, it offers seating both indoors and outdoors under umbrella-shaded tables. The entrées at dinner range from steaks and burgers to shrimp scampi, pork à la crème, breast of chicken with mushroom sauce, and vegetable lasagna. At lunchtime, soups, salads, and sandwiches are featured. Sit, relax, and watch all the activities of Howth from a front-row seat.

6

Out from Dublin

The scope of this chapter is more or less defined by what the distinguished Trinity geographer J. H. Andrews has labeled "the eastern triangle," a wedge of Ireland's east coast extending north to south from Co. Wicklow to Co. Louth and west to Co. Westmeath. Like a stage, compact and prominent, this relatively small space has witnessed and preserved more of the Irish drama than perhaps any other comparable part of Ireland.

The stretch of level coast from Dundalk to the Wicklows marks the greatest breach in Ireland's natural defenses, made worse—or better, depending on your perspective—by the inviting estuaries of the Liffey and the Boyne. These "opportunities" were not lost on explorers, settlers, and invaders across the millennia. Once taken, whether by Celts, Danes, Normans, or English, this area's strategic importance was soon recognized as the most likely command and control center for the whole of Ireland. Here lay Tara, the hill of kings; Dublin, the greatest of the Viking city-states; and the Pale, the English colonial fist holding the rest of Ireland in its grip. Here too are Newgrange and Knowth, marking one of the most profound prehistoric sites in the world; Kells, where Ireland's greatest treasure was fished from a bog; Mellifont, where the Irish Cistercian movement made its beginning; and the Valley of the Boyne, where the Irish finally lost their country to the English.

Rimmed by the Irish Sea, this eastern triangle —every point of which is an easy distance from Dublin city—has less rain, less bog, and more history than any other region of comparable concentration on the island. To the south, Co. Wicklow presents a verdant and varied panorama of gardens, lakes, mountains, and seascapes; to the east sit the flat plains of Co. Kildare, Ireland's prime horse country; and in the north are the counties of Meath and Louth, packed with historic sites. Pair all of this with the region's central location vis-à-vis the rest of the country and you have an area that is both a great hub from which to explore and a historical and geographic microcosm for those who don't have time to hit the four corners of the land.

AT&T

AT&T Direct℠ Service

How to call internationally from overseas:

1. Just dial the AT&T Access Number for the country you are calling from.
2. Dial the phone number you're calling.
3. Dial the calling card number listed above your name.

AT&T Access Numbers

Argentina ✱	001-800-200-1111	Costa Rica ■	0-800-0-114-114
Australia	1800-881-011	Czech Rep. ▲	00-42-000-101
Austria ○	022-903-011	Ecuador ● ▲	999-119
Bahamas	1-800-872-2881	Egypt ● (Cairo) †	510-0200
Belgium ●	0-800-100-10	France	0-800-99-0011
Brazil	000-8010	Germany	0130-0010
Canada ■	1-800-225-5288	Greece ●	00-800-1311
China, PRC ▲	10811	Guam	018-872
Colombia	980-11-0010	Guatemala ○	190

AT&T

AT&T Direct℠ Service

How to call internationally from overseas:

1. Just dial the AT&T Access Number for the country you are calling from.
2. Dial the phone number you're calling.
3. Dial the calling card number listed above your name.

AT&T Access Numbers

Argentina ✱	001-800-200-1111	Costa Rica ■	0-800-0-114-114
Australia	1800-881-011	Czech Rep. ▲	00-42-000-101
Austria ○	022-903-011	Ecuador ● ▲	999-119
Bahamas	1-800-872-2881	Egypt ● (Cairo) †	510-0200
Belgium ●	0-800-100-10	France	0-800-99-0011
Brazil	000-8010	Germany	0130-0010
Canada ■	1-800-225-5288	Greece ●	00-800-1311
China, PRC ▲	10811	Guam	018-872
Colombia	980-11-0010	Guatemala ○	190

AT&T Access Numbers

Country	Number	Country	Number
Honduras ■	123	Panama ●■	109
Hong Kong	800-1111	Philippines ●	105-11
Ireland	1-800-550-000	Saudi Arabia ◇	1-800-10
Israel	177-100-2727	Singapore	800-0111-111
Italy ●	172-1011	Spain ◇	900-99-00-11
Jamaica □	872	Sweden	020-795-611
Japan ●	0039-111	Switzerland ●	0-800-550011
Japan ●▲	0066-55-111	Taiwan ●	0080-10288-0
Korea, Republic ●	00-911	Thailand ✴	0019-991-1111
Mexico ▽	95-800-462-4240	U.K. ▲	0800-89-0011
Netherlands ●	06-022-9111	U.Arab Emirates ●■	800-121
New Zealand	000-911	Venezuela ▽	800-11-120

For a wallet card listing over 140 AT&T Access Numbers, dial the number for the country you're calling from, and ask the operator for customer service. In the U.S., call 1 800 331-1140, ext 704.

● Bold-faced countries permit country-to-country calling outside the U.S.
■ Public phones require coin or card deposit.
◇ Country-to-country calls can only be placed to this country.
✴ Calling available to most countries.
+ Not available from public phones.
▽ Dial "02" first, outside of Cairo.
○ May not be available from every phone/pay phone.
▲ Public phones require local coin payment through the call duration.
□ When calling from public phones, use phones marked "Ladtel."
◁ Calling card calls available from select hotels.

©1996, AT&T

AT&T Access Numbers

Country	Number	Country	Number
Honduras ■	123	Panama ●■	109
Hong Kong	800-1111	Philippines ●	105-11
Ireland	1-800-550-000	Saudi Arabia ◇	1-800-10
Israel	177-100-2727	Singapore	800-0111-111
Italy ●	172-1011	Spain ◇	900-99-00-11
Jamaica □	872	Sweden	020-795-611
Japan ●	0039-111	Switzerland ●	0-800-550011
Japan ●▲	0066-55-111	Taiwan ●	0080-10288-0
Korea, Republic ●	00-911	Thailand ✴	0019-991-1111
Mexico ▽	95-800-462-4240	U.K. ▲	0800-89-0011
Netherlands ●	06-022-9111	U.Arab Emirates ●■	800-121
New Zealand	000-911	Venezuela ▽	800-11-120

For a wallet card listing over 140 AT&T Access Numbers, dial the number for the country you're calling from, and ask the operator for customer service. In the U.S., call 1 800 331-1140, ext 704.

● Bold-faced countries permit country-to-country calling outside the U.S.
■ Public phones require coin or card deposit.
◇ Country-to-country calls can only be placed to this country.
✴ Calling available to most countries.
+ Not available from public phones.
▽ Dial "02" first, outside of Cairo.
○ May not be available from every phone/pay phone.
▲ Public phones require local coin payment through the call duration.
□ When calling from public phones, use phones marked "Ladtel."
◁ Calling card calls available from select hotels.

©1996, AT&T

love 0-800-99-0011
in the springtime.

Every country has its own AT&T Access Number which makes calling from France and other countries really easy. Just dial the AT&T Access Number for the country you're calling from and we'll take it from there. And be sure to charge your calls on your AT&T Calling Card. It'll help you avoid outrageous phone charges on your hotel bill and save you up to 60%.* 0-800-99-0011 is a great place to visit any time of year, especially if you've got these two cards. So please take the attached wallet card of worldwide AT&T Access Numbers.

AT&T Direct® Service
How to call internationally from overseas:
1. Just dial the AT&T Access Number for the country you are calling from.
2. Dial the phone number you're calling.
3. Dial the calling card number listed above your name.

AT&T Access Numbers
France	0-800-99-0011
Germany	0130-0010
Italy	172-1011
Philippines	105-11
Saudi Arabia	1-800-10

AT&T True Choice™ Calling Card
836 000 6780 1111
T BOFFA
International Number 891288 327 928 730 3   Auth. Code 50

All you need for the fastest, clearest connections home.

The East Coast

Castleblayney
Kilkeel
N1
1
Greenore
Carlingford Lough
N2
2
Carrickmacross
Dundalk
C A V A N
L O U T H
Dundalk Bay
Baileborough
Kingscourt
Ardee
Dunleer
Virginia
Clogher
Head
3
Clogher Head
Lough
Ramor
Collon
Baltray
25
Kells
M E A T H
4
5
Drogheda
Crossakiel
6
7
N2
Duleek
N1
I r i s h   S e a
Delvin
N51
Balbriggan
Athboy
Skerries
Trim
8
N3
Garristown
Rush
Kinnegad
Summerhill
Swords
Malahide
Enfield
D U B L I N
N4
Kilcock
Howth
Leixlip
Lucan
Prosperous
9
Liffey River
★ **Dublin**
Dun
Laoghaire
10
Dalkey
Bray
16
Edenderry
Newbridge
14
Enniskerry
12
15
Blessington
17
Monasterevan
11
13
N7
Kildare
K I L D A R E
Newtownmountkennedy
Roundwood
Stradbally
Ardscull
Rathnew
18
19
Laragh
Wicklow Head
W I C K L O W   M O U N T A I N S
N81
Rathdrum
20
Glenealy
Brittas Bay
21
W I C K L O W
23
Avoca
Carlow
22
Aughrim
Woodenbridge
Tinahely
Arklow
Tullow
Shillelagh
24
Castlecomer
N9
N80
Carnew
Gorey
N11
26
Kilkenny
Bunclody
W E X F O R D
0 ——— 9 mi
12 km
N

COUNTIES LOUTH & MEATH
Carrickmacross Lace **2**
Hill of Tara **8**
Holy Trinity Heritage Centre **1**
Knowth **6**
Loughcrew **25**
Mellifont Abbey **4**
Millmount Museum **5**
Monasterboice **3**
Newgrange **7**
Newgrange Farm **7**

COUNTY KILDARE
The Curragh **13**
Castletown House **9**
Irish National Stud **11**
Japanese Gardens **12**
Newbridge Cutlery **14**
Steam Museum **10**

COUNTY WICKLOW
Avoca Handweavers **23**
Avondale **21**

Glendalough **19**
Huntington Castle **26**
Killruddery House
& Gardens **16**
Mount Usher Gardens **20**
Noritake Arklow Pottery **24**
Powerscourt Waterfall
& Gardens **17**
Russborough House **15**
Vale of Avoca **22**
Wicklow Mountains
National Park **18**

183

1 County Wicklow: The Garden of Ireland

County Wicklow extends from Bray, 12 miles south of Dublin, to Arklow, 40 miles south of Dublin.

The borders of Co. Wicklow start just a dozen or so miles south of downtown Dublin, and within this county is some of Ireland's best rural scenery. If you're based in Dublin, you can easily spend a day or afternoon in Wicklow and still return to Dublin in time for dinner and the theater, but you'll probably want to linger overnight at one of the many fine country inns.

One quite accessible and charming gateway to Co. Wicklow is the small harbor town of Greystones, which I hesitate to mention because it is almost a secret. It is hands down one of the most unspoiled and attractive harbor towns on Ireland's east coast, with no special attractions except itself, and that's enough.

Wicklow's most stunning scenery and most interesting towns and attractions are to be found inland, between Enniskerry and Glendalough. The best way to see the Wicklow Hills is on foot, following the Wicklow Way past mountain tarns and secluded glens. In this region, don't miss the picturesque villages of Roundwood, Laragh, and Aughrim.

In the southernmost corner of Wicklow the mountains become hills and share with the villages they shelter an unassuming beauty, a sleepy tranquility that can be a welcome respite from the bustle of Wicklow's main tourist attractions. In the vicinity of Shillelagh village are lovely forests, great hill-walking, and the curious edifice of Huntington Castle.

GETTING THERE By Train Irish Rail (☎ **01/836-3333**) provides daily train service between Dublin and Bray and Wicklow.

By Bus Bus Eireann (☎ **01/836-6111**) operates daily express bus service to Arklow, Bray, and Wicklow towns. Both Bus Eireann and **Gray Line Tours** (☎ **01/661-9666**) offer seasonal (May to September) sightseeing tours to Glendalough, Wicklow, and Powerscourt Gardens.

By Car Take N11 south from Dublin City and follow turn-off signs for major attractions.

VISITOR INFORMATION For information about Co. Wicklow, contact the **Wicklow Tourist Office,** Fitzwilliam Square, Wicklow Town, Co. Wicklow (☎ **0404/69117**), open Monday to Friday year-round and Saturday during peak season.

AREA CODES Telephone numbers in the Co. Wicklow region use the area codes **0404, 045,** or **01.**

SEEING THE SIGHTS

Killruddery House & Gardens
Off the main Dublin-Wicklow road (N11), Killruddery, Bray, Co. Wicklow. ☎ **01/286-2777.** House and garden tour £2.50 ($3.75) adults, £1.50 ($2.25) seniors and students over 12; garden only £1 ($1.50) adults, 50p (75¢) seniors and students over 12. May, June, and Sept daily 1–5pm.

This estate has been the seat of the earl of Meath since 1618. The original part of its mansion, dating from 1820, features a Victorian conservatory modeled on the Crystal Palace in London. The gardens are a highlight here, with a lime avenue, a sylvan theater, foreign trees, exotic shrubs, twin canals, and a round pond with fountains that's edged with beech hedges. They are the only surviving 17th-century French style gardens in Ireland.

Powerscourt Waterfall and Gardens

Off the main Dublin-Wicklow road (N11), Enniskerry, Co. Wicklow. ☎ **01/286-7676.** Gardens £3 ($4.80) adults, £2.50 ($4) seniors and students, £2 ($3.20) children ages 5–16, free for children under 5; waterfall £1.50 ($2.40) adults, £1 ($1.60) seniors and students, 80p ($1.30) children ages 5–16, free for children under 5. AE, MC, V. Gardens, Mar–Oct daily 9:30am–5:30pm; waterfall, summer daily 9:30am–7pm, winter 10:30am–dusk.

On a 1,000-acre estate less than a dozen miles south of Dublin city sits one of the finest gardens in Europe, designed and laid out by Daniel Robertson between 1745 and 1767 and filled with splendid Greek- and Italian-inspired statuary, decorative ironwork, a petrified-moss grotto, lovely herbaceous borders, a Japanese garden, a circular pond and fountain with statues of winged horses, and the occasional herd of deer. Stories have it that Robertson, afflicted with gout, was pushed around the grounds in a wheelbarrow to oversee the work. This service is no longer offered, but I doubt you'll mind the walk around. An 18th-century manor house designed by Richard Cassels, the architect of Russborough House (see below) and the man credited with the design of Dublin's Parliament House, stood proudly on the site until it was gutted by fire in 1974. Current plans call for it to be rebuilt this year. In addition to its natural and artistic wonders, the Gardens offer a crafts center, garden center, children's play area, and restaurant. Nearby (4 miles) is the Powerscourt Waterfall, at 400 feet the highest waterfall in Ireland.

Russborough

Off N81, Blessington, Co. Wicklow. ☎ **045/865239.** Main rooms £3 ($4.80) adults, £2 ($3.20) seniors and students, £1 ($1.60) children under 12. Easter–May and Oct Sun 10:30am–5:30pm or by appointment; June–Aug daily 10:30am–5:30pm; Sept Mon–Sat 10:30am–2:30pm and Sun 10:30am–5:30pm.

Ensconced in this 18th-century Palladian house is the world-famous Beit Art Collection, with paintings by Vernet, Guardi, Bellotto, Gainsborough, Rubens, and Reynolds. The house is furnished with European pieces and decorated with bronzes, tapestries, and some fine Francini plasterwork. The maze and rhododendron garden may be viewed by prior appointment. Facilities include a restaurant, shop, and children's playground. It's 25 miles southwest of Dublin.

✪ Wicklow Mountains National Park

Glendalough, Co. Wicklow. ☎ **0404/45425.** Late Apr to late Aug daily 10am–6:30pm; Sept Sat–Sun 10am–6:30pm.

A large area of Co. Wicklow has been designated as a new national park. The core area of the park is centered around Glendalough, including the Glendalough Valley and Glendalough Wood Nature Reserves. An information point is found at the Upper Lake at Glendalough.

✪ Glendalough

Co. Wicklow. ☎ **0404/45325** or 0404/45352. Admission £2 ($3.20) adults, £1.50 ($2.40) seniors, £1 ($1.60) children/students under 16, £5 ($8) family. Sept–May daily 9:30am–6pm; June–Aug daily 9am–6:30pm. Bus: Two buses daily from Dublin year-round, departing from College of Surgeons, St. Stephen's Green. Located 7 miles east of Wicklow on T7 via Rathdrum.

Its name derived from the Irish phrase *Gleann Da Locha,* meaning "The Glen of the Two Lakes," this idyllically secluded setting was chosen in the 6th century by St. Kevin for a monastery. Over the centuries, it became a leading center of learning, with thousands of students from Ireland, Britain, and all over Europe. In the 12th century, St. Lawrence O'Toole was among the many abbots to follow Kevin and spread the influence of Glendalough. But, like so many early Irish religious sites, the glories of Glendalough came to an end by the 15th century at the hands of the plundering Anglo-Norman invaders.

Today, visitors can stroll from the upper lake to the lower lake and walk through the remains of the monastery complex, long since converted to a burial place. Although much of the monastic city is in ruins, the remains do include a nearly perfect round tower, 103 feet high and 52 feet around the base, as well as hundreds of timeworn Celtic crosses and a variety of churches, including St. Kevin's chapel, often called St. Kevin's Kitchen, a fine specimen of an early Irish barrel-vaulted oratory with its own miniature round belfry rising from a stone roof. A striking new visitor's center at the entrance to the site provides helpful orientation with exhibits on the archaeology, history, folklore, and wildlife of the area. There is no charge to walk around Glendalough, but there is a fee to view the center's exhibits and audio-visual presentation.

The main entrance to the monastic complex has been spoiled by a sprawling hotel and hawkers of various sorts, so you may want to cross the river at the visitor's center and walk along the banks, crossing back again at the monastic site and thus bypassing the trappings of commerce that St. Kevin himself once fled.

✪ Mount Usher Gardens

On the main Dublin-Wicklow road (N11), Ashford, Co. Wicklow. ☎ **0404/40116.** Admission £3 ($4.80) adults, £2.50 ($4) seniors, students, and children ages 5–12. Guided tours may be booked in advance for £20 ($32). Mar 17 to Oct Mon–Sat 10:30am–6pm, Sun 11am–6pm.

Encompassing 20 acres beside the River Vartry, this sylvan site is distinguished by its collection of more than 4,000 rare tree and plant species from all parts of the world, including spindle trees from China, North American swamp cypress, and Burmese juniper trees. Fiery rhododendrons, fragrant eucalyptus trees, meandering green creepers, pink magnolias, and snowy camellias also compete for your eye. A spacious tea room overlooks the river and gardens.

Avondale House & Avondale Forest Park

Rathdrum, Co. Wicklow. ☎ **0404/46111.** Admission £2.50 adults ($3.75), £1.50 ($2.25) seniors and children under 16. Daily May–Sept 10am–6pm, Oct–Apr 11am–5pm. Parking fee £1 ($1.60). Entrance to park and house signposted off R752.

In a fertile valley between Glendalough and the Vale of Avoca, this is the former home of Charles Stewart Parnell (1846–91), one of Ireland's great political leaders. Built in 1779, the house is now a museum to his memory. Set in the surrounding 523-acre estate and boasting signposted nature trails alongside the Avondale River, Avondale Forest Park is considered the cradle of modern Irish forestry.

Vale of Avoca

Route 755, Avoca, Co. Wicklow. Free admission.

Basically a peaceful riverbank, the Vale of Avoca was immortalized in the writings of 19th-century poet Thomas Moore. It's here at the "Meeting of the Waters" that the Avonmore and Avonbeg Rivers join to form the Avoca River. It's said that the poet sat under "Tom Moore's Tree," looking for inspiration and penned the lines "There is not in the wide world a valley so sweet, / as the vale in whose bosom the bright waters meet . . ." The tree is a sorry sight now, as it's been picked almost bare by souvenir hunters, but the place is worth a visit.

Huntington Castle

Clonegal, Co. Carlow (off N80, 4 miles from Bunclody). ☎ **054/77552.** Admission £2.50 ($4). Jun–Aug 2–6pm daily; other times by appointment.

Located at the confluence of the rivers Derry and Slaney, this castle was of great strategic importance from the time it was built in the early 17th century and was at the center of conflicts in the area up to the early 20th century, when it was briefly used as a headquarters by the IRA. The castle is unlike many others you will visit in that it has a lived-in feel, a magnificent decrepitude evoked not least by the sometimes overwhelming assortment of debris left by previous generations, an assortment in which some real treasures lurk. The house has many stories to tell, and young Alexander Durdin-Robertson, whose ancestors built the place, seems to know them all; he gives a great tour. Don't forget to visit the garden, which hides a lovely yew walk and one of the first hydroelectric facilities in Ireland among its waist-high weeds. The castle's basement is now home to a temple of the Fellowship of Isis, a religion founded here in 1976.

SPORTS & OUTDOOR PURSUITS

BIRD-WATCHING & BOTANY   Courses in ornithology and wildflowers, among other topics, are offered at the **Altamont Gardens,** Tullow, Co. Wicklow (☎ **0503/ 59128**). Mrs. North, the current owner, has left a personal imprint on the gardens, reflecting her extensive knowledge of and concern for the plant and animal species of Ireland. The cost of the weekend courses includes lodging in a 17th-century cottage and meals featuring organic produce from the adjacent farm and vegetable garden; prices are £185 to £200 ($296 to $320).

CANOEING & KAYAKING   There are weekend courses on white-water and flatwater streams at the **Tiglin Adventure Center,** Ashford, Co. Wicklow (☎ **0404/ 40169,** fax 0404/40701), a state-funded facility that provides training in a variety of outdoor activities. Basic equipment is provided; course fees are £70 to £110 ($112 to $176). The center caters to a young clientele, and lodging is in hostels unless you arrange otherwise.

FISHING   The streams in Wicklow are not renowned fishing waters, although brown trout and river trout can be found in such rivers as the Avoca and the Aughrim. Sea angling is popular all along the Wicklow coast, but there are not any opportunities in Wicklow to hire boats or fishing equipment.

GOLF   County Wicklow's verdant hills and dales provide numerous opportunities for golfing. Among the 18-hole courses welcoming visitors are the new **Rathsallagh Golf Club,** an 18-hole, par-72 championship course at Dunlavin, Co. Wicklow (☎ 045/53112), with greens fees of £20 ($30) on weekdays and £29 ($43.50) on weekends; the seaside **European Club,** Brittas Bay, Co. Wicklow (☎ 0404/47415), a championship links with greens fees of £25 ($40) on weekdays and £30 ($48) on weekends; the parkland **Glenmalure Golf Club,** Greenane, Rathdrumm, Co. Wicklow (☎ 0404/46679), with greens fees of £12 ($18) on weekdays and £15 ($22.50) on weekends; and the **Arklow Golf Club** (☎ 0402/32492), a seaside par-68 course with greens fees of £17 ($27.20) seven days a week.

HORSEBACK RIDING   With its valleys and glens and its secluded paths and nature trails, Co. Wicklow is a natural territory for horseback riding. More than a dozen stables and equestrian centers offer horses for hire and instructional programs. Rates for horse hire average £10 to £12 ($16 to $19.20) per hour. Among the leading venues are **Devil's Glen Equestrian Village,** Ashford, Co. Wicklow (☎ 0404/ 40637); **Calliaghstown Riding Centre,** Glenmore, Blessington, Co. Wicklow (☎ 045/65538); **Brennanstown Riding School,** Hollybrook, Kilmacanogue, Co. Wicklow (☎ 01/286-3778); and the **Laragh Trekking Centre,** Laragh East, Glendalough, Co. Wicklow (☎ 0404/45282). At the **Paulbeg Riding School,** Shillelagh, Co. Wicklow (☎ 055/29100), experienced riders can explore the beautiful surrounding hills while beginners can partake of expert instruction from Sally Duffy, a friendly woman who will give you an enthusiastic introduction to the sport.

Grandpa, Where Do Shillelaghs Come From?

Glad you asked. If you've ever wondered about the origin of the blackthorn walking stick known commonly as a "shillelagh" (pronounced shi-*lay*-lee), this is at least one story worth considering: About 15 miles southwest of Avoca is the village of Shillelagh. Local legend has it that the bushes of the Shillelagh Woods were cut down in the 13th century to be used as weapons in a local battle. At the time, these sturdy cudgels were called "Shillelagh sticks," and eventually this was shortened to just "shillelagh." In more recent times, they've become symbols of authority and been used for hunting and games. Not all the trees from this part of Co. Wicklow were made into sticks—the oak roofing of Dublin's St. Patrick's Cathedral is Shillelagh wood.

HUNTING   The **Broomfield Riding School,** Broomfield, Tinahely, Co. Wicklow (☎ 0402/38117), offers access to the hunt for those who can demonstrate adequate equestrian skills, including jumping. The riding school is open year-round for lessons and trail rides.

WALKING   The Wicklow Way is a signposted walking path that follows forest trails, sheep paths, and country roads from the hills south of Dublin to the trail's terminus in Clonegal. It takes about five to seven days to walk the whole of the Way, with overnight stops at B&Bs and hostels along the route. Most people choose to walk sections as day trips, and for this reason I've highlighted some of my favorites below. Information and maps can be obtained at the Wicklow National Park center in Glendalough or in any local tourist office.

Information on less strenuous walks can be found in a number of local publications. Check out the **"Wicklow Trail Sheets"** that are available at tourist offices. These provide a map and route description for several short walks. The **Ballyknocken House B&B** (see "Walking" section of Chapter 4) also publishes a list of walks beginning and ending at the house for their guests.

The most spectacular walks in Wicklow are found in the north and central parts of the county, an area traversed by the Wicklow Way and numerous short trails. One lovely walk on the Way begins at the Deerpark car park near the Dargle River, and continues to Luggala, passing Djouce Mountain; the next section, between Luggala and Laragh, traverses some wild country around Lough Dan.

You won't want to miss the southern section of the Wicklow Way, through Tinahely, Shillelagh, and Clonegal. Although not as rugged as the terrain in central Wicklow, the hills here are voluptuously round, with delightful woods and glens hidden in their folds. Through much of this section the path follows country roads that have been well chosen for their lack of vehicular traffic. Consider treating yourself to a night at **Park Lodge B&B,** Clonegal, Shillelagh, Co. Wicklow (☎ 055/29140), located near the trail's terminus; rooms are £15 to £20 ($24 to $32) per person. If you're on foot you can arrange with the exceedingly hospitable Osborne family to be picked up at one of several points along the trail between Shillelagh and Clonegal.

SHOPPING

Co. Wicklow offers a wide array of wonderful craft centers and workshops. Here is a small sampling:

✪ Avoca Handweavers
Avoca, Co. Wicklow. ☎ **0402/35105** or 0402/35284.

Dating from 1723, this cluster of whitewashed stone buildings and a weaving mill houses the oldest surviving hand-weaving company in Ireland, producing a wide range of tweed clothing, knitwear, and accessories. The dominant tones of mauve, aqua, teal, and heather reflect the landscape of Wicklow. Visitors are welcome to watch as craftspeople weave strands of yarn that has been spun from the wool of local sheep. A retail outlet and coffee shop are located on the complex. A second outlet/shop is on the main N11 road at Kilmacanogue, Bray, Co. Wicklow (☎ **01/286-7466**). Open Monday through Friday from 9:30am to 5:30pm and Saturday and Sunday from 10am to 6pm.

Bergin Clarke Studio
The Old Schoolhouse, Ballinaclash, Rathdrum, Co. Wicklow. ☎ **0404/46385.**

Stop into this little workshop and see Brian Clarke hand-fashioning silver jewelry and giftware or Yvonne Bergin knitting stylish and colorful apparel using yarns from Co. Wicklow. Open May through September daily from 10am to 8pm and October through April, Monday through Saturday, from 10am to 5:30pm.

Fisher's of Newtownmountkennedy
The Old Schoolhouse, Newtownmountkennedy, Co. Wicklow. ☎ **01/281-9404.**

This shop, located in a converted schoolhouse, stocks a wide array of men's and women's sporting clothes—quilted jackets, raincoats, footwear, blazers, and accessories. There's also a new tearoom. Open Monday through Saturday from 9:30am to 5:30pm.

Glendalough Craft Centre
Laragh, Co. Wicklow. ☎ **0404/45156.**

In a converted farmhouse, this long-established craft shop offers handcrafts from all over Ireland, such as Bantry Pottery and Penrose Glass from Waterford. Books, jewelry, and a large selection of hand knits from the area are also sold. Open daily from 10am to 6pm.

Noritake Arklow Pottery Ltd.
South Quay, Arklow, Co. Wicklow. ☎ **0402/31101.** Daily 9:30am to 4:45pm.

Situated in a busy seaside town, this is Ireland's largest pottery factory and the home of Noritake's Celt Craft and Misty Isle lines. The pottery produced here ranges from earthenware, porcelain, and bone china tableware to decorated teapots, casseroles, and gifts in both modern and traditional designs. Free tours are available mid-June through August with the exception of the last week of July and first two weeks of August, when the factory is closed for the staff's vacation.

ACCOMMODATIONS
EXPENSIVE

✪ Rathsallagh House
Dunlavin, Co. Wicklow. ☎ **800/223-6510** from the U.S., or 045/53112. Fax 045/53343. 14 rms. TV TEL. £110–£170 ($176–$272) double. No service charge. Rates include full breakfast. AE, DC, MC, V. Closed Dec 23–31.

On the western edge of Co. Wicklow, this rambling, ivy-covered country house sits amid 530 acres of parks, woods, and farmland. The original house on the property was built between 1702 and 1704 and owned by a horse-breeding family named Moody. It was burned down in the 1798 Rebellion, and the Moodys moved into the Queen Anne–style stables, which were converted into a proper residence and served as a private home until the 1950s. It was purchased in 1978 by Joe and Kay O'Flynn and opened as a country house ten years later. Each room is individually decorated and named accordingly, from the Yellow, Pink, and Blue Rooms to the Romantic, Over Arch, Loft Rooms, and so on. Most rooms have a sitting area, huge walk-in closet, and window seats, and some have a Jacuzzi. All have a hair dryer, tea/coffeemaker, vanity/desk, good reading lamps over the beds, and antique furnishings.

Dining/Entertainment: The dining room, under the personal supervision of Kay O'Flynn, is noted for its excellent food, using local ingredients and vegetables and herbs from the garden.

Facilities: 18-hole championship golf course, indoor heated swimming pool, sauna, hard tennis court, archery, croquet, billiards, two-acre walled garden.

✪ Tinakilly House

Off the Dublin-Wexford road, on R750, Rathnew, Co. Wicklow. ☎ **800/223-6510** from the U.S., or 0404/69274. Fax 0404/67806. 29 rms. TV TEL. £132–£160 ($211.20–$256) double, £160 ($256) junior suites, £200 ($320) admiral's suites with sea view. Rates include full breakfast. No service charge. AE, DC, MC, V. Closed Dec 23–31.

Dating from the 1870s, this was the home of Capt. Robert Charles Halpin, commander of the *Great Eastern,* who laid the first successful cable connecting Europe with America. With a sweeping central staircase said to be the twin of the one on the ship, Tinakilly is full of seafaring memorabilia and paintings, as well as Victorian antiques. Many of the individually furnished guest rooms have views of the Irish Sea. Opened as a hotel by the Power family in 1983, it is adjacent to the Broadlough Bird Sanctuary and a seven-acre garden of beech, evergreen, eucalyptus, palm, and American redwood trees.

Dining/Entertainment: The restaurant, known for fresh fish and local game, blends country house cooking with a nouvelle cuisine influence. Vegetables, fruits, and herbs come from the house gardens, and all breads are baked fresh daily on the premises.

EXPENSIVE/MODERATE

✪ Glenview Hotel

Glen o' the Downs, Delgany, Dublin-Wexford road (N11), Co. Wicklow. ☎ **800/528-1234** or 01/287-3399. Fax 01/287-7511. 42 rms. TV TEL. £96–£130 ($153.60–$208) double. AE, DC, MC, V.

With the Sugar Loaf Mountain in the background and nestled in an idyllic setting overlooking the Glen of the Downs, this hotel has been a popular stopping-off place on the main road for more than 50 years. Totally refurbished and enlarged in 1993, it has a striking new yellow facade and a bright and airy contemporary interior, yet still maintains much of its traditional charm in the guest rooms and public areas. The main dining room, the Malton Room, is noted for its wooden paneling and full set of Malton prints on the walls, while the Lodge Bar and Library Lounge enjoy panoramic views of the Co. Wicklow countryside, including the hotel's 30 acres of gardens and woodlands. A luxurious health and leisure club was recently added.

MODERATE

Glendalough Hotel

Glendalough, Co. Wicklow. ☎ **800/365-3346** from the U.S., or 0404/45135. Fax 0404/45142. 44 rms. TV TEL. £60–£66 ($96–$105.60) double. Rates include full breakfast. AE, DC, MC, V. Closed Dec and Jan.

If location is everything, this hotel scores high. It sits in a wooded glen at the entrance to Glendalough, beside the Glendasan River. Dating from the 1800s, it was refurbished and updated a few years ago with traditional Irish furnishings and every modern comfort. Public rooms include the Glendasan Restaurant overlooking the river and the Glendalough Tavern.

Vale View Hotel

Avoca, Co. Wicklow. ☎ **0402/35236.** Fax 0404/35144. 10 rms. TV TEL. £65 ($104) double. Rates include full breakfast. AE, DC, MC, V.

Set on a hillside in the heart of the Avoca valley, this small family-run hotel is a great place to get away from it all and relax amid the natural beauty of the hotel's gardens and surrounding Wicklow scenery. Many do—the place has a faithful following. The decor in the public rooms is homey, filled with local art and Parnell memorabilia, while the guest rooms have standard furnishings. There is a restaurant and bar, and a patio for outdoor sitting when the weather is good. Innkeepers Mahon and Maureen O'Brien provide a warm welcome.

INEXPENSIVE

Derrybawn House

Laragh, Co. Wicklow. ☎ **0404/45134.** Fax 0404/45109. 6 rms. £50 ($80) double (including full breakfast). No service charge. No credit cards.

This elegant, comfortable fieldstone manor house in an idyllic, pastoral parkland setting looks out over the surrounding hills. The rooms are spacious, bright, and tastefully furnished; public rooms include a sitting room, dining room, and rec room with snooker table and facilities for making tea and coffee. Located just outside Laragh village, convenient to fishing streams and hiking trails (including the Wicklow Way), this is a great place from which to explore Wicklow's natural wonders.

Slievemore

The Harbour, Greystones, Co. Wicklow. ☎ **01/287-4724.** 8 rooms, shower only. Cable TV. £38 ($60.80) double. Includes full Irish breakfast. No service charge. No credit cards. Open year-round. Free parking.

This mid–19th century harbor house offers white-glove cleanliness, spacious comfort, and (if you book early and request a seafront room) a commanding view of Greystones Harbor, Bray Head, and the Irish Sea. Proprietor Pippins Parkinson says that "people stumble on Greystones, find it by accident." Whether you're accident-prone or not, stay here and reserve a table for dinner at Coopers (see listing below), just paces away, and you won't forget the day you stumbled on Greystones.

DINING
MODERATE

✪ Coopers

The Harbour, Greystones, Co. Wicklow (above the Beach House). ☎ **01/287-3914.** Reservations recommended. Main courses £6.95–£14.95 ($12.65–$23.85); lunch menu £8.45–£12.95 ($13.50–$20.70). No service charge. AE, MC, V. Mon–Sat 5:30–11:30pm, Sun 5:30–10pm and Sun lunch 12:30–4pm. INTERNATIONAL/SEAFOOD.

Coopers is the perfect reward after making the cliff walk from Bray to Greystones. This is one of the most tasteful dining environments I've found in Ireland—vaulted beamed ceilings, exposed brick and stone walls, stained glass, three fireplaces, wrought-iron fixtures, and linen table settings; a warm, relaxed, and comfortable place for couples and families of any age. The menu is a rarity in that it understates its offerings, with quite ordinary descriptions like "smoked lamb" for quite extraordinary fare. The roast duckling and the steamed sea trout are two of the house specialties, enhanced by a fine wine list. There are spectacular views of the open sea on two sides, and a piano player on Friday and Saturday nights. Coopers is no secret to the locals, so book well ahead in order not to be disappointed.

❂ Mitchell's

Laragh, Glendalough, Co. Wicklow. ☎ **0404/45302.** Reservations recommended. Lunch main courses £4.50–£7.50 ($7.20–$12); fixed-price dinner £16.50–£18.50 ($26.40–$29.60); afternoon tea £3.75 ($6). AE, MC, V. Open Easter–Sept, 9am–9pm daily, Oct–Easter 9am–9pm Wed–Sun. Closed Good Friday and Christmas. IRISH/INTERNATIONAL.

A 200-year-old former schoolhouse serves as the setting for this small restaurant in a garden in sight of the mountains. The unique cut-granite facade opens to a country-kitchen atmosphere, with pine furnishings and open, log-burning fireplaces. In the summer, there is seating outdoors. The menu changes daily, but often includes rack of Wicklow lamb with honey and rosemary sauce, smoked salmon on a spiced saffron-scented sauce, grilled fillet of sea trout with sorrel sauce, and fillet of beef with red wine and mushroom sauce, as well as daily vegetarian entrées. All breads and scones are made on the premises, as is an assortment of ice cream.

❂ Roundwood Inn

Main St., Roundwood, Co. Wicklow. ☎ **01/282-8107** or 01/282-8125. Reservations not necessary for lunch, advised for dinner. Lunch main courses £3–£10 ($4.80–$16); dinner main courses £10–£16 ($16–$25.60). MC, V. Tues–Sat 1–2:30pm and 7:30–9:30pm. IRISH/CONTINENTAL.

Dating from 1750, this old coaching inn is the focal point of an out-of-the-way spot high in the mountains called Roundwood, said to be the highest village in Ireland. The old-world atmosphere includes open log fireplaces and antique furnishings. Menu choices range from steaks and sandwiches to traditional Irish stew, fresh lobster, and smoked salmon. It's located in the middle of the village on the main road (R755).

INEXPENSIVE

❂ The Opera House

Market Sq., Wicklow Town, Co. Wicklow. ☎ **0404/66422.** Reservations recommended Fri–Sun. Main courses £5.50–£10.95 ($8.80–$17.50). No service charge. EU, MC, V. Jun–Aug 11am–11pm, Sept–May 5–11pm. ITALIAN.

This Irish trattoria, beginning its second year, is a unique find in this traditional harbor town. Inside, the faux Mediterranean decor is warm and tasteful; outside, picnic tables provide street-side dining for nonsmokers. The smoked salmon and tagliatelle flamed in a cream and vodka sauce for £5.95 ($9.50) is a delicious bargain, and the house French table wine at £8.95 ($14.30) suits both wallet and palate. The service is enthusiastic though, on weekends, stretched a bit thin. For a delightful conclusion, treat yourself to the lemon brûlée.

Poppies Country Cooking

Enniskerry, Co. Wicklow. ☎ **01/282-8869.** Reservations not required. All items £1.50–£4.50 ($2.40–$7.20). No credit cards. Daily 9am–7pm. IRISH/SELF-SERVICE.

Situated in the middle of town opposite the main square, this small 10-table shopfront eatery is popular for light meals and snacks throughout the day. The menu ranges from homemade soups and salads to nut roast, baked salmon, vegetarian quiche, and lasagna. Poppies now has a second location, with the same wholesome, budget-saving menu, in Greystones, Co. Wicklow (☎ **01/287-4228**).

PUBS

Cartoon Inn

Main St., Rathdrum, Co. Wicklow. ☎ **0404/46774.**

With walls bedecked with the work of many famous cartoonists, this cottagelike pub claims to be Ireland's only cartoon-theme pub and is the headquarters for Ireland's Cartoon Festival, held in late May or early June each year. Pub grub is available at lunchtime.

The Coach House

Main St., Roundwood. ☎ **01/281-8157.**

Adorned with lots of colorful hanging flowerpots on the outside, this Tudor-style inn sits in the mountains in the heart of Ireland's highest village. Dating from 1790, it is full of local memorabilia, from old photos and agricultural posters to antique jugs and plates. It's well worth a visit, whether to learn about the area or to get some light refreshment.

The Meetings

Avoca, County Wicklow. ☎ **0402/35226.**

This Tudor-style country-cottage pub stands idyllically at the "Meeting of the Waters" associated with poet Thomas Moore. An 1889 edition of Moore's book of poems is on display. Good pub grub is served every day, with traditional Irish music every Sunday afternoon (from 4 to 6pm), compliments of the house.

2 County Kildare: Ireland's Horse Country

15 to 30 miles west of Dublin.

ESSENTIALS

Co. Kildare and horse-racing go hand in hand, or should we say neck and neck? It's home of the Curragh racetrack, where the Irish Derby is held each June, and other smaller tracks at Naas and Punchestown. Co. Kildare is also the heartland of Ireland's flourishing bloodstock industry. In this panorama of open grasslands and limestone-enriched soil, many of Ireland's 300 stud farms are found.

Kildare is famed as the birthplace of Brigid, Ireland's second patron saint. Brigid was a bit ahead of her time as an early exponent for women's equality—she founded a coed monastery in Kildare in the 5th or 6th century.

GETTING THERE   Irish Rail (☎ **01/836-3333**) provides daily train service to Kildare town.

Bus Eireann (☎ **01/836-6111**) operates daily express bus service to Kildare.

If you're traveling by car, take the main Dublin-Limerick road (N7) west of Dublin to Kildare or the main Dublin-Galway road (N4) to Celbridge, turning off on local road R403.

VISITOR INFORMATION   **For information about Co. Kildare, contact the **Wicklow Tourist Office, Wicklow Town (☎ **0404/69117**), open year-round Monday to Friday, and Saturdays during peak season. Seasonal information offices are located at Athy, Co. Kildare (☎ **0507/31859**) and in Kildare Town, Co. Kildare (☎ **045/22696**). Both are open June through mid-September.

AREA CODES   **The telephone area codes used in Co. Kildare are **01, 045, and **0503.**

SEEING THE SIGHTS

✪ Castletown House

R403, off the main Dublin-Galway road, Celbridge, Co. Kildare. ☎ **01/628-8582.** Admission £2.50 ($4) adults, £2 ($3.20) seniors and students, £1 ($1.60) children, £6 ($9.60) family. Apr–Sept Mon–Fri 10am–6pm, Sat 11am–6pm, Sun 2–6pm; Oct Mon–Fri 10am–5pm and Sun 2–5pm; Nov–Mar Sun 2–5pm.

Although a little removed from the heart of Kildare horse country, this great house, 10 miles northeast of Naas, deserves a detour. One of Ireland's architectural gems, Castletown is a 1722 Palladian-style mansion designed by Italian architect Alessandro Galilei for William Connolly, then speaker of the Irish House of Commons. The house is decorated with Georgian furniture and paintings and is known for its long gallery laid out in the Pompeian manner and hung with Venetian chandeliers, its main hall and staircase with elaborate Italian plasterwork, and its 18th-century print room.

Steam Museum

Off Dublin-Limerick road (N7), Straffan, Co. Kildare. ☎ **01/627-3155.** Museum: £3 ($4.80) adults; £2 ($3.20) seniors, children, and students; £10 ($16) family. Garden £2 ($3.20). Museum April–May Sun 2:30–5:30pm, June–Aug Tues–Sun 1–6pm, September Sun 2:30–5:30pm. Walled garden June–July 2–6pm, Aug Tues–Fri 2:30–5:30pm.

Housed in a converted church, this museum is a must for steam-engine buffs. It contains two collections: The Richard Guinness Hall has more than 20 prototypical locomotive engines dating from the 18th century, and the Power Hall has rare industrial stationary engines. The steam and garden shop stocks a variety of recent books and videos on the Irish Railway and serves as the sole outlet for National Trust Enterprises gifts, which can be excellent values. The walled garden is of 18th-century origin and features several garden rooms extending to a delightful rosery. Inquire ahead regarding when one or more engines will be in operation.

Newbridge Cutlery

Off Dublin-Limerick road (N7), Newbridge, Co. Kildare. ☎ **045/31301.** Free admission. Mon–Fri 9am–5pm, Sat 11am–5pm, Sun 2–5pm.

Look closely at the silverware when you sit down to eat at one of Ireland's fine hotels or restaurants—there's a good chance it'll be made by Newbridge, which for the past 60 years has been one of Ireland's leading manufacturers of fine silverware. In the visitor center, you can see a display of silver place settings, bowls, candelabras, trays, frames, and one-of-a-kind items. A video on silvermaking is also shown. Silver pieces are sold here, including "sale" items.

✪ The Curragh

Dublin-Limerick road (N7), Curragh, Co. Kildare. ☎ **045/441205.** Admission £6 ($9.60) for most races; £7–£25 ($11.20–$40) for Derby. AE, DC, MC, V. Hours vary; first race usually 2pm. Rail links with all major towns. Dublin-Curragh return "Racing by Rail" package for £15 ($24), including courtesy coach to main entrance.

Often referred to as the Churchill Downs of Ireland, this is the country's best-known racetrack, just 30 miles west of Dublin. Majestically placed at the edge of Ireland's central plain, it's home to the Irish Derby held each year in late June and early July. Horses race here at least one Saturday a month from March to October. The main stand has been extensively renovated, and new bars, a food hall, and a betting hall have been added.

✪ Irish National Stud & Japanese Gardens

Off the Dublin-Limerick road (N7), Tully, Kildare, Co. Kildare. ☎ **045/21617.** Admission £5 ($8) adults; £3 ($4.80) seniors, students, and children over 12; £2 ($3.20) children under 12;

£12 ($19.20) family. MC, V. Feb 12–Nov 12 daily 9:30am–6pm. Bus: Eireann stop. Buses from Dublin each morning, returning each evening.

Some of Ireland's most famous horses have been bred and raised on the grounds of this government-sponsored stud farm. A prototype for other horse farms throughout Ireland, it has 288 stalls to accommodate the mares, stallions, and foals. Visitors are welcome to walk around the 958-acre grounds and see the noble steeds being exercised and groomed.

A converted groom's house has exhibits on racing, steeplechasing, hunting, and show jumping, plus the skeleton of Arkle, one of Ireland's most famous horses.

The Japanese garden is considered to be among the finest Oriental gardens in Europe. Laid out between 1906 and 1910, its design symbolizes the journey of the soul from oblivion to eternity. The Japanese-style visitor center has a restaurant and craft shop.

SPORTS & OUTDOOR PURSUITS

GOLF   The flat plains of Kildare provide some lovely settings for parkland courses, including two new 18-hole championship courses. The par-72 **Kildare Country Club,** Straffan, Co. Kildare (☎ **01/627-3333**), charges £50 ($80) per day for greens fees to those staying at the hotel and £85 ($136) per day to day visitors. The par-70 **Kilkea Castle Golf Club,** Castledermot, Co. Kildare (☎ **0503/45156**), charges £25 ($40) every day of the week.

For a slightly less costly game, try the par-72 championship course at the **Curragh Golf Club,** Curragh, Co. Kildare (☎ **045/441238**), with greens fees of £15 ($24) weekdays and £20 ($32) on weekends.

HORSEBACK RIDING   Visitors who want to go horseback riding can expect to pay an average of £10 to £15 ($16 to $24) per hour for trekking or trail riding in the Kildare countryside. To arrange a ride, contact the **Donacomper Riding School,** Celbridge, Co. Kildare (☎ **01/628-8221**) or the **Kill International Equestrian Centre,** Kill, Co. Kildare (☎ **045/77208**).

ACCOMMODATIONS
Very Expensive

Kildare Hotel & Country Club

Straffan, Co. Kildare. ☎ **800/221-1074** from the U.S., or 01/627-3333. Fax 01/627-3312. 45 rms. MINIBAR TV TEL. £286–£316 ($457.60–$505.60) double. No service charge. Rates include full breakfast. AE, DC, MC, V.

Located 20 miles west of Dublin, this 330-acre resort is a favorite with Ireland's sporting set. The focal point of the estate is Straffan House, a 19th-century mansion that now serves as the core of the hotel, with an adjacent new west wing that is a replica of the original building. The bedrooms are spread out among the main hotel, courtyard suites, and a lodge. High ceilings, bow windows, wide staircases, antiques, and period pieces are all enhanced by hand-painted wall coverings and murals. The house overlooks a 1-mile stretch of the River Liffey.

Dining/Entertainment: The main restaurant is the Bryerley Turk, featuring French food, while lighter fare including afternoon tea is available in the Gallery; the Legends bar overlooks the golf course.

Services: 24-hour room service, nightly turndown, concierge, laundry/valet service.

Facilities: 18-hole Arnold Palmer–designed championship par-72 golf course, private access to salmon and trout fishing, two indoor and two outdoor tennis courts, two squash courts, gym, indoor swimming pool, sauna, solarium.

EXPENSIVE

✪ Kilkea Castle

Castledermot, Co. Kildare. ☎ **0503/45156** or 0503/45100. Fax 0503/45187. 40 rms. TV TEL. £140–£170 ($224–$272) double. Service charge 12.5%. AE, DC, MC, V.

Nestled beside the River Greese and surrounded by lovely formal gardens, this tall, multiturreted stone castle is a standout in the flat farmland of Co. Kildare. Considered the oldest inhabited castle in Ireland, it dates from 1180 and was built by Hugh de Lacy, an early Irish governor, for Walter de Riddlesford, a great warrior. The castle later passed into the ownership of the legendary Geraldines and it is still supposed to be haunted by the 11th earl of Kildare. Every seven years, the earl, dressed in full regalia and accompanied by his knights, is said to gallop around the castle walls.

Fully restored as a hotel in recent years, Kilkea is decorated with suits of armor and medieval banners, as well as a mix of Irish antiques and Oriental tables, chests, and urns. About a third of the bedrooms are in the original castle building, with the rest in a newer courtyard addition. The furnishings include dark woods, semi-canopy beds, armoires, chandeliers, brass fixtures, gilt-framed paintings and mirrors, and floral designer fabrics; each has a modern tile-and-brass bathroom. The castle is approximately 2½ miles from Castledermot and is well signposted from the town.

Dining/Entertainment: The main dining room is de Lacy's, specializing in innovative Irish cuisine. The Geraldine Bar conveys a 12th-century atmosphere, with original stone walls, stained-glass windows, and huge fireplace crowned by a copper flue.

Services: Room service, concierge, baby-sitting.

Facilities: 18-hole golf course, indoor heated swimming pool, exercise room, saunas, spa pool, steam rooms, sun bed, toning table, fishing for brown trout on the adjacent River Greese, two floodlit hard tennis courts, clay pigeon shooting, bicycle rental, archery range.

EXPENSIVE/MODERATE

Hotel Keadeen

Off Dublin-Limerick road (N7), Newbridge, Co. Kildare. ☎ **045/431666.** Fax 045/434402. 33 rms. TV TEL. £150 ($240) double. No service charge. Rates include full breakfast. AE, DC, MC, V.

Situated less than 2 miles east of The Curragh racetrack, this small country-style hotel is a favorite with the horse set. Although just off the main road, it is set back in its own eight acres of grounds in a quiet garden setting. Equestrian art dominates the public rooms. The guest rooms are up-to-date, with light woods, floral fabrics, and brass fixtures. Facilities include the Derby Room restaurant and lounge.

DINING
EXPENSIVE

Moyglare Manor

Maynooth, Co. Kildare. ☎ **01/628-6351.** Reservations required. Fixed-price dinner £24 ($38.40). Service charge 12.5%. AE, DC, V. Daily 7–9:30pm. Closed Good Friday and Dec 23–26. FRENCH.

A half-hour's drive on the Dublin-Galway road (N4) will deliver you to this grand Georgian mansion/inn, whose restaurant is surprisingly intimate. Elegance is the operative word here. The roast quail, baked plaice stuffed with shrimp, panfried brill, and steaks, all with fresh vegetables from the manor's own garden, are not known to disappoint.

MODERATE/INEXPENSIVE

Silken Thomas

The Square, Kildare, Co. Kildare. ☎ **045/22232.** Reservations not required for lunch. Lunch main courses £5–£8 ($8–$12.80); dinner main courses £6–£12 ($9.50–$19.20). AE, MC, V. Daily 12:30–3pm and 6–10pm. IRISH/INTERNATIONAL.

Formerly known as Leinster Lodge, this historic inn offers an old world–pub/restaurant with open fire and dark woods. It is named after a famous member of the Norman Fitzgerald family, whose stronghold was in Kildare. He led an unsuccessful rebellion against Henry VIII and some of the decor recalls his efforts. The menu offers a good selection of soups, sandwiches, burgers, and salads as well as steaks, roasts, mixed grills, and fresh seafood platters. It is located on the main square in Kildare town.

3 Counties Meath & Louth / The Boyne River Valley

30 to 50 miles north and west of Dublin.

ESSENTIALS

GETTING THERE   Irish Rail (☎ 01/836-3333) provides daily train service between Dublin and Drogheda.

Bus Eireann (☎ 01/836-6111) operates daily express bus service to Slane and Navan in Co. Meath, and Collon and Drogheda in Co. Louth. Both Bus Eireann and Gray Line Tours (☎ 01/661-9666) offer seasonal (March to October) sightseeing tours to Newgrange and/or the Boyne Valley.

If you're traveling by car, take N1 north from Dublin City to Drogheda and then N51 west to Boyne Valley; N2 northwest to Slane and east on N51 to Boyne Valley; or N3 northwest via Hill of Tara to Navan, and then east on N51 to Boyne Valley.

VISITOR INFORMATION   **For year-round information about counties Meath and Louth, contact the **Dundalk Tourist Office, Jocelyn Street, Co. Louth (☎ 042/35484). **Seasonal information offices** are also open at Newgrange (☎ 041/24274) from Easter to October and in Drogheda (☎ 041/37070) from June through August.

AREA CODES   **The telephone area code for Co. Louth is **041 and for Co. Meath, **042.**

COUNTY MEATH: THE ROYAL COUNTY

Less than 30 miles north of Dublin along Ireland's east coast runs the River Boyne, surrounded by the rich and fertile countryside of counties Meath and Louth. More than any other river in the country, this meandering body of water has been at the center of Irish history.

The banks of the Boyne are lined with reminders from almost every phase of Ireland's past, from the prehistoric passage tombs of Newgrange to the storied Hill of Tara, seat of the High Kings, to early Christian sites. This land was also the setting for the infamous Battle of the Boyne, when on July 1, 1690 (July 12 by modern calendars), King William III defeated the exiled King James II for the crown of England.

The southern portion of the Boyne belongs to Co. Meath, an area that consists almost entirely of a rich limestone plain, with verdant pasturelands and occasional low hills. Once a separate province that included neighboring Co. Westmeath, Meath was usually referred to as the Royal Co. Meath since it was ruled by the kings of pagan and early Christian Ireland, from the Hill of Tara near Navan.

While the chief town of Co. Meath is Navan, nearby Kells is better known to the traveler because of its association with the famous Book of Kells, the hand-illustrated gospel manuscript on display at Trinity College in Dublin. The town of Kells, known as Ceanannus Mor in Gaelic (meaning "Great Residence"), was originally the site of an important 6th-century monastic settlement founded by St. Columcille and occupied for a time by monks driven from Iona in the 9th century by the Vikings. These monks may have brought with them at least an incomplete Book of Kells. The book was stolen in 1007, only to be recovered months later from a bog. The monastery was dissolved in 1551, and today only ruins and a number of crosses survive.

Less than 25 miles southeast of Kells, beside the River Boyne, stand the luring ruins of Bective Abbey, a Cistercian monastery founded in 1147 and fortified in the 15th century. Today, the fortress aspect of the abbey prevails and it has more the feel of a castle than of a monastery. It is a great climbing ruin, with myriad staircases, passageways, and chambers—a favorite hide-and-seek venue for local children, and perfect for a family picnic.

A focal point of Co. Meath is Slane, a small crossroads village and gateway to prehistoric Newgrange. Nearby is the Hill of Slane, a lofty mound of 500 feet overlooking one of the loveliest parts of the Boyne Valley. On this hill, tradition has it, Patrick lit the Christian paschal fire in direct defiance of the Irish King Laoghaire, thus throwing down the gauntlet for a confrontation between the old and the new religious orders in Ireland.

Even though Meath is primarily an inland county, it is also blessed with a short, 6-mile stretch of Irish coastline and two fine sandy beaches, Bettystown and Laytown. History pops up everywhere in Co. Meath, even on the beach: It was at Bettystown in 1850 that the Tara Brooch was found. Often copied in modern jewelry designs, the brooch is one of Ireland's finest pieces of early Christian gold-filigree work embellished with amber and glass. It's on view at the National Museum in Dublin.

SEEING THE SIGHTS

✪ Hill of Tara

Off the main Dublin road (N3), Navan, Co. Meath. ☎ **046/25903.** Admission £1 ($1.50) adults, 70p ($1.05) seniors, 40p (60¢) children and students; no access to interior. May to mid-June daily 10am–5pm; mid-June to mid-Sept daily 9:30am–6:30pm; mid-Sept to end Oct daily 10am–5pm.

This glorious hill is best remembered as the royal seat of the high kings in the early centuries after Christ. Every three years a *feis* (a banquet reaching the proportions of a great national assembly) was held. It's said that more than 1,000 people—princes, poets, athletes, priests, druids, musicians, and jesters—celebrated for a week in a single immense hall. As the poet Thomas Moore wrote: "The harp that once through Tara's halls, / the soul of music shed . . ." A feis wasn't all fun and games, though: Laws were passed, tribal disputes settled, and matters of peace and defense decided.

The last feis was held in A.D. 560, and thereafter Tara went into a decline associated with the rise of Christianity. If you rally to Tara's halls today, you won't see any turrets or towers, nor moats and crown jewels—in fact, you won't even see any halls. All that remains of Tara's former glories are grassy mounds and some ancient pillar stones. All the wooden halls rotted long ago, so you'll have to rely on your imagination to fill in the glories. Nevertheless, it's still a magnificent spot, with the hill rising 300 feet above the surrounding countryside, and the views surely as awesome as they were 1,500 years ago.

A new visitor center, with exhibits and a stirring audiovisual presentation, is located in the old church beside the entrance to the archaeological area.

✪ Knowth

Slane, Co. Meath. ☎ **041/24824.** Admission £2 ($3.20) adults, £1.50 ($2.40) seniors, £1 ($1.60) students and children, £5 ($8) family. May to mid-June daily 10am–5pm; mid-June to mid-Sept daily 9:30am–6:30pm; mid-Sept to end Oct daily 10am–5pm. Signposted off N51.

Dating from the Stone Age and under seemingly perpetual excavation, this great mound is believed to have been a burial site for the high kings of Ireland. Archaeological evidence points to occupation from 3000 B.C. to A.D. 1200. Located 1 mile northwest of Newgrange (see below), between Drogheda and Slane, Knowth is more complex than Newgrange, with two passage tombs surrounded by another 17 smaller satellite tombs. The site has the greatest collection of passage tomb art ever uncovered in Western Europe.

✪ Newgrange

Off N51, Slane, Co. Meath. ☎ **041/24488.** Admission £3 ($4.80) adults, £2 ($3.20) seniors, £1.25 ($2) students and children over 12, £7.50 ($12) family. No credit cards accepted. Open daily Nov–Feb 10am–4:30pm; Mar–Apr 10am–5pm; May 9:30am–6pm; June to mid-Sept 9:30am–7pm; mid–end Sept 9:30am–6pm; Oct 10am–5pm.

Known in Irish as *Brugh na Boinne* (the Palace of the Boyne), Newgrange is Ireland's best-known prehistoric monument and one of the archaeological wonders of Western Europe. Built as a burial mound more than 5,000 years ago—long before the Great Pyramids and Stonehenge—it sits atop a hill near the Boyne, massive and impressive. The huge mound—36 feet tall and approximately 260 feet in diameter—consists of 200,000 tons of stone, a six-ton capstone, and other stones weighing up to 16 tons each, many of which were hauled from as far away as Co. Wicklow and the Mountains of Mourne. Each stone fits perfectly in the overall pattern and the result is a water-tight structure, an amazing feat of engineering. Carved into the stones are myriad spirals, diamonds, and concentric circles. Inside, a passage 60 feet long leads to a central burial chamber with a 19-foot ceiling.

Curiosity about Newgrange reaches a peak each winter solstice, when at 8:58am, as the sun rises to the southeast, sunlight pierces the inner chamber with an orange-toned glow for about 17 minutes. This occurrence is so remarkable that, as of this writing, the waiting list for viewing extends through the year 2004. Admission to Newgrange is by guided tour only. It's located 2 miles east of Slane, off N51. When the new Visitors Centre, across the Boyne from Newgrange, is completed this year, all visitors will be conveyed from there by bus to the monuments.

✪ Newgrange Farm

Off N51, Slane, Co. Meath. ☎ **041/24119.** Admission £2 ($3.20) per person, £8 ($12.80) family. Apr–Sept, Mon–Fri 10am–5:30pm and Sun 2–5:30pm.

A contrast to all the surrounding antiquity in the Boyne Valley, this busy 333-acre farm is very much a 20th-century attraction. Farmer Willie Redhouse and his family invite visitors on a 1¹⁄₂-hour tour of their farm, which grows wheat, oats, barley, oil seed rape, corn, and linseed (flax). You can throw feed to the ducks, groom a calf, or bottle-feed the baby lambs or kid goats. Children can hold a newborn chick, pet a pony, or play with the pigs. In the aviaries are pheasants and rare birds. In the fields romp horses, donkeys, and rare Jacob sheep.

Demonstrations of sheepdog-working, threshing, and horse-shoeing are given. The Redhouses spin and dye their own wool and have put together an exhibit of the fibers produced and the natural dyes used to color them. At the herb garden, visitors receive a lesson on picking edible plants and herbs. Many of the farm buildings are from the 17th century. There's a coffee shop (see below) and indoor and outdoor picnic areas. It's located 2 miles east of Slane, signposted off N51 and directly west of Newgrange monument.

Loughcrew

Outside Oldcastle, Co. Meath. Open site. From N3, take R195 through Oldcastle toward Mullingar. 1¹/₂ miles out of Oldcastle, look for a signposted left turn. The next left turn into Loughcrew is also signposted.

The 30 passage tombs of Loughcrew, also known as Slieve na Calliaghe or "the hill of the witch," crown three hilltops in western Meath. The views of the plains of Meath and of the lakelands of Cavan are spectacular on a clear day. Two of the cairns, ornamented with Neolithic carvings, can be entered with a key (see below). The wonder of this site is that, like the tombs of Carrowkeel, these are unattended and rarely visited, so it is possible to be alone with them. Why be alone with 5,000-year-old megalithic burial mounds? Bring this question with you to Loughcrew and you'll leave with the answer. A key to the two locked cairns can be gotten from Mrs. Basil Balfe (☎ 049/41256), whose home is the first house on your right after turning into the Loughcrew drive. A deposit of £5 ($8) is required.

SHOPPING

Mary McDonnell Craft Studio

Newgrange Mall Studio, Slane, Co. Meath. ☎ **041/24722.** July–Aug Mon–Sat 10am–6pm, Sun 2–6pm; Sept–June Tues–Sat 10am–6pm, Sun 2–6pm.

Mary McDonnell, textile artist, welcomes visitors to watch as she creates beautiful leather items, ceramics, jewelry, quilts, cushions, and wall hangings. Her shop also stocks the work of other local artisans. Dried flower art, candles, and lace are for sale. It's worth a detour.

ACCOMMODATIONS

Inexpensive

⑤ Conyngham Arms Hotel

Main St., Slane, Co. Meath. ☎ **800/447-7462** from the U.S., or 041/24155. Fax 041/24205. 16 rms (15 with bath). TV TEL. £47.50–£65 ($76–$104) double. No service charge. Rates include full breakfast. AE, DC, MC, V. Closed Jan–Mar.

In the heart of one of the Boyne Valley's loveliest villages, this three-story stone-faced inn dates from 1850 and has been run by the same family for more than 60 years. The current proprietors, Kevin and Vonnie Macken, work hard to blend old-world charm and personal attention with 20th-century efficiency and innovative innkeeping. The guest rooms offer traditional dark wood furnishings, some with part-canopy beds, rich primary-color fabrics, good reading lights, and wildlife art. Other features include writing desks, towel warmers, mirrored closets, and hair dryers, but, in keeping with the building's character, no elevator. Exceptionally good bar food is available all day in the lounge. Dinner is served in the adjacent Flemings restaurant, two rooms with a lot of character and Irish memorabilia.

DINING

Moderate

Hudson's Bistro

Railway St., Navan, Co. Meath. ☎ **046/29231.** Reservations required Fri–Sat. Main courses £7.50 ($12)–£12.50 ($20). 10% service charge. AE, CB, DC, EU, MC, V. Tues–Sat 6:30–11pm, Sun 6:30–10pm. NOUVELLE INTERNATIONAL.

This snappy little bistro, decked out in sunny colors and bright pottery, is a treat for travelers en route through the Navan area, especially couples or small groups of friends who enjoy quiet talk, wine, and terrific food. Try the tender Greek lamb kebabs with saffron rice, ratatouille chutney, and truly crisp salad, or the authentic and delicious spicy Thai curry with vegetables. The saffron fettucine with prawns boasts perfectly cooked fresh pasta, though the sauce was too obscure for my taste. Daily soup and entrée specials are also offered. Not to be missed are the desserts, such as "the Symphony," a house best that lives up to its name. The staff is friendly and the chefs gladly accommodate vegetarian requests and food allergies.

Inexpensive

ⓢ Newgrange Farm Coffee Shop

Off N51, Slane, Co. Meath. ☎ **041/24119.** Reservations not necessary. All items £2–£5.50 ($3.20–$8.80). No credit cards. Apr–June and Sept Sun–Fri 10am–5:30pm; July–Aug daily 10am–5:30pm. SELF-SERVICE/IRISH.

Located on the premises of a working farm (see Newgrange Farm listing, above), this family-run restaurant is housed in a converted barn, now whitewashed and skylit. It has an open fireplace and local art on the walls. Ann Redhouse and her family oversee the baking and food preparation each day, using many ingredients grown on the farm or locally. The ever-changing blackboard menu ranges from homemade soups and hot scones or biscuits to sandwiches, with tempting desserts like apple tart and cream, carrot cake, and fruit pies. Food can also be enjoyed in an outdoor picnic area and there is often live Irish traditional music in the summer months.

COUNTY LOUTH / CUCHULAINN COUNTRY

To the north and east of Meath is Louth, the smallest of Ireland's counties but possessing a diversity of historic treasures and early Christian landmarks. Carlingford, one of Ireland's heritage towns, is set on a spur of the Cooley Mountains, overlooking Carlingford Lough and the Irish Sea at the most northerly point of Ireland's east coast south of Northern Ireland. Established by the Vikings, it is still very much a medieval town dominated by a massive 13th-century castle. Legend has it that long before the Vikings came, Carlingford was part of the hunting grounds of warriors. On the heights above the town, folk hero Cuchulainn is said to have single-handedly defeated the armies of Ulster in an epic battle.

Louth is not a place of outstanding scenic beauty, and most visitors will choose to move on after exploring a few sites of historic interest.

ATTRACTIONS

Millmount Museum

Duleek St., off the main Dublin road (N1), Drogheda, Co. Louth. ☎ **041/36391** or 041/33097. Admission £1 ($1.60) adults, 50p (80¢) children under 12. May–Sept Tues–Sun 2–6pm; Oct–Apr Wed and Sat–Sun 3–5pm.

In the courtyard of 18th-century Millmount Fort, this museum offers exhibits on the history of Drogheda and the Boyne Valley area. A Bronze Age oracle, medieval tiles, and a collection of 18th-century guild banners are on display. Domestic items are showcased, too, such as spinning, weaving, and brewing equipment; antique gramophones; mousetraps; and hot-water jars. A geological exhibit contains specimens of stone from every county in Ireland, every country in Europe, and beyond.

Mellifont Abbey

Off T25, Collon, Co. Louth. ☎ **041/26459.** Admission £1.50 ($2.40) adults, £1 ($1.60) seniors, 60p (95¢) students and children under 12, £4 ($6.40) family. May to mid-June daily 10am–5pm; mid-June to mid-Sept daily 9:30am–6:30pm; mid-Sept to end Oct daily 10am–5pm.

"Old Mellifont"—as distinct from "New Mellifont," an existing Cistercian monastery several miles away—was established in 1142 by St. Malachy of Armagh. Although little more than foundations survive here, this tranquil spot is worth a visit for a few moments of quiet. Remnants of a 14th-century chapter house, an octagonal lavabo dating from around 1200, and several Romanesque arches remain. A new visitors center contains sculpted stones from the excavations. The abbey is on the banks of the Mattock River, 6 miles west of Drogheda.

Monasterboice

Off the main Dublin road (N1), near Collon, Co. Louth. Free admission. Daylight hours.

Once a great monastery and now little more than a peaceful cemetery, this site is dominated by Muiredeach's High Cross. At 17 feet tall, it's one of the most perfect crosses in Ireland. Dating from the year 922, the cross is ornamented with sculptured panels of scenes from the Old and New Testaments. On the monastery grounds are the remains of a round tower, two churches, two early grave slabs, and a sundial. It's located 6 miles northwest of Drogheda.

✪ Holy Trinity Heritage Centre

Carlingford, Co. Louth. ☎ **042/73454.** Admission £1 ($1.60) adults, 50p (80¢) for children under 16. Sept–May weekends noon–5pm, June–Aug 10am–7pm.

In a beautifully restored medieval church, this center has exhibits that detail the town's history from its Norman origins. If you book ahead, a visit here includes a guided walking tour of the town and a look at King John's Castle, the Mint, The Tholsel (the sole surviving, though altered, gate to the old medieval town), and a Dominican friary. The center overlooks the south shore of Carlington Lough, at the foot of Sliabh Foy, the highest peak of the Cooley Mountains.

ACCOMMODATIONS & DINING

Moderate

Ballymascanlon House

Off the Dublin-Belfast road (N1), Dundalk, Co. Louth. ☎ **800/528-1234** from the U.S., or 042/71124. Fax 042/71598. 56 rms. TV TEL. £75–£90 ($105–$112.50) double. Rates include full breakfast. No service charge. AE, DC, MC, V.

A stone-faced Victorian mansion dating from the early 1800s, Ballymascanlon was formerly the home of Baron Plunkett and in 1947 was converted into a hotel by the Quinn family, which has enlarged it several times since. It stands on 130 acres of award-winning gardens and grounds, a peaceful oasis just 3 miles south of the Northern Ireland border. Rooms vary in size, but are decorated in traditional style, with some Victorian or antique touches.

   Dining/Entertainment: The Dining Room specializes in local meats and seafood, using vegetables from the hotel gardens; the Cellar Bar offers light refreshment and (usually) traditional Irish music on weekends.

Facilities: Indoor heated swimming pool, two floodlit all-weather tennis courts, two squash courts, sauna, solarium, and gym. An 18-hole golf course was recently added.

Inexpensive

McKevitts Village Inn

Market Sq., Carlingford, Co. Louth. ☎ **800/447-7462** from the U.S., or 042/73116. Fax 042/73144. 13 rms. TV TEL. £50–£65 ($80–$104) double. Rates include full breakfast. No service charge. AE, DC, MC, V.

Situated right in the heart of a lovely medieval village, this is a great hotel for unwinding and taking long walks along the shores of Carlingford Lough. It's a vintage two-story property that has been updated and refurbished in recent years. Guest rooms vary in size and shape, but all have standard Irish furnishings and are very comfortable, with nice views of the town. The public areas include an old-world bar and a very good restaurant that specializes in local seafood and produce. It makes a great base for day trips into Northern Ireland and the surrounding Boyne Valley countryside.

AN EASY EXCURSION FROM COUNTY LOUTH

The town of Carrickmacross in Co. Monaghan has been famous for its tradition of lace making for more than 150 years. Five miles from Co. Louth's northwest border, it's well worth a detour to the Lace Gallery of the **Carrickmacross Lace Co-op** on Main Street, Carrickmacross (☎ **042/62506**). On view here are the beautiful and intricate handmade laces produced in the area. Demonstrations are given every once in a while; call to inquire.

It's open May through October on Monday, Tuesday, Thursday, and Friday from 9:30am to 12:30pm and 1:30 to 5:30pm, on Wednesday and Saturday from 9:30am to 12:30pm only.

Accommodations & Dining

Nuremore

Ashbourne-Slane-Ardee road (N2), Carrickmacross, Co. Monaghan. ☎ **042/61438.** Fax 042/61853. 69 rms. TV TEL. £110–£150 ($176–$240) double. No service charge. Rates include breakfast. V.

In a town famous for its lace, this modern three-story hotel is equally well known for its hospitality and high standards. Set amid 100 acres of parkland and woods (including three lakes), it has been totally refurbished and updated in recent years. The decor is traditional with dark woods, marble fireplaces, and antique framed prints of the area. Most of the bedrooms feature bright colors, reproduction furniture, and semicanopy beds; some have light woods and more contemporary styles. They all provide lake or garden views. Public areas include a restaurant and lounge bar. Facilities include an 18-hole championship golf course, heated indoor swimming pool, squash court, two tennis courts, sauna, steam room, gym, whirlpool, and trout fishing on the privately stocked hotel lake.

7

The Southeast

Wexford, Waterford, and Kilkenny are often referred to as Ireland's sunny southeast, because these counties usually enjoy more hours of sunshine than the rest of the country. No matter what the weather, they also provide a varied touring experience, from the world-famous Waterford Crystal Factory to the Viking streets of Wexford and the medieval buildings of Kilkenny.

1 County Wexford

Wexford Town is 88 miles S of Dublin, 39 miles E of Waterford, 56 miles S of Wicklow, 116 miles E of Cork, 133 miles SE of Shannon Airport.

GETTING THERE   Daily train service into Wexford and Rosslare Pier is provided by Irish Rail into **O'Hanrahan Station,** Redmond Place, Wexford (☎ **053/22522**).

Daily bus service to Wexford and Rosslare is operated by Bus Eireann, into O'Hanrahan Station and Bus Depot, Redmond Place, Wexford (☎ **053/22522**).

If you're driving from Dublin and points north, take N11 or N80 to Wexford; from the west, take N25 or N8. Two bridges lead into Wexford from points north—the Ferrycarrig Bridge from the main Dublin road (N11) and the Wexford Bridge from R741. The Ferrycarrig Bridge takes you into town from the west, while the Wexford Bridge leads right to the heart of town along the quays.

Ferry service from Britain to Rosslare Harbour, 12 miles south of Wexford Town, is operated from Fishguard by **Stena Line** (☎ **053/ 33115**) and from Pembroke by **Irish Ferries** (☎ **053/33311**). Irish Ferries also provides service from Le Havre and Cherbourg, France.

Within Ireland, the **Passage East Ferry Co. Ltd.,** Barrack Street, Passage East, Co. Waterford (☎ **051/382480** or 051/382488), operates a car ferry service across Waterford Harbour, linking Passage East, about 10 miles east of Waterford, with Ballyhack, about 20 miles southwest of Wexford. This shortcut saves about an hour's driving time between the two cities. Crossing time averages 10 minutes and service is continuous. It's a drive-on, drive-off service, with no reservations required. The fares are £4 ($6.40) one way and £6 ($9.60) round-trip for car and passengers, £1.00 ($1.60) round-trip for foot passengers, £1.50 ($2.40) one-way and £2 ($3.20) round-trip for cyclists. It operates April through September, Monday through Saturday, 7:20am until 10pm, and on Sunday, 9:30am until 10pm; October through March, Monday through Saturday, 7:20am until 8pm, and Sunday, 9:30am until 8pm.

VISITOR INFORMATION   Year-round information services are provided by the **Wexford Tourist Office,** Crescent Quay, Wexford (☎ **053/23111**), and the **Rosslare Harbour Tourist Office,** Ferry Terminal, Rosslare Harbour (☎ **053/ 33622**). The Wexford Town office is open April, May, September, and October Monday through Saturday, 9am to 6pm; January through March and November, Monday through Friday, 9am to 5:15pm; July and August Monday through Saturday, 9am to 6pm, and Sunday, 10am to 5pm. The Rosslare Harbour Office opens daily to coincide with ferry arrivals. **Seasonal offices,** open June through August, are maintained at Enniscorthy, Town Centre (☎ **054/34699**); Gorey, Town Centre (☎ **055/21248**); New Ross, Town Centre (☎ **051/21857**), and Rosslare (☎ **053/ 33232**).

TOWN LAYOUT   Rimmed by the River Slaney, Wexford is a small and compact town. Four Quays (Custom House, Commercial, Paul, and the semicircular Crescent) run beside the water, with Cresent Quay marking the center of town. One block inland is Main Street, a long, narrow thoroughfare that can be easily walked. Wexford's shops and businesses are on either North or South Main Street or on one of the many smaller streets that fan out from it.

GETTING AROUND   By Public Transport   Since Wexford is small and compact, with narrow streets, there is no local bus transport. **Bus Eireann** (☎ **053/ 22522**) operates daily service between Wexford and Rosslare. Other local services operate on certain days only to Kilmore Quay, Carne, and Gorey. If you need a taxi, call **Andrew's Hackney Service** (☎ **053/45933**), **Rory Conroy** (☎ **053/22934**), or **Wexford Taxi** (☎ **053/06666**).

By Car   To see Wexford Town, walk. Park your car along the Quays; parking is operated according to the disc system, at 30p (48¢) per hour. Discs are on sale at the tourist office or many of the shops. There is free parking off Redmond Square, beside the train/bus station. You'll need a car to reach Co. Wexford attractions outside of town.

If you need to rent a car, contact **Budget** at Rosslare Ferryport, Rosslare (☎ **053/ 33318**); **Murrays Europcar,** Wellington Place, Wexford (☎ **053/22122**) or at the Rosslare Ferryport, Rosslare (☎ **053/33634**); or **Hertz** at Ferrybank, Wexford (☎ **053/23511**) or at Rosslare Ferryport, Rosslare (☎ **053/33238**).

On Foot   The best way to see the town is by walking the entire length of North and South Main Street, taking time to detour up and down the various alleys and lanes that cross the street. The tourist office will supply you with a free map.

FAST FACTS: WEXFORD

Area Codes   The telephone area code for Wexford Town is **053;** the surrounding areas use **051, 053, 054,** and **055.**

Drugstores   Try **John Fehily / The Pharmacy,** 28 S. Main St., Wexford (☎ **053/23163**); **Sherwood Chemist,** 2 N. Main St., Wexford (☎ **053/22875**); and **Fortune's Pharmacy,** 82 N. Main St., Wexford (☎ **053/42354**).

Dry Cleaning and Laundry   Two good choices are **My Beautiful Launderette,** at St. Peter's Square, Wexford (☎ **053/24317**); and **Marlow Cleaners,** at 7 S. Main St., Wexford (☎ **053/22172**).

Emergencies   Dial **999.**

Hospital   **Wexford General Hospital** is located on Richmond Terrace, Wexford (☎ **53/42233**).

The Southeast

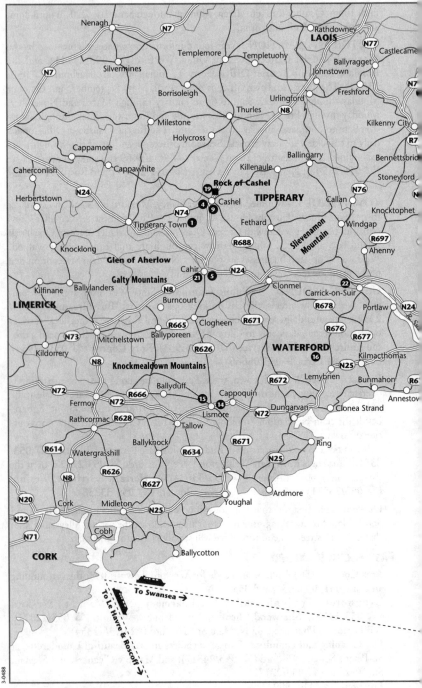

N9
Carlow Town
R726
Tullow   Woodenbridge
                  WICKLOW
            Shillelagh   Arklow
Leighlinbridge
d Leighlin

Muine Bheag
(Bagenalstown)   Gorey
                          Bunclody ❶❼
N9   R705 CARLOW
            Borris   Ferns
❻ Graiguenamanagh
Thomastown   ❽
                          Enniscorthy
R729
            St. Mullins   Blackwater
R. Nore   Clonroche   N11
❶❸   N79   Oylgate
ILKENNY   New Ross
            ❸ WEXFORD   ❶❽
        John F.
        Kennedy Park
N25   ❶❶   N25   Wexford
            Dunganstown   Harbour   St. George's
                    R738   Channel
Mullinavat   Wellington-Bridge Wexford Town
Cheekpoint ❷ Ballyhack   ❶❷
            R733   Rosslare Rosslare
5 Waterford Duncannon Duncormick R736 ❷❸ Harbour
City Passage East   Tomhaggard   To Fishguard →
amore   Waterford   Fethard-on-Sea   Lady's Island
         Harbour   Fornlorn Pt. Kilmore Quay
         HOOK
         PENINSULA   To Le Havre & Cherbourg →
                    ❷❶ SALTEE ISLANDS

                         Celtic Sea

Athassel Priory ❶
Ballyhack Castle ❷
Ballylane Farm ❸
Bru Boru ❹
Cahir Castle ❺
Duiske Abbey ❻
Dunmore Cave ❼
Enniscorthy Castle/Wexford
   County Museum ❽
GPA—Bolton Library ❾
Jerpoint Abbey ❿
John F. Kennedy Arboretum ⓫
Johnstown Castle Gardens &
   Irish Agricultural Museum ⓬
Kennedy Centre ⓭
Lismore Castle ⓮
Lismore Heritage Centre ⓯
Mahon Falls ⓰
Mount Leinster ⓱
Raven Nature Reserve ⓲
The Rock of Cashel ⓳
Saltee Islands ⓴
Swiss Cottage ㉑
Tipperary Crystal ㉒
Tola Farmstead ㉓

IRELAND

The
Southeast

0 ▭▭▭▭ 10 mi   N
         16 km

207

Newspaper　The *Wexford People* is the weekly newspaper covering town and county events and entertainment.

Photographic Services　Try the **Photo Centre,** at 6 N. Main St., Wexford (☎ **053/45502**).

Police　The **Garda Station** is located on Roches Road, Wexford (☎ **053/22333**).

Post Office　The **General Post Office** on Anne Street, Wexford (☎ **053/22587**), is open Monday through Saturday from 9am to 5:30pm.

A FEW WORDS ABOUT WEXFORD

County Wexford is most remarkable for the long stretches of pristine beach that line its coast, and for the evocative historic monuments to be found in Wexford Town and on the Hook Peninsula. The Blackstairs Mountains dominate the western border of the county, and provide excellent hill-walking. Bird-watchers will find an abundance of great sites, including Wexford Wildfowl Reserve and Great Saltee Island.

The modern English name of Wexford evolved from Waesfjord, which is what the Viking sea-rovers called it when they settled here in the 9th century. It literally means "the harbor of the mud-flats." Like the rest of Ireland, Wexford was under Norman control by the 12th century, and there still remain some reminders in stone of their dominance in this region.

ATTRACTIONS

✪ West Gate Heritage Tower

Westgate St., Wexford. ☎ **053/46506.** Admission £1.50 ($2.40) adults, £1 ($1.60) children and students. July–Aug Mon–Sat 9am–1pm and 2–5pm, Sun noon–4pm; May, June, Sept Mon–Sat 11am–1pm and 2–5pm, Sun noon–4pm.

West Gate once guarded the western entrance of Wexford Town. It was built in the 13th century by Sir Stephen Devereux on instructions of King Henry. Like other town gates, it consisted of a toll-taking area, cells for offenders, and accommodations for guards. Fully restored and reopened in 1992 as a heritage center, it presents artifacts, displays, and a 27-minute audiovisual presentation depicting Wexford's varied history.

Selskar Abbey

Off Temperance Row at Westgate St., Wexford.

Said to be one of the oldest sites of religious worship in Wexford, this abbey dates from at least the 12th century. It was often the scene of synods and parliaments. The first Anglo-Irish treaty was signed here in 1169, and it's said that Henry II spent the Lent of 1172 at the abbey doing penance for having Thomas à Becket beheaded. Although the abbey is mostly in ruins, its choir is now part of a Church of Ireland edifice, and a portion of the original tower is a vesting room. Check the sign on the often-locked gate for information on access.

Cornmarket

Off Upper George's St., Wexford.

Until a century ago, this central marketplace buzzed with the activity of cobblers, publicans, and more than 20 other businesses. Today it's just a wide street. The Wexford Arts Centre, in a structure dating from 1775, dominates the street.

The Bull Ring

Off N. Main St., Wexford. Free admission.

In 1798, the first declaration of an Irish Republic was made here, and a statue memorializes the Irish pikemen who fought for the cause. Earlier, in the 17th

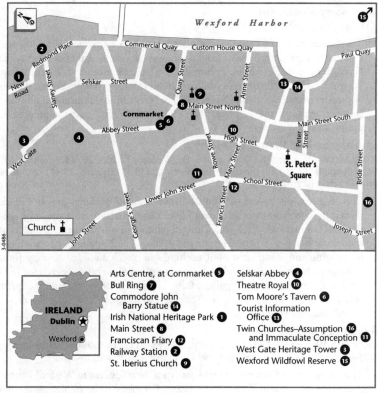

Arts Centre, at Cornmarket ⑤
Bull Ring ⑦
Commodore John
  Barry Statue ⑭
Irish National Heritage Park ①
Main Street ⑧
Franciscan Friary ⑫
Railway Station ②
St. Iberius Church ⑨

Selskar Abbey ④
Theatre Royal ⑩
Tom Moore's Tavern ⑥
Tourist Information
  Office ⑬
Twin Churches–Assumption ⑯
  and Immaculate Conception ⑪
West Gate Heritage Tower ③
Wexford Wildfowl Reserve ⑮

century, the town square was a venue for bull-baiting, a sport introduced by the butcher's guild. Tradition has it that, after a match, the hide of the ill-fated bull was presented to the mayor and the meat used to feed the poor. Currently, the activity at the ring is much tamer: a weekly outdoor market, open Friday and Saturday 10am to 4:30pm.

St. Iberius Church

N. Main St. ☎ **053/43013.** Free admission; donations welcome. May–Sept daily 10am–5pm; Oct–Apr Tues–Sat 10am–3pm.

Erected in 1660, St. Iberius was built on hallowed ground—the land had been used for previous houses of worship dating from Norse times. The church has a lovely Georgian facade and an interior known for its superb acoustics. Free guided tours are given according to demand.

✪ The Twin Churches: Church of the Assumption and Church of the Immaculate Conception

Bride and Rowe sts., Wexford. ☎ **053/22055.** Free admission; donations welcome. Daily 8am–6pm.

These twin Gothic structures (1851–58) were designed by architect Robert Pierce, a pupil of Augustus Pugin. Their spires rise 230 feet and dominate the skyline of Wexford. Cobbled on the main door of both churches are mosaics showing relevant names and dates.

John Barry Monument

Crescent Quay, Wexford.

This bronze statue, a gift from the American people in 1956, faces out to the sea as a tribute to John Barry, a favorite local son who became the father of the American Navy. Born at Ballysampson, Tacumshane, 10 miles southeast of Wexford Town, Barry emigrated to the colonies while still in his teens and volunteered for the cause of the American Revolution. One of the U.S. Navy's first commissioned officers, he became captain of the *Lexington*. In 1797, George Washington appointed him commander-in-chief of the U.S. Navy.

✪ Irish National Heritage Park

Off Dublin-Wexford road (N11), Ferrycarrig, Co. Wexford. ☎ **053/20733.** Admission £3.50 ($5.60) adults, £3 ($4.80) seniors and students, £2 ($3.20) children, £9 ($14.40) family. Mar–Oct daily 10am–7pm.

This 36-acre living history park on the banks of the River Slaney provides an ideal introduction for visitors of all ages to life in ancient Ireland, from the stone age to the Norman invasion. Each reconstructed glimpse into Irish history is beautifully crafted and has its own natural setting and wildlife. The 20-minute orientation video is engaging and informative, but nothing can match a guided tour by Jimmy O'Rourke, the park's head guide, who is an utter master in bringing each site to life, captivating children and intriguing adults. The park's nature trail and interpretive center, complete with gift shop and cafe, add to its appeal and argue for allowing several hours for your visit here.

Wexford Wildfowl Reserve

North Slob, Wexford. ☎ **053/23129.** Fax 053/24785. E-mail: cjwilson@iol.ie. Free admission. Mid-April to mid-Sept daily 9am–6pm; mid-Oct to mid-April daily 10am–5pm.

This national nature reserve is part of the North Slob adjacent to Wexford Harbour, 3 miles east of Wexford Town. About 10,000 Greenland white-fronted geese—more than one-third of the world's population—spend the winter here, as do brent geese, Bewick's swans, and wigeon. The area is immensely attractive to other wildfowl and birds, and more than 240 species have been seen here. The reserve has a visitor center, an audio-visual program, a new exhibition hall, and an observation tower and blinds.

SIGHTSEEING TOURS

✪ Walking Tours of Wexford

c/o Seamus Molloy, "Carmeleen," William St. ☎ **053/22663.** £3 ($4.80) adults, £1 ($1.60) children. Mon–Sat at 11:30am and 2:30pm.

Proud of their town's ancient streets and vintage buildings, the people of Wexford spontaneously started to give tours to visitors more than 30 years ago. Eventually

Impressions

I am glad to be here. It took 115 years to make this trip, and 6,000 miles, and three generations . . . In Ireland I think you see something of what is so great about the United States, and I must say that in the United States, through millions of your sons and daughters and cousins—25 million, in fact—you see something of what is great about Ireland . . . I am proud to have connected . . . the coat of arms of Wexford, the coat of arms of the kingly and beautiful Kennedys, and the coat of arms of the United States. That is a very good combination.

—Pres. John F. Kennedy, Wexford, June 1963

organized as the Old Wexford Society, this core of local folk has developed a real expertise over the years and continues to give tours on a regular basis. All tours depart from West Gate Heritage Tower.

NEARBY COUNTY WEXFORD ATTRACTIONS

✪ **SALTEE ISLANDS**   The Great Saltee Island is one of the best places in Ireland to watch seabirds, especially during the months of May, June, and July, when the place is mobbed with nesting parents and their young. Like something out of a Hitchcock feature, the cliffs on the island's southernmost point are packed to over-flowing with raucous avian residents, and the combined sound of their screeching, squawking, and chortling is nearly deafening at times. This is a place to get up close and personal with puffins, which nest in underground burrows, or the graceful guillemots. Other species include cormorants, kittiwakes, gannets, and Manx shear-waters. The island is privately owned, but visitors are welcome on the condition that they do nothing to disturb the bird habitat and the island's natural beauty. Boat rides out to the island and back are provided from the town of Kilmore Quay (about 10 miles south of Wexford Town) by **Declan Bates** (☎ **053-29684**); he charges £50 ($80) for the boat or £10 ($16) per person when there are at least five people.

MOUNT LEINSTER   The rounded granite form of this mountain, the highest in Wexford, is a familiar landmark throughout the region. One of the most popular hang-gliding spots in Ireland, the summit is always windy, and often shrouded in clouds. If you can get to the top on a clear day, however, it will be an experience you won't soon forget. To get there, follow signs for the Mount Leinster Scenic Drive from the sleepy town of Kiltealy on the eastern slopes of the mountain. Soon you will begin climbing the exposed slopes; don't be distracted by the dazzling views, as the road is twisting and quite narrow in places. There's a parking area at the highest point reached by the road, and a paved access road (closed to cars) continues approximately 1.5 miles to the summit. From the top you can scramble along the ridge to the east, known as Black Rock Mountain. To return, continue along the Scenic Drive, which ends a few miles outside the town of Bunclody.

✪ **John F. Kennedy Arboretum**
Dunganstown, New Ross, Co. Wexford. ☎ **051/388171.** Admission £2 ($3.20) adults, £1.50 ($2.40) seniors, £1 ($1.60) students and children, £5 ($8) family. Apr and Sept daily 10am–6:30pm; May–Aug daily 10am–8pm; Oct–Mar daily 10am–5pm.

Dedicated to the memory of the 35th U.S. president, this 600-acre arboretum is located near a hill known as Slieve Coilte. The arboretum overlooks the simple thatched cottage that was the birthplace of John F. Kennedy's great-grandfather. Opened in 1968, the arboretum was initiated with financial help from a group of Irish Americans, while its development and maintenance are funded by the Irish government. More than 4,500 species of plants and trees from five continents grow here. Facilities include an information center and a picnic area. A hilltop observation point (at 888 feet) presents a sweeping view of Co. Wexford and five neighboring counties, the Saltee Islands, the Comeragh Mountains, and parts of the Rivers Suir, Nore, and Barrow. It's located off Duncannon road (R733), about 20 miles west of Wexford.

Kennedy Centre
The Quay, New Ross, Co. Wexford. ☎ **051/25239.** Details not final at press time. Will open to the public in April 1998.

Housed in twin 18th-century grain mills, the center tells the story of the Irish Diaspora: their lives and achievements abroad, beginning with the Irish monks who went to Europe in the 6th century and continuing to the present day. A computerized data bank for tracing Co. Wexford roots is being developed with the Ellis Island Immigration Museum in New York and other immigration centers as far away as Australia and Argentina, and will contain more than four million names. A section of the Centre will be devoted to John F. Kennedy, descended from a Co. Wexford family and practically a sainted figure in Ireland.

Enniscorthy Castle / Wexford County Museum

Castle Hill, Enniscorthy, Co. Wexford. ☎ **054/35926.** Admission £2 ($3.20) adults, £ ($1.60) teenagers, 50p (80¢) children. June–Oct daily 10am–6pm, Nov–May daily 2–5:30pm.

Overlooking the River Slaney at Enniscorthy, 15 miles north of Wexford Town, this castle was built by the Prendergast family in the 13th century. It's said that it was once owned briefly by the poet Edmund Spenser. Remarkably well preserved and restored, it's now home to the Wexford County Museum, which focuses on the area's ecclesiastical, maritime, folk, agricultural, industrial, and military traditions. Displays include an old Irish farm kitchen, early modes of travel, nautical memorabilia, and items connected with Wexford's role in Ireland's struggle for independence.

At the eastern end of Enniscorthy is Vinegar Hill (390 feet), where the Wexford men of 1798 made their last stand. Now a scenic viewing point, it offers panoramas of Wexford from its summit.

Johnstown Castle Gardens and Irish Agricultural Museum

Bridgetown Rd., off Wexford-Rosslare road (N25), Wexford. ☎ **053/42888.** Admission to museum £2 ($3.20) adults, £1.25 ($2) children; gardens £1.50 ($2.40) adults, 50p (80¢) children. No credit cards. Museum, June–Aug Mon–Fri 9am–5pm, Sat–Sun 2–5pm; Apr–May and Sept–Nov 14 Mon–Fri 9am–12:30pm and 1:30–5pm, Sat–Sun 2–5pm; mid-Nov–Mar Mon–Fri 9am–12:30pm and 1:30–5pm. Gardens year-round daily 9am–5:30pm.

The importance of farming in Wexford's history is the focus at this museum, on the Johnstown Castle Demesne, four miles southwest of Wexford Town. In historic farm buildings, the museum contains exhibits relating to rural transport, planting, and the diverse activities of the farm household. There are also extensive displays on dairying, crafts, and Irish country furniture. Large-scale replicas illustrate the workshops of the blacksmith, cooper, wheelwright, harness maker, and basket maker. The 19th-century Gothic-Revival castle on the grounds is not open to the public except for its entrance hall, where tourist information is available. Visitors can enjoy the 50 acres of ornamental gardens that include more than 200 different kinds of trees and shrubs, three lakes, a tower house, hothouses, a statue walk, and a picnic area.

Ballyhack Castle

Off R733, Ballyhack, Co. Wexford. ☎ **051/89468.** Admission £1 ($1.60) adults, 50p (80¢) seniors, students, and children. Apr–June and Sept Wed–Sun noon–6pm; July–Aug daily 10am–6pm.

On a steep slope overlooking the Waterford estuary, about 20 miles west of Wexford, this castle is a large tower house thought to have been built around 1450 by the Knights Hospitallers of St. John, one of the two great military orders founded at the beginning of the 12th century during the Crusades. Hence, this building is considered a Crusader castle. It's currently being restored and turned into a heritage information center with displays on the Crusader knights, medieval monks, and Norman nobles, but remains open to the public while the work goes on.

Ballylane Farm

Signposted off New Ross-Wexford road (N25), New Ross, Co. Wexford. ☎ **051/21315.** Admission £2.50 ($4) adults, £1 ($1.50) students and children, £7 ($11.20) family. May–Sept daily 10am–6pm.

In the heart of Co. Wexford's verdant countryside, this 200-acre farm is owned by the Hickey family, who invite visitors to get a first-hand look at their farm life, which includes such activities as tillage, sheep-raising, and deer and pheasant husbandry. Guided tours, lasting about an hour, are given on a set route covering fields of crops, woodlands, bog lands, ponds, and farm buildings. A new tea room and improved shop and picnic area have been added. Located 27 miles west of Wexford Town and 3 miles east of New Ross.

Yola Farmstead

Wexford-Rosslare road (N25), Tagoat, Co. Wexford. ☎ **053/31177.** Admission £2 ($3.20) adults, £1.50 ($2.40) seniors, and £1 ($1.60) children. June–Sept daily 10am–5pm.

A voluntary community project, this theme park depicts a Wexford farming community as it would have been 200 years or more ago. Thatched-roof buildings have been constructed, including barns housing farm animals. Bread- and butter-making are demonstrated, and craftsmen can be seen at work blowing and hand-cutting crystal at Wexford Heritage Crystal, an on-site glass production enterprise. A small area is devoted to endangered species. Future plans call for a genealogy center. It's located about 10 miles south of Wexford Town.

SPORTS & OUTDOOR PURSUITS

BEACHES   Co. Wexford's beaches at Courtown, Curracloe, Duncannon, and Rosslare are ideal for walking, jogging, or swimming.

BICYCLING   Mountain bikes can be rented at **Black's Cycle Center** in Arklow, Co. Wicklow (☎ **0402/31898**), for £8 ($12.80) per day and £40 ($64) per week including helmet and panniers. This is a good starting point for excursions along the Wexford coastal roads, although a short section of the very busy N11 road will have to be followed before reaching the coast road—use extreme caution. There are also two Raleigh Rent-a-Bike locations in Wexford Town: **Hayes Cycle Shop,** 108 South Main St. (☎ **053/22462**); and **The Bike Shop,** 9 Selskar St. (☎ **053/22514**), which allows one-way rentals. From Wexford, the road north up the coast through Curracloe to Blackwater is a scenic day trip.

BIRD-WATCHING   A good starting place for bird-watching in the region is the Wexford Wildfowl Preserve (see description above), where warden Chris Wilson can direct you to other places of interest.

While driving south from Gorey toward Ballycanew on R741, keep an eye out for a reddish cliff on the left, about 1.5 miles out of Gorey; this is a well-known peregrine aerie, with birds nesting until the early summer. The land is private, but it is possible to watch the birds from the roadside.

The Saltee Islands offer one of the best summer bird-watching sites in Ireland, especially during May, June, and July when many species come here to nest (see listing above).

Hook Head is a well-known spot for watching the spring and autumn passerine migration—the lack of sizable cliffs means that it isn't popular with summer nesting seabirds. In addition to the swallows, swifts, and warblers, look out for the less common cuckoos, turtle doves, redstarts, and blackcaps.

Other places of interest are Lady's Island Lake near Carnsore Point, an important tern colony, and the neighboring Tacumshin Lake.

FISHING   One center for sea angling in Wexford is the town of Kilmore Quay, south of Wexford Town on R739. There are several people here who offer boats for hire, with all the necessary equipment; Dick Hayes runs **Kilmore Quay Boat Charters** (☎ **053/29704**) and is skipper of the *Cottage Lady.* The most popular rivers for fishing are the Barrow and the Slaney, where the sea trout travel upstream from mid-June to the end of August.

GOLF   In recent years, Wexford has blossomed as a golfing venue. The newest development is an 18-hole championship seaside par-72 course at **St. Helens Bay Golf Club,** Kilrane, Co. Wexford (☎ **053/33234**), with greens fees of £18 ($28.80 on weekdays and £22 ($35.20) on weekends. Tennis courts, sauna, and luxury cottages are available. Another course welcoming visitors is the **Enniscorthy Golf Club,** Knockmarshall, Enniscorthy, Co. Wexford (☎ **054/33191**), an inland par-70 course with greens fees of £10 ($16) on weekdays and £12 ($19.20) on weekends.

HORSEBACK RIDING   ✪ **Horetown House,** Foulksmills, Co. Wexford (☎ **051/565771**), offers riding lessons by the hour or packages that include meals and lodging. They cater particularly to families and children. For more experienced riders, lessons in jumping and dressage are available, as well as a game called polocross, which combines polo and lacrosse. Training in hunting and admission to the hunt can also be arranged. One day's accommodation, meals, and riding is £79 ($126.40). This is one of the better residential equestrian centers in Ireland.

Boro Hill, Clonroche, Enniscorthy, Co. Wexford (☎ **054/44117**), is a residential equestrian center offering instruction, trekking, hunting, and programs for children. A package with full board, room, and riding for one day is £80 ($128).

WALKING   The entire coastline in Co. Wexford is posted with brown signs indicating a man with backpack walking on water: This is the Wexford Coastal Path, which theoretically allows one to walk the whole coast on beaches and country roads. In reality, the roads are often too popular with cars, so I wouldn't recommend walking the entirety of the route, especially the bypass around Wexford Town. The markers are handy, however, for shorter walks along and between Wexford's clean beaches.

In the northern part of the county, the section of beach from Clogga Head (Co. Wicklow) to Tara Hill is especially lovely, as is the walk to the top of Tara Hill, which offers many viewpoints over sloping pastures to the sea. A good base for both these walks is **Carrigeen B&B,** Tara Hill, Gorey, Co. Wexford (☎ **055/21732**), which offers basic accommodations, a spectacular view of the sea, and a welcoming family (the Leonards) that is quite familiar with the local walks; double rooms are £30 to £34 ($48 to $54.40). Farther south, the path veers off the roads and sticks to the beach from Cahore Point south to Raven Point and from Rosslare Harbour to Kilmore Quay.

There's a lovely coastal walk near the town of Wexford in the **Raven Nature Reserve,** an area of forested dunes and uncrowded beaches. To get there, take R741 north out of Wexford, turn right on R742 to Curracloe just out of town, and in the village of Curracloe turn right and continue 1 mile to the beach parking lot. The nature reserve is now to your right. You can get there by car, driving another half mile south, or walk the distance along the beach. The beach extends another 3 miles to Raven Point, where at low tide you can see the remains of a shipwreck, half buried in the sand. The point is also a great place to watch migratory birds in the winter and spring—the flight of the white-fronted geese at dusk is an experience you shouldn't miss.

On the border between counties Wexford and Carlow is a long rounded ridge of peaks known as the Blackstairs Mountains, which offer a number of beautiful walks in an area remarkably unspoiled by tourism. A good guide is *Walking the Blackstairs* by Joss Lynam, available at Wexford tourist offices, which includes trail descriptions and information on local plants and wildlife. There is a road to the top of Mt. Leinster; for information see description above.

SHOPPING

Shops in Wexford are open Monday through Thursday from 9am to 5:30pm, Friday and Saturday from 9am to 6pm; some shops stay open until 8pm on Friday.

Barkers
36–40 S. Main St. ☎ **053/23159.**

Established in 1848, this has long been a mainstay in Wexford for a large selection of Waterford Crystal, Belleek China, and Royal Irish Tara China, as well as Irish linens and bronze and international products such as Aynsley, Wedgwood, and Lladro.

The Book Centre
5 S. Main St. ☎ **053/23543.**

This shop offers a wide selection of maps and books about Wexford, and on Ireland in general, and also carries cards, stationery, and music tapes and cassettes. There is a literary-theme coffee shop on the premises.

Faller's Sweater Shop
39 N. Main St. ☎ **053/24659.**

As its name implies, this shop specializes in Aran hand-knit sweaters (of which it carries a large selection) and mohair, cotton, and linen knits. To warm and accessorize other parts of your body, they also carry ties, scarves, wool socks, and tweed caps.

✪ Ferrycarrig Crystal
115 N. Main St. ☎ **053/43211.**

Ferrycarrig Crystal, a new name in an ancient craft, was conceived by a former Waterford craftsman and has quickly developed into one of Wexford's great enterprises. Visitors can watch as crystal is mouth-blown, hand-crafted, and hand-decorated into glasses, bowls, tankards, lamps, decanters, vases, bowls, and more.

✪ Wexford Silver
115 N. Main St. ☎ **053/43211.**

Pat Dolan, one of Ireland's leading silversmiths, plies his craft at this shop, along with his sons, creating gold, silver, and bronze pieces by hand using traditional tools and techniques. They are members of a long line of Dolans who trace their silversmithing connections back to 1647. A second workshop is located at Kinsale (see "Kinsale Silver" in Chapter 9).

The Wool Shop
39–41 S. Main St. ☎ **053/22247.**

In the heart of the town's main thoroughfare, this is Wexford's long-established best source for hand knits, from caps and tams to sweaters and jackets, as well as tweeds, linens, mohairs, and knitting yarns.

ACCOMMODATIONS
Very Expensive

✪ Marlfield House
Courtown Rd., Gorey, Co. Wexford. ☎ **800/223-6510** from the U.S., or 055/21124. Fax 055/21572. 19 rms. TV TEL. £158–£452 ($252.80–$723.20) double. Rates include full breakfast and service charge. AE, MC, V.

Originally a dower house and then the principal residence of the earl of Courtown, this splendid Regency manor home was built around 1850. Thanks to the current owners, Ray and Mary Bowe, it has been masterfully transformed into a top-notch country inn with award-winning gardens. Although guest rooms have every modern convenience (including fully carpeted bathrooms), they retain an old-world charm with individualized decor, many with four-poster or canopied beds, hand-carved armoires, and one-of-a-kind antiques. The public rooms and lounge have comfortable and inviting furnishings plus gilt-edge mirrors, crystal chandeliers, and marble fireplaces. Marlfield has earned many plaudits for its cuisine, using organically grown fruits and vegetables from the garden, served either in the main dining area or in a fanciful skylit Victorian-style conservatory room. Outdoor facilities include a tennis court and croquet lawn. It is located 40 miles north of Wexford Town in the northernmost part of the county.

EXPENSIVE

Ferrycarrig

P.O. Box 11, Wexford-Enniscorthy road (N11), Wexford, Co. Wexford. ☎ **053/20999.** Fax 053/20982. 59 rms and 16 suites. TV TEL. £40–£140 ($64–$224) double. No service charge. Rates include full breakfast. AE, DC, MC, V.

Situated next to the Ferrycarrig Bridge and opposite the Irish National Heritage Park about 2 miles north of town, this contemporary four-story hotel overlooks the River Slaney estuary and fertile Wexford countryside. Guest rooms are furnished in soft pastel tones with light woods and modern art, with picture windows that look out onto the river and well-cultivated gardens. Dining facilities include the Conservatory restaurant, noted for its seafood; the Boathouse Bistro for light fare; and the Dry Dock Bar. Tennis courts and a river walk are available, and a new leisure center with pool and two new restaurants are scheduled for completion in April 1997.

MODERATE

✪ The Talbot

Trinity St., Wexford, Co. Wexford. ☎ **800/223-6764** from the U.S., or 053/22566. Fax 053/23377. 96 rms. TV TEL. £80–£90 ($128–$144) double. Rates include full breakfast. No service charge. AE, DC, MC, V.

On the western end of the quays, this modern six-story hotel has the advantage of overlooking the harbor while still being within a block of the town's main shopping street. The guest rooms are outfitted with light woods and bright floral fabrics, many have river views, and all have extra amenities such as hair dryers and tea/coffeemakers. Room service, concierge, and valet/laundry services are available, and there is a hair-dressing salon on the premises. The Guillemot Restaurant offers formal dining for lunch or dinner, while lighter fare is available all day at the Pike Grill. For drinks with traditional music, try the Tavern; for jazz or '60s music, the Trinity Lounge. Exercise facilities include a gym, saunas, a squash court, solarium, table tennis, and an indoor heated swimming pool.

White's

George and Main sts., Wexford, Co. Wexford. ☎ **800/528-1234** from the U.S., or 053/22311. Fax 053/45000. 82 rms. TV TEL. £56–£136 ($89.60–$217.15). No service charge. Rates include full breakfast. AE, DC, MC, V.

Dating from 1779, this vintage hotel is situated right in the middle of town, with its older section facing North Main Street. Over the years it has been expanded and updated, resulting in lots of connecting corridors and bedrooms of varying size and standards, some with four-poster or canopy beds and others with modern light-wood furnishings. For the most part, the public rooms reflect the aura of an old coaching inn. Twenty-four-hour room service, one-day dry cleaning, and concierge services are available, and exercise facilities include a Jacuzzi, gym, sauna, steam room, and solarium.

Top-class meals are served in the main restaurant, Captain White's, and lighter fare is available all day in the Country Kitchen. There are two bars: the Shelmalier, where jazz and folk music is often on tap on weekends, and Speakers, a contemporary watering hole.

INEXPENSIVE

Clonard House

Clonard Great, Co. Wexford. ☎ **053/43141.** Fax 053/43141. 9 rms. TV. £36 ($57.60) double. No service charge. Rates include full breakfast. MC, V. Closed Nov 11–Easter.

Just a few miles out of Wexford Town, Clonard House is a great base for exploring the town and the southern Wexford coast. As you pass through the imposing gates you enter the peaceful pastoral world of this country estate, with its 18th-century Georgian farmhouse. Meals are served in the high-ceilinged, chandeliered dining room, with tea in a cozy parlor complete with fireplace. The rooms are simple and elegant; those in the front of the house look out over Wexford Harbour. The breakfast here is especially memorable, but dinner is not exceptional, so you're best off going into nearby Wexford Town.

✪ Clone House

Ferns, Enniscorthy, Co. Wexford. ☎ **054/66113.** Fax 054/66113. 5 rms (4 with bath, 3 with TV). £32–£37 ($51.20–$59.20) double. No service charge. Rates include full breakfast. No credit cards. Closed Oct–Feb.

You will receive a gracious welcome at this 300-acre working farm, the home of Tom and Betty Breen. The bedrooms are furnished with handsome antiques, as is the rest of the 250-year-old farmhouse. A courtyard opens onto an attractive garden in back, and you can walk through the fields to the bank of the River Bann. Tom prides himself on his knowledge of the local area, as well as Ireland as a whole, and will be glad to assist you in making plans for touring or outdoor activities. The whole house is nonsmoking.

McMenamin's Townhouse

3 Auburn Terrace, Redmond Rd., Wexford. ☎ **053/46442.** Fax 053/46442. 6 rms. TEL. £35 ($56) double. No service charge. Rates include full breakfast. MC, V.

Situated at the west end of town, opposite the railroad station, this lovely Victorian-style town house, one of the town's newest guest houses, offers up-to-date accommodations at an affordable price. Guest rooms are individually furnished with local antiques, including brass beds and caned chairs, and all have tea/coffee-making facilities. Not all of the rooms have televisions, so if this is important to you, ask. McMenamin's is operated by Seamus and Kay McMenamin, who formerly ran the Bohemian Girl pub/restaurant, so your stomach is in luck: Kay puts her culinary skills to work by providing gourmet breakfast for guests.

Rosslare Great Southern

Wexford–Rosslare Harbour road (N25), Rosslare Harbour, Co. Wexford. ☎ **800/44-UTELL** from the U.S., or 053/33233. Fax 053/33543. 99 rms. TV TEL. £50–£70 ($80–$112) double. Rates include full Irish breakfast and service charge. AE, DC, MC, V.

For travelers taking the ferry to or from Britain or France, or for anyone fond of sea views, this modern three-story hotel is an ideal overnight stop. It is positioned approximately 12 miles south of Wexford Town, on a cliff top overlooking the harbor, and is less than a mile away from the ferry terminals. With a bright and airy decor, it has lots of wide floor-to-ceiling windows and colorful contemporary furnishings in the guest rooms and public areas, and features sea views from the Norman Room Restaurant, which serves meals throughout the day. There is also a lounge that offers evening entertainment in the summer, and a conservatory, indoor heated swimming pool, sauna, gym, and tennis court.

Wexford Lodge

Wexford Bridge, Wexford, Co. Wexford. ☎ **800/365-3346** from the U.S., or 053/23611. Fax 053/23342. 18 rms. TV TEL. £25–£70 ($40–$112) single or double. No service charge. Rates include full breakfast. AE, MC, V.

Facing south on Wexford Harbour, this small family run two-story hotel is situated across from town on the River Slaney via the Wexford Bridge, off R471. A handy choice if you want to be close to town but in a more peaceful setting, it's next to a former U.S. Air Force station. The interior is furnished in contemporary style. Both the public rooms and guest rooms have lovely views of the river. Facilities include the Beann Abu restaurant, known for good local seafood, and a new River Bar.

DINING
EXPENSIVE/MODERATE

✪ Granary

West Gate, Wexford. ☎ **053/23935.** Reservations recommended. Main courses £10–£15 ($16–$24). AE, DC, MC, V. Mon–Sat 6–10pm. INTERNATIONAL.

Located in one of Wexford's most historic sections near the old city walls, and with a decor of beamed ceilings, wooden pillars, and copper kettles, this restaurant is rustic personified. The menu includes dishes such as roast Kilmore scallops poached in white wine; farmyard duck with honey and lime sauce; chicken Selskar, free-range chicken with Parmesan cheese and almonds baked in orange and thyme sauce; Slaney salmon baked in balsamic vinaigrette sauce; and a variety of steaks.

Lobster Pot

Carne, Co. Wexford. ☎ **053/31110.** Reservations recommended for dinner. Main courses £8.95–£14.95 ($14.30–$23.90), lobster dishes £18–£20 ($28.80–$32). AE, MC, V. June–Aug daily, Sept–May Tues–Sat noon–2pm and 6–9pm. Closed Jan. SEAFOOD.

Situated about 10 miles south of Wexford Town near the sea, this thatched-roof cottage restaurant is a popular spot for indoor and outdoor dining. The atmosphere is rustic, with a decor of local memorabilia such as crocks and kettles, framed newspaper clippings and pictures, and seafaring equipment. The menu, which is the same all day, features wild fresh salmon, panfried Dover sole, grilled trout meunière, baked crab or Kilmore scallops mornay, and a house special of Lobster Pot Pourri (lobster and seafood in a creamy white wine sauce). For nonseafood eaters, there are steaks, chicken Kiev, and roast duckling. Lighter items, popular at lunchtime, include seafood salads and chowders.

MODERATE

✪ The Neptune

Ballyhack Harbor, Ballyhack, Co. Wexford. ☎ **051/389284.** Reservations required. Main courses £9.50–£13 ($15.20–$20.80). AE, DC, MC, V. Mar 15–Nov 15 Tues–Sat 6–10pm; open Mon 6–10pm in July and Aug. INTERNATIONAL/SEAFOOD.

Situated in a sheltered harbor town on the western edge of Co. Wexford, about 20 miles from Wexford Town, this restaurant is located in an old house on the waterfront. The interior has an airy modern motif, with paintings and pottery by Irish artisans; tables are also set up outside for sunny days. Dinner options might include scallops in orange and ginger sauce, fillet of hake in citrus sauce, hot buttered lobster, Ballyhack wild salmon baked in cream, or the house signature dish, hot crab Brehat (crab sautéed in port and baked with mushrooms, béchamel sauce, and cheese). You can reach this little gem easily from Waterford (via the Ballyhack–Passage East car ferry) or by road from Wexford. It's worth the trip from any direction.

MODERATE/INEXPENSIVE

Bohemian Girl

North Main and Monck sts., Wexford. ☎ 053/24419. Reservations not necessary. All items £1.50–£6.50 ($2.40–$10.40). MC, V. Pub lunches 12:30–3pm. PUB GRUB.

Named for an opera written by William Balfe, a onetime Wexford resident, this is a Tudor-style pub, with hanging plants on the outside wall and an interior of lantern lights, barrel-shaped tables, and matchbook covers on the ceiling. It is known for excellent pub lunches including fresh oysters, pâtés, combination sandwiches, and homemade soups.

Cellar Restaurant

Cornmarket at Abbey St., Wexford. ☎ 053/24544. Reservations not accepted. All items £2–£6.50 ($3.20–$10.40). No credit cards. Daily 10am–6pm. IRISH/VEGETARIAN.

Housed in the Wexford Arts Centre, this charming eatery has a country kitchen atmosphere, with stone walls, pine furnishings, and home cooking prepared by Chef Caroline. Selections include salads, soups, quiches, pizzas, and chili, with particular emphasis on vegetarian items.

Robertino's

19 S. Main St., Wexford. ☎ 053/23334. Reservations recommended. Main courses £3–£10 ($4.80–$16). No credit cards. Mon–Thurs 10:30am–midnight, Fri–Sat 10:30am–12:30am, Sun 7pm–midnight. ITALIAN.

This informal restaurant prides itself as being an Italian oasis in the heart of Wexford, and is known for its freshly made pastas and pizzas. The menu also includes a fine selection of steaks, quiches, omelets, and curries. The wine list is particularly extensive.

WEXFORD AFTER DARK

Famed for its Opera Festival each October, Wexford is a town synonymous with music and the arts. Year-round performances are given at the **Theatre Royal,** High Street, Wexford (☎ 053/22400), a beautiful theater dating from 1832.

Alternatively, there is usually something going on at the **Wexford Arts Centre,** Cornmarket, Wexford (☎ 053/23764). Built as the market house in 1775 at the Cornmarket, this building has served as a dance venue, concert hall, and municipal office. Since 1974, it has provided a focal point for all of the arts in Wexford and now houses three exhibition rooms and showcases a range of theatrical and artistic events. The center's staff is particularly eager to meet visiting artists in all fields, with a view toward developing ongoing links with artists worldwide.

To see traditional Irish music and dancing, head 10 miles south of Wexford to the **Yola Farmstead,** Wexford-Rosslare road (N25), Tagoat, Co. Wexford (☎ 053/31177). It stages traditional ceili evenings of Irish music, song, dance, and recitations during July and August, on Thursday and Saturday at 7:30pm. Admission is £3 ($4.80) per person.

PUBS

Antique Tavern

14 Slaney St., Enniscorthy. ☎ 054/33428.

It's worth a 15-mile trip to Enniscorthy to see this unique Tudor-style pub, located off the main Dublin-Wexford road (N11). The walls are lined with memorabilia from the Wexford area—old daggers, pikes, farming implements, lanterns, pictures, and prints. You'll also see mounted elk's heads, an antique wooden bird cage, and a glass case full of paper money from around the world.

Con Macken's, The Cape of Good Hope
The Bull Ring, off North Main St., Wexford. ☎ 053/22949.

Long a favorite with photographers, this pub is unique for the trio of services it offers, aptly described by the sign outside the door: "Bar–Undertaker–Groceries." Hardly any visitor passes by without a second look at the windows, one displaying beer and spirit bottles, the other featuring plastic funeral wreaths. An alehouse for centuries, The Cape has always been at the center of Wexford political events, and the bar walls are lined with rebel souvenirs, old weapons, and plaques.

The Crown Bar
Monck St., Wexford. ☎ **053/24701.**

Once a stagecoach inn, this tiny pub in the center of town has been in the Kelly family since 1841. Besides its historical overtones, it is well known for its museumlike collection of antique weapons. You'll see 18th-century dueling pistols, pikes from the 1798 Rebellion, powder horns, and blunderbusses, as well as vintage prints, military artifacts, and swords. Unlike most pubs, it may not always be open during the day, so it's best to save a visit for the evening hours.

Oak Tavern
Wexford-Enniscorthy road (N11), Ferrycarrig, Wexford. ☎ **053/20945.**

Dating back over 150 years and originally a tollhouse on the River Slaney, this pub is situated 2 miles north of town, overlooking the River Slaney and near the Ferrycarrig Bridge. Bar lunches are served during the day, with the choices being of the beef and vegetable hot pot and shepherd's pie variety. There is a riverside patio for outside seatings on fine days, and traditional music sessions are held most evenings in the front bar.

Thomas Moore Tavern
The Cornmarket, Wexford. ☎ **053/24348.**

There's a good reason this pub is named for the famous Irish composer and poet Thomas Moore: His mother was born in the living quarters upstairs, when the pub was known as The Ark. Although Moore never lived here, he returned to his mother's town on many occasions to visit, and played music nearby. It's a good spot for a quiet drink in a literary ambience.

The Wren's Nest
Custom House Quay, Wexford. ☎ **053/22359.**

Situated along the harbor front near the John Barry Memorial, five minutes from the bus and train station, this pub has redesigned its front bar to include an old-style wood floor and ceiling and attractive pine tables and chairs. The varied pub grub includes Wexford mussel platters, house pâtés, soups, salads, and vegetarian entrées. There is free traditional Irish music on Tuesday and Thursday nights.

2 County Waterford

Waterford City is 40 miles W of Wexford, 33 miles W of Rosslare Harbour, 98 miles SW of Dublin, 78 miles E of Cork, and 95 miles SE of Shannon Airport.

GETTING THERE   Air service from Britain is operated into Waterford Airport, off R675, Waterford (☎ **051/75589**), by **Manx Airlines** from London (Stansted)

Waterford City

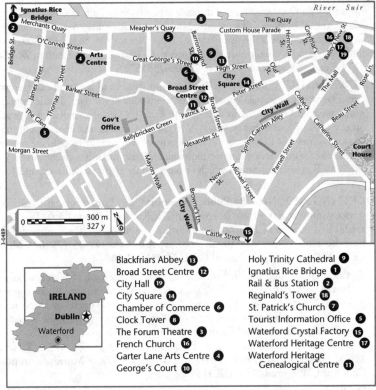

Blackfriars Abbey **13**
Broad Street Centre **12**
City Hall **19**
City Square **14**
Chamber of Commerce **6**
Clock Tower **8**
The Forum Theatre **3**
French Church **16**
Garter Lane Arts Centre **4**
George's Court **10**

Holy Trinity Cathedral **9**
Ignatius Rice Bridge **1**
Rail & Bus Station **2**
Reginald's Tower **18**
St. Patrick's Church **7**
Tourist Information Office **5**
Waterford Crystal Factory **15**
Waterford Heritage Centre **17**
Waterford Heritage
  Genealogical Centre **11**

and **British Airlines Express** from London (Stansted). Service is also available from Luton.

Irish Rail offers daily service from Dublin and other points into Plunkett Station, at Edmund Ignatius Rice Bridge, Waterford (☎ **051/73401**).

Bus Eireann operates daily services into Plunkett Station Depot, Waterford (☎ **051/73401**), from Dublin, Limerick, and other major cities throughout Ireland.

If you're coming by car, these major roads lead into Waterford: N25 from Cork and the south, N24 from the west, N19 from Kilkenny and points north, and N25 from Wexford.

The Passage East Ferry Co. Ltd., Barrack Street, Passage East, Co. Waterford (☎ **051/382480** or 051/382488), operates a car ferry service across Waterford Harbour, linking Passage East, about 10 miles east of Waterford, with Ballyhack, about 20 miles southwest of Wexford. This shortcut saves about an hour's driving time between the two cities. Crossing time averages 10 minutes and service is continuous. It's a drive-on, drive-off service, with no reservations required. The fares are £4 ($6.40) one way and £6 ($9.60) round-trip for car and passengers, £1 ($1.60) round-trip for foot passengers, £1.50 ($2.40) one way and £2 ($3.20) round-trip for cyclists. It operates April through September, Monday through Saturday, 7:20am until 10pm, and on Sunday, 9:30am until 10pm; October through March, Monday through Saturday, 7:20am until 8pm, and Sunday, 9:30am until 8pm.

VISITOR INFORMATION Year-round information services are provided by the Waterford Tourist Office, 41 The Quay, Waterford (☎ **051/875788**). It's open

April through October, Monday through Saturday, from 9am to 6pm; January to March and November to December, Monday through Friday from 9am to 5pm. In July and August, it's also open Sunday from 10am to 5pm. Seasonal offices, open mid-June through August, are maintained at Dungarvan Town Centre (☎ **058/ 41741**) and The Square at Tramore (☎ **051/381572**).

TOWN LAYOUT   Rimmed by the River Suir, Waterford is a small and compact city. The main commercial hub sits on the south bank of the river. Traffic from the north, west, and east enters from the north bank via the Ignatius Rice Bridge and onto a series of four quays (Grattan, Merchants, Meagher, and Parade), but most addresses simply say "The Quay." The majority of shops and attractions are concentrated near the quay area or on two thoroughfares that intersect with the quays: The Mall and Barronstrand Street, which changes names to Broad, Michael, and John streets.

GETTING AROUND   By Public Transport   Bus Eireann operates daily bus service within Waterford and its environs. The flat fare is 70p ($1.15). Taxi ranks are located outside of Plunkett Rail Station and along the Quay opposite the Granville Hotel. If you need to call a taxi, try **A.B. Cabs** (☎ **051/79100**), **Metro Cabs** (☎ **051/57157**), or **Parnell Cabs** (☎ **051/77710**).

By Car   To see most of Waterford's sights, with the exception of Waterford Glass, it's best to walk. Park your car along the Quays; parking is operated by machines at 30p (48¢) for two hours, or by the disc system at 40p (64¢) per hour. Discs are on sale at the tourist office or many of the shops. You'll need a car to reach the Waterford Glass Factory and Waterford County attractions outside of town.

If you need to rent a car, contact **Budget,** 41 The Quay, Waterford (☎ **051/ 21670**); **Hertz,** Dublin Road, Waterford (☎ **051/78737**); or **Murrays Europcar,** Cork Road, Waterford (☎ **051/73144**)

On Foot   The best way to see the city is by walking along the quays and taking a right at Reginald's Tower on The Mall (which becomes Parnell Street) and then turning right onto John Street (which becomes Michael, Broad, and Barronstrand streets), which brings you back to the quays. The tourist office will supply you with a free map.

Fast Facts: Waterford

Area Code   The telephone area code for Waterford City and the surrounding area is **051.** County Waterford area codes include **052** and **058.**

Drugstores   Try **Gallagher's Pharmacy,** at Barronstrand Street (☎ **051/78103**), and **Mulligan's Chemists,** with shops at 40-41 Barronstrand St. (☎ **051/75211**) and at Unit 12A of City Square Shopping Centre (☎ **051/53247**).

Dry Cleaning & Laundry   Two good spots are **Eddie's Dry Cleaners,** at 82 The Quay (☎ **051/77677**), and **Boston Cleaners,** at 6 Michael St. (☎ **051/74487**).

Emergencies   Dial **999.**

Gay & Lesbian Resource   Call the **Gay and Lesbian Line Southeast** (☎ **051/ 79907**).

Hospital   **Holy Ghost Hospital** is located on Cork Road (☎ **051/74397**).

Local Newspaper and Media   The weekly newspaper covering local events and entertainment is the *Waterford News & Star.* Waterford Local Radio (WLR) broadcasts on 97.5 FM and 95.1 FM.

Photographic Supplies   **Hennebry Camera,** 109 The Quay (☎ **051/75049**).

Police   Phone the **Garda Headquarters** (☎ **051/74888**).

Post Office   The **General Post Office** on Parade Quay (☎ 051/74444) is open Monday through Friday from 9am to 5:30pm and Saturday from 9am to 1pm.

A FEW WORDS ABOUT WATERFORD

Waterford City (pop. 50,000) is the main seaport of the southeast. Although the historic district around Reginald's Tower is quite attractive, the city is primarily a commercial center, and is dominated by its busy port. Since the rest of Co. Waterford is so beautiful, most travelers don't linger for long in the somewhat dingy capital city.

Coastal highlights south of Waterford include Dunmore East, a picturesque fishing village; Dungarvan, a major town with a fine harbor; Ardmore, a quiet beach resort; and Passage East, a tiny seaport from which you can catch a ferry across the harbor and cut your driving time from Waterford to Wexford in half. Ardmore, which in Irish means "the great height," is also the setting for a 7th-century monastic settlement, founded by St. Declan, which has on its grounds a 12th-century cathedral, numerous ancient grave sites, a holy well, and a 97-foot-tall round tower, one of the most perfect of its kind in this part of Ireland. Portally Cove, near Dunmore East, is the home of Ireland's only Amish-Mennonite community.

In northwest Co. Waterford, the Comeragh Mountains provide many opportunities for beautiful walks, including the short trek to Mahon Falls. These mountains also have highly scenic roads for bicycle excursions. Farther west, there's great fishing and bird-watching on the Blackwater estuary.

ATTRACTIONS

✪ Waterford Crystal Factory and Gallery

Cork Rd., Waterford. ☎ **051/73311.** Admission £2 ($3.20) per person for the tour; free for the audiovisual presentation and gallery. Apr–Oct Mon–Sat 8:30am–5pm, Sun 10am–5pm; Nov–Mar Mon–Fri 9am–5pm. Tours given on continuous first-come basis Apr–Oct Mon–Sat 8:30am–3:15pm, Sun 10am–3:15pm; Nov–Mar Mon–Fri 9am–3:15pm.

Without a doubt, this is Waterford's number-one attraction. Founded in 1783, this glass-making enterprise thrived, and Waterford became the crystal of connoisseurs. The factory was forced to close in 1851, due to the devastating effects of the Irish famine. Happily, it was revived in 1947, and Waterford has since regained the lead among prized glassware. With more than 2,000 employees, Waterford is now the largest crystal factory in the world and the major industry in Waterford.

Visitors are welcome to watch a 17-minute audiovisual presentation on the glass-making process and then take a 35-minute tour of the factory to see the process first-hand, from the mouth-blowing and shaping of the molten glass to the delicate hand-cutting. *Note:* Children under 10 are not permitted on the factory tour. Reservations are not required.

You can also stroll around the Waterford Crystal Gallery, a bilevel showroom containing the most comprehensive display of Waterford Crystal in the world, from all the glassware patterns to elaborate pieces like trophies, globes, and chandeliers. Crystal is on sale in the gallery.

Reginald's Tower

The Quay, Waterford. ☎ **051/73501.** Admission 75p ($1.20); combination ticket in conjunction with Waterford Heritage Centre, £1 ($1.60). Apr–Oct Mon–Fri 10am–8pm, Sat 10am–6pm.

Circular, topped with a conical roof, and having walls 10 feet thick, this mighty tower stands at the eastern end of the Quay beside the river. It's said to have been built in 1003 by a Viking governor named Reginald. Still dominating the Waterford skyline, it's particularly striking at night when fully floodlit. Over the centuries, it's been a fortress, prison, military depot, mint, and air-raid shelter, and now it's the home of Waterford's Civic Museum; on display are medieval charters.

City Hall

The Mall, Waterford. ☎ **051/73501.** Free admission. Mon–Fri 9am–1pm and 2–5pm.

Headquarters of the local Waterford city government, this late 18th-century building houses various local memorabilia, including information on the city's charter, which was granted in 1205. In addition, a display is dedicated to Thomas Francis Meagher, a leader in an 1848 Irish insurrection. Meagher was sentenced to death but he escaped to America, where he fought in the Civil War, earned the rank of brigadier general, and eventually became acting governor of Montana. City Hall's other treasures include an 18th-century Waterford glass chandelier, a complete dinner service of priceless antique Waterford glasses, and a painting of Waterford City in 1736 by the Flemish master William Van der Hagen.

Waterford Heritage Centre

Greyfriars St., Waterford. ☎ **051/71227.** Admission 75p ($1.20) adults; in conjunction with Reginald's Tower Museum £1 ($1.60) adults. Apr–May Mon–Fri 10am–1pm and 2–6pm, Sat 10am–1pm; June–Sept Mon–Fri 10am–8pm, Sat 10am–1pm and 2–5pm.

A half block away from Reginald's Tower at the former Greyfriars church, this center focuses on Waterford's early days of Viking and Norman settlements and houses a fine collection of Viking and medieval artifacts recovered from a recent archaeological dig.

Waterford Heritage Genealogical Centre

Jenkins Lane, Waterford. ☎ **051/76123.** Fax 051/50645. Free admission, but minimum search fee is £30 ($48). Mon–Thurs 9am–5pm, Fri 9am–2pm (5pm May–Sept).

Did your ancestors come from Waterford? Then follow the small lane between George's and Patrick's streets to this historic building adjoining St. Patrick's, one of Ireland's oldest churches. This center specializes in tracing Co. Waterford ancestry. Church registers dating from 1655 and other surveys, rolls, and census lists are used as resources. An audiovisual presentation examines the heritage of the people of the area.

Garter Lane Arts Centre

5 and 22a O'Connell St. ☎ **051/855038.** Free admission. Gallery Mon–Sat 10am–6pm.

One of Ireland's largest arts centers, the Garter Lane occupies two buildings on O'Connell Street: no. 5, the site of the former Waterford Library, and now the setting for exhibition rooms and artists' studios, and no. 22a, the former Friends Meeting House, now home of the Garter Lane Theatre, with an art gallery and outdoor courtyard. The gallery showcases works by contemporary and local artists. In December, a crafts fair usually takes place, with works by artists from all over Ireland. Show prices are £6 to £8 ($9.60 to $12.80).

SIGHTSEEING TOURS
WALKING TOURS OF HISTORIC WATERFORD

Waterford Tourist Services

Jenkins Lane, Waterford. ☎ **051/73711** or 051/51043. £3 ($4.80) adults, small children free. Mar–Oct daily noon and 2pm.

Local Waterford residents, well versed in the history, folklore, and wit of the city, conduct one-hour walking tours of Waterford that include two cathedrals and four national monuments. Tours depart from the Granville Hotel, The Quay.

Waterford Viking River Cruises
4 Gladstone St., Waterford. ☎ **051/72800.** £5 ($8) adults, £2.50 ($4) children age 14 and under. May–Sept daily 3:30pm and 8pm; June–Aug daily noon, 3:30pm, and 8pm.

See the Waterford sights from the water on board the *Viking I*, a luxury two-deck cruiser with bar and refreshment facilities. The trip leaves from the Waterford Quay opposite Reginald's Tower and goes downriver to Passage East and Ballyhack, passing rolling parkland, glens, fishing villages, cliffs, and the island where Waterford Castle is nestled, and returns in just under two hours. Details and reservations are available from the office or the tourist office.

ATTRACTIONS IN NEARBY COUNTY WATERFORD

✪ Lismore Castle
Lismore, Co. Waterford. ☎ **058/54424.** Admission £2.50 ($4) adults, £1.50 ($2.40) children under 16. End of April to mid-Sept daily 1:45–4:45pm. Lismore lies 4 miles W of Cappoquin on N72.

Perched high on a cliff above the River Blackwater, this multiturreted castle has a long history, dating back to 1185 when Prince John of England built a similar fortress on this site. Local lore says that Lismore Castle was once granted for £12 a year to Sir Walter Raleigh, although he never occupied it. One man who did choose to live here was Richard Boyle, the first Earl of Cork, who rebuilt the castle, including the thick defensive walls that still surround the garden, in 1626. Richard's son Robert, who was born at the castle in 1627, is the celebrated chemist whose name lives on in Boyle's Law. Most of the present castle was added in the mid-19th century. Today this 8,000-acre estate of gardens, forests, and farmland is the Irish seat of the Duke and Duchess of Devonshire, whose primary home is at Chatsworth in England. Although the castle itself is not open for tours, the public is welcomed in the splendid walled and woodland gardens.

The castle can be rented, complete with the duke's personal staff, to private groups (minimum five persons/four nights) for £159 ($255.40) per person, per night, which includes dinner, afternoon tea, breakfast, and laundry services.

Lismore Heritage Centre
Lismore. ☎ **058/54975.** Admission £2 ($3.20) adults, £1.50 ($2.40) seniors, £1 ($1.60) children. Apr and Oct Sun 2:30–5:30pm; May–Sept Mon–Fri 10am–5:30pm, Sat–Sun 2:30–5:30pm.

Where is the only Hindu Gothic bridge in Ireland located? Step inside this building and find out. This new interpretative center, housed in the town's Old Courthouse, will not only answer that question but also tell the history of Lismore, a charming town founded by St. Carthage in the year 636. The Lismore Experience is a multimedia presentation on the town's unique treasures including the Book of Lismore, dating back 1,000 years, and the Lismore Crozier from 1116, both of which were discovered hidden in the walls of Lismore Castle in 1814.

RING OF HOOK DRIVE   The Hook Peninsula in southwest Co. Wexford is a place of rocky headlands and secluded beaches. Located between Bannow Bay and Waterford Harbor, two of the most significant inlets in medieval times for travelers from Britain to Ireland, the strategic significance of this area is reflected in the great abundance of archaeological remains. The end of the peninsula is popular with birders as a site for watching the spring and fall passerine migration, and is tipped with a lighthouse reputed to be one of the oldest in Europe. The route described is appropriate for bicycling or driving, and most of the places listed can be seen by walkers from the Wexford Coastal Pathway.

An exploration of the peninsula begins at the town of Wellington Bridge. Just west of town on R733 is a roadside pull off on the left by a cemetery; from here you can look across Bannow Bay to the ruins of Clonmines, a Norman village established in the 13th century. This is one of the finest examples of a walled medieval settlement in Ireland, with remains of two churches, three tower houses and an Augustinian priory. It is possible to drive to the ruins: Follow R733 another mile west to a left turn posted for the Wicklow Coastal Pathway, and continue straight on this road where the Coastal Pathway turns right. The ruins are on private land, so you should ask permission at the farmhouse at the end of the road.

Continuing west on R733, turn left on R734 at the sign for the Ring of Hook, and turn right at the sign for Tintern Abbey. The abbey was founded by the monks of Tintern in South Wales in the 13th century, and has been much altered since then. Although it isn't possible to enter the abbey due to restoration work, the grounds are quite beautiful, and include a restored stone bridge spanning a narrow sea inlet.

At Baginbun Head there is a fine beach nestled against the cliffs, from which it is possible to see the outline of the Norman earthwork fortifications on the head. It is here that the Norman presence in Ireland was first established with the victory of Norman forces over the Irish at the Battle of Baginbun.

The tip of the peninsula has been famous for shipwrecks since Norman times, with its line of low cliffs, eroded in places to form blowholes. There has long been a lighthouse on this site, and the present structure consists of a massive base, built in the early 13th century, and a narrower top dating from the 19th century.

The Ring of Hook road returns along the western side of the peninsula, passing the beaches at Booley Bay and Dollar Bay. On a promontory overlooking the town of Duncannon is a fort built in 1588 to protect Waterford Harbour from the threat of attack by the Spanish Armada. Just north of Duncannon, along the coast, is the village of Ballyhack, where a ferry operates to Passage East in County Waterford, and a Knights Hospitallers castle stands on a hill over the harbor (see separate description for Ballyhack Castle, above).

A visit to the Hook Peninsula wouldn't be complete without a stop at Dunbrody Abbey, about 4 miles north of Duncannon. Situated in a field beside the road, the abbey is a magnificent ruin. It was founded in 1170, and is one of the largest Cistercian abbeys in Ireland. Despite its grand size, it bears remarkably little ornamentation. Tours are sometimes available; inquire at the visitor's center across the road.

WALK TO MAHON FALL   Located in the Comeragh Mountains, on R676 between Carrick-on-Suir and Dungarvan. At the tiny village of Mahon Bridge, 15.5 miles south of Carrick-on-Suir, turn west on the road marked for Mahon Falls, and continue to follow signs for the falls and the "Comeragh Drive." In about 3 miles you will reach a parking lot along the Mahon River (which is, in fact, a tiny stream); the trail begins across the road from the parking lot and is indicated by two boulders. Follow the stream along the floor of the valley to the base of the falls. From here you can see the fields of Waterford spread out below you and the sea a glittering mirror beyond. Walking time is about 30 minutes round-trip.

SPORTS & OUTDOOR PURSUITS

BEACHES   For walking, jogging, or swimming, visit one of Co. Waterford's wide sandy beaches at Tramore, Ardmore, Clonea, or Dunmore East.

BICYCLING   Neither of the rental venues in town offers helmets or panniers, so plan to bring your own or rent elsewhere. Bikes can be had for £7 ($11.20) daily and

£30 ($48) weekly at **Wright's Cycle Depot Ltd.,** Henrietta Street, Waterford (☎ **051/874411**), or **B 'n' B Cycles,** 22 Ballybricken, Waterford, (☎ **051/870356**). B 'n' B Cycles also offers an emergency repair service for travelers, whereby just about any repair is completed on the same day you bring the bike in. From Waterford you can ride 8 miles to Passage East and take the ferry (£1.50 [$2.40] with a bicycle) to Wexford and the beautiful Hook Peninsula. Alternately, you can continue on from Passage East to Dunmore East, a picturesque seaside village with a small beach hemmed in by cliffs. The road from there on to Tramore and Dungarvan is quite scenic.

FISHING   For sea fishing, picturesque Dunmore East, 8 miles south of Waterford, is a good bet. A boat can be chartered from **John O'Connor** (☎ **051/383397**) for reef, wreck, and shark fishing. Boat charter rates are £150 to £200 ($240 to $320) per day; rod and reel can also be rented. The species you're likely to encounter in this area during the summer include blue shark, cod, bass, whiting, conger, and ling.

GOLF   County Waterford's golf venues include three 18-hole championship courses: **Faithlegg Golf Club,** Faithlegg House, Co. Waterford (☎ **051/382241**), a par-72 parkland course beside the River Suir, with greens fees of £18 to £25 ($28.80 to $40), depending on the time of day; **Dungarvan Golf Club,** Knocknagranagh, Dungarvan, Co. Waterford (☎ **058/41605**), a par-72 parkland course with greens fees of £14 ($22.40) on weekdays and £17 ($27.20) on weekends; and **Waterford Castle Golf and Country Club,** The Island, Ballinakill, Waterford (☎ **051/871633**), a par-72 parkland course with greens fees of £22 ($35.20) weekdays and £25 ($40) weekends for overnight guests at the castle or £50 ($80) for visitors. In addition, there is the 18-hole par-71 inland course at **Waterford Golf Club,**Newrath, Waterford (☎ **051/74182**), a mile from the center of the city, with greens fees of £19 ($30.40) on weekdays and £22 ($35.20) on weekends.

HORSEBACK RIDING   County Waterford is filled with trails for horseback riding, with fees averaging £10 ($16) per hour. You can arrange to ride at **Killoteran Equitation Centre,** Killoteran, Waterford (☎ **051/384158**) or **Melody's Riding Stables,** Ballmacarberry, Co. Waterford (☎ **052/36147**).

SAILING, WINDSURFING & SEA KAYAKING   Courses are offered from May to September at the **Dunmore East Adventure Center,** Dunmore East, Co. Waterford (☎ **051/383783;** fax 051/383786). Courses last one to four days and are priced at £18 to £30 ($28.80 to $48) per day, including equipment rental. Summer programs for children are also available. This is a great spot for an introductory experience, but there isn't much wave action for veteran windsurfers seeking thrills.

SHOPPING

Most people come to Waterford to buy Waterford crystal, but there are many other fine products in the shops and in the three multilevel enclosed shopping centers— **George's Court,** off Barronstrand Street, **Broad Street Centre** on Broad Street, and **City Square** off Broad Street. Hours are usually Monday through Saturday from 9 or 9:30am to 6 or 6:30pm. Some shops are open until 9pm on Thursday and Friday.

Aisling
Barronstrand St. at George's Court. ☎ **051/873262.**

Located opposite the city's Catholic cathedral, this small and interesting shop (whose name means "dream" in Gaelic) offers an assortment of unique crafts, from quilts, tartans, and kilts to floral art and miniature paintings and watercolors of Irish scenes and subjects.

The Book Centre
25 Broad St. ☎ **051/73823.**

This huge, four-level bookstore sells all types of books, newspapers, and magazines, as well as posters, maps, and music tapes and CDs. You can also make a quick photocopy here, or zap off a fax if you need to.

Joseph Knox
4 Barronstrand St. ☎ **051/75307.**

For visitors to Waterford, this store has long been a focal point, offering a large selection of Waterford crystal, particularly in specialty items like chandeliers.

Kelly's
75/76 The Quay. ☎ **051/73557.**

Dating from 1847, this store offers a wide selection of Waterford crystal, Aran knitwear, Belleek china, Royal Tara china, Irish linens, and other souvenirs.

Penrose Crystal
John St., Waterford. ☎ **051/76537.**

Established in 1786 and revived in 1978, this is Waterford's other glass company, turning out delicate hand cut and engraved glassware. The craftsmen here practice the stipple engraving process, the highest art form in glass. A retail sales outlet is also located at Unit 8 of the City Square Shopping Centre. Both the factory and the retail shop are open usual hours, but the factory is also open on Sunday from June to August from 2 to 5:30pm.

Woolcraft
11 Michael St., Waterford. ☎ **051/74082.**

For more than 100 years, the Fitzpatrick family has operated this midcity shop, a reliable source for quality Irish knitwear. The focus here is on hand-loomed and hand-knit Aran sweaters—2,000 square feet of 'em—at exceptionally low prices.

ACCOMMODATIONS
VERY EXPENSIVE

Jurys
Ferrybank, Waterford, Co. Waterford. ☎ **800/843-3311** from the U.S., or 051/832111. Fax 051/832863. 98 rms. TV TEL. £96 ($153.60) double. Service charge 10%. AE, DC, MC, V. Closed Dec 24–27.

Set amid 38 acres of gardens and lawns, this modern six-story hotel is perched on a hill along the River Suir's northern banks. With such a commanding position, each guest room enjoys a sweeping view of Waterford City. Recently refurbished, the rooms offer a Victorian-style decor of frilly floral fabrics, dark woods, and brass trim. In-room amenities include a hair dryer, luggage rack, and tea/coffee-making facilities.

Dining/Entertainment: Bardens Restaurant and the Conor Bar face the river and city.

Services: 24-hour room service, concierge, same-day dry-cleaning/laundry, baby-sitting service.

Facilities: Indoor heated swimming pool, Jacuzzi, two saunas, steam room, gymnasium, two floodlit outdoor tennis courts, hairdressing salon.

✪ Waterford Castle
The Island, Ballinakill, Waterford, Co. Waterford. ☎ **800/221-1074** from the U.S., or 051/878203. Fax 051/79316. 19 rms. TV TEL. £150–£205 ($240–$328) double, £275 ($440) suites. No service charge. MC, V. Open year-round.

Dating back 800 years, this is the most secluded of Ireland's castles, situated on a private 310-acre island in the River Suir, 2 miles south of Waterford and reached by private chain-link car ferry. Comprising an original Norman keep and two Elizabethan-style wings, it is built entirely of stone with a leaded roof, mullioned windows, granite archways, ancient gargoyles, and fairy-tale turrets, towers, and battlements. Fully restored and refurbished in 1988, the castle's interior is full of oak-paneled walls, ornate plaster ceilings, colorful tapestries, spacious sitting areas with huge stone fireplaces, original paintings, and antiques. Each guest room is decorated with four-poster or canopied beds, hand-carved armoires, designer fabrics, and other regal accessories.

Dining/Entertainment: Choices include The Munster Room restaurant and the Fitzgerald Room bar.

Services: 24-hour room service, concierge, laundry and valet service.

Facilities: 18-hole championship golf course, indoor heated pool and fitness center, tennis court, horseback riding, fishing, watersports.

EXPENSIVE

Granville

Meagher Quay, Waterford, Co. Waterford. ☎ **800/538-1234** from the U.S., or 051/855111. Fax 051/870307. 74 rms. TV TEL. £88–£100 ($140.80–$160) double, £124 ($198.40) executive suites. No service charge. Rates include full breakfast. AE, DC, DISC, MC, V. Closed Dec 24–27.

Located along the quayside strip of Waterford's main business district, this historic hotel looks out onto the south side of the River Suir. The Granville was originally a coaching inn, and an adjacent section was the home of Irish patriot Thomas Francis Meagher and a meeting place for Irish freedom fighters. In 1980 it was purchased by the Cusack family, who totally restored, refurbished, and enlarged it. Today the Granville is a member of Best Western International. The architecture is a blend of many centuries, but the furnishings are modern and functional. The bedrooms are bedecked with bright floral fabrics and the front rooms look out onto the river. Parking is in nearby public lots for 80p ($1.30) per hour, £1($1.60) overnight.

Dining/Entertainment: Amenities include Bells, a small gourmet restaurant, the Bianconi grill room, and a large lounge bar that's popular with a local clientele.

Services: Room service, concierge, laundry, valet.

MODERATE

The Bridge

1 The Quay, Waterford, Co. Waterford. ☎ **800/221-2222** from the U.S., or 051/77222. Fax 051/77229. 80 rms. TV TEL. £66–£88 ($105.60–$140.80) double. Includes full Irish breakfast and service charge. AE, DC, MC, V.

Taking its name from its location, right on the waterfront at the foot of the Ignatius Rice Bridge, this three-story vintage hotel is one of the city's oldest, but it has been updated in recent years. Rooms have light wood furnishings and bright floral fabrics. Facilities include the Ignatius Rice Restaurant for formal dining, the Kitchen for light meals in an Irish country-kitchen setting, and Crokers Bar and Timber Toes Lounge for liquid refreshment.

Tower

The Mall, Waterford, Co. Waterford. ☎ **051/75801**. Fax 051/70129. 141 rms. TV TEL. £96–£104 ($153.60–$264) single or double. Includes full Irish breakfast and service charge. AE, DC, MC, V.

In a historic section of the city overlooking the River Suir, this contemporary four-story hotel is named after Reginald's Tower across the street and is within walking distance of all major downtown attractions. A popular base for bus tours, it was completely refurbished and enlarged in 1991. The bedrooms are standard but comfortable, with an eclectic mix of colors and furnishings. The public rooms have been recently extended, with emphasis on lovely wide-windowed views of the harbor. Amenities include a full-service restaurant, lounge overlooking the river, and a leisure center with indoor swimming pool, whirlpool, steam room, saunas, and exercise room.

INEXPENSIVE

Aglish House

Aglish, Cappoquin, Co. Waterford. ☎ **024/96191.** Fax 024/96482. 4 rms (3 with bath). TV TEL. £45–£60 ($72–$96) double. No service charge. Rates include full breakfast. EU, MC, V.

This corner of the Waterford countryside possesses a mix of pastoral charm and wild beauty, and Aglish House is a perfect base from which to explore the area. The breakfast here is especially good. The Moore family are generous hosts, and their home is comfortable and spacious. As numerous photos and trophies attest, this is a family of avid cyclists, and they are well versed in the local bicycling routes. A short walk from the house are the Kiltera Ogham stones, inscribed pillars dating from pre-Christian times; also nearby is the lovely Blackwater estuary. A short drive brings you to the coast or the Knockmealdown Mountains.

Cliff House Hotel

Ardmore, Co. Waterford. ☎ **024/94106.** Fax 024/94496. 13 rms. TEL. £76 ($121.60) double. No service charge. Rates include full breakfast. AE, DC, MC, V. Closed Nov–Feb.

Perched above the breakers, this hotel has spectacular views of the bay at Ardmore and a long stretch of rocky coast. The rooms are modern and bright; all but one are on the sea side of the building. There is a restaurant and pub on the building's lower level, and a terrace permits outdoor dining. A beautiful walk around the point begins at the edge of the parking lot, taking in the Ardmore chapel and round tower as well as the majestic sea cliffs; a leaflet published by the hotel describes this and other local walks. There are also two bikes for hire at the hotel, and good cycling roads run from here along the coast.

✪ Foxmount Farm

Passage East Rd., Waterford, Co. Waterford. ☎ **051/874308.** Fax 051/854906. 6 rms (4 with bath) £45 ($72) double. 25% off for children under 12. No service charge. Rates include full breakfast. No credit cards. Closed Nov–Feb.

This elegant, secluded 17th-century country home is the perfect place to relax and collect yourself after a busy day of sightseeing. Margaret and David Kent are superlative hosts and do all they can to assure that your stay here will be a memorable one. Dinner is offered for £16 ($25.60), with tea following in the spacious and comfortable sitting room; the dining room is nonsmoking, but smoking is allowed in the sitting room. The floor plan of the house provides for two adjacent bedrooms in a separate alcove, perfect for a family, and four double rooms with private bath; all have views of the fields around the house. A guide to walks in the area is available. Jack Meades pub (see below) is within walking distance.

✪ Three Rivers Guesthouse

Cheekpoint, Co. Waterford. ☎ **051/382520.** Fax 051/382542. 15 rms. TEL. £36–£60 ($51–$75) double. 2- and 3-night specials available. No service charge. Rates include full breakfast. AE, DC, MC, V.

This relatively new guest house enjoys a serene waterfront setting, yet it's just 7 miles from downtown Waterford. Aptly named, it sits on the harbor at the point where three rivers meet: the Suir, Nore, and Barrow. The guest rooms are bright and contemporary, with pastel tones, rattan furnishings, framed prints, and floral fabrics and comforters. Most rooms have lovely views of the water, and all are nonsmoking. Award-winning breakfasts are served in the bright, multiwindowed dining room overlooking the rivers, and there's a large, plant-filled, conservatory-style TV/reading room for relaxation. Proprietors Stan and Mailo Power enthusiastically provide local sightseeing guidance.

DINING
MODERATE

✪ Dwyer's
8 Mary St., Waterford. ☎ **051/77478** or 051/71183. Reservations recommended. Main courses £12.50–£14.50 ($18–$19.50). Early bird (6–7:30pm) 4-course fixed-price dinner £14 ($22.40) AE, DC, MC, V. Mon–Sat 6–10pm. IRISH/INTERNATIONAL.

Situated on a quiet back street near the northern entrance to the city at Ignatius Rice Bridge, this small restaurant is owned and operated by Martin and Sile Dwyer, who cook everything to order in a homey 30-seat setting. The menu changes often, but choices often include wild salmon in filo pastry with cucumbers and fennel, roast squab pigeon with port wine sauce, roast marinated brill with Gremolata sauce, and honey-glazed breast of duck with lemon sauce.

✪ Jade Palace
3 The Mall, Waterford. ☎ **051/55611.** Reservations recommended. Fixed-price lunch £6.95 ($11.10); dinner main courses £8–£14 ($12.80–$22.40). MC, V. Mon–Fri noon–2:30pm; daily 6–10pm. CHINESE/IRISH.

Some of Waterford's best cuisine is served at this reliable restaurant, on the upstairs level above a Victorian-style bar. The menu, which has garnered several awards, is attentively served amid a setting of pink linens, red velvet seats, Oriental statuary, library books, gilt-framed paintings, fresh flowers, and silver cutlery (or chopsticks, if you prefer). Dishes include king prawns, duck Cantonese, fillet steak cooked at the table, lemon chicken, sweet-and-sour pork, baked lobster, and steamed fish with ginger.

The Olde Stand
Michael St., Waterford. ☎ **051/79488.** Reservations recommended. Dinner main courses £8–£12 ($12.80–$19.20); bar food all items £2–£8 ($3.20–$12.80). MC, V. Mon–Sat bar food 12:30–2:30pm, restaurant 5:30–10:15pm, Sun 12:30–9:30pm. IRISH/SEAFOOD.

Overlooking the busy center of the city at the corner of Lady Lane, this upstairs restaurant is part of a Victorian-style pub with a decor of old paintings and maps of Waterford. The restaurant, open only for dinner and Sunday lunch, features steaks

Readers Recommend

Brown's Town House, 29 South Parade, Waterford, Co. Waterford. ☎ **051/870594.** *Brown's Town House is just the place you want to end up after a hard day's touring. Located in Waterford within walking distance of everything, Brown's B&B offers impeccably clean rooms with old-world charm and all the modern conveniences. . . . [Breakfast] included salmon, gourmet coffee, and home-mixed cereal. Mr. Brown has traveled and worked around the world. . . . There was plenty of interesting conversation to be had around the breakfast table.*

—Nicholas S. Murphy, Williamsburg, VA

and seafood, with choices including surf-and-turf, salmon in pastry, and seafood pancakes. The lower-level pub also offers morning coffee, a self-service carvery lunch, and snacks throughout the day.

Prendivilles

Cork Rd., Waterford. ☎ **051/78851.** Reservations recommended. Fixed-price lunch £8.35–£10.75 ($13.35–$17.20); main courses £10.50–£15 ($16.80–$24). AE, DC, MC, V. Mon–Fri 12:30–2:15pm; Mon–Sat 6:30–9:45pm. IRISH/INTERNATIONAL.

Located midway between downtown and the Waterford Crystal Factory, this restaurant is housed in a 19th-century Gothic-style stone gate lodge. The light and airy interior is enhanced by modern Irish art, and the menu blends innovative cuisine with fresh local ingredients, offering dishes such as venison sausage with homemade black pudding, fresh basil pasta with creamy chive sauce, poached wild salmon with peach cream and mint sauce, and loin of new season lamb.

The Reginald

The Mall, Waterford. ☎ **051/55087.** Reservations recommended for dinner. Bar food £2–£7 ($3.20–$11.20) all items; main courses £8.50–£15 ($13.60–$24). DC, MC, V. Daily 11am–10:30pm. IRISH.

One of the city's original walls (ca. 850) is part of the decor at this pub/restaurant next to Reginald's Tower. In keeping with its Viking-inspired foundations, the Reginald is laid out in a pattern of caverns, alcoves, and arches. The restaurant offers innovative choices using local ingredients, such as fillet steak Aoife topped with avocado, chives, tomatoes, and green peppercorn sauce; fillet of pink trout with vermouth sauce; half of roast duck with three peppercorns; and pork steak and sorrel sauce. Buffet-style pub grub is available in the bar at lunchtime (Monday to Saturday), and jazz is on tap during Sunday afternoon lunch from 12:30 to 2:30pm.

The Seanachie

Waterford-Cork road (N25), Pulla, Ring, Dungarvan, Co. Waterford. ☎ **058/46285.** Reservations recommended for dinner. Lunch main courses £3–£7.95 ($4.80–$12.72); dinner main courses £11–£15 ($17.60–$24). Apr to mid-Nov daily noon–10pm. IRISH.

Located 5 miles west of Dungarvan and about 32 miles west of Waterford City, this cozy thatched-roof pub sits off the main road in a farmyard setting. It takes its name from the Irish word meaning storyteller, and storytelling as well as Irish music is usually on tap here, day and night. This pub/restaurant is also known for its good food. Lunch or snack choices include soups, sandwiches, omelets, seafood salads, and Irish stew. Entrées at dinner have more of a gourmet flair, with dishes such as noisettes of lamb with apple mint or red wine sauce, panfried rainbow trout, chicken mornay, seafood pancake, stuffed breast of duck, and a variety of steaks.

✪ The Strand Seafood Restaurant

Dunmore East, Co. Waterford. ☎ **051/383174.** Reservations recommended. Main courses £10.95–£13.50 ($17.50–$21.60). No service charge. EU, MC, V. Apr–Oct daily 7am–10pm. SEAFOOD.

This intimate restaurant, set within the Strand Inn and attached to two pubs, has its own independent reputation for outstanding cuisine. If you manage to look up from your plate, the views of Waterford Harbour and the Celtic Sea are stunning. The excellent menu is augmented daily by four or five seafood specials. The grilled wild salmon with green gooseberry sauce sounds risky but generously rewards all takers, while the fresh lemon sole stuffed with seafood mousse is gorgeous. Plates of crisp sautéed vegetables are liable to appear all by themselves, so be forewarned. A most alluring dessert cart lies in wait at the end of your meal.

INEXPENSIVE

Bewley's

Broad St., Waterford. ☎ **051/70506.** Reservations not necessary. All items 80p–£4.95 ($1.30–$7.90). Mon–Sat 8am–6pm. IRISH/SELF-SERVICE.

Located on the second level of the Broad Street Shopping Centre, this is a branch of the famous Dublin coffeehouse of the same name. It's open for breakfast, lunch, and coffee and tea all day. Homemade scones, fresh pastries, and soups are a specialty.

Poppy's

25 Barronstrand St., Waterford. ☎ **051/70008.** Reservations not necessary. Breakfast £1.50–£3.50 ($2.40–$5.60); all lunch/snack items £1.50–£5.50 ($2.40–$8.80). No credit cards. Mon–Sat 9–11am and noon–6pm. INTERNATIONAL.

Poppy's is located on the fifth floor above the four-story Book Centre, and yes, there is an elevator. Tables overlook the book shop or, on the outdoor roof, have views of the city. All food is prepared and cooked on the premises, including soups, breads, pastries, biscuits, and cakes. The menu offers an eclectic array of choices such as Italian-style stuffed mushrooms filled with three cheeses and served with pasta, California meat loaf stuffed with bacon and cheddar cheese, and spinach and mushrooms wrapped in puff pastry.

A CRUISING RESTAURANT

✪ Galley Cruising Restaurants

New Ross Quay, New Ross, Co. Wexford. ☎ **051/21723.** Reservations required. Lunch £13 ($20.80); afternoon tea £6 ($9.60); dinner £20–£24 ($32–$38.40); cruise only £6 ($9.60) at 12:30pm, £5 ($8) at 3pm, and £10 ($16) at 7pm. Apr–Oct daily from New Ross at 12:30pm (lunch), Apr–Sept daily from New Ross at 5:30pm or 7pm (dinner); June–Aug from Waterford and New Ross at 3pm (afternoon tea or cruise only). IRISH.

This is Ireland's only cruising restaurant, newly refurbished throughout, based 15 miles northeast of Waterford at New Ross, Co. Wexford, but considered part of the Waterford experience. Capt. Dick Fletcher welcomes guests aboard to enjoy a full bar service and a meal while cruising the sylvan waters of the Rivers Suir, Nore, or Barrow. The menu is limited in choice, but the food is freshly prepared, and the views can't be equaled. Cruises last from two to three hours and are timed for lunch, afternoon tea, or dinner departures. Boats normally leave from New Ross, but during the summer months trips are also scheduled from Waterford.

WATERFORD AFTER DARK

Waterford has two main entertainment centers. Housed in one of Ireland's largest arts centers, the **Garter Lane Theatre,** 22a O'Connell St. (☎ 051/855038), presents the work of local production companies such as the Red Kettle and Waterford Youth Drama. Visiting troupes from all over Ireland also perform contemporary and traditional works at this 170-seat theater. Performances are usually Tuesday through Saturday, and tickets average £3 to £8 ($4.80–$12.80) for most events. The box office is open Monday to Saturday from 10am to 6pm and 7 to 9pm. Accepts AE, V.

When big-name Irish or international talent comes to Waterford, they usually perform at **The Forum Theatre** at The Glen (☎ 051/871111), a 1,000-seat house off Bridge Street. Tickets average £8 to £15 ($12.80 to $24) depending on the event. The box office is open Monday through Friday, 11am to 1pm and 2 to 4pm. The Forum presents a late-night bar, "Deja Vu," every Friday and Saturday. No cover. Clientele mostly mid- to late 30s.

Aside from these two venues, Waterford's nightlife is centered in the hotel lounges and in the city's interesting assortment of pubs.

PUBS

T.&H. Doolan
32 George's St. ☎ 051/72764.

Once a stagecoach stop, this 170-year-old pub in the center of town claims to be Waterford's oldest public house. It is a favorite venue for evening sessions of ballad, folk, and traditional music. It is lantern lit, with whitewashed stone walls and a collection of old farm implements, crocks, mugs, and jugs.

Egan's
36/37 Barronstrand St. ☎ 051/75619.

Situated in the heart of the city center, this friendly pub is a showcase of Tudor style and decor, from its neat black-and-white facade to its cozy interior.

The Kings
8 Lombard St. ☎ 051/70949.

Situated just off The Mall, this pub dates from 1776 when it was called the Packet Hotel because of its proximity to the Waterford docks and the packet ships sailing to England. It was often a send-off point for people leaving Ireland to emigrate to new shores. Today, it retains its original Georgian-style facade and the interior reflects an old-world charm, particularly in the cozy 20-seat front bar. Check out the mid–19th-century bar counter—it has panels that used to hold sandpaper for customers to strike a match.

✪ Jack Meades
Cheekpoint Rd., Halfway House, Ballycanavan, Co. Waterford. ☎ 051/50950.

Waterford's most unusual pub is not in the city at all, but is nestled beneath an old stone bridge in an area known as Halfway House, 4 miles south of Waterford. Dating from 1705, this old pub is widely known by the locals as Meade's Under the Bridge, or "Ireland's only fly over pub." As a public house with a forge, it was a stopping-off point for travelers between Waterford and Passage East in the old days. The facade and interior haven't changed much in the intervening years—wooden beams, historical paintings, antiques, and open, crackling fireplaces. All year-round there is music with sing-along sessions on Wednesday, Friday, Saturday, and Sunday evenings. The grounds include an icehouse, corn mill, lime kilns, a viaduct, and a beer garden / barbecue area. On Sundays in summer, barbecues with outdoor music are held from 5pm. From May through September bar food is served daily.

The Munster
Bailey's New St. ☎ 051/74656.

The flavor of old Waterford prevails in this 300-year-old building, which also can be entered from The Mall. Often referred to as Fitzgerald's (the name of the family that owns it), this pub has a decor rich in etched mirrors, antique Waterford glass sconces, and dark wood walls, some of which are fashioned out of timber from the old Waterford Toll Bridge. Among the many rooms are an original "Men's Bar" and a lively modern lounge, which often features traditional Irish music on weekends.

EASY EXCURSIONS FROM WATERFORD TO TIPPERARY

It's not such a long way to Tipperary from Waterford. In fact, it's less than 50 scenic miles from Waterford City to Cashel. Deep in the Irish inland countryside,

Cashel is not to be missed. Since it's right on the main N8 road, most people pass through en route from Dublin to Cork. If your travels don't take you to Cashel, then a side trip from Waterford is worth the drive. In particular, two scenic routes are well worth a detour:

At Cahir, embark in a northerly direction through the ✪ **Galtee Mountains** to the Glen of Aherlow. Often called Ireland's Greenest Valley, the 7-mile Glen of Aherlow is a secluded and scenic area that was an important pass between the plains of counties Tipperary and Limerick.

If you're trekking south after a visit to Cashel, then head for the Vee. This 11-mile-long road winds through the Knockmealdown Mountains from Clogheen to Lismore and Cappoquin in Co. Waterford, and is one of the most scenic drives in the Southeast.

ATTRACTIONS

✪ The Rock of Cashel

Cashel, Co. Tipperary. ☎ **062/61437.** Admission £2.50 ($4) adults, £1.75 ($2.80) seniors, £1 ($1.60) students and children, £6 ($9.60) family. Mid-Sept to mid-Mar daily 9:30am–4:30pm; mid-Mar to mid-June daily 9:30am–5:30pm; mid-June to mid-Sept daily 9am–7:30pm.

When you reach the town of Cashel, look for signs to the Rock of Cashel, which dominates the Tipperary countryside for miles. An outcrop of limestone reaching 200 feet into the sky, "the Rock" tells the tales of 16 centuries: It was the castled seat of the kings of Munster at least as far back as A.D. 360, and it remained a royal fortress until 1101, when King Murtagh O'Brien granted it to the church. Among Cashel's many great moments was the legendary baptism of King Aengus by St. Patrick in 448. Remaining on the rock are the ruins of a two-towered chapel, a cruciform cathedral, a 92-foot round tower, and a cluster of other medieval monuments. The views of and from the Rock are spectacular.

Bru Boru

Rock Lane, Cashel, Co. Tipperary. ☎ **062/61122.** Free admission to center; £5 ($8) per person for music performances. Daily 10am–6pm or later; evening music shows May–Sept Tues–Sat at 9pm.

At the foot of the Rock of Cashel, this modern complex adds a musical element to the historic Cashel area. Operated by Comhaltas Ceoltoiri Eireann, Ireland's foremost traditional music organization, Bru Boru presents daily performances of authentic Irish traditional music at an indoor theater, and on many summer evenings concerts are given at an open-air amphitheater. A heritage center, gift shop, restaurant, and self-service snack bar are also on hand here.

Impressions

Then came Cashel! . . . 'the great vision of the guarded mount' stood directly poised on the chimney-pots of the gay painted street. Below everything was Georgian; shadowed, solid, decorous and domestic to the last degree, and above each outline from the lifted finger-tip of the belfry to the toy towers of Cormac's Chapel was remote, romantic and insubstantial. It was all grey, the cathedral with its angle tower, the belfry with its conical top, even the steep flagged roof of Cormac's Chapel was remote; a pure, pearly, translucent grey which seemed to float and melt into the evening sky, as though it were in another dimension; an Irish Olympus.

—Frank O'Connor, *Irish Miles* (1903–66)

GPA–Bolton Library

John St., Cashel. ☎ **062/61944.** Admission £1.50 ($2.40) adults, £1 ($1.60) seniors and students, 50p (80¢) children. Mar–Oct Mon–Sat 9:30am–5:30pm, Sun 2:30–5:30pm.

In this library you'll see the smallest book in the world as well as other rare, antiquarian, and unusual books dating from the 12th century. Ensconced here are works by Dante, Swift, Calvin, Newton, Erasmus, and Machiavelli. Also on display are some silver altar pieces from the original cathedral on the Rock of Cashel. It is located on the grounds of St. John the Baptist Church.

✪ Cahir Castle

Cahir, Co. Tipperary. ☎ **052/41011.** Admission £2 ($3.20) adults, £1.50 ($2.40) seniors, £1 ($1.60) students and children, £5 ($8) family. April to mid-June and mid-Sept to mid-Oct daily 10am–6pm; mid-June to mid-Sept daily 9am–7:30pm; mid-Oct–Mar daily 10am–1pm and 2–4:30pm.

On a rock in the middle of the River Suir, this is one of Ireland's largest medieval fortresses. Its origins can be traced from the 3rd century when a fort was built on the rock—hence the town's original name, City of the Fishing Fort. The present structure, which belonged to the Butler family from 1375 to 1961, is Norman and dates to the 13th and 15th centuries. It has a massive keep, high walls, spacious courtyards, and a great hall, all fully restored. The interpretive center offers an engaging 20-minute video introduction to the major historical sites of the region, as well as guided tours of the castle grounds. Be sure to find your own way through the castle buildings, not included in the tour.

Swiss Cottage

Off Dublin-Cork road (N8), Cahir. ☎ **052/41144.** Admission £2 ($3.20) adults, £1.50 ($2.40) seniors, £1 ($1.60) students and children, £5 ($8) family. Apr Tues–Sun 10am–5pm; May–Sept daily 10am–6pm; Oct–Nov Tues–Sun 10am–1pm and 2–4:30pm.

The Swiss Cottage was used as a hunting and fishing lodge by the earls of Glengall as far back as 1812. It's a superb example of "cottage orné": a rustic house embodying the ideal of simplicity that so appealed to the Romantics of the early 19th century. The thatched-roof cottage has extensive timber work, usually not seen in Ireland, and is believed to have been designed by John Nash, a royal architect. The interior has some of the first wallpaper commercially produced in Paris. Access is by guided tour only.

✪ Tipperary Crystal

Waterford-Limerick road (N24), Ballynoran, Carrick-on-Suir, Co. Tipperary. ☎ **051/41188.** Free admission. Mon–Sat 8am–7pm, Sun 10am–6pm.

If you're nearby, don't miss this crystal factory, laid out in the style of traditional Irish cottages, complete with a thatched roof. Visitors are welcome to watch master craftsmen as they mouth-blow and hand-cut crystal. Unlike at other crystal factories, there's no restrictions on photographs and video recorders here. The facility includes a showroom and restaurant.

Athassel Priory (Open site)

This is the largest medieval priory in Ireland, spread out over four acres, and although it is in ruins, many delightful details from the original structure remain. Take the signposted road about 2 miles south from the town of Golden, which is located between Tipperary and Cashel on N74; the priory is located in a field just east of the road, and its many pinnacles offer a strikingly picturesque scene. This was an Augustinian priory, founded in the late 12th century; the remaining structures date from that time until the mid–15th century. The main approach is over a low stone bridge and through a gatehouse that was the focal point of the outer fortifications. The church is entered through a beautifully carved doorway at its west end. To the south of the church is the cloister, whose graceful arches have been largely eroded away by time. Don't miss the carved face protruding from the southwest corner of the chapel tower, about 30 feet above ground level.

SPORTS & OUTDOOR PURSUITS

HORSEBACK RIDING   Bansha House, Bansha, Co. Tipperary (☎ **062/54194;** fax 062/54215), is one of the best equestrian centers in Ireland for trail rides, located as it is at the foot of the Galty Mountains. They offer a sequence of rides beginning and ending at the house, covering some great trails and beautiful countryside. The horses are extremely well trained and cared for, and are capable of making even a rank beginner feel at ease; the safety precautions here are particularly good. Children are welcome, as long as they have some previous experience on horseback. The package of meals, accommodations, and riding for three days is £200 ($320). Admission to the hunt can be arranged for experienced riders.

WALKING   R668 between Clogheen and Lismore is one of the most scenic stretches of road in the southeast, and there are some great walks beginning at the Vee Gap, a dramatic notch in the Knockmealdown Mountains. About 1.5 miles north of R669 and R668 you will reach the highest point in the gap; there is a parking lot here, and a dirt road continuing down to a lake nestled into the hillside below. This is Bay Lough, and the dirt road used to be the main thoroughfare over the gap; it now offers a fine walk to the shores of the lake, with outstanding views of the valley to the north. For a truly panoramic perspective of the region, start walking due east from the gap parking lot to the summit of Sugarloaf Hill; the way is extremely steep, but well worth the effort, as the views from the ridge are superb.

The Galty Mountains, located just northwest of the Knockmealdowns, offer some great long and short walks. One beautiful walk on a well-defined trail is the circuit of Lake Muskry, on the north side of the range. To get there, take R663 west out of Bansha and follow signs for the town of Rossadrehid. To get to the trail, ask for directions in Rossadrehid; there are several turns to be made, and the landmarks change frequently due to logging in the region. The trail leads you up a glaciated valley to the base of a ring of cliffs, where lie the crystalline waters of Lake Muskry; from here you can walk around the lake, take in the tremendous views of the valley, and return the way you came. Walking time to the lake and back is three hours. Another option on this walk is to continue on up past the lake to the top of the ridge, and from there along the ridge top to Galtymore, a prominent dome-shaped peak about 3.1 miles west of Lake Muskry. This is a beautiful but extremely demanding walk, about six hours to Galtymore and back.

ACCOMMODATIONS
VERY EXPENSIVE

Cashel Palace

Main St., Cashel, Co. Tipperary. ☎ **800/221-1074,** 800/223-6510 from the U.S., or 062/61411. Fax 062/61521. 20 rms. TV TEL. £175–£225 ($280–$360) double. Includes full Irish breakfast and service charge. AE, DC, MC, V.

Originally built in 1730 as a residence for Church of Ireland archbishops, this stately red-brick Palladian mansion has been a hotel for the last 30 years. It has an ideal location, right in the middle of Cashel town yet within its own walled grounds, and recent owners have thoroughly updated the property and filled it with antiques and designer-coordinated fabrics. Its well-tended back garden includes mulberry bushes planted in 1702 to commemorate the coronation of Queen Anne, and a private pathway known as the Bishop's Walk that runs up a hill to the Rock of Cashel. The house itself is a proud display of Corinthian pillars, mantelpieces of Kilkenny marble, and a paneled early Georgian staircase of red pine.

Dining/Entertainment: The Four Seasons restaurant offers splendid views of the revered Rock, especially at night when it is floodlit. Other choices include the lower-level coffee shop/pub, The Buttery, and the Cellar Bar.

MODERATE

Dundrum House

Dundrum, Co. Tipperary. ☎ **800/447-7462** from the U.S., or 062/71116. Fax 062/71366. 55 rms. TV TEL. £90.20–£96.80 ($144.30–$154.90) double. Includes full Irish breakfast and service charge. AE, DC, MC, V.

Located 6 miles northwest of Cashel, this impressive Georgian country manor is nestled in the fertile Tipperary countryside, surrounded by 100 acres of grounds and gardens, with the River Multeen running through the property. Originally built as a residence in 1730 by the earl of Montalt, then used as a convent school, it was renovated, updated, and turned into a hotel in 1978 by local residents Austin and Mary Crowe. It is furnished with assorted heirlooms, vintage curios, Victorian pieces, and reproductions. Each bedroom is individually decorated, some with four-poster beds or hand-carved headboards, armoires, vanities, and other traditional furnishings. Dining choices include the elegant high-ceiling dining room and a unique bar/lounge with stained-glass windows (formerly a chapel). Exercise facilities include a championship 18-hole golf course, two tennis courts, riding stables, and trout fishing privileges.

MODERATE/INEXPENSIVE

✪ Kilcoran Lodge

Dublin-Cork road (N8), Cahir, Co. Tipperary. ☎ **800/447-7462** from the U.S., or 052/41288. Fax 052/41994. 22 rms. TV TEL. £50–£70 ($80–$112) double. Service charge 10%. Rates include full breakfast. AE, DC, MC, V.

A former hunting lodge nestled on 20 acres of wooded grounds, this old Victorian treasure is on a hillside set back from the main road a few miles west of Cahir. It's been totally renovated and refurbished in recent years, but still retains its old-world charm in the public areas. Step inside and relax amid the open fireplaces, grandfather clocks, antique tables and chairs, brass fixtures, and tall windows that frame expansive views of the Suir Valley and Knockmealdown Mountains. Each of the guest rooms is outfitted with traditional furnishings as well as modern conveniences such as a hair dryer, tea/coffeemaker, and garment press. Hotel dining choices include a formal restaurant with lovely views of the countryside and a bar/lounge noted for its daytime pub grub, which includes Irish stew, traditional boiled bacon and cabbage, homemade soups, and hot scones. Indoor swimming pool, Jacuzzi, sauna, and solarium are available to guests.

Rectory House

Dundrum, Co. Tipperary. ☎ **800/528-1234** from the U.S., or 062/71266. Fax 062/71115. 10 rms. TV TEL. £55–£75 double ($88–$120). No service charge. Rates include full breakfast. MC, V. Closed Dec–Feb.

Located about 5 miles northwest of Cashel, this mid–19th century house is surrounded by ancient trees and lovely gardens. It has a storied past, having been built by Viscount Hawarden and then used as a Church of Ireland pastor's house until a few years ago. Totally renovated and redecorated by owners Stephanie and Paul Deegan, it is outfitted with all the modern conveniences and is a very homey place to stay. The candlelit dining room has earned a reputation for fine French/Irish cuisine, and the bar is full of old-world atmosphere, a favorite gathering spot for the locals.

INEXPENSIVE

Ballyowen House

Dualla, Cashel, Co. Tipperary. ☎ **062/61265** or 062/61895. 3 rms (2 with bath). £50 ($80) double. No service charge. Rates include full breakfast. No credit cards. Closed Oct–Apr.

This is a secluded retreat from which to explore Cashel, Cahir, and the immediate area. The rather imposing manor house, dating from 1750, is both elegant and charmingly antiquated. Surrounding the house are vast fields dotted with sheep and beautiful old trees. The rooms are extravagantly large, and furnished with handsome antiques. Tea is available upon arrival, and breakfast is served in the spacious dining room. The McCan family offer a warm welcome and knowledgeable advice on walks and nearby sightseeing.

Bansha House

Bansha, Co. Tipperary. ☎ **062/54194**. Fax 062/54215. 8 rms (5 with bath). £40 ($64) double. No service charge. Rates include full breakfast. EU, MC, V. Closed Dec 20–Jan 1.

The Marnanes have won many well-deserved awards during 25 years of offering accommodation in their elegant and comfortable Georgian manor farmhouse. The town of Bansha sits at the base of the magnificent Galtee Mountains, which dominate the skyline on a clear day and make this house a great base for walking and bicycling or just taking in the beautiful scenery. Five years ago an equestrian program was added, which is now quite top-notch (see description above). Mary and John Marnane can also direct you to walks, bike rides, and drives in the area.

DINING
EXPENSIVE

Chez Hans

Rockside, Cashel, Co. Tipperary. ☎ **062/61177**. Reservations required. Fixed-price dinner £22–£25 ($35.20–$40). MC, V. Tues–Sat 6:30–9:30pm. Closed Jan. FRENCH/IRISH.

It's not surprising that the Rock of Cashel, a pivotal landmark in the course of Irish royal and ecclesiastical history, would inspire a great restaurant within its shadow. Entirely appropriate, too, that the restaurant be housed in a former Gothic chapel at the foot of the path that leads to the mighty Rock. The cathedral-style ceiling, original stone walls, lyrical background music, and candlelight atmosphere of Chez Hans provide the perfect setting for the cooking of chef-owner Hans Pieter Mataier, whose repertoire includes such dishes as quenelles of sea bass, sole meunière, succulent herb-encrusted roast lamb, and free-range duckling with honey and thyme.

MODERATE

Spearman

97 Main St., Cashel, Co. Tipperary. ☎ **062/61143**. Reservations recommended. Dinner main courses £9–£14 ($14.40–$22.40). MC, V. Daily 12:30–3pm and 6–9:30pm. IRISH/INTERNATIONAL.

Until recently a grocery store, this attractive new restaurant offers an excellent, sophisticated menu at a very reasonable price; by combining the freshest local produce and some culinary imagination, it's rapidly gaining a fine reputation. The menu includes such entrées as baked chicken with Gruyère cheese and Dijon mustard, poached salmon in a creamy tarragon sauce, and steak with red pepper and mushroom sauce. It is located in the center of Cashel, behind the Tourist Office.

A PUB

The Ronald Reagan

Main St., Ballyporeen, Co. Tipperary. ☎ **052/67133.**

Yes, there really is a pub named after the former U.S. president, right in the middle of the town that was home to his great-grandfather, Michael Reagan. Filled with pictures and mementos of the president's June 3, 1984, visit to Ballyporeen, and with a mural of the original Reagan homestead cottage on the back wall, the bar is part of the pub-cum-gift-shop complex of local entrepreneur John O'Farrell. Partisan politics aside, it's worth a stop for a toast or at least a picture.

3 County Kilkenny

Kilkenny City is 30 miles N of Waterford, 50 miles NW of Wexford, 75 miles SW of Dublin, 85 miles SE of Shannon Airport, 92 miles NE of Cork, and 38 miles NE of Cashel.

GETTING THERE   Irish Rail provides daily service from Dublin into the Irish Rail McDonagh Station, Dublin Road, Kilkenny (☎ 056/22024).

Daily bus services from Dublin and all parts of Ireland are operated by **Bus Eireann,** McDonagh Station, Dublin Road (☎ **056/64933**).

Many roads lead to inland Kilkenny, including N9/N10 from Waterford and Wexford, N8 and N76 from Cork and the southwest, N7 and N77 from Limerick and the west, and N9 and N78 from Dublin and points north and east.

VISITOR INFORMATION   For year-round information, maps, and brochures about Kilkenny and the surrounding area, contact the **Kilkenny Tourist Office,** Shee Alms House, Rose Inn Street, Kilkenny (☎ **056/51500**). It is open May through September, Monday through Saturday from 9am to 6pm and Sunday from 10am to 5pm; April and October, Monday through Saturday from 9am to 6pm; and January to March and November to December, Tuesday through Saturday from 9am to 5pm.

CITY LAYOUT   The main business district of Kilkenny sits on the west banks of the River Nore. A mile-long north-south thoroughfare, High Street, runs the entire length of the city, although it changes its name to Parliament Street at midpoint. It starts at The Parade, on the south end near Kilkenny Castle, and continues through the city to St. Canice's Cathedral at the northern end. Most of the city's attractions are to be found along this route or on offshoot streets such as Patrick, Rose Inn, Kieran, and John. The tourist office will supply you with a good street map.

GETTING AROUND   By Public Transport   There is no downtown bus service in Kilkenny, but local buses do run to nearby towns on a limited basis, departing from The Parade. Check with Bus Eireann (☎ **056/64933**) for details.

If you need a taxi, call **Seamus Brett Taxi** (☎ **056/63000**), **Billy Delaney Cabs** (☎ **056/22457**), **Liam Dwyer Taxis** (☎ **056/51717**), **Mick Howe Taxis** (☎ **056/ 65874**), or **Phonecab** (☎ **056/63017**).

By Car   Don't attempt to drive—Kilkenny's narrow medieval streets make for extremely slow-moving traffic, and you'll almost certainly get stuck. If you have a car, park it at one of the designated parking areas at The Parade, the rail station, or at one of the shopping centers. Some parking is free and other parking is subject to coin-operated machines, usually charging 20p (32¢) per hour. If you need to rent a car

Kilkenny City

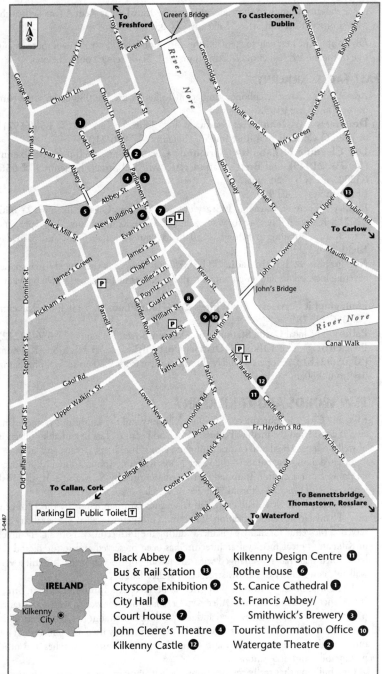

Parking **P** Public Toilet **T**

IRELAND

Kilkenny City

Black Abbey **5**
Bus & Rail Station **13**
Cityscope Exhibition **9**
City Hall **8**
Court House **7**
John Cleere's Theatre **4**
Kilkenny Castle **12**

Kilkenny Design Centre **11**
Rothe House **6**
St. Canice Cathedral **1**
St. Francis Abbey/
  Smithwick's Brewery **3**
Tourist Information Office **10**
Watergate Theatre **2**

to see the surrounding countryside, check at the **EuroDollar Rent A Car** desk at the tourist office, Rose Inn Street, Kilkenny (☎ **056/63994**).

On Foot   The best way to see Kilkenny City is on foot. Plot your own route or join one of the guided Kilkenny Walking tours (see "Sightseeing Tours," below).

FAST FACTS: KILKENNY

Area Codes   Most telephone numbers in Kilkenny use the **056** code; some parts of the county use **0505.**

Drugstores   Try **John Street Pharmacy,** at 47 John St., Kilkenny (☎ **056/65971**), or **John O'Connell,** at 4 Rose Inn St., Kilkenny (☎ **056/21033**).

Dry Cleaning & Laundry   Ormonde Cleaners, at 29 High St., Kilkenny (☎ **056/21949**), and **Brett's Launderette,** Michael Street, Kilkenny (☎ **056/ 63200**), are two good spots.

Emergencies   Dial **999**.

Library   There's a **Carnegie Library** in town, at John's Quay, Kilkenny (☎ **056/ 22021**). It's open Tuesday to Wednesday from 10:30am to 1pm, 2 to 5pm, and 7 to 9pm; Thursday to Friday 10:30am to 1pm and 2 to 5pm; and Saturday 10:30am to 1:30pm.

Newspapers & Local Media   The *Kilkenny People* is the weekly newspaper covering local events and entertainment. **Radio Kilkenny** broadcasts on 96.6 FM and 96 FM.

Photographic Services   Try **White's One-Hour Photo,** at 5 High St., Kilkenny (☎ **056/21328**).

Police   The local **Garda Station** is on Dominic Street, Kilkenny (☎ **056/22222**).

Post Office   The **Kilkenny District Post Office,** at 73 High St., Kilkenny (☎ **056/21813**), is open Monday through Friday from 9:30am to 5:30pm, Saturday from 9:30am to 1pm.

A FEW WORDS ABOUT KILKENNY

Kilkenny City, the centerpiece of County Kilkenny and the southeast's prime inland city, is considered the medieval capital of Ireland because of its remarkable collection of well-preserved medieval castles, churches, public buildings, streets, and lanes.

Situated along the banks of the River Nore, Kilkenny (population 11,000) takes its name from a church founded in the 6th century by St. Canice. In the Irish language, *Cill Choinnigh* means "Canice's Church."

Like most Irish cities, Kilkenny had fallen into Norman hands by the 12th century. Thanks to its central location, it became a prosperous walled medieval city and served as the venue for many parliaments during the 14th century. Fortunately, much of Kilkenny's great medieval architecture has been preserved and restored, and the basic town plan has not changed with the passing of the centuries: It's still a very walkable community of narrow streets and arched lanes.

The oldest house in town is purported to be **Kyteler's Inn** on St. Kieran Street. It was once the home of Dame Alice Kyteler, a lady of great wealth who was accused of witchcraft in 1324. She escaped and forever disappeared, but her maid, Petronilla, was burned at the stake. Now restored, the inn is currently used as a pub/restaurant, but it retains an eerie air, with appropriately placed effigies of witches and other memorabilia and decorations.

One building that really stands out on the Kilkenny streetscape is the **Tholsel** on High Street, with its curious clock tower and front arcade. Otherwise known as the town hall or city hall, it was erected in 1761 and served originally as the tollhouse or exchange. Milk and sugar candy were sold at the Tholsel, and dances, bazaars, and political meetings were held here, too. Today, completely restored after a fire in 1987, it houses the city's municipal archives.

Kilkenny is often referred to as the Marble City. Fine black marble used to be quarried on the outskirts of town. Up until 1929, some of the city streets also had marble pavements.

Primarily a farming area, the surrounding Co. Kilkenny countryside is dotted with rich river valleys, rolling pasturelands, gentle mountains, and picture-postcard towns. Don't miss **Jerpoint Abbey,** on the River Nore and just southwest of Thomaston on N9, one of the finest of Ireland's Cistercian ruins. Also on the Nore is the village of **Inistioge,** about 15 miles southeast of Kilkenny City. Inistioge has an attractive tree-lined square and an 18th-century bridge of nine arches spanning the river.

The town of Graiguenamanagh—its name means "village of the monks"—is home to **Duiske Abbey.** Surrounded by vistas of Brandon Hill and the Blackstairs Mountains, Graiguenamanagh is situated at a bend of the River Barrow, about 20 miles to the southeast of Kilkenny City.

Kells, about 6 miles south of Kilkenny City, is the only completely walled medieval town in Ireland. The extensive curtain walls, seven towers, and some of the monastic buildings have been well preserved.

ATTRACTIONS

✪ Kilkenny Castle
The Parade, Kilkenny. ☎ **056/21450.** Admission £2 adults ($3.20), £1.50 ($2.40) seniors, £1 ($1.60) children and students. Apr–May daily 10:30am–5pm; June–Sept daily 10am–7pm; Oct–Mar Tues–Sat 10:30am–12:45pm and 2–5pm, Sun 11am–12:45pm and 2–5pm.

Majestically standing beside the River Nore on the south side of the city, this landmark castle remained in the hands of the Butler family, the dukes of Ormonde, from 1391 until 1967, when it was given to the Irish government to be preserved as a national monument. From its sturdy corner towers (three of which are original and date from the 13th century) to its battlements, Kilkenny Castle retains the lines of an authentic medieval fortress and duly sets the tone for the entire city. The well-preserved interior features a fine collection of Butler family portraits, some from as far back as the 14th century. On the grounds are a riverside walk and extensive gardens.

St. Canice Cathedral
Coach Rd., Irishtown, Kilkenny. ☎ **056/21516.** Free admission, donations welcome. Easter–Oct Mon–Sat 9am–1pm and 2–6pm, Sun 2–6pm; Oct–Apr Mon–Sat 10am–1pm and 2–4pm, Sun 2–4pm.

At the northern end of the city, this is the church that gave Kilkenny its name. The St. Canice's Cathedral that stands today is actually a relative newcomer, built in the 13th century on the site of the 6th-century church of St. Canice. The cathedral, which has benefited from much restoration work in recent years, is noteworthy for its interior timber and stone carvings, its colorful glasswork, and for the structure itself: Its roof, which dates from 1863; its marble floor, composed of the four marbles of Ireland; and its massive round tower, 100 feet high and 46 feet in circumference, which is believed to be a relic of the ancient church, although its original conical top has been replaced by a slightly domed roof. The steps that lead to the cathedral were constructed in 1614. The library contains 3,000 volumes from the 16th and 17th centuries.

Black Abbey

Abbey St. (off Parliament St.), Kilkenny. ☎ **056/21279.** Free admission, donations welcome. March–Sept Mon–Sat 7:30am–7pm, Sun 9am–7pm; Oct–March Mon–Sat 7:30am–5:30pm. No visits during worship.

Why is this Dominican church founded in 1225 named Black Abbey? Two possible reasons are given: First, the Dominicans wore black capes over their white habits; second, the Black Plague claimed the lives of eight priests in 1348. The Black Abbey's darkest days came in 1650, when it was used by Oliver Cromwell as a courthouse; by the time he left, all that remained were the walls.

The abbey was reopened in 1816 for public worship, a new nave was constructed by 1866, and the entire building was fully restored in 1979. Among the elements remaining from the original abbey are an alabaster sculpture of the Holy Trinity that was carved about 1400 and a pre-Reformation statue of St. Dominic carved in Irish oak, which is believed to be the oldest such piece in the world. The huge Rosary Window, a stained-glass work of nearly 500 square feet and representing the 15 mysteries of the rosary, was created in 1892 by Mayers of Munich.

✪ Rothe House

Parliament St., Kilkenny. ☎ **056/22893.** Admission £2 ($3.20) adults, £1.50 ($2.40) seniors and students, £1 ($1.60) children. Apr–Oct Mon–Sat 10:30am–5pm, Sun 3–5pm; Nov–Mar Mon–Sat 10:30am–5pm, Sun 3–5pm and by appointment.

This fine Tudor-style merchant's home, built in 1594, consists of three stone build-ings divided by three cobbled courtyards. It has an arcaded front and a remarkable timber ceiling. Purchased in 1961 by the Kilkenny Archeological Society, it was restored and opened to the public in 1966. Inside is a museum of Kilkenny artifacts and a collection of period costumes. A family history research service for Kilkenny city and county has its offices here.

Cityscope Exhibition

Shee Alms House, Rose Inn St., Kilkenny. ☎ **056/51500.** Admission £1 ($1.60) adults, 80p ($1.28) seniors and students, and 50p (80¢) children. May–Sept Mon–Sat 9am–6pm, Sun 11am–5pm; Oct–Apr Tues–Sat 9am–5pm.

In the same restored building as the city's tourist office, this imaginative presenta-tion uses an architectural scale model and lighting and sound effects to re-create the town of Kilkenny in 1640. The show lasts 20 minutes. Also exhibited are dolls and miniature paintings. The building itself was erected in 1582 by a rich merchant to provide housing for the poor of the city.

St. Francis Abbey Brewery

Parliament St., Kilkenny. ☎ **056/21014.** Free admission. June–Aug Mon–Fri, visits at 3pm.

Established in 1710 by John Smithwick, the brewery occupies a site that orig-inally belonged to the 12th-century Abbey of St. Francis. A local beer called Smithwick's (pronounced *smith*-icks) is produced here, as are Budweiser and Land Kilkenny Irish Beer. A video presentation and free samples are offered in the summer months.

Dunmore Cave

Off Castlecomer road (N78), Ballyfoyle, Co. Kilkenny. ☎ **056/67726.** Admission £2 ($3.20) adults, £1.50 ($2.40) seniors, £1 ($1.60) students and children, £5 ($8) family. Mid-Mar to mid-June daily 10am–5pm, mid-June to mid-Sept daily 10am–7pm; mid-Sept to Oct daily 10am–5pm, winter Sat, Sun, and holidays 10am–5pm.

Known as one of the darkest places in Ireland, this underground cave, a series of chambers formed over millions of years, contains some of the finest calcite formations found in any Irish cave. Known to humans for many centuries, the cave may have been the site of a Viking massacre in A.D. 928. Exhibits at the visitor center tell the story of the cave. It's about 7 miles from Kilkenny City.

✪ Jerpoint Abbey

Waterford road (N9), Thomastown, Co. Kilkenny. ☎ **056/24623.** Admission £2 ($3.20) adults, £1.50 ($2.40) seniors, £1.00 ($1.60) students and children, £5 ($8) family. Mid-Apr to mid-June 10am–1pm and 2–5pm; mid-June to end of Sept daily 9:30am–6:30pm; and end of Sept to mid-Oct daily 10am–1pm and 2–7pm.

About 11 miles southeast of Kilkenny, the ruins of this 12th-century Cistercian monastery offer a splendid array of artifacts from medieval times, from unique stone carvings on walls and tombs to a 14th- or 15th-century tower and cloister, as well as Irish Romanesque details of a late 12th-century Abbey church.

Duiske Abbey

Graiguenamanagh, Co. Kilkenny. ☎ **0505/24238.** Free admission, donations welcome. Mon–Fri 10am–5pm, Sat–Sun 2–5pm.

The Duiske Abbey (1207) has a long and colorful history. It was suppressed in 1536, but its monks continued to occupy the site for many years. In 1774 the tower of the ruined abbey church collapsed. Things took a turn for the better in 1813, when the missing roof was replaced and religious services returned to the church, but the abbey didn't approach its former glory until the 1970s, when a group of local people pooled their time and talents to mount a major reconstruction effort. Now, with its fine Lancet windows and a large effigy of a Norman knight, the abbey is the pride and joy of Graiguenamanagh. The adjacent visitor center has an exhibit of Christian art and artifacts.

SIGHTSEEING TOURS

Tynan's Walking Tours

10 Maple Dr., Kilkenny. ☎ **056/65929.** £2.50 ($4) adults, £2 ($3.20) seniors and students, 60p (96¢) children. Mar–Oct Mon–Sat 9:15am, 10:30am, 12:15pm, 1:30pm, 3pm, 4:30pm; Sun 11am, 12:15pm, 3pm, 4:30pm; Nov–Feb Tues–Sat 10:30am, 12:15pm, 3pm.

Walk the streets and lanes of medieval Kilkenny, accompanied by local historian Pat Tynan. Tours depart from the Tourist Office, Rose Inn Street.

SPORTS & OUTDOOR PURSUITS

BICYCLING   Rent a bike to ride around the outskirts of Kilkenny, especially along the shores of the River Nore. Rates average £7 ($10.50) per day. Contact **J. J. Wall,** 88 Maudlin St., Kilkenny (☎ **056/21236**); **Raleigh Cycle Centre,** 5 John St., Kilkenny (☎ **056/62037**); or **Kilkenny Rent-A-Bike,** Avonmore House, Castle Street, Kilkenny (☎ **056/51399**).

FISHING   The River Nore and the nearby River Barrow are known for good salmon and trout fishing. For advice, permits, and supplies, visit the **Sport Shop,** 82 High St., Kilkenny (☎ **056/21517**).

GOLF   The annual Irish Open Golf Tournament, the pinnacle of the Irish golfing year, took place two years in a row (1993/1994) at the **Mount Juliet Golf and Country Club,** Thomastown, Co. Kilkenny (☎ **056/24725**), situated 10 miles south of Kilkenny City. You too can play a round on this 18-hole par-72 championship course designed by Jack Nicklaus, for greens fees of £65 to £70 ($104 to $112). The price drops to £35 to £45 ($56 to $72) if you are overnighting at Mount Juliet. Alternatively, try the 18-hole championship course at the **Kilkenny Golf Club,** Glendine, Co. Kilkenny (☎ **056/65400**), an inland par-71 layout 1 mile from the city. Greens fees are £20 ($32) on weekdays and £22 ($35.20) on weekends.

SHOPPING

A haven for artisans, Kilkenny City and its surrounding area is known for good shopping. To assist visitors in discovering some of the smaller workshops, the local tourist office provides a free **Craft Trail map** and information on local craft workers.

Kilkenny shopping hours are normally Monday through Saturday from 9am to 6pm; however, many shops stay open until 9pm on Thursday and Friday. The newest addition to the Kilkenny shopping scene is **Market Cross,** a new shopping center off High/Parliament Street (☎ 056/65534), with its own multistory parking lot.

The Book Centre
10 High St., Kilkenny. ☎ 056/62117.

This shop offers a fine selection of books about Kilkenny and the local area, as well as books of Irish interest. Current best-sellers, maps, stationery, cards, and posters are sold. You can grab a quick daytime snack at the Pennefeather Cafe, upstairs.

Kilkenny Crystal
19 Rose Inn St. ☎ 056/21090.

Established in 1969, this is the retail shop for Kilkenny's own hand-cut crystal enterprise, specializing in footed vases, rose bowls, bells, ring holders, wine glasses, carafes, and decanters. The factory is on the Callan Road (☎ 056/25132), 10 miles outside of town, and also welcomes visitors.

✪ Kilkenny Design Centre
Castle Yard, The Parade, Kilkenny. ☎ 056/22118.

The 18th-century stables of Kilkenny Castle were converted in 1965 into a workshop for craftspeople from all over Ireland. The adjacent shop, in the original coach house with an arched gateway and topped by a copper-domed clock tower, has become a showcase for the country's top hand-crafted products: jewelry, glassware, pottery, clothing, candles, linens, books, leather work, and furniture. An excellent coffee shop / restaurant is on the upstairs level. In addition to the normal hours listed above, this shop is open on Sundays, April to September, from 10am to 6pm.

Liam Costigan
Colliers Lane, off High St. ☎ 056/62408.

Hand-crafted jewelry is produced in this tiny shop by a fellow named Liam, who's an alumnus of the Kilkenny Design Centre; as you browse, you can watch him work.

Nicholas Mosse Pottery
Bennettsbridge, Co. Kilkenny. ☎ 056/27126.

In a former flour mill on the banks of the River Nore, this enterprise is the brainchild of Nicholas Mosse, a potter since age seven. Using water power from the river to fire the kilns, he produces colorful earthenware from Irish clay, including jugs, mugs, bowls, and plates. All are hand-slipped and hand-turned, then decorated by hand with cut sponges and brushes. An on-site museum displays antique Irish earthenware made with this process.

P. T. Murphy
85 High St., Kilkenny. ☎ 056/21127.

The sign above the entrance says it all: Watchmaker, Jeweler, Optician, and Silversmith. This is Kilkenny's master jeweler. The shop is a very good source for Irish Claddagh and Heraldic jewelry.

Yesterdays

30 Patrick St., Kilkenny. ☎ **056/65557.**

Porcelain dolls and miniatures, lace, teddy bears, miniframes, perfume bottles, jewelry, and doll-house furniture are found at this curiosity shop. It's definitely worth a browse.

ACCOMMODATIONS
VERY EXPENSIVE

✪ Mount Juliet Estate

Thomastown, Co. Kilkenny. ☎ **800/447-7462** from the U.S., or 056/24455. Fax 056/24522. 53 rms. TV TEL. £135–£250 ($216–$400) double. No service charge. Rates includes full breakfast. AE, DC, MC, V.

Kilkenny's top lodging facility is not in Kilkenny City at all, but 10 miles south in a little country village. A winding 2-mile path wends its way beside the pastures of the Ballylinch Stud Farm to this hotel, an 18th-century manor house set on a hillside overlooking the River Nore and surrounded by 1,500-acres of formal gardens, lawns, woodlands, and parklands. Built in the 1760s, the house was named after Juliana (also known as Juliet), wife of the 8th Viscount Ikerrin, the first earl of Carrick. It was later owned by the McCalmont family, leaders in the Irish horse-breeding industry. Guests may choose between the manor house, the Hunters Yard, or the Rose Garden lodges. Guest rooms are individually decorated with traditional dark woods, designer fabrics, and antiques, and public areas are full of antiques, period pieces, and original art.

Dining/Entertainment: The Lady Helen McCalmont Room offers formal dining amid a Wedgwood blue decor overlooking the river; lighter fare is served in the Old Kitchen, a basement-level bistro, and in the Loft, a chalet-style lodge in the sporting complex. The bar has an equestrian theme.

Service: 24-hour room service, concierge, valet and laundry service.

Facilities: 18-hole championship golf course designed by Jack Nicklaus; golf clubhouse with indoor swimming pool, indoor and outdoor tennis courts, badminton, squash, gym, sauna, and Jacuzzi; golf and fishing academies for on-site sports instruction; riding stables and 10 miles of bridle paths; salmon and trout fishing on exclusive 1.5-mile stretch of River Nore; pheasant shooting; and fox hunting with the Kilkenny Hunt, which is headquartered on the estate. Mount Juliet is also the home of Ireland's oldest cricket club.

EXPENSIVE

Hotel Kilkenny

College Rd., Kilkenny, Co. Kilkenny. ☎ **056/62000.** Fax 056/65984. 80 rms. TV TEL. £82.50–£100 ($132–$160) double. No service charge. Rates includes full breakfast. AE, DC, MC, V.

In a residential neighborhood on the southwest edge of the city, this hotel combines a gracious country house dating back to 1830 with a block of modern bedrooms. The main house, once the private residence of Sir William Robertson, the architect who rebuilt Kilkenny Castle, is today comprised of Gingers restaurant and the Rose Inn Bar, which features a sporting motif. The modern wing lacks the charm of the main building, but the bedrooms are comfortable and close to a health complex with indoor swimming pool, sauna, hot tub, sun beds, gym, and two hard tennis courts.

MODERATE

Butler House

16 Patrick St., Kilkenny, Co. Kilkenny. ☎ **056/65707.** Fax 056/65626. 14 rms. TV TEL. £69–£99 ($110.40–$158.40) double. No service charge. Rates include full breakfast. AE, DC, MC, V.

Built in 1770 by the 16th earl of Ormonde as a dower house for Kilkenny Castle, this elegant three-story house has a front door facing busy Patrick Street and a backyard overlooking lovely secluded gardens and the Kilkenny Castle stables / craft center. Converted into a guest house in the late 1980s, it offers individualized bedrooms of various sizes and eclectic furnishings. Amenities include VCRs and video rental. There's a free private parking lot, and the house is only a 15-minute walk from the bus and train station.

✪ Cullintra House

The Rower, Inistioge, Co. Kilkenny. ☎ **051/423614.** 6 rms (3 with bath). £40–£50 ($64–$80) double. Dinner £16 ($25.60). No service charge. Rates include full breakfast. No credit cards.

Atmosphere is of primary importance at this quaint country farmhouse, presided over by the energetic Mrs. Cantlon and her several cats. Dinner begins between 9 and 9:30pm, announced by the sound of a gong, and guests sometimes don't depart from the candlelit dining room until the small hours of the morning. A lovely art studio/conservatory has tea-making facilities and a piano; food is set here for the neighborhood foxes in the evening. Morning brings a relaxed breakfast schedule (served between 9 and noon), and perhaps a walk to Mt. Brandon or the nearby cairn (prehistoric burial mound); a trail departs from the back gate. Mrs. Cantlon is an enthusiastic hostess, and clearly enjoys entertaining her guests and making them feel at home. If you enjoy candles, cats, and good food, this place is for you.

✪ The Newpark

Castlecomer Rd., Kilkenny, Co. Kilkenny. ☎ **800/528-1234** or 056/22122. Fax 056/61111. 94 rms. TV TEL. £82–£104 ($131.20–$166.40) double. Rates include full Irish breakfast and service charge. AE, DC, MC, V.

A warm and friendly atmosphere pervades this lovely hotel, situated about a mile north of the city center. Set amid 50 acres of gardens and parklands, it was opened as a small Victorian-style country hotel more than 35 years ago and has been growing in size and gaining in reputation ever since. The bedrooms are decorated in light woods with colorful Irish furnishings, and the public areas have an old-world charm, especially in the Damask Restaurant. The grill room and lounge feature a more contemporary style. Hotel facilities include an indoor heated swimming pool, sun lounge, Jacuzzi, gym, steam room, saunas, and two tennis courts.

INEXPENSIVE

✪ Lacken House

Dublin-Carlow road, Kilkenny, Co. Kilkenny. ☎ **056/65611.** Fax 056/61085. 8 rms. TV TEL. £50–£60 ($80–$96). No service charge. Rates include full breakfast. AE, CB, MC, V.

A husband and wife duo, Eugene and Breda McSweeney, has made this restored Georgian home into one of the area's best guest houses. Breda supervises the lodging end and keeps the rooms in tiptop shape, while Eugene, an award-winning chef, oversees the restaurant (see below). Guest rooms are small but are comfortably decorated with colorful Irish furnishings. Lacken is situated on its own grounds with gardens, in the northeast corner of the city, about ten minutes walking distance from High Street and within a long block of the rail/bus station.

DINING
EXPENSIVE

✪ Lacken House
Dublin Rd., Kilkenny. ☎ 056/61085. Reservations required. Fixed-price dinner £23 ($36.80). AE, CB, DC, MC, V. Tues–Sat 7–10:30pm. IRISH/INTERNATIONAL.

A stately Georgian house is the setting for this restaurant, on the northeast edge of the city. Chef Eugene McSweeney, who earned international laurels as chef of the Berkeley Court Hotel in Dublin during its early years, has carved out his own niche in this lovely setting. The menu changes daily but often includes dishes such as breast of pigeon served with lentils and smoked bacon, baked crab au gratin, and fillet of Nore salmon with galette of potato and celeriac with sage butter sauce.

The Maltings
Bridge House, Inistioge, Co. Kilkenny. ☎ 056/58484. Reservations required. Fixed-price dinner £22 ($35.20). MC, V. Mon–Sat 7–9:30pm. IRISH.

Overlooking the River Nore about 10 miles southeast of Kilkenny City, this venerable restaurant offers simple but well-prepared food in an idyllic and romantic county-house setting. The menu changes daily but usually includes Nore salmon, fillet steak, stuffed breast of chicken bonne femme, duckling with brandy sauce, rosettes of pork, and minted lamb cutlets.

MODERATE

Parliament House Restaurant
Parliament St., Kilkenny. ☎ 056/63666. Reservations recommended. Fixed-price lunch £4.50–£9.50 ($7.20–$15.20); dinner main courses £7.50–£13.95 ($12–$22.32). AE, MC, V. Daily noon–3pm and 6:30–10:30pm. IRISH/CONTINENTAL.

Overlooking busy Parliament Street, this upstairs restaurant has a distinctive Edwardian decor, with high ceilings, chandeliers, and floral wallpaper. The menu offers a fine selection of local beef, veal, and lamb, as well as tasty combination dishes such as prawns and mussels with hazelnuts, Nore salmon in pastry with lobster sauce, duckling in wine and garlic butter, and chicken Parliament stuffed with seafood mousse and lobster sauce.

✪ Ristorante Rinuccini
1 The Parade, Kilkenny. ☎ 056/61575. Reservations recommended. Lunch main courses £3.95–£7.95 ($6.30–$12.70); dinner main courses £7.95–£14.95 ($12.70–$23.90). AE, DC, MC, V. Daily noon–2:30pm and 6–10:30pm. ITALIAN/IRISH.

Situated opposite Kilkenny Castle, this romantic candlelight restaurant specializes in the best of Irish seafood and locally produced beef in dishes such as steak Diane with brandy and prawns Rinuccini with cream sauce, mushrooms, and brandy. Chef Antonio Cavaliere also presents a full range of homemade Italian pastas and specialties, including spaghetti, fettuccine Alfredo, ravioli al pomodoro, lasagne al forno, and chicken cacciatore.

MODERATE/INEXPENSIVE

The Italian Connection
38 Parliament St., Kilkenny. ☎ 056/64225. Reservations recommended. Lunch main courses £3–£4.95 ($4.80–$7.90); dinner main courses £4.95–£12.95 ($7.90–$20.70). MC, V. Daily noon–midnight. ITALIAN/INTERNATIONAL.

Located just half a block from the Watergate Theatre, this small shop-front restaurant is popular for pre- and posttheater dining. The decor is appealing, with dark woods, wine casks, and crisp pink linens, and the menu is noted for pasta and pizza dishes prepared on the premises. In addition, there are steaks, five variations of veal, seafood, and curries.

Lautrec's

9 St. Kieran St., Kilkenny. ☎ **056/62720.** Reservations recommended. Main courses £4.95–£12.95 ($7.90–$20.70). AE, MC, V. Mon–Sat 5:30pm–12:30am and Sun 1–11pm. FRENCH/INTERNATIONAL.

With a skylit and plant-filled decor, this informal bistro-style restaurant offers an eclectic menu ranging from char-grilled salmon and brochette of lamb to a range of Tex-Mex, pasta, and curry dishes.

⑤ Kilkenny Design Restaurant

The Parade, Kilkenny. ☎ **056/22118.** Reservations not accepted. All items £1.25–£4.95 ($2–$7.90). AE, DC, MC, V. Apr–Sept Mon–Sat 9am–6pm, Sun 10am–6pm; Oct–Mar Mon–Sat 9am–5pm. IRISH/SELF-SERVICE.

Located above the Kilkenny Design shop, this spacious Georgian-style restaurant is an attraction in itself, with whitewashed walls, circular windows, beamed ceilings, framed art prints, and fresh and delicious food. The ever-changing menu often includes local salmon, chicken and ham platters, salads, and homemade soups. Pastries and breads offer some unique choices, such as cheese and garlic scones.

KILKENNY AFTER DARK

Kilkenny is home to one of Ireland's newest theaters (opened in 1993), the **Watergate Theatre,** Parliament Street (☎ **056/61674**). This modern, 328-seat showplace presents both local talent and visiting professional troupes performing a variety of classic and contemporary plays, concerts, opera, ballet, one-person shows, and choral evenings. Ticket prices average £4 to £10 ($6.40 to $16), depending on the event. Most evening shows start at 8 or 8:30pm; matinees at 2pm or 3pm.

Across the street is **John Cleere's Theatre,** 28 Parliament St. (☎ **056/62573**), a small pub theater presenting a variety of local productions, including the "Cat Laughs" comedy fest. It is also a venue for the Kilkenny Arts Week. Tickets average £3 to £6 ($4.80 to $9.60), and most shows start at 8:15 or 9:30pm.

PUBS

Caislean Ui Cuain (The Castle Inn)

Castle St., Kilkenny. ☎ **056/65406.**

A striking facade with a mural of Old Kilkenny welcomes guests to this pub, founded in 1734 as a stagecoach inn. The interior decor is equally inviting, with dark wood furnishings, globe-style lights, a paneled ceiling, and local memorabilia. Both scheduled and spontaneous Irish traditional music are often on tap, and Irish is spoken by patrons and staff.

Kyteler's Inn

St. Kieran St., Kilkenny. ☎ **056/21064.**

If you are in a medieval mood, try this stone-walled tavern in the center of town. An inn since 1324, it was once the home of Dame Alice Kyteler, a colorful character who was accused of being a witch. The decor suggests caverns and arches, and the art and memorabilia has a witchcraft theme.

✪ Edward Langton

69 John St., Kilkenny. ☎ **056/65133.**

A frequent Pub of the Year winner. Pub enthusiasts delight in Edward Langton's rich wood tones, etched mirrors, stained-glass windows, brass globe lamps, and green velour banquettes. On cool evenings the hand-carved limestone fireplace is warming, and for summer days there's a conservatory / garden area backed by the old city walls. Pub meals are a specialty here.

Marble City Bar
66 High St., Kilkenny. ☎ **056/62091.**

One of the best shop-front facades in Ireland belongs to this pub in the middle of the city. Its exterior is a showcase of carved wood, wrought iron, polished brass, and globe lamps, with flower boxes overhead—and the interior is equally as inviting. Even if you don't stop for a drink here, you'll certainly want to take a picture.

✪ Tynan's Bridge House
2 Horseleap Slip, Kilkenny. ☎ **056/21291.**

The Tynan family cheerfully welcomes all comers to this award-winning 225-year-old pub, situated along the River Nore next to St. John's Bridge, on a street that was once used as an exercise run for horses. The interior is fitted with a horseshoe-shaped marble bar, gas lamps, shiny brass fixtures, and silver tankards, and side drawers marked "mace," "citron," and "sago" are not filled with exotic cocktail ingredients, but remain from the years when the pub also served as a grocery and pharmacy. Shelves display 17th-century weighing scales, shaving mugs, and teapots; there is even a tattered copy of Chaucer's *Canterbury Tales* for rainy days.

8

Cork City

It's been said that Cork City is the Irish version of Manhattan. It's also been said that the earth is flat. True, both cities are built on islands, but that's about where the similarity ends. That said, Cork is not exactly a backwater burg, either. Stuck in the middle, neither as cosmopolitan as Dublin nor as scenic and historic as West Cork, it's nevertheless the sporting, brewing, and university center of the southwest, and thus definitely a spot to consider visiting.

St. Finbarr is credited with laying the foundation of the city by starting a church and school here in the 6th century. At that point, the area was a wetland and St. Finbarr, flush with imagination, identified it as Corcaigh, or "the marshy place." In time, the school flourished and a considerable town grew up.

Because of its relatively remote location and the spunky attitude of its citizens, Cork asserted a remarkable independence from outside authority over the years, gradually earning the title "Rebel Cork." This was carried through to the 1919–21 Irish War of Independence, when Corkmen figured prominently in the struggle.

Today, as the Republic of Ireland's second largest city, Cork (population 136,000) is a busy commercial hub for the south of Ireland. Be warned that the traffic moves fast and the people talk even faster, even with their almost sing-song accent. Be sure to taste the local brews, Beamish and Murphy's, and if you care for tea, ask for Barry's, blended in Cork since 1901.

Oh, yeah: This is where they keep the Blarney Stone, the rock that launched a thousand kisses (and a heck of a lot of tourist revenue). To kiss or not to kiss is a deeply personal decision that no guidebook could hope to help with. Look deep within yourself, and check out "What's the Deal with the Rock?" later in this chapter.

1 Orientation

Cork is 160 miles SW of Dublin, 128 miles SE of Galway, 63 miles S of Limerick, 76 miles S of Shannon Airport, 78 miles W of Waterford, and 54 miles E of Killarney.

GETTING THERE Flights via **Aer Lingus** from Dublin are scheduled regularly into Cork Airport, Kinsale Road (☎ **021/313131**), 8 miles south of the city. From Britain, there is service into Cork via **British Airways** from Birmingham, Bristol, Manchester, and Plymouth; via **Orient Air** from Coventry; via **Manx Airlines** from Jersey; via **Ryanair** from London; and via **Air South West** from

Cornwall. From the Continent, there is service to Cork via **Aer Lingus** from Amsterdam, Paris, and Rennes; via **Brit Air** from Brest and Nantes; via **KLM** from Amsterdam.

Bus Eireann (☎ 021/508188) provides bus service from the airport to Parnell Place Bus Station in the city center; the fare is £2.50 ($4) one way, £3.50 ($5.60) round-trip.

Car ferry routes into Cork from Britain include service from Swansea via **Swansea/ Cork Ferries** (☎ 021/378036); and from the Continent from LeHavre and Roscoff via **Irish Ferries** (☎ 021/378111) and from Roscoff and St. Malo via **Brittany Ferries** (☎ 021/378401). All ferries arrive at Cork's Ringaskiddy Ferryport.

Locally, there is a car-ferry service operating in Cork Harbour, linking Glenbrook, east of Cork City, and Carrigaloe, outside of Cobh. It saves at least an hour's driving time between the east and west sides of Cork Harbour, avoiding Cork City traffic. The trip lasts less than five minutes, with continuous service daily from 7:15am to 12:30am. Fare is £2.50 ($4) one way and £3.50 ($5.60) round-trip; no reservations are required. For more information, contact **Cross River Ferries, Ltd.,** Atlantic Quay, Cobh (☎ 021/811223).

Trains from Dublin, Limerick, and other parts of Ireland arrive at **Kent Station,** Lr. Glanmire Road, Cork (☎ 021/506766), on the city's eastern edge.

Buses from all parts of Ireland arrive into **Bus Eireann's Passenger Depot,** Parnell Place, Cork (☎ 021/508188), in the downtown area, three blocks from Patrick Street.

If you're driving, many main national roads lead into Cork, including N8 from Dublin, N25 from Waterford, N20 from Limerick, N22 from Killarney, and N71 from West Cork.

VISITOR INFORMATION   For brochures, maps, and other information about Cork, visit the **Cork Tourist Office,** Tourist House, 42 Grand Parade, Cork (☎ 021/273251). It's open in July and August on Monday through Saturday from 9am to 7pm and Sunday from 3 to 5pm; September through June it's open Monday through Friday from 9:30am to 5:30pm and Saturday from 9:30am to 1pm.

CITY LAYOUT

Cork is divided into three sections:

SOUTH BANK   Running south of the River Lee, South Bank encompasses the grounds of St. Finbarr's Cathedral, the site of St. Finbarr's 6th-century monastery, and also includes 17th-century city walls, the remains of Elizabeth Fort, and City Hall, built in 1936 and Cork's chief administrative center.

FLAT OF THE CITY   This is the downtown core of Cork, surrounded on both north and south sides by channels of the River Lee. This area includes the South Mall, a wide tree-lined street with mostly Georgian architecture and a row of banks, insurance companies, and legal offices; the Grand Parade, a spacious thoroughfare that blends 18th-century bow-fronted houses and the remains of the old city walls with modern offices and shops; and a welcome patch of greenery, the Bishop Lucey Park, a fairly new (1986) addition to the cityscape.

Extending from the northern tip of the Grand Parade is the city's main thoroughfare, St. Patrick Street. Referred to simply as Patrick Street by Corkonians, this broad avenue was formed in 1789 by covering in an open channel in the river. It is primarily a shopping street, but it is also a place for the Cork folks to stroll and be seen and to greet friends. Patrick Street is also the site of one of the city's best-known meeting places: the statue of 19th-century priest Fr. Theobald Matthew, a crusader against drink who is fondly called the apostle of temperance. The statue—or "the stacha," as the locals call it—stands at the point where Patrick Street reaches St. Patrick's Bridge, and is the city's most central point of reference.

NORTH BANK   St. Patrick's Bridge (or Patrick's Bridge), opened in 1859, leads over the river to the north side of the city, a hilly and terraced section where the continuation of Patrick Street is called St. Patrick's Hill. And is it ever a hill, with an incline so steep that it is nearly San Franciscan. If you climb the stepped sidewalks of St. Patrick's Hill, you will be rewarded with a sweeping view of the Cork skyline.

To the east of St. Patrick's Hill is MacCurtain Street, a busy commercial thoroughfare that goes one way in an easterly direction, leading to Summerhill Road and up into the Cork hills to the residential districts of St. Luke's and Montenotte. To the west of St. Patrick's Hill is one of the city's oldest neighborhoods, home of St. Ann's Shandon Church and the city's original Butter Market building.

2 Getting Around Cork City

BY PUBLIC TRANSPORT   Bus Eireann operates bus service from Parnell Place Bus Station (☎ **021/508188**) to all parts of the city and its suburbs, including Blarney and Kinsale. Service is frequent and the flat fare is 70p ($1.15). Buses from 7am to 11pm Monday through Saturday, and slightly shorter hours on Sunday.

BY TAXI   Taxis are readily available throughout Cork. The chief taxi ranks are located along St. Patrick's Street, the South Mall, and outside of major hotels. To call for a taxi, try ABC Taxis (☎ 021/961961), Shandon Cabs (☎ 021/502255), Supercabs (☎ 021/500511), or Tele-Cabs (☎ 021/505050).

BY CAR   Most hotels have parking lots or garages for guests' use, so if you drive into Cork, it's best to take advantage of this and explore the city on foot or by public transport. If you end up having to park your car in public areas, it will cost 40p (64¢) per hour, whether you park in one of the city's two multistory parking lots, at Lavitt's Quay and Merchant's Quay, or on the street, where the disc system is in use. Parking discs are sold singly or in books of 10 for £4 ($6.40), available at many shops and newsstands. There are also at least a dozen ground-level parking lots throughout the city.

Many international car-rental firms maintain rental desks at Cork Airport including **Avis/Johnson and Perrott** (☎ **021/281169**), **Budget** (☎ **021/314000**), **Hertz** (☎ **021/965849**), and **Europcar** (☎ **021/966736**). Avis/Johnson and Perrott also has a large depot in Cork City at Emmet Place (☎ **021/281166**).

ON FOOT   As I said, the best way to see Cork is on foot, but don't try to do it all in one day. The South Bank and the central part, or flat, of the city can easily take a day to explore; save the Cork Hills and the North Bank for another day. You may wish to follow the signposted Tourist Trail to guide you to all of the major sights.

FAST FACTS: CORK CITY

Area Codes   The area code for most Cork City numbers is **021,** unless indicated otherwise.

Drugstores   If you're in need of pharmaceutical aid, try **Duffy's Dispensing Chemists,** 95/96 Patrick St. (☎ **021/272566**); **Hayes Conyngham and Robinson,** Merchants Quay Shopping Centre (☎ **021/272230**); or **Murphy's Pharmacy,** 48 N. Main St. (☎ **021/274121**).

Emergencies   For emergencies, dial **999.**

Gay & Lesbian Resource   For information and aid, call the **Lesbian and Gay Resource Group and Community Centre,** The Other Place, 7–8 Augustine St. (☎ **021/278470**).

Hospitals   Try **Bon Secours Hospital,** College Road (☎ **021/542807**), or **Cork Regional Hospital,** Wilton Road (☎ **021/546400**).

Information   See "Visitor Information," above.

Laundry & Dry Cleaning   Nasty Guinness stain on your Armani? Try **Castle Cleaners,** 90 N. Main St. (☎ **021/277603**) or **Winthrop Cleaners,** Winthrop Street (☎ **021/276383**).

Library   **Cork Central Library,** Grand Parade (☎ **021/277110**), is a good bet.

Local Newspapers & Media   The *Cork Examiner* is Cork's daily morning newspaper; the *Evening Echo* is a daily afternoon paper. Local Cork radio stations are Radio Cork, 89 FM, 96 FM, and 103 FM.

Photographic Needs   For film and other supplies, try **Cork Camera Services,** 16 Academy St. (☎ **021/270937**), or **John Roche Ltd.,** 55A Patrick St. (☎ **021/ 272935**).

Police   The local **Garda Headquarters** is located on Barrack Street (☎ **021/ 271220**).

Post Office   The **General Post Office** on Oliver Plunkett Street (☎ **021/272000**) is open Monday through Saturday from 9am–5:30pm.

3 Accommodations

MODERATE

Arbutus Lodge

St. Luke's Hill, Montenotte, Cork, Co. Cork. ☎ **021/501237.** Fax 021/502893. 20 rms (16 with bath). Luxury rooms/suites available. TV TEL. £85 ($136) double. No service charge. Rates include full breakfast. AE, DC, MC, V.

The views of Cork City are hard to beat from the vantage point of this restored 1802 Georgian town house, perched high in the hills overlooking the north bank of the River Lee. Taking its name from the arbutus tree that grows in its prize-winning gardens, it was once the home of the lord mayor of Cork, and was converted by the Ryan family into a comfortable hotel with antique furnishings, modern Irish art, and Wedgwood trim.

Dining/Entertainment: This hotel's main claim to fame is its award-winning restaurant (see "Dining," below). Other facilities include the Gallery bar and patio for lighter meals.

✪ Fitzpatrick Silver Springs

Dublin Rd., Tivoli, Cork, Co. Cork. ☎ **800/367-7701** or 021/507533. Fax 021/507641. 109 rms. TV TEL. £96–£121 ($153.60–$193.60) double. Service charge 12.5%. AE, DC, MC, V.

Set on a hillside overlooking the River Lee and surrounded by 42 acres of gardens and grounds, this modern seven-story hotel is 2 miles east of the main business district. Like its sister properties in Dublin and Bunratty, it is personally managed by the Fitzpatrick family, so in spite of its size, a friendly and attentive atmosphere prevails. Guests are transported from the lobby to their rooms via a glass-walled elevator that offers views of the surrounding countryside, and each guest room, furnished with handcrafted Irish furniture and designer fabrics, has lovely views of the river, city, or gardens, plus little extras such as hair dryers and tea/coffeemakers.

Dining/Entertainment: Choices include Truffles Restaurant for gourmet dining; the Waterfront Grill for meals or snacks all day; the Flyover Bar; and Thady Quill's, a pub that offers live music Thursday through Saturday nights and a jazz brunch on Sunday mornings.

Services: Concierge, room service, laundry and dry cleaning, courtesy minibus service.

Facilities: Indoor heated Olympic-size swimming pool, Jacuzzi, sauna, steam room, gym, aerobics room, indoor and outdoor tennis courts, squash court, 9-hole golf course, heliport.

Imperial Hotel

South Mall, Cork, Co. Cork. ☎ **800/44-UTELL** from the U.S., or 021/274040. Fax 021/275375. 101 rms. TV TEL. £85–£110 ($136–$176) double. Service charge 10%. AE, DC, MC, V.

Within easy walking distance of Cork's major attractions and shops, this vintage four-story lodging is conveniently situated in the heart of the city's business district. With Waterford crystal chandeliers, marble floors, and brass fittings, the reception area and public rooms exude an aura of 19th-century grandeur, while the bedrooms are a mix of contemporary and traditional, some with light woods and striped pastel tones and others with dark woods, antique fixtures, and semicanopy beds. Each room has a tea/coffeemaker, a garment press, and a VCR.

Dining/Entertainment: Facilities include The Orangery coffee shop, Clouds Restaurant and bar, and the nautical Captains Bar.

✪ Jurys

Western road (N22), Cork, Co. Cork. ☎ **800/44-UTELL** from the U.S., or 021/276622. Fax 021/274477. 185 rms. TV TEL. £100 ($160) double. Service charge 12.5%. AE, DC, MC, V. Free parking.

Situated on the western edge of town, this is the only five-star hotel in this busy southern coastal city. Built on the site of the former Muskerry Railway station, it is well positioned in its own gardens, next to University College of Cork and along the banks of the River Lee, yet just a five-minute walk from the city center. A modern two-story multiwinged structure, it was recently refurbished. The public areas are light and open and include a skylit atrium and a wall-length mural of Cork characters in the lobby. Guest rooms are furnished in traditional dark woods with designer fabrics, and have views of either the central courtyard gardens or the river and city.

Dining/Entertainment: Choices include the Fastnet, a seafood restaurant with a nautical theme open only for dinner; the Glandore for meals throughout the day; the skylit, atrium-like Pavilion piano bar; and Corks Bar, an in-house pub that combines views of the river with an Old Cork ambience, with free ballad music entertainment performed by The Weavers, a local group, Wednesday through Sunday nights.

Services: Concierge, 24-hour room service, laundry and dry cleaning.

Facilities: Indoor-outdoor heated swimming pool, sauna, gym, squash court.

Morrison's Island Hotel

Morrison's Quay, Cork, Co. Cork. ☎ **800/44-UTELL** from the U.S., or 021/275858. Fax 021/275833. 40 suites. TV TEL. £115 ($184) double. No service charge. AE, CB, DC, MC, V. Free private parking.

Situated in the downtown area, overlooking the River Lee just off the South Mall, this six-story property is Cork's first all-suite hotel. The guest rooms, decorated with contemporary furniture and modern art, have views of the river, cityscape, and the nearby bridges. Each unit contains a hallway, sitting room, dining area, kitchen, bathroom, and one or two bedrooms. The public area includes the River Bank restaurant and lounge.

INEXPENSIVE

⊖ Forte Travelodge

Airport road (R600), Blackash, Cork, Co. Cork. ☎ **800/CALL-THF** from the U.S., or 021/310730. Fax 021/310707. 40 rms. TV. £36.50 ($58.40) per room. No service charge. AE, DC, MC, V.

Located in a grassy hillside setting 1¹/₂ miles south of downtown, this contemporary brick-faced, two-story motel is on the main road to Kinsale and the airport. The first representative of this no-frills chain in Ireland, it offers standard rooms with basic furnishings and tea/coffee-making facilities, providing accommodations (a double bed and a sofa bed) for up to four people for one flat rate. The public area is confined to a small reception desk, but there is an adjacent Little Chef chain restaurant.

⑤ Jurys Cork Inn

Anderson's Quay, Cork, Co. Cork. ☎ **800/44-UTELL** from the U.S., or 021/276444. Fax 021/276144. 133 rms. TV TEL. £53 ($84.80) per room. No service charge. AE, DC, MC, V.

Opened in August 1994, this five-story hotel is situated in the busy heart of the city overlooking the River Lee, next to the bus station and three blocks from Patrick Street. The brick facade, with mansard-style roof, blends in with Cork's older architecture, yet the interior is bright and modern, with contemporary light-wood furnishings. Since the flat-rate room price covers one or two adults and two children, it offers amazingly good value for a city center hotel. Facilities include Arches Restaurant and The Inn Pub.

❁ Lotamore House

Dublin-Waterford road (N8/N25), Tivoli, Co. Cork. ☎ **021/822344.** Fax 021/822219. 20 rms. TV TEL. £50 ($80) double. No service charge. Rates include full breakfast. AE, MC, V.

Overlooking the River Lee on four acres of wooded grounds and gardens 2 miles east of Cork City, this Georgian manor is one of the county's best guest houses. Owned by two doctors, Mareaid and Leonard Harty, it is an exceptionally well run facility, furnished with antiques, crystal chandeliers, and a fireplace dating from 1791. Extra comforts such as orthopedic beds, garment presses, and hair dryers have been provided in the guest rooms. Breakfast is the only meal served, but it is exceptional, with freshly squeezed juices and fruits on the menu every day.

4 Dining

EXPENSIVE

❁ Arbutus Lodge

St. Luke's Hill, Montenotte, Cork. ☎ **021/501237.** Reservations required. Fixed-price lunch £12.50 ($20); fixed-price dinner £22 ($35.20); dinner main courses £14–£18 ($22.40–$28.80). AE, DC, MC, V. Mon–Sat 1–2:30pm and 7–9:30pm. INTERNATIONAL.

Overlooking the city skyline from a hilltop vantage point, this lovely Georgian town house restaurant has long been synonymous with gourmet cuisine in Cork. The menu includes such entrées as roast quail à l'Armagnac, veal kidney with mustard sauce, chicken in tomato and basil, or rib of beef with sauce Beaujolais, as well as your choice of lobster from the tank. On some evenings, the chef also prepares a tasting menu, eight courses incorporating the best of many dishes. In addition to the quality of their meals, the Ryan family, who own and operate this restaurant, have also earned a reputation for maintaining one of the best wine lists in Ireland and beyond.

❁ Cliffords

18 Dyke Parade, Cork. ☎ **021/275333.** Reservations required. Fixed-price lunch £14 ($22.40); fixed-price dinner £30 ($48). MC, V. Tues–Fri 12:30–2:30pm; Tues–Sat 7–10:30pm. FRENCH.

Housed in the old County Library Building, this art deco–style restaurant offers a relaxing setting of dark woods and light lemon tones. Gastronomically, it is a trendsetter in the city, thanks to the creative cuisine of chef/owner Michael Clifford, who gained previous experience in the kitchen of the French Troisgros brothers. The menu changes daily and all dishes are cooked to order, but some favorites include ragout of veal, breast of farmyard duck with mushroom mousse, and warm salad of fresh shellfish.

MODERATE

✪ Jacques

9 Phoenix St., Cork. ☎ **021/277387.** Reservations recommended. Lunch main courses £3.50–£6.50 ($5.60–$10.40); dinner main courses £8.90–£13.90 ($14.25–$22.25). AE, MC, V. Lunch Mon–Fri noon–3pm; dinner Mon–Sat 6–10:30pm. IRISH/INTERNATIONAL.

Decorated with modern art on cheery lemon, tangerine, and green walls, this small bistro is the creation of two sisters, Eithne and Jacqueline Barry. It is situated in the heart of town, on a side street near the South Mall and General Post Office. Innovative cuisine is the keynote, with featured dishes such as roast duck with an apricot and potato stuffing; rack of lamb topped with Dijon mustard and garlic bread crumbs; and vegetable polenta with Parmesan cheese, field mushrooms, tomatoes, chili, and garlic.

⊛ Michael's Bistro

4 Mardyke St., Cork. ☎ **021/276887.** Reservations required. Main courses £7–£14 ($11.20–$22.40). MC, V. Lunch Tues–Fri noon–3pm; dinner Mon–Sat 6–10:30pm. BISTRO/IRISH.

An offshoot of the revered Clifford's restaurant next door, this small shop-front eatery embodies the true bistro ethos—quick service and low prices—while still providing Michael Clifford's creative cuisine. Decorated with a simple black-and-white decor, it matters little that the room is tightly packed and noisy, with small tables clustered close together, because the food is fresh, simple, and delicious. The same menu applies all day, with straightforward choices such as Irish Stew and hamburger of prime beef with braised red onions on garlic croutons as well as inventive combinations such as potato and crab cakes in parsley cream sauce.

✪ Oyster Tavern

4 Market Lane (off 56 St. Patrick St.), Cork. ☎ **021/272716.** Reservations recommended. Main courses £9–£16 ($14.40–$25.60). DC, MC, V. Mon–Sat 12:30–2pm and 6–9:30pm. IRISH.

Nestled in a narrow alley in the heart of the city, this Cork institution is known for its seafood. With an equestrian-theme decor and old-world ambience, it's very popular with the locals. As its name implies, oysters are a specialty, but it also offers such seafood dishes as salmon, sole, and panfried prawns. In addition, the menu features honey-roasted breast of duck, rack of lamb with herb crust, and a variety of steaks. Be prepared to sip an aperitif and wait in the bar area, even if you have a reservation—it's part of the tradition.

Ristorante Rossini

34/35 Princes St., Cork. ☎ **021/275818.** Reservations recommended. Lunch main courses £4–£5 ($6.40–$8); dinner main courses £6–£12 ($9.60–$19.20). MC, V. Mon–Sat noon–3pm and 6pm–12:30am, Sun 5pm–midnight. ITALIAN.

If you're in Ireland and suddenly want to be in Italy, this shop-front restaurant is the place for you. Vaulted ceiling, dark wood furnishings, an open fireplace, fresh flowers, and pictures on the walls transport your mind to Bella Italia, while the menu does the same for your stomach: steaks and lamb chops, a variety of pasta dishes, pollo Regina (chicken with asparagus, artichokes, and butter sauce), and the house special, sirloin Rossini (steak prepared with prawns, cream, white wine, and peppercorns).

INEXPENSIVE

ⓢ Bewley's Oriental Cafe

4 Cook St., Cork. ☎ 021/270660. Reservations not required. All items 95p–£6 ($1.50–$9.60). MC, V. Mon–Sat 8am–6pm. IRISH/SELF-SERVICE.

A branch of the famous Dublin coffee and tea emporium of the same name, this dependable restaurant serves breakfast, lunch, snacks, or freshly brewed coffee or tea at any time of day. It also offers a new carvery with daily specials and pasta dishes. A favorite meeting spot for Corkonians, it is located just off Patrick Street.

Bully's Restaurant and Wine Bar

40 Paul St., Cork. ☎ 021/773555. Reservations suggested. Main courses £3–£12 ($4.80–$19.20). MC, V. Mon–Sat noon–11:30pm, Sun 5–11pm. IRISH/ITALIAN.

Located on one of Cork's best shopping streets near antique row, this small shop-front eatery has a modern decor of black and white furnishings enhanced by colorful plants. It offers pizzas, pastas, and burgers as well as seafood omelets and charcoal-grilled steaks. Bully's has two other Cork locations, at Bishopstown and Douglas.

✪ Crawford Gallery Cafe

Emmet Place, Cork. ☎ 021/274415. Reservations suggested for parties of 6 or more. All items £2–£7.50 ($3.20–$12). V. Mon–Fri 10am–5pm, Sat 10am–4:30pm. IRISH.

Ensconced amid oil paintings and statuary in a ground floor room at the Crawford Art Gallery, this restaurant is run by the Allen family of Ballymaloe House fame (see East Cork). Serving breakfast, lunch, and afternoon tea, their menu includes such traditional dishes as stuffed fillet of pork and steak and kidney pie, and more contemporary open sandwiches such as a wonderful smoked salmon, cheese, and pickle combination. All fish is brought in fresh daily from Ballycotton Bay and breads and baked goods are from Ballymaloe kitchens.

Gingerbread House

Paul St. Plaza, Cork. ☎ 021/276411. Reservations recommended for dinner. All items £1.50–£3 ($2.40–$4.80); dinner entrées £5.50–£11.80 ($8.80–18.90). AE, MC, V. Mon–Wed 8:15am–9:30pm, Thurs–Sat 8:15am–10:30pm. SELF-SERVICE/SNACKS/ITALIAN.

Conveniently located between Patrick and Paul Streets in the main shopping area, this patisserie and casual restaurant is popular with Corkonians for its wide array of delicious baked goods, freshly roasted coffees and teas, soups, and light Italian fare. You can choose from their wine list or bring your own wine for a £2 ($3.20) "corkage" fee.

Gino's

7 Winthrop St., Cork. ☎ 021/274485. Reservations not necessary. Main courses £2.35–£9 ($3.75–$14.40). No credit cards. Mon–Sat noon–midnight, Sun 1pm–midnight. ITALIAN.

Shoppers from nearby Patrick Street flock to this bright and airy cafe, which specializes in pizzas with all the toppings you've come to expect, from salami, spinach, or pepperoni to things you once thought were weird but now aren't sure about, like pineapple. Fresh homemade Italian-style ice cream with exotic flavors and toppings is the other menu feature.

✪ Isaac's

48 MacCurtain St., Cork. ☎ 021/503805. Reservations advised for dinner. Lunch main courses £1.85–£5.90 ($2.95–$9.45); dinner main courses £4.20–£11.20 ($6.70–$17.90). AE, CB, MC, V. Mon–Sat 10am–10:30pm, Sun 6:30–9:30pm. IRISH.

Situated on the city's north side, this restaurant is housed in a vintage warehouse-style building with stone arches, brick walls, big globe lights, tall ceilings supported by columns, and modern art. It can be noisy when busy, but the din never disturbs the enthusiastic patrons who come for the trendy food. The menu offers choices ranging from freshly prepared salads, burgers and steaks, and seafood chowders to international dishes such as beef bourguignonne, gratin of smoked salmon and potato, and spinach tagliatelle with salmon, fennel, and cream. Daily blackboard specials add to the variety.

5 Attractions

From May to September, **Bus Eireann,** Parnell Place Bus Station (☎ **021/508188**), offers narrated tours to all of Cork's major landmarks and buildings with fares from £8 ($12.80). Open-top bus tours of Cork City, lasting 2¹/₂ hours, operate in July and August for a flat fare of £4 ($6.40).

IN TOWN

✪ St. Anne's Shandon Church

Church St. ☎ **021/505906.** Church, tower, and bells £1.50 ($2.40) per person. Open year-round Mon–Sat 10am–5pm.

Famous for its giant pepperpot steeple and its eight melodious bells, this is Cork's prime landmark. No matter where you stand in the downtown area, you can usually see the 1722 church's stone tower, crowned with a gilt ball and a fish weathervane. Visitors are often encouraged to climb to the belfry and play a tune, so you might hear the bells of Shandon ringing at all times of the day.

✪ St. Finbarr's Cathedral

Bishop St. ☎ **021/963387.** Free admission; donations welcome. Mon–Fri 10am–1pm and 3–5:30pm.

This Church of Ireland cathedral sits on the spot St. Finbarr chose in A.D. 600 for his church and school. The current building dates from 1880 and is a fine example of early French Gothic style; its three giant spires dominate the skyline. The interior is highly ornamented with unique mosaic work. The bells were inherited from the 1735 church previously on this site.

Cork Museum

Fitzgerald Park, Cork. ☎ **021/270679.** Free admission except Sun 75p ($1.20) per person, £1.50 ($2.40) family. Mon–Fri 11am–1pm and 2:15–5pm, Sun 3–5pm. July–Aug closes at 6pm. Bus: 8.

In a magnificent Georgian building set in a park on the western edge of the city, this museum has models depicting early medieval times; artifacts recovered from excavations within the city, some dating as far back as 4,000 years; a working model of an early flour mill with an unusual horizontal water wheel; and an archive of photographs and documents relating to Cork-born Irish patriots Terence McSwiney, Thomas MacCurtain, and Michael Collins. Antique Cork silver, glass, and lace are displayed. A new extension is currently underway.

✪ University College, Cork (U.C.C.)

Western Rd., Cork. ☎ **021/902758.** Free admission. Mon–Fri 9am–5pm; tours are conducted by arrangement—☎ 021/902371; fax 021/277004.

A component of Ireland's National University, with about 7,000 students, this center of learning is housed in a quadrangle of Gothic Revival–style buildings. Lovely gardens and wooded grounds grace the campus, tours of which include the Crawford Observatory, the lovely Harry Clarke stained glass windows in the Honan Chapel,

Cork City Attractions

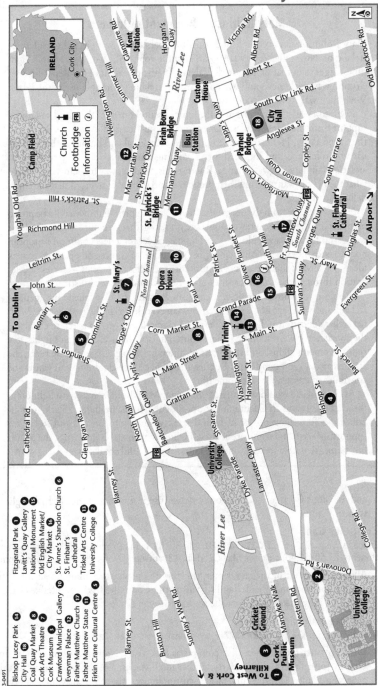

Bishop Lucey Park ⑭
City Hall ⑱
Coal Quay Market ⑧
Cork Arts Theatre ⑦
Cork Museum ③
Crawford Municipal Gallery ⑫
Everyman Palace ⑫
Father Matthew Church ⑰
Father Matthew Statue ⑪
Firkin Crane Cultural Centre ⑤

Fitzgerald Park ①
Lavitt's Quay Gallery ⑨
National Monument ⑮
Old English Market/
City Market ⑯
St. Anne's Shandon Church ⑥
St. Finbarr's
Cathedral ④
Triskel Arts Centre ⑬
University College ②

Mary Robinson: President of Ireland

Mary Robinson, an accomplished constitutional lawyer, was elected president of Ireland on November 7, 1990, by 52.8% of the voters. She won by a margin eight times larger than that of Eamon de Valera, the first president of the Republic. Her election was world news and was compared in Ireland to the collapse of the Berlin Wall, such was its magnitude.

Robinson began her campaign in the more obscure corners of the island and found support from the three smallest parties: the Labour Party, the Worker's Party, and the Green Party. Her campaign emphasized individual and human rights, pluralism and tolerance, and the need for "a working, caring presidency" responsive to an Ireland undergoing vast change. Robinson listened her way to victory. She heard what the people wanted from their president, and she was convinced that she could deliver just that.

"I got a message from the people that they wanted a president they could be proud of, but more than that, that we could take pride together—in our Irishness and our wonderful heritage and culture . . . . The stage is set for a new common European home based on respect for human rights, pluralism, tolerance and openness to new ideas . . . . I want this presidency to promote the telling of stories—stories of celebration through the arts and stories of conscience and of social justice."

Robinson is known for firsts. Before she became the first female president of Ireland, she was at age 25 the youngest woman ever elected to the Irish Senate. With her stellar education at Trinity College and Harvard, she was prepared to challenge the courts and government on issues of birth control, divorce, children's rights, gay rights, women's rights, and the rights of itinerant people. During these years, she also married a Protestant, Nick Robinson, and had three children, with whom she continues to enjoy a vibrant home life.

As she said she would during her campaign, Mary Robinson keeps a light on in the kitchen of Áras an Uachtaráin, the presidential home in Phoenix Park, to symbolize the 70 million people of Irish descent who look to Ireland and to her for support. Mary Robinson's presidency, including who she is and what she stands for, points to a new Ireland, one she both listens to and speaks for.

and the Stone Corridor, a collection of stones inscribed with the ancient Irish Ogham style of writing.

Cork City Gaol

Sunday's Well Rd., Cork. ☎ **021/542478.** Admission £3 ($4.80) adult, £2 ($3.20) seniors and students, £1.50 ($2.40) children. Mar–Oct daily 9:30am–8pm; Nov–Feb Sat–Sun 10am–4pm.

About a mile west of the city center, this restored prison was infamous in the 19th century, housing many of Ireland's great patriots. Sound effects and lifelike characters inhabiting the cells recreate the social history of Cork.

Crawford Municipal Gallery

Emmet Place, Cork. ☎ **021/273377.** Free admission. Mon–Sat 10am–5pm.

Works by such well-known Irish painters as Jack Yeats, Nathaniel Grogan, William Orpen, John Lavery, James Barry, and Daniel Maclise are the focal point of this gallery in Cork's 18th-century former customhouse. Also on display are sculptures and handcrafted silver and glass pieces, and there's a fine restaurant and bookstore on the premises. It's next to the Opera House.

Lavitts Quay Gallery
16 Lavitts Quay, Cork. ☎ **021/277749.** Free admission. Tues–Sat 10:30am–2pm and 3–5:30pm.

Operated by the Cork Arts Society, this gallery promotes the contemporary visual arts of the Cork area. It's in an early 18th-century Georgian house that overlooks the River Lee. The ground floor presents a variety of work by established artists, and the upper floor showcases up-and-coming talent.

✪ Old English Market / City Market
Grand Parade, Cork. Free admission. Mon–Sat 9am–6pm. Enter from Patrick St., Grand Parade, Oliver Plunkett St., or Princes St.

A Cork tradition from 1610, this marketplace unfolds in a building dating from 1786. Stands brim with meats, fish, vegetables, and fruit, and you'll also see such traditional Cork foods as tripe (animal stomach), crubeens (pig's feet), and drisheens (local blood sausage). The market's name is a holdover from the days of English rule.

Coal Quay Market
Cornmarket St., Cork. Free admission. Mon–Sat 9am–5pm.

This is Cork's open-air flea market, a treasure trove of secondhand clothes, old china, used books, and memorabilia. It all happens on a street, now a little ragged, that was once Cork's original outdoor market. Happily, Cornmarket Street has been earmarked for urban renewal to the tune of £2.5 million ($4 million), more than half of which is being provided by the European Community (EC).

Cork Heritage Park
Bessboro Rd., Blackrock, Cork City. ☎ **021/358854.** Admission £2 ($3.20) adults, £1.50 ($2.40) children. May–Sept daily 10:30am–5pm, Oct–April Sat–Sun 10am–5pm.

Two miles south of the city center, this new park is set in a 19th-century courtyard on lovely grounds beside an estuary of Cork Harbour. The site was originally part of the estate of the Pike family, Quakers who were prominent in banking and shipping in Cork in the 1800s. The center's exhibits trace the maritime and shipping routes of Cork as well as the history of the Pike family, in a series of colorful tableaux. There is also an environmental center, an archaeology room, a small museum dedicated to the history of Cork fire fighting from 1450 to 1945, and stables that house models of a saddler and blacksmith.

NEARBY: BLARNEY CASTLE & MORE

Blarney Castle and Stone and Blarney House
Blarney, Co. Cork. ☎ **021/385252.** Castle £3 ($4.80) adults, £2 ($3.20) seniors and students, £1 ($1.60) children; house £2.50 ($4) adults, £2 ($3.20) seniors and students, £1.50 ($2.40) children; combination ticket to both castle and house £4.50 ($7.20) adults, £3 ($4.80) seniors and students, £2 ($3.20) children. Castle, May and Sept Mon–Sat 9am–6:30pm, Sun 9:30am–5:30pm; June–Aug Mon–Sat 9am–7pm, Sun 9:30am–5:30pm; Oct–Apr Mon–Sat 9am–sundown, Sun 9:30am–5:30pm. House, June to mid-Sept Mon–Sat noon–6pm. 5 miles NW of Cork City on R617. Bus: 154 from bus station on Parnell Place, Cork City.

What remains of this impressive castle today is a massive square tower, or keep, with a parapet rising 83 feet. The infamous Blarney Stone is wedged far enough underneath the battlements to make it uncomfortable to reach but not far enough that countless tourists don't, for reasons inexplicable, abandon all concern for health to kiss it.

After bypassing the stone, you should stroll through the gardens and a nearby dell beside Blarney Lake. The Badger Cave and adjacent dungeons, penetrating the rock at the base of the castle, can be explored by claustrophobics with the aid of a flashlight. You may also wish to visit the neighboring Blarney House, a Scottish baronial

The Blarney Stone; or, What's the Deal with the Rock?

Say the words *Blarney Stone* to the average person, and if they don't think of a string of bars by that name in midtown Manhattan they'll think of a rock wedged under a wall high atop Blarney Castle in County Cork. Now ask them what the significance of that rock is, and as often as not you'll be greeted with blank stares or stuttered explanations. It's a rock, they'll say. You kiss it when you're in Ireland. Something to do with heritage.

OK, then, here's the deal: Back in the 1830s, a fella named Father Prout wrote these immortal lines: "There's a stone there / That whoever kisses / Oh! he never misses / To grow eloquent." That did it: instant tourist attraction. "But," you ask, "where did Prout get this idea?" For the answer to that, we have to go all the way back to the first Queen Elizabeth, who in trying to elicit an oath of fealty from one Cormac McCarthy, lord of Blarney, ran smack into the stone wall of Irish dissimulation. The silver-tongued McCarthy smiled and flattered and nodded his head, all the while keeping a firm hold on his own sovereignty, until the queen, finally exasperated beyond all queenly reserve, reportedly exclaimed, "This is nothing but Blarney—what he says, he never means!"

And that's why people kiss the Blarney Stone.

---

mansion dating from 1874, which was recently restored. It contains a fine collection of ancestral paintings and heraldic decorations.

Royal Gunpowder Mills

Ballincollig, Co. Cork. ☎ **021/874430.** Admission £2.50 ($4) adults, £2 ($3.20) seniors and students, £1.50 ($2.40) children. Apr–Sept daily 10am–6pm. About 5 miles west of Cork City on the main Cork-Killarney road (N22).

Set beside the River Lee, this industrial complex was a hub for the manufacture of gunpowder from 1794 to 1903, a time of wars between Britain and France. In its heyday as Cork's prime industry, it employed about 500 men as coopers, millwrights, and carpenters. Visitors can tour the restored buildings. Exhibits and an audiovisual presentation tell the story of gunpowder production in the Cork area.

6 Spectator Sports & Outdoor Pursuits

SPECTATOR SPORTS

GREYHOUND RACING   Go to the dogs, as they say in Cork, at **Cork Greyhound Track,** Western Road, Cork (☎ 021/543013), on Monday, Wednesday, and Saturday evenings at 8pm. Admission is £3 ($4.80).

GAELIC GAMES   Hurling and Gaelic football are both played on summer Sunday afternoons at Cork's **Pairc Ui Chaoimh Stadium,** Marina Walk (☎ 021/963311). Check the local newspapers for details.

HORSE RACING   The nearest racetrack is **Mallow Race Track,** Killarney Road, Mallow (☎ 022/21338), approximately 20 miles north of Cork. Races are scheduled in mid-May, early August, and early October.

RECREATION

BICYCLING   Although walking is probably the ideal way to get around Cork, if you want to rent a bike, try **The Bike Store,** 48 MacCurtain St., Cork (☎ 021/

500011). It costs £7 ($11.20) per day or £30 ($48) per week. Open Monday to Saturday, 9am to 6pm.

FISHING   The River Lee, which runs through Cork, the nearby Blackwater River, and the many lakes in the area present fine opportunities for fishing. Salmon licenses and lake fishing permits, as well as tackle and equipment, can be obtained from **T. W. Murray and Co.,** 87 Patrick St., Cork (☎ **021/271089**), and **The Tackle Shop,** Lavitt's Quay, Cork (☎ **021/272842**).

GOLF   Corkonians welcome visitors to play on the following 18-hole courses, all within a 5-mile radius of the city: **Cork Golf Club,** Little Island, Cork (☎ **021/353451**), 5 miles east of Cork, with greens fees of £25 ($40) weekdays and £28 ($44.80) weekends; **Douglas Golf Club,** Maryboro Hill, Douglas (☎ **021/895297**), 3 miles south of Cork, with greens fees of £19 ($30.40) weekends, £12 ($19.20) weekdays; and **Harbour Point,** Little Island (☎ **021/353094**), 4 miles east of Cork, with greens fees of £22 ($35.20).

7 Shopping

Patrick Street is the main shopping thoroughfare of Cork, and many other stores are scattered throughout the city on side streets and in lanes. In general, shops are open from 9:30am to 6pm, Monday through Saturday, unless indicated otherwise. In the summer, many shops remain open until 9:30pm on Thursday and Friday and some are open on Sunday.

The city's antique row is **Paul's Lane,** an offshoot of Paul Street, which sits between Patrick Street and the Quays. There are three shops along this lane, each brimming with old Cork memorabilia and furnishings: **Anne McCarthy,** 2 Paul's Lane (☎ **021/273755**); **Mills,** 3 Paul's Lane (☎ **021/273528**); and **O'Regan's,** 4 Paul's Lane (☎ **021/509141**).

The main multilevel mall is **Merchant's Quay Shopping Centre,** Merchant's Quay and Patrick Street. This enclosed complex houses large department stores, such as **Marks and Spencer** (☎ **021/275555**), as well as small specialty shops, such as **Laura Ashley** (☎ **021/274070**).

Cork's legendary department store is **Cash's,** 18 St. Patrick St. (☎ **021/276771**). Dating back to 1830, it offers three floors of wares and gift items, including Waterford crystal, Irish linen, and all types of knitwear and tweeds.

BOOKS & MUSIC

✪ The Living Tradition
40 MacCurtain St. ☎ **021/502040.**

Located on the city's north bank, this small shop specializes in Irish traditional music—CDs, cassettes, books, videos, sheet music, and song books—as well as instruments such as bodhrans (Irish frame drums) and tin whistles. In addition, there is a good selection of recordings of musicians from around the world, along with handcrafted goods. Open Monday to Saturday from 9am to 6pm.

✪ Mainly Murder
2A Paul St. ☎ **021/272413.**

Tucked between French Church and Academy streets, this tiny book shop is a huge treasure trove of whodunits for amateur sleuths or anyone looking for a good read. It stocks volumes on murder, mystery, and mayhem from Ireland, England, and many other English-speaking lands. It's well worth a visit to stock up for a rainy day. Open Monday to Saturday from 10am to 5:30pm.

✪ Mercier Bookshop
5 French Church St. ☎ **021/275040.**

Long a part of Cork's literary tradition, this shop stocks a variety of books, including those published by Cork-based Mercier Press, founded in 1944 and now Ireland's oldest independent publishing house. In particular, this shop had an extensive Irish-interest section, including volumes on Irish history, literature, folklore, music, art, humor, drama, politics, current affairs, law, and religion.

Waterstone's
69 Patrick St. and 12 Paul St. ☎ **021/276522.**

With entrances on two streets, this large British-owned bookshop is always busy. It has a good selection of books about Cork and of Irish interest, as well as sections on art, antiques, biography, religion, and travel. Mailing service is available. Open Monday to Thursday from 9am to 8pm, Friday 9am to 9pm, Saturday 9am to 7pm, and Sunday noon to 7pm.

CRAFTS

✪ Crafts of Ireland
11 Winthrop St. ☎ **021/275864.**

Just a block off Patrick Street, this well-stocked shop presents an array of local crafts including weavings, wrought iron, batik hangings, candles, glass, graphics, leather work, pottery, toys, Irish wildlife mobiles, and Irish floral stationery. Open Monday to Saturday from 9:30am to 5:30pm.

Cork Candles
36–37 Princes St. ☎ **021/275562.**

Festive and decorative candles of all sizes and styles are produced in this shop, with ongoing demonstrations of candle-dipping and candle-carving. This shop also specializes in home fragrance products such as incense and sachets, and unusual gifts and crafts.

House of James
20 Paul St. ☎ **021/272324.**

Formerly a tea warehouse and candy factory, this store is a multilevel artistic showcase for the pottery products of Stephen Pearce from nearby Shanagarry, as well as the wares of at least 50 other local craftspeople, from tweeds and tiles to candles and cards, not to mention wooden toys and natural soaps.

✪ Shandon Craft Centre
Cork Exchange, John Redmond St. ☎ **021/508881.**

Cork's original Butter Market, a commercial exchange begun in 1730, is the site of this unique sightseeing and shopping experience: an enclosed emporium where 20th-century artisans practice a range of traditional trades and display their wares for sale. The crafts include porcelain dolls, jewelry, clothing, crystal, pottery, and handmade violins, cellos, and violas. In the months of June through August, musicians offer free lunchtime concerts from 1 to 2pm, playing folk, traditional, jazz, or classical music.

TWEEDS & WOOLLENS

Blarney Woollen Mills
Blarney, Co. Cork. ☎ **021/385280.**

Located about 6 miles northwest of Cork City near the famous castle of the same name, this Kelleher family enterprise is housed in an old mill dating from 1824. It is a one-stop source for all kinds of Irish products, from cashmeres to crystal glass-ware, hats to heraldry, and tweeds to tee shirts, as well as the distinctive Kelly green Blarney Castle–design wool sweaters, made on the premises. Best of all, it's open until 10pm every night in summer.

Carraig Donn
Cook St. ☎ **021/274050.**

This shop, which has branches all over Ireland, is known for its wide selection of knitwear, particularly Aran sweaters. In addition, the stock includes mohair garments, Irish tweeds, and fashion knitwear, as well as glassware and china, jewelry, and pottery. For markdowns and seconds, there's a bargain loft.

House of Donegal
7 Paul St. ☎ **021/272447.**

"Tailoring to please" is the theme of this showroom/workshop, located one block north of St. Patrick Street, off the Grand Parade. You can buy ready-made or spe-cially tailored raincoats, classic trench coats, jackets, suits, and sportswear for men and women. The handsome rainwear, with Donegal tweed linings, is a special find.

Quills
107 Patrick St. ☎ **021/271717.**

For tweeds, woollens, and knits at the best prices, don't miss this family run enterprise on Cork's busy main thoroughfare. It is a branch of a woollen shop that started small more than 20 years ago at Ballingeary, in the heart of the West Cork Gaeltacht, and has since grown to have similar shops in Killarney, Kenmare, and Sneem.

8 Cork After Dark

PUBS

An Bodhran
42 Oliver Plunkett St. ☎ **021/274544.**

Irish traditional music is on tap at this friendly pub Monday through Thursday nights at 9pm. The old-world decor includes stone walls, dark woods, and a huge stained-glass window with Book of Kells–inspired designs depicting Irish monks playing traditional Irish instruments.

Henchy's
40 St. Luke's. ☎ **021/501115.**

It's worth a walk up the steep Summerhill Road, a northeast continuation of busy MacCurtain Street, to reach this classic and well-maintained pub located near the Arbutus Lodge Hotel. Originally established by John Henchy in 1884, it looks just the same as it did then, with lots of polished brass fittings, leaded-glass windows, silver tankards, thick red curtains, and a small snug. The original Henchy family grocery store still operates adjacent to the pub.

Le Chateau
93 Patrick St. ☎ **021/270370.**

Established in 1793, this is one of Cork's oldest pubs of great character, located right in the middle of the city's main thoroughfare. As pubs go, it's a large specimen, with a choice of various rooms and alcoves filled with Cork memorabilia. Irish Coffee is a specialty here.

Maguire's Warehouse Bar

Daunt Sq., Grand Parade. ☎ **021/277825.**

Located just off Patrick Street in the heart of town, this Edwardian-style pub has a conversation-piece decor of vintage bicycles, unicycles, and lots of old brass fixtures.

✪ Mutton Lane Inn

3 Mutton Lane, off Patrick St., Cork. ☎ **021/273471.**

Old Cork is alive and well at this tiny pub down an alley that was first trod as a pathway for sheep going to market. Begun in 1787 as a public house by the Ring family, who used to make their own whiskey, it is now the domain of Maeva and Vincent McLoughlin, who have preserved the old-world aura, which includes lantern lights, dark wood-paneled walls, exposed-beam ceilings, and an antique cash register.

✪ An Spailpin Fanac (The Loft)

28–29 S. Main St. ☎ **021/277949.**

For traditional Irish music, this place is one of the choice spots in Cork, Sunday through Friday nights starting at 9:30pm. Situated opposite Beamish's Brewery, it was established in 1779, making it one of Cork's oldest pubs. The decor retains many of the furnishings of yesteryear, including brick walls, flagstone floors, open fireplaces, and an authentic snug.

THE HOTEL BAR SCENE

Half Moon

Cork Opera House, Emmet Place. ☎ **021/270022.** Cover £5–£7 ($8–$11.20). Wed–Sun 11:30pm–3am.

After the main stage empties, the Cork Opera House Bar swings into action with an ever-changing program of contemporary music from blues and ragtime to pop and rock, with comedy gigs on occasion.

The Lobby Bar

1 Union Quay. ☎ **021/311113.** Cover £2–£6 ($3.20–$9.60), depending on the act. Nightly, with music starting at 9pm for most performances.

Situated opposite City Hall, this bar presents a variety of musical entertainment, from folk, traditional, bluegrass, and blues to jazz, gypsy, rock, classical, and New Age.

PERFORMING ARTS CENTERS

Cork Opera House

Emmet Place. ☎ **021/270022.** Tickets £6–£12.50 ($9.60–$20). Box office 10:15am–7pm; curtain 8 or 8:30pm; matinees on Sat at 3pm; schedule varies.

Situated just off Lavitt's Quay along the River Lee, this is the major venue in southwest Ireland for opera, drama, musicals, comedies, dance, concerts, and variety nights.

Firkin Crane Cultural Centre

John Redmond St., Shandon, Cork. ☎ **021/507487.** Tickets £5–£10 ($8–$16). Most events 8pm, traditional music July–Aug 9pm.

Dating from the 1840s, this unique rotunda was part of Cork's original Butter Market, and the building's name is derived from Danish words pertaining to measures of butter. Although destroyed by fire in 1980, the site was completely rebuilt and opened as a cultural center in 1992. It is now a venue for live theater, ballet, concerts, dance, poetry readings, and art exhibitions. In the summer, the center hosts evenings of Irish traditional music.

Triskel Arts Centre

Tobin St., off S. Main St. ☎ **021/272022.** Tickets £2–£6 ($3.30–$9.60), depending on act. Box office Mon–Sat 10:30am–5:30pm; performances Tues–Sun 8pm, Sat–Sun matinees 1:15 or 1:30pm.

This ever-growing arts center presents a variety of entertainment, from drama to poetry readings, musical recitals, opera, and popular Irish and traditional music concerts. There is also a full program of daytime art workshops and gallery talks.

THEATERS

Cork Arts Theatre

Knapp's Sq. ☎ **021/508398.** Tickets £5 ($8) adults, £4 ($6.40) seniors. Shows Tues–Sat at 8pm.

Situated across the river from the Opera House, this busy theater presents a wide variety of contemporary dramas, comedies, and musical comedies, to full houses. A multistory parking garage and the city center main street are a 10-minute walk away.

Everyman Palace

17 MacCurtain St. ☎ **021/501673.** Tickets £5–£7 ($8–$11.20). Box office Mon–Fri 10am–5pm; curtain at 8pm.

This lovely, refurbished historic theater is well known as a showcase for new plays, both Irish and international. The Irish National Ballet also performs here regularly. Two minutes from bus and train station.

9

Out from Cork

Once the haunt of outlaws, Cork long had a reputation as an inaccessible and unruly corner of the country, and aside from a drastic decrease in the number of outlaws, not much has changed—it's still adamantly unconventional and countercultural, and its populace continues to make waves. The landscape has hardly been tamed either, and West Cork holds some of Ireland's most remote and wild coastal regions.

There's no better place to start a tour of County Cork than in Kinsale, a small harbor town directly south of Cork City.

1 Kinsale

18 miles S of Cork, 54 miles SE of Killarney, 97 miles SE of Shannon Airport, 177 miles SW of Dublin, and 20 miles E of Clonakilty

GETTING THERE   **Bus Eireann** (☎ **021/506066**) operates regular daily service from Cork City to Kinsale. The arrival/departure point is on Pier Road, opposite the Tourist Office.

Kinsale is 18 miles south of Cork City via the Airport Road; if you're coming by car, it's reached from the west via N71. From East Cork, the Cross River Ferries provide regular service via Cork Harbour (see Chapter 8, "Cork City").

GETTING AROUND   Kinsale's streets are so narrow that walking is the best way to get around. There is no local transport, but if you need a taxi to take you to outlying areas, call **O'Dea & Sons** (☎ **021/774900**).

VISITOR INFORMATION   **The Kinsale Tourist Office,** Pier Road, Kinsale (☎ **021/774026** or 021/772234) is open March through October.

AREA CODE   The telephone code for Kinsale numbers is **021.**

KINSALE IN 250 WORDS OR LESS

Less than 20 miles south of Cork City, Kinsale is a small seaside fishing village with a sheltered semicircular harbor rimmed by hilly terrain. Considered the gateway to the western Cork seacoast, this compact little town of 2,000 residents has also made a big name for itself as the "gourmet capital of Ireland." Home to more than a dozen award-winning restaurants and pubs, Kinsale draws lovers of good food year-round but particularly each October during a three-day Gourmet Festival.

County Cork

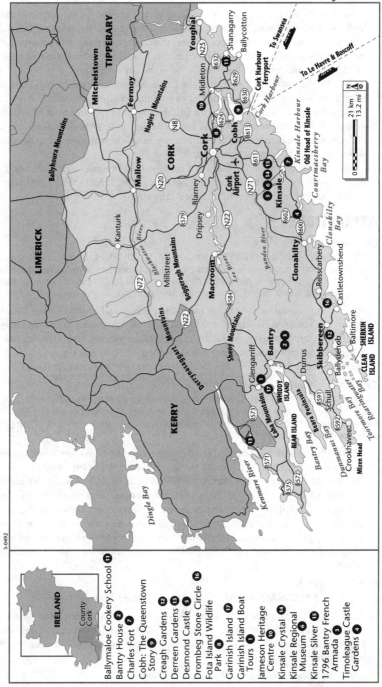

Ballymaloe Cookery School **9**
Bantry House **2**
Charles Fort **7**
Cobh: The Queenstown Story **9**
Creagh Gardens **12**
Derreen Gardens **13**
Desmond Castle **5**
Drombeg Stone Circle **16**
Fota Island Wildlife Park **8**
Garinish Island **17**
Garinish Island Boat Tours **1**
Jameson Heritage Centre **10**
Kinsale Crystal **14**
Kinsale Regional Museum **6**
Kinsale Silver **15**
1796 Bantry French Armada **3**
Timoleague Castle Gardens **4**

IRELAND
County Cork

Kinsale fits the picture-postcard image of what a charming Irish seaport should look like—narrow, winding streets, well-kept 18th-century houses, imaginatively painted shop fronts, windowboxes and street stanchions brimming with colorful flowers, and a harbor full of sailboats. Consequently, Kinsale has become a tourist mecca, so add traffic jams and tour buses to the list of the city's sights.

In 1601 the town was the scene of the Battle of Kinsale, a turning point in Irish history. This defeat of the Irish helped to establish English domination. After the battle, a new governor representing the British crown was appointed—a fella named William Penn. For a time, Penn had his namesake son serve in Kinsale as clerk of the admiralty court, but Penn Jr. did not stay long—he was soon off to the New World to found the state of Pennsylvania.

Just off the coast of the Old Head of Kinsale—about five miles west of the town—the *Lusitania* was sunk by a German submarine in 1915. More than 1,500 people were killed, and many are buried in a local cemetery.

ATTRACTIONS

✪ Charles Fort

Off the Scilly Rd. ☎ **021/772263.** Admission £2 ($3.20) adults, £1.50 ($2.40) seniors, £1($1.60) students. Tours available upon request. Mid-Apr to mid-June Mon–Sat 9am–5pm, Sun 9:30am–5:30pm; mid-June to mid-Sept daily 9am–6pm; mid-Sept to late Oct Mon–Sat 9am–5:30pm, Sun 10am–5pm; last admission 40 min. before closing.

Southeast of Kinsale, at the head of the harbor, this coastal landmark dates back to the late 17th century. A classic star-shaped fort, it was constructed to prevent foreign naval forces from entering the harbor of Kinsale, then an important trading town. Additions and improvements were made throughout the 18th and 19th centuries, and the fort remained garrisoned until 1921. Across the river is James Fort (1602).

✪ Desmond Castle

Cork St. ☎ **021/774855.** Admission £1.50 ($2.40) adults, £1 ($1.60) seniors and students, 50p (80¢) children. Mid-June to mid-Sept daily 9am–6pm; mid-Sept to early Oct Mon–Sat 9am–5pm, Sun 10am–5pm; mid-Apr to mid-June Tues–Sun 10am–1pm and 2–5pm; last admission 45 minutes before closing.

A customhouse built by the earl of Desmond around 1500, this tower house has had a colorful history. It was occupied by the Spanish in 1601 and later used as a prison for captured American sailors during the War of Independence. Locally, it's known as "French Prison" because 54 French seamen prisoners died here in a 1747 fire. During the years of the Great Famine, the castle became a workhouse for the starving populace. At various times, the vaults of the castle have also been used as a wine storage depot. The castle has recently undergone considerable restoration and been designated a Heritage site, and in April 1997 it became the home of the International Museum of Wine.

Kinsale Crystal

Market St. ☎ **021/774463.** Free admission. Mon–Sat 9:15am–1pm and 2–6pm.

Started in 1991 by a former Waterford Crystal master-craftsman, this small workshop produces a traditional full-lead, mouth-blown and hand-cut crystal, with personalized engraving. Visitors are welcome to watch the entire fascinating process and admire the sparkling results.

Kinsale Regional Museum

Market Sq. ☎ **021/772044.** Admission 50p (80¢) adults, 20p (32¢) children. Daily 10am–6pm.

This museum tells the town's story from its earliest days, with exhibits, photos, and memorabilia. It's in the Market House (1600), to which an arched facade was added in 1706.

Kinsale Silver
Pearse St. ☎ **021/774359.** Free admission. Daily 9:30am–6pm.

Silvermaking is a craft that traces its origins back more than 300 years; this local silversmithing workshop is run by the Dolan family (see Chapter 7, Wexford shopping). Visitors can watch as each piece is wrought and forged by hand, using tools of yesteryear.

SPORTS & OUTDOOR PURSUITS

BICYCLING   Biking along Kinsale Harbour is an exhilarating experience. To rent a bike, contact **Deco's Cycles,** 18 Main St., Kinsale (☎ **021/774884**). A day's rental averages £7 ($11.20), depending on equipment. Open Monday through Saturday from 9am to 6pm.

FISHING   Kinsale is one of the sea-angling centers of the southern Irish coast. There are numerous shipwrecks in the area for wreck fishing, including the *Lusitania,* near the Old Head of Kinsale. The **Castlepark Marina Centre,** Kinsale, Co. Cork (☎ **021/774959,** fax 021/774958) has a 43 foot purpose-built sea angling boat that can be chartered for £245 to £275 ($392 to $440) per day. A full day's fishing with rod hire is £30 ($48) per person. **Kinsale Holiday Activities,** 8 Main St. (☎ **021/ 774355**), arranges sea fishing from Kinsale Harbour or game fishing for salmon and trout in nearby rivers (contact Kevin Wilyman). The fee for sea fishing averages £20 ($32) per day (3-person minimum), and river fishing is £39 ($62.40) per day. It's open May through September daily from 9:30am to 8pm; October to April Monday through Saturday from 10am to 6pm.

For fishing tackle or to rent a rod and other equipment, try **Deco's Fishing Tackle,** 18 Main St., Kinsale (☎ **021/774884**). Open Monday through Saturday from 9am to 6pm.

GOLF   Kinsale boasts a new 18-hole, par-71 golf course at Farrangalway, 3 miles north of town. This new course is an addition to the existing nine-hole Ringenane course, dating back to 1930. Greens fees are £20 ($32) on weekends and £15 ($24) Monday through Friday, with an early bird special of £10 ($16). Open daily 9am to 9pm. For full information, contact the **Kinsale Golf Club,** Kinsale (☎ **021/772197,** fax 021/773114).

The new 18-hole, 6,650-yard, par-72 **Old Head Golf Links** (☎ **021/778444**) is scheduled to open on June 1, 1997. Designed by Joe Carr and Ron Kirby, the course runs along the sea, offering a spectacular backdrop for your game. It will be open year-round daily from 8:30am, with greens fees of £50 in summer and £45 in winter.

SAILING   Yacht charters are available from **Sail Ireland Charters,** Trident Hotel, Co. Cork (☎ **021/772927,** fax 021/774170). From Kinsale it is possible to sail to Bantry Bay and back on a one-week charter, or to the Dingle Peninsula on a two-week charter. Prices for a six-berth yacht begin at £650 ($1040) per week, not including outboard or skipper; during peak season (July 6 to August 24) the base rate almost doubles to £1275 ($2040). Weekend charters are offered, beginning at £375 ($600).

WALKING   There is a pedestrian path along the sea in Scilly, the community across the harbor from Kinsale, which continues almost all the way to Charles Fort; this is signposted as the Scilly Walk. If you continue to walk south along the sea from Charles Fort you'll find another path, which follows the headland to the tip of Frower Point, which offers great views across the harbor to the Old Head of Kinsale. The complete walk from Kinsale to Frower Point is five miles each way, although any part of the walk will be quite rewarding.

WATERSPORTS   Kinsale Harbour is favored by boaters. **Kinsale Holiday Activities,** 8 Main St., Kinsale (☎ 021/774355), offers scuba diving from £30 ($48) per dive (minimum 3 persons), and canoeing, windsurfing, or dinghy sailing from £8 ($12.80) per hour. They also offer pleasure yacht hire from £60 ($96) per half day. Open May through September daily from 9:30am to 8pm; October through April Monday to Saturday from 10am to 6pm.

SHOPPING

Boland's Irish Craft Shop
Pearse St. ☎ 021/772161.

This is a good spot to buy a traditional Kinsale smock, as well as Aran knit vests, local pottery, Ogham plaques, woolly and ceramic sheep, quilts, Irish leather belts, and miniature paintings by Irish artists. Open daily 8am to 6:30pm. Closes 9pm July to August.

Granny's Bottom Drawer
53 Main St. ☎ 021/774839.

Ireland's traditional linens and lace are the focus of this small shop. It's well stocked with tablecloths, pillowcases, and hand-crocheted place mats. Open Monday through Saturday from 10am to 6pm and Sunday from noon to 2pm.

Irish Arts & Crafts
8 Main St. ☎ 021/774355.

This shop features hand-crafted items produced by artisans in Counties Cork and Kerry, such as needlepoint art, handmade shoes, pottery, scenic prints and art cards, candles, jewelry, and kites. Open May through September daily from 9:30am to 8pm, and October through April Monday through Saturday from 9:30am to 8pm.

ACCOMMODATIONS
MODERATE

Actons
Pier Rd., The Waterfront, Kinsale, Co. Cork. ☎ 021/772135. Fax 021/772231. 56 rms. TV TEL. £75–£110 ($120–$176) double. No service charge. Rates include full breakfast. AE, DC, MC, V.

This Trusthouse Forte hotel is actually six 3-story harbor-front houses that have been joined, renovated, expanded, and refurbished over the years. Consequently, the guest rooms vary in size, but most are large and airy, with standard furniture; the best part is that most of the rooms overlook the marina and the well-tended rose gardens. Amenities include The Captain's Table restaurant; the Ships' Tavern, with a nautical theme; and an adjacent health center and leisure club with swimming pool, saunas, sunbeds, and billiard room.

✪ The Blue Haven
3 Pearse St., Kinsale, Co. Cork. ☎ 021/772209. Fax 021/774268. 21 rms. TV TEL. £70–£120 ($112–$192) double. No service charge. Rates include full breakfast. AE, DC, MC, V.

In the heart of town on the old Fish Market, the Blue Haven is an old-world inn meticulously run by Brian and Anne Cronin. This hardworking duo has won accolades for their top-notch seafood restaurant (see "Dining," below). In 1994, the Cronins expanded their inn to include an adjacent building, adding 11 new rooms, an elevator, a ground-floor residents' lounge, and a roof garden. All the guest rooms are individually furnished in a bright and contemporary decor, with local crafts and artwork. Views are of the town or the back gardens. Rooms in the new wing are named for the Irish exiles who left Kinsale and established wineries in Europe, such as Chateau McCarthy or Chateau Dillon. These rooms have a more traditional decor with canopy beds, window seats, armoires, and brass fixtures. Dining facilities include the aforementioned Blue Haven restaurant, a pub with a nautical theme, and a wine and cheese shop.

The Moorings

Scilly, Kinsale, Co. Cork. ☎ **021/772376.** Fax 021/772675. 8 rms. TV TEL. £80–£90 ($128–$144) double. No service charge. Rates include full breakfast. DC, MC, V.

Overlooking the harbor and marina, this new two-story guest house has a bright and contemporary decor with lots of wide-windowed views of the water. The guest rooms are individually furnished with brass beds, pastel-colored quilts, light woods, and modern art, plus the added convenience of over-the-bed reading lamps and a tea/coffeemaker. Five rooms with balconies face the harbor, while the rest overlook the garden. Guests enjoy use of a cozy traditional parlor and a large sunlit conservatory with wraparound views of the water. Pat and Irene Jones are the innkeepers.

✪ Scilly House Inn

Kinsale, Co. Cork. ☎ **021/772413.** Fax 021/774629. 7 rms. TEL. £80 ($128) double. No service charge. Rates include full breakfast. AE, MC, V.

The entrance to the house is rather inauspicious, but once within the door you are enveloped in an entrancing atmosphere of casual elegance. An extensive garden with many secluded corners slopes down to the seaside pedestrian path. Common rooms include a sitting room and library with self-service bar and piano. Bedrooms are decorated in bright colors with wicker and pine furniture. One bedroom is located in a separate cottage and includes a small private sitting room; there is also a luxury suite available for £115 ($184). Scilly House is said to have a spectral visitor, the White Lady, who lived in the house and was the daughter of a captain stationed at Charles Fort. The story goes that she was engaged to an officer; one night her fiancé was filling in for a soldier on guard duty, and fell asleep at his post. Her father, finding the sleeping guard, shot him on the spot, not realizing until it was too late who he had punished so severely. Upon receiving this news, the daughter threw herself from the cliffs by Charles Fort; her ghost has since been seen dressed in white, and is a well-known figure in the Kinsale area.

Trident

World's End, Kinsale, Co. Cork. ☎ **021/772301.** Fax 021/774173. 58 rms. TV TEL. £50–£118 ($80–$188.80) double. No service charge. Rates include full breakfast. AE, DC, MC, V.

Situated on the harbor at the west end of the marina, this modern three-story hotel has been updated and refurbished in recent years. The bedrooms feature wide-window views of the harbor, with modern furnishings of light woods, floral fabrics, and art deco–style fixtures. Two luxurious suites with views of Kinsale Harbour are available. Facilities include the Savannah Restaurant overlooking the water, Fisherman's Wharf Bar, and a health center with sauna, steam room, gym, and Jacuzzi.

INEXPENSIVE

Ducey House

Denis Quay, Kinsale, Co. Cork. ☎ **021/774592.** 4 rms (3 with bath). £32–£40 ($51.20–$64) double. No service charge. Rates include full breakfast. No credit cards.

Situated in the center of town on a small square facing the sea, this unpretentious B&B offers a cozy alternative to the neighboring hotels. A comfortable sitting room and secluded patio provide a tranquil respite from the bustle of Kinsale's busy streets. The rooms are simply furnished and bright; several look out over the harbor. Enticing vegetarian breakfast options such as buttermilk pancakes and omelets are a welcome alternative to the usual bacon and rasher fry.

DINING
EXPENSIVE/MODERATE

✪ Blue Haven

3 Pearse St., Kinsale. ☎ **021/772209.** Reservations recommended. Bar, lunch main courses £1.85–£9.90 ($2.95–$15.85), dinner main courses £4.25–£12.50 ($6.80–$29); restaurant, dinner main courses £9–£16.50 ($14.40–$26.40). AE, MC, V. Bar, 12:15–3pm and 5:30–9:30pm; restaurant, 7–10pm. SEAFOOD/IRISH.

Of all the restaurants in Kinsale, this one is the benchmark, and it has a huge following. To suit every budget and appetite, there are two menus, one for the top-of-the-line pub food in the atmospheric bar and a full à la carte menu for the lovely skylit restaurant. The bar food includes smoked seafood quiches, seafood pancakes, oak-smoked salmon, steaks, pastas, and a lamb stew that's to die for. The restaurant offers a wide array of fresh seafood, including a house special of salmon slowly cooked over oak chips. Other specialties include brill and scallop bake, farmyard duck with sage and onion stuffing, and local venison (in season). Wines served at the Blue Haven have Irish connections—they come from many of the French wineries that were started by Irish exiles, such as Chateau Dillon, McCarthy, Barton, Kirwan, Lynch, and Phelan. These wines are also on sale in the Blue Haven's adjacent wine and cheese shop.

✪ The Vintage

50/51 Main St., Kinsale. ☎ **021/772502.** Reservations recommended. Main courses £15.50–£22 ($24.80–$35.20). AE, MC, V. Mar–Apr and Nov–Jan 15 Wed–Mon 6:30–10pm; May–Oct daily 6:30–10:30pm, Sun lunch. CONTINENTAL/IRISH.

Located in a charming 200-year-old house in the heart of Kinsale, this landmark restaurant has recently changed hands. Raoul and Seiko de Gendre, the new proprietors, have thoroughly redecorated, retaining the restaurant's old charm and enhancing its elegance. House specialties include fillets of black sole sautéed belle meunière, oven-roasted barbary duck, and sautéed tenderloin steak of Irish venison.

MODERATE

Chez Jean-Marc

Lower O'Connell St., Kinsale. ☎ **021/774625.** Reservations recommended. Dinner main courses £14–£16 ($22.40–$25.60). AE, DC, MC, V. Daily 7–10:30pm. INTERNATIONAL.

Although most of the cooking at this restaurant is French and continental, chef Jean-Marc Tsai offers an occasional stir-fry entrée. The regular evening menu includes dishes such as duck with black-currant liqueur, turbot filled with vegetable salsa and smoked salmon and baked in pastry, salmon poached in court bouillon with crab toes and vermouth butter-cream sauce, and fillet of beef in red wine sauce. It is located on the upper west end of town, near the Trident Hotel.

Cottage Loft

6 Main St., Kinsale. ☎ **021/772803.** Reservations recommended. Main courses £5.50–£15.95 ($8.80–$25.50); fixed-price dinner £16.50 ($26.40). AE, MC, V. May–Oct, daily 5:30–10:30pm; Nov–Apr, Tues–Sun 6:30–10:30pm. IRISH/INTERNATIONAL.

Housed in a 200-year-old building in the heart of town, this shop-front restaurant has a cottage-style decor, with pink linens, antiques, caned chairs, leafy hanging plants, and wooden ceiling beams. The eclectic menu includes such items as delicious rack of lamb, farmyard duck in apple brandy sauce, fillet of lemon sole rolled in smoked salmon, prawns with lobster sauce, and a house specialty of seafood Danielle salmon stuffed with crab, prawns, and peppers with a prawn or nettle sauce.

○ Jim Edwards

Market Quay, off Emmet Place, Kinsale. ☎ **021/772541.** Reservations recommended for dinner. Lunch main courses £5–£8 ($8–$12.80); dinner main courses £10–£16 ($16–$25.60). AE, MC, V. Daily 12:30–3pm and 6–10:30pm. IRISH.

A classy nautical theme dominates the decor of this pub/restaurant, with colored-glass windows, ship's wheels, sailing-ship art, plush red cushioned seating, and a clock over the door that tells time by letters instead of numbers. Located in a lane between the Methodist Church and the Temperance Hall, it is known for its good food, including such dishes as boneless duck with cassis and red-currant sauce, rack of lamb, king prawns in light basil cream sauce, medaillons of monkfish with fresh herbs, and a variety of steaks.

Man Friday

Scilly, Kinsale. ☎ **021/772260.** Reservations recommended. Main courses £9–£15 ($14.40–$24). AE, MC, V. Daily 7–10:30pm. INTERNATIONAL.

Situated in a hilly area overlooking Kinsale Harbour, this restaurant, with its bamboo-covered entrance and profusion of leafy plants, exudes a tropical garden ambience. The bar area is rustic with its exposed-beam ceilings, stone walls, and tree-stump stools, while the dimly lit pine-paneled restaurant has a romantic display of fine artwork. The menu offers six varieties of steak and beef, as well as rack of lamb and dishes such as black sole on the bone, Swiss veal with Gruyère cheese sauce, and farmyard duck with nectarine and brandy sauce.

Seasons

Milk Market St., Kinsale. ☎ **021/772244.** Reservations recommended. Lunch main courses £3.95–£7.95 ($6.25–$12.70); dinner main courses £9.50–£17.50 ($15.20–$28). AE, DC, MC, V. Mar–Sept, dinner nightly 6:30–10:30pm, Sun lunch 12:30–3pm; Sept–Mar closed Tues. IRISH/INTERNATIONAL.

Nestled in the old market area of Kinsale in a 16th-century building, this restaurant is known for fine Irish cuisine and features a varied and tasty menu, with dishes that include vegetable pancakes, farmyard duck, salmon filled with scallops and fresh herbs, and hickory-flavored cod topped with bacon, cheddar, and herbs.

INEXPENSIVE

Max's

Main St., Kinsale. ☎ **021/772443.** Reservations recommended. Lunch main courses £3–£6 ($4.80–$9.60); dinner main courses £6.50–£12.50 ($10.40–$20). MC, V. Daily 12:30–3pm and 6:30–10:30pm. Closed Nov–Feb. INTERNATIONAL.

For more than 20 years, this old-world town house with an outdoor patio has been a local favorite for a light snack as well as for a full meal. Grilled mussels are a specialty here, as are hamburgers. Other dishes offered include scallops poached in vermouth and cream, duck with orange and ginger sauce, and rack of lamb.

PUBS

The Dock
Castlepark, Kinsale. ☎ **021/772522.**

On the outskirts of town, this pub overlooks the inner harbor. The walls are lined with fishing-theme posters and equipment, and the windows give views of the water. If the weather is nice, you can step out onto the front deck with its row of inviting tables and chairs.

The Greyhound
Marian Terrace, Kinsale. ☎ **021/772889.**

Photographers are enchanted with the exterior of this pub, with its neat flower boxes, rows of stout barrels, and handmade signs depicting its namesake, the swift Irish racing dog. The interior rooms are cozy and known for hearty pub grub such as farmhouse soups, seafood pancakes, shepherd's pie, and Irish stew.

Lord Kingsale
Main St. and Market Quay, Kinsale. ☎ **021/772371.**

A touch of elegance prevails at this handsome pub, decorated with lots of polished horse brass and black and white Tudor-style trappings. It takes its name (and ancient spelling) from the first Anglo-Norman baron who took charge of this Irish port in 1223. You'll often find evening sing-alongs here, and the soup-and-sandwich pub grub is very good. Live entertainment nightly in summer.

The Shanakee
Market St., Kinsale. ☎ **021/774472.**

With an Anglicized name (derived from the Irish word *seanachie,* which means storyteller), this vintage pub is known for its music—traditional tunes and ballads nightly—and has recently added a full restaurant.

The Spaniard
Scilly, Kinsale. ☎ **021/772436.**

Named for Don Juan de Aguila, who rallied his fleet with the Irish in a historic but unsuccessful attempt to defeat the British in 1601, this old pub is full of local seafaring memorabilia. It has a much-photographed facade, a great location in the hills overlooking Kinsale, and tables outside for sunny day snacks, and it draws large crowds for live music nightly in the summer months and on weekends at other times of the year. On Sunday afternoons year-round there is a jazz/blues session at 5pm.

The White House
End of Pearse St. ☎ **021/772125.**

With its Georgian facade and distinctive name over the front entrance, this is one pub that tempts nearly every American visitor to take a photograph. Inside, you will find a popular new bistro, the Antibes Room, with bright decor and a comfortable bar.

2 East Cork

GETTING TO EAST CORK   If you're coming by car from Cork City, take the main Waterford road (N25) eastward, exiting at R624 for Fota and Cobh, or R632 for Shanagarry and Ballycotton. Midleton and Youghal have their own signposted exits. To bypass Cork City (a capitol idea during rush hour), take the car ferry operated by **Cross River Ferries Ltd.,** Atlantic Quay, Cobh (☎ **021/811485**). It links Carrigaloe near Cobh with Glenbrook south of Cork City. Ferries run daily from 7:15am to 12:45am, with average crossing time of five minutes. No reservations are necessary and the fares, payable on the ferry, are £2 ($3.20) one way and £3 ($4.80) round-trip.

Irish Rail (☎ **021/506766** or 021/811655) operates daily train service between Cork City and Cobh via Fota Island; the fare is £2 ($3) one way or £2.40 ($3.60) round-trip. **Bus Eireann** (☎ **021/506066**) also provides daily service from Cork City to Cobh and other points in East Cork.

VISITOR INFORMATION   Seasonal (May or June to September) **tourist offices** operate at Cobh Harbour (☎ **021/813591**); 4 Main St., Midleton (☎ **021/613702**); and Market Square, Youghal (☎ **024/92390**).

AREA CODES   Telephone area codes for East Cork are **021** and **024.**

A FEW WORDS ABOUT EAST CORK

The east end of County Cork is notably more tame than the west. What the region lacks in rugged splendor it makes up for in sophisticated amenities: Ballymaloe House is famed throughout Ireland for its fine cuisine, and Crosshaven holds the world's most venerable yacht club.

Lying 15 miles east from Cork City is the harbor town of Cobh (pronounced *cove* and meaning "haven" in the Irish language). In the days before airline travel, Cobh was Ireland's chief port of entry, with about three or four transatlantic liners calling here a week. For thousands of Irish emigrants, particularly during the famine years and in the early part of this century, Cobh was the last sight of Ireland they'd ever see. Cobh is still an important, heavily industrialized port. The new visitor attraction, "Cobh: The Queenstown Story," tells the city's history, which includes the construction of a magnificent Gothic revival cathedral, completed in 1915.

The county's major coastal town is Youghal (pronounced *yawl*), 30 miles to the east of Cork City, near the Waterford border. A leading beach resort and fishing port, Youghal is loosely associated with Sir Walter Raleigh, who was once the town mayor and is said to have planted Ireland's first potatoes here. From a tourist's-eye view, present-day Youghal is a moderately attractive, congested town with a grand stretch of beach just beyond the town center.

ATTRACTIONS

✪ Cobh: The Queenstown Story

Cobh Railway Station, Cobh. ☎ **021/813591.** Admission £3.50 ($5.60) adults, £2 ($3.20) children. Daily 9:30am–6pm.

This new heritage center commemorates the days when Cobh (then known as Queenstown) was a vital link in transatlantic liner traffic, particularly in the years of high emigration. Because more than $2^1/_2$ million people from all over Ireland departed from Cobh for new lives in the United States, Canada, and Australia, the city became synonymous with emigration. In the former railway station, the heritage center tells the story of the city, its harbor, and the exodus of the Irish in a series of displays, with an audiovisual presentation. The center also offers exhibits that recreate the age of luxury-liner travel and events such as the sinking of the *Titanic* and the *Lusitania*. A new genealogical referral service is currently in the works.

✪ Fota Island Wildlife Park & Arboretum

Fota Island, Carrigtwohill. ☎ **021/812678.** Admission £3.80 ($6.10) adults, £3.40 ($5.45) students, £2.20 ($3.50) seniors and children age 14 and under. Tour train, 40p (60¢) per ride. Apr to early Oct, Mon–Sat 10am–5pm, Sun 11am–5pm. Parking £1 ($1.50) per car. Accessible by rail via the Cork-Cobh line from Cork City to Fota station.

Located 10 miles east of Cork on the Cobh Road, this wildlife park was established in 1983. It's home to rare and endangered types of giraffe, zebra, ostrich, antelope, cheetah, flamingo, penguin, and peafowl. The animals and birds roam in natural wildlife settings, with no obvious barriers. Monkeys swing through the trees, and kangaroos, macaws, and lemurs have the complete run of the 40 acres of grasslands. Only the cheetahs are bounded by conventional fencing. Admission charges include entrance to the adjacent Fota Arboretum. First planted in the 1820s, it contains trees and shrubs from the temperate and subtropical regions of the world, from China to South America and the Himalayas. A coffee shop, a tour train, picnic tables, and a gift shop are on the grounds.

Jameson Heritage Centre

Distillery Rd., off Main St., Midleton. ☎ **021/613594.** Admission £3.50 ($5.60) adults, £1.50 ($2.40) children. Mar–Nov, daily 10am–4pm.

If you've always wanted to know what makes Irish whiskey different from Scotch, you can find out at this hub of whiskey making, the production center for John Jameson Whiskey and other leading Irish brands. On hand are the largest pot still in the world (it has a capacity of more than 30,000 gallons) and many of the original 1825 structures, which have been meticulously preserved—the mill building, maltings, corn stores, still houses, warehouses, kilns, a water wheel, and the last copper stills manufactured in Ireland.

High-tech methods are now used in a modern distillery, but the production areas are closed to visitors. If you'd like a taste (so to speak) of the whiskey-making process, the center offers an audiovisual presentation, photographs, working models, and a demonstration. If you'd like a *real* taste, a whiskey tasting follows a tour. There is also a lunch restaurant at the center that serves up traditional Irish fare.

Ballymaloe Cookery School

Kinoith, Shanagarry. ☎ **021/646785.** One- to five-day courses from £69 to £365 ($110.40–$584); 12-week certificate courses £3,575 ($5,720). New half-day gardening courses are available. Accommodations are £12–£14.50 ($19.20–$23.20) per night extra. Year-round; schedule varies.

Come to Ireland and learn to cook? Yes, if you head to this mecca of fine food, offering more than 35 different courses a year. The success of the Ballymaloe restaurant (see "Accommodations & Dining," below) led to the founding of this cooking school more than a dozen years ago. Courses, which range from a day to 12 weeks, appeal to all types of amateur and professional chefs, with topics such as breadmaking, weekend entertaining, hors d'oeuvres, seafood, vegetarian cuisine, family food, barbecue, mushrooms, and Christmas cooking. There are also courses for absolute beginners, on new trends in cooking, and for chef certificates. There are beautiful and extensive gardens on the grounds, which visitors can enjoy from April to October.

ACCOMMODATIONS & DINING

✪ Aherne's

163 N. Main St., Youghal. ☎ **800/223-6510** from the U.S., or 024/92424. Fax 024/93633. 10 rms. TV TEL. £70–£100 ($112–$160) double. No service charge. Rates include full breakfast. AE, DC, MC, V.

Located in the heart of a busy seaside resort 30 miles east of Cork City, this cozy inn has long been a focal point because of its top-class seafood, served in both the restaurant and the nautically themed pub. Now the FitzGibbon family, who have owned Aherne's for three generations, have added some excellent and very spacious bedrooms. Each unit is individually decorated in the finest hotel style, with traditional

Bellevue, Myrtleville (near Crosshaven), Co. Cork. ☎ **021/831640.** Fax 021/831138. *This one is SUPERLATIVE! Homemade jam and bread, French toast, lovely simple modern rooms, view over the sea, 100-year-old grape arbor in the breakfast room (room built around it), outstanding view of Cork Harbor, a couple (Gaby and Benny Neff: he's Irish; she's Swiss) who have retired from 23 years in the travel business—they love people . . . I have traveled the world and have never been so impressed with ordinary real goodness and caretaking—nothing overdone—truly real, heartfelt and professional.*
— Elizabeth A. Hin, Santa Fe, N.M.

furnishings including antiques and designer fabrics, oversized six-foot-long beds, and extra amenities such as a hair dryer and garment press. Guest facilities include two bars and a library-style sitting room, but the main reason to stay here is to be close to the restaurant, known for concentrating on the best of the local catch, including Blackwater salmon, giant prawn tails, rock oysters, and lobsters from the tank. Even the daytime bar food is worth a detour—seafood pies, chowders, crab sandwiches, and crisp salads.

✪ Ballymaloe House

Ballycotton Rd., Shanagarry, Co. Cork. ☎ **800/223-6510** from the U.S., or 021/652531. Fax 021/652021. 29 rms. TEL. £110–£130 ($176–$208) double. No service charge. Rates include full breakfast. AE, DC, MC, V.

Combining a Georgian farmhouse facade with the tower of a 14th-century castle, this ivy-covered enclave of hospitality run by the Allen family is situated on a 400-acre farm, complete with grazing sheep and cows. The only road sign you'll see is one that alerts you to the importance of four-legged traffic: "Drive Slow: Lambs Crossing." The bedrooms are furnished in an informal, comfortable style, and the guest facilities include a heated outdoor swimming pool, hard tennis courts, trout pond, nine-hole golf course, and a craft shop emphasizing local wares.

The biggest draw to Ballymaloe, however, is the dining room, a trendsetter for much of Ireland's imaginative cookery, relying on local seafood and produce, accompanied by fresh vegetables from the garden. The success of the kitchen also spawned Ireland's first year-round, country-inn cooking school (see "Attractions," above), and a shelf-load of Allen family cookbooks. Ballymaloe is located about 20 miles southeast of Cork City, less than 2 miles from Ballycotton Bay.

Bayview Hotel

Ballycotton, Midleton, Co. Cork. ☎ **021/646746.** Fax 021/646824. 35 rms. TV TEL. £110 ($176) double. No service charge. Rates include breakfast. AE, DC, MC, V. Open Apr–Oct.

If location is everything, then this hotel has a lot to offer. Set high on a hillside overlooking Ballycotton Bay, this sprawling three-story property is an ideal waterside retreat, yet is within 25 miles of Cork City. Recently refurbished and updated from top to bottom, it offers a spacious lobby, restaurant, and lounge with wide-windowed views of the bay, traditional furnishings, and contemporary art. Guest rooms have modern light-wood furniture and pastel and sea-toned fabrics, and most have panoramic views.

3 West Cork

GETTING THERE   N71 is the prime road leading into West Cork from north and south; from Cork and points east, N22 also leads to West Cork.

Bus Eireann (☎ 021/518188) provides daily bus service to the principal towns in West Cork.

VISITOR INFORMATION   For information on West Cork, contact the **Skibbereen Tourist Office,** North Street, Skibbereen, Co. Cork (☎ 028/21766). It is open year-round, Monday through Friday from 9am to 6pm and on Saturday from 9am to 1pm, with expanded hours in the summer, according to demand. There are seasonal (May/June to August/September) **tourist offices** in The Square, Bantry (☎ 027/50229); Rossa Street, Clonakilty (☎ 023/33226); and Main Street, Glengariff (☎ 027/63084).

AREA CODES   Telephone area codes for West Cork include **023, 026, 027,** and **028.**

WEST CORK IN 250 WORDS OR LESS

For many, West Cork is the ultimate destination in Ireland, not so heavily touristed as Kerry yet just as alluring. It shares with Kerry the kind of craggy topography and jagged coastline that combine to create many hidden corners and seldom-explored byways. Though the amenities available to the traveler are not always so copious as in other parts of the country, those willing to rough it a little will be amply rewarded.

Some of the most beautiful coastal scenery (and severe weather) is to be found on the islands, several of which have frequent ferry service. Cape Clear is home to a bird-watching observatory, and is a well-known *gaeltacht:* Many schoolchildren come here to work on their Gaelic each summer. Dursey Island, off the tip of the Beara Peninsula, is accessible by means of a rickety cable car. Garinish Island in Glengarriff is the site of Ilnacullen, an elaborate Italianate garden.

West Cork is known for its enticing towns. Ballydehob has an artistic flair thanks to a cluster of artists in residence. At the local butcher, colorful drawings of cattle, pigs, and chickens indicate what meats are available, and a mural on the outside wall of a pub depicts a traditional music session. Other notable enclaves include Schull, an old-world yachting town, and Barleycove, a remote windswept resort that's the last stop before Mizen Head and the sheer cliffs at the southernmost tip of Ireland.

ATTRACTIONS

Timoleague Castle Gardens

Timoleague, Bandon, Co. Cork. ☎ **023/46116.** Admission £2.50 ($4) adults, £2 ($3.20) seniors and students. June–Aug, Mon–Sat 11am–5:30pm, Sun 2–5:30pm.

On the banks of the River Argideen, 15 miles west of Kinsale, these gardens have been cultivated by five generations of the Travers family since 1818. A feast of palm trees and other frost-tender plants are nurtured by the Gulf Stream. Resident peacocks wander around the ruins of a 13th-century tower and a 1920s house.

Drombeg Stone Circle

Open site. Off R597 between Rosscarbery and Glandore.

This ring of 17 standing stones is the finest example of a stone circle in Co. Cork. From this site the hills slope gently toward the sea, a short distance away, and the builders could hardly have chosen a more picturesque spot. The circle has been dated to sometime between 153 B.C. and A.D. 127, but little is known about its ritual purpose. Just west of the circle are the remains of two huts and a cooking place; it is thought that heated stones were placed in a water trough that can be seen adjacent to the huts, the hot water then being used for cooking. The cooking place dates from between A.D. 368 and 608.

✪ Creagh Gardens

Creagh, Skibbereen, Co. Cork. ☎ **028/22121.** Admission £2.50 ($4). Daily 10am–6pm. On R595, 3.5 miles south of Skibbereen.

This is one of the most beautifully situated gardens in Ireland, hemmed in by colorful meadows and the waters of an exquisitely picturesque estuary. Serpentine paths wind among magnificent old oaks, maples, and beeches, with occasional prospects through meadow and wood to the weathered facade of Creagh House. In the early summer the garden is loud with the drone of bees and the blazing colors of the massive rhododendrons, fuchsia, and hydrangeas. A walled garden encloses a greenhouse, vegetable garden, and collection of domestic fowl. Despite its modest size (somewhat over 20 acres) this garden contains many surprises and hidden corners, and really shouldn't be missed.

Cape Clear Island

Located 8 miles off the mainland, this is the southernmost inhabited point in Ireland. Irish is spoken by most of the islanders, and many students come here each summer to study the language. The place can be bleak, with a rugged rocky coastline and no trees to break the rush of sea wind, but this same barrenness will appeal to many for its stark beauty, rough and irregular but not without solace and grace. In early summer the landscape is brightened by wildflowers, and in October the air is filled with passerine migrants, some on their way from North America and Siberia; sea birds are present in abundance during the nesting season, especially from July to September. There are three pubs on the island, two of which are within sight of the north harbor; here you'll see most of the people you've met during the day, and hear some good music if you're lucky. **Mary and Ciarán O'Driscoll** (☎ 028/39153) operate a B&B (£15 [$24] per person) and self-catering apartments (starting at £20 [$32] per night); their house is on a hill overlooking the sea to the north and to the south. Ferries leave from Baltimore or Schull (£7 [$11.20] round-trip) one to three times daily; check local tourist offices for times of departure. A map and guide to Cape Clear is available in any of the island shops.

Mizen Head

☎ **028/35225.** Admission £2 ($3.20) adults, £1 ($1.60) children. June–Sept daily 11am–5pm. Call for winter hours. Take R591 to Goleen, and follow the signs for Mizen Head.

At the tip of the Mizen Head Peninsula the land falls precipitously into the Atlantic breakers in a line of spectacular sea cliffs. A suspension bridge permits access to the lighthouse on a small rock promontory; from here there are great views of the surrounding cliffs and nearby Three Castle Head. This place is worth a visit even if the bridge isn't open. For a cliff-side walk from the suspension bridge parking lot, see "Walking" under the "Sports & Recreation" section below. On the way out to Mizen Head you'll pass Barleycove Beach, one of the most beautiful beaches in southwest Ireland, and a great place to explore.

Dursey Island

This barren promontory extending into the sea at the tip of the Beara Peninsula offers no amenities for the tourist, but the adventuresome will find great seaside walks and a memorable passage from the mainland on Ireland's only operating cable car. To get there, take R571 past Cahermore to its terminus. As you sway wildly in the rickety wooden cable car, reading the text of psalm 91, which has kindly been posted to comfort the nervous, you may wonder whether a ferry might not be a wiser option. It wouldn't be. Apparently the channel between island and mainland is often too treacherous to permit regular crossing by boat. There is no accommodation on the island, so be sure that you know when the last cable car departs for the mainland; for more information on the schedule call **027/73017.**

✪ Bantry House

Bantry, Co. Cork. ☎ **027/50047.** Admission £5 ($8) adults, £3.50($5.60) seniors and students, children under 12 free. Admission includes gardens. June–Sept, daily 9am–7pm; Oct–May, 9am–5:30pm.

Set on the edge of town, this house was built around 1750 for the earls of Bantry. It has a mostly Georgian facade with Victorian additions. Open to the public since 1946, it contains many items of furniture and objets d'art from all over Europe, including four Aubusson and Gobelin tapestries said to have been made for Marie Antoinette. Today, Bantry House is the home of Mr. and Mrs. Egerton Shelswell-White, descendants of the 3rd earl of Bantry. The gardens, with original statuary, are beautifully kept and well worth a stroll. Climb the steps behind the house for a panoramic view of the house, gardens, and Bantry Bay.

1796 Bantry French Armada Exhibition Centre

East Stables, Bantry House, Bantry, Co. Cork. ☎ **027/51796.** Admission £3 ($4.80) adults, £1.75 ($2.80) seniors and students, £1 ($1.60) children under 14. Daily 10am–6pm.

This center commemorates Bantry Bay's role in the battle of 1796, when a formidable French Armada—inspired by Theobold Wolfe Tone and the United Irishmen—sailed from France to expel the British. Almost 50 warships carried nearly 15,000 soldiers to this corner of southwest Ireland. Thwarted by storms and a breakdown in communications, the invasion never came to pass. Ten ships were lost. Too storm-damaged to return to France, the frigate *Surveillante* was scuttled off Whiddy Island, to lay undisturbed for almost 200 years. The remains of that ship are now the centerpiece here. A combination ticket covering both the Exhibition Centre and Bantry House is available for £4.50 ($7.20).

✪ Garinish Island

Glengarriff, Co. Cork. ☎ **027/63333.** Admission to island, £2.50 ($4), adults, £1.75 ($2.80) seniors, £1 ($1.60) children and students, £6 ($9.60) family; boat trips, £5 ($8) per person. Island, Mar and Oct, Mon–Sat 10am–4pm, Sun 1–4:30pm; Apr–June and Sept, Mon–Sat 10am–6:30pm, Sun 1–7pm; July–Aug, Mon–Sat 9:30am–6:30pm, Sun 11–7pm.

Officially known as Ilnacullin, but usually referred to as "Garinish," this balmy island was once barren. In 1919 it was transformed into an elaborately planned Italianate garden with classical pavilions and myriad unusual plants and flowers from many continents. It's said that George Bernard Shaw wrote parts of *St. Joan* under the shade of the palm trees here.

The island is reached by covered ferry operated by **Blue Pool Ferry,** The Blue Pool, Glengarriff (☎ **027/63333**), or one of the other local services. Boats operate every 30 minutes during the island's visiting hours.

Derreen Gardens

Lauragh, Co. Kerry. ☎ **064-83103.** Admission £2.50 ($4). Apr–Oct, daily 10am–6pm. Signposted: 1 mile off R571 in Lauragh.

This subtropical informal garden is located on a site of great natural beauty, a hilly promontory on the breathtaking north coast of the Beara Peninsula. In the late 19th century the garden was planted with American species of conifer, many of which have become venerable giants during the intervening years. One garden path follows the sweep of the shoreline, through tunnels of rhododendron, while others wind through the dense foliage of the promontory, opening occasionally to a view of the mountains or an entrancing rocky glen. The garden is home to several rarities, most notably the

New Zealand tree ferns that flourish in a small glade, among giant blue gum and bamboo.

SPORTS & OUTDOOR PURSUITS

BEACHES   Barleycove Beach offers vast expanses of pristine sand and a fine view out toward the Mizen Head cliffs; despite the trailer park and holiday homes on the far side of the dunes, large parts of the beach never seem to get crowded. Take R591 to Goleen, and follow signs for Mizen Head. There is a public parking lot at the Barleycove Hotel.

BICYCLING   The Mizen Head, Sheep's Head, and Beara Peninsulas offer fine roads for cycling, with great scenery and few cars. Of these, the Beara Peninsula is the most spectacular, whereas the other two are less likely to be crowded with tourists during peak season. The loop around Mizen Head, starting in Skibbereen, is a good two- to three-day trip, while a loop around the Beara Peninsula from Bantry, Glengarriff, or Kenmare is at least three days at a casual pace. In Skibbereen, bicycles with panniers, helmet, and accessories can be rented from **Roycroft's Stores** (☎ 028/ 21235) for £45 ($72) per week; if you call ahead, a lightweight mountain bike with toe clips can be arranged at no extra cost, an *enormous* advantage over the leaden, battleship-like bicycles rented at most stores. One-way riding from Skibbereen to Killarney or Kenmare can be arranged for an additional £10 ($16).

BIRD-WATCHING   Cape Clear Island is the prime birding spot in West Cork, and one of the best places in Europe to watch seabirds and passerine migrants. The best time for sea birds is July to September, while October is the busiest month for passerines (and also for bird-watchers, who flock to the island in droves during this month). There is a bird observatory at the North Harbour, with a warden in residence from March to November, and accommodations for bird-watchers; to arrange a stay, write **Kieran Grace,** 84 Dorney Court, Shankhill, Co. Dublin. **Ciarán O'Driscoll** (☎ 028/39153), who operates a B&B on the island, also runs boat trips for bird-watchers around the island, and has a keen eye for vagrants and rarities.

DIVING   **The Baltimore Diving Centre** in Baltimore, Co. Cork (☎ 028/20300; fax 028/20300), provides equipment and boats to certified divers for exploring the many shipwrecks, reefs, and caves in this region; £25 ($40) per dive with equipment. Courses are available for all levels of experience; beginners can take a 2- to 3-hour snorkeling course for £10 to £15 ($16 to $24) or a scuba diving course for £22 to £30 ($35.20 to $48).

FISHING   The West Cork Coast is known for its many shipwrecks, which are quickly taken over by all manner of marine life after they hit the ocean floor. Wreck fishing is popular all along the Irish coast, and this is one of the best places for it. **Mark and Patricia Gannon** of Woodpoint House, Courtmacsherry (☎ 023/ 46427), offer packages including accommodation in their idyllic stone farmhouse, full board, and sea angling aboard one of their purpose-built fishing boats (starting at £50 [$80] per person per day). Boats can be chartered for £140 ($224) per day, and take up to 10 people. For sea angling in Baltimore, contact **Michael Walsh** (☎ 028/20352) or **Kieran Walsh** at the Algiers Inn (☎ 028/20145).

KAYAKING   With 100 islands in the vicinity of Baltimore, numerous inviting inlets, and a plethora of sea caves, the coast of West Cork is a sea kayaker's paradise. Lough Ine offers warm, still waters for beginners, a tidal rapid for the more intrepid, and access to a nearby headland riddled with caves demanding exploration. Day trips are offered throughout the year by ✪ **Jim Kennedy** (☎ 028/33002), a top competitor in flat-water racing and an expert sea kayaker. With his knowledgeable and friendly instruction, even rank beginners will soon feel at ease in a sea kayak. He operates from Maria's Schoolhouse (see listing under "Accommodations," below) near the seaside village of Union Hall; the charge is £5 ($8) per hour. The Schoolhouse is a fabulous base from which to explore the nearby coast by sea kayak.

Lessons and day trips are also available at the **Courtmacsherry Leisure Center,** a summertime operation with minimal facilities but great location and enthusiastic instructors; package deals including instruction, lodging, and meals are available through **Brookhill House,** Courtmacsherry, Cork (☎ 023/46177). The hourly fee is £5 ($8), and packages range from £30 to £40 ($48 to $64) per person per day.

SAILING   The Glenans Sailing Club was founded in France and now has three centers in Ireland, of which two are in Co. Cork, on Bear Island in Bantry Bay and on Baltimore Harbour. The centers provide weeklong courses at all levels using either dinghies, cruisers, catamarans, or Windsurfers; prices are £239 to £285 ($382.40 to $456). The living facilities are spartan, with dorm-style accommodation and meals cooked by participants. The clientele is mostly middle-aged and younger, from Ireland and the Continent. Day sailing is available in Baltimore on Saturdays in June, July, and August for £21 ($33.60) per person; call **028/20289** to make an advance booking.

WALKING   One of the most beautiful coastal walks in West Cork begins along the banks of Lough Ine, the largest saltwater lake in Europe. Connected to the sea by a narrow isthmus, the lake is situated in a lush valley of exceptional beauty. To get there, follow signs for Lough Ine along R595 between Skibbereen and Baltimore; there is a parking lot at the northwest corner of the lake. The wide trail proceeds gradually upward from the parking lot through the woods on the west slope of the valley, with several viewpoints toward the lake and the sea beyond. Once you reach the hilltop, there is a sweeping view of the coast from Mizen Head to Galley Head. Walking time to the top and back is about 1 1/2 hours.

At the mesmerizingly high cliffs of Mizen Head it is possible to follow the sheep paths that skirt the rim of the precipice—only for the nonacrophobic, though, and only on clear, dry days. Start at the parking lot for the suspension bridge at Mizen Head, and instead of entering the gate leading to the bridge and lighthouse, cut up the hill heading toward two high electrical towers. Continue to climb the hill past the towers, keeping to the left of the old lighthouse, a small abandoned stone structure on a small hill overlooking the sea. From here, continue along the cliffs, keeping a safe distance from the edge. From the parking lot to the old lighthouse is a 15-minute walk, and from there you can continue on another 30 minutes to the end of the headland, returning the way you came.

Near Lauragh on the Beara Peninsula is the abandoned town of Cummingeera, situated at the base of a cliff in a wild and remote valley. The walk to the village gives you a taste for the rough beauty of the Caha Mountains, and a sense for the lengths to which people would go in prefamine Ireland to find a patch of arable land. To get to the start of the walk, take the road posted for Glanmore Lake south from R571; this road is .8 miles west of the turnoff for Healy Pass. Follow the Glanmore Lake road .6 miles, then turn right at the road posted for "stone circle"; continue 1 1/3 miles to the point at which the road becomes dirt, and park on the roadside. From here there is no trail—one must simply walk up the valley to its terminus, about 1 1/4 miles away, where the ruins of a village hug the cliff's base. Where the valley is blocked by a headland, take the route around to the left, which is less steep. Return the way you came; the whole walk is 2¹/₂ miles, and takes about two hours—moderate in difficulty.

An easy seaside walk on the Beara Peninsula begins at Dunboy Castle, just over a mile west of Castletownbere on R572; this stretch of trail is part of the O'Sullivan Beara trail, which may eventually extend from Castletownbere to Leitrim. You can park your car along the road, by the castellated gatehouse, or drive up to the castle itself; the entry fee is 50p (80¢) for pedestrians or £2 ($3.20) for a car. The castle is a ruined 19th-century manor house overlooking the bay, with some graceful marble arches spanning the grand central hall. Just down the road are the sparse ruins of a medieval fortress, and beyond this the trail continues to the tip of Fair Head through overarching rhododendrons, with fine views across to Bear Island. From the gatehouse parking lot to the tip of Fair Head and back is about two hours.

WINDSURFING   Lessons and equipment rental are available at the Court-macsherry Leisure Center (☎ 023/46177; see listing in "Kayaking," above); rates are £8 ($12.80) per hour. There is a sheltered beach in town where beginners can get started, and another beach that's good for wave jumping nearby.

SHOPPING

The Bandon Pottery Shop
St. Finbarr's Place, Bandon, Co. Cork. ☎ 023/43525.

Right in the town center, this attractive shop produces a colorful line of hand-thrown tableware, vases, bowls, and other accessories. Open Monday through Saturday 9:30am to 1pm and 1:30 to 5:30pm.

Courtmacsherry Ceramics
Main St., Courtmacsherry, Co. Cork. ☎ 023/46239.

Overlooking the sea, this studio/shop offers an array of porcelain animals, birds, butterflies, and tableware, all inspired by the flora and fauna of West Cork. Visitors are welcome to watch potter Peter Wolstenholme at work on new creations. Open mid-March to October daily from 10am to 6pm.

Prince August Ltd.
Kilnamartyra, Macroom, Co. Cork. ☎ 026/40222. Sept–June Mon–Fri 10am–5pm; July–Aug Mon–Fri 10am–5pm and Sat 10am–4pm.

Prince August is Ireland's only toy soldier factory. The shop produces and displays a huge collection of metal miniatures based on J. R. R. Tolkien's classic books *The Hobbit* and *The Lord of the Rings*. Located off the main N22 road, northwest of Kinsale.

ACCOMMODATIONS
EXPENSIVE/MODERATE

Ballylickey Manor House
Bantry-Glengarriff road (N71), Ballylickey, Co. Cork. ☎ 800/223-6510 from the U.S., or 027/50071. Fax 027/50124. 11 rms. TV TEL. £88–£165 ($140.80–$264) double. 10% service charge. Rates include full breakfast. AE, MC, V. Mid-Mar to early Nov.

Overlooking Bantry Bay in a 10-acre setting of lawns and gardens, this well-established retreat offers a choice of accommodations in a 300-year-old manor house or in modern wooden cottages that surround the swimming pool. The units in the main house have a separate sitting room. All are decorated with country-style furnishings. This inn has an international ambience, thanks to the influence of its owners, the French-Irish Graves family, and a largely European clientele.

❖ Longueville House

Killarney road (N72), Mallow, Co. Cork. ☎ **800/223-6510** from the U.S., or 022/47156. Fax 022/47459. 18 rms. TV TEL. £110–£164 ($176–$262.40) double. 10% service charge. AE, DC, MC, V. Mar–Dec 23.

No discussion of the Co. Cork area would be complete without mentioning Longueville House. Geographically it's hard to classify—it's not really in West Cork, but northwest of Cork City. Built about 1720 and situated on a 500-acre farmland estate with its own winery, this convivial country retreat is the pride and joy of the O'Callaghan family. It produces a fine white wine, unique in this land known for its beers and whiskies, and is a very welcoming and homey place to stay, convenient to both Cork City and West Cork. Guest rooms are furnished in old-world style, with family heirlooms and period pieces, and most have bucolic views of the gardens, grazing pastures, or vineyards. Most of all, this house is distinguished by its award-winning restaurant, The Presidents' Room, adorned with portraits of Ireland's past heads of state. The menu offers produce and vegetables from the hotel's own farm and gardens. In the summer months, meals are also served in a festive and skylit Victorian conservatory.

MODERATE

❖ Sea View

Bantry-Glengarriff road (N71), Ballylickey, Co. Cork. ☎ **800/447-7462** from the U.S., or 027/50073. Fax 027/51555. 17 rms. TV TEL. £65–£110 ($96–$176) double. Suites are available. Service charge 10%. Rates include full breakfast. AE, CB, MC, V. Mid-Mar to mid-Nov. Free parking.

This handsome and comfortable hotel, aptly named Sea View, is homey and full of heirlooms, antiques, lots of tall windows, and a cheery decor, with guest rooms individually furnished with traditional dark woods and designer fabrics. The establishment is best known for the award-winning cuisine of proprietor Kathleen O'Sullivan. Besides the restaurant, there is also a cozy lounge bar and an outdoor patio. It is located off the main road, 3 miles from Bantry.

West Lodge

Off Bantry-Glengarriff road (N71), Bantry, Co. Cork. ☎ **027/50360.** Fax 027/50438. 104 rms. TV TEL. £60–£80 ($96–$128) double. Service charge 12.5%. Rates include full breakfast. AE, DC, MC, V. Open Jan to mid-Dec.

Set on a hillside overlooking Bantry Bay, this modern three-story hotel is surrounded by gardens and woodlands. The public areas and guest rooms are bright and airy, enhanced by wide windows, light wood furnishings, and colorful Irish fabrics. The facilities include a restaurant, tavern, indoor heated swimming pool, tennis and squash courts, sauna, and gym.

INEXPENSIVE

Lettercollum House

Timoleague, Co. Cork. ☎ **023/46251.** Fax 023/46270. 8 rms (5 with bath). £16–27 ($25.60–$43.20) double. No service charge. AE, DC, MC, V.

This is a place of interesting contrasts, where backpackers rub shoulders with businesspeople and an elegant Victorian home provides comfortable but somewhat spartan quarters. A spacious and well-equipped kitchen is provided for guests to make their own meals, although no one should stay here without sampling the extraordinary food from the in-house restaurant (see "Dining" below). Rooms are bright and clean; some have great views of the surrounding hills. A walled garden provides organic vegetables for the restaurant. The surroundings are pastorally idyllic, and the pervading atmosphere is one of tranquility. For those who don't mind a highly laid-back approach to service and the sometimes rowdy clientele attracted by a hostel on the premises, Lettercollum House is a real treasure.

✪ Maria's Schoolhouse

Cahergal, Union Hall, Co. Cork. ☎ **028/33002.** Fax 028/33002. 8 rms. £18–30 ($28.80–$48) double. No service charge. MC, V. Closed Jan–Feb.

The austere and handsome fieldstone exterior of this renovated schoolhouse gives way inside to nontraditional decor in bright purple and pink. The rooms are very comfortable, and each has its own unique character. A sunny and spacious hall is the scene of innovative dinners that focus on ethnic and vegetarian cuisine, and elaborate breakfasts. Every other Saturday there is an acoustic music concert in conjunction with dinner. These events feature top musicians and are well worth attending. Maria Hoare is an amiable and outgoing host, as is Jim Kennedy, who runs his excellent sea kayaking program from here.

DINING
EXPENSIVE

✪ Blair's Cove

Barley Cove Rd., Durrus, Co. Cork. ☎ **027/61127.** Reservations required. Dinner with starter buffet, £28 ($44.80); buffet and dessert only, £22 ($35.20). AE, DC, MC, V. Mar–June and Sept–Oct, Tues–Sat 7–9:30pm; July–Aug, Mon–Sat 7–9:30pm. INTERNATIONAL.

A grassy country lane leads you to this romantic restaurant overlooking Dunmanus Bay, less than 10 miles from Bantry. Owners Philip and Sabine de Mey have converted a stone barn with a 250-year-old Georgian courtyard and terrace into one of the best dining experiences in southwest Ireland. Amid high ceilings, stone walls, open fireplaces, and contemporary art, each meal starts with a buffet of appetizers (perhaps salmon fume, prawns, oysters, or mousse), a display large enough to satisfy some dinner appetites. But, if you decide to have an entrée as well, rack of lamb, grilled rib of beef, or monkfish fillet flambéed in Pernod will appear. For dessert, step up to the grand piano that doubles as a sweets trolley.

Chez Youen

The Pier, Baltimore, Co. Cork. ☎ **028/20136.** Reservations required. Fixed-price lunch £12.50 ($20); fixed-price dinner £21.50 ($34.40); dinner main courses £9.50–£32 ($15.20–$51.20). AE, DC, MC, V. Mar–May and Sept–Oct, 6:30–11pm; June–Aug, 12:30–4pm and 6:30–midnight. BRETON/SEAFOOD.

Set overlooking the marina of this small harbor town, Brittany-born Youen Jacob's restaurant has been drawing people to West Cork since 1978. The decor is relaxing, with beamed ceilings, candlelight, floral pottery, and an open copper fireplace. Lobster is the specialty, fresh from local waters, but the steaks, poached wild salmon in fennel, and leg of lamb are also very good. The chef's signature dish (and the one that commands the £32 price tag) is a gourmet shellfish platter, piled high with rare specimens not usually seen on ordinary menus: galley head prawns, Baltimore shrimp, and velvet crab, as well as local lobster and oysters, all served in a shell.

MODERATE

The Altar

Toormore, Schull, Co. Cork. ☎ **028/35254.** Reservations recommended. Bar food items £1.50–£8 ($2.40–$12.80); set traditional lunch £8 ($12.80); dinner main courses £7.50–£13 ($12–$20.80). AE, DC, MC, V. May–Oct, Mon–Sat noon–midnight, Sun noon–3pm. IRISH/SEAFOOD.

Situated deep in the West Cork countryside, this rustic cottage seems to appear out of nowhere on the horizon. It has all the trappings of a rustic retreat inside, including the requisite open, glowing fireplace and stone walls. The menu, which changes daily, emphasizes local seafoods, with choices such as seafood chowder, crab salad, oysters, and seafood plates. On Sundays, a traditional Irish lunch is served, and there is Irish music on Wednesday nights.

Casey's Cabin

Baltimore, Co. Cork. ☎ **028/20197.** Reservations recommended for dinner. All items £1.50–£28 ($2.40–$44.80). AE, DC, MC, V. Daily noon–3pm and 6–9:30pm. Bar snacks Mon–Sat noon–9:30pm. SEAFOOD/IRISH.

Overlooking Church Strand Bay, this nautical pub/restaurant has lovely views of the water, a beer garden, and a cottagelike interior with open peat fires. It specializes in simple fare such as fresh local seafood and steaks.

✪ Lettercollum House

Timoleague, Co. Cork. ☎ **023/46251.** Main courses £9–£14 ($14.40–$22.40). V, MC, DC. Apr–Oct Tues–Sun 7:30pm–9:30pm. Weekends only Nov–Mar. INNOVATIVE CONTINENTAL.

Owner and chef Con McLoughlin creates simple and original dishes based on organic produce from the adjacent walled garden, pigs raised on the premises, and locally caught fish. The menu changes daily, and there is always at least one vegetarian entrée, but your choices may include grilled wild salmon with sorrel sauce, cannelloni of sea spinach and brie with tomato butter sauce, or organic lamb tahini. The dining room was once a chapel, and the stained-glass windows remain. The service is rather informal, but the food is so good that it's best to overlook such shortcomings. This is a place where backpackers dine side by side with businesspeople, all united for the moment in their enjoyment of a truly great meal. (See also "Accommodations," above.)

Mary Ann's

Castletownshend, Skibbereen, Co. Cork. ☎ **028/36146.** Reservations recommended for dinner. Bar food £1.50–£14.50 ($2.40–$23.20); main courses £12–£18.50 ($19.20–$29.60). MC, V. Open daily 12:30–2pm and 6–10pm. Closed holidays. IRISH.

Dating from 1844, this rustic pub is decorated with ship's wheels, lanterns, and bells. The menu offers salads and West Cork cheese plates, as well as more ambitious dishes such as scallops meunière, sirloin steak with garlic butter, chicken Kiev, and deep-fried prawns. On fine days, patrons can sit in the pleasant outside courtyard.

Wine Vaults

73 Bridge St., Skibbereen, Co. Cork. ☎ **028/22743.** Reservations not required. All items £1.50–£7 ($2.40–$11.20). No credit cards. Year-round, daily noon–8pm for food; open until 11:30pm for music and drinks. INTERNATIONAL.

Situated in the heart of a busy market town, this restaurant has a classy winery-style decor. It is a handy place for lunch or a light meal in transit. The menu includes soups, sandwiches on pita bread, and pizzas, including a house-special pizza topped with mushrooms, peppers, onions, ham, and salami. There is live traditional music or jazz and blues offered nightly.

The Southwest: County Kerry

Kerry is a place of disorienting contrasts, where the tackiest tourist attractions coexist with some of Ireland's most spectacular scenic wonders. It's a rugged place for the most part, some of it so rugged that it's seldom visited and remains quite pristine; Ireland's two highest mountains, Carrantuohill and Mount Brandon, are examples of such places. You could be driving along—say, on the famous and popular Ring of Kerry, which traces the shores of the Iveragh Peninsula—make one little detour from the main road, and be in wild and unfrequented territory. The transition can be startling.

Thanks to its remoteness, Co. Kerry has always been an outpost of Gaelic culture. Poetry and music are intrinsic to Kerry lifestyle, as is a love of the outdoors and sports. Gaelic football is an obsession in this county, and Kerry wins most of the national championships. You'll also find some of Ireland's best golf courses here, and the fishing for salmon and trout is equally hard to resist.

1 The Iveragh Peninsula

GETTING THERE   **Bus Eireann** (☎ 064/34777) provides limited daily service from Killarney to Caherciveen, Waterville, Kenmare, and other towns on the Ring of Kerry. The best way to get to the Ring is by car, via the N70 and N71 roads. Some Killarney-based companies provide daily sightseeing tours of the Ring (see Killarney section).

VISITOR INFORMATION   For year-round information, stop in at the **Killarney Tourist Office,** Town Hall, Main Street, Killarney (☎ 064/31633), before you explore the area (for hours open, see the Killarney section, below). The **Kenmare Tourist Office,** Market Square, Kenmare (☎ 064/41233), is open from May through September.

AREA CODES   Most telephone numbers on the Iveragh Peninsula use the **064** or **066** code.

ACTIVITIES

✪ **THE RING OF KERRY**   Undoubtedly Ireland's most popular scenic drive, the Ring of Kerry is a 110-mile panorama of seacoast, mountain, and lakeland vistas. Bicyclists usually avoid this route, since the scores of tour buses that thunder through here every day in the summer aren't always generous about sharing the road. For the most part, the Ring follows N70 and circles the Iveragh Peninsula; it starts and finishes at Killarney, but you can also use Kenmare as a base. The drive can be undertaken in either direction, but we recommend a counterclockwise route.

Although it's possible to circle the peninsula in as little as four hours, the only way to get a feel for the area and the people is to leave the main road, get out of your car, and explore some of the inland and coastal towns. Portmagee is a lovely seaside town, connected by a bridge to Valencia Island, which houses the informative Skellig Heritage Centre. In Caherdaniel, there is a museum devoted to Daniel O'Connell, one of Ireland's great historical figures.

The most memorable and magical site to visit on the Iveragh Peninsula is Skellig Michael, a rocky pinnacle towering over the sea, where medieval monks built their monastery in ascetic isolation. The crossing to the island can be rough, so you'll want to choose as clear and calm a day for your trip as possible. Sea birds nest here in abundance, and more than 20,000 pairs of gannets inhabit neighboring Little Skellig during the summer nesting season.

Departing Killarney, follow the signs for Killorglin. When you reach this little town, you're on N70. You may wish to stop and walk around Killorglin, a spot that's known far and wide for its annual mid-August horse, sheep, and cattle fair. It's officially called the Puck Fair, because the local residents capture a wild goat (symbolizing the *puka* or *puki,* a mischievous sprite) from the mountains and enthrone it in the center of town as a sign of unrestricted merry-making.

Continue on N70 and soon vistas of Dingle Bay appear on your right. Carrantuohill, at 3,414 feet Ireland's tallest mountain, is to your left. The open bogland constantly comes into view. From it, the local residents dig pieces of peat, or turf, to burn in their fireplaces for warmth. Formed thousands of years ago, these boglands are mainly composed of decayed trees. They tend to be bumpy if you attempt to drive over them too speedily, so do be cautious.

The Ring winds around cliffs and the edges of mountains, with nothing but the sea below—another reason that you will probably average only 30 miles an hour, at best. As you go along, you'll notice the remains of many abandoned cottages. These date from the famine years, in the mid-1840s, when the Irish potato crop failed and millions of people starved to death or were forced to emigrate. This peninsula alone lost three-fourths of its population.

The next town on the Ring is Glenbeigh, a palm tree–lined fishing resort with a lovely, duned beach called Rossbeigh Strand. You may wish to stop here or continue the sweep through the mountains and along the sea's edge to Cahirciveen. From Cahirciveen, you can make a slight detour to see Valentia, an offshore island 7 miles long and one of the most westerly points of Europe. Connected to the mainland by a bridge at Portmagee, this was the site from which the first telegraph cable was laid across the Atlantic in 1866. In the 18th century, the Valentia harbor was famous as a refuge for smugglers and privateers; it's said that John Paul Jones, the Scottish-born American naval officer in the War of Independence, also anchored here quite often.

Head next for Waterville, an idyllic spot wedged between Lough Currane and Ballinskelligs Bay off the Atlantic. For years, it was known as the favorite retreat of Charlie Chaplin, but today it's the home of the only Irish branch of Club Med.

If you follow the sea road north of town out to the Irish-speaking village of Ballinskelligs, at the mouth of the bay, you can also catch a glimpse of the two Skellig Rocks. Continuing on N70, the next point of interest is Derrynane at Caherdaniel,

County Kerry

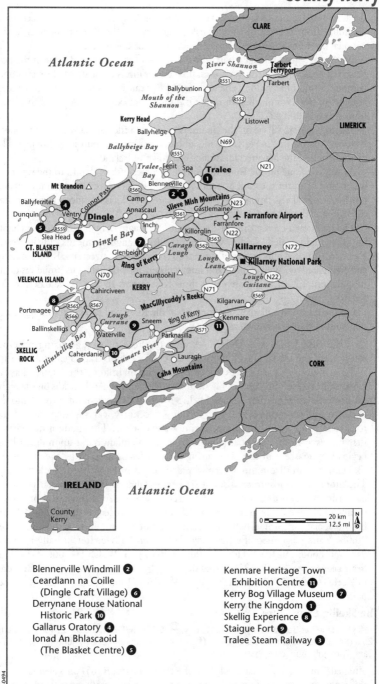

Blennerville Windmill **2**
Ceardlann na Coille
 (Dingle Craft Village) **6**
Derrynane House National
 Historic Park **10**
Gallarus Oratory **4**
Ionad An Bhlascaoid
 (The Blasket Centre) **5**

Kenmare Heritage Town
 Exhibition Centre **11**
Kerry Bog Village Museum **7**
Kerry the Kingdom **1**
Skellig Experience **8**
Staigue Fort **9**
Tralee Steam Railway **3**

3-0494

the home of Daniel O'Connell, remembered as "the Liberator" who freed Irish Catholics from the last of the English Penal Laws in 1829. Derrynane is now a national monument and park, and a major center of Gaelic culture.

Watch for signs to Staigue Fort, about 2 miles off the main road. One of the best preserved of all ancient Irish structures, this circular fort is constructed of rough stones without mortar of any kind. The walls are 13 feet thick at its base, and the diameter is about 90 feet. Not much is known of its history, but experts think it probably dates from around 1000 B.C.

Sneem, the next village on the circuit, is a colorful little hamlet with twin parklets. Its houses are painted in vibrant shades of blue, pink, yellow, purple, and orange, like a little touch of the Mediterranean plunked down in Ireland.

As you continue on the Ring, the foliage becomes lusher, thanks to the warming waters and winds of the Gulf Stream. When you begin to see lots of palm trees and other subtropical vegetation, you'll know you are in Parknasilla, once a favorite haunt of George Bernard Shaw.

The final town on the Ring of Kerry route, Kenmare, is by far the most enchanting. Originally called Neidin, which in the Irish language means "Little Nest," Kenmare is indeed a little nest of verdant foliage nestled between the River Roughty and Kenmare Bay. Well laid out and immaculately maintained by its proud residents (population: 1,200), Kenmare easily rivals Killarney as an alternative base for Co. Kerry sightseeing.

On the return to Killarney, the final lap of the Ring road takes you through a scenic mountain stretch known as Moll's Gap.

✪ **THE SKELLIG ISLANDS**   A visit to these two crags rising precipitously from the sea, about 10 miles off the coast of the Iveragh Peninsula, is sure to be a memorable experience. Seen from the mainland, the islands have a fantastic aspect, seeming impossibly steep and sharp-angled. And yet it is on the highest pinnacle of the larger island, Skellig Michael, that a community of monks chose to build a monastery in the 6th or 7th century, carving steps out of the rock to provide access from the stormy waters below. The modern-day visitor first makes a 45-minute boat passage from the mainland, and upon embarking begins a long ascent of the island using the same steps trodden by the monks for six centuries, until the monastery was abandoned in the 12th or 13th century. The monastic enclosure consists of six beehive-shaped huts of mortarless stone construction, two oratories, and a church; there is also a collection of carved stones that have been found on the island. The smaller of the Skellig Islands has no space for human habitation, but is home during nesting season to over 20,000 pairs of gannets. Ferries leave daily from Ballyferriter, usually between 9am and noon; call **Joe Roddy** (☎ 066/74268), **J. B. Walsh** (☎ 066/79147), or **Sean Feehan** (☎ 066/79182). Ferries departing from Portmagee are run by **Brendan O'Keefe** (☎ 066/77103) and **Murphy's** (☎ 066/77156). The cost is £20 ($32) per person.

The Skellig Experience

Skellig Heritage Centre, Valentia Island, Co. Kerry. ☎ **066/76306.** Admission £3 ($4.80) adults, £2.70 ($4.30) seniors and students, £1.50 ($2.40) children under 12. May–June and Sept, daily 10am–7pm; July–Aug, daily 9:30am–7pm.

Situated 7 miles off the mainland Ring of Kerry route (via R765) on Valentia Island, this new attraction blends right in with the terrain, with a stark stone facade framed by grassy mounds. Inside, through a series of displays and audiovisuals, the center presents a detailed look at birds and plant life of the Valentia area. In particular, it gives the story of the Skellig Rocks, Skellig Michael and Little Skellig.

Derrynane House National Historic Park

Caherdaniel, Co. Kerry. ☎ **066/75113.** Admission £2 ($3.20) adults, £1.50 ($2.40) seniors, £1 ($1.60) students and children, £5 ($8) family. Oct–Apr, Tues–Sun 1–5pm; May–Sept, Mon–Sat 9am–6pm, Sun 11am–7pm.

Situated on a 320-acre site along the Ring of Kerry coast between Waterville and Caherdaniel, this is where Ireland's Great Liberator, Daniel O'Connell, lived for most of his life. The house is maintained as a museum by Ireland's Office of Public Works. It's filled with all kinds of documents, illustrations, and memorabilia related to O'Connell's life. Visitors can also watch a 25-minute audiovisual about the great leader entitled *Be You Perfectly Peaceable.*

Kenmare Heritage Town Exhibition Centre

The Square, Kenmare, Co. Kerry. ☎ **064/41233.** Admission £2 ($3.20) adults, £1.50 ($2.40) seniors and students, £1 ($1.60) children under 12, £5 ($8) family. Mon–Sat 10am–6pm, Sun 11am–5pm.

To learn more about the delightful town of Kenmare, the Ring of Kerry's "little nest," step inside this new visitor center. Exhibits recount Kenmare's history as a planned estate town that grew up around the mineworks founded in 1670 by Sir William Petty, ancestor of the Landsdownes, the local landlords. The center also displays locally made Kenmare lace, and the story of the woman who originated the craft is told. A scripted walking trail around the town is also under development.

Kerry Bog Village Museum

Ring of Kerry road (N71), Ballycleave, Glenbeigh, Co. Kerry. ☎ **066/69184.** Admission £2.50 ($4) adults, £1.50 ($2.40) students, £1 ($1.60) children. MC, V. Mar–Nov daily 9am–6pm, Dec–Feb by appointment.

This little cluster of thatched-roof cottages shows what life was like in Kerry in the early 1800s. This museum village has a blacksmith's forge and house, a turf-cutter's house, a laborer's cottage, a thatcher's dwelling, a tradesman's house, and a stable and dairy house. Stacks of newly cut turf sit piled high beside the road. There's also a football pitch and other recreational facilities. The interiors are furnished with authentic pieces gathered from all parts of Kerry.

SIGHTSEEING CRUISES

Seafari Scenic & Wildlife Cruises

Kenmare Pier, Kenmare, Co. Kerry. ☎ **064/83171.** £8 ($12.80) adults, £6 ($9.60) seniors and students, £5 ($8) children. May–Sept, daily every 2 hours between sunrise and sunset.

See the sights of Kenmare Bay on board this 50-foot covered boat. The two-hour cruises cover 10 miles and are narrated by well-versed guides who provide information on local history, geography, and geology. Sightings of sea otters, gray seals, herons, oyster catchers, and kingfishers are pointed out. Boats depart from the pier next to the Kenmare suspension bridge. Reservations recommended.

SPORTS & OUTDOOR PURSUITS

GOLF Home to myriad seascapes and sand dunes, the Ring of Kerry is known for its great golf courses, particularly **Waterville Golf Links,** Waterville (☎ **064/74102**) on the edge of the Atlantic. On huge sand dunes and bounded on three sides by the sea, this 18-hole championship course is one of the longest in Ireland (7,234 yards). Visitors are welcome; greens fees are £30 ($48) weekdays.

Other challenging 18-hole courses on the Ring include **Dooks Golf Club,** Glenbeigh (☎ **066/68205**), a seaside par-70 course on the Ring of Kerry road, with a fee of £15 ($24); and the newly expanded **Kenmare Golf Club,** Kenmare (☎ **064/41291**), a parkland par-71 course with greens fees from £10 ($16).

WALKING Ireland's longest low-level, long-distance path, the **Kerry Way,** traverses the Ring of Kerry. The first stage from Killarney National Park to Glenbeigh is inland through wide and scenic countryside, while the second stage provides a circuit of the Iveragh Peninsula, linking Cahirciveen, Waterville, Caherdaniel, Sneems, and Kenmare, with a farther inland walk along the old Kenmare Road back to Killarney, for a total of 125 miles. The route consists primarily of paths and "green" (unsurfaced) roads, such as old driving paths, butter roads, and routes between early Christian settlements. A leaflet outlining the route is available from the Killarney or Kenmare tourist office.

SHOPPING

Many good craft and souvenir shops are found along the Ring of Kerry, but those in **Kenmare** offer the most in terms of variety and quality. Kenmare shops are also open year-round, usually Monday through Saturday from 9am to 6pm. From May through September, many shops remain open till 9 or 10pm and some open on Sunday from noon to 5 or 6pm.

Avoca Handweavers at Moll's Gap
Ring of Kerry road (N71), Moll's Gap, Co. Kerry. ☎ **064/34720.**

Located in one of the most scenic of settings, this shop is set on a high mountain pass (960 feet above sea level) between Killarney and Kenmare. It's a branch of the famous tweed makers of Avoca, Co. Wicklow, dating back to 1723. The wares range from colorful handwoven capes, jackets, throws, and knitwear to pottery and jewelry. There's an excellent coffee shop on the premises, staffed by chefs trained at the Ballymaloe Cookery School. Closed November to mid-March.

Cleo
2 Shelbourne Rd., Kenmare. ☎ **064/41410.**

A branch of the long-established Dublin store of the same name, this trendy women's wear shop is known for its colorful tweed and linen fashions, as well as specialty items like Kinsale cloaks.

D. J. Cremin & Sons
20 Henry St., Kenmare. ☎ **064/41597.**

Founded in 1906 as a general drapery store, this family run business is a haven for limited Waterford Crystal items like lamps, globes, candelabras, wall brackets, and chandeliers. You will also find unusual Irish dolls, locally made hand knits, and other giftware.

Kenmare Book Shop
Shelbourne St., Kenmare, Co. Kerry. ☎ **064/41578.**

This shop specializes in books on Ireland, particularly Irish biographies and books by Irish writers, as well as guides and maps about the local area. There are also art cards and craft items relating to the Book of Kells. In an upstairs room, there is a display and audiovisual presentation on the Book of Kells for those who can't get to Dublin to see the real thing; there's an admission charge of £2 ($3.20) adults, £1 ($1.60) children for the upstairs exhibit.

Nostalgia
27 Henry St., Kenmare, Co. Kerry. ☎ **064/41389.**

In a town known for its lace, it's a natural to stop into this shop and view the new and antique lace, table and bed linens, traditional teddy bears, and accessories.

Quills Woolen Market

Market Sq. and Main St., Kenmare, Co. Kerry. ☎ **064/41078**; and North Sq., Sneem, Co. Kerry. ☎ 064/45277.

This is a branch of the store of the same name in Killarney, known for Aran hand knits, Donegal tweed jackets, Irish linen, Celtic jewelry, and colorful hand-loomed knitwear.

ACCOMMODATIONS
VERY EXPENSIVE

✪ The Park

Kenmare, Co. Kerry. ☎ **800/223-6764** from the U.S., or 064/41200. Fax 064/41402. 48 rms. TV TEL. £210–£302 ($336–$483.20) double. No service charge. Rates include full breakfast. AE, DC, MC, V. Closed mid-Nov to mid-Dec and Jan to mid-Apr.

Dating from 1897, this Victorian-style chateau is a haven of impeccable service and luxurious living. Augustly ensconced amid palm tree–lined gardens beside Kenmare Bay, it originally served as a Great Southern Railway hotel, but was totally restored and refurbished about 20 years ago under the masterful ownership and management of Francis Brennan. The interior is rich in high-ceilinged sitting rooms and lounges, crackling open fireplaces, original oil paintings, tapestries, plush furnishings, and museum-worthy antiques, including an eye-catching cistern decorated with mythological figures and supported by gilded sea horses and dolphins. The individually decorated bedrooms are decked out in a mix of Georgian and Victorian styles, many with four-poster or canopy beds, hand-carved armoires, china lamps, curios, and little extra touches like telephones in the bathroom and towel warmers. Most have views of river and mountain vistas. Amid all of the elegance, this hotel exudes an intrinsically welcoming atmosphere. It's not surprising that it is considered by some to be Ireland's best hotel.

Dining/Entertainment: The elegant dining room, with romantic views of the water and the palm tree–lined gardens, is one of the most highly acclaimed hotel restaurants in Ireland, meriting a Michelin star. Other public areas include a hexagonal-shaped bar and a drawing room where a pianist plays each evening.

Services: Concierge, 24-hour room service, laundry and dry cleaning, nightly turn-down.

Facilities: 18-hole golf course, joggers' trail, tennis court, croquet lawn, salmon fishing.

Sheen Falls Lodge

Kenmare, Co. Kerry. ☎ **800/221-1074** from the U.S., or 064/41600. Fax 064/41386. 40 rms. TV TEL. £160–£240 ($256–$384) double. No service charge. AE, DC, MC, V. Closed Jan to mid-Mar.

Originally the 18th-century home of the earl of Kerry, this relatively new resort sits beside a natural waterfall amid 300 acres of lawns and semitropical gardens where the River Sheen meets the Kenmare Bay estuary. The public areas are spacious and graceful with pillars and columns, open fireplaces, traditional furnishings, and original oil paintings. The guest rooms are large and spacious, decorated in contemporary style; each overlooks the falls or bay. The hotel also maintains a vintage 1922 Buick to provide local excursions for guests.

Dining/Entertainment: The Cascades is a wide-windowed restaurant facing the falls, which are floodlit at night.

Services: 24-hour room service, concierge, laundry and dry cleaning, nightly turn-down.

Facilities: Leisure center with Jacuzzi, sauna, and steam room; billiard room; 1,000-volume library; a 15-mile stretch of private salmon fishing; horseback riding; tennis; croquet; golf on a nearby course; helicopter pad.

VERY EXPENSIVE / EXPENSIVE

✪ Parknasilla Great Southern

Ring of Kerry road (N70), Sneem, Co. Kerry. ☎ **800/44-UTELL** from the U.S., or 064/45122. Fax 064/45323. 84 rms. TV TEL. £136–£170 ($217.60–$272) single or double. Includes full Irish breakfast and service charge. AE, DC, MC, V. Closed Mar 1–10.

Facing one of the loveliest seascape settings in Ireland, this chateau-style hotel is nestled amid 300 acres of lush subtropical foliage, palm trees, and flowering shrubs. Thanks to the warming influence of the Gulf Stream, it enjoys a year-round temperate climate. The present structure, an outgrowth and expansion of a former private mansion, was built with a fanciful Victorian stone facade in 1896. Over the years, it has been a favorite with visiting royalty and celebrities, including Nobel prize–winning dramatist George Bernard Shaw. Today's traveler enjoys such amenities as a private nine-hole golf course, heated indoor saltwater swimming pool, saunas, horseback riding, tennis, fishing, boating, indoor and outdoor sundecks, a pubby lounge bar, and an award-winning restaurant. The bedrooms, which vary in size, are individually furnished with reproduction pieces, and most look out onto broad vistas of the Kenmare River and the Atlantic.

MODERATE

Butler Arms

Waterville, Co. Kerry. ☎ **066/74144.** Fax 800/447-7462 from the U.S., or 066/74520. 30 rms. TV TEL. £80–£110 ($128–$176). Includes full Irish breakfast and service charge. AE, DC, MC, V. Closed late Oct to mid-April.

Once a favorite vacation retreat of Charlie Chaplin, this grand old inn is now run by the third generation of the Huggard family. Located on the edge of town and partially facing the sea, it has a sprawling and semiturreted white facade. The refurbished guest rooms are functional and pleasant, and many have views of the water or the palm tree–studded gardens. An old-world charm emanates from the public rooms and bars, most of which have open turf fireplaces. Other facilities include a full-service restaurant, a nautically themed bar, sun lounge, tennis court, and free salmon and sea trout fishing on Lough Currane and private lakes.

Club Med

Off Ring of Kerry road (N70), Waterville, Co. Kerry. ☎ **800/CLUB-MED** from the U.S., or 066/74133. Fax 066/74483. 80 rms. TV TEL. £50–£100 ($80–$160) double. Includes full Irish breakfast and service charge. AE, DC, MC, V. Closed late Oct to mid-Apr.

Located on the western sweep of the Iveragh Peninsula, just south of the village of Waterville and on the shores of Lough Currane, this is Club Med's first venture into Ireland. It is a well-kept and up-to-date two-story hotel with a bright and airy decor, and lots of wide windows to show off the surrounding lake and mountain views. The public areas include a restaurant, piano bar, pub, bridge room, and shop. As for outdoor activities, there is an 18-hole championship golf course (greens fees extra), heated indoor swimming pool, thermal spa pool, sauna, solarium, three tennis courts, bicycling, guided nature walks, aerobics classes, and exercise room. The hotel also holds exclusive rights to some of the best salmon and sea-trout fishing in Ireland.

Derrynane Hotel

Off Ring of Kerry road (N71), Caherdaniel, Co. Kerry. ☎ **800/528-1234** or 066/75136. Fax 066/75160. 75 rms. TV TEL. £60.40–£77 ($96.65–$123.20) double. Includes full Irish breakfast and service charge. AE, DC, MC, V. Closed Nov to mid-Apr.

You can really get away from it all at this contemporary style three-story hotel, set deep in the outer reaches of the Ring of Kerry between Waterville and Sneem on the edge of the Atlantic. It is surrounded by beautiful beaches, hills, and the nearby Derrynane National Historic Park. The standard furnishings of the guest rooms are enhanced by the great views from every window. The public areas include a restaurant and lounge, while a heated swimming pool is available outside.

Dromquinna Manor Hotel

Blackwater Bridge P.O., off Ring of Kerry road (N71), P.O. Kenmare, Co. Kerry. ☎ **064/41657.** Fax 064/41791. 27 rms. TV TEL. £59–£120 ($94.40–$192) double; £100–£150 ($160–$240) tree house suite. No service charge. Rates include full Irish breakfast. AE, DC, MC, V.

Situated a little over 2 miles west of Kenmare, this newly opened Victorian-style hotel dates from 1850 and was originally a private home. It is situated on 42 acres of woodland with almost a mile of land facing the Kenmare River. Totally refurbished in recent years, it still retains an old-world ambience, with log fireplaces, original oak paneling, ornate ceilings, and authentic bric-a-brac. Each bedroom is individually furnished, some with four-poster beds or Victorian-style beds, and some modern with light woods and frilly floral fabrics; some face the water. Suites with two bedrooms, bathroom, and large balcony are available in the tree house, said to be the only one in Ireland or Britain, situated 15 feet above ground. Public areas offered include a restaurant and boathouse-style bistro, while sporting facilities include a tennis court, croquet, and rowboats for hire (£12 [$19.20] per day).

INEXPENSIVE

⑤ Kenmare Bay

Sneem Rd., Kenmare, Co. Kerry. ☎ **800/528-1234** from the U.S., or 064/41300. Fax 064/41541. 136 rms. TV TEL. £56–£70 ($89.60–$112) double. Rates include full breakfast and service charge. AE, DC, MC, V. Closed Nov–Mar.

Situated on a hillside at the edge of town, just off the main road that winds around the Ring of Kerry, this modern hotel was recently expanded and refurbished. The guest rooms are furnished with light woods and tweedy or quilted fabrics, with large windows that look out onto the mountainous countryside. Facilities include a full-service restaurant and a spacious lounge bar that is the setting for traditional Irish music sing-alongs on most evenings.

Towers

Ring of Kerry road (N70), Glenbeigh, Co. Kerry. ☎ **800/447-7462** or 066/68212. Fax 066/68260. 28 rms. TV TEL. £50–£60 ($80–$96) double. Service charge 12.5%. Rates include full breakfast. AE, DC, MC, V. Closed Jan–Mar.

If you'd like to be right in the heart of one of the Ring of Kerry's most delightful towns, then this vintage brick-faced country inn is for you. Shaded by ancient palms, it sits in the middle of a small fishing village, yet is within a mile of the sandy Rossbeigh Strand and only 20 miles west of Killarney. Recently refurbished and updated, most of the guest rooms are in a contemporary-style new wing with lovely views of the nearby waters. Facilities include a lively old-fashioned pub and a good seafood restaurant.

DINING
MODERATE

The Blue Bull
South Sq., Ring of Kerry road (N70), Sneem, Co. Kerry. ☎ **064/45382.** Reservations recommended. Main courses £8.95–£13.95 ($14.30–$22.30). AE, DC, MC, V. Daily Mar–Dec 6–10pm. SEAFOOD/INTERNATIONAL.

With a blue straw bull's head resting over the doorway, this old pub/restaurant has long been a favorite on the Ring of Kerry route. There are three small rooms, each with an open fireplace and walls lined with old prints of Co. Kerry scenes and people, plus a skylit conservatory room in the back. The menu offers dishes such as salmon Hollandaise, salmon stuffed with spinach and smoked salmon in white wine sauce, Valencia scallops in brandy, chicken stuffed with prawns, chicken Kiev, steaks, and Irish stew. Bar food available daily, 11am to 8pm year-round, and traditional Irish entertainment most evenings.

D'Arcy's Old Bank House
Main St., Kenmare, Co. Kerry. ☎ **064/41589.** Reservations recommended. Main courses £9.50–£15.50 ($15.20–$24.80). MC, V. Mar–Oct, daily 6–10:30pm; Nov–Feb, Wed–Sat 7–9:30pm. Closed Mondays Sept–June. IRISH.

Situated in a two-story stone house at the top end of Kenmare, this restaurant has a homey atmosphere, with a big open fireplace. The chef/owner, Matt d'Arcy, who formerly presided at the kitchens of the nearby Park Hotel, has branched out to make his own culinary mark in this restaurant-rich town. Using fresh local ingredients, the creative menus include dishes such as baked sea trout in pastry with smoked salmon; fillet of beef in pastry with a stuffing of mushrooms, roast garlic, and shallots; veal with mushroom timbale and caper sauce; and loin of Kerry lamb with eggplant, tomato, and garlic.

The Huntsman
The Strand, Waterville, Co. Kerry. ☎ **066/74124.** Reservations recommended. Lunch/bar food items £2.50–£10 ($4–$16); dinner main courses £7.95–£16.95 ($12.70–$27.10). AE, DC, MC, V. Apr and Oct, Wed–Sun noon–4pm and 6–10pm; May–Sept, daily noon–4pm and 6–10pm. Closed Nov–Mar. INTERNATIONAL.

It's worth a trip to Waterville just to dine at this contemporary restaurant on the shores of Ballinskelligs Bay. The Huntsman has sweeping picture-window vistas of the Atlantic and a welcoming decor of plush red-cushioned seating, wrought-iron fixtures, and lots of leafy plants. The menu concentrates on using the freshest of the local catch, including Skellig lobster and Kenmare Bay scampi, but also offers a wide choice of meat dishes such as chateaubriand, rack of lamb, Irish stew, and seasonal pheasant, rabbit, and duck.

✪ Lime Tree
Shelbourne Rd., Kenmare, Co. Kerry. ☎ **064/41225.** Reservations recommended. Main courses £8.95–£14.50 ($14.30–$23.20). MC, V. Apr–Oct daily 6:30–10pm. IRISH.

Innovative cuisine is the focus at this restaurant in an 1821 landmark renovated schoolhouse next to the grounds of the Park Hotel. The decor includes a skylit gallery and stone walls lined with paintings by local artists, and the menu offers such dishes as breast of chicken with apple rosemary marmalade; lambs liver with bacon, shallots, and crumb stuffing; twice-seared pork chop with ginger rhubarb chutney; warm smoked salmon salad with gingered starfruit and lime; and vegetarian stir-fry in pastry.

The Smuggler's Inn

Cliff Rd., Waterville, Co. Kerry. ☎ **066/74330.** Reservations recommended for dinner. Main courses £11.95–£17.50 ($19.10–$28). MC, V. Mar–Oct, daily 8:30–10:30pm. SEAFOOD.

Positioned a mile north of the town along the Ballinskelligs Bay beach, this renovated farmhouse is on a sandy beach and across the road from the entrance to the Waterville Golf Course. The decor is nautical, with fine sea views from the dining room windows. The menu offers the freshest of seafood with dishes such as sea trout in capers and lemon butter, Ballinskelligs Bay black sole, sweet seafood curry, and steaks. Snacks and pub food available throughout the day and evening.

MODERATE/INEXPENSIVE

Packie's

Henry St., Kenmare, Co. Kerry. ☎ **064/41508.** Reservations recommended. Main courses £7.90–£15.70 ($12.65–$25.10). MC, V. Easter to mid-Nov, Mon–Sat 5:30–10pm. IRISH.

With window boxes full of colorful seasonal plantings, this informal, bistro-style restaurant in the middle of town exudes a welcoming atmosphere. The interior has a slate floor, stone walls, and dark oak tables and chairs. On the walls is a collection of wonderful contemporary Irish art, and on the menu are tried-and-true favorites: Irish stew and rack of lamb. Also offered are creative combinations such as gratin of crab and prawns, beef braised in Guinness with mushrooms, and blackboard fish specials. Chef/owner Maura Foley uses herbs from her own garden to enhance each dish.

Red Fox Inn

Ring of Kerry road (N71), Ballycleave, Glenbeigh, Co. Kerry. ☎ **066/69184.** Reservations recommended for dinner. Main courses £4.95–£13.75 ($7.90–$22). MC, V. Daily noon–3pm and 6–9pm. IRISH.

Situated adjacent to the Kerry Bog Museum, this restaurant has an old Kerry cottage atmosphere, with open turf fireplaces, family heirloom pictures on the walls, and local memorabilia. There are picnic tables outside for good weather dining. The menu includes hearty traditional dishes such as Irish stew, seafood pie, chicken and ham, leg of lamb, and steaks. In the summer (May to September), there is Irish ceili band entertainment Wednesday through Sunday from 9:30 to 11:30pm. Snacks are served all day in the bar.

The Vestry

Ring of Kerry road (N71), Templenoe, Kenmare, Co. Kerry. ☎ **064/41958.** Reservations recommended for dinner. Main courses £8.50–£16.25 ($13.60–$26). MC, V. Daily 6–10pm. Closed Mon Sept–June. MODERN IRISH.

As its name implies, this building is a former Church of Ireland edifice, constructed between 1790 and 1816, and in use for services until 1987. In 1993, it was tastefully converted into a restaurant, retaining many of its original decorations and fixtures. The menu, along with dishes such as scalloped salmon with prawn sauce and duck with black cherry sauce, offers more unusual items such as ostrich, pheasant, and wild boar. The Vestry is situated on Kenmare Bay about 4 miles west of Kenmare.

INEXPENSIVE

Purple Heather

Henry St., Kenmare, Co. Kerry. ☎ **064/41016.** Reservations not necessary. All items £2–£9.95 ($3.20–$15.90). No credit cards. Mon–Sat 11am–7pm. Closed Christmas week. IRISH.

Situated in the heart of town, this dependable pub/restaurant is a great place to stop for a snack or for a light meal with a gourmet flair, such as wild smoked salmon or prawn salads, smoked trout pâté, vegetarian omelets, and Irish cheese platters, as well as homemade soups.

2   Killarney

Killarney is 84 miles SW of Shannon, 192 miles SW of Dublin, 54 miles W of Cork, 69 miles SW of Limerick, and 120 miles SW of Galway.

GETTING THERE   **Aer Lingus** offers nonstop flights from Dublin, Dusseldorf, and Frankfort into Kerry County Airport, Farranfore, Co. Kerry (☎ **066/64644**), about 10 miles north of Killarney. **Manx Airlines** flies direct from London Luton to Kerry, as do Charter Kreutzer from Munich and Zurich Charter ICS and Cosmopolitan from Zurich.

Irish Rail services from Dublin, Limerick, Cork, and Galway arrive daily at the **Killarney Railway Station,** Railway Road, off East Avenue Road (☎ **064/31067** or 066/26555).

Bus Eireann operates regularly scheduled bus services into Killarney from all parts of Ireland. The bus depot is adjacent to the train station at Railway Road, off East Avenue Road (☎ **064/34777**).

The Kerry people like to say that all roads lead to Killarney, and at least a half dozen major national roads do go there, including N21 and N23 from Limerick, N22 from Tralee, N22 from Cork, N72 from Mallow, and N70 from the Ring of Kerry and West Cork.

VISITOR INFORMATION   The **Killarney Tourist Office** is located in Town Hall, Church Place, off Main Street, Killarney (☎ **064/31633**). It's open Monday to Saturday from 9:15am to 6pm in June, 9:15am to 8pm in July and August, and 9:30am to 5pm during the rest of the year. It offers many helpful booklets, including the *Tourist Trail* walking-tour guide and the Killarney Area Guide with maps.

Useful local publications include *Where: Killarney,* a quarterly magazine distributed free at hotels and guest houses. It is packed with all types of current information on tours, activities, events, and entertainment.

TOWN LAYOUT   Killarney is small, with a year-round population of approximately 7,000. The town is built around one central thoroughfare, Main Street, which changes its name to High Street at midpoint. The principal offshoots of Main Street are Plunkett Street, which becomes College Street at midpoint, and New Street, which, as its name implies, is still growing. The Deenagh River edges the western side of town and East Avenue Road rims the eastern side. It's all very walkable in an hour or two.

The busiest section of town is at the southern tip of Main Street, where it meets East Avenue Road. Here the road curves and heads southward out to the Muckross road and the entrance to the Killarney National Park.

GETTING AROUND   Killarney Town is so small and compact that there is no local bus service; the best way to get around is on foot.

By Taxi   Taxi cabs line up at the rank on **College Square** (☎ **064/31331**). You can also phone for a taxi from **Dero's Taxi Service** (☎ **064/31251**) or call **Donal O'Connell** (☎ **064/32415**).

By Car   In Killarney Town, it's best to park your car and walk. Most hotels and guest houses offer free parking to their guests. If you must park on the street for any reason, you must buy a parking disk and display it on your car; parking costs 30p (48¢) per hour and disks can be purchased at hotels or shops. A car is necessary to

Killarney

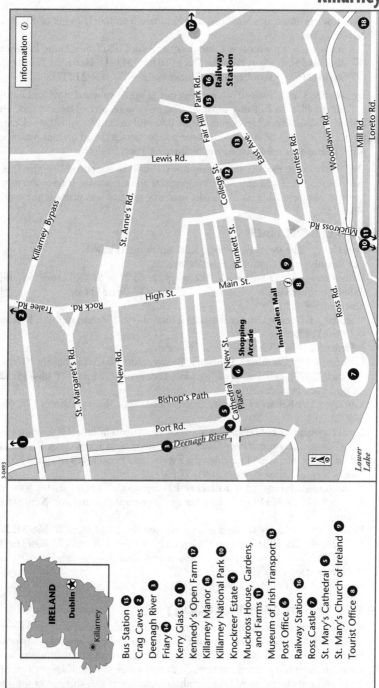

Bus Station **15**
Crag Caves **2**
Deenagh River **3**
Friary **14**
Kerry Glass **12**
Kennedy's Open Farm **17**
Killarney Manor **18**
Killarney National Park **10**
Knockreer Estate **4**
Muckross House, Gardens, and Farms **11**
Museum of Irish Transport **13**
Post Office **6**
Railway Station **16**
Ross Castle **7**
St. Mary's Cathedral **5**
St. Mary's Church of Ireland **9**
Tourist Office **8**

drive from town on the Muckross and Kenmare road (N71) to get to Killarney National Park.

If you need to rent a car in Killarney, contact **Avis,** c/o Killarney Autos, Park Road (☎ **064/36655**); **Budget,** Kenmare Place (☎ **064/34341**); **Hertz,** 28 Plunkett St. (☎ **064/34216**); or **Randles Bros.,** Muckross Road (☎ **064/31237**).

By Jaunting Car   Horse-drawn jaunting cars (a light, two-wheeled vehicle) line up at Kenmare Place in Killarney town, offering rides to Killarney National Park sites and other scenic areas. Depending on the time and distance required, prices range from £12 to £32 ($19.20 to $51.20) per ride per person, based on four passengers participating. (For more details, see "Sightseeing Tours," below.)

On Foot   To see the best of Killarney town, follow the signposted "Tourist Trail," encompassing the highlights of the main streets and attractions. It takes about two hours to complete the walk. A booklet outlining the trail is available at the tourist office.

FAST FACTS: KILLARNEY

Area Code   The area code for most Killarney numbers is **064.**

Car Rentals   See "Getting Around," above.

Drugstores   Try **O'Sullivan's Pharmacy,** at 81 New St., Killarney (☎ **064/ 35866**), or **Sheahans,** at 34 Main St., Killarney (☎ **064/31113**).

Emergencies   Dial **999.**

Hospital   **Killarney District Hospital** is located on St. Margaret's Road, Killarney (☎ **064/31076**).

Information   See "Visitor Information," above.

Laundry & Dry Cleaning   **Gleeson's,** Brewery Lane, off College Square, Killarney (☎ **064/33877**), and **The Washing Line,** Park Road, Killarney (☎ **064/35282**), are both good bets.

Library   The **Killarney Library** is located on Rock Road, Killarney (☎ **064/ 32972**).

Local Newspapers & Media   Local weekly newspapers include *The Kerryman* and *The Killarney Advertiser. Where: Killarney,* a quarterly magazine, is chock-full of helpful, up-to-date information for visitors; it is distributed free at hotels and guest houses. The local radio station is Radio Kerry, 97 FM.

Photographic Needs   Try **Killarney Photographic Centre,** at 105 New St., Killarney (☎ **064/32933**), or Moriarty Photographic Stores, on New Street, Killarney (☎ **064/31225**).

Police   The **Killarney Garda Station** is on New Road, Killarney (☎ **064/31222**).

Post Office   The **Killarney Post Office,** on New Street, Killarney (☎ **064/31051**), is open 9am to 5:30pm Monday, Tuesday, and Thursday through Saturday, and 9:30am to 5:30pm on Wednesday.

Shoe Repairs   Try **The Cobbler,** at 24 High St., Killarney (no phone).

A FEW WORDS ABOUT KILLARNEY

Killarney is the Grand Central Station of tourism in the southwest. If you've never seen a traffic jam of battling tour buses or been besieged by a bevy of pushy jaunting car drivers, this is the place to seek out such curious and unusual spectacles of nature. If that's not your bag, however, it's easy enough to resist Killarney's gravitational pull and explore instead the incredibly scenic hinterlands that border the town on all sides, perhaps sneaking into town at some point to sample the best of what this tourist megalopolis has to offer.

The lakes are Killarney's main attraction. The first of these, the Lower Lake, is sometimes called "Lough Leane" or "Lough Lein," which means "the lake of learning." It's the largest, more than 4 miles long, and is dotted with 30 small islands. The second lake is aptly called the Middle Lake or Muckross Lake, and the third simply Upper Lake. The last is the smallest and is full of storybook islands covered with a variety of trees—evergreens, cedars of Lebanon, Juniper, Holly, and Mountain Ash.

The lakes and the surrounding woodlands are all part of the 25-square-mile Killarney National Park. Found within its borders are two major estates, the Muckross and Knockreer demesnes, and the remains of major medieval abbeys and castles. Blossoming in season is a profusion of foliage such as rhododendrons, azaleas, magnolias, camellias, hydrangeas, and tropical ferns. At almost every turn, you'll see Killarney's own botanical wonder, the arbutus, or strawberry tree, plus eucalyptus, redwoods, and native oak.

The most noteworthy of Killarney's islands is Innisfallen, which seems to float peacefully in the Lower Lake and which you can reach by rowboat, available for rental at Ross Castle. St. Fallen founded a monastery here in the 7th century, and it flourished for 1,000 years. It's said that Brian Boru, the great Irish chieftain, and St. Brendan the Navigator were educated here. From 950 to 1320, the "Annals of Innisfallen," a chronicle of early Irish history, was written at the monastery; it's now in the Bodlein Library at Oxford University. Traces of an 11th-century church and a 12th-century priory can still be seen today.

ACCOMMODATIONS
VERY EXPENSIVE / EXPENSIVE

Aghadoe Heights
Off Tralee road (N22), Aghadoe, Killarney, Co. Kerry. ☎ **800/44-UTELL** from the U.S., or 064/31766. Fax 064/31345. 57 rms, 3 suites. TV TEL. £120–175 ($192–$280) double, £175–£225 ($280–$360) suite. No service charge. Rates include full breakfast. AE, DC, MC, V.

For viewing the whole Killarney perspective—town, lakes, mountains, and surrounding countryside—this hotel couldn't be in a better spot. It is situated on 8¹/₂ acres of high ground 2 miles northwest of Killarney Town. Guest rooms offer contemporary furnishings with floor-to-ceiling window views of the Killarney kaleidoscope.

Dining/Entertainment: The main dining room is Frederick's, a rooftop restaurant with great views and an adjacent bar.

Facilities: Indoor heated swimming pool with waterfall, Jacuzzi, sauna, steam room, solarium, tennis court, salmon and trout fishing on a private stretch of river.

EXPENSIVE

✪ Killarney Park Hotel
Kenmare Place, Killarney, Co. Kerry. ☎ **064/35555.** Fax 064/35266. 67 rms, 8 suites. TV TEL. £110–£150 ($176–$240) double. No service charge. Rates include full breakfast. AE, DC, MC, V.

With a striking yellow neo-Georgian facade, this new four-story property is located on its own grounds on the eastern edge of town, between the railway station and the tourist office. Public rooms are posh and spacious, with brass fixtures, oil paintings, wainscot paneling, deep-cushioned seating, open fireplaces, and a sunlit conservatory-style lounge overlooking the gardens. Guest rooms are decorated in a contemporary style with dark and light wood furnishings, quilted designer fabrics, and marble-finished bathrooms. Public areas include a restaurant, piano bar, patio, indoor heated swimming pool, gym, and steam room.

☺ Killeen House

Aghadoe, Killarney, Co. Kerry. ☎ **064/31711.** Fax 064/31811. 19 rms. TV TEL. £80–£110 ($128–$176) double. Service charge 10%. Rates include full breakfast. AE, DC, MC, V.

Dating from 1838 and set on high ground overlooking Killarney's lakes and golf courses, this rambling country manor house is surrounded by mature gardens in a quiet residential area about 2 miles northwest of town. Completely refurbished and opened for guests in 1992, it offers a relaxed and homey feeling, with all the comforts of a hotel. The bedrooms, which vary in size and decor, feature semi-orthopedic beds and standard furniture. The public areas include a restaurant, fireside lounge, and a golf-themed bar that is the only pub in the world to accept golf balls as legal tender.

EXPENSIVE/MODERATE

Clarion Hotel Randles Court

Muckross road (N71), Killarney, Co. Kerry. ☎ **800/4-CHOICE** from the U.S., or 064/35333. Fax 064/35206. 37 rms. TV TEL. £60–£120 ($96–$192) double. Service charge 12.5%. Rates include full breakfast. DC, MC, V. Closed Jan–Feb.

A former rectory dating from the turn of the century, this multigabled four-story house sits on its own grounds in a raised site off the main road outside of Killarney Town on the road to Muckross House. Totally restored, enlarged, and refurbished, it opened as a hotel in 1992. The public areas hark back to the house's earlier days, with a decor of marble floors, mantled fireplaces, chandeliers, gilt mirrors, tapestries, and old prints. Of the bedrooms, three are in the original building and the rest in a new wing, all with distinctive furnishings, including armoires, antique desks, or vanities. Facilities include a restaurant, lounge, and outdoor patio.

☺ Great Southern

Railway Rd., off East Avenue Rd., Killarney, Co. Kerry. ☎ **800/44-UTELL** from the U.S., or 064/31262. Fax 064/31642. 180 rms. Executive rooms and suites also available. TV TEL. £81.50–£129 ($130.40–$206.40) single or double. Service charge 12.5%. AE, DC, MC, V. Closed Jan–Feb.

Set amid 36 acres of gardens and lush foliage on the eastern edge of town, this four-story, ivy-covered landmark is the grande dame of Killarney hotels. Dating from 1854, it was built around the time of Queen Victoria's visit to Killarney and has since been host to presidents, princes, and personalities from all over the world, as well as many a modern-day travel group. The guest rooms offer every modern convenience, including garment press, hair dryer, and sometimes a minibar. The public areas retain the charm of yesteryear, with high ceilings rimmed by ornate plasterwork, tall paned windows looking out onto nearby mountain vistas, glowing open fireplaces, and Waterford crystal chandeliers. The lobby and all bedrooms have been recently renovated. Train and bus terminals are located opposite the hotel.

Dining/Entertainment: The classic main dining room overlooks the gardens, while the smaller Malton Room provides à la carte service in a clubby setting (dinner only). Light refreshments and snacks are available in The Lounge and The Punch Bowl Bar.

Services: Concierge, room service, laundry, dry cleaning.

Facilities: Indoor heated swimming pool, sauna, Jacuzzi, steam room, gym, two tennis courts, hairdressing salon, gift shop.

Hotel Dunloe Castle

Off Killorglin Rd., Beaufort, Killarney, Co. Kerry. ☎ **800/221-1074** from the U.S., or 064/44111. Fax 064/44583. 120 rms. TV TEL. £98–£132 ($156.80–$211.20) double. No service charge. Rates include full breakfast. AE, DC, MC, V. Closed Oct to mid-Apr.

Located on its own extensive tropical grounds about 6 miles west of town near the entrance to the Gap of Dunloe, this is not really a castle, in the medieval sense. Instead, it's a contemporary-style five-story hotel that takes its name from a ruined 15th-century fortress nearby. Entirely renovated in 1993, it has traditional-style furnishings with many valuable antiques. Surrounded by broad mountain vistas, the Dunloe has a certain agrarian ambience, with horses, ponies, and cows grazing in the adjacent fields. It's a place to come to unwind and to spend a few days; you'll need a car to get to town or to sightsee in the area.

Dining/Entertainment: Restaurant and cocktail bar.

Facilities: Heated indoor swimming pool, sauna, tennis courts, horseback riding, fishing, putting green, fitness track.

Hotel Europe

Off Killorglin Rd., Fossa, Killarney, Co. Kerry. ☎ **800/221-1074** from the U.S., or 064/31900. Fax 064/32118. 205 rms. TV TEL. £98–£132 ($156.80–$211.20) double. No service charge. Rates include full breakfast. AE, DC, MC, V. Closed Nov–Feb.

One of the most picturesque settings in Killarney belongs to this modern five-story property sitting right on the shores of the Lower Lake, 3 miles west of town, adjacent to Killarney's two 18-hole championship golf courses, and surrounded by dozens of mountain peaks. The hotel's public areas are spacious, open, and filled with antiques, while the guest rooms offer contemporary furnishings, all enhanced by spectacular lakeside vistas; most of the bedrooms have private balconies. The hotel also has its own stables with Haflinger horses.

Dining/Entertainment: Choices include the aptly named Panorama Restaurant, an alpine-themed Lakeside cafe, and two lounges for light refreshment.

Facilities: Olympic-size indoor pool, saunas, gym, tennis, boating, fishing, horseback riding, bicycling, hairdressing salon.

MODERATE

Cahernane Hotel

Muckross road (N71), Killarney, Co. Kerry. ☎ **800/552-6676** from the U.S., or 064/31895. Fax 064/34340. 48 rms. TEL. £97.50–£125 ($156–$200) double. No service charge. Rates include full breakfast. AE, DC, MC, V. Closed Nov–Mar.

Originally built in 1877 as a manor home for the Herbert family (the earls of Pembroke), this country house hotel is situated less than a mile from town, along the shores of the Lower Lake in a sylvan setting of ancient trees and well-tended rose gardens. As befits its Victorian heritage, it is furnished with antiques and period furniture both in its public areas and in most of its guest rooms. Dining and entertainment choices include The Herbert, a gracious old-world main dining room, and The Pembroke, for lighter fare. For recreation there are two tennis courts, pitch and putt, croquet, and privileges for salmon and trout fishing.

Castlerosse

Killorglin Rd., Killarney, Co. Kerry. ☎ **800/528-1234** from the U.S., or 064/31114. Fax 064/31031. 65 rms. TV TEL. £76–£102 ($121.60–$163.20) double. Includes full Irish breakfast and service charge. AE, DC, MC, V. Closed Dec–Feb.

Set on its own parklands between the Lower Lake and surrounding mountains, this modern, rambling, ranch-style inn is 2 miles from the heart of town and next to Killarney's two golf courses. The guest rooms, recently refurbished, offer contemporary furnishings and views of the lake. Facilities include a restaurant, lounge, a new leisure center, two tennis courts, putting green, walking paths, and jogging trails.

✪ Kathleen's Country House

Madam's Height, Tralee road (N22), Killarney, Co. Kerry. ☎ **064/32810.** Fax 064/32340. 16 rms. TV TEL. £45–£75 ($72–$120) double. No service charge. Rates include full breakfast. AE, MC, V. Closed early Nov to mid-Mar.

Of the many guest houses in this area, this one stands out. Located about a mile north of town on its own grounds next to a dairy farm, it is a two-story contemporary house with a modern mansard-style roof and many picture windows. Enthusiastic and efficient hostess Kathleen O'Regan-Sheppard has also outfitted all the bedrooms with orthopedic beds, hair dryers, and tea/coffeemakers. Quite recently, all rooms have been totally refurbished in antique pine, and a new library / drawing room has been added.

✪ Muckross Park Hotel

Muckross Rd., Killarney, Co. Kerry. ☎ **064/31938.** Fax 064/31965. 27 rms. TV TEL. £80–£120 ($128–$192) double. No service charge. Rates include full breakfast. AE, DC, MC, V. Closed Dec to mid-Mar.

Located just off the main road, about 2 miles outside of town, this hotel takes its name from the fact that it sits across the road from Muckross House and Killarney National Park. Although fairly new, it incorporates parts of the oldest hotel in Killarney, dating from 1795, and is furnished in an old-world, country-house style with paneled walls, open fireplaces, and equestrian-theme oil paintings. The rooms, which vary in size and decor, have period furniture, including some semi-canopy beds, quilted fabrics, frilly draperies, and Victorian-style ceiling fixtures, plus modern amenities such as a garment press and hair dryer. Facilities include an old-world–style restaurant and Molly Darcy's, a traditional thatched-roof pub (see "Evening Entertainment & Pubs," below).

INEXPENSIVE

Killarney Town House

31 New St., Killarney, Co. Kerry. ☎ **064/35388.** Fax 064/35382. 11 rms. TV TEL. £40–£45 ($64–$72) double. No service charge. Rates include full breakfast. V.

This recently built three-story guest house is situated in the heart of town on one of the busiest streets. It's ideal for those who want a good clean room and don't need a bar or restaurant on the premises. The guest rooms, newly refurbished in 1996–97 and identified by Killarney flowers rather than by numbers, offer all the basic comforts. Breakfast is served in a bright and airy ground-floor dining room. It's a 10-minute walk from the bus and train station.

DINING
EXPENSIVE

✪ Gaby's

27 High St., Killarney. ☎ **064/32519.** Reservations recommended. Lunch main courses £4–£6 ($6.40–$9.60); dinner main courses £11.50–£26 ($18.40–$41.60). MC, V. Tues–Sat 12:30–2:30pm; Mon–Sat 6–10pm. SEAFOOD.

One of Killarney's longest established restaurants, this nautically themed place is a mecca for lovers of fresh seafood. It is known for its succulent lobster, served grilled or in a house sauce of cognac, wine, cream, and spices. Other choices include turbot, haddock in wine, local salmon, and a giant Kerry shellfish platter, a veritable feast of prawns, scallops, mussels, lobster, and oysters.

✪ Strawberry Tree

24 Plunkett St., Killarney. ☎ **064/32688.** Reservations recommended. Main courses £13.95–£16.95 ($23.30–$27.10). AE, DC, MC, V. June–Aug, daily 6–10pm; Feb–May and Sept–Nov, Mon–Sat 6–10pm. NEW IRISH.

Named for Killarney's signature plant, this lovely shop-front restaurant is in the heart of town, yet it has a serene old-fashioned atmosphere, with a decor of soft pastel tones and an open hearth. The menu blends the organic produce of local farmers and suppliers with creative sauces and presentation. Entrées include farm duck; free-range beef from Thady Crowley's farm; free-range chicken from Michael Barry's farm, with wild-nettle mousse stuffing; sole baked in crisp potato crust and smoked salmon sauce; and rack of mountain lamb with wild garlic sauce.

MODERATE

Dingles

40 New St., Killarney. ☎ **064/31079.** Reservations suggested. Main courses £9.50–£15 ($15.20–$24). AE, DC, MC, V. Mar–Oct, daily 6–10pm. INTERNATIONAL.

Located near St. Mary's Cathedral, this bistro-style restaurant is furnished with recycled church pews, wooden benches, and choir stalls, enhanced by arches and alcoves and an open turf fireplace. The menu includes such dishes as chicken curry, beef stroganoff, Irish stew, vegetable casserole, Dingle Bay prawns in creole sauce, and other seafood dishes.

Foley's

23 High St., Killarney. ☎ **064/31217.** Reservations recommended for dinner. Main courses £8.80–£14.50 ($14.10–$23.20). AE, DC, MC, V. Daily 12:30–3pm and 5–10pm. Closed Dec 22–27. IRISH.

A Georgian country home atmosphere prevails at this restaurant in the heart of town. The ever-changing menu features such items as Dingle Bay scallops mornay, rainbow trout, and fresh salmon, as well as breast of pheasant in port wine, duck in black-currant sauce, steaks, and Kerry mountain lamb. Don't pass up the home-baked brown bread scones that accompany each meal.

MODERATE/INEXPENSIVE

✪ Bricín

26 High St., Killarney. ☎ **064/34902.** Reservations suggested for dinner. Snacks £1.50–£5 ($2.40–$8); dinner main courses £6.90–£12.50 ($11.04–$20). MC, V. Mon–Sat 10am–10pm; Sun 6–10pm. IRISH.

Traditional Kerry boxty dishes (potato pancakes with various fillings, such as chicken, seafood, curried lamb, or vegetables) are the trademark of this upstairs restaurant, one floor above a very good craft and bookshop. The menu also offers a variety of fresh seafood, pastas, Irish stew, and specials such as medaillons of beef in peppercorn sauce, fillet of pork with sage and apricot stuffing, and chicken Bricin (breast of chicken in red-currant and raspberry sauce). This eatery is housed in one of Killarney's oldest buildings, dating from the 1830s. It sports original stone walls, pine furniture, turf fireplaces, and, something very rare in Ireland, a completely nonsmoking room seating 40. Snacks and light fare are served during the day. In addition to the book and craft shop downstairs, the locale also houses the Bricín Art Gallery, exhibiting oils and watercolors by local artists.

Robertino's

9 High St., Killarney. ☎ **064/34966.** Reservations recommended. Main courses £6–£15 ($9.60–$24). MC, V. Daily 6–10:30pm. ITALIAN.

Step through the wrought-iron gates of this restaurant and experience the ambience of Italy—operatic arias playing in the background and a Mediterranean-style decor of statues, murals, marble columns, palms and hanging plants, and brick walls. There are five separate dining areas including a "green zone" for nonsmokers. The menu offers dishes such as veal saltimbocca, roast rib of lamb flamed in Marsala wine sauce, steaks, and a variety of local seafood and homemade pastas.

Swiss Barn

17 High St., Killarney. ☎ **064/36044.** Reservations recommended. Fixed-price lunch main courses £4–£7.95 ($6.40–$12.70); dinner main courses £9–£21 ($14.40–$33.60); 4-course early bird special 5:30–7:30pm £7.70 ($12.30); 5-course tourist menu £10.75 ($17.20). AE, DC, MC, V. Mon and Wed–Sun 12:30–3pm and 5:30–10:30pm. SWISS/CONTINENTAL.

With a rustic alpine decor, this restaurant aims to bring the taste of Switzerland and the Continent to Killarney. The menu offers Swiss favorites such as émincé of veal Zurichoise, pork fillet in morel sauce, and fondue bourguignonne, as well as veal cordon bleu, beef stroganoff, steaks, seafood, and vegetarian platters.

MAJOR ATTRACTIONS

✪ Killarney National Park

Kenmare road (N71), Killarney. ☎ **064/31440.** Fax 064/33926. Free admission. Year-round daylight hours.

This is Killarney's centerpiece: a 25,000-acre area of natural beauty. You'll find three storied lakes—the Lower Lake (or Lough Leane), the Middle Lake (or Muckross Lake), and the Upper Lake—myriad waterfalls, rivers, islands, valleys, mountains, bogs, and woodlands, and lush foliage and trees including oak, arbutus, holly, and mountain ash. There's also a large variety of wildlife, including a rare herd of red deer. No automobiles are allowed within the park, so touring is best done on foot, bicycle, or via horse-drawn jaunting car. The park offers four signposted walking and nature trails along the lakeshore.

Access is available from several points along the Kenmare road (N71), with the main entrance being at Muckross House, where there is a new visitor center featuring background exhibits on the park and a 15-minute film titled *Killarney: A Special Place.*

✪ Muckross House & Gardens

Kenmare road (N71), Killarney. ☎ **061/31440.** Admission £3.30 ($5.28) adults, £2.20 ($3.52) seniors, £1.50 ($2.40) children. *Note:* A combination ticket covering both Muckross House and Muckross Traditional Farms is available for approximately £1 ($1.60) extra per person. Jan–June and Sept–Dec, daily 9am–6pm; July–Aug, daily 9am–7pm. Closed during Christmas holidays.

The focal point of the Middle Lake and, in many ways, of the entire national park, is the Muckross Estate, often called "the jewel of Killarney." It consists of a gracious ivy-covered Victorian mansion and its elegant surrounding gardens.

Dating from 1843, the 20-room Muckross House has been converted into a museum of Co. Kerry folklife, showcasing locally carved furniture, prints, maps, paintings, and needlework. Imported treasures like Oriental screens, Venetian mirrors, Chippendale chairs, Turkish carpets, and curtains woven in Brussels are also displayed.

The house's cellars have been converted into craft shops with local artisans demonstrating traditional trades such as bookbinding, weaving, and pottery. The adjacent mature gardens, known for their fine collection of rhododendrons and azaleas, are also worth exploring.

✪ Muckross Traditional Farms

Kenmare road (N71), Killarney. ☎ **064/31440.** Admission £3.30 ($5.30) adults, £2.20 ($3.50) seniors, £1.50 ($2.40) children. *Note:* A combination ticket covering both Muckross Traditional Farms and Muckross House is available for approximately £1 ($1.60) extra per person. May–Oct, daily 11am–7pm; March 17–April 30 weekends and bank holidays 11am–6pm.

Located near the Muckross House estate, this 70-acre park is home to displays of traditional farm life and artisans' shops. The various farmhouses and buildings are so authentically detailed that visitors feel they are dropping in on working farms and lived-in houses. The animals and household environments are equally fascinating for children and adults, making for a great family exploration.

Visitors can watch sowing and harvesting or potato-picking and haymaking, depending on the season. Farmhands work in the fields and tend the animals, while the blacksmith, carpenter, and wheelwright ply their trades in the old manner. Women draw water from the wells and cook meals in traditional kitchens with authentic utensils, crockery, and household items.

Ross Castle

Ross Rd., off Kenmare road (N71), Killarney. ☎ **064/35851.** Admission £2.50 ($4) adults, £1.75 ($2.80) seniors , £1 ($1.60) students and children, £6 ($9.60) family. Apr daily 11am–6pm, May daily 10am–6pm, June–Sept daily 9am–6pm, Oct daily 9am–5pm.

Newly restored, this 15th-century fortress sits on the edge of the Lower Lake, 2 miles outside of Killarney Town. Built by the O'Donoghue chieftains, this castle distinguished itself in 1652 as the last stronghold in Munster to surrender to Cromwell's forces. All that remains today is a tower house, surrounded by a fortified bawn with rounded turrets. The tower has been furnished in the style of the late 16th and early 17th centuries and offers a magnificent view of the lakes and islands from its top. Access is by guided tour only. A lovely lakeshore walk stretches for two miles between Killarney and the castle.

Knockreer Estate

Cathedral Place, off New St., Killarney. ☎ **064/31440.** Free admission. Daily, daylight hours.

Lovely views of the Lower Lake can be enjoyed in this setting, a part of the National Park grounds most recently opened to the public (1986). Once the home of Lord Kenmare, the estate has a turn-of-the-century house, a pathway along the River Deenagh, and gardens mixing 200-year-old trees with flowering cherries, magnolias, and azaleas. The house, not open to the public, is now a field study center for the National Park. Main access to Knockreer is via Deenagh Lodge Gate, opposite the cathedral, in town.

St. Mary's Cathedral

Cathedral Place, off Port Rd., Killarney. ☎ **064/31014.** Free admission, donations welcome. Daily 10:30am–6pm.

Officially known as the Catholic Church of St. Mary of the Assumption, this limestone cathedral is the town's most impressive building. Designed in the Gothic Revival style by Augustus Pugin, and cruciform in shape, its construction was begun in 1842, interrupted by the Irish famine years, and finished in 1855. The magnificent central spire was added in 1912. The entire edifice was extensively renovated from 1972 to 1973. It's situated at the edge of town on the far end of New Street.

MORE ATTRACTIONS

Museum of Irish Transport

East Ave. Rd., Killarney. ☎ **064/34677.** Admission £2.50 adults ($4), £2 ($3.20) seniors and students, £1 ($1.60) children. Daily 10am–6pm or later.

This museum presents a unique collection of vintage and classic cars, motorcycles, bicycles, carriages, and fire engines, including an 1825 hobby horse bicycle; a 1907 Silver Stream, the only model ever built; a 1904 Germain, one of four remaining in the world; a 1910 Wolseley Siddeley, once driven by the poet William Butler Yeats;

and an ill-fated DeLorean, a futuristic, stainless-steel car that was manufactured over its short life at a plant in Ireland. Lining the walls are early motoring and cycling periodicals and license plates from all over the world.

St. Mary's Church

Church Place, Killarney. ☎ **064/31832.** Free admission, donations welcome. Year-round 9:30am–5pm.

It's commonly believed that St. Mary's, an 1870 neo-Gothic church, stands on the site of the original "Church of the Sloe Woods" (in Irish called *Cill Airne*—the Anglicization of which is Killarney). It's located in the heart of town, across from the Tourist Office.

○ Kerry Glass Studio & Visitor Centre

Killorglin Rd., Fossa, Killarney. ☎ **064/44666.** Free admission. Daily 9am–4:30pm.

This studio produces Killarney's distinctive colored glass. Visitors are welcome to watch and photograph the artisans firing, blowing, and adding color to the glass as it is shaped into vases, paperweights, candleholders, and figurines. Free guided tours are conducted according to demand. The center includes a factory shop and snack bar. Located 4 miles west of the town.

Kennedy's Open Farm

Brewsterfield, Glenflesk, Killarney. ☎ **064/54054.** Admission £3 adults ($4.80), £2 ($3.20) children. Daily. Six miles east of Killarney, off the main Cork road (N22).

This 75-acre dairy and sheep farm is surrounded by mountain vistas. Visitors can see cows being milked, piglets being fed, and peacocks strutting their stuff. Horse-drawn machinery is displayed.

Crag Caves

Off Limerick road (N21), Castleisland, Co. Kerry. ☎ **066/41244.** Admission £3 ($4.50) adults, £1.50 ($2.25) children over 6. Mar–June and Sept–Nov, daily 10am–6pm; July–Aug, daily 10am–7pm.

Believed to be more than a million years old, these limestone caves were discovered and first explored in 1983. Guides accompany you 12,510 feet into the passage on a well-lit tour revealing some of the largest stalactites in Europe. Exhibits, a crafts shop, and a restaurant are on the premises, 15 miles north of Killarney.

SIGHTSEEING TOURS

BUS TOURS　　To get your bearings in Killarney, consider one of these sightseeing tours:

Killarney Highlights

Dero's Tours, 7 Main St., Killarney. ☎ **064/31251** or 064/31567. £7.50 ($12). May–Sept daily at 10:30am, but schedules vary, so check in advance.

Besides showing off Killarney's Lakes from the best vantage points, this three-hour tour takes you to Aghadoe, the Gap of Dunloe, Ross Castle, Muckross House and Gardens, and Torc Waterfall.

Lakeland Tour

Castlelough Tours, 7 High St., Killarney. ☎ **064/32496.** £10 ($16). May–Sept, daily at 10:30am and 2pm.

This tour, approximately 3½ hours long, includes a visit to Muckross House and Gardens by bus and a tour of the lakes via Killarney Water Bus.

MORE BUS TOURS　　In addition to Killarney's main sights, some bus tours also venture into the two prime scenic areas nearby: the Ring of Kerry and Dingle

Peninsula. In the May-to-September period, tours are offered daily; prices average £10 ($16) per person. Check the following companies if that's the kind of tour for you: **Bus Eireann,** Bus Depot, Railway Road, off East Avenue Road (☎ **064/34777**); **Castlelough Tours,** 7 High St. (☎ **064/32496**); **Corcoran's Tours,** 10 College St. (☎ **064/36666**); and **Dero's Tours,** 7 Main St. (☎ **064/31251**).

JAUNTING CAR TOURS   If you enjoy walking or bicycling, just say no to the numerous drivers who will inevitably offer their services as you make your way around the Killarney lakes. These quaint horse-driven buggies are one of the main features of the landscape here, and if at some point you decide to give them a try, keep in mind that jaunting car rates are set and carefully monitored by the Killarney Urban District Council. Current rates, all based on four persons to a jaunting car, run £3 ($4.80) per person for a round-trip to Ross Castle; £6 per person ($9.60) for a round-trip to Muckross House & Gardens and Torc Waterfall; and £8 per person ($12.80) for round-trips to Muckross Abbey, Dinis Island, and Torc Waterfall, or for a round-trip to Kate Kearney's Cottage, gateway to the Gap of Dunloe.

✪ Gap of Dunloe

Amid mountains and lakelands, the winding and rocky Gap of Dunloe is situated about 6 miles west of Killarney. The route through the gap passes a kaleidoscope of craggy rocks, massive cliffs, meandering streams, and deep valleys. The road through the gap ends at Upper Lake. One of the best ways to explore the gap is by bicycle (see "Bicycling" section, below). Horse fanciers may want to take one of the horse-back excursions offered by **Castlelough Tours,** 7 High St. (☎ **064/32496**); **Corcoran's Tours, Kilcummin** (☎ **064/43151**); and **Dero's Tours,** 22 Main St. (☎ **064/31251**). A tour will cost about £20 to £30 ($32 to $48).

BOAT TOURS   There is nothing quite like seeing the sights from a boat on the Lakes of Killarney. Two companies operate regular boating excursions, with full commentary:

M.V. Pride of the Lakes Tours

Scotts Gardens, Killarney. ☎ **064/32638.** £5 ($8) adults; £2.50 ($4) children. Apr–Oct, 11am, 12:30pm, 2:30pm, 4pm, and 5:15pm.

This enclosed water bus offers daily sailings from the pier at Ross Castle. The trip lasts just over an hour and reservations are suggested.

M.V. Lily of Killarney Tours

3 High St., Killarney. ☎ **064/31068.** £5 ($8) adults; £2.50 ($4) children. Apr–Oct 10:30am, noon, 1:45pm, 3:15pm, 4:30pm, and 5:45pm.

Departing from the pier at Ross Castle, this enclosed water bus cruises the lakes for just over an hour. Reservations are suggested.

SPECTATOR SPORTS & OUTDOOR PURSUITS
SPECTATOR SPORTS

GAELIC GAMES   The people of Killarney are passionately devoted to the national sports of hurling and Gaelic football. Games are played almost every Sunday afternoon during the summer at **Fitzgerald Stadium,** Lewis Road, Killarney (☎ **064/31700**). For complete details, consult the local *Kerryman* newspaper or the Killarney tourist office.

HORSE RACING   Killarney has two annual horse-racing events in early May and mid-July. Each event lasts for three or four days and is very heavily attended. For more information, contact the **Killarney Racecourse,** Ross Road, Killarney (☎ **064/31125**) or the Killarney tourist office.

RECREATION

BICYCLING   The **Killarney National Park,** with its many lakeside and forest pathways, trails, and byways, is a paradise for bikers. Various types of bikes are available for rent, from 21-speed touring bikes and mountain bikes to tandems. Rental charges average £5 ($8) per day or £25 ($40) per week. Bicycles can be rented from the following shops: **Killarney Rent-a-Bike,** High Street (☎ 064/32578); **O'Neill Cycle Shop,** 6 Plunkett St., Killarney (☎ 064/31970); and **O'Sullivan's Bike Shop,** High Street, Killarney (☎ 064/31282). Most shops are open year-round from 9am to 6pm daily, with extended hours until 8 or 9pm in the summer months.

One great ride beginning in Killarney takes you through the Gap of Dunloe along a dirt forest road, where you'll see some of the best mountain scenery in the area; this can be made into a 35-mile loop if you return on N71.

FISHING   Fishing for salmon and brown trout is a big attraction in Killarney's unpolluted lakes and rivers. Brown trout fishing is free on the lakes, but a permit is necessary for the Rivers Flesk and Laune. A trout permit costs £2 to £5 ($3.20 to $8) per day.

Salmon fishing anywhere in Ireland requires a license; the cost is £3 ($4.80) per day or £10 ($16) for 21 days. In addition, some rivers also require a salmon permit, which will cost you £8 ($12.80) per day. Permits and licenses can be obtained at the Fishery Office at the **Knockreer Estate Office,** New Street, Killarney (☎ 064/31246).

For fishing tackle, bait, rod rental, and other fishing gear, as well as permits and licenses, try **O'Neill's,** 6 Plunkett St., Killarney (☎ 064/31970). This shop also arranges the hire of boats and ghillies (fishing guides). Gear and tackle can also be purchased from **Handy Stores,** Kenmare Place, Killarney (☎ 064/31188) and from Michael O'Brien at **Angler's Paradise,** Loreto Road, Killarney (☎ 064/33818).

GOLF   Visitors are always welcome at the twin 18-hole championship courses of the **Killarney Golf & Fishing Club,** Killorglin Road, Fossa, Killarney (☎ 064/31034), located 3 miles west of the town center. Widely praised as the most scenic golf setting in the world, these courses, known as "Killeen" and "Mahony's Point," are surrounded by lake and mountain vistas. Greens fees are £35 ($56) on either course.

HORSEBACK RIDING   Many trails in the Killarney area are suitable for horseback riding. The cost of hiring a horse ranges from £8 to £10 ($12.80 to $16) per hour at the following establishments: **Killarney Riding Stables,** R562, Ballydowney, Killarney (☎ 064/31686); **O'Donovan's Farm,** Mangerton Road, Muckross, Killarney (☎ 064/32238); and **Rocklands Stables,** Rockfield, Tralee Road, Killarney (☎ 064/32592). Lessons and week-long trail rides can also be arranged.

WALKING   Killarney is ideal for walking enthusiasts. On the outskirts of town, the **Killarney National Park** offers four signposted nature trails. The Mossy Woods Nature Trail starts near Muckross House near Muckross Lake and rambles 1 1/2 miles through yew woods along low cliffs. Old Boat House Nature Trail begins at the 19th-century boathouse below Muckross Gardens and leads half a mile around a small peninsula by Muckross Lake. Arthur Young's Walk (3 miles) starts on the road to Dinis, traverses natural yew woods, and then follows a 200-year-old road on the Muckross Peninsula. The Blue Pool Nature Trail goes from Muckross village through woodlands and past a small lake known as the Blue Pool (1 1/2 miles). Leaflets with maps of these four trails are available at the park visitor center.

Rising steeply from the south shore of Muckross Lake, Torc Mountain provides spectacular views of the Killarney Lakes and nearby MacGillycuddy's Reeks. Start at the Torc Waterfall parking lot, about 4 miles south of Killarney, and follow the trail to the top of the falls. At a "T" intersection turn left toward the top parking lot, and almost immediately turn right on the Old Kenmare Road, which follows a small stream along the south slopes of Torc Mountain. After leaving the woods, you will see Torc Mountain on your right. Look for a crescent-shaped gouge in the side of the road, about 30 feet across, with a small cairn at its far edge—this is the beginning of the path to the ridge top, marked somewhat erratically by cairns along the way. Return the way you came; the whole trip is 6 miles, takes about four hours, and is moderate in difficulty.

In addition to walking independently, visitors to the Killarney area can avail of a range of guided walks varying in grade and duration (from one day to a weekend or a full week). Priced from £12 ($19.20) per person, per day, these walks are operated by **Kerry Country Rambles,** P.O. Box 60, Killarney, Co. Kerry (☎ **064/35277;** fax 064/31903), which organizes and guides walks throughout Ireland for small parties and groups. Reservations are required.

For long-distance walkers, there is the 125-mile "Kerry Way," a signposted walking route that extends from Killarney around the Ring of Kerry (see "The Ring of Kerry," above).

SHOPPING

Vying for the business of tourists, the shops of Killarney keep their prices competitive. Shopping hours are usually Monday through Saturday 9am to 6pm, but during May through September or October most stores are open every day till 9 or 10pm. Almost all stores carry Kerry Glass products, a unique Killarney-made souvenir.

Although there are more souvenir and craft shops in Killarney than you can shake a stick (or shillelagh) at, here are a few of the best.

Anu Crafts
8 Main St. No phone.

This little shop specializes in jewelry, stationery, and clothing with Celtic design imprints and engravings inspired by the original art of Newgrange, the Book of Kells, and other historic symbols. The items range from T-shirts and art cards to jewelry made from stone, brass, ceramics, bronze, and silver.

Blarney Woollen Mills
10 Main St. ☎ **064/33222.**

A branch of the highly successful Co. Cork–based enterprise, this large store occupies a beautiful shop-front on the corner of Plunkett Street in the center of town. The wares range from hand-knit or hand-loomed Irish-made sweaters to tweeds, crystal, china, pottery, and souvenirs of all sizes, shapes, and prices.

Frank Lewis Gallery
6 Bridewell Lane. ☎ **064/34843.**

Housed in one of Killarney's enchanting lanes in a restored artisan's dwelling near the post office, this gallery shows and sells a wide variety of contemporary and traditional paintings, sculptures, and photographic work of the highest quality by some of Ireland's most acclaimed emerging artists. Exhibits change monthly.

Kerry Glass
College St. ☎ **064/32587.**

If you can't get to the Kerry Glass Studio outside of town (see "More Attractions," above), then stop at this outlet store for Killarney's colorful and distinctive glass, available in paperweights, figurines, vases, bowls, pendants, and more.

Killarney Art Gallery
52 High St. ☎ **064/34628.**

This shop-front gallery features original paintings from leading Irish artists, both from the Killarney area and elsewhere, as well as art supplies, Irish prints, and engravings.

Killarney Book Shop
32 Main St. ☎ **064/34108.**

Stop into this shop for books and maps on the history, legends, and lore of Killarney and Kerry, as well as for good maps of the area and other books of Irish and international interest. Catalogue available on request.

Quill's Woollen Market
1 High St. ☎ **064/32277.**

This is one of the best spots in town for hand-knit sweaters of all colors, sizes, and types, plus tweeds, mohair, and sheepskins. If you miss this one, there are also branches in Sneem and Kenmare on the Ring of Kerry, in Cork City, and the original shop at Ballingeary, Co. Cork.

Serendipity
15 College St. ☎ **064/31056.**

The shelves of this tidy shop feature a wide range of unusual crafts from local artisans, such as hand-thrown pottery, N. Mosse pottery, Stephen Pearce pottery, Jepoint glass, and handcrafted jewelry.

EVENING ENTERTAINMENT & PUBS

At the **Killarney Manor Banquet,** Loreto Road, Killarney (☎ **064/31551**) you can have a five-course dinner in 19th-century style with a complete program of songs, ballads, and dance. It's held in a stately 1840s stone-faced mansion that was built as a hotel and later served as a convent and school. The mansion is set on a hillside 2 miles south of town overlooking the Killarney panorama. Open from April through October, the banquet is staged five nights a week (usually closed on Sunday and Thursday) starting at 8pm. The price is £26 ($41.60) per person for complete banquet and dinner. It's also possible to attend the entertainment segment only for £9 ($14.40) from 9pm to 10:30pm. Reservations are required. AE, DC, MC, V.

Dero's Tours, 22 Main St., Killarney (☎ **064/31251**) offers a special bus and theater ticket to **Siamsa Tire,** the National Folk Theatre of Ireland, located at Town Park, Tralee, 20 miles northwest of Killarney. (See "Tralee After Dark" in the Tralee section, below.)

PUBS

Dunloe Lodge
Plunkett St. ☎ **064/32502.**

This simple pub in the heart of town has a friendly and comfortable atmosphere. Don't be surprised if some of its local patrons spontaneously pull out a harmonica, an accordion, a banjo, or a fiddle and start to play. You'll hear anything from Irish ballads to folk or rock music.

Kate Kearney's Cottage
Gap of Dunloe. ☎ **064/44146.**

Almost everyone who ventures through the famous Gap first visits this former coaching inn, which is named for a woman who was believed to be a witch. Today this outpost, 9 miles west of town, is a refreshment stop at the start of the Gap, with souvenirs on sale. From May through September, traditional music is performed on Sunday, Wednesday, and Friday evenings from 9 to 11:30pm.

The Laurels

Main St. ☎ **064/31149.**

The rafters ring here to the lilt of Irish song each evening. Ballad singers are slated nightly from April through October, starting at 9pm.

Molly Darcy's

Muckross Village, Muckross Rd. ☎ **064/31938.**

Located across from Muckross House, this is one of Killarney's best traditional pubs, with a thatched roof, stone walls, an oak-beamed ceiling, open fireplaces, alcoves, snugs (private rooms), and lots of Killarney memorabilia. There's dancing on Sunday evenings.

Scotts Beer Garden

College St. ☎ **064/31060.**

On a warm summer's night, this is the place to enjoy a drink in an outdoor beer garden. Music ranges from ballads to piano or jazz.

Tatler Jack

Plunkett St. ☎ **064/32361.**

This traditional pub is a favorite gathering place for followers of Gaelic football and hurling. Traditional music or ballads are on tap from June through September, nightly from 9:30pm.

3 The Dingle Peninsula

Dingle Town is 30 miles W of Tralee and 50 miles NW of Killarney.

GETTING THERE Bus Eireann (☎ 066/23566) provides daily coach service to Dingle from all parts of Ireland. The boarding and drop-off point is on Upper Main Street.

If you're driving from Tralee to Dingle, follow R559, or take R561 from Castlemaine.

GETTING AROUND By Public Transport Dingle Town has no local bus service, although **Bus Eireann** (☎ 066/23566) provides service from Dingle to other towns on the peninsula. For local taxi transport, contact **V. Flannery** (☎ 066/51163) or **John Sheehy** (☎ 066/51301).

On Foot The best way to get around Dingle Town, with its narrow, winding, and hilly streets, is to walk. The town is small and compact and easy to get to know.

By Car To see the sights beyond the town, you will need to drive westward along R559 or to take one of the sightseeing tours suggested below.

VISITOR INFORMATION The Dingle Tourist Office is located on Main Street, Dingle (☎ 066/51188). It is open seasonally, usually mid-April through June Monday through Saturday 9:30am to 6pm and Sunday 11am to 5pm, July to August Monday through Saturday 9:30am to 7pm and Sunday 11am to 5pm, and September Monday through Saturday 9:30am to 6pm.

FAST FACTS: THE DINGLE PENINSULA

Area Code The area code for most Dingle numbers is 066.

Hospital The **Dingle District Hospital** is on Upper Main Street, Dingle (☎ 066/51455).

Library   The Dingle District Library is on Green Street, Dingle (☎ 066/51499).
Local Newspapers & Media   *In & About Dingle Peninsula* is a newspaper-style
publication distributed free at hotels, restaurants, shops, and at the tourist office. It
lists events, attractions, activities, and more.
Police   The local **Garda Station** is at Holy Ground, Dingle (☎ 066/51522).

A FEW WORDS ABOUT DINGLE

Like the Iveragh Peninsula, Dingle has a spectacularly scenic peripheral road, along
which there has blossomed over time a substantial tacky tourist trade. As soon as you
veer off the main roads, however, or penetrate to such far hinterlands of the peninsula as the Blasket Islands or Brandon Head, you'll discover extraordinary desolate
beauty seemingly worlds away from the tour buses and shamrock-filled shops.

Don't miss Slea Head, at the southwestern extremity of the Dingle peninsula, a
place of pristine beaches, great walks, and fascinating archaeological remains. The
village of Dunquin is stunningly situated between Slea Head and Clogher Head, and
is home to the Blasket Centre. Dunbeg Fort sits on a rocky promontory just south
of Slea Head, its walls rising from the cliff edge, and although much of the fort
has fallen into the sea since it was built, the place is well worth a visit at the bargain-
basement rate of £1 ($1.60) per person. From Slea Head, the Dingle Way contin-
ues east to Dingle town (15 miles) or north along the coast toward Ballyferriter.

Just offshore from Dunquin are the seven Blasket Islands; a ferry (☎ 066/56455)
connects Great Blasket with the mainland when the weather permits. The islands
were abandoned by the last permanent residents in 1953, and now are only inhabited by a few summer visitors who share the place with the seals and seabirds. There
is a magnificent 8-mile walk to the west end of Great Blasket and back, passing sea
cliffs and ivory beaches; you can stop along the way at the only cafe on the island,
which serves lunch and dinner.

East of Ballyferriter is **Gallarus Oratory,** one of the best-preserved early Christian
church buildings in Ireland. With a shape much like an overturned boat, it's constructed
of unmortared stone, yet is still completely watertight after more than 1,000 years.

ATTRACTIONS

✪ Ionad An Bhlascaoid Mhoir / The Blasket Centre
Dunquin, Co. Kerry. ☎ 066/56371. Admission £2 ($3.20) adults, £1.50 ($2.40) seniors,
£1 ($1.60) children and students. Easter–Sept, daily 10am–6pm.

This newly opened T-shaped heritage center is perched on the westerly tip of the
Dingle Peninsula, overlooking the Atlantic waters and the distant vistas of the remote
Blasket Islands. The Great Blasket was once an outpost of Irish civilization and
nurturing ground for a small group of great Irish-language writers, but its inhabitants abandoned the island in 1953. Through a series of displays, exhibits, and a video
presentation, this center celebrates the cultural and literary traditions of the Blaskets
and the history of Corca Dhuibhne, the Gaeltacht area. This center also has a research
room, a bookshop specializing in local literature, and a wide-windowed restaurant
with views of the Blaskets.

✪ Ceardlann Na Coille
The Wood, Dingle. ☎ 066/51778. Free admission. Daily 10am–6pm.

Just west of the Dingle Marina, this cluster of traditional cottages is a circular craft
village, set on a hillside above the town and harbor. Each workshop is staffed by a
local craft worker who produces and sells his or her craft. Handmade felts, fun jewelry and mosaics, and Irish traditional music are offered, as well as silver jewelry and

ceramic pictures. A cafe on the premises serves excellent homemade soups, salads, and hot dishes.

SIGHTSEEING TOURS

Sciuird Tours

Holy Ground, Dingle. ☎ **066/51937.** £7 ($11.20) per person. May–Sept, daily 11am, 2pm, and 5pm.

These archaeological tours, lasting two to three hours, are led by a local expert. They involve a short bus journey and some easy walking. Four or five monuments from the Stone Age to medieval times are visited. All tours start from the top of the Pier. Reservations suggested.

Fungie the Dolphin Tours

The Pier, Dingle. ☎ **066/51967** or 066/51163. £6 ($9.60) adults, £3 ($4.80) children under 12. Year-round daily 10am–5pm.

Visitors are ferried out into the nearby waters via fishing boats to see the famous Dingle dolphin, Fungie. Trips last about one hour and depart on the hour. Early morning swimming-with-Fungie trips can be arranged.

Hidden Ireland Tours

Dingle. ☎ **066/51868.** £10–£35 ($16–$56) depending on tour. May–Sept, daily half-day walks from 9:30am–1:30pm and 2–6pm; full-day walks from 10am–5pm.

Con Moriarty, a local exponent of active travel, conducts a variety of walking tours around the cliff walks, hills, mountains, woods, and lakelands of Dingle, interspersing commentaries on local history, archaeology, folklore, and culture along the way. Participants are advised to bring sturdy footwear and rain/windproof clothing. Tours can be custom-designed for those who prefer to travel by bike or car. Reservations necessary.

SPORTS & OUTDOOR PURSUITS

BICYCLING   Mountain bikes can be rented at **The Mountain Man,** Strand Street, Dingle (☎ **066/51868**), for £6 ($9.60) per day or £30 ($48) per week; rear panniers are included. Mike Shea knows the area well, and can suggest a number of one-day or overnight touring options on the Dingle Peninsula. A great day trip is the road out to the tip of the Peninsula past Slea Head and Clogher Head, which is outrageously beautiful and not too hilly. Touring and mountain bikes are also available year-round from **Foxy John Moriarty,** Main Street, Dingle (☎ **066/51316**), from £5 ($8) per day or £25 ($40) per week.

BIRD-WATCHING   Great Blasket Island is of some interest for the fall passerine migration, and in summer there is a great abundance of nesting seabirds on the small, uninhabited islands surrounding Great Blasket, including more than 20,000 pairs of Storm Petrels. From Clogher Head north of Dunquin at the western extremity of the Dingle Peninsula, rare autumn migrants can sometimes be seen. Inch Peninsula, extending into Castlemaine Harbour south of Inch town, is a wintering ground for Brent geese, which arrive here in late August and move on in April; there is also a large wigeon population during the fall.

HORSEBACK RIDING   At **Milltown House,** Dingle, Co. Kerry. (☎ **066/ 52018;** fax 066/51095), rides are available along nearby beaches or through the mountains; cost is £15 ($24) for a one-hour ride. Three-day packages including accommodation, meals, and riding are offered for £300 ($480) per person, assuming double occupancy.

DIVING The **Dingle Diving Centre,** Milltown, Dingle, Co. Kerry (☎ **066/ 51325**), has lessons for beginners and boat dives for the experienced. A one-hour pool lesson followed by an ocean dive is £40 ($64); boat dives start at £15 ($24) per dive.

GOLF Situated 10 miles west of Dingle town on the western edge of the Dingle Peninsula, overlooking the waters of the Atlantic, the **Dingle Golf Club** (Golf Chumann Ceann Sibeal), Ballyferriter (☎ **066/56255**), welcomes visitors to play its 18-hole, par-72 course. Greens fees are £20 ($32) per round.

SAILING Sailing the beautiful waters of Dingle Bay is a relaxing way to enjoy the coastline. **John Doyle,** 3 John St., Dingle (☎ **066/51174**), offers skippered sailing trips from Dingle Marina on board his 32-foot sailing cruiser, *Canna.* The price is £60 ($96) for a half day and £120 ($192) for a full day, for up to four persons. All cruises are dependent on the weather and advance reservations are required.

Capt. Michael O'Connor, The Old Stone House, Cliddaun, Dingle (☎ **066/ 59882**), offers seven-hour trips from the Marina on board the *Kimberly Laura,* a 41-foot cutter-rigged sailing yacht. The Dingle price is £40 ($64) per person including lunch and snacks, for up to eight persons. Reservations are required.

SWIMMING WITH A DOLPHIN A unique watersport in Dingle Bay is to swim with the resident dolphin, known as Fungie. Although Fungie can swim about 25 miles per hour, he seems willing to slow down and romp at slower speeds in the waters with human visitors. To arrange a dolphin encounter, contact **Seventh Wave,** Milltown, Slea Head Road, Dingle (☎ **066/51548**). They will advise and outfit you in preparation for a dolphin encounter. You can rent a wetsuit, mask, snorkel, foot fins, and duffel bag for £10 ($16) for three hours or £15 ($24) overnight. The office, which is open year-round daily from 10am to 2pm and 3 to 6pm, also includes an exhibition center on dolphins and whales and their place in our environment.

WALKING The **Dingle Way** begins in Tralee and circles the peninsula, covering 95 miles of gorgeous mountain and coastal landscape. The most rugged section is along Brandon Head, where the trail passes between Mount Brandon and the ocean; the views are tremendous, but the walk is long (about 15 miles, averaging nine hours) and strenuous, and should only be attempted when the sky is clear. The section between Dunquin and Ballyferriter (also 15 miles) follows an especially lovely stretch of coast. For more information see *The Dingle Way Map Guide,* available in local tourist offices and shops.

Mount Eagle rises steeply from the sea at the western tip of the Dingle Peninsula, and the summit commands tremendous views of the sweeping Dingle coastline and the nearby mountains of the Iveragh Peninsula. There is a road which extends most of the way to the summit from the south side; it is signposted off the R559 between Fahan and Ventry. Park your car at the television broadcasting tower and walk up a steep path to the summit.

There are several good walks in the vicinity of Conor Pass. From Dingle, R560 climbs steeply to the top of a high ridge, rimmed on the north side by a line of crags and cliffs. The road is extremely narrow and serpentine, so this isn't a good place to be driving on a stormy or foggy day. At the pass (about 5 miles outside Dingle town) there is a parking lot, and paths extending along the ridge in both directions. The paths peter out after a while, but finding your way on the ridge is quite easy on a clear day; be sure to keep a safe distance from the cliff edge. To the northwest are the massive slopes of Mount Brandon, the second highest mountain in Ireland, and to the northeast the waters of Brandon Bay. One mile north of the pass on R560 there is another parking lot; leave your vehicle here and walk 100 yards uphill to the edge of a small lake rimmed by a crescent-shaped ridge. This is a great spot for a picnic lunch or a walk around the lake (about one hour).

The Inch Peninsula offers miles of walking along the east-side beach or through the dunes; there is a parking lot off R561 just west of Inch town.

SHOPPING

Annascaul Pottery
Green St. Courtyard, off Green St., Dingle. ☎ **066/57186.**

Colorful locally made pottery and ceramics, with wildflower designs, are on sale here, in all sizes and shapes, including jewelry. Open daily Easter through October from 10:30am to 6pm. The factory at nearby Annascaul is open year-round.

Brian De Staic
The Wood, Dingle. ☎ **066/51298.**

Considered by many as Ireland's leading goldsmith, Brian de Staic plies his trade in his workshop, located just west of the Dingle Pier. He specializes in unusual Irish jewelry, handcrafted and engraved with the letters of the Ogham alphabet, an ancient Irish form of writing dating from the 3rd century. His collection includes pendants, bracelets, earrings, cuff links, brooches, and tie clips. There are two other retail shops: Green Street, Dingle (☎ 066/51298), and 18 High St., Killarney (☎ 064/33822). Shop hours are November to May, Monday to Saturday 9am to 6pm; June to October, daily 9am to 6pm.

Green Lane Gallery
Green St., Dingle. ☎ **066/52018.**

This gallery/shop offers a wide selection of modern painting and sculpture created by leading Irish artists. Open daily 11am to 7pm.

✪ Holden Leathergoods / Sparan Sioda (The Silk Purse)
Main St., Dingle, Co. Kerry. ☎ **066/51896.**

Established in 1989 by Jackie and Conor Holden, this shop offers beautiful handcrafted suede- and silk-lined leather handbags, suede and leather pouches, and duffel and travel bags, as well as briefcases, belts, wallets, key cases, and billfolds. Visitors are also welcome to visit their workshop in a converted schoolhouse, 4 miles west of town on the Ventry road (R559), Baile an Ghoilin, Dingle Harbour (☎ 066/51796). Open Easter to May, Monday to Saturday 9:30am to 6pm and Sunday, noon to 5pm; June, Monday to Saturday 9am to 7pm, Sunday 11am to 6pm; July and August, Monday to Saturday, 9am to 9pm, Sunday 11am to 6pm; September through March, Monday to Saturday 10am to 6pm.

Leac A Re
Strand St., Dingle. ☎ **066/51138.**

This new shop features dolphin arts and crafts, as well as a unique array of local crafts, from woollens and blankets to pottery and posters. You may find use for a local specialty footwarmer sold here and known as "The Brandon sock."

✪ Lisbeth Mulcahy / The Weavers' Shop
Green St., Dingle. ☎ **066/51688.**

One of Ireland's leading weavers, Lisbeth creates fabrics and tapestries inspired by seasonal changes in the Irish landscape and seascape. Pure wool, Irish linen/cotton, and alpaca are used in the weaving of scarves, shawls, knee rugs, wall hangings, tapestries, table mats, and napkins. Open October through May, Monday through

Saturday 9am to 6pm; June to September, Monday through Saturday 9am to 9pm and Sunday 10am to 6pm.

Louis Mulcahy Pottery

Clogher, Ballyferriter, Co. Kerry. ☎ **066/56229.**

Located north of Dunquin, this is a large working pottery studio, producing a range of pottery made from local clay and glazes devised at the shop. The finished products include giant vases, teapots, platters, and huge lamps. Complementary furniture and hand-decorated silk and cotton lamp shades are available, as well as a selection of Lisbeth Mulcahy's tapestries and weavings. Open Monday thorough Saturday 9am to 6pm, Sunday 10am to 6pm, except December 25 to 27.

ACCOMMODATIONS
MODERATE

Benner's Hotel

Main St., Dingle, Co. Kerry. ☎ **066/51638.** Fax 066/51412. 25 rms. TV TEL. £60–£90 ($96–$144) double. Includes full Irish breakfast and service charge. AE, DC, MC, V.

One of the few hostelries that is open year-round, this hotel is in the heart of town. The lovely Georgian doorway with fanlight at the front entrance sets the tone for guests checking in. Dating from more than 250 years ago and totally updated in recent years, the hotel is a blend of old-world charm and modern comforts, and is furnished with Irish antique pine furniture throughout, including four-poster beds and armoires in the guest rooms. Facilities include a restaurant with tall and wide-paned windows overlooking a walled garden, and two bars, including the Boston Bar.

Dingle Sceilig (Ostan Na Sceilge)

Annascaul Rd., Dingle, Co. Kerry. ☎ **800/528-1234** from the U.S., or 066/51144. Fax 066/51501. 100 rms. TV TEL. £106 ($169.60) double. Service charge 10%. Rates include full breakfast. AE, MC, V. Closed mid-Nov to mid-Mar.

Named for the fabled Sceilig (or Skellig) Rocks off the coast, this modern three-story hotel enjoys an idyllic location next to Dingle Bay on the eastern edge of town. Expanded and totally refurbished in recent years by the Cluskey family, it has a pleasing facade with a mansardlike roof that fits well in the local panorama of mountain and sea. The public areas are decorated with Irish pine and brass touches, and the guest rooms, with lovely views of the bay and countryside, are modern with light woods and pastel-toned fabrics and wall coverings. The Coastguard Conservatory Restaurant and Gallarus Lounge both offer good views of Dingle Bay, the Bistro Restaurant serves bar food all day, and a nautical atmosphere pervades The Blaskets Bar. For recreation, the hotel has an indoor heated swimming pool, sauna, tennis court, table tennis, and a snooker room. A new leisure center is under construction. There's a guest laundry on the premises.

✪ Doyle's Townhouse

5 John St., Dingle, Co. Kerry. ☎ **800/223-6510** from the U.S., or 066/51174. Fax 066/51816. 12 rms and 4 suites. TV TEL. £66 ($105.60) double. Service charge 10%. Rates include full breakfast. DC, MC, V. Closed mid-Nov to mid-Mar.

An outgrowth of the successful Doyle's Seafood Restaurant next door, this three-story guest house is a favorite Dingle hideaway. Designed to reflect an old-world ambience, it has a lovely Victorian fireplace in the main sitting room area and many of the antique fixtures date from 250 years or more. Period pieces and country pine predominate in the bedrooms, although the accouterments are totally up-to-date, with semi-orthopedic beds, bathrooms of Italian marble, towel warmers, and hair dryers. Front rooms look out onto the town while the back rooms have either a balcony or patio and face a garden, with mountain vistas in the background.

INEXPENSIVE

Bambury's Guest House

Mail Rd., Dingle, Co. Kerry. ☎ **066/51244.** Fax 066/51786. 12 rms. TV TEL. £26–£45 ($41.60–$72) double. No service charge. Rates include full breakfast. MC, V. Open year-round.

This lovely two-story pink-toned guest house stands out as you enter Dingle from the east. It has a modernized Tudor-style facade, with wide-paned windows. Guest rooms are bright and contemporary, with lovely views of the town or bay. It's an easy two-minute walk to the center of town.

Barnagh Bridge Country Guesthouse

Cappalough, Camp, Dingle, Co. Kerry. ☎ **066/30145.** Fax 066/30299. 5 rms. TV TEL. £36–£44 ($57.60–$70.40) double. No service charge. Rates include full breakfast. MC, V. Closed Dec.

Opened in 1993 on a hillside overlooking Tralee Bay, almost equidistant between Tralee and Dingle, this stunning two-story modern house was built as a guest house by the Williams family, and is an ideal touring base for those who prefer a country setting to a town. Each guest room is named and furnished with the theme and colors of flowers from the surrounding gardens, such as Fuschia, Blue Bell, and Rose. The newly redecorated rooms have modern light wood furnishings, and most have views of the mountains and sea.

✪ Greenmount House

John St., Dingle, Co. Kerry. ☎ **066/51414.** 12 rms. TV TEL. £32–£50 ($51.20–$80) double. No service charge. Rates include full breakfast. No credit cards. Closed last week of Dec.

Perched on a hill overlooking Dingle Bay and town, this modern bungalow-style bed-and-breakfast home is a standout in its category. It has all the comforts of a hotel at bargain prices, including bedrooms decorated with contemporary furnishings, a public sitting room with an open fireplace, and a sunlit conservatory filled with plants. The breakfasts, ranging from smoked salmon omelets to ham-and-pineapple toasties, have garnered many an award for enthusiastic proprietors Mary and John Curran.

Slea Head Farm

Couminole, Dunquin, Ventry, Co. Kerry. ☎ **066/56120.** 5 rms (2 with bath). £26–£30 ($41.60–$48) double. No service charge. Rates include full breakfast. EU, MC, V. Open May–Oct. On R559, first house on left past Slea Head.

The waters of the Atlantic wash the rocks immediately below this cozy stone farmhouse, which has private access to the glorious Couminole Strand. All the rooms have great sea views, looking out over Dunmore Head and the Blasket Islands; the two in the older part of the house are small, but have more character than the somewhat bland new rooms. The house is on the Dingle Way, a day's walk from Dingle town, and is often used as a base by hikers. The Blasket Island Ferry is 1 1/2 miles away.

The house itself provides merely adequate accommodation, but it is situated in the midst of one of the most beautiful and unspoiled stretches of seacoast in Ireland, a fact which more than compensates for its slight austerity.

DINING

EXPENSIVE/MODERATE

Beginish

Green St., Dingle. ☎ **066/51588.** Reservations recommended. Lunch main courses £3.50–£6.95 ($5.60–$11.10), dinner main courses £10–£15 ($16–$24). AE, MC, V. Tues–Sun 12:30–2:15pm and 6–10pm. Closed mid-Nov to mid-Mar. SEAFOOD.

Situated in a Georgian town house in the heart of Dingle, this restaurant is named for one of the Blasket Islands off the coast, and the paintings on the walls show the seascapes that surround the island. There are two dining rooms, one a traditional room with a fireplace and the other a conservatory overlooking the back gardens. The varied menu offers dishes such as seafood à la nage (salmon, mussels, prawns, scallops, monkfish in Pernod-scented juice), black sole on the bone, scalloped wild salmon with tarragon sauce, and fillet of beef with cognac and grilled peppercorn sauce. For dessert, chef Pat Moore's hot rhubarb soufflé tart is legendary in these parts.

✪ Doyle's Seafood Bar

4 John St., Dingle. ☎ **066/51174.** Reservations necessary. Main courses £11.50–£18 ($18.40–$28.80). DC, MC, V. Mon–Sat 6–10pm. Closed mid-Nov to mid-Mar. SEAFOOD.

It is almost 25 years since John and Stella Doyle left Dublin and settled in Dingle to open the town's first seafood bar. With John meeting the fishing boats each morning and bringing in the best of the day's catch, and Stella plying her culinary skills in the kitchen, this winning combination has achieved international acclaim and is the benchmark of all of Dingle's eateries. The atmosphere is homey, with stone walls and floors, sugan (a kind of straw) chairs, tweedy place mats, and old Dingle sketches. All the ingredients come either from the sea, the Doyles' own gardens, or nearby farms—and the Doyles even smoke their own salmon. Specialties include baked fillet of lemon sole with prawn sauce, salmon fillet with puff pastry with sorrel sauce, rack of lamb, and a signature platter of seafood (sole, salmon, lobster, oysters, and crab claws).

The Half Door

3 John St., Dingle. ☎ **066/51600.** Reservations recommended. Lunch main courses £5–£20 ($8–$32); dinner main courses £11–£20 ($17.60–$32). AE, MC, V. Easter–Oct, Wed–Mon 12:30–2:30pm and 6–10pm. Closed Nov–Easter. SEAFOOD/INTERNATIONAL.

Aptly named, with a traditional half-door at the entrance, this restaurant exudes a country cottage atmosphere, with exposed-brick walls, low ceilings, arches, and vintage furnishings that include copper pots and an original stove, yet there is also a bright and airy conservatory at the back. The menu combines old and new, with dishes such as lobster thermidor, salmon en croûte, fillet of plaice in savory crust with mustard sauce, and roast farm duck with honey and lime sauce.

✪ Lord Baker

Main St., Dingle. ☎ **066/51277.** Reservations suggested for dinner. Bar food £2–£10 ($3.20–$16); dinner main courses £10–£20 ($16–$32). AE, MC, V. Daily 11:30am–2:30pm and 6–10pm. Closed Christmas. IRISH/SEAFOOD.

Named after a 19th-century Dingle poet, politician, and publican, this restaurant is part of a building that is supposed to be the oldest pub in Dingle. The decor blends an old-world stone fireplace and cozy alcoves with a sunlit conservatory and art deco touches. The menu offers standard bar food as well as crab claws or prawns in garlic butter, fried scampi, Kerry oysters, seafood Mornay, and steaks. The full dinner specialties include sole stuffed with smoked salmon and spinach in cheese sauce, lobster thermidor, and rack of lamb.

MODERATE

Fenton's

Green St., Dingle. ☎ **066/51209.** Reservations recommended. Lunch main courses £2.50–£5.95 ($4–$9.50), dinner main courses £8.95–£14.95 ($14.30–$23.90), and early bird (6–7pm) 3-course dinner for £11.50 ($18.40). AE, DC, MC, V. Tues–Sun 12:30–3:30pm and 6–10pm. Closed Nov to mid-Mar. INTERNATIONAL.

Situated in the heart of town, this restaurant combines a country cottage interior of pine furniture and stone walls with a bright and airy garden courtyard patio setting that seats 12 people for alfresco dining. The diverse menu offers dishes such as hot buttered lobster, mussels in garlic with white wine sauce, and medaillons of fillet steak on a garlic croûte topped with Cashel blue cheese.

Waterside

Strand St., Dingle. ☎ **066/51458.** Reservations recommended for dinner. Cafe items £2–£10 ($3.20–$16); restaurant main courses £9–£13 ($14.40–$20.80). MC, V. Easter–Sept, cafe daily 10am–6pm; restaurant June–Aug, 7–10pm. Closed Oct–Easter. INTERNATIONAL.

For a daytime snack with a Dingle ambience, this restaurant offers a setting opposite the busy town marina. It is a bright and airy place with a decor of blue and white, enhanced by seasonal flowers and plants. There is seating in a sunlit conservatory-style room as well as on an outdoor patio. It operates as a cafe by day and as a full-service restaurant on summer nights. The choices include oysters on the half-shell, cockles and mussels sandwiches, prawn and crab seafood salads, and soups, as well as quiches, omelets, crepes, and pastries. The evening menu concentrates on local seafood and steaks.

INEXPENSIVE/BUDGET

✪ An Cafe Liteartha

Dykegate St., Dingle. ☎ **066/51388.** Reservations not necessary. All items £1–£6 ($1.60–$9.60). No credit cards. Mon–Sat 9am–6pm with extended hours in summer. IRISH/SELF-SERVICE.

A combination bookstore and cafe, this is a treasure trove for all types of books and maps of Irish interest, and particularly on life in this corner of Co. Kerry. The cafe section features soups, salads, seafoods, and freshly baked scones and cakes, as well as traditional dishes such as Irish stew. It's an ideal spot to browse and to enjoy a quick lunch or snack in the middle of town.

Old Smokehouse

Main St., Dingle. ☎ **066/51147.** Reservations not necessary. All items £1.50–£8 ($2.40–$12.80). MC, V. Apr–May noon–6pm, closed Tues; June–Oct daily noon–10pm; Nov–Jan 15 daily noon–6pm. INTERNATIONAL.

Situated in the heart of town beside a flowing stream, this restaurant is housed in an old stone building with a country kitchen decor, including a turf fireplace, pinewood hutch with antique crockery, and paintings of the Dingle area. There is also an outdoor patio for alfresco dining in good weather. Breakfast, snacks, morning coffee, evening meals, lunch, and take-out service are all available. The menu ranges from freshly made salads and seafood sandwiches to hot dishes such as beef in Guinness, chicken Kiev, beef lasagna, or deep-fried cod.

PUBS

An Droichead Beag / The Small Bridge

Lower Main St., Dingle. ☎ **066/51723.**

With an old-Dingle decor and a friendly atmosphere, this pub, right in the heart of town, draws crowds each night throughout the year for its spontaneous sessions of traditional Irish music, usually starting at 9:30pm. Be sure to arrive early if you want even standing room!

Dick Macks

Green St., Dingle. ☎ **066/51070.**

Although Richard "Dick" Mack died a few years ago, his family keeps on the traditions of this unique pub where Dick handcrafted leather boots, belts, and other items in between his pub chores. The small leather shop is still on the left, opposite a tiny bar. The walls are lined with old pictures, books, and mugs, all part of the Dick Mack legend. This pub is a favorite with the locals.

Kruger's Guest House and Bar

Ballinaraha, Dunquin, Co. Kerry. ☎ 066/56127.

Deep in the outer reaches of the Dingle Peninsula, this pub is a social center of the Irish-speaking district. The unusual name is attributed to its former owner, Muiris "Kruger" Kavanagh, a local man who was known as a fighter at school, and so was nicknamed "Kruger" after Paulus Kruger, a famous Boer leader. The local Kruger eventually emigrated to the United States, where he worked variously as a bodyguard, truck driver, male nurse, journalist, and then as PR man of the Schubert Theater Company of New York City. After 16 years, he returned to Dunquin and opened this pub, to which he then drew his great circle of friends from the entertainment field on visits. Although Kruger is gone now, his pub is still an entertainment hub, with nightly performances of the "sean-nos" Irish singing (an old, unaccompanied style) plus traditional music and step dancing on weekends.

O'Flaherty's

Bridge St., Dingle. ☎ **066/51461.**

The true flavor of the Dingle Peninsula is reflected in this rustic pub. The walls are lined with old posters, prints, clippings, and photos of Irish literary figures of long ago. You'll also see poems on the Dingle area by local authors and favorite Gaelic phrases, many of which are just tacked up and curling at the edges. In the evenings, traditional music sessions are usually on tap.

4 Tralee

20 miles NW of Killarney.

GETTING THERE   **Aer Lingus** operates daily nonstop flights from Dublin into **Kerry County Airport,** Farranfore, Co. Kerry (☎ **066/64644**), about 15 miles south of Tralee.

Buses from all parts of Ireland arrive daily at the **Bus Eireann Depot,** John Joe Sheehy Road, Tralee (☎ **066/23566**).

Rail services from major cities into Tralee arrive at the **Irish Rail Station,** John Joe Sheehy Road, Tralee (☎ **066/23522**).

Four major national roads converge on Tralee: N69 and N21 from Limerick and the north, N70 from the Ring of Kerry and points south, and N22 from Killarney, Cork, and the east.

GETTING AROUND   The best way to get around Tralee's downtown area is to walk. If you prefer to take a taxi, call the **Taxi Rank** (8am to midnight), Denny Street (☎ **066/23259**); **Kingdom Cabs,** Boherbee, Tralee (☎ **066/27828**); or **Tralee Radio Cabs,** Monavelley, Tralee (☎ **066/25451**).

VISITOR INFORMATION   The **Tralee Tourist Office,** Ashe Memorial Hall, Denny Street, Tralee (☎ **066/21288**), offers information on Tralee and the Dingle Peninsula. It is open year-round Tuesday through Saturday 9am to 1pm and 2 to 5pm, with extended hours in the summer season. There is also a first-rate cafe on the premises.

FAST FACTS: TRALEE

Area Code   The area code for most numbers in the Tralee area is **066.**

Drugstore   Try **Kelly's Chemist,** The Mall, Tralee (☎ **066/21302**).

Dry Cleaning & Laundry   The Laundry, Pembroke Street, Tralee (☎ **066/ 23214**), and **True Care Dry Cleaners,** 3 High St. (☎ **066/23245**), are good bets.

Hospital   Bon Secours Hospital is located on Strand Street, Tralee (☎ **066/21966**), and **Tralee General Hospital** is on Killarney road (N22), Tralee (☎ **066/26222**).

Library   The **County Kerry Library** is on Moydewell Road, Tralee (☎ **066/ 21200**).

Newspapers & Local Media   The weekly newspaper, *The Kerryman,* covers all local events. The local radio station, Radio Kerry/97 FM, broadcasts from Park View, Tralee (☎ **066/23666**).

Police   The local **Garda Station** is located off High Street, Tralee (☎ **066/22022**).

Photographic Supplies   Try **Kennelly's Photocentre, Ltd.,** 6 Castle St. (☎ **066/ 23966**).

A FEW WORDS ABOUT TRALEE

Tralee is the commercial center of Co. Kerry, and with its population of 22,000 it's three times the size of Killarney. This is more a functioning town than a tourist center, and locals outnumber visitors except during the ever-popular "Rose of Tralee" festival in August. The town is the permanent home of the National Folk Theatre of Ireland, Siamsa Tire, open year-round but most active during July and August.

The harbor of Tralee is located 4 miles northwest of the town, at Fenit. A major sailing center, Fenit is the spot where St. Brendan the Navigator was born in 484, or so it's said. Brendan is credited with sailing the Atlantic in a small leather boat known as a coracle, and discovering America long before Columbus.

ATTRACTIONS

Kerry the Kingdom

Ashe Memorial Hall, Denny St., Tralee. ☎ **066/27777.** Admission £4 adults ($6.40); £2.50 ($4) children. Daily July–Aug 9:30am–6pm; Sept–June 3–5pm.

One of Ireland's largest indoor heritage centers, the Kingdom offers three separate attractions that give an in-depth look at 7,000 years of life in Co. Kerry. A 10-minute video, *Kerry in Colour,* presents the seascapes and landscapes of Kerry; the Kerry County Museum chronologically examines the county's music, history, legends, and archaeology through interactive and hands-on exhibits; and the exhibit on Gaelic football is unique. Many items of local origin that were previously on view at the National Museum in Dublin are now here. Complete with lighting effects and aromas, a theme park–style ride called Geraldine Tralee takes you through a re-creation of Tralee's streets, houses, and abbeys during the Middle Ages.

Blennerville Windmill

R559, Blennerville, Co. Kerry. ☎ **066/21064.** Admission £2.50 ($4) adults, £2 ($3.20) seniors and students, £1.50 ($2.40) children over 5. Mar–Oct Mon–Sat 1–6pm, Sun 1–6pm (8pm in Aug).

Located just 3 miles west of Tralee and reaching 65 feet into the sky, this landmark mill is the largest working windmill in Ireland or Britain. Built in 1800 by Sir Rowland Blennerhasset, it flourished until 1850. After decades of neglect, it was restored in the early 1990s and is now fully operational, producing five tons of ground whole meal flour per week. The visitor complex has an emigration exhibition center, an audiovisual theater, craft workshops, and a cafe.

✪ Tralee Steam Railway

Ballyard, Tralee. ☎ 066/28888. £2.50 ($4) adults; £1.50 ($2.40) children. Apr Sun 11am–5:30pm, May and Sept daily noon–5:30pm, June–Aug daily 11am–5:30pm. Closed on second Monday of each month for maintenance.

Europe's most westerly railway, this restored steam train offers narrated, scenic 2-mile trips from Tralee's Ballyard Station to Blennerville. It uses equipment that was once a part of the Tralee and Dingle Light Railway (1891–1953), one of the world's most famous narrow-gauge railways. Trains run on the hour from Tralee and on the half-hour from Blennerville.

SIGHTSEEING TOURS

During July and August, **Tralee Tourism,** Ostendia, Oakpark, Tralee (☎ 066/25364) sponsors guided walks around Tralee, taking in the local churches, the Square, Market Lane, Ashe Hall, Siamsa Tire, the Town Park, and principal streets. Departures are at 10am and 4 and 9pm. After the 9pm walks, participants are taken to the local pubs to enjoy folk and traditional music. Cost is £2 ($3.20).

SPECTATOR SPORTS & OUTDOOR PURSUITS

SPECTATOR SPORTS

HORSE RACING   Horse racing takes place twice a year (in early June and late August) at Ballybeggan Park, Racecourse Road, Tralee (☎ 066/36148 and, on race days, 066/26188). Post time is usually 2:30pm. Admission is £7 ($11.20) adults, £3.50 ($5.60) seniors and students, and free for children under 14.

DOG RACING   Greyhounds race year-round on Tuesday and Friday nights from 8pm at the **Kingdom Greyhound Racing Track,** Oakview, Brewery Road, Tralee (☎ 066/24033). Admission is £3 ($4.80) per person, including program.

RECREATION

GOLF   Like its neighbor Killarney, Tralee is great golfing turf, particularly at the **Tralee Golf Club,** Fenit/Churchill Road, West Barrow, Ardfert (☎ 066/36379). Overlooking the Atlantic 8 miles northwest of Tralee, this was the first Arnold Palmer–designed golf course in Europe. One of Ireland's newer courses, it's expected in time to rank among the great courses of the world. Greens fees are £30 ($48) on weekdays and £40 ($64) on weekends.

About 25 miles north of Tralee in the northwest corner of Co. Kerry is the famous **Ballybunion Golf Club,** Ballybunion, Co. Kerry (☎ 068/27146). This facility offers visitors a new clubhouse and the chance to play on two challenging 18-hole seaside links, both on the cliffs overlooking the Shannon River estuary and the Atlantic. The "old" course is rated by Tom Watson as one of the finest in the world, while the "new" one was designed by Robert Trent Jones. Greens fees are £30 ($48) on the New Course, £45 ($72) on the Old Course, or £65 ($104) to play both courses.

HORSEBACK RIDING   If you'd like to see the Tralee sights from horseback, you can hire a horse from **El Rancho Riding Stables,** Ballyard, Tralee (☎ 066/21840). Prices start at £10 ($16) per hour for one- or two-hour rides on the Slieve Mish Mountains and Queen Scotia's Glen. El Rancho also offers extended three-day or one-week trail rides.

A Rose Is a Rose Is a Rose

She was lovely and fair as the rose of the summer,
Yet 'twas not her beauty alone that won me;
Oh no, 'twas the truth in her eyes ever dawning,
that made me love Mary, the Rose of Tralee.

A carnival-like atmosphere prevails at the annual five-day **Rose of Tralee Festival,** with a full program of concerts, street entertainment, and horse races leading up to a beauty/talent pageant in which women from Irish communities around the world vie to be crowned "the Rose of Tralee." In 1997, the festival will run from August 22 to 29. For information, contact Eileen Kenny or Eleanor Carrick, **Rose of Tralee Festival Office,** Ashe Memorial Hall, Denny Street, Tralee, Co. Kerry (☎ **066/21322** or 066/23227; fax 066/22654), or E-mail Liam Looney at llooney@staffmail.rtc-tralee.ie.

ACCOMMODATIONS
EXPENSIVE

Ballyseede Castle Hotel

Tralee-Killarney road, Tralee, Co. Kerry. ☎ **800/223-5695** from the U.S., or 066/25799. Fax 066/25287. 12 rms. TV TEL. £95–£150 ($152–$240) double. Service charge 12.5%. MC, V.

Ballyseede Castle—a 15th-century, multiturreted, four-story castle complete with live-in ghost—was once the chief garrison of the legendary Fitzgeralds, the Earls of Desmond. Later, the Blennerhassett family occupied it until 1966 and, in 1985, turned it into a hotel. The lobby has Doric columns and a hand-carved oak staircase. Decorated with cornices of ornamental plasterwork, two drawing rooms are warmed by marble fireplaces. Residents feel like royalty in the elegant bedrooms and in the Regency Restaurant, with its huge oil paintings and fabric-lined walls. A library and piano lounge are open to guests. The castle is 2 miles east of Tralee, on 30 acres of parkland.

MODERATE

Abbey Gate Hotel

Maine St., Tralee, Co. Kerry. ☎ **066/29888.** Fax 066/29821. 100 rms. TV TEL. £56–£90 ($89.60–$144) double. No service charge. Rates include full breakfast. AE, DC, MC, V.

This new three-story hotel brings much-needed quality accommodation and a broader dimension of social activity to the center of Tralee Town. The guest rooms, like the public areas, are furnished with new reproductions and fabrics, art, and accessories that convey an air of Georgian/Victorian Tralee. The Vineyard Restaurant has a decorative theme that matches its name, and the Old Market Place Bar is a convenient place to have a pint of Guinness. The hotel is ideally located within walking distance of Tralee's prime attractions, shops, and pubs.

Brandon Hotel

Princes St., Tralee, Co. Kerry. ☎ **800/44-UTELL** from the U.S., or 066/23333. Fax 066/25019. 158 rms. TV TEL. £70–£100 ($112–$160) double. No service charge. Rates include full breakfast. AE, DC, MC, V. Closed Dec 24–28.

Named for nearby Mount Brandon, this is a modern and dependable five-story hotel at the west edge of town, with vistas of the Dingle Peninsula in the distance. There is nothing unique about the guest rooms, but they are functional and well kept. The facilities include the Galleon restaurant, a coffee shop, two bars, and a leisure center with indoor heated swimming pool, sauna, steam room, and gym. Best of all, the hotel is just a block from the National Folk Theatre and tourist office, and within easy strolling distance of all the shops and downtown restaurants. Convenience is the word here.

INEXPENSIVE

Ballygarry House Hotel

Tralee-Killarney road, Leebrook, Tralee, Co. Kerry. ☎ **066/21233.** Fax 066/27630. 16 rms. TV TEL. £56–£70 ($89.60–$112) double. Includes full Irish breakfast and service charge. AE, MC, V. Closed Dec 20–28.

Located 1 mile south of town, this country inn is on the edge of a residential neighborhood, surrounded by well-tended gardens and sheltering trees. Recently updated, the bedrooms vary in size; each is individually furnished and decorated to reflect different aspects of Co. Kerry. Each has a name to match, such as Arbutus, Muckross, Valentia, and Slea Head. The public areas have a horsey theme, with pictures of prize-winning thoroughbreds, horse brass, and other equestrian touches. Amenities include the Monarchs restaurant and old-world–style lounge bar.

DINING
MODERATE

✪ Larkins

Princes St., Tralee, Co. Kerry. ☎ **066/21300.** Main courses £9–£13 ($14.40–$20.80). AE, MC, V. Mon–Sat 12:30–2pm and 6–9pm (Sunday hours July–Aug). IRISH/SEAFOOD/VEGETARIAN.

This bright, welcoming Irish-country restaurant with antique pine furnishings is conveniently located and widely acclaimed for its catch of the day and its roast rack of Irish lamb. Modestly priced and immodestly tasty, Larkins' offerings are well worth a stop. As a bonus, proprietor Michael Fitzgibbon greets his guests personally and generously provides information on the area.

The Tankard

Kilfenora, Fenit. ☎ **066/36164.** Reservations recommended. Main courses £8–£15 ($12.80–$24). AE, DC, MC, V. Daily 6–10pm. SEAFOOD/IRISH.

Located 6 miles northwest of Tralee, this is one of the few restaurants in the area that capitalizes on sweeping views of Tralee Bay. Situated right on the water's edge, it is outfitted with wide picture windows and a sleek contemporary decor. The straightforward menu primarily features local shellfish and seafood such as lobster, scallops, prawns, and black sole, but also includes rack of lamb, duck, quail, and a variety of steaks. Bar food is available all day, but this restaurant is at its best in the early evening, especially at sunset.

TRALEE AFTER DARK

Siamsa Tire, the National Folk Theatre of Ireland, is located at Town Park, Tralee (☎ **066/23055,** or 066/23049 for credit cards). Founded in 1974, Siamsa (pronounced Sheem-sha) offers a mixture of music, dance, and mime, and its programs focus on three different themes: Fado Fado / The Long Ago; Sean Agus Nua / Myth and Motion; and Ding Dong Dedero / Forging the Dance. The scenes depict old folk tales and farmyard activities such as thatching a cottage roof, flailing sheaves of corn, and twisting a sugan (straw) rope.

In addition to these folk theater entertainments, Siamsa presents a full program of drama and musical concerts (from traditional to classical) performed by visiting amateur and professional companies. Admission is £9 ($14.40) for adults, £7 ($11.20) for seniors and children, £28 ($44.80) for a family of two adults and up to four children. The schedule is Tuesday, Thursday, and Saturday in May; Monday, Tuesday, Thursday, and Saturday in June and September; and Monday through Saturday in July and August; curtain time is 8:30pm. The schedule in October through April varies.

PUBS

An Blascaod (The Blasket Inn)
Castle St., Tralee. ☎ 066/23313.

Named for the Blasket Islands, this pub has a lovely modern facade and interior using a stark red-and-black color scheme. The inside includes a two-story atrium with an open fireplace, plus shelves lined with old books and plates.

Harty's Lounge Bar
Castle St., Tralee. ☎ 066/25385.

This pub is celebrated as the original meetinghouse where the Rose of Tralee festival was born. It is also known for its traditional pub grub such as steak and kidney pie, shepherd's pie, and Irish stew.

Kirby's Olde Brogue Inn
Rock St., Tralee. ☎ 066/23221.

This pub has a barnlike layout, with an interior that incorporates agricultural instruments, farming memorabilia, and rush-work tables and chairs. Good pub grub, specializing in steaks, is served.

Oyster Tavern
Fenit Rd., Spa, Tralee. ☎ 066/36102.

The nicest location of any pub in the Tralee area belongs to this tavern, just 3 miles west of downtown, overlooking Tralee Bay. The pub grub available includes seafood soups and platters.

In the west of Ireland, between almost-tropical Kerry and the rugged austerity of the northwest, lie four counties: Limerick, Clare, Galway, and Mayo. Unlike Galway (the county and the town), Limerick, Clare, and Mayo, for all that they have to offer, are not principal tourist destinations—but neither are they well-kept secrets. Westport, in Co. Mayo, for instance, is justifiably one of the most popular resort towns in Ireland, while the Burren in Co. Clare is a unique spectacle, with seldom a tour bus in sight.

Leaving Galway aside for now (we'll get to it in Chapters 12 and 13), this chapter focuses on its less prestigious yet surprising western neighbors in the hope of encouraging and guiding you to explore beyond the bus-beaten track.

1 Limerick City & Environs

Limerick is 15 miles E of Shannon Airport, 123 miles SW of Dublin, 65 miles N of Cork, 69 miles NE of Killarney, and 65 miles S of Galway.

GETTING THERE   From the United States, Aer Lingus, Aeroflot, and Delta Airlines provide regularly scheduled flights into **Shannon Airport,** off the Limerick-Ennis road (N18), Co. Clare (☎ **061/471444**), 15 miles west of Limerick. From Britain, flights into Shannon are provided from London by Aer Lingus (from Heathrow) and Ryanair (from Stansted). From the Continent, flights to Shannon are operated by Aer Lingus from **Dusseldorf, Paris, and Zurich. Bus Eireann** (☎ **061/313333**) provides bus service from Shannon Airport to Limerick's Railway Station. The fare is £3.50 ($5.60). A taxi will cost about £14 ($22.40).

Irish Rail operates direct trains from Dublin, Cork, and Killarney, with connections from other parts of Ireland, arriving at Limerick's **Colbert Station,** Parnell Street (☎ **061/315555**).

Bus Eireann provides bus services from all parts of Ireland into Limerick's Colbert Station, Parnell Street (☎ **061/313333**).

If you're driving, Limerick City can be reached via N7 from the east and north; N20, N21, N24, and N69 from the south; and N18 from the west and north.

VISITOR INFORMATION   The **Limerick Tourist Information Office** is located on Arthurs Quay, Limerick (☎ **061/317522**). It is open Monday through Friday from 9am to 6pm and Saturday from 9am to 1pm, with extended hours in the summer season. Ask for a free copy of the *Shannon Region Visitors Guide,* which is packed with helpful information about activities and events in Limerick and the surrounding areas. A seasonal tourist office is also operated May to October in the **Adare Heritage Centre,** Main Street, Adare (☎ **061/396255**).

GETTING AROUND   By Public Transport   Bus Eireann (☎ **061/313333**) operates local bus service around Limerick and its environs; flat fare is 80p ($1.30). Buses depart from Colbert Station, Parnell Street.

By Taxi   Taxis line up outside of Colbert Station, at hotels, and along Thomas and Cecil streets, off O'Connell Street. To reserve a taxi, call **Economy Taxis** (☎ **061/411422**); **Speeditaxis** (☎ **061/318844**); or **Top Cabs** (☎ **061/417417**).

By Car   Driving around Limerick can be a little confusing due to the profusion of one-way streets. It is best to park your car and walk to see the sights, although you may want to drive to King's Island for King John's Castle and the other historic sights (there's a free parking lot opposite the castle). If you must park downtown, head for the multistory parking lot at Arthur's Quay, very convenient to all sightseeing and shopping and well signposted. Parking is 60p (96¢) per hour.

If you need to rent a car in Limerick, contact Alamo/Treaty Rent A Car (☎ **061/416512**) or Thrifty Irish Car Rentals, Ennis Road, Limerick (☎ **061/453049**). In addition, all major international car-rental firms maintain desks at Shannon Airport (see "County Clare" section, below).

On Foot   The best way to get around Limerick is to walk. Follow the signposted "Tourist Trail" to see most of the city's main attractions; a booklet outlining the trail is available at the tourist office or in bookshops. Guided walking tours are also available in the summer months (see "Attractions," below).

FAST FACTS: LIMERICK CITY

Area Code   The telephone area code for most numbers in the Limerick area is **061.** Some Co. Limerick numbers have the codes **063, 068,** or **069.**

Drugstores   Try **Hogan's Pharmacy,** at 45 Upper William St., Limerick (☎ **061/415195**).

Emergencies   Dial **999.**

Gay & Lesbian Resource   Gay and Lesbian Switchboard Limerick (☎ **061/310101**).

Hospital   St. John's Hospital is located on St. John's Square, Limerick (☎ **061/415822**).

Information   See "Visitor Information," above.

Laundry & Dry Cleaning   Try **Gaeltacht Cleaners,** 58 Thomas St. (☎ **061/415124**), or **Speediwash Laundrette & Dry Cleaners,** 11 St. Gerard St., Limerick (☎ **061/319380**).

Library   Limerick County Library is located at 58 O'Connell St., Limerick (☎ **061/318477**).

Local Newspapers & Media   Local papers include *The Limerick Leader,* published four times a week, and the *Limerick Chronicle,* a weekly. The weekly *Clare Champion,* published in Ennis, is also widely read in Limerick. *The Limerick Events Guide,* issued free every two weeks, gives news of entertainment. Radio Limerick broadcasts on 95 FM.

Parks   Limerick's People's Park is located on Pery Square off Upper Mallow Street, one block east of O'Connell Street. Other smaller parks include Arthur's Quay Park at Arthur's Quay and the Custom House Park on the south side of Matthew Bridge.

Photographic Needs   Try **Whelan's Cameras,** 30 O'Connell St. (☎ 061/415246), or **Photo World,** 3 William St. (☎ 061/417515), for all your shutterbug needs. **Police**   The local **Garda Headquarters** is located on Henry Street (☎ 061/414222). **Post Office**   The **General Post Office** is on Post Office Lane, off Lower Cecil Street, Limerick (☎ 061/314636). There is a branch of the post office at Arthur's Quay Shopping Centre, Patrick Street (☎ 061/415538).

LIMERICK IN 250 WORDS OR LESS

Situated along the midwest coast of Ireland, Limerick is the third largest city in the Republic, with a population approaching 80,000. As a river port on the Shannon, Limerick has long been of strategic and commercial importance, and during the years that transatlantic flights were required to land at Shannon Airport, the city profited mightily from its proximity.

Very little of Limerick's ancient past strikes the eye of the visitor apart from its 12th-century cathedral, its 13th-century castle, and remnants of Norman fortifications. What does strike the eye is a small, struggling, hard-working city with few resources and little energy to expend on polishing and preening itself for visitors. Apart from its historic area, the "Heritage Precinct," Limerick City has little with which to attract tourists. Neither its proud past nor its likely renaissance can make it, for the moment, a major tourist destination.

The countryside around Limerick, however, has a number of interesting sites to offer. Southwest of Limerick, the village of Adare is worth a visit, as are Glin Castle, Lough Gur, and Rathkeale. In addition to the attractions described below, see "Easy Excursions from Limerick City," later in this chapter for more suggestions about sightseeing when based in Limerick City.

ATTRACTIONS

✪ King John's Castle

Nicholas St., Limerick. ☎ **061/411201.** Admission £3.50 ($5.60) adults, £2 ($3.20) students and children. Daily 9:30am–5:30pm.

Strategically built on the banks of the Shannon River, this royal fortress is the centerpiece of Limerick's historic area. It is said to date from 1210, when King John of England visited and was so taken with the site that he ordered a "strong castle" to be built here. It survives today as one of the oldest examples of medieval architecture in Ireland, with rounded gate towers and curtain walls. Thanks to a recent $7 million restoration, the interior includes an authentic on-site archaeological excavation dating back to Hiberno/Norse times, as well as gallery displays and an audio-visual presentation portraying Limerick's 800 years of history. On the outside, the impressive facade has battlement walkways along the castle's walls and towers, offering sweeping views of the city.

✪ St. Mary's Cathedral

Bridge St., Limerick. ☎ **061/416238.** Donation £1 ($1.60). June–Sept Mon–Sat 9am–5pm, Oct–May Mon–Sat 9am–1pm.

Founded in the 12th century on a hill on King's Island, this site originally held a palace belonging to one of the kings of Munster, Donal Mor O'Brien. In 1172, he donated it for use as a church. Currently undergoing restoration, the building contains many fine antiquities including a Romanesque doorway, a pre-Reformation stone altar, and a huge stone coffin lid said to be that of Donal Mor O'Brien himself. Features added in later years include 15th-century misericords (supports for standing worshippers) with carvings in black oak, and a reredos (ornamental partition) on the high altar carved by the father of Irish patriot Patrick Pearse. Now a

Limerick City

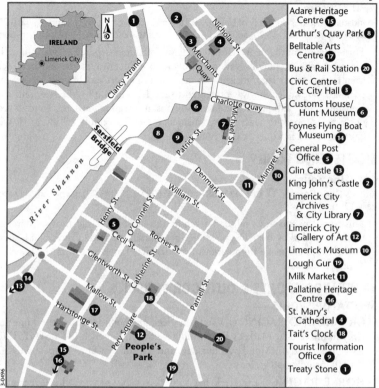

Adare Heritage Centre 15
Arthur's Quay Park 8
Belltable Arts Centre 17
Bus & Rail Station 20
Civic Centre & City Hall 3
Customs House/ Hunt Museum 6
Foynes Flying Boat Museum 14
General Post Office 5
Glin Castle 13
King John's Castle 2
Limerick City Archives & City Library 7
Limerick City Gallery of Art 12
Limerick Museum 10
Lough Gur 19
Milk Market 11
Pallatine Heritage Centre 16
St. Mary's Cathedral 4
Tait's Clock 18
Tourist Information Office 9
Treaty Stone 1

Church of Ireland property, St. Mary's is the site of nightly *son et lumière* (sound and light) presentations during the summer season (see "Pubs & Other Evening Entertainment," below).

Limerick Museum

St. John's Sq., Limerick. ☎ **061/417826.** Free admission. Tues–Sat 10am–1pm and 2–5pm.

Housed in two stone town houses dating from 1751, this museum provides an insight into the history of Limerick. It contains displays on Limerick's archaeology, natural history, civic treasures, and traditional crafts of lace, silver, furniture, and printing, plus historical paintings, maps, prints, and photographs. Of particular interest are the city's original charters from Oliver Cromwell and King Charles II, and the civic sword presented by Queen Elizabeth I. Building repairs are underway at present and some of the exhibits will be closed in 1997, so call ahead.

Limerick City Gallery of Art

Pery Sq., Limerick. ☎ **061/310633.** Free admission. Mon–Wed and Fri 10am–1pm and 2–6pm; Thurs 10am–1pm and 2–7pm; Sat 10am–1pm.

Founded in 1948 and expanded in 1985 to occupy the whole of the neo-Romanesque Carnegie Building (built in 1903), this gallery is situated in the People's Park, on the corner of Mallow Street. It houses a permanent collection of 18th-, 19th-, and 20th-century art, and also plays host to a wide range of traveling contemporary art exhibitions, including touring exhibitions from the Irish Museum of Modern Art. On some evenings, the gallery holds literary readings or traditional or classical music concerts at 8pm.

Hunt Museum

Foundation Building, University of Limerick, off the main Dublin road (N7), Limerick. ☎ **061/ 202661.** Admission £2 ($3.20) adults, £1 ($1.60) students and children. Mon–Sat 10am–5pm.

This museum collection of Celtic to medieval treasures is reputed to be the finest in Ireland outside of Dublin's National Museum. It includes antiquities and art objects from Europe and Ireland, ancient Irish metalwork, and medieval bronzes, ivories, and enamels. The collection was presented to the Irish nation by the late John and Gertrude Hunt, antiquarians and art historians. As we go to press, this entire collection is being moved to newly restored quarters at the 18th-century Palladian-style Old Custom House in Limerick City center.

SIGHTSEEING TOURS

Gray Line Tours

Arthur's Quay, Limerick. ☎ **061/413088** or 061/416099. £27 ($43.20) per person. May–Oct, daily 10am.

This company operates a full-day, seven-hour tour of the scenic areas surrounding Limerick, including the Cliffs of Moher, the Burren, Bunratty Castle, and Galway Bay. Pickups are made from various Limerick area hotels and from the Limerick Tourist Office.

SPECTATOR SPORTS & OUTDOOR PURSUITS

SPECTATOR SPORTS

GREYHOUND RACING   Watch the sleek greyhounds race at the **Limerick Greyhound Track,** Market's Field, Mulgrave Street, Limerick (☎ **061/415170**). Races are slated on Monday, Thursday, and Saturday at 8pm. Admission is £3 ($4.80) including program.

HORSE RACING   Limerick has two racetracks nearby: the **Greenpark Race Course,** South Circular Road, Dooradoyle, Limerick (☎ **061/229377**), and **Tipperary Race Course,** Limerick Junction (☎ **062/51357**), about 20 miles southeast near Tipperary. There is racing throughout the year; check the local newspapers for exact fixtures and times. Admission averages £5 to £6 ($8 to $9.60) for most events.

RECREATION

FISHING   Visitors are welcome to cast a line in the River Shannon for trout and other freshwater fish. For information and equipment, contact **Steve's Fishing Tackle,** 19 Catherine St., Limerick (☎ **061/413484**).

GOLF   The Limerick area has three 18-hole golf courses, including a championship par-72 parkland layout at the **Limerick County Golf & Country Club,** Ballyneety (☎ **061/351881**), 5 miles east of Limerick, with greens fee of £25 ($40). In addition, there is the par-72 inland course at the **Limerick Golf Club,** Ballyclough (☎ **061/415416**), 3 miles south of Limerick, charging greens fees of £22.50 ($36); and the par-69 inland course at **Castletroy Golf Club,** Castletroy, Co. Limerick (☎ **061/335753**), 3 miles east of Limerick, with greens fees of £25 ($40).

HORSEBACK RIDING   County Limerick's fertile fields provide good turf for horseback riding and pony trekking, at rates starting at about £25 ($40) per hour. The **Clonshire Equestrian Centre,** Adare, Co. Limerick (☎ **061/396770**), offers riding for all levels of ability, horsemanship classes and instruction for cross-country riding, dressage, and jumping. Clonshire is also home to the Limerick Foxhounds and in the winter months is a center for hunting in the area.

Above All: We Were Wet

People everywhere brag and whimper about the woes of their early years, but nothing can compare with the Irish version: the poverty; the shiftless loquacious alcoholic father; the pious defeated mother moaning by the fire; pompous priests; bullying schoolmasters; the English and the terrible things they did to us for eight hundred long years.

Above all: we were wet.

Out in the Atlantic Ocean great sheets of rain gathered to drift slowly up the River Shannon and settle forever in Limerick. The rain dampened the city from the Feast of the Circumcision to New Years Eve. It created a cacophony of hacking coughs, bronchial rattles, asthmatic wheezes, consumptive croaks. It turned noses into fountains, lungs into bacterial sponges. It provoked cures galore; to ease the catarrh you boiled onions in milk blackened with pepper; for the congested passages you made a paste of boiled flour and nettles, wrapped it in a rag, and slapped it, sizzling, on the chest . . . .

The rain drove us into the church—our refuge, our strength, our only dry place. At Mass, Benediction, novenas, we huddled in great damp clumps, dozing through priest drone, while steam rose again from our clothes to mingle with the sweetness of incense, flowers and candles.

Limerick gained a reputation for piety, but we knew it was only the rain.

—Frank McCourt, *Angela's Ashes* (Simon & Schuster, 1996)

Rathcannon Equestrian Centre, Kilmallock, Co. Limerick (☎ **063/90557**), offers horseback riding, trekking, cross-country riding, and hunting, as well as instruction in the art of show-jumping.

SHOPPING

Shopping hours in Limerick are Monday through Saturday from 9:30am to 5:30pm. Many stores, particularly in the Arthurs Quay Centre, also stay open until 9pm on Thursday and Friday nights.

✪ Arthurs Quay Centre

Arthurs Quay, Limerick. ☎ **061/419888.**

With a striking four-story brick facade, this shopping complex overlooks Arthurs Quay park and the Shannon River. It houses more than three dozen shops and services, ranging from Irish handcrafts to fashions, casual wear, shoes, music recordings, and books. Open Monday to Wednesday from 9am to 7pm, Thursday and Friday 9am to 9pm, and Saturday 9am to 6pm.

✪ Cruises Street Shopping Centre

Cruises St., Limerick.

This is the centerpiece of Limerick's retail downtown shopping district, situated just off Patrick Street. Taking an original city street, the developers spent £18 million ($27 million) and turned it into an old-world village–style pedestrianized shopping mall, with a total of 55 retail outlets and 20 residential apartments and offices.

Heirlooms

Cruises St., Limerick. ☎ **061/419111.**

Long established in downtown Limerick, this shop moved to the new Cruises Street Shopping Centre for more space to show off its vast stock of local collectibles, which includes old books and maps, dolls and puppets, and biscuit tins, as well as frames, wood carvings, pottery, clocks, sculptures, jewelry, and candles.

Irish Handcrafts
26 Patrick St., Limerick. ☎ **061/455504.**

Dating back more than 100 years, this family run business specializes in products made by people from the Limerick area, with particular emphasis on women's hand-knit and hand-loomed sweaters of all types, colors, and styles. There are also linen and lace garments. Open daily 9am to 6pm.

Leonards
23 O'Connell St., Limerick. ☎ **061/415721.**

This long-established shop is a good source of men's tweed jackets, hats, caps, ties, and cravats, as well as silk ties and cashmere and lambswool knitwear.

Todd's
O'Connell St., Limerick. ☎ **061/417222.**

For more than 100 years, this has been Limerick's leading department store, selling a wide array of Waterford crystal, Aran knitwear, Donegal tweeds, and ready-to-wear clothing of all types.

White and Gold
34 O'Connell St. at Roches St., Limerick. ☎ **061/419977.**

Irish Dresden figurines, the delicate porcelain pieces made at nearby Drumcollogher, are the special attraction of this chic gift shop. Other wares include fanciful European Christmas ornaments, intricate wind chimes, and Hummels.

ACCOMMODATIONS
EXPENSIVE/MODERATE

✪ Jurys
Ennis road (N18), Limerick, Co. Limerick. ☎ **800/44-UTELL** from the U.S., or 061/327777. Fax 061/326400. 95 rms. TV TEL. £129.80 ($207.70) double. Includes full Irish breakfast and service charge. AE, DC, MC, V.

Situated on the banks of the Shannon across the Sarsfield Bridge in a residential section of the city, this contemporary-style hotel is just a three-minute walk from O'Connell Street. Recently renovated, it is laid out in a bright and airy style, with a skylit, atrium-style foyer. The up-to-date bedrooms are spacious and practical, with traditional dark-wood furniture and brass fixtures, and wide-windowed views of the gardens and river.

Dining/Entertainment: The choices include The Copper Room, a gourmet restaurant open only for dinner; an all-day coffee shop; and Limericks Bar, a pub with walls full of quotable and lyrical limericks.

Facilities: Indoor heated swimming pool, sauna, steam room, Jacuzzi, tennis court.

Limerick Inn
Ennis road (N18), Limerick, Co. Limerick. ☎ **800/223-0888** or 061/326666. Fax 061/326281. 153 rms. TV TEL. £114–£125 ($182.40–$200) double. Includes full Irish breakfast and service charge. AE, DC, MC, V.

A country-club atmosphere permeates this rambling and modern hotel, located in a pastoral setting 3 miles west of the city. It is handsomely decorated with bright-toned designer furnishings and fabric-textured wall coverings. Guest facilities include a leisure center with swimming pool, fitness equipment, hairdressing salon, and a billiards room. There is also a full-service restaurant, The Burgundy Room, plus a coffee shop, piano lounge, and spacious drawing rooms with views of the nearby grassy hills.

MODERATE

Castle Oaks House

Off Dublin road (N7), Castleconnell, Co. Limerick. ☎ **800/223-6510** from the U.S., or 061/ 377666. Fax 061/377717. 20 rms. TV TEL. £60–£90 ($96–$144) double. Service charge 10%. Rates include full breakfast. AE, DC, MC, V.

Six miles east of Limerick City and set on 25 acres of mature oak woodlands along the Shannon River, this two-story Georgian manor house is more than 150 years old and has seen use as a private residence, a convent, and, since 1987, a hotel. Among the original fittings are classic bow windows, a decorative staircase, and a skylit central dome, and left over from its convent days are stained-glass windows and a chapel that is now used as a banqueting room. The comfortable bedrooms are furnished with crown-canopy beds, soft pastel fabrics, and choice antiques from the area. Facilities include a restaurant, lounge bar, tennis court, and health club with indoor pool.

Limerick Ryan Hotel

Ennis road (N18), Limerick, Co. Limerick. ☎ **800/44-UTELL** from the U.S., or 061/453922. Fax 061/326333. 166 rms. TV TEL. £40–£120 ($64–$192) double. No service charge. AE, DC, MC, V.

Situated on the main (N18) road a mile west of the city center, this hotel combines one of Limerick's oldest buildings, Ardhu House, dating from 1780, with a modern wing of new bedrooms. The public areas, part of the original manor house, are decorated in classic Georgian style. Facilities include the Ardhu Restaurant, Ardhu Bar, and a sports bar with giant screen for viewing all major sporting events.

INEXPENSIVE

Shannon Grove

Athlunkard, Killaloe road (R463), Limerick. ☎ **061/345756.** Fax 061/343838. 9 rms. TEL. £38 ($60.80) double. Rates include full Irish breakfast. No credit cards. Closed Christmas week.

Situated in a quiet residential area a mile north of the city center, this modern two-story guest house is surrounded by lovely gardens and is just a quarter-mile walk from a curve of the Shannon River. The bedrooms, individually decorated in light tones of pink, blue, and peppermint, have contemporary furnishings. Facilities include a TV lounge with tea/coffeemaker and two cheery breakfast rooms. There are also tables and chairs for outdoor seating in fine weather. Proprietor Noreen Marsh provides a particularly warm welcome and will help you plan an insider's tour of Limerick. If you don't have a car, local bus service stops nearby.

DINING

EXPENSIVE/MODERATE

De La Fontaine

12 Upper Gerald Griffin St., Limerick. ☎ **061/414461.** Reservations recommended. Main courses £11–£16 ($17.60–$25.60); fixed-price six-course dinner £22 ($35.20). DC, MC, V. Mon–Sat 7–10pm. FRENCH.

Situated on the east end of the downtown area, this upstairs restaurant brings the aromas and ambience of France to Limerick. Chef Alain Bras-White changes the menu often, depending on the season and what is fresh in local markets, but his specialty dishes include breast of duck with walnut-scented sauce, breast of chicken stuffed with smoked salmon and topped by a whiskey and hazelnut cream sauce, farm-venison T-bone with balsamic vinegar, and fillet of beef flambéed with peppercorns and foie gras.

✪ Finnegans Basement Restaurant

74 O'Connell St., Limerick. ☎ **061/316311.** Reservations required. Main courses £8–£14 ($12–$21). MC, V. Daily 5:30–11pm. INTERNATIONAL.

Situated in the heart of Limerick's Georgian streetscape, this small, 40-seat restaurant occupies the basement of a restored 18th-century town house near the Crescent and Pery Square. Fireplaces warm the exposed brick and stonework, and the atmosphere is cozy. The menu emphasizes seafood, with such specialties as lobsters from the tank and wild Shannon salmon, along with meat choices such as rack of Adare lamb and medaillons of beef au poivre.

MODERATE/INEXPENSIVE

✪ Patrick Punchs

O'Connell Ave. (N20), Punchs Cross, Limerick. ☎ 061/229588. Reservations suggested for dinner. Main courses £8.25–£12.75 ($13.20–$20.40). MC, V. Daily 10:30am–11:30pm. IRISH/INTERNATIONAL.

Situated on the southern edge of town, this popular pub-restaurant is on the main road, surrounded by gardens, ancient trees, and lots of parking. It offers a variety of settings in which to dine, ranging from a three-tier lounge area and a glass-enclosed conservatory overlooking the gardens to a clubby main room with an eclectic decor of Tiffany-style lamps, dark woods, an open turf fireplace, and old photos of movie stars. The menu is equally varied, and changes often, with dishes such as fillet of beef Wellington, chicken Cleopatra with lemon and prawn sauce, and vegetable lasagna.

⑤ Piccola Italia

55 O'Connell St., Limerick. ☎ **061/315844.** Reservations recommended. Main courses £5–£12 ($8–$19.20). Daily 6pm–midnight. ITALIAN.

With a name that means "Little Italy," this basement ristorante adds a touch of the Mediterranean to the heart of Limerick. The tables have red-and-white check cloths, and Chianti baskets hang from the ceiling. The menu is also unmistakably Italian, from mushroom soup, cannelloni, lasagna, and fettuccine to scampi, salmon alla griglia, and steak pizzaiola.

PUBS & OTHER EVENING ENTERTAINMENT
PUBS

The Locke

3 Georges Quay, Limerick. ☎ 061/413733.

Established in 1724, this is one of Limerick's oldest pubs, situated beside the east bank of the Shannon, just off Bridge Street. Although it started as a haven for sea captains visiting the port of Limerick, today it's known for its traditional Irish music—played on Sunday and Tuesday, year-round—and for its outdoor riverside seating.

Matt the Thresher

Dublin road (N7), Birdhill, Co. Tipperary. ☎ 061/379227.

Situated about 15 miles northeast of Limerick but well worth the drive, this roadside tavern is a replica of a 19th-century farmers' pub. A rustic, cottagelike atmosphere prevails inside, with antique furnishings, agricultural memorabilia, traditional snugs (private rooms), and lots of cozy alcoves. A new patio and small restaurant have been added recently, and there's music on many evenings.

M. J. Finnegans

Dublin road (N7), Annacotty. ☎ 061/337338.

Dating from 1776, this wonderfully restored and newly renovated alehouse takes its name from James Joyce's *Finnegans Wake* and the decor reflects a Joycean theme, albeit with appropriate Limerick overtones. Special features include Irish ceili music on weekends, and picnic tables for sitting by the rose garden on warm summer days. Good pub grub is to be had here. It's located on the main road about 5 miles east of Limerick City.

Nancy Blake's

19 Denmark St., Limerick. ☎ 061/416443.

Situated downtown just off Patrick Street, this cozy old-world pub is known for its free traditional music sessions, year-round Sunday through Wednesday from 9pm.

Vintage Club

9 Ellen St., Limerick. ☎ 061/410694.

Located in one of Limerick's older sections near the quays, this pub used to be a wine cellar and the decor reflects it: barrel seats and tables, oak casks, and dark-paneled walls.

PERFORMING ARTS CENTERS

Belltable Arts Centre

69 O'Connell St., Limerick. ☎ 061/319866. Tickets £5–£10 ($8–$16). Mon–Sat 8pm for most shows; check in advance. Five-minute walk from bus and train station.

Dramas, musicals, and concerts are staged year-round at this midcity theater and entertainment center. The summer program includes a season of professional Irish theater. By day, the building is also open for gallery exhibits, showing the works of modern Irish artists as well as local crafts.

University Concert Hall

University of Limerick, Plassey, Co. Limerick. ☎ 061/331549. Tickets £6–£15 ($9.60–$24). Most performances start at 8pm.

On the grounds of the University of Limerick, this hall presents a broad program of national and international solo stars, variety shows, and ballet, as well as the Irish Chamber Orchestra, RTE Concert Orchestra, University of Limerick Chamber Orchestra, the Limerick Singers, and the European Community Orchestra. It publishes a monthly list of events, available from the tourist office.

SHOWS

✪ Son et Lumière

St. Mary's Cathedral, Merchant's Quay, Limerick. ☎ 061/416238. Tickets £2.50 ($4) adults, £1.50 ($2.40) seniors and students. Mid-June to mid-Sept nightly at 9:15pm.

Housed in the historic setting of the city's oldest cathedral, this is Limerick's long-running sound-and-light show. It is comprised of a 45-minute program that uses quadraphonic sound and spectacular lighting to tell the story of Limerick and the cathedral; it's produced by actors and lighting experts from Irish television. Reservations are not necessary.

Jurys Summer Show

Jurys Hotel, Ennis road (N18), Limerick. ☎ 061/327777. £8 ($12.80) show only, £16 ($25.60) for show and traditional meal; £20 ($32) full dinner and show. June, Thurs at 8pm; July–Sept, Wed–Thurs at 8pm.

Patterned after the famous long-running Jurys Cabaret of Dublin, this show presents the best of comedy, drama, music, song, and dance with a midwest-of-Ireland slant and starring Limerick-based entertainers. For those who wish to eat, there are two options: a meal of traditional Irish stew, apple pie, and Irish coffee, or a full-course dinner of choice.

EASY EXCURSIONS FROM LIMERICK CITY

Dotted about the Co. Limerick countryside within a 25-mile radius of Limerick City are many historic and cultural attractions. Here are a few suggestions:

✪ Adare Heritage Centre

Main St., Adare, Co. Limerick. ☎ 061/396666. Admission £2 ($3.20) adults, £1 ($1.60) seniors, students, and children. May–June and Sept–Oct, daily 9am–6pm; July–Aug, daily 9am–7pm.

Adare is one of Co. Limerick's special places, with thatched-roof and Tudor-style houses, beautiful gardens, and ivy-covered medieval churches in wooded surroundings on both sides of the street beside the River Maigue. For those who want to linger and learn more about this bucolic enclave's history, a new heritage center opened in 1994. Housed in a stone building with traditional courtyard, it offers a walk-through display on Adare's colorful history, along with a model of the town as it looked in medieval times. There is also a 20-minute audiovisual presentation illustrating the many facets of Adare today. The center also houses a cafe, craft shop, knitwear shop, and library with books on the local area.

Lough Gur

Lough Gur, Co. Limerick. ☎ 061/361511. Museum and audiovisual presentation £1.90 ($3.05) adults, £1 ($1.50) students. Mid-May to Sept, daily 10am–6pm. Situated 7 miles southeast of Limerick City via N24 and R513.

Lough Gur is one of Ireland's principal archaeological sites. Excavations have shown that it was occupied continuously from the Neolithic period to late medieval times, and the natural caves nearby have yielded the remains of extinct animals such as reindeer, giant Irish deer, and bear. The current site includes the foundations of a small farmstead built circa A.D. 900, a lake island dwelling built between A.D. 500 and 1000, a wedge-shaped tomb that was a communal grave circa 2,500 B.C., and the Grange Stone Circle, the largest and finest of its kind in Ireland. The lake and its shores, access to which is free, are quite lovely and are a great place to explore and maybe set out a picnic. The museum and audiovisual program, however, are worth neither the time nor the fee. They represent an opportunity missed to bring this most important site alive for the visitor. Better to explore on your own and to use your imagination.

Irish Palatine Heritage Centre

Limerick-Killarney road (N21), Rathkeale, Co. Limerick. ☎ 069/64397. Admission £2 ($3.20) adults, £1 ($1.60) children, £5 ($8) family. June–Sept, daily 10am–noon, 2–5pm, Sun 2–6pm and by appointment.

Ireland's unique links with Germany are the focus of this new museum, located 18 miles south of Limerick off the main road. Reflecting on the history of the several hundred Palatine families who emigrated from Germany and settled in this part of Ireland in 1709, it includes an extensive display of artifacts, photographs, and graphics. In addition, the museum seeks to illustrate the Palatines' innovative contributions to Irish farming life and their formative role in the development of world Methodism.

Foynes Flying Boat Museum

Foynes, Co. Limerick. ☎ **069/65416.** Admission £3 ($4.80) adults, £2.50 ($4) seniors, £1 ($1.60) children, £8 ($12.80) family. Apr–Oct, daily 10am–6pm. Located 20 miles east of Limerick via N69.

For aviation buffs, this museum is a must. This is the "first" Shannon Airport, the predecessor to the modern jetways of Shannon Airport in Co. Clare. It has now been restored and reopened as a visitor attraction, to commemorate an era begun on July 9, 1939, when Pan Am's luxury flying boat *Yankee Clipper* landed at Foynes, marking the first commercial passenger flight on the direct route between the United States and Europe. This was followed on June 22, 1942, when Foynes was the departure point for the first nonstop commercial flight from Europe to New York. This was also the airport where Irish coffee was invented in 1942 by bartender Joe Sheridan. The complex includes a 1940s-style cinema and cafe, the original terminal building, and the radio and weather rooms with original transmitters, receivers, and Morse Code equipment.

✪ Glin Castle

Limerick-Tarbert road (N69). ☎ **068/34112.** Admission £3 ($4.80) adults, £1.50 ($2.40) seniors and students. May–June, 10am–noon, 2–4pm, and by appointment. Approximately 25 miles east of Limerick City, via the main road (N69).

Lilies of the valley and ivy-covered ash, oak, and beech trees line the driveway leading to this gleaming white castle, home to the knights of Glin for the last 700 years. Sitting on the south bank of the Shannon Estuary, this sprawling estate contains 400 acres of gardens, farmlands, and forests. Although there were earlier residences on the site, the present home was built in 1785. It is more of a Georgian house than a castle, with added crenellations and Gothic details. The current (29th) knight of Glin, Desmond FitzGerald, a noted historian and preservationist, maintains a fine collection of 18th-century Irish furniture and memorabilia. The house features elaborate plasterwork, Corinthian columns, and a unique double-ramp flying staircase, and is protected by three sets of toy fort lodges, one of which houses a craft shop and cafe. In addition, B&B and castle rental can be arranged.

ACCOMMODATIONS

Very Expensive / Expensive

✪ Adare Manor

Adare, Co. Limerick. ☎ **800/462-3273** from the U.S., or fax 201/425-0332 from the U.S., or 061/396566. Fax 061/396124. 64 rms. TV TEL. £195–£295 ($312–$472) double. Service charge 15%. AE, DC, MC, V.

Most people wouldn't expect to find a five-star hotel in a village as tiny and secluded as Adare, 10 miles south of Limerick, but Ireland is surprising, with little gems tucked in all corners. This gem is a 19th-century Tudor Gothic mansion, nestled on the banks of the River Maigue amid an 840-acre estate. The former home of the earls of Dunraven, it has been masterfully restored and refurbished as a deluxe resort, with original barrel-vaulted ceilings, 15th-century carved doors, Waterford crystal chandeliers, ornate fireplaces, and antique-filled bedrooms. The facilities include an oak-paneled restaurant with views of the river and gardens, heated indoor swimming pool, gym, sauna, riding stables, salmon and trout fishing, horseback riding, fox hunting, clay pigeon shooting, a variety of nature trails for jogging and walking, and an 18-hole golf course designed by Robert Trent Jones.

Moderate

✪ Dunraven Arms

Main St. (N21), Adare, Co. Limerick. ☎ **800/447-7462** or 061/396633. Fax 061/396541. 66 rms. Luxury suites available. TV TEL. £86–£106 ($137.60–$169.60). Service charge 12.5%. AE, CB, DC, DISC, MC, V.

Nestled on the banks of the River Maigue, this small 19th-century inn is a charming country retreat just 10 miles south of Limerick City. The public areas have an old-world ambience with open fireplaces and antiques. Half of the rooms are in the original house and the other half are in a new wing, but all are furnished in traditional style with Victorian accents and period pieces. A new leisure center offers pool, gym, and steam room. The hotel's gardens supply fruit and vegetables for its award-winning restaurant.

DINING

Expensive

✪ The Mustard Seed at Echo Lodge

Ballingarry, Co. Limerick. ☎ **069/68508.** Reservations recommended. Fixed-price 4-course dinner £30 ($48). AE, MC, V. Tues–Sat 7–10pm. Closed mid-Jan to Feb. Eight miles from Adare off the Newcastle West road from the center of Ballingarry. IRISH.

Creativity is the keynote at this lovely restored country house restaurant set on seven acres of gardens. The menu presents a creative mix of dishes such as roulade of spinach encasing a pepper and tomato filling on warm salad of tomato and spinach, or maybe chicken coated in honey, garlic, and green peppercorns with scallion cream sauce. Organic produce and cheeses are included in the food preparation, and the atmosphere is peaceful and lovely.

Moderate

Inn Between

Main St., Adare, Co. Limerick. ☎ **061/396633.** Reservations recommended. Main courses £6.75–£11.95 ($10.80–$19.10). AE, CB, DC, DISC, MC, V. Apr–Oct, Thurs–Mon 12:30–2:30pm and 6:30–9:30pm. IRISH.

Tucked in a row of houses and shops, this thatched-roof brasserie-style restaurant has a surprisingly airy skylit decor dominated by bright red and yellow tones, and a back courtyard for outdoor seating. The menu offers choices ranging from homemade soups and traditional dishes to innovative concoctions such as medaillons of beef fillet with green peppercorn sauce, wild salmon on leek fondue with tomato and chive butter sauce, and the classic Inn Between Burger with homemade relish and french fries.

2 County Clare

GETTING THERE From the United States, Aer Lingus, Aeroflot, and Delta Airlines provide regularly scheduled flights into **Shannon International Airport** (☎ **061/471444;** flight arrival and departure information ☎ 061/471582). From Britain, flights into Shannon are provided from London by Aer Lingus (Heathrow). From the Continent, flights to Shannon are operated by Aer Lingus from Dusseldorf, Paris, and Zurich. From Russia, Aeroflot flies to Shannon from Moscow and St. Petersburg.

Irish Rail provides service to **Ennis Rail Station,** Station Road (☎ **065/40444**), and Limerick's **Colbert Station,** Parnell Street (☎ **061/315555**), 15 miles from Shannon.

County Clare

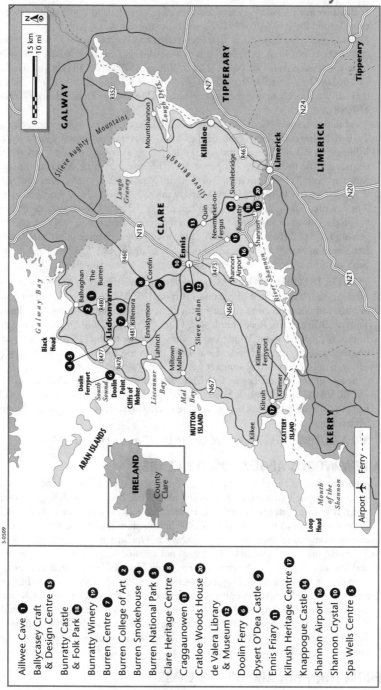

N
15 km
10 mi
0

GALWAY

TIPPERARY

Slieve Aughty Mountains

Lough Derg

R352

N7

Mountshannon

Killaloe

CLARE

R463

Limerick

LIMERICK

Lough Graney

Slieve Bernagh

N24

Tipperary

N18

Slieve Callan

Quin

Newmarket-on-Fergus

Sixmilebridge

Bunratty

Shannon

Shannon Airport

River Shannon

N20

Galway Bay

The Burren

Ballvaghan

R480

Lisdoonvarna

Kilfenora

R481

Ennistymon

Corofin

R460

Ennis

R473

N21

Black Head

R477

R478

Doolin Ferryport

Doolin Point

Cliffs of Moher

South Sound

Lahinch

Miltown Malbay

Liscannor Bay

Mal Bay

N67

N68

Killimer Ferryport

Kilrush

Killimer

Kilkee

Kilrush

SCATTERY ISLAND

KERRY

ARAN ISLANDS

MUTTON ISLAND

IRELAND

County Clare

Mouth of the Shannon

Loop Head

Airport ✈ Ferry - - - -

Aillwee Cave ❶
Ballycasey Craft & Design Centre ⓯
Bunratty Castle & Folk Park ⓲
Bunratty Winery ⓳
Burren Centre ❼
Burren College of Art ❷
Burren Smokehouse ❹
Burren National Park ❸
Clare Heritage Centre ⓭
Craggaunowen ⓭
Cratloe Woods House ⓴
de Valera Library & Museum ⓬
Doolin Ferry ❻
Dysert O'Dea Castle ❾
Ennis Friary ⓫
Kilrush Heritage Centre ⓱
Knappogue Castle ⓮
Shannon Airport ⓰
Shannon Crystal ❿
Spa Wells Centre ❺

Bus Eireann provides bus services from all parts of Ireland into **Ennis Bus Station,** Station Road (☎ 065/24177), and other towns in Co. Clare.

If you're coming by car, Co. Clare can be reached via N18. At Shannon Airport, cars can be rented from the following international firms: **Alamo** (☎ 800/522-9696 or 061/472342); **Avis** (☎ 061/471094); **Budget** (☎ 061/471361); **EuroDollar** (☎ 061/472633); and **Hertz** (☎ 061/471369). Several local firms also maintain desks at the airport; among the most reliable is **Dan Dooley Rent A Car** (☎ 061/471098).

From points south, Co. Clare can be reached directly, bypassing Limerick, via the **Tarbert-Killimer car ferry,** crossing the Shannon River from Tarbert, Co. Kerry, to Killimer, Co. Clare. Crossing time is 20 minutes, via a drive-on/drive-off service; no reservations are needed. Ferries operate April through September, Monday through Saturday from 7 or 7:30am until 9 or 9:30pm, Sunday from 9 or 9:30am until 9 or 9:30pm; October through March, Monday through Saturday from 7 or 7:30am to 7 or 7:30pm, Sunday from 10 or 10:30am to 7 or 7:30pm. Crossings from Tarbert are on the half-hour and from Killimer on the hour. The fares for cars with passengers are £7 ($11.20) one way and £10 ($16) round-trip. For more information, contact **Shannon Ferry Ltd.,** Killimer/Kilrush, Co. Clare (☎ 065/53124). The Killimer Ferry terminal offers a new gift shop and restaurant. Open daily 9am to 9pm.

VISITOR INFORMATION   As soon as you land in Ireland, you will find a **tourist office** in the Arrivals Hall of Shannon Airport (☎ 061/471644). It's open year-round, with hours timed to coincide with flight arrivals and departures. The **Ennis Tourist Office,** Clare Road, Ennis, Co. Clare (☎ 065/28366), is also open year-round. It's located about 1 mile south of town on the main N18 road. Hours are normally Monday through Friday from 9am to 6pm and Saturday from 9am to 1pm, with extended hours during summer.

Seasonal tourist offices in Co. Clare are maintained at the Cliffs of Moher (☎ 065/81171); O'Connell Street, Kilkee (☎ 065/56112); and at Town Hall, Kilrush (☎ 065/51577). These offices are usually open May or June through early September.

AREA CODES   Telephone area codes for Co. Clare are **061** and **065.**

A FEW WORDS ABOUT COUNTY CLARE

After stepping off the plane at Shannon, your first sight of Ireland will be the vistas of Co. Clare: rich green fields and rolling hills joined by the meandering Shannon River. If you turn left off the main road, the barren rocky Atlantic coast of Clare will await you; if you continue north, you'll be heading into the historic town of Ennis and then onward to the rocky outpost known as The Burren.

Among the counties of Ireland, Clare is not a major celebrity. It is less dramatic and less touristed than its neighbors, Kerry and Galway. Clare can and does boast, however, of some quite dazzling sites, such as the Cliffs of Moher and the Burren, and it's the proud heir to a number of impressive ancient sites and monuments, from the Poulnabrone Dolmen to Bunratty Castle with its a-lot-better-than-you-would-think folk park. The wildflowers and butterflies of the Burren, the birds of the cliffs from Hags Head to Loop Head, the silent dolmens, and the pounding bodhrans of Doolin all contribute to Clare's appeal.

FROM SHANNON AIRPORT TO ENNIS

The 15-mile road from Shannon Airport to Ennis, a well-signposted section of the main Limerick-Galway road (N18), is one the most traveled roads in Ireland. It has the feel of a superhighway—a feel you won't often encounter in Ireland and a misleading introduction to the land of *boreens* (country lanes). The whole point in Ireland, unless you know exactly where you must arrive in a hurry, is to turn off the straight and wide and get lost.

Now that you're on N18, turn right, proceed for 5 miles, and the village of Bunratty is before you, with its 15th-century medieval castle and theme park. Turn left, heading toward Ennis, and you pass through the charming river town of Newmarket-on-Fergus, home of Dromoland Castle.

The main town of Co. Clare, Ennis (population 6,000) is a compact enclave of winding narrow streets on the banks of the River Fergus. The original site was an island on the river and hence the name Ennis, an Anglicized form of the Gaelic word *inis,* meaning "island." Easily explored on foot, Ennis offers a walking trail developed by the Ennis Urban District Council. A leaflet outlining the route is available free throughout the town.

ATTRACTIONS

✪ Bunratty Castle and Folk Park

Limerick-Ennis road (N18), Bunratty, Co. Clare. ☎ **061/361511.** Admission £5 ($8) adults, £4.50 ($7.20) students and seniors, £2.50 ($4) children. Sept–May, daily 9:30am–5:30pm, June–Aug, daily 9:30am–7pm.

Long before you reach the village of Bunratty, vistas of this striking 15th-century fortress stand out along the main road from the airport. Nestled beside the O'Garney River, Bunratty Castle was built in 1425 and is today Ireland's most complete medieval castle. This ancient stronghold has been carefully restored, with authentic furniture, armorial stained glass, tapestries, and works of art. By day, the building's inner chambers and grounds are open for public tours; at night, the castle's Great Hall serves as a candlelit setting for medieval banquets and entertainment (see "Dining," below).

Bunratty Castle is the focal point of a 20-acre theme park, appropriately known as Bunratty Folk Park. This re-creation of a typical 19th-century Irish village includes thatched cottages, farmhouses, and an entire village street with school, post office, pub, grocery store, print shop, and a hotel—all open for browsing and shopping. Fresh scones are baked in the cottages, and craftspeople ply such trades as knitting, weaving, candle-making, pottery, and photography.

Bunratty Winery

Bunratty, Co. Clare. ☎ **061/362222.** Free admission. Daily 9:30am–5:30pm.

Housed in a coach house dating from 1816, this winery produces mead, a medieval drink made from honey, fermented grape juice, water, matured spirits, and a selection of herbs. In days long ago, it was served by the jugful at regal gatherings and at weddings. In fact, custom required that a bride and groom continue to drink mead for one full moon in order to increase the probability of a happy marriage. (Some speculate that this is where the term *honeymoon* came from.) Today, the Bunratty Winery produces mead primarily for consumption at Bunratty Castle's medieval-style banquets. Visitors are welcome to stop by this working winery, watch the production in progress, and taste the brew. Also available is traditional Irish potcheen, the first of this heady moonshine to be legally made and bottled in Ireland since it was banned in 1661.

✪ Knappogue Castle

Quin, Co. Clare. ☎ **061/361511.** Admission £2.40 ($3.85) adults, £1.60 ($2.55) children. Daily year-round 9:30am–5:30pm.

Located approximately midway between Bunratty and Ennis, this castle was built in 1467 and was the home of the McNamara clan, who dominated the area for more

Knowing Your Castles

Ireland, as even the most casual visitor will notice, has no shortage of stones. When the first Irish farmers began to turn over the soil, these stones merely got in their way. Eventually, the stones were put to use, to build walls. The first walls were built to keep nature out (animals and the elements). Eventually, however, what had to be kept out were other human beings. In the world of walls, you can't miss the difference between walls raised to deter wolves and those raised to deter warriors.

The earliest stone fortifications in Ireland—round forts, often on hilltops—date from the Iron Age, sometime after 500 B.C. Dún Aengus on the Aran Islands, Staigue Fort in Co. Kerry, and the newly restored Lisnagun Ring Fort are among the survivors of as many as 30,000 stone forts that once protected the Irish from each other. On a smaller scale, individual families seem to have fortified their homes with mud and stone bulwarks. Another form of fortification was the crannóg, a stone and mud island, complete with palisades.

Later, in the early Christian period, when the centers of Irish civilization, the monastic communities, came under attack from Vikings, round towers that often climbed to nearly 100 feet in height were constructed to lift life, limb, and everything else precious out of harm's reach. This strategy, however, depended on the enemy's going away, like a dog that becomes tired of waiting for a treed cat to come down. Vikings, however, preferred to stay, and smoke or burn or starve the monks down from their towers.

With the Normans came the first Irish castles constructed with massive rectangular keeps. Trim Castle in Co. Meath and Carrickfergus Castle in Co. Antrim are impressive reminders of Norman clout. Cahir Castle in Co. Tipperary—complete with eight towers in its encircling battlements—has no equal in Ireland for sheer scale. Next came the tower house, a fortified residence. Needless to say, these were residences worthy of and requiring fortification. Bunratty Castle in Co. Clare and Dunguaire Castle in Co. Galway are splendidly restored examples of this kind of "safe house," which remained in vogue for several centuries. Wealthy merchants and others with less to protect built semifortified mansions, of which a well-preserved example is Rothe House in Kilkenny.

Nearly all of the above might loosely be called castles. After all, a man's (or woman's) house is reputedly his or her castle, a point made then as now by walls, towers, dead bolts, motion detectors, and alarm systems.

than 1,000 years. The original Norman structure includes elaborate late-Georgian and Regency wings that were added in the mid–19th century. Now fully restored, it is furnished with authentic 15th-century pieces and, like Bunratty Castle, serves as a venue for nightly medieval banquets in the summer season.

Cratloe Woods House

Cratloe, Co. Clare. ☎ **061/327028.** Admission £2.50 ($4) adults, £1.75 ($2.80) seniors and students, £1.50 ($2.40) children. June to mid-Sept, Mon–Sat 2–6pm.

This 17th-century house is a fine example of an Irish longhouse, an almost obsolete type of Irish architecture. Steeped in history and long associated with the O'Brien clan, who trace their ancestry back to Brian Boru, the house is still lived in, filled with family portraits, works of art, and curios, and the grounds feature a collection of horse-drawn farming machinery. The primeval Garranon Oak Wood, which provided timbers for the Westminster Hall in London, is also part of the estate.

Ballycasey Craft & Design Centre

Airport road (N19), Shannon Airport, Co. Clare. ☎ **061/362105.** Free admission. Mon–Sat 9:30am–6pm. Signposted within the airport complex, 3 miles from the main terminal, en route to the main road.

Housed in the courtyard of a restored Georgian manor house, these workshops feature an array of handcrafted items ranging from pottery, jewelry, and metalwork to knitwear and fashions. Watch the artisans as they work and learn more about their trades.

✪ Ennis Friary

Abbey St., Ennis, Co. Clare. ☎ **065/29100.** Admission £1 ($1.60) adults, 70p ($1.12) seniors, 40p (64¢) children and students. Late May to late Sept, daily 9:30am–6:30pm.

Founded in 1241 and a famous seat of learning in medieval times, this Franciscan abbey made Ennis a focal point of western Europe for many years. Records show that in 1375 it buzzed with the activity of no fewer than 350 friars and 600 students. Although it was finally forced to close in 1692 and thereafter fell into ruin, the abbey still contains many interesting sculpted tombs, decorative fragments, and carvings, including the famous McMahon tomb. The nave and chancel are the oldest parts of the friary, but other structures, such as the 15th-century tower, transept, and sacristy, are also rich in architectural detail.

Craggaunowen Bronze-Age Project

Quin, Co. Clare. ☎ **061/367178.** Admission £4 ($6.40) adults, £2.75 ($4.40) children. AE, DC, MC, V. Open daily Apr–May 19 and Aug 19–Sept 15 10am–6pm, May 20–Aug 18 9am–6pm, Sept 16–Oct 28 10am–5pm; Nov Fri–Sat 10am–4pm. Located about 10 miles east of Ennis, signposted off R469.

Making use of an actual castle, crannog (fortified island), and ring fort, the Craggaunowen Project has attempted to reconstruct and present glimpses of Ireland's ancient past, from the Neolithic period to the Christian middle ages. In addition, a special glass house has been created to house and to exhibit Tim Severin's sea-proven replica of the curragh in which Brendan and his brother monks may have sailed to America in the 5th century. This project must have been launched with great vision and enthusiasm, but much of the original wind seems to have left its sails. As a "living history" project, it is currently on life-support. The possibilities here are exciting, but the reality is disappointing.

de Valera Library & Museum

Harmony Row, off Abbey St., Ennis, Co. Clare. ☎ **065/21616.** Free admission. Mon and Wed–Thurs 11am–5:30pm, Tues and Fri 11am–8pm.

Housed in a renovated 19th-century Presbyterian church, this museum/library pays tribute to Ireland's American-born freedom fighter and president, Eamon de Valera (1882–1975). It contains many of de Valera's personal possessions, including his private car. There is also an art collection and interesting area relics, such as a door from a Spanish Armada galleon that sank off the Clare coast in 1588 at a place now known as Spanish Point. A bronze statue of de Valera stands several blocks away at the Ennis Courthouse.

Shannon Crystal

Sandfield Rd., Ennis, Co. Clare. ☎ **065/21250.** Free admission. Daily 9am–6pm.

Situated on the north end of town, on the approach to Galway road, this is the Shannon area's own crystal-making enterprise, producing original hand-cut glassware on the premises. The showroom is open to visitors, who can watch daily demonstrations by the master cutter.

Readers Recommend

Adare Lodge, Kildimo Road, Adare, Co. Limerick. ☎ **061/396629.** *Agnes Fitzpatrick, the proprietor, provides immaculate rooms which are beautifully decorated, coordinating prints and solids and colors. Tea-making facilities and TVs are in each room and all rooms are en-suite. Every need is met. Breakfast is superb with fresh home-baked breads, fruit, and yogurts as well as a delicious traditional Irish breakfast. You may help yourself to as much as you'd like. Most importantly, Agnes genuinely cares about her guests. She is delightful and takes time to talk with you and offer suggestions for places to dine, sightseeing, etc. Agnes and her husband work very hard and take personal pride in their business.*

—Kevin and Gerry Boyle, Landenburg, Pa.

SHOPPING

Avoca
Limerick-Ennis road (N18), Bunratty, Co. Clare. ☎ **061/364029.**

This pink, thatched-roof cottage shop is a branch of the legendary Co. Wicklow-based Avoca Handweavers, the oldest company of its kind in Ireland, dating from 1723. Like its sister shops, this one carries all the colorful tweeds and mohairs that have made the Avoca line famous, plus linen-cotton fashions, stylish sweaters, tweed totes, and a wide array of hats. A coffee shop, serving lunches and snacks, is on the premises. Open daily from 9:30am to 5:30pm.

Belleek Shop
36 Abbey St., Ennis. ☎ **065/22607.**

Located in the heart of Ennis, overlooking the 16th-century Franciscan Abbey, this shop is more than 90 years old and was the first Belleek china outlet in southern Ireland. The shop is renowned for its extensive range of Waterford, Galway, and Tipperary crystals, fine china, tableware, and figurines. In recent years, it has expanded to include other Irish products such as handmade character dolls and turf crafts, pewter, jewelry, and fashionable tweeds. Open Monday through Saturday from 9am to 6pm.

Custy's Traditional Music Shop
Francis St., Ennis. ☎ **065/21727.**

If you'd like to bring back the melodious sounds of Co. Clare, this is the place to shop. The wares include a full range of traditional and folk music tapes and CDs as well as books, photos, paintings, and crafts pertaining to traditional music. You can also buy your own fiddle, tin whistle, banjo, concertina, accordion, or flute here. Open Monday through Saturday from 9:30am to 6:00pm.

Shannon Duty Free Shops
Shannon Airport, Co. Clare. ☎ **061/471444.** Fax 061/472680.

Founded in 1947, this huge airport complex is known throughout the world as the mother of all duty-free shops. It offers tax-free bargains to shoppers passing through or departing from the airport. Most of the products are Irish, such as Waterford crystal, Belleek china, Donegal tweeds, Aran knitwear, Connemara marble, ceramic leprechauns, shillelaghs, and smoked salmon, but you'll also find names like Wedgwood, Bing and Grondahl, Lladro, Anri, Limoges, Orrefors, and Pringle. Open daily from 9:30am to 5:30pm.

SPORTS & OUTDOOR PURSUITS

GOLF   Where else but in Ireland can you step off a plane and step up to the first tee? The 18-hole, par-72 championship course at the **Shannon Golf Club,** Shannon Airport (☎ **061/471020**), welcomes visitors to play, for greens fees of £24 to £28 ($38.40 to $44.80). Located within a half mile of the main terminal, it is surrounded by scenic vistas of Co. Clare and the Shannon River, as well as of the busy jetways.

Other choices in the area include the newly expanded 18-hole, par-71 **Dromoland Golf Club,** Newmarket-on-Fergus, Co. Clare (☎ **061/368444**), with greens fees of £22 to £24 ($35.20 to $38.40); and the par-69 parkland course at the **Ennis Golf Club,** Drumbiggle, Ennis, Co. Clare (☎ **065/24074**), with greens fees of £17 ($27.20).

HORSEBACK RIDING   Horseback riding over 40 acres of County Clare can be arranged at the **Smithtown Riding Centre,** Ennis Road, Newmarket-on-Fergus, Co. Clare (☎ **061/3611494**). It's located 2 miles north of Shannon Airport. An hour's ride averages £10 to £12 ($13 to $19.20).

ACCOMMODATIONS

Very Expensive / Expensive

✪ Dromoland Castle

Limerick-Ennis road (N18), Newmarket-on-Fergus, Co. Clare. ☎ **800/346-7007** from the U.S., or 061/368144. Fax 061/363355. 73 rms. TV TEL. £116–£202 ($185.60–$323.20) single or double, £245–£414 ($392–$662.40) suite. No service charge. AE, DC, MC, V.

You can vacation like royalty in a fairy-tale setting of turrets and towers (and every 20th-century luxury) at this impressive castle hotel located just 8 miles from Shannon Airport. The castle was built in 1686 by the O'Briens, the high kings of Ireland, and was restored and refurbished 30 years ago as a hotel. It's nestled beside the River Rine, amid 400 acres of parklands and gardens that are home to varied species of wildlife, including a deer herd. As befits its royal exterior, the castle's drawing rooms and stately halls are full of splendid wood and stone carvings, medieval suits of armor, rich oak paneling, and original oil paintings. The guest rooms are individually decorated with designer fabrics and reproduction furniture; many look out onto the water or the romantic walled gardens.

Dining/Entertainment: The Earl of Thomond restaurant is known for French cuisine served in a regal setting overlooking the lake. There's also a relaxing bar/lounge.

Services: Concierge, 24-hour room service, laundry and dry cleaning.

Facilities: 18-hole golf course, two tennis courts, walking/jogging trails, equipment for fishing and boating.

Expensive/Moderate

West County Conference and Leisure Hotel

Clare road (N18), Ennis, Co. Clare. ☎ **800/528-1234** from the U.S., or 065/28421. Fax 065/28801. 110 rms. TV TEL. £88–£100 ($140.80–$160) double. No service charge. AE, DC, MC, V.

This modern three-story hotel is set on its own grounds on the southern edge of Ennis, 17 miles from Shannon. The decor makes use of wide-windowed facades and skylights in many of the public areas. The guest rooms are roomy and newly refurbished, and many have views of the nearby Clare hills. The new health and leisure club offers three swimming pools plus a sauna, steam room, Jacuzzi, solarium, and gym. Dining and entertainment facilities include The Pine Room candlelit

---

Readers Recommend

Laurel Lodge, Adare Rd., Newboro, Patrickswell, Co. Limerick. ☎ **061/355059.** ¹/₄ mile off the main road, only minutes from Adare. *Our room was modern, bright and spaciously comfortable. We looked out onto beautiful gardens and landscaping front and back. The entire home was immaculately clean. The bathroom was modern and large enough to move around in and the shower water was piping hot and came out of the fixture in a strong, steady flow. There were convenient places in the room to hang and store clothing. The breakfasts were delicious and one of our nicest memories of Ireland is the last rainy afternoon when we sat with other guests on the glass-enclosed porch overlooking the magnificent gardens and were served tea and biscuits. Laurel Lodge was the best of all the B&Bs we stayed in. Mr. and Mrs. Buckley were most welcoming and pleasant hosts.*

—Mr. and Mrs. Frank W. Vincent III, Canterbury, Conn.
(The Vincents operate their own B&B, Woodchuck Hill, in Connecticut.)

---

restaurant; the County Grill for a light meal; the Ivory Bar, a piano bar; and an Irish cabaret show in summer (see "Evening Entertainment," below).

Moderate

Clare Inn Golf and Leisure Hotel

Limerick-Ennis road (N18), Newmarket-on-Fergus, Co. Clare. ☎ **800/473-8954** or 061/ 368161. Fax 061/368622. 121 rms. TV TEL. £88–£100 ($140.80–$160) double. AE, DC, MC, V. No service charge. Closed Jan–Feb.

Panoramic views of the River Shannon and the Clare hills are part of the scene at this contemporary Tudor-style hotel, within 8 miles of Shannon Airport and surrounded by the Dromoland Castle golf course. The public areas are bright and airy, with large picture windows framing the countryside vistas. The guest rooms are newly renovated. Dining and entertainment choices include Deerfields restaurant, Castlefergus Bar, and the Coffee Dock cafe. For recreation, there's an 18-hole championship golf course, indoor heated swimming pool, Jacuzzi, gym, sauna, solarium, two tennis courts, jogging track, pitch and putt, and a games room.

✪ Fitzpatrick Bunratty Shamrock Inn

Limerick-Ennis road (N18), Bunratty, Co. Clare. ☎ **800/367-7701** from the U.S., or 061/ 361177. Fax 061/471252. 118 rms. TV TEL. £90–£121 ($144–$193.60) double. Service charge 12.5%. AE, DC, MC, V.

Ideally located 5 miles from Shannon Airport, this rambling two-story ranch-style hotel sits on its own wooded grounds, set back from the main road and next to Bunratty Castle and Folk Park. The guest rooms are contemporary, with beamed ceilings, light woods, multitoned Irish fabrics and furnishings, and tall windows offering views of the gardens and Bunratty Castle. In-room extras include a hair dryer, an ironing board and iron, and a luggage rack; some units have Jacuzzis. The public areas include a plant-filled sunlit conservatory and a spacious lobby/lounge. Like its sister hotels, Fitzpatrick's Castle in Dublin and Fitzpatrick's Silver Springs in Cork, this inn exudes a friendly atmosphere, brimming with the pervasive Fitzpatrick family finesse and hospitality. Concierge, valet/laundry service, room service, and a courtesy minibus service to and from the airport are all available, and for recreation, there's a new leisure center, completed in 1996, that includes an indoor heated swimming pool and sauna.

Seafood and game are the specialties of Truffles Restaurant, where there is also an efficient breakfast buffet each morning; An Bruion Bar is a lively lounge with musical entertainment most evenings.

Old Ground

O'Connell St., Ennis, Co. Clare. ☎ **065/28127.** Fax 065/28112. 58 rms. TV TEL. £80–£125 ($128–$200) double. No service charge. Rates include full breakfast. AE, DC, MC, V.

Long a focal point in the busy marketing town of Ennis, this ivy-covered two-story hotel dates from 1749. According to a citation at the front entrance, it has been known variously as the Great Inn of Jayl Street and the Kings Arms; part of the hotel was once used as the Town Hall and the Town Jail. Many of the furnishings are antiques—you'll find vintage tea chests in the halls, and there's even a 1553 fireplace that once warmed the interior of nearby Lemaneagh Castle. By 1997, a complete upgrading and refurbishment should be completed. Amenities include a restaurant, a grill room, and a very atmospheric pub called The Poet's Corner. In summer, cabaret-style entertainment is provided on many evenings.

Moderate/Inexpensive

Queens Hotel

Abbey St., Ennis, Co. Clare. ☎ **800/365-3346** from the U.S., or 065/28963. Fax 065/28628. 52 rms. TV TEL. £40–£80 ($64–$128) double. No service charge. Rates include full breakfast. MC, V.

James Joyce fans will feel especially comfortable in this hotel, since the author referred to it as "delightful" in *Ulysses.* It is no surprise that the hotel uses this literary connection to the hilt, with a Victorian-style restaurant named Joyce's and a bar called Bloom's. Nestled in the heart of Ennis next to the old friary, it is more than 100 years old but was recently updated and expanded to contemporary standards, while still preserving its old-world quality. The guest rooms are furnished in traditional style, with dark woods and frilly floral fabrics, along with the modern additions of garment presses, hair dryers, and tea/coffeemakers.

Inexpensive

☉ Cill Eoin House

Killadysert Cross, Clare road, Ennis, Co. Clare. ☎ **065/41668.** Fax 065/41668. 14 rms. TV TEL. £32–£40 ($51.10–$64) double. No service charge. Rates include full breakfast. AE. Closed Dec 24–Jan 8.

Situated just off the main N18 road at the Killadysert Cross a half mile south of Ennis, this newly built two-story guest house is a real find. It offers bright and comfortable guest rooms with hotel-quality furnishings at a very affordable price, capped by attentive service from the McGann family. Although it's within walking distance of Ennis, the rooms offer lovely views of the countryside. The house is named after the nearby medieval Killone Abbey (Killone being the Anglicization of *Cill Eoin*).

DINING

Medieval Banquets & Traditional Meals with Music

The medieval banquets at Bunratty Castle and Knappogue Castle and the traditional evening at Bunratty Folk Park can be booked in advance in the United States through a travel agent or by calling **800/CIE-TOUR.**

☉ Bunratty Castle

Limerick-Ennis road (N18), Bunratty, Co. Clare. ☎ **061/361511.** Reservations required. Dinner and entertainment £30 ($48). AE, DC, MC, V. Daily year-round; two sittings, 5:30 and 8:45pm. MEDIEVAL BANQUET.

Built in 1425, this splendid structure is the most complete and authentic example of a medieval castle in Ireland. Each evening, a full medieval banquet is re-created with music, song, and merriment. Seated at long tables in the castle's magnificent baronial hall, you'll feast on ancient recipes using modern Irish ingredients, all served in strictly medieval use-your-fingers style. For refreshment, there's mulled wine, claret, and mugs of mead (the traditional honey-based drink). To add to the fun, at each banquet a "lord and lady" are chosen from the participants to reign over the three-hour proceedings, and someone else is thrown into the dungeon.

✪ Knappogue Castle

Quin, Co. Clare. ☎ **061/361511.** Reservations required. Dinner and entertainment £29.50 ($47.20). AE, DC, MC, V. May–Oct daily; two sittings, 5:30 and 8:45pm. MEDIEVAL BANQUET.

Once the stronghold of the McNamara clan, this castle was built in 1467. Now fully restored, it's the setting for authentic medieval banquets during the summer season. This castle is smaller and more intimate than Bunratty, but you'll still feast on a medieval meal, followed by a colorful pageant of Irish history celebrating the influential role of women in Celtic Ireland. The program includes rhyme and mime, song and dance.

✪ Traditional Irish Night

Bunratty Folk Park, off the Limerick-Ennis road (N18), Bunratty, Co. Clare. ☎ **061/361511.** Reservations required. Dinner and entertainment £24 ($40). AE, DC, MC, V. May–Sept daily; two sittings, 5:30 and 8:45pm. TRADITIONAL IRISH.

Irish country life of yesteryear is the focus of this "at home" evening in a thatched farmhouse cottage. You'll dine on a traditional meal of Irish stew, homemade breads, and apple pie and fresh cream. Then the music begins: the flute and fiddle, accordion, bodhran, and spoons—all at a spirited, foot-tapping pace.

Expensive

✪ MacCloskey's

Bunratty Mews House, Bunratty, Co. Clare. ☎ **061/364082.** Reservations required. Fixed-price dinner £26 ($39). AE, DC, MC, V. Tues–Sat 7–9:30pm. Closed 3 weeks in February. IRISH/FRENCH.

Located in the former mews and wine cellars of Bunratty House, a restored 1804 Georgian mansion, this award-winning candlelight restaurant is the creation of a hard-working duo, Gerry and Marie MacCloskey. There are four dining rooms, each with original whitewashed walls, archways, and polished slate floors. Rack of lamb, black sole, mussels in champagne, duck à l'orange, crab crepes, and wild salmon are specialties. You can also get a masterful Caesar salad or pickled herring here, plus desserts like hot Cointreau soufflé, chocolate mousse with brandy, or baked pear puffs. It's the best in the area—don't miss it.

Moderate

✪ The Cloister

Club Bridge, Abbey St., Ennis. ☎ **065/29521.** Reservations recommended. Bar food all items £2–£8 ($3.20–$12.80); dinner main courses £11–£16 ($17.60–$25.60). AE, MC, V. Daily noon–10:30pm. IRISH.

Next to the remains of a 13th-century abbey, this old-world gem offers innovative Irish cuisine. The decor is warmly elegant, with open turf fireplaces and stoves, beamed ceilings, and reproductions from the Book of Kells adorning the walls. The menu includes poached monkfish with red-pepper sauce, wild venison with juniper-and-Armagnac sauce, and suprême of chicken layered with Carrigline cheese and Irish Mist. A house specialty starter is Inagh goat cheese laced with port-wine sauce. Pub-style lunches are served in the skylit Friary Bar, adjacent to the old abbey walls.

Moderate/Inexpensive

Brogan's

24 O'Connell St., Ennis. ☎ **065/29859.** Reservations recommended for dinner. Main courses £5.75–£12 ($9.20–$19.20). MC, V. Daily noon–11pm. IRISH.

An old-timer in the center of town, this pub is known for its hearty meals, including Irish stew, beef stroganoff, and chicken curry. In addition, there is roast duck, Dover sole, and local salmon. The atmosphere is casual and the decor cozy, with brick walls, a copper-fluted fireplace, and ceiling fans. On Tuesday and Thursday nights ballad music is usually offered.

Cruise's Pub Restaurant

Abbey St., Ennis. ☎ **065/41800.** Reservations recommended for dinner. Bar food £1.25–£8.50 ($2–$13.60); dinner main courses £5.50–£12.50 ($8.80–$20). MC, V. Daily noon–3pm and 5:30–10:30pm. IRISH.

Housed in a 1658 building, this relatively new eatery has low beamed ceilings, timber fixtures and fittings, crackling fires in open hearths, lantern lighting, a rough flagstone floor strewn with sawdust, memorabilia from crockery to books, and a snug appropriately dubbed "The Safe Haven." On warm days, seating is extended into an outdoor courtyard overlooking the friary. The menu offers a good selection of pub grub, including a specialty dish called Friars Irish Stew plus steaks, club sandwiches, and seafood soups and sandwiches. There are often impromptu music sessions. Evening meals range from seafood and steaks to vegetarian stir-fry or chicken Kiev.

EVENING ENTERTAINMENT

In addition to the medieval banquets and traditional ceili evenings that are synonymous with this area, Co. Clare offers much to delight the visitor in the evenings. Many hotels, such as the **West County,** Clare Road, Ennis (☎ 065/28421), present music or shows, particularly in the high season. It offers Summer Cabaret, 2½ hours of traditional music, drama, comedy, and step dancing. Running each Tuesday from June through September, the show can be enjoyed with or without dinner. Dinner starts at 7:30pm, the show at 8:30pm. Admission is £5 ($8) for the show only, £15 ($24) for dinner and the show.

For pure traditional entertainment, try **Cois na hAbhna** (pronounced *cush*-na *how*-na), Gort Road, Ennis (☎ 065/20996). This center stages sessions of music, song, and dance, followed by ceili dancing with audience participation. Tea and brown bread are served. Sessions run year-round from 8:30 to 11:30pm. Admission ranges from £2 to £4 ($3.20 to $6.40), depending on the event.

This region has many fine pubs, but there's one you definitely shouldn't miss: **Durty Nelly's,** Limerick-Ennis road (N18), Bunratty, Co. Clare (☎ 061/364861). Established in 1620 next door to Bunratty Castle, this cottage tavern was originally a watering hole for the castle guards. Now, with a mustard-colored facade and palm trees at its entrance, it's a favorite before-and-after haunt of locals and of tourists who join the nightly medieval banquets at the castle. With mounted elk heads and old lanterns on the walls, sawdust on the floors, and open turf fireplaces, the decor hasn't changed much over the centuries. This is also a good spot for a substantial pub lunch or for a full dinner in one of Durty Nelly's two restaurants. Spontaneous Irish music sessions erupt here on most evenings.

THE BURREN

Moving westward from Ennis into the heart of Co. Clare, you'll come to an amazing district of 100 square miles called The Burren. The word *burren* is derived from the Irish word *boirreann,* which means "a rocky place."

It is a strange, lunarlike region of bare carboniferous limestone, roughly bordered by the towns of Corofin, Ennistymon, Lahinch, Lisdoonvarna, and Ballyvaughan. Massive sheets of rock, jagged and craggy boulders, caves, and potholes are visible for miles in a moonscapelike pattern, yet this is also a setting for little lakes and streams and an amazing assemblage of flora. There is always something in bloom, even in winter, from fern and moss to orchids, rock roses, milkwort, wild thyme, geraniums, violets, and fuchsia. The Burren is also famous for its butterflies, which thrive on the rare flora. Such animals as the pine martin, stoat, and badger, rare in the rest of Ireland, are also common here.

The story of The Burren began more than 300 million years ago, when layers of shells and sediment were deposited under a tropical sea, only to be thrust above this surface many millions of years later and left open to the erosive power of Irish rain and weather, producing the limestone landscape that appears today.

As early as 7,000 years ago, humans began to leave their mark on this landscape in the form of Stone Age burial monuments such as the famed Poulnabrone Dolmen and Gleninsheen wedge tomb.

In addition to rock, The Burren area does have other unique attractions. Lisdoonvarna, on the western edge, is a town known for its spa of natural mineral springs. Each summer it draws thousands of people to bathe in its therapeutic waters of sulfur, chalybeate (iron), and iodine. Lisdoon, as the natives call it, is also known worldwide for hosting an annual matchmaking festival.

One of the most scenic Burren drives is along R480, a corkscrew-shaped road that leads from Corofin to Ballyvaughan, a delightful little village overlooking Galway Bay.

ATTRACTIONS

✪ Burren National Park
The Burren, Co. Clare.

Currently under development as a national park, the confines of this park encompass the entire Burren area (100 square miles), a remarkable limestone plateau dotted with ruined castles, cliffs, rivers, lakes, valleys, green road walks, barren rock mountains, and plant life that defies all of nature's conventional rules. The area is particularly rich in archaeological remains from the Neolithic through the medieval periods—dolmens and wedge tombs (approximately 120), ring forts (500), round towers, ancient churches, high crosses, monasteries, and holy wells. In recent years there has been some local controversy with regard to the defining of the park and the placement of a permanent visitor/interpretative center along the lines of those at Connemara and Glenveagh National Parks. Until these issues are resolved, the park remains without an official entrance point, with no admission charges or restrictions to access.

The Burren Centre
Kilfenora, Co. Clare. ☎ **065/88030.** Admission £2.20 ($3.50) adults, £1.60 ($2.55) seniors, £1 ($1.60) children over age 8. AE, MC, V. Mar–May and Sept–Oct, daily 10am–5pm; June–Aug, daily 9:30am–6pm. R476 to Kilfenora.

Established in 1975 in the heart of The Burren as a community development cooperative, this building is the best place to acquaint yourself with all facets of this area. The facility includes a 25-minute audiovisual presentation plus landscape models and interpretive displays that highlight the unique features of the region's geology, geography, flora, and fauna. Also here are tearooms, a shop stocked with Burren-made crafts and products, and picnic tables outside.

⊙ Aillwee Cave

Ballyvaughan, Co. Clare. ☎ **065/77036.** Admission £4 ($6.40) adults, £2.25 ($3.60) children aged 4–16. Daily mid-Mar to June and Sept to early Nov, 10am–5:30pm; July–Aug, 10am–6:30pm.

One of Ireland's oldest underground sites, Aillwee was formed millions of years ago but remained hidden until it was discovered less than 50 years ago by local farmer Jacko McGann. The cave has more than 3,400 feet of passages and hollows running straight into the heart of a mountain. Its highlights are bridged chasms, deep caverns, a frozen waterfall, and the Bear Pits—hollows scraped out by the brown bear, one of the cave's original inhabitants. Guided tours, which last approximately half an hour, are conducted continuously. Among facilities are a cafe and craft shop; a unique farmhouse cheese-making enterprise called Burren Gold Cheese, located near the cave's entrance; and an apiary where honey is produced.

Clare Heritage Centre

Corofin, Co. Clare. ☎ **065/37955.** Admission £2 ($3.20) adults, £1 ($1.60) children under 12. Apr–Oct, daily 10am–6pm. R476 to Corofin.

If you have Clare family roots, you'll be especially fascinated by this heritage museum and genealogical research center, but even if you don't have Clare ancestry, this center is worth a visit to learn about the history of the county. Housed in a former Church of Ireland edifice built by a first cousin of Queen Anne in 1718, it has exhibits on Clare farming, industry, commerce, education, forestry, language, and music, all designed to reflect life in Co. Clare during the last 300 years. There's also a tearoom and gift shop. The genealogical research facility is open year-round.

Dysert O'Dea Castle and Archaeology Centre

Corofin, Co. Clare. ☎ **065/37722.** Admission £2 ($3.20) adults, £1.50 ($2.40) seniors and students, £1 ($1.60) children, £5 ($8) family. May–Sept, daily 10am–6pm. R476 to Corofin.

Built in 1480 by Diarmaid O'Dea on a rocky outcrop of land, this castle was badly damaged during the Cromwellian years but was restored and opened to the public in 1986 as an archaeology center and museum, with exhibitions on the history of the area, plus an audiovisual show. The castle is also the starting point for a signposted trail leading to 25 sites of historical and archaeological interest within a 2-mile radius, including a church founded by St. Tola in the 8th century that contains a unique Romanesque doorway surrounded by a border of 12 heads carved in stone. The O'Deas, who were chieftains of the area, are buried under the church. Also at the center are a round tower from the 10th or 12th century, a 12th-century high cross, a holy well, a 14th-century battlefield, and a stone fort believed to date back to the Iron Age. The castle bakery is currently under excavation.

Spa Wells Centre

Kincora Rd., Lisdoonvarna, Co. Clare. ☎ **065/74023.** Free admission. June–Oct, daily 10am–6pm.

Nestled in a shady parkland on the edge of town, this is Lisdoonvarna's famous Victorian-style spa complex, dating from the 18th century. The sulfur-laced mineral waters are served hot or cold in the pump room, drawn from an illuminated well. Sulfur baths can also be arranged. Videos of the Burren and the Shannon area are shown continuously in the visitor center.

Burren College of Art

Newtown Castle, Ballyvaughan, Co. Clare. ☎ **065/77200.** Fax 065/77201. Admission fees vary according to courses. Year-round. N67 to Ballyvaughan.

If there ever was a great place for an artist to paint or a photographer to take a picture, it has to be The Burren. Bearing this in mind, this new center of artistic learning has sprung up in the midst of the dramatic Burren landscapes. Set on the grounds of a 16th-century castle, this newly constructed college was opened in 1993. Although geared to 15-week semester programs and to granting full four-year bachelor of fine arts degrees, it also offers a range of weekend and one-week courses ideal for a visitor. The facilities include bright modern studios for sculpture, painting, photography, and drawing, plus a lecture theater, exhibition area, library, cafeteria, and shop.

The Burren Smokehouse Ltd.

Kincora Rd., Lisdoonvarna, Co. Clare. ☎ 065/74432. Free admission. Daily Mar–Oct 9am–7pm.

Aficionados of smoked salmon flock to this place to see the fish-smoking process firsthand and to buy right from the source. Visitors are welcome to watch as fresh Atlantic salmon is sorted, hand-treated, salted, and then slowly smoked over Irish oak chips in the traditional way. Each side of salmon is then vacuum sealed and chilled. Tours are given continually. Smoked mackerel, eels, and trout are also produced here.

WALKING THE BURREN

With its unique terrain and pathways, The Burren lends itself to walking. Visitors who want to amble through the hills and turloughs (dry lakes that sometimes take on water), limestone pavements and terraces, shale uplands and inland lakes, should follow **The Burren Way,** a 26-mile signposted route stretching from Ballyvaughan to Liscannor. An information sheet outlining the route is available from any tourist office.

SHOPPING

Manus Walsh Art Gallery & Craft Workshop

Main St., Ballyvaughan, Co. Clare. ☎ 065/77029.

This shop in the center of town features a wide range of colorful handcrafted enamel jewelry of Celtic and early Irish designs. Visitors are welcome to watch Manus work as they browse or buy. Items for sale include Manus-made pendants, brooches, earrings, ornate boxes, dishes, and plaques, as well as crafts by other local artisans. Open April through October, Monday through Saturday from 10am to 6pm.

ACCOMMODATIONS

Expensive

✪ Gregans Castle Hotel

Ballyvaughan-Lisdoonvarna road (N67), Ballyvaughan, Co. Clare. ☎ 800/223-6510 from the U.S., or 065/77005. Fax 065/77111. 22 rms. TEL. £120 ($192) double. Service charge 12.5%. Rates include full breakfast. MC, V. Closed Nov–Mar.

Located in the northern part of Co. Clare, just over 3 miles outside of Ballyvaughan, this two-story country house is in the heart of the rocky Burren country, and provides distant views of Galway Bay. Although not strictly a castle, it is built on the site of the ancient family estates of the Martyn family and the O'Loughlens, princes of The Burren. Owned and managed by the Hayden family, it's surrounded by beautiful gardens. The public areas, which include a newly renovated traditional drawing room and library, are furnished with heirlooms and period pieces, antique

Impressions

Stoney seaboard fair and foreign
Stoney hills poured over space,
Stoney outcrop of the Burren,
Stones in every fertile place. . . .

—Sir John Betjeman (1906–84)

books, and Raymond Piper's mural paintings of Burren flora. The Corkscrew Bar is a particular delight, with copper and brass hangings and an open turf fireplace. Each bedroom is individually decorated in country-house style, with designer fabrics, dark woods, and brass accents; some have four-poster or canopied beds. The restaurant has a reputation for fine seafood and creative cookery.

Inexpensive

Carrigann Hotel

Lisdoonvarna, Co. Clare. ☎ **800/989-7676** from the U.S., or 065/74036. Fax 065/74567. 20 rms. TV TEL. £50–£64 double ($80–$102.40). Rates include full breakfast. MC, V. Closed Nov–Feb.

Situated on a hillside just off the main road on the outskirts of town, this country house hotel is surrounded by rose bushes and flower-filled gardens. Most of the guest rooms, which have standard furnishings, are enhanced by views of the gardens. Facilities include a restaurant, lounge bar, and sun lounge. The Carrigann also offers its own one-week Burren Walking Holidays.

✪ Rusheen Lodge

Knocknagrough, Ballyvaughan, Co. Clare. ☎ **065/77092.** Fax 065/77152. 6 rms. TV TEL. £40–£50 double ($64–$80). No service charge. Rates include full breakfast. AE, MC, V. Closed mid-Dec to Feb.

On the main road just south of Ballyvaughan village, this modern two-story bungalow-style guest house is surrounded by flowers, both in the garden and hanging from baskets in front of the house. The innkeepers are Rita and John McGann, whose father, Jacko McGann, discovered the nearby Aillwee Caves, one of the area's most remarkable natural attractions. The guest rooms are individually furnished with light woods, semicanopied beds, and floral fabrics, and include a tea/coffeemaker and hair dryer. Breakfast, served in a cheery pastel-toned room overlooking the gardens, presents freshly caught local fish as an option. Dried and fresh Burren flowers enhance the decor throughout the house.

DINING

Moderate

Claire's

Main St., Ballyvaughan, Co. Clare. ☎ **065/77029.** Reservations required. Main courses £9.95–£12.95 ($15.90–$20.70). MC, V. May–Sept, Mon–Sun 7–10pm; and Mar–Apr, weekends 7–10pm. IRISH.

A favorite with regular visitors to The Burren, this homey and intimate restaurant in the middle of the village is the domain of Claire Walsh, whose husband, Manus, operates an adjacent craft shop (see "Shopping," above). Just as Manus is creative with enamel designs, so Claire is with food in the kitchen. The chef's specials include monkfish Provençale, pigeon breasts flamed in brandy with a red-currant and cream sauce, and baked Barbary duck breasts with a raspberry cream sauce.

✪ Whitethorn

Galway road (N67), Ballyvaughan. ☎ **065/77044.** Reservations recommended for dinner. Main courses at lunch £4.50–£6.95 ($7.20–$11.10), at dinner £8.95–£14.50 ($14.30–$23.20). MC, V. Daily 10am–6pm. Mar–May and Oct, Thurs–Sat 6:30–9pm; June–Sept, Tues–Sat 6:30–9pm. IRISH.

With a sailboat-shaped weathervane on the roof, this site was once a coast guard station and then a fish-processing factory. Totally rebuilt in 1989 as a restaurant, its stone facade blends right in with The Burren's terrain. The interior has a refreshing decor of ketchup-colored paneling, black tables and chairs, old photographs, fresh Burren flowers, and floor-to-ceiling slanted windows that provide spectacular views of Galway Bay and distant shores. There is seating outside as well. Lunch items, served buffet style, include fresh seafood salads, pastas, soups, and meat casseroles or platters. The dinner menu offers such choices as rack of lamb with rosemary-and-almond sauce, grilled sirloin steak with Irish whiskey sauce, roast stuffed pheasant with a red-currant glaze, and couscous with eggplant and goat cheese. It's located about a mile east of the village on the main road.

Moderate/Inexpensive

Bofey Quinn's

Main St., Corofin, Co. Clare. ☎ **065/37321.** Reservations not necessary. Main courses £4.35–£14.50 ($6.95–$23.20). V. Jan–May and Oct–Dec noon–9pm; June–Sept 10:30am–10pm. IRISH.

An informal atmosphere prevails at this pub/restaurant in the center of town. Dinner specialties include fresh wild salmon and cod as well as a variety of steaks, chops, and mixed grills. Pub grub lunches are also available throughout the day.

THE CLARE COAST

One of Ireland's most photographed scenes, the Cliffs of Moher draw busloads and carloads of visitors to Clare's remote reaches every day of the year. Rising sheer above the Atlantic Ocean to heights of over 700 feet and extending about 5 miles along the coast, these cliffs are Co. Clare's foremost natural wonder.

The Cliffs are only the beginning, however. Other highlights of the Clare Coast include the world-renowned golf resort at Lahinch, praised by ace golfers as the "St. Andrews of Ireland" and the paradigm of Irish links golf.

Farther up the coast is the secluded fishing village of Doolin, often referred to as the unofficial capital of Irish traditional music. Doolin, like Galway to the north, is also a departure point for the short boat trip to the Aran Islands.

The Clare Coast is dotted with a variety of seaside resorts, such as Kilrush, Kilkee, Miltown Malbay, and Ennistymon, that are particularly popular with Irish families. As you drive around this craggy coastline, you'll find many other off-the-beaten-path delights, with intriguing place names: Pink Cave, Puffing Hole, Intrinsic Bay, Chimney Hill, Elephant's Teeth, Mutton Island, Loop Head, and Lovers Leap.

ATTRACTIONS

✪ Cliffs of Moher

R478, Co. Clare. ☎ **065/81171.** Free admission to cliffs; £1 ($1.60) to O'Brien's Tower. Cliffs visitor center, daily 10am–6pm; O'Brien's Tower, May–Oct, daily 10am–6pm.

Hailed as one of Ireland's natural wonders, these 760-foot cliffs stretch for over 5 miles along Clare's Atlantic coast. They offer panoramic views, especially from the 19th-century O'Brien's Tower at the northern end. On a clear day you can see the Aran Islands, Galway Bay, and many distant vistas. The visitor center includes a tearoom, an information desk, and a craft and souvenir shop. The Cliffs are located about 7 miles north of Lahinch.

Kilrush Heritage Centre

Town Hall, Market Sq., off Henry St., Kilrush. ☎ **065/51577** or 065/51047. Admission £2 ($3.20) adults, £1 ($1.60) children. May–Sept, Mon–Sat 10am–5:30pm, Sun noon–4pm.

Housed in the town's historic Market House, this center provides historic and cultural background on Kilrush—often called the "capital of West Clare"—and the south Clare coast. An audiovisual presentation, *Kilrush in Landlord Times,* tells of the struggles of this area's tenant farmers during the 18th and 19th centuries and particularly during the Great Famine years. The museum is also the focal point of a signposted heritage walk around the town. The building itself, erected in 1808 by the Vandeleur family, the area's chief landlords, was burned to the ground in 1892 and rebuilt in its original style in 1931.

TRIPS TO THE ARAN ISLANDS

Doolin Ferry Co.

The Pier, Doolin, Co. Clare. ☎ **065/74455.** Inisheer £15 ($24) round-trip, Inishmore £20 ($32) round-trip. Mid-Apr to mid-May, daily 11am to both islands; rest of May, daily 10am, 11:30am, and 6:30pm to Inisheer, 10am and 11am to Inishmore; June–Aug, daily 9:30am, 11am, 1pm, 2:30pm (July–Aug only), 5:15pm, 6:30pm, and 7:30pm to Inisheer, 10am and 11am to Inishmore; Sept, daily 10am and 11:30am to both islands.

Although many people come to Doolin to see the local sights and enjoy the music, they also come to board this ferry to the Aran Islands. The three fabled islands, sitting out in the Atlantic, are closer to Doolin than they are to Galway (a short 5-mile/30-minute journey). Service is provided to both Inisheer and Inishmore. (For more information about excursions to the Aran Islands, see Chapter 12, "Galway City.")

SPORTS & OUTDOOR PURSUITS

BIRD-WATCHING   The Bridges of Ross on the north side of Loop Head is one of the prime autumn bird-watching sites in Ireland, especially during northwest gales when several rare species have been seen with some consistency. The lighthouse at the tip of the Head is also a popular spot for watching sea birds.

BOATING & FISHING   The waters of the lower Shannon estuary and the Atlantic coastline are known as a good place to fish for shark, skate, turbot, ray, conger eel, tope, pollack, and more. The new Kilrush Creek Marina, an attraction in itself, is the base for **Atlantic Adventures Sea Angling,** Cappa, Kilrush, Co. Clare (☎ **065/52133;** fax 065/51720), a company that offers boat charters and rentals for fishing in these waters. Prices start at £30 ($48) per person for a day's fishing or £220 ($350) for an eight-hour boat charter. Rods and reels can be hired for £5.50 ($8.80) per day.

DOLPHIN WATCHING   The Shannon Estuary is home to about 70 bottlenose dolphins, one of four such resident group of dolphins in Europe. Dolphin-watching cruises leave from Carrigaholt with **DOLPHINWATCH** (☎ **065/58156**), and from **Kilrush Creek Marina** (☎ **065/51327**) daily. Advance booking is essential. £8 ($12.80) adults, £4 ($6.40) children.

GOLF   For golfers coming to Clare's Atlantic coast, a day at **Lahinch Golf Club,** Lahinch (☎ **065/81003**), is not to be missed. There are two 18-hole courses here, but the longer championship links course is the one that has given Lahinch its farreaching reputation. This course's elevations, such as the 9th and 13th holes, reveal open vistas of sky, land, and sea; they also make the winds an integral part of the scoring. Watch out for the goats: They're Lahinch's legendary weather forecasters. If they huddle by the clubhouse, it means a storm is approaching. Visitors are welcome to play any day, especially on weekdays; greens fees range from £25 ($40) on weekdays to £30 ($48) on weekends.

SHOPPING

Doolin Craft Gallery

Ballyvoe, Doolin, Co. Clare. ☎ 065/74309.

Since 1982 this has been an oasis of fine craftsmanship in the heart of the Clare coast. Surrounded by gardens on the edge of the village next to the churchyard, this shop is the brainchild of two artisans: Matthew O'Connell, who creates batik work with Celtic designs on wall hangings, cushion covers, ties, and scarves; and Mary Gray, who hand-fashions contemporary gold and silver jewelry, inspired by The Burren's rocks, flora, and wild flowers. There are also products by other Irish craftspeople. A good coffee shop is on the premises. Open daily from 8:30am to 8pm.

Traditional Music Shop

Doolin, Co. Clare. ☎ 065/74407.

In this town known for its traditional music, this small shop is a center of attention. It offers all types of Irish traditional music on cassette tape and compact disc, as well as books and instruments including tin whistles and bodhrans. Open Easter to mid-October daily from 10am to 6pm or later.

ACCOMMODATIONS

Moderate

Aberdeen Arms

Main St., Lahinch, Co. Clare. ☎ **065/81100.** Fax 065/81228. 55 rms. TV TEL. £70–£90 ($112–$144) double. Includes full Irish breakfast and service charge. AE, DC, V.

In the heart of town yet within view of the golf course that has made Lahinch famous, this hotel is more than 140 years old and is said to be the oldest golf links hotel in Ireland. It's an ideal base for golfers and for vacationers touring the Clare coast. The bedrooms are contemporary and functional, and the public rooms have a country-inn atmosphere. Facilities include a restaurant, coffee shop, and golf-theme lounge bar where the chat is usually centered on golf. For nongolfers, there's a tennis court, squash court, and gym.

Aran View House

Doolin, Co. Clare. ☎ **065/74061** or 065/74420. Fax 065/74540. 19 rms. TV TEL. £50–£80 ($80–$128) double. Rates include full breakfast. AE, DC, MC, V. Closed Nov–Mar.

Dating from 1736, this three-story Georgian-style stone house stands on a hill on the main road, overlooking panoramic views of the Clare coastline and, on a clear day, the Aran Islands. Recently, innkeepers John and Theresa Linnane have updated and refurbished it as a hotel in traditional Irish style. The guest rooms are decorated with dark woods, and some have four-poster beds and armoires. Facilities include a restaurant and lounge. It's situated on 100 acres of farmland just north of town.

Inexpensive

Doolin House

Doolin, Co. Clare. ☎ **065/74259.** Fax 065/74474. 6 rms. TEL. £30–£32 ($48–$51.20) single or double. No service charge. Rates include full breakfast. MC, V. Closed Dec 20–26.

Built as a guest house in 1991, this two-story traditional stone house sits on the main road on the edge of Doolin, with views of the countryside and the sea. The guest rooms have traditional dark-wood furnishings, with floral and pastel fabrics and accessories. Two rooms are on the ground floor. Facilities include a TV lounge for guests.

Doonmacfelim House

Doolin, Co. Clare. ☎ **065/74503.** Fax 065/74129. 8 rms. TEL. £30–£36 ($48–$57.60) double. No service charge. Rates include full breakfast. MC, V.

Situated on the main street a few hundred feet from the famous Gus O'Connor's Pub (see "A Pub," below), this modern two-story guest house is a great value in the heart of Doolin. Although it's in the center of everything, the house is also surrounded by a dairy farm. Guest rooms have standard furnishings and nice views of the neighboring countryside and town. Facilities include a hard tennis court.

DINING

Expensive/Moderate

Barrtra Seafood Restaurant

Barrtra, Lahinch, Co. Clare. ☎ **065/81280.** Reservations recommended. Fixed-price lunch £8 ($12.80), fixed-price dinner £20 ($32); à la carte available. AE, DC, MC, V. Mar–Sept, Tues–Sat 12:30–2:30pm, Mon–Sat 6–10pm. SEAFOOD/VEGETARIAN.

Set in a country house overlooking Liscannor Bay, this wide-windowed restaurant is one of the few good coastal eateries with ocean views that serves lunch as well as dinner. The menu changes daily. Lunch items include mussels, oysters, soups, and salads, while dinner choices include turbot with mushroom and sherry sauce and wild Irish salmon with white-wine sauce. In the vegetarian category are tomato-and-zucchini roulade Mornay and stuffed eggplant with fresh tomato sauce. The menu also features house-smoked salmon and such local Clare cheeses as Kilshanny (in five flavors: garlic, pepper, herb, cumin, plain), Poolcoin (Burren goat cheese), and Cratloe Hills Gold (sheep's cheese).

Moderate

✪ Manuel's

Corbally, Kilkee, Co. Clare. ☎ **065/56211.** Reservations required. Main courses £9.75–£19.75 ($15.60–$31.60). DC, MC, V. Easter to mid-Sept, daily 6:30–10:30pm. INTERNATIONAL.

With wide windows on two sides looking out onto the Atlantic coast, this restaurant has a nautical ambience and decor. It's on high ground off the main road, about a mile north of Kilkee. Chef Manuel di Lucia relies heavily on local seafood, with choices like Clare lobster, baked Atlantic salmon stuffed with seafood mousseline in pastry with tomato-butter sauce, chicken fillet in tarragon sauce, and a selection of steaks.

Moderate/Inexpensive

Ivy Cottage, Ilsa's Kitchen

Doolin, Co. Clare. ☎ **065/74244.** Reservations required. Main courses £8.90–£11.90 ($14.25–$19.05). MC, V. May–Sept, daily 6–9pm. IRISH.

Located just a few doors from Gus O'Connor's famous pub, this restaurant is housed in an ivy-covered, thatched-roof stone cottage dating from 1901, with a skylight, sugan chairs, a turf fireplace, and pictures of Burren flora on the inside. The simple menu concentrates on local seafood, including such dishes as lemon sole steamed with herbs and cream-wine sauce; fisherman's casserole of cod with leeks, tomato, and cheese; Burren lamb chops; and vegetarian lasagna.

Bruach na hAille

Roadford, Doolin, Co. Clare. ☎ **065/74120.** Reservations recommended. Main courses £7.50–£12 ($12–$19.20). No credit cards. Apr–Oct, daily 6–9:30pm. IRISH/SEAFOOD.

Beside the bridge over the River Aille, this restaurant's name means "bridge of the River Aille." It's a cozy, cottage-style place with an emphasis on seafood, including lobster, crab, and other local fish. Signature dishes include fillet of sole in cider with shellfish cream sauce, ragout of seasonal fish and shellfish, and baked seafood au gratin. In addition, there's a choice of steaks, chicken, lamb, and veal dishes.

A PUB

No description of the Clare coast would be complete without mention of ✪ **Gus O'Connor's Pub,** Doolin, Co. Clare (☎ **065/74168**). Situated in a row of thatched fishermen's cottages less than a mile from the roaring waters of the Atlantic, this simple pub beckons people from many miles each evening. Besides its historic charm (it dates from 1832), its big draw is music: This is *the* spot in north Co. Clare for Irish traditional music sessions. If your hunger extends beyond music, the pub is now serving meals, specializing in seafood.

3 County Mayo

Mayo's chief town (Ballina) is 63 miles N of Galway, 120 miles N of Shannon Airport, 153 miles NW of Dublin, and 193 miles NW of Cork.

GETTING TO & AROUND COUNTY MAYO   By Air   Aer Lingus provides daily service from Dublin into **Knock International Airport,** Charlestown, Co. Mayo (☎ **094/67222**). In addition, charter flights operate in the summer from the United States.

From Britain, air service to Knock is provided by **Logan Air** from Glasgow and Manchester, and **Ryan Air** from London's Stansted and Luton as well as from Liverpool.

By Public Transport   Irish Rail and **Bus Eireann** (☎ **096/21011**) provide daily service from Dublin and other cities into Ballina, Westport, and Castlebar, with bus connections into smaller towns. There is also express service from Galway into most Mayo towns.

By Car   From Dublin and points east, the main N5 road leads to many points in Co. Mayo; from Galway, take N84 or N17. From Sligo and points north, take N17 or N59. To get around Co. Mayo, it's best to rent a car. Two firms with outlets at Knock International Airport are **Diplomat Rent a Car** (☎ **094/67252**) and **Murrays Europcar** (☎ **094/33029**).

VISITOR INFORMATION   For year-round information, visit or contact the **Westport Tourist Office,** The Mall, Westport (☎ **098/25711**). It's open June through September, Monday through Friday from 9am to 6pm, and from October to May, Monday through Friday from 9am to 5:15pm. The **Knock Airport Tourist Office** at Knock International Airport (☎ **094/67247**) is also open year-round, but only to coincide with flight arrivals.

Seasonal tourist offices, open from May/June to September/October, are the **Ballina Tourist Office,** Cathedral Road, Ballina, Co. Mayo (☎ **096/70848**); **Castlebar Tourist Office,** Linenhall Street, Castlebar, Co. Mayo (☎ **094/21207**); **Knock Village Tourist Office,** Knock (☎ **094/88193**); **Cong Village Tourist Office** (☎ **092/46542**); **Achill Tourist Office,** Achill Sound (☎ **098/45384**); and **Newport Tourist Office** (☎ **098/41895**).

AREA CODES   Area codes for Co. Mayo are **094, 096, 097,** and **098.**

A FEW WORDS ABOUT COUNTY MAYO

Rimmed by Clew Bay and the Atlantic Ocean, Co. Mayo boasts many diverse attractions, although it has been most widely identified as *The Quiet Man* country ever since the classic movie was filmed here in 1951. The exact setting for the film was

County Mayo

Ballintubber Abbey ❶
Ceide Fields ❷
Granuaile Centre ❸
Foxford Woollen Mills ❹
Knock Folk Museum ❺
National Shrine of
Our Lady of Knock ❻
N. Mayo Family History
Research & Heritage Centre ❼
Salmon World ❽
Westport House ❾

Cong, a no-longer-so-quiet village wedged between Lough Mask and Lough Corrib and backed up against the Co. Galway border. Much of Mayo, however, has resisted the pull of Hollywood and still provides remote bogs and beaches, cliffs and crags where quiet splendor prevails.

Among Mayo's other attractions are the 5,000-year-old farmstead settlement at Ceide Fields, the Marian shrine at Knock, and some of Europe's best fishing waters at Lough Conn, Lough Mask, and the River Moy. Ballina, Mayo's largest town, calls itself the home of the Irish salmon.

ATTRACTIONS

Unlike counties Galway, Limerick, Cork, and others, Co. Mayo does not have one central city, although Westport is rapidly approaching such stature. It's a county of many towns, from large market and commercial centers such as Castlebar, Claremorris, and Ballinrobe in the southern part of the county to Ballina in the northern reaches. Most of the attractions of interest to visitors lie in the hinterlands, in smaller communities like Knock, Foxford, Ballycastle, Louisburgh, and Newport.

County Mayo's loveliest town, **Westport,** is nestled on the shores of Clew Bay. Once a major port, it is one of the few planned towns of Ireland, designed by Richard Castle with a splendid tree-lined mall, rows of Georgian buildings, and an octagonal central mall.

Southeast of Westport is **Croagh Patrick,** a 2,500-foot mountain dominating the vistas of western Mayo for many miles. It was here in A.D. 441 that St. Patrick is said to have prayed and spent the 40 days of Lent. To commemorate this belief, each year on the last Sunday of July, thousands of Irish people make a pilgrimage to the site, which has become known as St. Patrick's Holy Mountain.

The rugged, bog-filled, and thinly populated coast of Mayo provides little industry for the locals but many scenic drives and secluded outposts to intrigue visitors. Leading the list is **Achill Island,** a heather-filled bogland with sandy beaches and great cliffs dropping into the Atlantic. It's linked by a bridge to the mainland. Clare Island, once the home of Mayo's amazing pirate queen, Grace O'Malley, sits south of Achill in Clew Bay.

The drive from Ballina along the edge of the northern coast to Downpatrick Head is particularly scenic and includes a visit to **Killala,** a small and secluded harbor village that came close to changing the course of Ireland's history. In August 1798, France's General Humbert landed at Killala in an abortive attempt to lead the Irish in a full-scale rebellion against the British. For this reason, the phrase "The Year of the French" is part of the folk memory of Mayo. The incident was used by novelist Thomas Flanagan as the basis for his best-selling novel of the same name.

National Shrine of Our Lady of Knock

Knock, Co. Mayo. ☎ **094/88100.** Free admission to shrine; museum £1.50 ($2.25) adults, 75p ($1.08) seniors and children over age 5. Shrine and grounds, year-round, daily 8am–6pm or later; museum, May–Oct, daily 10am–6pm. On the N17 Galway road.

It's said that here, in 1879, local townspeople witnessed an appearance of Mary, the mother of Jesus. Considered the Lourdes or Fatima of Ireland, Knock came to the world's attention in 1979 when Pope John Paul II visited the shrine. Knock's centerpiece is a huge circular basilica seating 7,000 people and containing artifacts or furnishings from every county in Ireland. The grounds also contain a folk museum and a religious bookshop.

✪ Ballintubber Abbey

Ballintubber, Co. Mayo. ☎ **094/30934.** Free admission; donations welcome. Year-round daily 9am–midnight. Off the main Galway-Castlebar road (N84), about 20 miles west of Knock.

This abbey is known as the abbey that refused to die, because it is one of the few Irish churches that's been in continuous use for almost 800 years. Founded in 1216 by Cathal O'Connor, king of Connaught, it survived early fires and other tragedies. Even though the forces of Oliver Cromwell took off the church's roof in 1653 and attempted to suppress services, clerics persisted in discreetly conducting religious rites through the centuries. Completely restored in 1966, the interior includes a video display and an interpretative center, and the grounds are landscaped to portray spiritual themes.

Westport House

Westport, Co. Mayo. ☎ **098/25430.** Admission £6 ($9.60) adults, £3 ($4.80) children. Mid-May to June and Sept, daily 2–6pm; July–Aug, Mon–Sat 10:30am–6pm, Sun 2–6pm.

At the edge of town you can visit Westport House, a late 18th-century residence that's home of Lord Altamont, the marquis of Sligo, who is still in residence with his family. The work of Richard Cassels and James Wyatt, the house is graced with a staircase of ornate white Sicilian marble, unusual art nouveau glass and carvings, family heirlooms, and silver. Admission includes access to all the house's grounds and a zoo.

Granuaile Centre

Louisburgh, Co. Mayo. ☎ **098/66195.** Admission £2 ($3.20) adults, £1.25 ($2) seniors and students, £1 ($1.60) children. May and Sept–Oct, Mon–Fri 10am–5pm; June, Mon–Sat 10am–5pm; July–Aug, daily 10am–6pm.

Using an audiovisual display and graphic exhibits, this center tells the story of one of Ireland's great female heroes, Granuaile (Grace) O'Malley (1530–1600). Known as the pirate queen, Grace led battles against the English and ruled the Baronies of Burrishoole and Murrisk around Clew Bay. Her extraordinary exploits are recounted in Elizabethan state papers. The center also includes a craft shop and coffee shop.

Salmon World

Farran Laboratory, Furnace, Newport, Co. Mayo. ☎ **098/41107.** Admission £1.50 ($2.40) adults, £1 ($1.60) students, 50p (80¢) seniors and children. June–Aug, daily 10am–1pm and 2–6pm.

In this county of great salmon fishing, it is only natural that a center would open up to provide insight on the background and life cycle of the Atlantic salmon. Operated on the shores of Lough Furnace by the Salmon Research Agency of Ireland, it presents a video show as well as freshwater and marine aquariums, fish-feeding areas, and exhibits.

✪ Foxford Woollen Mills

St. Joseph's Place, Foxford, Co. Mayo. ☎ **094/56756.** Admission £3 ($4.80) adults, £2 ($3.20) seniors and students. Year-round, Mon–Sat 10am–6pm, Sun 2–6pm. Off the Foxford-Ballina road (N57).

Founded in 1892 by a local nun, Mother Agnes Morrogh-Bernard, to provide work for a community ravaged by the effects of the Irish famine, Foxford Woollen Mills brought prosperity to the area through the worldwide sales of beautiful tweeds, rugs, and blankets. Using a multimedia presentation, the center tells the story of this local industry, then provides an on-site tour of the working mills to see the production of the famous Foxford woollen products. Tours run every 20 minutes. A restaurant, a shop, an exhibition center, an art gallery, a heritage room, and other craft units (including a doll-making and -restoration workshop and a jewelry designer) enrich a visit.

✪ North Mayo Family History Research & Heritage Centre

Enniscoe, Castlehill, Ballina, Co. Mayo. ☎ **096/31809.** Admission to museum £2 ($3.20) adults, £1 ($1.60) seniors and students, £5 ($8) family. Oct–Apr, Mon–Fri 9am–4pm, June–Sept, Mon–Fri 9am–6pm, Sat–Sun 2–6pm. Situated on Lough Conn, about 2 miles south of Crossmolina, off R315.

If your ancestors came from Mayo, this center will help you trace your family tree. The data bank includes indices to church registers of all denominations plus school roll books, leases, and wills. Even if you have no connections in Mayo, you'll enjoy the adjacent museum with its displays of rural Mayo household items, farm machinery, and farm implements, including the gowl-gob, a spadelike implement exclusive to this locality. The center also offers a new blacksmithing course of five to 10 days. (*Note:* If your ancestors were from the southern part of the county, try the **South Mayo Family Research Centre** at Town Hall, Neale Road, Ballinrobe, Co. Mayo; ☎ **092/41214.** It's open Monday through Friday from 9am to noon and Saturday and Sunday from 2 to 4pm.)

✪ Ceide Fields

Ballycastle, Co. Mayo. ☎ **096/43325.** Admission £2.50 ($4) adults, £1.75 ($2.80) seniors, £1 ($1.60) students and children, £6 ($9.60) family. Mid-Mar to May and Oct daily 10am–5pm; June–Sept daily 9:30am–6:30pm; Nov daily 10am–4:30pm. For winter hours call ☎ **01/ 661-3111,** ext. 2386. Situated on R314, the coastal road north of Ballina, between Ballycastle and Belderrig.

Here, in a dramatic sea-edge setting, lies the oldest enclosed landscape in Europe, revealing a pattern of once-tilled fields as they were laid out and lived in fifty centuries ago. Preserved for millennia beneath the bog to which it had been lost, this Neolithic farming settlement, home to the builders of the nearby megalithic tombs, now shows its face again. Admittedly, it's a nearly inscrutable face, requiring all the resources of the interpretive center to make meaningful eye-contact with the visitor. The visitors center offers a 20-minute video presentation and conducts tours of the site.

SPORTS & OUTDOOR PURSUITS

FISHING   The Co. Mayo waters of the River Moy and Loughs Carrowmore and Conn offer some of the best fishing in Europe, and some of Ireland's premier sources for salmon and trout. For general information about fishing in Co. Mayo, contact the **North Western Regional Fisheries Board,** Ardnaree House, Abbey Street, Ballina (☎ **096/22788**).

To arrange a day's fishing, contact ✪ **Cloonamoyne Fishery,** Castlehill, near Crossmolina, Ballina (☎ **096/31851**). Managed by an Irish-born former New Yorker, Barry Segrave, this professional angling service will advise and equip you to fish the local waters—for brown trout on Loughs Conn and Cullin; for salmon on Loughs Beltra, Furnace, and Feeagh; and for salmon and sea trout on the Rivers Moy and Deel. Services include the rental of fully equipped boats, fly-casting tuition, tackle hire, and transport to and from all fishing. Daily rates average £10 ($16) for a boat, £20 ($32) for a boat with engine, and £45 to £50 ($72 to $80) for a boat with engine and *ghillie* (guide).

County Mayo is also home to the **Pontoon Bridge Fly Fishing School,** Pontoon, Co. Mayo (☎ **094/56120**). This school offers various one- to four-day courses in the art of fly casting, as well as fly tying, tackle design, and other background information necessary for successful game fishing. Fees range from £25 to £85 ($40 to $136), depending on the duration of the course. Courses run daily from April to late September.

Permits and state fishing licenses can be obtained at the **North Mayo Angling Advice Centre** (Tiernan Bros.), Upper Main St., Foxford, Co. Mayo (☎ **094/ 56731**).

For fishing tackle, try **Jones Ltd., General Merchants,** Main Street, Foxford, Co. Mayo (☎ **094/56121**), or **Walkins Fishing Tackle,** Tone Street, Ballina, Co. Mayo (☎ **096/22442**).

GOLF   County Mayo has three 18-hole golf courses: a par-72 links course at **Carn Golf Course,** Carn, Belmullet, Co. Mayo (☎ **097/82292**), with greens fees of £12 ($19.20); a par-71 inland course at **Castlebar Golf Club,** Rocklands, Castlebar, Co. Mayo (☎ **094/21649**), also with greens fees of £12 ($19.20); and a par-73 championship course at **Westport Golf Club,** Co. Mayo (☎ **098/28262**), with greens fees of £15 ($22.50) on weekdays and £22.50 ($36) on weekends. Set on the shores of Clew Bay, the last course winds its way around the precipitous slopes of Croagh Patrick Mountain. It's one of western Ireland's most challenging and scenic courses.

ACCOMMODATIONS

Very Expensive / Expensive

✪ Ashford Castle

Cong, Co. Mayo. ☎ **800/346-7007** from the U.S., or 092/46003. Fax 092/46260. 83 rms. TV TEL. £121–£430 ($193.60–$688) double. Service charge 15%. Open year-round with special packages offered for Christmas and New Years. AE, DC, MC, V.

From turrets and towers to drawbridge and battlements, this castle is indeed a fairy-tale resort, dating from the 13th century, when it was first the home of the De Burgo (Burke) family and later the country residence of the Guinnesses. A hotel since 1939, over the years it has been enlarged and updated and was the focus of worldwide media attention in 1984 when Pres. Ronald Reagan stayed here during his visit to Ireland. Situated on the shores of Lough Corrib amid 450 forested and flowering acres, it sits in the heart of the scenic territory that provided the setting for the film classic *The Quiet Man.*

The interior is rich in baronial furniture, medieval armor, carved oak paneling and stairways, objets d'art, and masterpiece oil paintings. Guest rooms are decorated with designer fabrics and traditional furnishings, some with canopied or four-poster beds.

Dining/Entertainment: Choices include the 130-seat main dining room for contemporary Irish cuisine and the smaller 40-seat Connaught Room, a French restaurant. Sip a cocktail in the vaulted basement-level dungeon bar.

Services: Concierge, room service, laundry and dry-cleaning service.

Facilities: Nine-hole golf course, tennis court, salmon and trout fishing, boating.

Expensive/Moderate

✪ Newport House

Newport, Co. Mayo. ☎ **800/223-6510** or 800/44-UTELL from the U.S., or 098/41222. Fax 098/41613. 19 rms. TEL. £100–£132 ($160–$211.10) double. No service charge. Rates include full breakfast. AE, DC, MC, V. Closed Oct to mid-Mar.

Close to the Clew Bay coast, this ivy-covered Georgian mansion sits at the edge of town along the Newport River, making it a favorite base for salmon anglers. Originally part of the estate of the O'Donnell family, ancient Irish chieftains, it has been a country-house hotel only in recent decades. The interior boasts splendid examples of ornate plasterwork and high ceilings, and a skylit dome crowns a curved central staircase. The public areas are filled with antique furnishings, oil paintings, and cases of fishing trophies. Guest rooms are spread among the main house and two smaller courtyard buildings.

Dining: The restaurant is known for its fish dishes, of course, including salmon smoked on the premises. If you catch a salmon, the chef will cook it for your dinner or smoke it for you to take home. There is also a small bar.

Facilities: Private salmon and sea-trout fishing on the Newport River and Lough Beltra.

Moderate

Breaffy House

Claremorris Rd., Castlebar, Co. Mayo. ☎ **800/528-1234** from the U.S., or 094/22033. Fax 094/22276. 38 rms. TV TEL. £76.50–£83 ($122.40–$132.80) double. No service charge. Rates include full breakfast. AE, DC, MC, V.

A long paved driveway leads into this sprawling three-story château-style hotel, picturesquely ensconced amid 60 acres of gardens and woodlands. The public areas are furnished with traditional and period pieces. Guest rooms vary in size and shape, each with individual furnishings and character. Facilities include a restaurant and bar.

The Downhill

Ballina, Co. Mayo. ☎ **800/221-1074** or 800/223-6510 from the U.S., or 096/21033. Fax 096/21338. 50 rms. TV TEL. £108–£125 ($172.80–$200) double. No service charge. Rates include full breakfast. AE, DC, MC, V. Closed Dec 22–27. Situated off Sligo road (N59).

Incorporating a gracious 19th-century manor house with a modern new wing, this three-story hotel sits amid 40 acres of wooded grounds on the banks of the Brosna River, a tributary of the River Moy, at the northern edge of town. The public areas exude traditional charm, while guest rooms vary from contemporary to traditional, with thoughtful extras like tea/coffeemakers and hair dryers. For dining and entertainment, The Brosna restaurant overlooks Brosna Falls; a bilevel piano bar, Frogs Pavilion, has a unique brass dance floor. Hotel facilities include an indoor heated swimming pool, two squash courts, sauna, Jacuzzi, gym, three all-weather tennis courts, hair salon, and game room.

✪ Enniscoe House

Castlehill, near Crossmolina, Ballina, Co. Mayo. ☎ **800/223-6510** from the U.S., or 096/31112. Fax 096/31773. 7 rms. £80–£104 ($128–$166.40) double. No service charge. Rates include full breakfast. AE, MC, V. Closed mid-Oct to Apr 1. Located 2 miles south of Crossmollina off R315, next to the North Mayo Heritage Centre.

Overlooking Lough Conn and surrounded by a wooded estate with more than 3 miles of nature walks, this two-story Georgian country inn has been described as the last great house of North Mayo. Owned and managed by Susan Kellett, a descendant of the original family that settled on the lands in the 1660s, Enniscoe is filled with family portraits, antique furniture, early drawings and pictures of the house and surrounding area, and open crackling fireplaces. Guest rooms are individually furnished, with huge hand-carved armoires and canopied or four-poster beds, and have views of parkland or lake. In the dining room, fish from local rivers, produce from the house's own farm, and vegetables and herbs from the adjacent garden are daily pleasures. Enniscoe also has its own Fishery (see Cloonamoyne Fishery under "Fishing" in "Sports and Outdoor Pursuits," above).

Mount Falcon Castle

Foxford road (N57), Ballina, Co. Mayo. ☎ **800/223-6510** from the U.S. or 096/21172. Fax 096/71517. 10 rms (8 with private bath). £98 ($156.80) single or double. Rates include full breakfast. Dinner available to guests £20 ($32). AE, DC, MC, V. Closed Feb–Mar and Christmas week.

Built in 1876 by the same man who did much of the exterior work at Ashford Castle in Cong, this multigabled Victorian-style structure has been owned and managed as a country house inn by the Aldridge family since 1932. The decor in both the public areas and the guest rooms is an eclectic blend of comfortable old furniture with fluffy pillows, carved chests, and gilded mirrors. If you're fond of fishing, this is a real find, because a stay here entitles you to salmon and trout fishing on Lough Conn and to fishing in a salmon preserve on the River Moy. The management enthusiastically caters to all the needs of fishing folk, and will prepare and serve you your day's catch for dinner. Set in a 100-acre wooded estate 4 miles south of Ballina, Mount Falcon has fine walking trails and an all-weather tennis court.

The Olde Railway Hotel

The Mall, Westport, Co. Mayo. ☎ **091/25166.** Fax 091/25605. 25 rms, half with bath. TV TEL. £65 ($104) standard double; £80 ($128) superior double. Service charge 10%. AE, CB, DISC, EU, JCB, MC, V.

William Thackeray's description of this hotel in 1834—"one of the prettiest, comfortablist inns in Ireland"—remains true. The Olde Railway Hotel, built in 1780 by Lord Sligo to accommodate his "overflow" house guests, has been tastefully restored by the Rosenkranz family. Outside, its bright yellow facade is warm and welcoming; inside, it exudes charm and a touch of elegance. No two rooms are alike; each has been given a distinctive character. Twenty-two rooms face the tree-lined Carrowbeg River. The "superior" rooms are more spacious and include a sitting area with sofa. Most mattresses are new and back-friendly, but not all, so if it matters, ask for a firm one. In addition to the delightful, glass, conservatory-style dining room, there is a bar and a function room, both offering weekend entertainment.

Westport Woods

Louisburg Rd., Westport, Co. Mayo. ☎ **098/25811.** Fax 098/26212. 95 rms. TV TEL. £76–£98 ($121.60–$156.80) double. No service charge. Full breakfast is included. AE, DC, MC, V.

Nestled in a quiet woodland setting, this two-story chalet-style hotel is conveniently situated midway between the historic town center and the quay area, which overlooks Clew Bay. The public rooms are woody, bright, and airy, with contemporary furnishings. The well-maintained bedrooms offer standard comforts plus hair dryer and garment press. Recently expanded facilities include a full-service restaurant, a lounge, and a tennis court.

Inexpensive

○ Suantrai

Ballycastle, Co. Mayo (on R314 at the east edge of town). ☎ **096/43040.** 3 rooms. £30 ($48) double with bath. Includes full Irish breakfast. No service charge. No credit cards. June–Aug 15.

Suantrai means "lullaby," and if you don't sleep soundly here you'd best consult a physician. The rooms are spacious, bright, meticulously clean, and mercifully uncluttered, requiring only minutes of habitation to feel comfortably familiar. This modest, welcoming home sets a standard rarely met by home-style B&Bs. The Chamberses (both teachers in the local school) and their family truly enjoy their guests—and the feeling's mutual.

DINING

Expensive/Moderate

The Asgard Tavern

The Quay, Westport, Co. Mayo. ☎ **098/25319.** Reservations recommended for dinner. Bar food main courses £3.50–£9 ($5.60–$14.40); dinner main courses £6–£14 ($9.60–$22.40), fixed-price dinner £17.50 ($28) and £18 ($29.30). AE, CB, DC, MC, V. Tues–Sun bar food noon–9pm, dinner 6:30–10pm. INTERNATIONAL.

Located in the center of the harbor strip opposite Clew Bay, this nautical pub/restaurant consists of an informal ground-floor pub and an upstairs candlelit 50-seat restaurant. Bar food, available throughout the day in the pub, includes very fresh fish dishes, Irish stew, beef stroganoff, and steaks. In the evening, the restaurant offers a range of dishes from a creamy coquille St-Jacques to medaillons of beef in garlic sauce.

Moderate

○ Ardmore House

The Quay, Westport Harbour, Westport, Co. Mayo. ☎ **098/25994.** Reservations recommended for dinner. Lunch main courses/bar food £1.70–£8.95 ($2.70–$14.30); dinner main courses £8.95–£13.95 ($14.30–$22.30). AE, MC, V. Mid–Aug to mid–July Mon–Sat bar food 4–9pm, dinner 6:30–10pm. CONTINENTAL/IRISH.

On high ground at the edge of town overlooking the harbor, Ardmore House enjoys grand views of Clew Bay, from which come the ingredients for the lunchtime

---

Readers Recommend

Mellotte's Restaurant, The Neale, Ballinrobe, Co. Mayo (2 miles NE of Cong). ☎ 092/41032. *The concierge at Ashford Castle recommended Mellotte's. . . . Excellent food in a tiny restaurant. At the next table were an American family who stay at Ashford Castle regularly, and they said that this was the best food in the area. You should try it.*
—Mark McGannon, Orangeburg, S.C.

special, Clew Bay seafood chowder. Also on the menu are burgers, cottage pies, steaks, and hot seafood shells. Entrées at dinner are varied and include fresh seafood crepes and moist roast duck.

✪ The Quay Cottage

The Quay, Westport. ☎ **096/26412.** Reservations recommended for dinner. Lunch main courses £2–£5 ($3.20–$8); dinner main courses £7.90–£15.50 ($12.64–$24.80). AE, MC, V. Daily 6–10pm, Sun 1–9:30pm. Closed Christmas and Jan. SEAFOOD/INTERNATIONAL.

Overlooking Westport Harbour, little Quay Cottage is awash with nautical bric-a-brac. The menu presents fresh and beautifully prepared seafood such as lemon sole beurre blanc or wild local salmon with an array of daily specials; a request for a plain steak will also be fulfilled. You can take a waterside stroll after your meal.

Inexpensive

⑤ The Old Mill

St. Joseph's Place, Foxford, Co. Mayo. ☎ **094/56756.** Reservations not necessary. All items £1–£4.50 ($1.60–$7.20). MC, V. Mon–Sat 11am–6pm, Sun 1–6pm. IRISH.

On the grounds of the Foxford Woollen Mills (see "Attractions," above), The Old Mill serves a wide array of light meals and snacks in a historic setting that's bright and airy. On the menu: freshly prepared soups, salads, sandwiches, and cold meat plates, as well as quiche, lasagna, sausage rolls, scones, muffins, and desserts. There are also daily hot meal specials.

Galway City

Galway City is the focal point and gateway of Co. Galway and the west of Ireland. Situated beside the River Corrib and at the mouth of Galway Bay off the Atlantic, it's just a little over an hour's drive from Shannon Airport. With a population of more than 50,000, it is by Irish standards a major city and yet retains much of the accessibility and congeniality of a town.

In recent years Galway has grown and developed dramatically without losing its character. It is said to be the fastest growing city in Europe, but its "boom" has meant only more and better of the same, not uncontrolled expansion and disfigurement. Galway is perhaps the most prosperous city in Ireland and arguably the most immediately appealing, and it's managed to attract droves of outsiders, either to visit or to settle, without alienating its own long-standing population. The result is a city that feels lived in, a real place that at the same time attracts and accommodates masses of visitors. Its university community and its well-rooted and lively arts scene surely contribute to its vitality and appeal.

Some say that Galway was named after the foreigners—*na Gall,* or the Galls—who had settled in the region. If so, then *Gaillimh,* or Galway, would mean "the place of the foreigners." The earliest historically dated references to the area date from A.D. 1124 and describe it as a Gaelic hinterland.

Because of its position on the Atlantic, Galway emerged as a thriving seaport and developed a brisk trade with Spain. Close to the city docks, you can still see the area where Spanish merchants unloaded cargo from their galleons. The Spanish Arch was one of four arches built in 1594, and the Spanish Parade is a small open square where the visitors would stroll in the evening.

Tradition has it that Christopher Columbus attended mass at Galway's St. Nicholas Collegiate Church before setting sail for the New World in 1492. Originally built in 1320, the church has been enlarged, rebuilt, and embellished over the years. It has also changed denominations at least four times.

From medieval times, Galway has been known as the City of Tribes, thanks to 14 wealthy merchant families—the Athys, Blakes, Bodkins, Brownes, Darcys, Deanes, Fonts, Frenchs, Joyces, Kirwans, Lynches, Martins, Morrises, and Skerrets—mostly of Welsh and Norman origins, who ruled the town for many years as an oligarchy.

By far the most important of these families was the Lynches, who gave the city not only its first mayor, in 1484, but an additional 83 other mayors during the next 169 years. In the center of town, on Shop Street, is Lynch's Castle, dating from 1490 and renovated in the 19th century. It remains the oldest Irish medieval town house used daily for commercial purposes (it's now a branch of the Allied Irish Bank). The exterior is full of carved gargoyles, impressive coats of arms, and other decorative stoneworks. If you walk northwest one block to Market Street, you'll see the Lynch Memorial Window embedded in a wall above a built-up Gothic doorway, commemorating the day in the 16th century when Mayor James Lynch FitzStephen, having condemned his own son to death for the murder of a Spanish merchant but finding no one to carry out the deed, acted as executioner himself, thereafter retreating into seclusion, broken-hearted.

In more recent centuries, two developments in the city have earned it a place of prominence in the west: the founding of the Queens' College (now University College, Galway) in 1848, and the establishment of a permanent rail link with Dublin in 1854.

Today, the activity of the city revolves around a pedestrian park at Eyre (pronounced "air") Square, originally a market area known as the Fair Green. It's officially called the John F. Kennedy Park in commemoration of his visit here in June 1963, and a bust of the president shares space in the park with a statue of a man sitting on a limestone wall—a depiction of Galway-born local hero Padraig O'Conaire, a pioneer in the Irish literary revival of the early 20th century and the epitome of a Galway Renaissance man.

Next to the downtown area, on the west bank of the River Corrib, is the Claddagh, originally a fishing village, once with its own fleet, laws, and king. Its name is taken from the Irish *An Cladach,* which means "a flat stony shore." The people of Claddagh were descendants of early Gaelic families and spoke only Irish. Their stone streets were haphazardly arranged, with small squares rimmed by thatched mud-walled houses. This old-world scene came to an end in 1934 with the construction of a modern housing development.

One Claddagh tradition, however, survives: the Claddagh ring, worn facing out for engagement and facing in for marriage. The ring's clasped hands representing friendship are a symbol dating from Roman times. The earliest known Claddagh ring, with the crown added for loyalty and the heart for love, was made in the 17th century by a Galway goldsmith named Richard Joyce. No longer widely worn as a wedding band, it is mostly either a souvenir or a token of friendship.

1 Orientation

Galway is 57 miles N of Shannon Airport, 136 miles W of Dublin, 65 miles NW of Limerick, 130 miles NW of Cork, and 120 miles N of Killarney.

GETTING THERE   Aer Lingus operates daily service from Dublin into **Galway Airport,** Carnmore (☎ **091/752874**), about 10 miles east of the city.

Irish Rail trains from Dublin and other points arrive daily into **Ceannt Station** (☎ **091/561444**), off Eyre Square, Galway.

Buses from all parts of Ireland arrive daily into **Bus Eireann Travel Centre,** Ceannt Station, Galway (☎ **091/562000**).

As the gateway to the West of Ireland, Galway is the terminus for many national roads, leading in from all parts of Ireland, including N84 and N17 from northerly points, N63 and N6 from the east, and N67 and N18 from the south.

Galway City

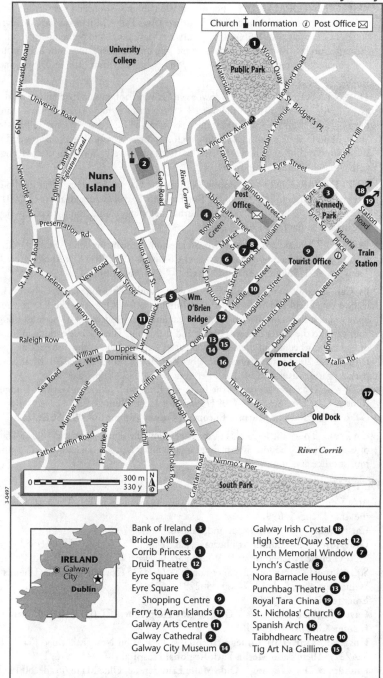

Church ✝ Information ⓘ Post Office ✉

IRELAND
Galway City
Dublin

Bank of Ireland ③
Bridge Mills ⑤
Corrib Princess ①
Druid Theatre ⑫
Eyre Square ③
Eyre Square
　Shopping Centre ⑨
Ferry to Aran Islands ⑰
Galway Arts Centre ⑪
Galway Cathedral ②
Galway City Museum ⑭

Galway Irish Crystal ⑱
High Street/Quay Street ⑫
Lynch Memorial Window ⑦
Lynch's Castle ⑧
Nora Barnacle House ④
Punchbag Theatre ⑬
Royal Tara China ⑲
St. Nicholas' Church ⑥
Spanish Arch ⑯
Taibhdhearc Theatre ⑩
Tig Art Na Gaillime ⑮

375

VISITOR INFORMATION For information about Galway and the surrounding areas, contact or visit **Ireland West Tourism** (Aras Failte), Victoria Place, off Eyre Square, Galway (☎ **091/563081**). Hours are May, June, and September Monday through Sunday from 8:30am to 5:45pm; July and August daily from 8:30am to 7:45pm; and, the rest of the year, Monday through Friday from 9am to 5:45pm and Saturday from 9am to 12:45pm.

TOWN LAYOUT The core of downtown Galway lies between Eyre Square on the east and the River Corrib on the west. To the west of Eyre Square, Galway's main thoroughfare begins—a street that changes its name four times (from William to Shop, Main Guard, and Bridge), before it crosses the River Corrib and changes again. If that sounds confusing, don't worry. The streets are all very short, well marked, and, with a map in hand, easy to follow.

GETTING AROUND By Public Transport Galway has an excellent local bus service, with buses running from the **Bus Eireann Travel Centre,** Galway (☎ **091/562000**) or Eyre Square to various suburbs, including Salthill and the Galway Bay coastline. The flat fare is 70p ($1.10).

By Taxi There are taxi ranks at Eyre Square and all the major hotels within the city. If you need to call a cab, try **Galway Taxi Co-op** (☎ **091/561111**), **Apollo-Corrib Taxis** (☎ **091/564444**), or **Big O Taxis** (☎ **091/566166**).

By Car A town of medieval arches, alleyways, and cobblestone lanes, Galway is at its best when explored on foot (with comfortable shoes). Once you check in to your hotel or guest house, it's best to leave your car and tour by walking. If you must bring your car into the center of town, park it and then walk. There is free parking in front of Galway Cathedral but the majority of street parking follows the disc parking system. It costs 20p (32¢) for one hour; a book of 10 disks costs £2 ($3.20). Multistory parking garages average £1 ($1.60) per hour or £8 ($12.80) per day.

To rent a car, contact one of the following firms with offices in Galway: **Budget Rent-A-Car,** Eyre Square (☎ **091/566376**); **Hertz Rent-A-Car,** Galway Airport (☎ **091/752502**); or **Murrays Europcar,** Galway Airport (☎ **091/562222**).

On Foot To see the highlights of the city, follow the signposts on the Tourist Trail of Old Galway. The tour is explained in a handy 32-page booklet available at the tourist office and at most bookshops.

Fast Facts: Galway City

Area Code The area code for most Galway city numbers is **091.** The area code for the Aran Islands is **099.**

Car Rentals See "Getting Around," above.

Drugstores Try **Commins Pharmacy,** at 32 Shop St., Galway (☎ 091/562924); **Matt O'Flaherty Chemist,** at 16 William St., Galway (☎ 091/561442), and 39 Eyre Sq., Galway (☎ 091/562927; after hours ☎ 091/525426; and **Whelan's Chemist,** Williamsgate St., Galway (☎ 091/562291).

Emergencies Dial **999.**

Gay & Lesbian Resources Galway Gay Help Line, (☎ 091/566134); **Galway Lesbian Line** (☎ 091/564611).

Hospital University College Hospital is located on Newcastle Road (☎ 091/524222). There's also **Merlin Park Regional Hospital** (☎ 091/757631).

Laundry & Dry Cleaning Olde Malte Launderette, Olde Malte Arcade, off High Street, Galway (☎ 091/564990), or **Heaslips Dry Cleaners,** William Street and Prospect Hill, Galway (☎ 091/568944), can get your spots out for you.

Library The **Galway Library / An Leabhar,** located in the Hynes Building, Augustine Street, Galway (☎ 091/561666), is open Monday 2 to 5pm, Tuesday to Thursday 11am to 8pm, Friday 11am to 5pm, Saturday 9am to 1pm, and 2–5pm.

Local Newspapers & Media The weekly *Connaught Tribune,* published in Galway, is the largest newspaper covering the west of Ireland. Other weeklies include the *City Tribune* and the *Connaught Sentinel.* Free weekly publications that cover the arts and entertainment include the *Galway Advertiser, Galway Observer,* and *Entertainment Weekly.* Local radio stations are Galway Bay FM 95.8 and FM 96.8, and Raidio na Gaeltachta, an Irish language and music station broadcasting on M.W. 556.

Photographic Needs Try **Fahyfoto Camera Shop,** 13 High St., Galway (☎ 091/562283); **Galway Camera Shop,** 58 Dominick St., Galway (☎ 091/565678); or **One Hour Photo,** Eglinton Street, Galway (☎ 091/562682).

Police The local **Garda Station** is on Mill Street, Galway (☎ 091/563161).

Post Office The **Post Office,** on Eglinton Street, Galway (☎ 091/562051), is open 9am to 5:30pm, Monday through Saturday.

Shoe Repairs To save your sole, consult **Heffernan Shoe Repairs,** 9 Sea Rd. (☎ 091/569228), or **Mister Minit,** U4 Corbetts Ct. Williamsgate St. (☎ 091/565056).

2 Accommodations

VERY EXPENSIVE

✪ Glenlo Abbey

Bushy Park, Galway, Co. Galway. ☎ **091/526666.** Fax 091/527800. 45 rms. TV TEL. £159–£174 ($254.40–$278.40) double. No service charge. Rates include full breakfast. AE, DC, MC, V.

Situated about 2 miles outside of Galway on the main Clifden road, this secluded five-star hotel overlooks Lough Corrib in a tranquil and sylvan setting, surrounded by a 9-hole golf course. Dating from 1740, it was originally the ancestral home of the French and Blake families, two of Galway's 14 great tribes who ruled over the city for centuries. Totally restored and opened as a hotel in 1993, it has retained its aura of grandeur in all of the public areas, with hand-carved wood furnishings, hand-loomed carpets, ornate plasterwork, and an extensive collection of Irish art and antiques. The guest rooms, which have lovely views of Lough Corrib and the surrounding countryside, are similarly decorated with traditional furnishings as well as marbled bathrooms; each room has a personal safe and garment press.

Dining/Entertainment: Choices include the French Room for fine dining; the Kentfield Bar, decorated with a unique collection of pen-and-ink drawings of Irish writers; and the Oak Cellar Bar.

Services: Concierge, room service, laundry and dry cleaning.

Facilities: New extensive golf course, fishing in Lough Corrib.

EXPENSIVE/MODERATE

Corrib Great Southern Hotel

Dublin road (N6), Galway, Co. Galway. ☎ **800/44-UTELL** from the U.S., or 091/755281. Fax 091/751390. 180 rooms. TV TEL. £80–£134 ($128–$214.40) double. Includes full Irish breakfast and service charge. AE, DC, MC, V.

Set on high ground 2 miles east of Galway City, this modern five-story hotel offers panoramic views of Galway Bay, from its skylit atrium-style lobby to the wide wrap-around windows in all of the public areas. Guest rooms are equally bright and airy, with lovely bay views enhanced by contemporary furnishings, pastel-toned fabrics, and modern art.

Dining/Entertainment: Enjoy views of Galway Bay while dining in The Currach, the hotel's main restaurant, or at O'Malley's Pub.

Services: Concierge, room service, laundry and dry cleaning, baby-sitting, children's program (July and August).

Facilities: Indoor heated swimming pool, sauna, Jacuzzi, steam room, table tennis.

✪ Galway Great Southern Hotel

15 Eyre Sq., Galway, Co. Galway. ☎ **800/44UTELL** from the U.S., or 091/564041. Fax 091/566704. 115 rms. TV TEL. £98–£146 ($156.80–$233.60) double. Includes full Irish breakfast and service charge. AE, DC, MC, V.

Dating from 1845, this handsome five-story hotel is truly the grande dame of the Galway area. Positioned in the heart of the city overlooking landmark Eyre Square, it's next to the bus/rail station and within walking distance of all the major sights. The spacious public areas have high ceilings, elaborate plasterwork, crystal chandeliers, and original Connemara marble fireplaces. Recently refurbished, the guest rooms have traditional dark woods, semicanopy beds, designer fabrics, and brass accoutrements, with extras such as hair dryer, garment press, and tea/coffeemaker. Rooms overlooking Eyre Square have views of the whole city and beyond.

Dining/Entertainment: Choices include the Oyster Room restaurant for fine dining and O'Flaherty's Pub, an Old Galway bar that serves excellent pub grub.

Services: Concierge, room service, dry cleaning and laundry, baby-sitting.

Facilities: Rooftop indoor heated swimming pool, sauna, steam room.

MODERATE

Ardilaun House

Taylor's Hill, Galway, Co. Galway. ☎ **800/44-UTELL** from the U.S., or 091/521433. Fax 091/521546. 89 rms. TV TEL. £70–£105 double ($112–$168). Service charge 10%. Rates include full breakfast. AE, DC, MC, V. Closed Dec 23–28.

This Georgian-style country-house hotel takes its name from the Irish place name *Ard Oilean,* meaning "high island" and referring to a picturesque island nearby in Lough Corrib. Built in 1840 as a town house for a prominent Galway family, it was converted into a hotel in 1962. With ancient trees and extensive gardens, it is located in a hilly residential section about a mile west of the downtown area. It has been expanded and updated in recent years, and most of the guest rooms, situated in a modern three-story addition, are decorated with traditional furnishings, dark woods, and quilted fabrics. The atmosphere of an old mansion prevails in the public areas, especially in the Camilaun dining room, and in The Blazers, a hunting-theme bar that's a favorite local rendezvous. Facilities include a sauna and steam room.

Brennan's Yard Hotel

Lr. Merchant's Rd., Galway, Co. Galway. ☎ **800/44-UTELL** from the U.S., or 091/568166. Fax 091/568262. 24 rms. TV TEL. £70–£95 ($112–$152) double. No service charge. Rates include full breakfast. AE, MC, V.

One of the cleverest restorations in Galway's historic area, this four-story stone building was formerly a stone warehouse. Opened as a hotel in 1992, it offers compact but skylit public areas enhanced by modern Irish art. Guest rooms overlook the city's Spanish Arch area and are decorated in contemporary style with Irish pine furnishings, designer fabrics, and locally made pottery. In-room extras include hair dryer and tea/coffeemaker. The restaurant specializes in European and seafood dishes and the Oyster Bar offers bar food and snacks all day.

Seaview, 7 Beach Ct., Grattan Rd., Salthill, Galway. ☎ **091/582109.** *Seaview, the home of Tom and Breda Treacy, is a great place. The house is immaculately kept. The location is ideal—facing Galway Bay yet easy walking distance to town. The breakfasts are of the hearty Irish variety and served in a pleasant sitting room.*

—Bob and Nancy Bernstein, Lewisburg, PA

Victoria Hotel

Victoria Place, Eyre Sq., Galway, Co. Galway. ☎ **091/567433.** Fax 091/565880. 57 rms. TV TEL. £70–£75 ($112–$120) double. No service charge. DISC, V.

Tucked in a peaceful corner of the city, opposite the tourist office and just a block from Eyre Square, this new hotel has a great location. The interior is designed in a modern art deco style, enhanced by lots of plants and mirrors. Guest rooms are compact and contemporary, with light wood furnishings and pastel-toned fabrics, as well as in-room amenities such as tea/coffeemaker, hair dryer, and garment press. There is a restaurant/bar and 24-hour room service.

INEXPENSIVE

Adare Guest House

9 Fr. Griffin Place, Galway, Co. Galway. ☎ **091/566421** or 091/562638. Fax 091/563963. 9 rms. TV TEL. £40–£44 ($64–$70.40) double. No service charge. Rates include full breakfast. V.

Situated west of the River Corrib in a quiet residential area, this modern three-story guest house is within comfortable walking distance (two blocks) of the Wolf Tone Bridge and the Spanish Arch area of the city. It offers modern accommodations with orthopedic beds and standard furnishings. Breakfast is served in a cheery dining room, using Royal Tara china and other Galway-produced accessories. Innkeepers are Padraic and Grainne Conroy.

❸ Jurys Inn

Quay St., Galway, Co. Galway. ☎ **800/44-UTELL** from the U.S., or 091/566444. Fax 091/568415. 128 rooms. TV TEL. £42–£60 ($67.20–$96) single, double, or triple. No service charge. AE, DC, MC, V.

Situated beside the River Corrib and opposite the Spanish Arch, this is a new four-story hotel designed in keeping with the area's historic character. Geared to the cost-conscious traveler, it's the first of its kind for Galway's downtown area, providing quality hotel lodgings at guest-house prices. The guest rooms look out on expansive views of the river or nearby Galway Bay; each room is decorated in modern art deco style, with light wood furniture and pink- and gray-toned fabrics, enhanced by pictures of Old Galway and Connemara. There are tea/coffeemakers in the rooms, and ice machines, a rarity in Ireland, on the first and third floors. Facilities include a moderately priced restaurant, The Arches, and the Inn Pub.

3 Dining

EXPENSIVE

Casey's Westwood

Dangan, Upper Newcastle Rd. ☎ **091/21442.** Reservations recommended. Lunch main courses £5–£10 ($8–$16); dinner main courses £12–£22 ($19.20–$35.20). AE, MC, V. Daily 12:30–2:30pm and Mon–Sat 5:30–10:15pm Oct–Easter. INTERNATIONAL.

Situated on Clifden road (N59) about 1 1/2 miles from Eyre Square, this restaurant is set back from the main road amid flowering gardens and tall trees. Owner Bernie Casey has converted an old brick house into a modern Georgian-style dining experience. The creative Irish menu includes parcel of turbot wrapped in pastry with spring onions, ravioli of lobster and Galway Bay prawns, fillet of salmon with herbs and crab claws, steak Diane, and guinea fowl wrapped in pastry. Light pub meals are available all day in the Elm bar, including a stew of the day.

✪ deBurgos

15/17 Augustine St. ☎ **091/562188.** Reservations recommended. Fixed-price lunch £9.50 ($15.20) or bar menu items £1.85–£9.85 ($5.45–$15.75); dinner main courses £10.50–£14.75 ($16.80–$23.60) or set menu £17.50 ($28). AE, MC, V. Mon–Sat noon–2:30pm and 6:30–10:15pm. INTERNATIONAL.

Named after one of Galway's most important Norman tribes, deBurgos is found in what was originally the wine vault of a 16th-century merchant's house. It has an impressive interior of whitewashed walls, caverns, arches, turreted dividers, Oriental carpets, and medieval-style wall hangings, all enhanced by flickering candles, fresh flowers, pink linens, and Irish music playing in the background. The imaginative menu offers dishes such as deBurgos three fillets (pork, veal, beef) on a confit of shallots and chicken Nicole and stuffed with farci of chicken, shrimp, and chervil cream sauce, as well as an array of seafood and vegetarian offerings. The chef will happily cater to celiac diets. The bar lunch menu includes sandwiches, salads, seafood, and steaks.

Park House Hotel & Eyre House Restaurant

Forster St., Eyre Sq., Galway. ☎ **091/564924.** Reservations recommended. Fixed-price lunch £6–£8 ($9.60–$12.80); fixed-price dinner Eyre House £16.75–£18.75 ($26.80–$30). AE, DC, MC, V. Daily noon–4pm and 6–10pm. INTERNATIONAL.

Just a half block east of Eyre Square, this fine restaurant and new hotel pair are housed in a lovely old five-story stone building. Eyre House has an old-world decor of stained glass, dark woods, oil paintings, and plants, while Park House is more elegant, with Georgian-style windows, pink walls, and modern Art Deco fittings. The exquisite entrées include sirloin steak au poivre, roast duckling with peach and brandy sauce, fresh Carna scallops Mornay, and Dublin Bay prawns thermidor.

MODERATE

Bridge Mills Restaurant

O'Briens Bridge. ☎ **091/566231.** Reservations recommended. Dinner main courses £6.95–£11.95 ($11.10–$19.10). AE, MC, V. Sept–June daily 9am–6pm, July–Aug daily 9am–10:30pm. INTERNATIONAL.

Located on the lower ground floor (riverbank level) in a restored mill building beside the Corrib, this restaurant allows the diner the charm of sitting beside the rhythmic flow of the river or by the gently turning mill wheel. Menu choices include such dishes as poached salmon with beurre blanc, and hearty beef in Guiness with crisp vegetables.

The Grapevine

2 High St. ☎ **091/562438.** Reservations recommended. Lunch main courses £2–£4.50 ($3.20–$7.20); dinner main courses £10.95–£16.50 ($17.50–$26.40). MC, V. Daily lunch May–Sept 12:30–2:30pm and year-round dinner 6:30–10:30pm. IRISH/EUROPEAN.

Situated above the Bunch of Grapes pub, this small, 10-table restaurant has an elegant decor of natural stone and whitewashed walls, lantern and candle lighting, fresh and dried flower arrangements, and a nautical theme. The freshest ingredients are employed here. Moist grilled ray in a fennel and mint sauce might tempt you, as may loin of lamb in blackberry gravy. Lunch items include Irish stew, smoked salmon plate, seafood chowder, and fresh local oysters or mussels.

✪ The House of Bards

2 Market St. ☎ **091/568414.** Reservations recommended. Lunch main courses £2–£5 ($3.20–$8), dinner main courses £6.95–£15.95 ($11.10–$25.50). MC, V. Daily 12:30–2:30pm and 6–11pm. IRISH.

One of Galway's newest restaurants, the House is lodged in one of the city's oldest buildings, with a fireplace oven dating from 1589. The crest over the fireplace is the marriage stone of Joyce and Skerret, two of Galway's 14 tribes. Whitewashed walls, arches, flagstone floors, candle wall sconces, medieval art, and the menu itself add to the 16th-century atmosphere. What choices! There's Lady Jane Darcy's fancy (chicken with Irish cheese stuffing); the Chieftain's Choice (pork filled with cheese and apples in rosemary sauce); Knight's Armour (sirloin steak with Irish whiskey sauce); Jester's Leap (salmon stuffed with creamy dill sauce); and King's Ransom (seafood trio of baked scallops, mussels, and prawns in white wine cheese sauce). Lunch items range from soups and salads to a medley of seafood au gratin, chicken cordon bleu, or lasagna.

Tigh Neachtain

2 Quay St. and 17 Cross St. ☎ **091/566172.** Reservations required. Main courses £7.50–£14.50 ($12–$23.20). MC, V. Mon–Sat 6:30–10:30pm. IRISH/INTERNATIONAL.

Situated above a vintage pub of the same name, this restaurant exudes an intimate old-fashioned atmosphere, with a glowing open fireplace, paneled walls, and Victorian-style furnishings, all enhanced by live guitar music. The menu offers a variety of fresh seafood as well as breast of chicken in saffron sauce, medaillons of pork in onion cream sauce, marinated fillet of beef in brandy sauce, and vegetable chili.

MODERATE/INEXPENSIVE

Conlon & Sons

3 Eglinton St., Galway. ☎ **091/562268.** Reservations not accepted. Seafood bar items £1.20–£7.95 ($1.80–$11.95); main courses £4.90–£9.90 ($7.35–$14.85). Service charge 10%. MC, V. Daily 11am–midnight. SEAFOOD.

Located in the heart of the city opposite the post office, this restaurant, known for its fresh fish, serves its meals in a ground-level cafe/take-out bar and pleasant restaurant. Treasures of the deep await: grilled wild salmon, steamed Galway Bay mussels, and fishermen's platters (smoked salmon, mussels, prawns, smoked mackerel, oysters, crab claws). Conlon & Sons plans a move just down the street this year and will keep the same phone number.

⊘ G.B.C. / Galway Bakery Company

7 Williamsgate St. ☎ **091/563087.** Reservations not necessary. Coffee shop all items £2–£6 ($3.20–$9.60); lunch main courses £2.50–£6.50 ($4–$10.40); dinner main courses £4.50–£13 ($7.20–$20.80). AE, DC, MC, V. Coffee shop Mon–Sat 8am–9pm, Sun 9am–9pm; restaurant daily noon–10pm. INTERNATIONAL.

With a distinctively Old Galway shop-front facade, this building is two eateries in one: a ground level self-service coffee shop and a full-service restaurant upstairs. On the restaurant menu a variety of dishes appear, priced to every budget, from steaks and seafood dishes to chicken Kiev or cordon bleu, as well as quiches, omelets, salads, and stir-fried vegetable platters. Baked goods, particularly the homemade brown bread, are an added attraction.

Hooker Jimmy's Steak & Seafood Bar

The Fishmarket, Spanish Arch. ☎ 091/568351. Reservations recommended for dinner. Main courses £4.85–£16.50 ($7.75–$26.40). AE, DC, MC, V. Daily noon–10:30pm. SEAFOOD/IRISH.

Housed in an old stone building beside the Spanish Arch and the River Corrib, this informal restaurant offers the same menu all day in a nautical atmosphere: mussels in cream sauce, lobster thermidor, west coast platter (crab claws, lobster tail, salmon, mussels), Galway Bay salmon with stir-fry vegetables, smoked salmon platter with prawns, and a variety of steaks and pastas. There is a terrace dining area overlooking the river.

⑤ McDonagh's Seafood Bar

22 Quay St. ☎ 091/565001. Reservations not accepted. Main courses £5.75–£14 ($9.20–$22.40). AE, MC, V. Daily 11am–10pm. SEAFOOD.

For fresh seafood in an authentically seagoing atmosphere, Galway's best choice is this little shop-front eatery, divided into a fish market, a fish-and-chip shop, and a full-service restaurant. The McDonagh family, fishmongers for more than four generations, buy direct from local fishers every day—and it shows, as crowds line up every night to get in. The choices usually include salmon, trout, lemon and/or black sole, turbot, and silver hake, all cooked to order. In addition, you can crack your own prawns' tails and crab claws in the shell, or tackle a whole lobster.

INEXPENSIVE

⑤ Bewley's Cafe

The Cornstore, Middle St. ☎ 091/565789. Reservations not accepted. All items £1–£5 ($1.60–$8). MC, V. Oct–May, Mon–Sat 8:30am–6pm; June–Sept, Mon–Sat 8:30am–8:30pm, Sun noon–6pm. IRISH/SELF-SERVICE.

For a cup of coffee or a snack, this is a favorite spot for Galwegians and visitors. A branch of the famous Dublin institution established in the 1840s, this new location has been designed to re-create the 19th century with rounded Georgian windows, dark wood furnishings, and brass fixtures. The menu, though, is modern: sandwiches, salads, soups, and quiches, as well as the famous Bewley's cakes and sticky buns.

Grainstore Cafe

Lower Abbeygate St. ☎ 091/566620. Reservations not accepted. All items £1–£5 ($1.60–$8). No credit cards. Oct–May, Mon–Sat 9:30am–5:30pm, June–Sept, 9:30am–9pm. IRISH/SELF-SERVICE.

Set amid a gallery of contemporary Irish art, this little cafe offers snacks and light meals, with choices including homemade soups, pastries, pastas, and stir-fry dishes, as well as stuffed eggplant, pizzas, quiches, salads, and hummus plates. Traditional fare, such as bacon and cabbage, is also prepared. Downstairs you can enjoy the lovely Design Ireland Plus shop.

4 Attractions

Some of Galway's top attractions are outdoors and free of charge. Leading the list is Galway Bay; and no one should miss a stroll around the Spanish Arch and Spanish Parade, through Eyre Square and the John F. Kennedy Park, or on the banks of the River Corrib.

For a change of pace, or if it rains, here are some of Galway's indoor attractions:

Galway Cathedral

University and Gaol rds. ☎ 091/563577. Free admission; donations welcome. Daily 8am–6pm.

Dominating the city's skyline, Galway Cathedral is officially known as the "Cathedral of Our Lady Assumed into Heaven and St. Nicholas." Mainly in the Renaissance style, it's constructed of fine-cut limestone from local quarries with Connemara marble floors. Completed in 1965, it took eight years to build. Contemporary Irish artisans designed the statues, stained-glass windows, and mosaics. It's beside the Salmon Weir Bridge on the west bank of the River Corrib.

◐ St. Nicholas' Collegiate Church

Lombard St. ☎ **091/566784.** Free admission to the church, but donations welcome; tours £1.50 ($2.40) adults, £1 ($1.60) students. May–Sept, daily 9am–5:30pm.

It's said that Christopher Columbus prayed here before setting out to discover the New World. Established about 1320, it has changed from Roman Catholic to Church of Ireland (Episcopal) at least four times and is currently under the aegis of the latter denomination. Highlights include an authentic crusader's tomb dating from the 12th or 13th century, with a rare Norman inscription on the grave slab. In addition, there is a free-standing benitier (a holy-water holder) that's unique in Ireland, as well as a carved font from the 16th or 17th century and a stone lectern with barley-sugar twist columns from the 15th or 16th century. The belfry contains 10 bells, some of which date from 1590. Guided tours, conducted by Declan O Mordha, a knowledgeable and enthusiastic church representative, depart from the south porch according to demand, except on Sunday mornings.

Nora Barnacle House

Bowling Green. ☎ **091/564743.** Admission £1 ($1.60) per person. May–Sept, Mon–Sat 10am–5pm.

Opposite St. Nicholas' church clock tower, this restored terrace house was once the home of Nora Barnacle, wife of James Joyce. It contains letters, photographs, and other exhibits on the lives of the Joyces and their connections with Galway. Call to confirm times open.

Tig Art Na Gaillime

Flood St. ☎ **091/563553.** Free admission. Mon–Sat 9:30am–5:30pm.

Located near the Spanish Arch, this is Galway's House of Art, displaying oils, watercolors, and pen and pencil work by native artists. Many pieces are on display for the first time.

Galway Arts Centre

47 Dominick St. and 23 Nuns Island. ☎ **091/565886.** Free admission to exhibits, concerts £2–£6 ($3.20–$9.60). Mon–Sat 10am–5:30pm.

Originally the town house of W. B. Yeats's patron, Lady Augusta Gregory, then for many years the offices of the Galway Corporation, this arts center offers excellent concerts, readings, and exhibitions by Irish and international artists.

Galway City Museum

Off Spanish Arch. ☎ **091/567641.** Admission £1 ($1.60) adults, 50p (80¢) students and children. Daily 10am–1pm and 2:15–5:15pm.

Located next to the Spanish Arch, this little museum offers a fine collection of local documents, photographs, city memorabilia, examples of medieval stonework, and revolving exhibits.

◐ Galway Irish Crystal Heritage Centre

Merlin Park. ☎ **091/757311.** Free admission. May–Sept Mon–Fri 9am–8pm, Sat 9am–6pm, Sun 10am–6pm; Oct–Apr Mon–Fri 9am–6pm, weekends 10am–6pm.

Visitors to this distinctive crystal manufacturer are welcome to watch the craftsmen at work—blowing, shaping, and hand-cutting the glassware as part of a great tour through the new heritage center. Demonstrations are continuous weekdays. The shop and new restaurant are open daily. It's located east of the city on the main road (N6).

○ Royal Tara China Ltd.

Tara Hall, Mervue. ☎ **091/751301.** Free admission. Oct–June daily 9am–6pm; July–Sept daily 8am–8pm; free tours Mon–Fri 9:30am to 3:30pm hourly.

One of Galway's oldest enterprises, this company manufactures fine bone china gift and tableware, distinguished by delicate shamrock patterns and designs inspired by the Book of Kells, the Tara brooch, and the Claddagh ring. The showrooms are quite beautiful. Look for their sign a mile east of Galway City off the main Dublin Road.

SIGHTSEEING TOURS & CRUISES

Western Heritage Sightseeing

Galway Tourist Office, Victoria Place, off Eyre Sq., Galway. ☎ **091/563081.** Walking tour of Galway City, £3.50 ($5.60) adults, £3 ($4.80) students. June–Aug daily.

Walking tours of Galway are conducted by local guides, with emphasis on the city's medieval history and connections. Tours last for 1¹/₂ hours and depart at 2:30pm from the Galway Tourist Office.

Western Heritage also offers an array of bus tours, field trips, and guided walks to such nearby destinations as The Burren, the Cliffs of Moher, and the Aran Islands. Prices range from £10 to £26 ($16 to $41.60) for adults; prices for students and seniors are £2 ($3.20) less.

○ *Corrib Princess*

Woodquay, Galway. ☎ **091/568903.** £6 ($9.60) per person. May–Sept daily 2:30 and 4:30pm.

See the sights of Galway from afloat aboard this 157-passenger two-deck boat that cruises along the River Corrib, with a commentary on all points of interest. The trip lasts 90 minutes, passing castles, various sites of historical interest, and assorted wildlife. There is full bar and snack service. Tickets can be bought at the dock or at the *Corrib Princess* desk at the Tourist Office.

5 Spectator Sports & Outdoor Pursuits

SPECTATOR SPORTS

GREYHOUND RACING   The hounds race year-round every Tuesday and Friday at 8:15pm at the Galway Greyhound Track, College Road, off Eyre Square, Galway (☎ **091/562273**). The admission price of £3 ($4.80) includes a racing card.

HORSE RACING   For six days each year at the end of July, thoroughbreds ply the track at the Galway Racecourse, Ballybrit, Galway (☎ **091/753870**), less than 2 miles east of town. Shorter two-day race meetings are scheduled in early September and late October. Admission is £5 to £8 ($8–$12.80), depending on the event.

RECREATION

BICYCLING   To rent a bike, contact **The Bike Store,** the Great Western Hostel, Frenchville Lane, Eyre Square (☎ **091/566941**), or Richard Walsh Cycles, Headford Road, Woodquay (☎ **091/565710**).

FISHING   Sitting beside the River Corrib, Galway City and nearby Connemara are popular fishing centers for salmon and sea trout in the west of Ireland. For the latest information on requirements for licenses and local permits, check with the **Western Regional Fisheries Board,** Weir Lodge, Earl's Island, Galway (☎ **091/563118**). For gear and equipment, try **Duffy's Fishing,** 5 Mainguard St., Galway (☎ **091/562367**); **Freeney's Sport Shop,** 19–23 High St., Galway (☎ **091/568794**); or **Great Outdoors Sports Centre,** Eglinton Street, Galway (☎ **091/562869**).

GOLF   Less than 5 miles east of Galway is the 18-hole, par-72 championship **Galway Bay Golf & Country Club,** Renville, Oranmore, Co. Galway (☎ **091/ 590500**), with greens fees of £25 ($40), and less than 2 miles west of the city is the 18-hole, par-69 seaside course at **Galway Golf Club,** Blackrock, Galway (☎ **091/ 522033**), with greens fees of £15 ($24).

HORSEBACK RIDING   Riding enthusiasts head to **Aille Cross Equitation Centre,** Aille Cross, Loughrea, Co. Galway (☎ **091/841216**), about 20 miles east of Galway. Run by personable Willy Leahy (who has appeared often on American television programs), this facility is one of the largest in Ireland, with 50 horses and 20 Connemara ponies. For about £10 ($16) an hour, you can arrange to ride through nearby farmlands, woodlands, forest trails, and mountain lands. Week-long trail rides in the scenic Connemara region are also a specialty of this riding center, as is hunting with the Galway Blazers in the winter months.

6 Shopping

Galway offers malls of small shops clustered in some of the city's well-preserved and restored historic buildings, such as the **Cornstore** on Middle Street, the **Grainstore** on Lower Abbeygate Street, and the **Bridge Mills,** a 430-year-old mill building beside the River Corrib.

Eyre Square Centre, with 50 shops the downtown area's largest shopping mall, has incorporated a major section of Galway's medieval town wall as part of its complex.

Most shops are open Monday through Saturday from 9 or 10am to 5:30 or 6pm. In July and August, many shops stay open late, usually till 9pm on weekdays, and some also open on Sunday from noon to 5pm.

Here's a sampling of some of Galway's best shops.

ANTIQUES & CURIOS

Cobwebs
7 Quay Lane. ☎ **091/564388.**

Established almost 25 years ago, this little shop is located across from the Spanish Arch. It offers a variety of antique toys and rarities from all parts of Ireland.

Curiosity Corner
Cross St. No phone.

Located on a corner opposite the Spanish Arch, this shop has a wide variety of unusual Irish-made gifts, from curios and ceramics to scents, potpourri, and dried flowers.

BOOKS

Charlie Byrne's Bookshop
4 Middle St. ☎ **091/561766.**

Situated opposite the Cornstore, this small but well-organized shop presents a large selection of second-hand books on Irish literature and poetry.

Hawkins House Bookshop
14 Churchyard St. ☎ **091/567507.**

Visit this shop for new books concentrating on Irish poetry, drama, fiction, history, art, archaeology, genealogy, mythology, and music, as well as for its great selection of children's books. It's located beside the Collegiate Church of St. Nicholas, off Shop Street.

✪ Kennys Book Shop and Gallery
Middle and High sts. ☎ **091/562739.**

A Galway fixture for more than 50 years, this shop is a sightseeing attraction unto itself. You'll find old maps, prints, and engravings. Books on all topics—many on local history, as well as whole sections on Yeats and Joyce—are wedged on shelves and window ledges and piled in crates and turf baskets. Lining the walls are signed photos of more than 200 writers who have visited the shop over the years. In addition, Kennys is famous for its antiquarian department, its book-binding workshop, and an ever-changing gallery of watercolors, oils, and sculptures by local talent. Enough goes on here to keep eight members of the Kenny family busy. Reconstruction completed in June 1996 has considerably expanded and enhanced the gallery and book rooms.

CRYSTAL, CHINA & SOUVENIRS

Moons
William St., at Eglinton St. ☎ **091/565254.**

This is Galway's long-established midcity department store, with crystal, china, linens, and gifts, as well as clothing and household items.

✪ Treasure Chest
31 William St. at Castle St. ☎ **091/563862.**

For more than 25 years, this attractive shop with a Wedgwood-style exterior has been a treasure trove of top quality crafts, fashions, and gifts. You'll find everything from Waterford Crystal chandeliers to Royal Tara and Royal Doulton china, Irish Dresden figurines, Lladro figures, and Belleek China, as well as Irish designer clothing, Aran knitwear, lingerie, and swimwear, not to mention handmade leprechauns and Irish whiskey marmalade.

HANDCRAFTS

✪ Design Ireland Plus
The Cornstore, Middle St. ☎ **091/567716.**

Ceramics, pottery, linen, lace, jewelry, leather bags, rainwear, blankets, stationery, candlesticks, multicolored sweaters and capes, and handcrafted batik ties and scarves—all designed and made in Ireland—are sold here. Open September through June, Monday through Saturday from 9am to 6pm; in July and August they're also open Sundays from noon to 6pm.

Judy Greene Pottery
11 Cross St. ☎ **091/561753.**

Don't miss this small shop for hand-thrown pottery painted by hand with colorful Irish floral designs. Wares include goblets, vases, candleholders, dinner and tea services, garden pots, cut-work lamps, miniatures, and jewelry. Pieces can be specially commissioned.

Kevin McGuire & Son
Prospect Hill. ☎ **091/568733.**

Housed in a whitewashed cottage and a gray stone building one block from Eyre Square, this specialty leather shop offers Celtic and modern handbags, briefcases, music cases, wallets, watch straps, belts, pendants, and sheepskin rugs.

Meadows & Byrne

Castle St., Galway. ☎ 091/567776.

Earthenware pottery and hand-blown glass have long been featured at this store, as well as wooden ware, textiles, tableware, scented beeswax candles, and Irish preserves and honey.

JEWELRY

Hartmann's

27–29 William St. ☎ 091/562063.

The Hartmann family, which began in the jewelry business in the late 1800s in Germany, brought their skills and wares to Ireland in 1895, eventually opening this Galway shop in 1942. They still enjoy a far-reaching reputation as watchmakers, goldsmiths, and makers of Claddagh rings. This store also stocks Celtic crosses, writing instruments, crystal, silverware, and unusual clocks. It's in the heart of town, just off Eyre Square.

✪ Fallers of Galway

Williamsgate St., Galway. ☎ 091/561226 or 800/229-3892 from the U.S. for catalogues.

Dating from 1879, Fallers has long been a prime source of Claddagh rings, many of which are made on the premises. It also sells Celtic crosses, some inlaid with Connemara marble, as well as gold and silver jewelry and crystal. Open Monday to Saturday from 9am to 9pm.

MUSIC & MUSICAL INSTRUMENTS

Mulligan's

5 Middle St. Court, Middle St. ☎ 091/564961.

Mulligan's boasts of having the largest stock of Irish and Scottish traditional records, CDs, and cassettes in Ireland. There is also a good selection of folk music from all over the world, including Cajun, Latin American, and African, as well as country music, blues, and jazz. They're open from 9:30am to 7pm Monday through Thursday, close at 9pm on Fridays and 6pm on Saturdays, and are open noon to 4pm on Sundays.

✪ P. Powell & Sons / The Music Shop

The Four Corners, William St. ☎ 091/562295.

Located opposite Lynch's Castle, where William Street meets Abbeygate Street, this shop is known for Irish traditional music. In addition to cassettes and CDs, tin whistles, flutes, bodhrans, accordions, and violins are sold, as are sheet music and a full range of music books. Open daily from 9am to 5:30pm.

TWEEDS, WOOLLENS & CLOTHING

✪ O Maille (O'Malley)

Dominick St. ☎ 091/562696.

Established in 1938, this family run shop is located on the west side of the River Corrib, slightly off the beaten track, but customers from far and near flock here for quality Irish clothing, including Irish-designed knitwear, traditional Aran knits, and tweeds for men and women. There is always a good selection of sweaters, jackets, coats, suits, capes, kilts, caps, and ties. Open Monday through Saturday from 9am to 6:30pm.

Mac Eocagain / Galway Woollen Market
21/22 High St. ☎ **091/562491.**

This shop brims with traditional Aran hand-knits and colorful hand-loomed sweaters and capes, as well as linens, lace, sheepskins, jewelry, and woolen accessories. Each item has two prices, one including value-added tax (VAT) and one tax-free for non–European Community (EC) residents. Open Monday through Saturday from 9am to 6pm, Sunday from noon to 5pm; in July and August the hours are 9am to 9pm and Sunday from 10am to 6pm.

7 Pubs & Evening Entertainment

PUBS

An Pucan
11 Forster St. ☎ **091/561528.**

Located a block east of Eyre Square, this old-fashioned nautical-theme pub features free traditional Irish music nightly from 9pm.

Busker Browns
Cross St., Galway. ☎ **091/563101.**

Alcoves, nooks and crannies, and a choice of bars fill this pub and busy bistro, one of the city's newest but with an Old Galway ambience. Traditional music is performed throughout the week and the place swings to Dixieland jazz on Sunday from noon to 2pm.

Crane Bar
2 Sea Rd. ☎ **091/567419.**

In the southwestern part of Galway at the corner of an open market area called "the Small Crane," this rustic pub is known for its nightly musical entertainment. From 9pm every night, it's country/western downstairs and traditional Irish tunes upstairs.

Hole in the Wall
Eyre St. ☎ **091/565593.**

Topped with a thatched roof, this old-world pub stands out on a busy shopping street one block from Eyre Square. The interior has a low beamed ceiling, open fireplaces, old sporting prints, and an old-fashioned juke box. Cable TV screens show major sports events in this regular gathering spot for fans of Gaelic football and horse racing. In between the sports talk, traditional Irish music starts nightly in the summer months at 9:30pm.

O'Malleys
30 Prospect Hill. ☎ **091/564595.**

Claiming to be Galway's oldest music pub, this informal watering hole has traditional Irish and folk music sessions with special guests on Fridays from October to March (cover charge £3 to £5; $4.80 to $8) and music with dancing in the summer.

The Quays
Quay St. and Chapel Lane. ☎ **091/568347.**

This little treasure is in the heart of the city, a half block from the Druid Theatre. The decor is decidedly nautical, with pictures of sailing ships and other seafaring memorabilia. The bar area is quite small, but there is also an enclosed skylit back courtyard. Evening music ranges from traditional Irish to Dixieland and usually starts at 9pm.

Rabbitt's
23–25 Forster St. ☎ **091/566490.**

Dating from 1872, this pub is much the way it was a century ago. Old lanterns hang in the corners, skylights brighten the bar area, and the walls are lined with pictures of Galway in horse-and-carriage days. A hefty bucket of ice sits on the counter and a hearty Irish stew awaits in the kitchen. Run by the fourth generation of the Rabbitt family, it's located just a block east of Eyre Square.

A MEDIEVAL BANQUET

On the shores of Galway Bay, **Dunguaire** is a splendid 16th-century castle that features a medieval banquet with a literary-themed show. Located in south Co. Galway on Ballyvaughan road (N67), Kinvara, Co. Galway (☎ **091/37108**), the castle is a nightlife option for people staying in Galway City—just a half-hour drive away (see "Side Trips from Galway City," below). The show features the work of Synge, Yeats, Gogarty, and other Irish writers who knew and loved this area of western Ireland. Banquets are staged from May to September, twice nightly at 5:30 and 8:45pm, priced at £28 ($44.80). Reservations can be made by calling the castle directly or the **Shannon Medieval Castle Banquets** (☎ **800/CIE-Tour** from the U.S., or 061/360788).

THEATERS

Druid Theatre
Chapel Lane. ☎ **091/568617.** Tickets, evening £6–£8 ($9.60–$12.80); Mon–Sat, box office noon to 8pm; evening shows at 8pm.

Irish folk dramas, modern international dramas, and Anglo-Irish classics are the focus at this professional theater in the heart of Galway. Started in 1975, it is housed in a converted grain warehouse, configured with 65 to 115 seats, depending on the production. Lunchtime performances are often staged during the summer months.

Punchbag Theatre
Quay Lane. ☎ **091/565422.** Tickets £7 ($11.20). Box office, Mon–Sat noon–6pm; shows, Tues–Sun 8pm.

Located opposite the Spanish Arch in the city's historic section, this newly renovated theater presents contemporary plays from Ireland and abroad. From May through September, the emphasis is on staging the works of new writers.

✪ An Taibhdhearc Theatre
Middle St. ☎ **091/562024.** Tickets £7 ($10.50). Box office, daily 11am–6pm; shows nightly, 8pm; Siamsa, July–Aug, Mon–Fri 8:45pm.

Pronounced *Thive-yark* and officially known as An Taibhdhearc na Gaillimhe (the Theatre of Galway), this is Ireland's national stage of the Irish language. Founded in 1928, it is a 108-seat, year-round venue for both Irish plays and visiting troupes (such as ballet). In the summer months, the theater presents Siamsa, a program of traditional music, song, dance, and folk drama.

8 Side Trips from Galway City

THE ARAN ISLANDS

West from the mouth of Galway Bay, 30 miles out at sea, the storied Aran Islands—Inis More (Inishmore), Inis Meain (Inishmaan), and Inis Oirr (Inisheer)—are outposts of Gaelic culture and language, where the rugged islanders immortalized in John Millington Synge's play *Riders to the Sea* and Robert Flaherty's film *Man of Aran* still maintain their hardscrabble traditional life, clinging like moss to the islands' harsh rocks and fishing from currachs, small craft made of tarred canvas stretched over a timber frame.

The island's 1,500 inhabitants live in stone cottages, get around in pony-drawn transport, and speak Irish among themselves, breaking into English when necessary to converse with nonislanders. Inevitably, tourism has altered things somewhat, and many distinctively Aran traditions hang on more as curios than as everyday elements of life. Among them are the *crios,* finger-braided belts made of colored wool that traditionally held up the islanders' heavy wool trousers but are now more commonly made for the tourist trade. The classic hand-knit bainin sweaters that originated here are still used, of course, as there's nothing better for keeping out the chill. You'll see plenty of them if you drop in to one of the islands' pubs, where my editor says he had the best pint of Guinness ever drawn by the hand of man.

Most visitors end up debarking from the ferries at Kilronan, Inishmore's main town and possibly the easiest place in the world in which to arrange or rent transportation. The mode is up to you: Jaunting cars can almost be hailed like taxis as you step off the boat, and bicycle rentals are within sight.

Among the attractions on the Arans is **Dún Aengus,** a stone cliff fortress on Inishmore that extends over more than 11 acres. Dating back to the 5th century, the fort is believed to have been of great maritime significance. It's set on the edge of a cliff that drops 250 feet to the sea, and it offers a spectacular view of Galway Bay.

The new heritage center, Ionad Arann, Kilronan, Inishmore (☎ **099/61355**), tells the history and culture of these islands. Exhibits examine the harsh yet beautiful landscape, the Iron Age forts, and the churches of the first Christians. It's open from April through September daily from 10am to 7pm. Admission is £2.50 ($4) adults, £2 ($3.20) students and seniors, £1.50 ($2.40) children, £6 ($9.60) family.

Here are the best ways to arrange an excursion to the Aran Islands:

Aer Arann

Connemara Airport, Inverin, Co. Galway. ☎ **091/593034.** Fax 091/593238. £35 ($56) round-trip, £18 ($28.80) one-way per person. MC, V. June–Sept daily at 9:30am, 11am, 2pm, and 5pm, returning at 9:45 and 11:15am, 4:15 and 5:15pm; Oct–May schedule varies.

The fastest way to get from the mainland to the Aran Islands is via this local airline, which departs from a new airport approximately 18 miles west of Galway City. Flight time is only 10 minutes, and bus service between Galway City and the airport is available. Flights can be booked at the Galway Tourist Office and at Aer Arann Reservations.

Aran Ferries

Galway Tourist Office, Eyre Sq., Galway. ☎ **091/568903.** Round-trip approximately £18 ($28.80) from Galway (90 min); round-trip approximately £15 ($24) from Rossaveal (20 min).

Galway Bay, a triple-decker, 290-passenger ferry, cruises to Kilronan on Inishmore in a 90-minute trip from the Galway Docks. From Rossaveal in Connemara— 23 miles west of the city, accessible from downtown Galway via a connecting bus— the *Aran Flyer,* a double-decker, 218-passenger ferry, will take you to Kilronan in 20 minutes. Both ships have a bar, snack service, and sundeck. Call for exact schedules and advance booking.

Island Ferries

Victoria Place, off Eyre Sq., Galway. ☎ **091/561676.** Approximately £15 ($24) per person. Year-round from Rossaveal; check for times.

The double-decker *Aran Seabird* ferries year-round, between Rossaveal, 23 miles west of downtown Galway, and the Aran Islands. The trip takes 35 minutes. Buses depart for Rossaveal from the ferry office opposite the tourist office in Galway an hour before each sailing. The boat has indoor and outdoor seating for all passengers. The snack bar serves alcohol.

O'Brien Shipping

Galway Docks, Galway. ☎ **091/567283.** £15 ($2.40) per person round-trip; £8 ($12.80) one-way; fly/sail £26 ($41.60) per person. From Galway, June and Sept at 10am, July–Aug 10:30am; from Aran, June and Sept at 5:30pm, July–Aug at 5pm. Oct–May schedule varies.

The M.V. *Oileain Arann,* a 240-passenger, air-conditioned, three-deck ship launched in 1993, is the newest on the Galway / Aran Islands route. It has a full bar, snack bar, TV, and public telephone on board. Sailing time is 90 minutes. Booking office is at the Galway Tourist Office. *Note:* this company also operates a "fly/sail" arrangement in conjunction with Aer Arann, offering a boat/plane combination trip.

OYSTER COUNTRY

South of Galway on the main road south (N18) are the two small fishing villages, Clarenbridge and Kilcolgan. Each year at the end of September, these two villages host the annual Galway Oyster Festival. Launched in 1954, this five-day festival is packed with traditional music, song, dancing, sports, art exhibits, and, above all, oyster-tasting events and oyster-opening competitions. A Galway beauty is crowned Oyster Pearl, and she reigns over the festival.

Even if you can't be there for the September festival, you can still enjoy some of Ireland's best oysters during any other month with an "r" in it.

If you continue southward on N18 for another 10 miles, you'll see signs to **Coole Park** (☎ 091/31804). This national forest is inhabited by Irish red deer, pine martens, red squirrels, and badgers. Coole House was once the home of Lady Augusta Gregory, dramatist and folklorist. Along with W. B. Yeats and Edward Martyn, she founded the Abbey Theatre. Her house no longer stands, but an "autograph tree" bears the sets of initials carved by George Bernard Shaw, Sean O'Casey, John Masefield, Oliver St. John Gogarty, W. B. Yeats, and Douglas Hyde, the first president of Ireland. The restored courtyard has a visitor center, tearooms, picnic tables, and a garden with nature trails to the lake. Admission is £2 ($3.20) adults, £1.50 ($2.40) seniors, £1 ($1.60) students and children. It's open from mid-April to mid-June and September, Tuesday through Sunday from 10am to 5pm, and mid-June to the end of August daily from 9:30am to 6:30pm with last admission 45 minutes before closing.

Also in Gort on the N18 is **Thoor Ballylee** (☎ 091/31436). This restored 16th-century Norman tower house was the summer home of the Nobel Prize–winning poet William Butler Yeats. Yeats described the house as "a tower set by a stream's edge"; it served as the inspiration for his poems "The Winding Stair" and "The Tower." In the interpretative center, an audio-visual presentation examines the poet's life. Also on the grounds are the original Ballylee Mill, partially restored, and a bookshop specializing in Anglo-Irish literature. Admission is £3 ($4.80) adults, £2.50 ($4) seniors and students, 75p ($1.20) children, £6 ($9.60) family. It's open from Easter to September daily from 10am to 6pm.

West off the main road, between Gort and Kilcolgan is **Dunguaire Castle,** Kinvara (☎ 091/37108). Reached via R347, this tower house and bawn sits on the south shore of Galway Bay. It was erected in the 16th century by the O'Heynes family at the royal seat of the 7th-century King Guaire of Connaught. The castle was later the country retreat of Oliver St. John Gogarty, Irish surgeon, author, poet, and wit. Admission is £2.50 ($4) adults, £2 ($3.20) seniors, and £1.50 ($2.40) students and children. It's open daily from late April through September from 9:30am to 5:30pm.

Medieval banquets are held here in the evenings (see "Pubs and Evening Entertainment," above).

ACCOMMODATIONS

Hazelwood House

Creganna, Oranmore, Co. Galway (signposted on N18, 15 minutes south of Galway). ☎ 091/794275. Fax 091/794608. 6 rooms (one without bath). £32 ($51.20) double with bath. Includes full Irish breakfast. No service charge. AE, DC, MC, V. Closed Dec–Jan.

If you've just arrived at Shannon or if you're on your way in or out of Galway, this is a perfect haven, close enough for convenience and remote enough for tranquility. Hazelwood House is set back, surrounded by trees, a house of character and comfort. The rooms are spacious, immaculate, and are equipped with orthopedic beds and personal coffeemakers. The Irish breakfast here takes an extra step and offers the option of kippers, herring, or trout. Fixed-price dinners are available for £16 ($25.60) and must be booked by 3pm. Patricia Kavanaugh, your host, is a fine cook who accommodates the needs of vegetarians and anyone with particular allergies or sensitivities, and she is fully certified by the Wine and Spirit Education Trust of London. Brace yourself for a pleasant stay.

WHERE TO EAT OYSTERS

✪ Moran's Oyster Cottage

The Weir, Kilcolgan, Co. Galway. ☎ 091/796113. Reservations not required. Main courses, lunch and dinner £1.80–£10.20 ($2.90–$16.30). AE, MC, V. Daily 10:30am–11pm. SEAFOOD.

If you miss the signpost for Moran's on N18, turn around and go back, because this is not a place to be missed. Presidents, prime ministers, movie stars, and locals who know their fish make a point of finding their way here. Their food is simply legendary. For six generations the Morans have been catching salmon and shucking oysters, and preparing them to perfection here on the weir. In fact, in 1960 Willie Moran caught 105 wild salmon in one day on the Dun Killen River in front of the family pub and went on to win the world title in oyster-opening. Two of his staff, Vincent Graham and Gerry Grealish, are also world champions. In short, they know their oysters. The wild smoked salmon is exquisite—sheer velvet. Willie Moran believes in a small menu, fresh and wild and with nothing in the way. Ambience? Thatched cottage with 36 swans and a blue heron outside the front door the night we were here.

Paddy Burkes

Ennis-Galway road (N18), Clarenbridge, Co. Galway. ☎ 091/796226. Reservations recommended for dinner. Lunch main courses £3–£12 ($4.80–$19.20), dinner main courses £8.95–£16 ($14.30–$25.60). AE, DC, MC, V. Daily 10:30am–11pm. SEAFOOD.

Platters of local oysters and mussels are served throughout the day at this homey tavern, with its lemon color and thatched roof, situated on the main road 10 miles south of Galway City. You can pick your favorite spot to relax amid a half-dozen rooms and alcoves with original stone walls, open fireplaces, pot-belly stoves, fishing nets on the walls, and traditional sugan chairs. In good weather, there is also seating in a back garden beside a weir bridge. Lunch and other snack items range from seafood soups and chowders to sandwiches, salads, and omelets. In the evening, you can also order full meals with choices such as whole black sole, baked salmon, Atlantic plaice and crab with prawn sauce, honey roast duck with mead sauce, and medaillons of beef with whiskey and mustard.

SHOPPING

Clarenbridge Crystal and Fashion Shop
Clarenbridge, Galway. ☎ **091/796178.**

This shop features all types and styles of Clarenbridge crystal, a local glass product that has been hand-cut, engraved, and decorated at a factory a mile away. In addition, a beautiful range of classic quality ladies fashions and men's country clothing is available alongside framed prints, watercolors, and jewelry. It's located 10 miles south of Galway on N18, and is open Monday through Friday from 9am to 7pm, Saturday from 10am to 6pm, and Sunday from noon to 6pm.

13 Out from Galway

Situated along the rocky western coast, Galway is Ireland's second-largest county, forming (with Mayo—see Chapter 11) the heart of the province of Connaught. "To hell or Connaught!" were the limited options offered by Cromwell to the Irish in the 17th century. Like a firestorm, Cromwell and his armies ravaged everything in their path and sent the native population running to the western edge of Ireland, where there was nothing much worth coveting or destroying. It was here that the displaced Irish were left to eke out a living on minute, rock-infested farms. It was also here, where it seemed people had little left to lose, that the famine of 1845–49 took its greatest toll, as masses of people either starved or took off on ships sailing westward, never to return.

History aside, this bleak western outpost is stunningly beautiful—a fact you can appreciate if you don't have to eat the scenery to survive. It is indeed a feast, and, as it happens, it's a feast that provides for everyone, since tourism is bringing a prosperity to the west that the potato never did.

1 The Galway Bay Coast

From Galway City to Inverin is 20 miles.

GETTING TO & AROUND   The best way to see the sights along the Galway Bay coast is to drive, departing Galway City and following the Coast road (R336).

VISITOR INFORMATION   Contact or visit the **Ireland West Tourist Office,** Aras Failte, Victoria Place, Galway, Co. Galway (☎ **091/563081**), open year-round (see Chapter 12, "Galway City," for hours). In addition, a seasonal office, open from late May to mid-September, is maintained at Salthill (☎ **091/ 563081**).

AREA CODE   Most numbers in this region have the area code **091.**

ATTRACTIONS

It's certainly worth a trip to see Galway Bay's wide blue waters, with the Aran Islands sitting 30 miles off the coast like three giant whales at rest. With vistas of Galway Bay on your left, the drive along the coast from Galway City is quite spectacular.

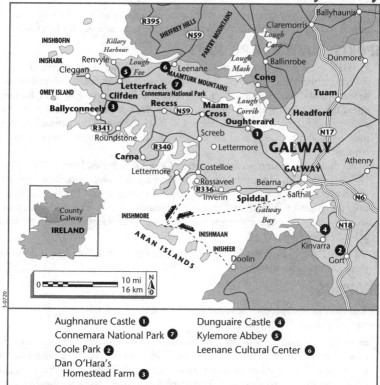

Aughnanure Castle ❶
Connemara National Park ❼
Coole Park ❷
Dan O'Hara's
    Homestead Farm ❸
Dunguaire Castle ❹
Kylemore Abbey ❺
Leenane Cultural Center ❻

Head west, following the signs for the Coast road (R336). Within 2 miles you'll be in Salthill, a modern Irish beach resort that's somewhat along the lines of the Jersey shore in the United States, with a boardwalk and fine beach plus lots of bars, fast food, amusement rides, and arcades of games. This is a summer mecca for Irish families, but you will likely prefer to continue on this scenic road to the little towns like Barna and Spiddal, both of which are considered to be Irish-language towns. Spiddal, 12 miles west of Galway City, is also an ideal spot to shop for locally made Aran knit sweaters and other handcrafts made by the people in the surrounding cottages.

The road continues as far as Inverin and then turns northward, with signposts for **Rossaveal.** From Rossaveal, you can make the shortest sea crossing from the Galway mainland to the Aran Islands (see "Side Trips from Galway City," in Chapter 12). You may wish to combine this coastal drive with a trip to the islands.

If you continue on R336, you'll leave the Galway Bay coast and travel amid the rocky and remote scenery approaching the center of Connemara. **Casla (Costelloe)** is the home of Raidio na Gaeltachta, the Irish-language radio station, and **Rosmuc** is the site of the **Padraic Pearse Cottage.** This simple thatched-roof cottage served as a retreat for Dublin-based Pearse, who was one of the leaders of Ireland's 1916 Rising. He used his time here to improve his knowledge of the Irish language. Now a national monument, the cottage contains various documents, photographs, and other Pearse memorabilia. Admission is £1 ($1.60) for adults, 70p ($1.12) for seniors, and 40p (64¢) for students and children. It's open from mid-June until mid-September, daily from 9:30am to 1:30pm and 2 to 6:30pm.

At this point you can continue northward into the heartland of Connemara or retrace your route back to Galway, setting out afresh the next day for Connemara.

SPORTS & OUTDOOR PURSUITS

FISHING   Rimmed by the waters of Galway Bay and the Atlantic, this area is prime territory for sea fishing, especially for mackerel, pollock, cod, turbot, and shark. **Spiddal Sea Angling,** Craigmore, Greenhill, Spiddal (☎ 091/83535), offers fishing trips on board the *Thresher 1,* a 33-foot catamaran designed especially for sea fishing. The price averages £30 ($48) per person per day and includes rods, reels, and bait. The boat leaves from Spiddal Pier; advance reservations are required.

For those who prefer trout fishing, there's **Crumlin Fisheries,** Inverin, Co. Galway (☎ 091/593105). This fishery has a lake stocked with sea-reared rainbow trout and allows two fish per person to be taken per day. Prices range from £10 ($16) for fishing from the bank to £25 ($40) for fishing with a boat; ghillies (fishing guides) are available for £25 ($40) extra. Fishing is from 9am daily, but reservations must be made at least a day in advance.

SWIMMING   The Silver Strand at Barna and the beach at Spiddal are clean and sandy, and ideal for swimming.

SHOPPING

✪ Ceardlann an Spideil / Spiddal Craft Centre
Coast road, Spiddal. ☎ 091/553376.

In a setting overlooking Galway Bay, this is a cluster of cottage shops where craftspeople ply their trades each day. Browse around and watch crafts in the process of being made. The selection includes pottery, weaving, knitwear, screen printing and design, jewelry, and wood-turning. The art galleries feature original hand-carved stone craft, sculpture, paintings, prints, posters, and cards, and there's a very good coffee shop on the premises. Open Monday through Saturday from 9:30am to 5:30pm and Sunday 2 to 5:30pm.

✪ Mairtin Standun
Coast road, Spiddal, Co. Galway. ☎ 091/553102.

A fixture on the Connemara coast since 1946, this shop has long been known as a good source for traditional bainin sweaters, handcrafted by local women from the nearby Aran Islands and the surrounding Connemara countryside. Recently enlarged, it also offers colorful knits, tweeds, sheepskins, linens, glassware, china, pottery, jewelry, books, and maps. In addition, there's a new wide-windowed cafe facing Galway Bay and the Aran Islands. Open March through December, Monday through Saturday from 9:30am to 6:30pm.

ACCOMMODATIONS

✪ Connemara Coast Hotel
Coast road, Furbo, Co. Galway. ☎ 091/592108. Fax 091/592065. 112 rms. TV TEL. £85–£130 ($136–$208) double. No service charge. Rates include full breakfast. AE, DC, MC, V.

If you want to see the sun go down on Galway Bay, this is the place to stay. Located 6 miles west of Galway City, it's nestled right along the shores of the famous bay, with unobstructed views of the coast as well as of the Aran Islands. Recently refurbished and expanded, the guest rooms are decorated in a colorful tweedy or floral style, each with a picture-window view of the water. Some units have turf-burning fireplaces and private verandas.

Dining/Entertainment: The bilevel Gallery restaurant has views of the bay, and the Players bar and local pub have traditional entertainment nightly in summer and on weekends during the rest of the year.

Facilities: Indoor heated swimming pool, Jacuzzi, steam bath, gym, two all-weather tennis courts.

✪ Delphi Lodge

The Delphi Estate and Fishery, Co. Galway. ☎ **095/42211.** Fax 095/42296. E-mail **delfish@iol.ie.** 12 rms, 4 cottages. £74 ($118.40) standard double; £100 ($160) lakeside double. Includes full Irish breakfast. No service charge. £25 ($40) fixed-price dinner daily. £395 ($632) per week 2-bedroom self-catering cottages. CB, EU, MC, V. Closed Christmas/New Year holidays.

Delphi Lodge is a dream destination, so much so that you'll pinch yourself every now and then to be sure you're not dreaming. Built in the early 19th century as a sportsman's hideaway for the marquis of Sligo, it sits tranquilly amid a landscape that almost defies description—crystalline lakes and rivers, hardwood forests, unspoiled ocean beaches, and luminous velveteen mountain slopes. All that and salmon and sea trout out the front door, waiting to be caught! The rooms are luxuriously simple and spacious, furnished in antique and contemporary light pine and featuring orthopedic mattresses. Fishing permits and registration are available at the lodge for £50 ($80), and another £5 ($8) will rent you the equipment you'll need. At dinner, the lodge will prepare your own personal catch of the day, or send it to you at home, smoked, after your return. Special three-day weekend packages, including courses in fly-tying, watercolors, wine appreciation, and other diversions, are available in the off season. If you're not going to spend October in Vermont, this is the place to be. All reservations must be made in writing or by fax. Detailed directions are provided with reservations.

DINING
MODERATE

✪ Boluisce

Coast road, Spiddal, Co. Galway. ☎ **091/83286.** Reservations recommended for dinner. Lunch main courses £2–£7 ($3.20–$11.20); dinner main courses £6–£20 ($9.60–$32). MC, V. Daily noon–10:30pm. SEAFOOD.

The name of this restaurant comes from an old Irish phrase meaning "patch of grazing by the water." And, if you're fond of seafood, this is one patch where you'll want to graze on scallops, prawns, lobster, smoked salmon, or crab plate (or try the West Coast platter, which includes prawns, crab, lobster, mussels, and salmon). The house chowder is a meal in itself, brimming with salmon, prawns, monkfish, mussels, and more. Home-baked brown bread, made with whole meal, bran, and buttermilk, accompanies every meal; it's rich and nutty, and genial proprietor John Glanville will gladly share the recipe with you.

Twelve Pins

Coast road, Barna, Co. Galway. ☎ **091/592368.** Reservations recommended for dinner. Lunch main courses £2–£9 ($3.20–$14.40); dinner main courses £5.50–£12 ($8.80–$19.20). MC, V. Daily 12:30–3pm and 6:30–10pm. IRISH.

Named for the famous mountains of Connemara, this old-world inn by the side of the road is a good place to come for fresh oysters or a seafood platter (oysters, mussels, smoked salmon, and prawns), and other creatively prepared seafood choices such as scallops en croûte and trout Oisin (stuffed with almonds and seafood). For non–fish-eaters, the menu offers a traditional roast of the day, plus steaks, rack of lamb, duckling, vegetarian stir-fry, and lasagne.

INEXPENSIVE

An Caife

Ceardlann an Spideil / Spiddal Craft Centre, Coast road, Spiddal, Co. Galway. ☎ **091/83443.**
Reservations not accepted. All items 80p–£6 ($1.30–$9.60). No credit cards. Apr–Oct Mon–Sat
9:30am–6pm, Sun noon–6pm. IRISH/SELF-SERVICE.

Housed in a rustic cottage at the Spiddal Craft Centre, overlooking Galway Bay, this
place is ideal for a snack or light meal. The menu includes home-baked scones and
pies and freshly prepared soups, salads, sandwiches, pizza, quiches, and sausage rolls.

2 Connemara

Clifden is 40 miles W of Galway City.

GETTING TO & AROUND CONNEMARA   From Galway City, **Bus Eireann**
(☎ **091/562000**) provides daily service to Clifden and other small towns en route.
The best way to get around Connemara is to drive, following the N59 route from
Moycullen and Oughterard. Alternatively, you can take a guided tour (see "Sightseeing Tours," below).

VISITOR INFORMATION   Contact or visit the **Ireland West Tourist Office,**
Aras Failte, Victoria Place, Galway, Co. Galway (☎ **091/563081**). It's open May,
June, and September, Monday through Saturday from 8:30am to 5:45pm; July and
August, daily from 8:30am to 7:45pm; and the rest of the year, Monday through
Friday from 9am to 5:45pm and Saturday from 9am to 12:45pm. The **Oughterard
Tourist Office,** Main Street, Oughterard (☎ **091/82808**), is also open year-round,
Monday through Friday from 9am to 5:30pm with extended hours in the summer
season. In addition, a seasonal office, open from May through September, is main-
tained at Clifden (☎ **095/21163**).

AREA CODES   Telephone area codes for numbers in the Connemara area are **091**
or **095.**

ATTRACTIONS

If you look at an average map or road sign, you won't usually see a marking or di-
rectional for Connemara. That's because it's not a city or a town or county, but rather
an area or region, such as the Burren is in Co. Clare. In general, Connemara constitutes the section west of Galway City, starting out from Oughterard and continuing
toward the Atlantic. It is an area of astounding barrenness and beauty.

The "capital," or largest town, in Connemara is **Clifden**—if you follow the signs
for Clifden, you can't go wrong. The road marked N59 will take you around the
heart of Connemara and then onward to Co. Mayo. You can also follow many of the
smaller roads and wander around Connemara for days. In fact, many people choose
to stay in this region for a week or so, usually basing themselves in one or more of
the fine resorts and inns that dot the countryside, especially in places like Cashel,
Ballynahinch, Renvyle, and Clifden itself.

In recent years Clifden has exploded into a major tourist center, and it shows.
B&Bs, pubs, and shops arm-wrestle for space in the town center, which for the first
time in its history experiences gridlock. Even so, it remains an attractive town, whose
past and present can be seen on the two sides of its buildings—their backs gray and
worn, their fronts bright and alluring. For a slower, more remote, yet still pleasing
taste of Connemara town life, you might give the small, active fishing port of
Roundstone a try.

The coastline is indented with little bays and inlets, small harbors, and beaches. At almost every turn are lakes, waterfalls, rivers, and creeks, while a dozen glorious mountains, known as the **Twelve Bens,** rise at the center. All of this is interspersed with rock-strewn land and flat fields of open bog, rimmed with gorse and heather, rhododendrons, and wildflowers. The tableau presents a dramatic panorama of sea and sky, land and bog.

Connemara's **boglands** began forming 2,500 years ago. During the Iron Age, the Celts preserved their butter in the bog. Today, with one-third of Connemara classified as bog, the turf (or peat) that's cut from the bog remains an important source of fuel. Cutting and drying turf is an integral part of the rhythm of the seasons in Connemara. Cutting requires a special tool, a spade called a slane, which slices the turf into elongated bricks about 18 inches long. These are spread out to dry and stiffen so that they can be stacked in pyramids to permit air circulation for further drying. Finally they're piled up along the roadside for transport. You can always tell when a family is burning turf in a fireplace—the smoke coming out of the chimney is blue and sweet-scented.

As you drive around Connemara you're sure to notice the absence of trees, felled and dragged off long ago for building English ships, houses, and furniture. More of Cromwell's handiwork. In recent years, however, the Irish government has undertaken an aggressive reforestation program, and vast areas of land have been set aside for planting trees, mostly pines, as a crop.

A trademark of this region is the **donkey,** still a worker on the farms. In some places you'll see a sturdy little horse known as the **Connemara pony,** the only horse breed native to Ireland (though it's had an infusion of Spanish blood over the centuries). Often raised in tiny fields with limestone pastures, these animals have great stamina and are invaluable for farming and pulling equipment. The Connemara pony is also noted for its gentle temperament, which makes it ideal for children's riding activities.

A major part of Connemara is designated as a **Gaeltacht,** or Irish-speaking area, so you may hear many of the people conversing in their native tongue. Traditional music thrives in this part of the countryside, as do handcrafts and cottage industries.

The much-imitated **Aran knit sweaters** are synonymous with this region of Ireland. Made of an oatmeal-colored wool from the native sheep, these semiwaterproof sweaters were first knit by the women of the nearby Aran Islands for their fishermen husbands and sons—each family would have a different stitch or pattern. Years ago, the patterns were not only a matter of aesthetics; they served as the chief way to identify men who had drowned in the treacherous waters off the coast. Today these sweaters are knit in the homes of Connemara and the nearby Aran Islands and then sold in the many craft shops throughout the region.

✪ Connemara National Park

Clifden-Westport road (N59), Letterfrack, Co. Galway. ☎ **095/41054.** Admission £2 ($3.20) adults, £1.50 ($2.40) groups and seniors £1 ($1.60) children and students, £5 ($8) family. Park, year-round; visitor center, daily May and Sept 10am–5:30pm, June 10am–6:30pm, July–Aug 9:30am–6:30pm.

This stunning national park incorporates 3,800 acres of Connemara's mountains, bogs, heaths, and grasslands. The grounds are home to herds of Connemara ponies and Irish red deer, as well as a variety of birds and smaller mammals. To orient and acquaint visitors with all of the aspects of the park, the handsome exhibition center offers a series of displays and an informative 20-minute audiovisual presentation. Tea, coffee, soup, sandwiches, and freshly baked goods are on hand in the tea room.

If you're up to it, test your willpower against the cheesecake. During July and August, Tuesdays and Thursdays are "nature days" for children while Mondays, Wednesdays, and Fridays offer guided walks for the whole family. Call the center for specific information on these and other special programs.

✪ Kylemore Abbey

Kylemore, Co. Galway. ☎ **095/41146.** Admission £1.50 ($2.40) adults, £1 ($1.60) seniors and students, 50p (80¢) children. Easter–Oct daily 9:30am–6pm.

Originally a private residence (circa 1868), this castellated house overlooking Kylemore Lake is a splendid example of Neo-Gothic architecture. In 1920 it was turned over to the Benedictine nuns, who have since opened the grounds and part of the house to the public. The highlight is the recently restored Gothic chapel, considered a miniature cathedral. The complex also includes a cafe, serving produce grown on the nuns' own farm, a shop with a working pottery studio, and a visitor center where a video presentation gives you an overview of life at Kylemore, both past and present. The abbey is most atmospheric when the bells are rung for midday office, or vespers at 6pm.

Leenane Cultural Center

Clifden-Westport road (N59), Leenane, Co. Galway. ☎ **095/42323.** Admission £2.50 ($4) adults, £1.50 ($2.40) seniors, students, and children over age 8. Mar–Oct daily 10am–7pm.

Overlooking Killary Harbour, this center focuses on the history of wool and the 20 breeds of sheep in Connemara. In particular, it presents exhibits on the local wool industry, including carding, spinning, weaving, and using natural dyes. Daily demonstrations of sheep-shearing are given from June through August, and visitors are invited to try their hand at it or at spinning or weaving. In addition, a 13-minute audiovisual presentation provides background on the local history and places of interest in the area. Facilities include a wool craft shop and an octagonal cafe.

Dan O'Hara's Homestead Farm

Lettershea, Clifden, Co. Galway. ☎ **095/21246.** Admission £2.75 ($4.40) adults, £2.25 ($3.60) seniors and students, £1.75 ($2.80) children. March–Nov daily 10am–6pm.

If you're wondering how Connemara farmers find soil to farm on this rocky land, head to this small farm about 4 miles east of Clifden off the main N59 road. As the name implies, it was once owned by Dan O'Hara, who was forced to emigrate to the United States because of the harsh conditions and high taxes of the time. Today, the newly expanded center incorporates an eight-acre prefamine farm and reflects how life here operated in the 1840s, with local people using traditional tilling and farming methods. The land also contains a reconstructed crannog (fortified lake dwelling), an authentic megalithic tom, and a dolmen.

Aughnanure Castle

Clifden Rd., Oughterard, Co. Galway. ☎ **091/82214.** Admission £2 ($3.20) adults, £1.50 ($2.40) seniors, £1 ($1.60) students and children, £5 ($8) family. Mid-June to mid-Sept, daily 9:30am–6:30pm. 20 miles (32km) W of Galway City off N59 (signposted).

Standing on a rocky island close to the shores of Lough Corrib, this castle is a well-preserved example of a six-story Irish tower house, with an unusual double bawn (a fortified enclosure) and a watchtower. It was built around A.D. 1500 as a stronghold of the O'Flaherty clan.

SIGHTSEEING TOURS

Several companies provide sightseeing tours of Connemara from Galway or Clifden.

Bus Eireann

Ceannt Station, Galway. ☎ **091/562000.** £10 ($15) adults, £5 ($7.50) children. Mid-June to late June and late Aug to mid-Sept on Sun, Tues, and Thurs 9:45am; end of June to end of Aug, daily Mon–Sat 9:45am.

Departing from the bus station in Galway, this eight-hour tour of Connemara takes in Maam Cross, Recess, Roundstone, and Clifden, as well as Kylemore Abbey, Leenane, and Oughterard.

Connemara Walking Centre

The Island House, Market St., Clifden, Co. Galway. ☎ **095/21379.** £10–£20 ($16–$32) depending on itinerary. June to mid-Sept, call for departure times.

Walking tours of Connemara with expert local guides are offered by this company, with an emphasis on history and archaeology as well as scenery. The walks cover different sections of Connemara—from the Renvyle Peninsula and Roundstone Bog to the Kylemore Valley, Maumturk Mountains, and the Sky Road. The tour to Inishbofin Island includes a 45-minute boat trip. All walks assemble at Island House in Clifden and include bus transportation to the walking site. Advance reservations are required.

Corrib Ferries

Oughterard, Co. Galway. ☎ **091/82644.** £5 ($8) to island; £8 ($12.80) to Cong. May–Sept daily 11am and 2:45pm.

Departing from the pier at Oughterard, this company's sightseeing boat cruises across Lough Corrib, Ireland's second-largest lake, with a stop at Inchagoill Island, home of a 12th-century monastery that was inhabited until the 1940s. Two round-trips are offered: one to the island only, the other to the island and continuing on to Cong in Co. Mayo, site of Ashford Castle and the area where the movie *The Quiet Man* was filmed.

Inishbofin Island Tours

Kings of Cleggan, Cleggan, Co. Galway. ☎ **095/44642.** £10–£12 ($16–$19.20) per person.

This company's boat tours explore the island of Inishbofin, about 3 miles off the northwest Connemara coast. A haunt of artists, poets, and philosophers, this still-inhabited island holds the ruins of a 7th-century monastery.

Western Heritage Sightseeing

Galway Tourist Office, Victoria Place, off Eyre Sq., Galway. ☎ **091/521699.** £10 ($16) adults, £9 ($14.40) seniors and students; boat trip extra. May–Sept, daily.

This full-day tour of Connemara includes a visit to Cong, with an optional boat trip to the early Christian site of Inchagoill, followed by an afternoon bus tour through the Maam Valley to Leenane, Kylemore Abbey, and Connemara National Park.

SPORTS & OUTDOOR PURSUITS

In terms of location, facilities, and quality of instruction, ✪ **Delphi Adventure Center,** Leenane, Co. Galway (☎ **095/42307**), is the best of the many adventure centers in Ireland. Courses are available in a wide range of watersports, as well as in mountaineering, pony trekking, tennis, and archery. Accommodation is in bright, simply furnished single or dorm-style rooms. The food in the dining room is good and plentiful, and vegetarian meals can be arranged. Residential adventure holidays for children are offered. Prices for room, full board, and activities per person per day begin at £43 ($66.65) for an adult and £25 ($40) for a child; there are also special prices for weekend and week-long stays. This place caters primarily to people in their 20s and 30s.

BICYCLING   Bicycles can be hired year-round from **John Mannion & Son,** Bridge Street, Clifden, Co. Galway (☎ 095/21160). The rate for a regular touring bike is £7 ($11.20) per day. Mountain bikes can be hired from May through October at the **Little Killary Adventure Centre,** Salruck, Renvyle, Co. Galway (☎ 095/43411), at a charge of £5 ($8) per day.

DIVING   You can rent equipment and receive instruction at **Scubadive West,** Lettergesh, Renvyle, Co. Galway (☎ 095/43922; fax 095/43923).

FISHING   Lough Corrib is renowned for brown trout and salmon fishing, with the brown trout fishing usually good from the middle of February and salmon best from the end of May. The Mayfly fishing commences around the middle of May and continues up to three weeks. Angling on Lough Corrib is free, but a state license is required for salmon. For expert advice and rental equipment, contact the **Cloonnabinnia Angling Centre,** Moycullen, Co. Galway (☎ 091/85555).

GOLF   Visitors are welcome at the 18-hole, par-72 championship seaside course of the **Connemara Golf Club,** Ballyconneely, Clifden (☎ 095/23502), nestled in the heart of Connemara and looking out into the waters of the Atlantic. Greens fees from May to September are £25 ($40); other months they're £16 ($25.60).

The **Oughterard Golf Club,** Oughterard, Co. Galway (☎ 095/552131), is an 18-hole, par-70 inland course. The greens fees are £15 ($24).

HORSEBACK RIDING   **Cashel Equestrian Centre,** Cashel, Co. Galway (☎ 095/31082), conducts treks of one, two, or three hours through the mountains. Beach trekking and jaunting-car (horse-drawn buggy) rides are also available. Minimum charges average £10 ($16) per hour.

WALKING   There is a plethora of beautiful walks in the vicinity of Killary Harbor, a narrow fjord cutting into the mountainous mainland along the border between Galway and Mayo. From the Killary Harbour Youth Hostel (where the German philosopher Ludwig Wittgenstein once stayed for a time, before it was a hostel) it is possible to continue southeast along the shore on a minor road, with great views across the fjord to Mweelrea Mountain. From the town of Leenane there is a walk that takes in the major peaks of the Maumturk Mountains—*Best Irish Walks* by Joss Lynam (Passport Books, 1995) includes a great description of this walk.

WATERSPORTS   Dinghy sailing and sailboarding can be arranged at the **Little Killary Adventure Centre,** Salruck, Renvyle, Co. Galway (☎ 095/43411). Daily rates are £22–£30 ($34.10–$46.50) per day, which entitles you to use the watersports equipment and participate in all the center's supervised sporting activities, including kayaking, hill and coastal walking, rock climbing, archery, and more.

SHOPPING

Clifden Heritage Crystal
Main St., Clifden. ☎ 095/21989.

This crystal enterprise produces patterns that reflect the beauty of the surrounding countryside. All glass is mouth-blown and hand-cut in this workshop, which is led by a former Waterford Crystal master cutter. Open Monday through Saturday from 9am to 6pm, with extended hours in summer.

Avoca Handweavers
Clifden-Leenane road (N59), Dooneen Haven, Letterfrack, Co. Galway. ☎ 095/41058.

Situated 6 miles north of Clifden on an inlet of the bay and surrounded by colorful flower gardens, this shop has one of the loveliest and most photographed locations in Ireland. Colorful tweeds are featured here, as are all sorts of Connemara-made marble souvenirs, candles, jewelry, books, music, wood carvings, pottery, and knits. A snack shop is on the premises. Open mid-March through October, daily from 9:30am to 6pm or later.

Connemara Marble Industries Ltd.

Galway-Clifden road (N59), Moycullen, Co. Galway. ☎ 095/85102.

Connemara's unique green marble—diverse in color, marking, and veining—is quarried, cut, shaped, and polished here. Estimated by geologists to be about 500 million years old, the marble shows twists and interlocking bands of serpentine in various shades, ranging from light lime green to dark emerald. On weekdays, you'll see craftspeople at work hand-fashioning marble jewelry, paperweights, ashtrays, Celtic crosses, and other giftware. The shop and showroom, on the main road 8 miles west of Galway City on N59, are open daily, May through October, from 9am to 5:30pm, with a reduced schedule in the off-season.

✪ Fuchsia Craft

The Square, Oughterard, Co. Galway. ☎ 091/552644.

Wedged in the center of Oughterard's main thoroughfare, this small shop is a treasure trove of unusual and hard-to-find crafts, produced by more than 100 craftspeople throughout Ireland. The items range from handmade fishing flies and products made from pressed Irish peat to bronze sculptures, recycled art cards of Connemara scenes, decorative metal figurines fashioned from nails, and lithographs of early Ireland—as well as pottery, crystal, jewelry, knitwear, and much more. It's open from May through September, daily from 9am to 10pm, and from October through April, Monday through Saturday from 9:30am to 6pm.

✪ Millar's Connemara Tweed Ltd.

Main St., Clifden, Co. Galway. ☎ 095/21038.

This is the home of the colorful Connemara tweeds, an industry started in 1900 by Robert Millar as a small mill to process wool from local mountain sheep. Although most people travel to Clifden just to buy Millar's skeins of wool or hand-woven materials—plus ready-made ties, hats, caps, scarves, blankets, and bedspreads—today's shop is more than just an outlet for wool. You'll also find Irish patchwork, rush baskets, Aran crios belts, embroidery work, handmade miniature currachs, tin whistles, and blackthorn pipes, plus an art gallery of regional paintings. Open Monday through Saturday from 9am to 6pm, with extended hours in summer.

✪ Roundstone Musical Instruments

I.D.A. Craft Centre, Roundstone, Co. Galway. ☎ 095/35808.

Devotees of Irish traditional music come from far and near to buy a handmade bodhran (goatskin-headed frame drum) at this small shop in a cottagelike setting on the grounds of a former monastery. Malachy Kearns, often fondly called "Malachy Bodhran," handcrafts and hand-decorates all instruments on the premises, with the help of his wife, Anne, an artist. Drums from the shop were used in the popular *Riverdance* show. In addition to bodhrans, you can buy a flute or tin whistle and choose from a fine selection of Irish music CDs, tapes, books, and videos, as well as crafts. A new exhibition area on the history of Irish folk instruments is due to appear soon. Open June through October, daily from 9am to 6:30pm, November through May, Monday through Friday from 9am to 6pm.

Sila Mag Aoide Designs (Shelagh Magee)

I.D.A. Craft Centre, Roundstone, Co. Galway. ☎ 095/35912.

Situated in a stone belltower on the grounds of a former monastery and claiming to be the smallest shop in Ireland, this wee place displays the creations of resident artist Shelagh Magee. The unusual, one-of-a-kind works include watercolor prints and art cards of Connemara scenes, jewelry, baskets, handmade wooden pencils, and miniature frames. It's open daily from 10am to 10pm from May through September, with shorter hours in the off-season.

Weavers Workshop

Main St., Clifden, Co. Galway. ☎ **095/21074.**

Hand-weaving and design work are carried on at this small shop for visitors and passersby to watch or to buy. The finished products include colorful sweaters, vests, scarves, and hats, as well as rugs and wall hangings. Open Easter through October, Monday through Saturday from 9am to 6pm.

ACCOMMODATIONS
EXPENSIVE/MODERATE

✪ Cashel House

Cashel Bay, Cashel, Co. Galway. ☎ **800/223-6510** or 800/44-UTELL from the U.S., or 095/31001. Fax 095/31077. 32 rms. TV TEL. £90–£140 ($156–$224) double. Service charge 12.5%. Rates include full breakfast. AE, DC, MC, V. Open Feb 10–Jan 10.

Set on 50 acres of exotic gardens and woodlands, this 100-year-old country house is nestled deep in the mountains and lakelands of Connemara. Established as a hotel in 1968 by enthusiastic innkeepers Dermot and Kay McEvilly, it has attracted a wide range of discerning guests over the years, including President and Madame de Gaulle, who spent two weeks here in 1969 and really put Cashel House on the map. Among the public rooms are an old-world lounge, a well-stocked library, and a conservatory-style restaurant that has won many awards for innovative cuisine. Guest rooms, which have wide-windowed views of the bay or the gardens, are decorated with a blend of Irish floral fabrics, European antiques, sheepskin rugs, rattan pieces, vintage paintings, and local heirlooms. Facilities include a private beach on the bay, a tennis court, fishing, boating, and signposted walking paths. On the grounds is a helipad—or, if you prefer to stay closer to the sod, a Connemara pony stable.

Hotel Ardagh

Ballyconneely Rd., Clifden, Co. Galway. ☎ **800/447-7462** from the U.S., or 095/21384. Fax 095/21314. 17 rms. TV TEL. £95–£130 ($152–$208) double. No service charge. Rates include full breakfast. AE, DC, MC, V. Closed Nov–Mar.

Overlooking Ardbear Bay, about 2 miles south of Clifden, this modern two-story inn reflects a chalet-style atmosphere, with a decor of light woods and expansive windows. Many of the rooms face the sea, including the newly renovated second-floor restaurant, and five guest rooms have individual balconies. A solarium and lovely gardens are added pleasures.

Rosleague Manor

Clifden-Leenane road (N59), Letterfrack, Co. Galway. ☎ **800/223-6510** from the U.S., or 095/41101. Fax 095/41168. 15 rms. TEL. £80–£130 ($128–$208) double. No service charge. Rates include full breakfast. AE, MC, V. Closed Nov–Easter.

Occupying a sheltered spot with views of Ballinakill Harbor and the Twelve Bens Mountains, this two-story Georgian house is surrounded by 30 acres of lush gardens and well-trimmed lawns. Brother/sister owners Paddy and Ann Foyle have decorated the interior with all sorts of antiques, polished heirloom silver, Waterford crystal chandeliers, and paintings of local scenes. The bedrooms have comfortable furnishings, mostly floral patterns, and many enjoy views of the bay. Among facilities are a fine restaurant that uses produce from the garden, plus a tennis court and sauna. The manor is situated 7 miles north of Clifden near the entrance to Connemara National Park.

Zetland Country House

Cashel Bay, Cashel, Co. Galway. ☎ **800/447-7462** from the U.S., or 095/31111. Fax 095/31117. 19 rms. TEL. £100–£150 ($160–$240) double. Service charge 12.5%. Rates include full breakfast. AE, MC, V. Closed mid-Oct through Mar.

Built in 1850 as a sporting lodge, this three-story manor house was named for the earl of Zetland, a frequent visitor during the 19th century. Surrounded by lush gardens and ancient trees, Zetland was converted into a hotel in the mid-1980s under its current owner, John Prendergast, a Paris-trained hotelier. The guest rooms, many of which look out onto the bay, have antique or reproduction furnishings. The dining room is known for its local seafood and lamb dishes, and its vegetables and fruit come from the inn's own kitchen garden. If you enjoy fishing, take note that the Zetland owns the Gowla Fishery, one of the best private sea-trout fisheries in Ireland, comprised of 14 lakes and four miles of river. The hotel staff is extraordinarily fisher-friendly. Other facilities include a tennis court, croquet, and a billiards room.

MODERATE

Ballynahinch Castle

Ballynahinch, Recess, Co. Galway. ☎ **095/31006.** Fax 095/31085. 28 rms. TEL. £80–£120 ($128–$192) double. Luxury suites available. Service charge 10%. Rates include full breakfast. AE, DC, MC, V. Closed first three weeks in Feb.

Set on a 350-acre estate at the base of Ben Lettery, one of the Twelve Bens mountains, this turreted and gabled manor house overlooks the Owenmore River. Dating back to the 16th century, it has served over the years as a base for such diverse owners as the O'Flaherty chieftains and the sea pirate Grace O'Malley, and as the sporting residence of the Maharajah Jans Sahib Newanagar, better known as Ranjitsinhgi, the famous cricketer. The guest rooms are individually named and decorated, many with individual fireplaces and four-poster or canopy beds. The restaurant, with its impressive Connemara marble fireplace, offers sweeping views of the countryside and the river. Most of all, this is a place for top-notch sea-trout and salmon fishing. Each evening, the day's catch is weighed in and recorded at the Fishermen's Bar, usually making a nightly cause for celebration. Other facilities include a tennis court and lovely gardens.

✪ Connemara Gateway

Galway-Clifden road (N59), Oughterard, Co. Galway. ☎ **091/552328.** Fax 091/552332. 62 rms. TV TEL. £75.50–£110 ($120.80–$176) double. Rates include full breakfast. AE, CB, MC, V.

Situated on its own grounds, less than a mile from the village of Oughterard and 16 miles west of Galway City, this contemporary two-story inn is well positioned near the upper shores of Lough Corrib and across the road from an 18-hole golf course. Although it has a rambling modern exterior, a hearthside ambience permeates the interior, with leafy plants and homey bric-a-brac in the corridors. Guest rooms are warmly furnished with local tweed fabrics and hangings, oak dressers and headboards, and scenes of Connemara. The hotel restaurant is enhanced by a fine collection of original paintings by landscape artists John MacLeod and Kenneth Webb, while the lounge has a village pub atmosphere. Facilities include a heated swimming pool, sauna, sun lounge, tennis court, putting green, croquet lawn, and 10 acres of walking trails.

Renvyle House

Renvyle, Co. Galway. ☎ **095/43511.** Fax 095/43515. 56 rms. TV TEL. £65–£130 ($104–$208) double. Includes full Irish breakfast and service charge. AE, DC, MC, V. Closed Jan–Feb.

Originally the residence of the Blake family, this grand old house sits on a 200-acre estate along the Atlantic shoreline in the wilds of Connemara. It was purchased in 1917 by Oliver St. John Gogarty, a leading Irish poet, wit, surgeon, and politician, who fondly called this secluded seascape and mountain setting "the world's end." And that's putting it mildly: It really is off the beaten track, not ideal for a quick overnight but perfect for a few days' stay or longer. Updated and refurbished in recent years by current owner Hugh Coyle, it retains a turn-of-the-century ambience, particularly in its public areas. Guest rooms vary in size and decor—from rooms with balconies to attic rooms with dormer windows. Facilities include a restaurant, a lounge bar, an outdoor heated swimming pool, horseback-riding stables, a nine-hole golf course, two all-weather tennis courts, fishing, and boating.

Rock Glen Manor House

Ballyconneely Rd., Clifden, Co. Galway. ☎ **095/21035.** Fax 095/21737. 29 rms. TV TEL. £100–£120 ($160–$192) double. Service charge 12.5%. Rates include full breakfast. AE, DISC, MC, V. Closed Oct to mid-Mar.

Originally an 18th-century hunting lodge, this rambling country house sits amid lovely gardens about $1\frac{1}{2}$ miles south of Clifden. Expanded over the years and now in the hands of John and Evangeline Roche, Rock Glen is set back from the road, with views of Ardbear Bay and the Atlantic Ocean. It's a restful spot, with tastefully furnished bedrooms and homey public areas. Most rooms, including the restaurant, face the sea, and half the bedrooms are on the ground floor. Facilities include a tennis court, a putting green, and fishing privileges.

✪ Sweeney's Oughterard House

Galway-Clifden road (N59), Oughterard, Co. Galway. ☎ **091/82207.** Fax 091/82161. 20 rms. TV TEL. £112 ($179) double. No service charge. Rates include full breakfast. AE, DC, MC, V. Closed late Dec to mid-Jan.

A favorite with fishers, this ivy-covered, 200-year-old Georgian house has been run by the Sweeney-Higgins family since 1913. Situated across the road from the rushing and babbling salmon-filled waters of the Owenriff River, the inn is surrounded by flowering gardens and ancient trees on the quiet western end of the village. The public rooms have an old-world charm thanks to multipaned bow windows and a decor that includes comfortable deep-cushioned original furnishings and paintings by Irish artists. The guest rooms vary in size and decor—from antique-filled to modern light-wood styles—but all include such extras as a hair dryer and tea/coffeemaker; some have four-poster or king-size beds. It's a great spot for fishing, taking long country walks, or catching up on your reading. Amenities include a good dining room with an extensive wine cellar.

Readers Recommend

Failte, Ardbear (off Ballyconneely Rd.), Clifden, Connemara, Co. Galway. ☎ **095/21159.** *This was one of the best B&Bs we stayed at in all of Ireland. Mr. Sean Kelly was an outstanding host. And the breakfast was the best breakfast we had at any B&B! I do not recall exactly how much we paid but it was around £15 and worth every penny. The showers were very good and the beds were very comfortable. I highly recommend this B&B.*

—Robert A. Windham, Greenbelt, Md.

MODERATE/INEXPENSIVE

Abbeyglen Castle

Sky Rd., Clifden, Co. Galway. ☎ **800/447-7462** from the U.S., or 095/21201. Fax 095/21797. 46 rms. TV TEL. £67–£99 ($107.20–$158.40) double. No service charge. Rates include full breakfast. AE, DC, MC, V. Closed early Jan–Feb.

Located on a hilltop overlooking Clifden and the bay, this property has a history dating from the 1820s, although the castlelike facade was added only within the last 20 years. Happily, the turrets and battlements blend in well with the Connemara countryside, and are enhanced within by public areas with brass candelabra chandeliers, arched windows, and vintage settees, as well as a Gothic-themed restaurant and guest rooms with crown canopies. Twelve acres of gardens and parklands, a heated outdoor swimming pool, sauna, solarium, and hard tennis court add to the enjoyment. Personable proprietor Paul Hughes will arrange fishing trips, packed lunches, and a host of other local activities.

DINING

EXPENSIVE/MODERATE

✪ Drimcong House

Moycullen, Co. Galway. ☎ **091/85115** or 091/85585. Reservations required. Fixed-price dinner £17.50–£24 ($28–$38.40). AE, DC, MC, V. Tues–Sat 7–10:30pm. Closed Sun–Mon and Christmas–March. IRISH/INTERNATIONAL.

In a 300-year-old lakeside house on the main Clifden road, just under 10 miles west of Galway City, this restaurant is the perfect setting for the quintessential Irish dining experience. As your order is taken, you relax in a book-filled drawing room/lounge with an open fireplace, then you're escorted into one of two elegant dining rooms (the back room looks out onto the lake while the front windows have garden views). All the little touches await at your table—fresh flowers, candlelight, fine Irish silver and glassware, and hot brown scones with butter twirls. The five-course dinners, to be sure, live up to the setting. Entrées range from roast local lamb with ratatouille and herbs or baked chicken breast with parsley mousse to *bollito misto* (Drimcong's version of an Italian dish with beef) or a vegetarian dinner such as herb and vegetable soufflé or smoked-cheese-and-apple ravioli.

O'Grady's

Market St., Clifden, Co. Galway. ☎ **095/21450.** Reservations recommended for dinner. Fixed-price lunch £10.95 ($17.50); dinner main courses £7.50–£20 ($12–$32). AE, MC, V. Mon–Sat 12:30–2:30pm and 6–10pm. Dinner only Nov–Mar. Closed Dec–Jan. IRISH/SEAFOOD.

Ever since the mid-1960s, this shop-front restaurant has been drawing seekers of great seafood to Clifden. The menu features all that is freshest from the sea on a daily basis, with such choices as Clifden lobster with lemon or garlic butter or a fillet of Cleggan brill. For non–fish-eaters there's fillet of beef with radish sauce, pork with peach stuffing in peppercorn cream sauce, and lamb with rosemary sauce.

Water Lily

Bridge St., Oughterard, Co. Galway. ☎ **091/82737.** Reservations suggested for dinner. Lunch main courses £4.50–£9 ($7.20–$14.40); dinner main courses £9.50–£22 ($15.20–$35.20), lobster £22 ($35.20). AE, DC, MC, V. Daily noon–3pm and 6–10pm. SEAFOOD/IRISH.

Set on the edge of town beside a stream of the Corrib, this yellow-and-green cottage is a delightful stopping place en route to or from Connemara. Bilevel and flower-filled, the restaurant offers wide-windowed river views and lunch items that range from platters of oysters and other seafoods to sandwiches, soups, and salads. The frequently changing dinner menu offers such creative entrées as suprême of chicken filled with Camembert and whole grain mustard sauce, duck with herb stuffing and peach sauce, and a variety of lobsters and steaks.

MODERATE

✪ High Moors

Off the Ballyconeely road, Dooneen, Clifden, Co. Galway. ☎ **095/21342.** Reservations recommended. Main courses £7.90–£11.90 ($12.65–$19.05). AE, MC, V. Wed–Sun 6:30pm–9:30pm. Closed Nov–Easter. IRISH.

Less than a mile from Clifden, a narrow country road leads to this modern bungalow-style restaurant, set high on a hill with panoramic views of the Atlantic and the surrounding wild Connemara countryside. A homey ambience prevails inside—and well it should since this is the home of Hugh and Eileen Griffin, host and chef, respectively. The food and menu are simple, based on what is fresh at the markets and what vegetables and herbs are in season in Hugh's gardens. Eileen's specialties include breast of chicken with basil and tomato; fillet of pork with three spices; wild salmon with sorrel butter sauce; ragout of salmon, sole, and scallops; and roast leg of Connemara lamb with red-currant and rosemary. Try to book a table for sunset—if you can tear your attention away from the food, the views are incredible.

Mitchell's

Market St., Clifden, Co. Galway. ☎ **095/21867.** Reservations suggested for dinner. Lunch/snack main courses £1.35–£6.95 ($2.15–$11.10); dinner main courses £6.50–£10.95 ($10.40–$17.50). MC, V. Mid-Mar through mid-Nov noon–10:30pm. IRISH/SEAFOOD.

Housed in a shop-front building in the center of town, this restaurant has a turn-of-the-century decor, with brick and stone walls, local furnishings and memorabilia, and an open fireplace. The menu offers a variety of dishes from traditional Irish stew, steak au poivre, and panfried grilled Atlantic salmon to lighter fare, available throughout the day, such as smoked salmon quiche, salads, crab claws, and seafood pastas.

MODERATE/INEXPENSIVE

✪ Destry's

The Square, Clifden, Co. Galway. ☎ **095/21722.** Reservations recommended for dinner. Lunch main courses £4.95–£6.95 ($7.90–$11.10); dinner main courses £7.95–£13.95 ($12.70–$22.30). MC, V. Tues–Sun noon–3pm and 6:30–10pm. Closed Christmas to Feb. INTERNATIONAL.

Borrowing its name from the classic Western starring James Stewart and Marlene Dietrich, this small 30-seat restaurant has a fun, funky, movie-inspired decor. But decor is not all; its menu is innovative and varied, ranging from baked crabmeat in coconut and Thai spices to steaks charcoal grilled over high flames. The grilled eggplant with red pepper, goat cheese, and basil is just one of the vegetarian selections. All meals are accompanied by a unique olive bread served with aromatic olive oil.

Fogertys

Market St., Clifden, Co. Galway. ☎ **095/21427.** Reservations recommended for dinner. Main courses £4.90–£12.90 ($7.85–$20.65). MC, V. Apr–Oct noon–10pm, Nov–Mar 5–10pm. INTERNATIONAL.

Occupying one of the oldest houses in town, this small shop-front restaurant has a charming decor of whitewashed walls, natural woods, old pictures, and fresh flowers. On the menu are such dishes as grilled tuna with Provençale sauce and Asian curry with vegetables, alongside pastas, pizzas, and bacon and cabbage.

The Northwest 14

f you're looking for a landscape of majestic wildness and splendor, Donegal is the place to go, although its austere beauty can become rather bleak when the weather turns gray and rainy. Several of Ireland's greatest natural wonders are to be found here, such as the Slieve League cliffs and Horn Head, and the most remote, pristine, and beautiful beaches in the country are tucked into the bays and inlets of Donegal's sharply indented coast.

The towns of Donegal are for the most part functional rather than beautiful—no doubt good places to live and work but offering few amenities to the tourist. It isn't so easy to settle into this county, where the people aren't always accustomed to tourism and tend to be more reticent than folks in the tourist centers of the southeast and southwest. With some effort you will find your way, but it may be hard work at times; in addition to dealing with the locals' ambivalence toward visitors, you have to contend with the road signs, which are cryptic or nonexistent on all but the national roads. In my experience, Donegal is affected by the political climate of Northern Ireland more directly than any other common tourist destination in the Republic, and the prevailing mood of the people may have a lot to do with the status of the peace talks at the moment.

Like Donegal, the main appeal of Co. Sligo is not in its towns but out in the countryside. The county does possess a wealth of historic sites, though, and fans of Yeats will enjoy visiting the plethora of sites associated with the poet and his writings.

1 Sligo & Yeats Country

136 miles NE of Shannon Airport, 135 miles NW of Dublin, 47 miles NE of Knock, 37 miles NE of Ballina, 87 miles NE of Galway, 73 miles N of Athlone, and 209 miles N of Cork.

GETTING THERE   **Aer Lingus** operates daily flights into Sligo Airport, Strandhill, Co. Sligo (☎ 071/68280), 5 miles southwest of Sligo Town.

Irish Rail, Lord Edward Street, Sligo (☎ 071/69888), operates daily service into Sligo from Dublin and other points.

Bus Eireann, Lord Edward Street, Sligo (☎ 071/60066), operates daily bus service to Sligo from Dublin, Galway, and other points, including Derry in Northern Ireland.

If you're driving, three major roads lead to Sligo: N4 from Dublin and the east, N17 from Galway and the south, and N16 from Northern Ireland.

VISITOR INFORMATION   For information about Sligo and the surrounding area, contact the **North West Tourism Office,** Aras Reddan, Temple Street, Sligo (☎ **071/61201**). It's open on Monday through Saturday in June from 9am to 6pm; in July and August until 8pm and Sunday from 10am to 2pm; and September through May on Monday through Friday from 9am to 5pm.

TOWN LAYOUT   Edged by Sligo Bay to the west, Sligo Town sits beside the Garavogue River, with most of the city's commercial district on the south bank of the river. **O'Connell Street** is the main north-south artery of the downtown district. The main east-west thoroughfare is **Stephen Street,** which changes its name to Wine Street and then to Lord Edward Street. The **Tourist Office** is in the southwest corner of the town on Temple Street, two blocks south of O'Connell Street. Three bridges span the river, but the **Douglas Hyde Bridge,** named for Ireland's first president, is the main link between the two sides.

GETTING AROUND   **By Public Transport**   There is no public transport in the town of Sligo, but during July and August **Bus Eireann** (☎ **071/60066**) runs from Sligo Town to Strandhill and Rosses Point. The fare is £2 ($3.20) round-trip.

By Taxi   Taxis line up looking for fares at the Sligo taxi rank on Quay Street. If you prefer to call for a taxi, try **ABC Cabs** (☎ **071/43000**), **Ace Cabs** (☎ **071/44444**), **Cab 55** (☎ **071/42333**), or **Sligo Cabs** (☎ **071/44998**).

By Car   You'll need a car to see the sights outside of Sligo Town. If you need to hire a vehicle locally, contact **Avis** at Sligo Airport, Strandhill (☎ **071/68280**), or **Hertz,** 1 Teeling St., Sligo (☎ **071/60111**).

On Foot   The best way to see Sligo Town is on foot. Follow the signposted route of the Tourist Trail. The walk takes approximately 90 minutes.

Usually during July and August, guided walking tours depart from the **Tourist Office,** Temple Street, Sligo (☎ **071/61201**) on Monday through Saturday at 11am and 7pm. The tour lasts 1¹⁄₂ hours and costs £2 ($3.20) per person. For further information, check at the tourist office.

FAST FACTS: SLIGO

Area Code   The area code for most Sligo telephone numbers is **071.** Some numbers in the county use **074.**

Emergencies   For emergencies, dial **999.**

Hospital   Try **Sligo General Hospital,** Malloway Hill (☎ **071/71111**).

Library   **County Sligo Library** is located on Stephen Street (☎ **071/42212**), and is open Tuesday through Friday from 10am to 5pm, Saturday from 10am to 1pm and 2 to 5pm.

Newspapers and Local Media   The weekly *Sligo Champion* covers most news and entertainment of the area, and the local North West Radio broadcasts from Sligo on FM 102.5 and FM 96.3.

Police   The local **Garda Station** is on Pearse Road (☎ **071/42031**).

Post Office   The **Sligo General Post Office,** Wine Street (☎ **071/42646**), is open Monday through Saturday from 9am to 5:30pm.

Although **Sligo Town** (population 18,000) is ideally located, nestled as it is in a valley between two mountains—Ben Bulben on the north and Knocknarea on the south—it's more a commercial center than a tourist attraction and has little to recommend it to the visitor. You'd be well advised to pass through here briefly,

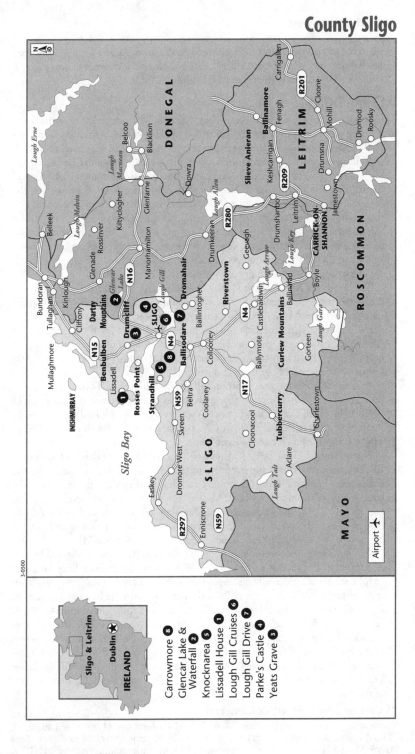

County Sligo

Carrowmore **8**
Glencar Lake &
Waterfall **2**
Knocknarea **5**
Lissadell House **1**
Lough Gill Cruises **6**
Lough Gill Drive **7**
Parke's Castle **4**
Yeats Grave **3**

IRELAND

Sligo & Leitrim

Dublin ★

411

exploring instead the countryside surrounding the town. As you'll quickly discover, this is Yeats country, and every hill, rill, cottage, vale, and lake seems to bear a plaque indicating its relation to the poet or his works.

ATTRACTIONS

Sligo's great antiquity can be counted in the seemingly numberless grave mounds, standing stones, ring circles, and dolmens still marking its starkly stunning landscape. In fact, Sligo contains the greatest concentration of megalithic sites in all of Ireland.

A fitting place to begin exploring ancient Sligo is at **Carrowmore** (see listing below), a vast Neolithic cemetery once containing perhaps as many as 200 passage tombs, some of which predate Newgrange by 500 years. From Carrowmore, the Neolithic mountaintop cemetery of **Carrowkeel** is visible in the distant south. Less than an hour's drive (ask for detailed directions at the Carrowmore Visitors Centre) will take you there for an experience beyond any account: After a breathtaking ascent on foot, you'll find yourself alone with the past. The tombs, facing Carrowmore below and aligned with the summer solstice, are unattended and infrequently visited. To this writer, even the memory of them brings chills of wonder.

To the west is **Knocknarea** (1,078 feet), on whose summit sits a gigantic unexcavated cairn (grave mound) known as **Miscaun Meadhbh** (Maeve's Mound) even though it predates Maeve, an early Celtic warrior queen who plays a central role in the Taín Bó Cuilnge, the Celtic epic, by millennia. Legend has it that she's buried standing, in full battle gear, spear in hand, facing her Ulster enemies even in death. This extraordinary tomb is 630 feet around at its base, 80 feet high, and 100 feet in diameter, and can be seen for miles.

At the foot of Knocknarea is **Strandhill,** 5 miles from Sligo Town. This delightful resort area stretches out into Sligo Bay, with a sand-duned beach and a patch of land nearby called Coney Island, which is usually credited with lending its name to the New York beach amusement area. Across the bay, about 4 miles north of Sligo Town, is another beach resort, Rosses Point.

Northwest of Sligo Bay, 4 miles offshore, lies the uninhabited island of **Inishmurray,** containing the haunting ruins of one of Ireland's earliest monastic settlements. Founded in the 6th century and destroyed by the Vikings in 807, the circular walls of the monastery of St. Molaise contain the remains of several churches, beehive cells, altars, and an assemblage of "cursing stones" once used to bring down ruin on those who presumably deserved it. For conveyance to the island call Joe McGowan (☎ **071/66267**) or Brendan Merrifield (☎ **071/41874**).

In Sligo Town, the earliest history can be traced to the ruins of **Sligo Abbey** on Abbey Street. Founded as a Dominican house in 1252 by Maurice Fitzgerald, earl of Kildare, it was accidentally destroyed by fire in 1414, then rebuilt two years later. It flourished in medieval times and was the burial place of the kings and princes of Sligo. After many raids and sackings, the abbey was eventually closed in 1641. Much restoration work has been done in recent years, however, and the cloisters are now considered to be outstanding examples of stone carving; the 15th-century altar is one of the few medieval altars still intact in Ireland.

Most of Sligo's attractions are associated in some way with the poet William Butler Yeats. If you visit the places described below, you'll have a thorough Yeatsean tour of the area.

✪ Carrowmore Megalithic Cemetery

Carrowmore Visitors Centre, Co. Sligo. ☎ **071/615341.** Admission £1.50 ($2.40) adults, £1 ($1.60) seniors, 60p (96¢) students and children, £4 ($6.40) family. No credit cards. May–Sept daily 9:30am–6:30pm. From Sligo, signposted on N15; from the south, signposted on N4.

Sligo Town

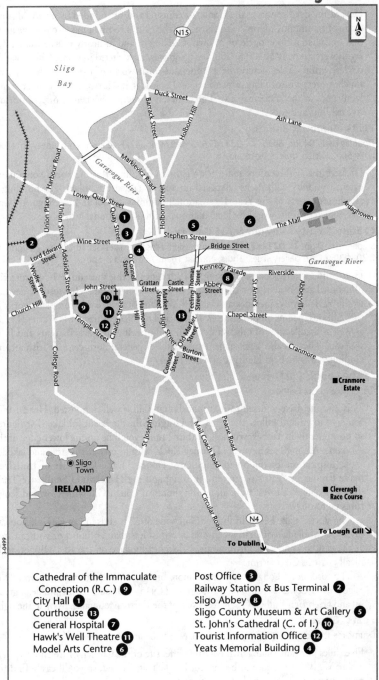

N

Sligo Bay

N15

Duck Street
Barrack Street
Holborn Hill
Ash Lane

Markievicz Road
Garavogue River
Harbour Road
Union Place
Lower Quay Street
Quay Street
Holborn Street
Stephen Street
The Mall
Ardaghowen

1
3
2
Wine Street
Union Street
Lord Edward Street
Adelaide Street
Wolfe Tone Street
O'Connell Street
4
5
Bridge Street
6
7

8
Kennedy Parade
Riverside
Garavogue River
Abbeyville

Church Hill
John Street
Grattan Street
Castle Street
Abbey Street
St Anne's
10
9
11
Harmony Hill
Market Street
Teeling Street
13
Chapel Street
Cranmore

Temple Street
12
Charles Street
High Street
Old Market Street
Burton Street
Connolly Street

College Road

St Joseph's

Mail Coach Road
Pearse Road
Circular Road

■ Cranmore Estate

● Sligo Town
IRELAND

■ Cleveragh Race Course

N4
To Lough Gill ↘
To Dublin ↓

3-0499

Cathedral of the Immaculate
  Conception (R.C.) 9
City Hall 1
Courthouse 13
General Hospital 7
Hawk's Well Theatre 11
Model Arts Centre 6

Post Office 3
Railway Station & Bus Terminal 2
Sligo Abbey 8
Sligo County Museum & Art Gallery 5
St. John's Cathedral (C. of I.) 10
Tourist Information Office 12
Yeats Memorial Building 4

Here at the dead center of the Coolera Peninsula and surrounded by a natural stone circle of mountains topped with cairns sits the giant's tomb, a massive passage grave that once had a stone circle of its own. Circling it, and in nearly every instance *facing* it, were as many as 100 to 200 passage graves, each circled in stone. Circles within circles within circles describing a stone-and-spirit world of the dead whose power touches every visitor who stops to see and consider it—it's one of the great sacred landscapes of the ancient world. The cemetery's interpretive center offers informative exhibits and tours.

Yeats Memorial Building

Douglas Hyde Bridge, Sligo. ☎ **071/42693** or 071/45847. Free admission. June–Aug, Mon–Fri 2–5pm. Gallery open year-round.

Located in a 19th-century red-brick Victorian building, this memorial contains an extensive library with items of special interest to Yeatsean scholars. The building is also headquarters of the Yeats International Summer School and the Sligo Art Gallery, which exhibits works by local, national, and international artists.

✪ Sligo County Museum & Art Gallery

Stephen St., Sligo. ☎ **071/42212.** Free admission. Museum, Tues–Sat 10:30am–12:30pm and 2:30–4:30pm. Art gallery, Tues, Thurs, and Sat 10am–noon and 2–5pm.

Housed in a church manse of the mid–19th century, this museum exhibits material of national and local interest dating back to pre-Christian times. One section, devoted to the Yeats family, includes a display of William Butler Yeats's complete works in first editions, poems on broadsheets, letters, and his Nobel Prize for literature (1923), as well as a collection of oils, watercolors, and drawings by Jack B. Yeats and John B. Yeats. There is also a permanent collection of general 20th-century Irish art, including works by Paul Henry and Evie Hone.

✪ The Lough Gill Drive

Co. Sligo and Co. Leitrim.

This 26-mile drive-yourself tour around Lough Gill is well signposted. Head 1 mile south of town and follow the signs for **Lough Gill,** the beautiful lake that figured so prominently in Yeats's writings. Within 2 miles you'll be on the lower edge of the shoreline. Among sites to see are **Dooney Rock,** with its own nature trail and lakeside walk (inspiration for the poem "Fiddler of Dooney"); the **Lake Isle of Innisfree,** made famous in Yeats's poetry and in song; and the **Hazelwood Sculpture Trail,** unique to Sligo, a forest walk along the shores of Lough Gill with 13 wood sculptures en route.

The storied Lake Isle of Innisfree is only one of 22 islands in Lough Gill. You can drive the whole lakeside circuit in one sweep in less than an hour, or you can stop at the east end and visit **Dromahair,** a delightful village on the River Bonet, technically part of Co. Leitrim.

The road along Lough Gill's upper shore brings you back to the northern end of Sligo Town. Continue north on the main road (N15) and you'll see the profile of graceful and green **Ben Bulben** (1,730 feet), one of the Dartry Mountains, rising to the right.

Yeats' Grave

Drumcliffe Churchyard, Drumcliffe, Co. Sligo. N15 to Drumcliff.

Five miles north of Sligo Town is Drumcliffe, site of the Church of Ireland cemetery where W. B. Yeats chose to be buried. It's well signposted, so you'll easily find the poet's grave with the simple headstone bearing the dramatic epitaph he composed: "Cast a cold eye on life, on death; Horseman, pass by." This cemetery also contains the ruins of an early Christian monastery founded by St. Columba in A.D. 745.

Impressions

Down at Sligo, one sees the whole world in a day's walk.
—William Trevor (b. 1928), Irish novelist

Lissadell House

Off the main Sligo-Donegal road (N15), Drumcliffe, Co. Sligo. ☎ **074/63150.** Admission £2.50 ($4) adults, 50p (80¢) children. June to mid-Sept, Mon–Sat 10:30am–12:15pm and 2–4:15pm.

Situated on the shores of Sligo Bay, 8 miles north of Sligo, this large neoclassical building was another of Yeats's favorite haunts. Dating from 1830, it has long been the home of the Gore-Booth family, including Yeats's friends Eva Gore-Booth, a fellow poet, and her sister Constance, who became the Countess Markievicz after marrying a Polish count. One of the first truly liberated women, Constance took part in the 1916 Irish Rising and was the first woman elected to the British House of Commons and the first woman cabinet member in the Irish Daíl. The house is full of such family memorabilia as the travel diaries of Sir Robert Gore-Booth, who mortgaged the estate to help the poor during the famine. At the core of the house is a dramatic two-story hallway lined with Doric columns leading to a double staircase of Kilkenny marble.

Glencar Lake

Off N16, Glencar, Co. Leitrim.

This Yeats Country attraction is not in Sligo at all, but just over the border in Co. Leitrim. Lovely Glencar Lake stretches eastward for 2 miles along a verdant valley, highlighted by two waterfalls, one of which rushes downward for 50 feet. Yeats's "The Stolen Child" speaks wondrously of this lake.

✪ Parke's Castle

Lough Gill Dr., Co. Leitrim. ☎ **071/64149.** Admission £2 ($3.20) adults, £1.50 ($2.40) seniors, £1 ($1.60) students and children, £5 ($8) family. St. Patrick's weekend (near March 17), 10am–5pm; mid-April to late May, Tues–Sun 10am–5pm; June–Sept, daily 9:30am–6:30pm, Oct daily 10am–5pm.

On the north side of the Lough Gill Drive, within the Co. Leitrim border, Parke's Castle stands out as a lone outpost amid the natural tableau of lakeview and woodland scenery. Named after an English family that gained possession of it during the 1620 plantation of Leitrim, this castle was originally the stronghold of the O'Rourke clan, rulers of the kingdom of Breffni. Beautifully restored using Irish oak and traditional craftsmanship, it exemplifies the 17th-century fortified manor house. In the visitors center, informative exhibits and a truly splendid audiovisual show illustrate the history of the castle and introduce visitors to the rich and diverse sites of interest in the surrounding area, making this an ideal place from which to launch your own local explorations. As icing on the cake, the tearoom offers fresh and exceptionally enticing pastries.

Model Arts Centre

The Mall, Co. Sligo. ☎ **071/41405.** Free admission. Readings/lectures £3–£5 ($4.80–$8). No credit cards. Mon–Sat, 11am–6pm; evening events 8pm, dates vary.

Although this is a relatively new development in Sligo (opened in 1991), it carries on the Yeatsean literary and artistic traditions. Housed in an 1850 Romanesque-style stone building that was originally a school, it offers nine rooms for touring shows and local exhibits by artists, sculptors, writers, and musicians. In the summer, there are often poetry readings or arts lectures.

SIGHTSEEING TOURS & CRUISES

JH Transport
57 Mountain Close, Carton View, Sligo. ☎ **071/42747.** Morning tour is £6 ($9.60) for adults and £3.50 ($5.60) for children ages 6–16; afternoon tour, £7 ($11.20) adults, and £3.50 ($5.60) for children ages 6–16. July–Aug, 9:45am–12:45pm, 2–5:45pm.

This company operates narrated minibus tours of the Sligo area, departing daily from the Sligo Tourist Office. The morning tour follows the Lough Gill Drive, while the afternoon tour goes to Yeats's grave, Lissadell House, and Glencar Lake and Waterfall.

Lough Gill Cruises
Blue Lagoon, Riverside, Sligo. ☎ **071/64266.** Lough Gill cruise, £5 ($8) adults, £2 ($3.20) children over age 10; Innisfree cruise, £4 ($6.40) adults, £2 ($3.20) children over age 10. June–Sept, Lough Gill cruise 2:30 and 4:30pm; Innisfree tour, 12:30, 3:30, and 6:30pm. Apr, May, and Oct, Sun schedule subject to demand.

Cruise on Lough Gill and the Garavogue River aboard the 72-passenger *Wild Rose* waterbus as the poetry of Yeats is recited. Trips to the Lake Isle of Innisfree are also scheduled. An on-board bar is open for refreshments.

SPORTS & OUTDOOR PURSUITS

BEACHES   For walking, jogging, or swimming, there are safe sandy beaches with promenades at Strandhill, Rosses Point, and Enniscrone on the Sligo Bay coast.

BICYCLING   With its lakes and woodlands, Yeats Country is particularly good biking territory. To rent a bike, contact **Gary's Cycles Shop,** Quay Street, Sligo (☎ **071/45418**), or **Woods,** Castle Street, Sligo (☎ **071/42021**).

GOLF   With its seascapes, mountain valleys, and lakesides, County Sligo is known for challenging golf courses. Leading the list is **County Sligo Golf Club,** Rosses Point Road, Rosses Point (☎ **071/77134**), overlooking Sligo Bay under the shadow of Ben Bulben mountain. It's an 18-hole, par-71 championship seaside links famed for its wild, natural terrain and constant winds; greens fees are £15 ($24) on weekdays and £20 ($32) on weekends.

Five miles west of Sligo Town is **Strandhill Golf Club,** Strandhill (☎ **071/ 68188**), a seaside par-69 course with greens fees of £10 ($16) on weekdays and £12 ($19.20) on weekends.

In the southwestern corner of the county, about 25 miles from Sligo Town and overlooking Sligo Bay, the **Enniscrone Golf Club,** Enniscrone (☎ **096/36297**), is a seaside par-72 course with greens fees of £15 ($24).

HORSEBACK RIDING   An hour's or a day's riding on the beach, in the countryside, or over mountain trails can be arranged at **Sligo Riding Centre,** Carrowmore (☎ **071/61353**), or at the **Celtic Farm,** Derry Cross, Grange (☎ **071/63337**). Both are within 7 miles of Sligo Town. Riding charges average £10 to £12 ($16–$19.20) per hour or £40 ($64) per day.

SHOPPING

Most Sligo shops are open Monday through Saturday from 9am to 6pm, although some may have extended hours during July and August, according to demand.

The Cat & the Moon
25 Market St., Sligo. ☎ **071/43686.**

This shop offers uniquely designed crafts from throughout Ireland, ranging from beeswax candles and baskets to modern art, metal and ceramic work, wood-turning, hand-weaving, Celtic jewelry, and furniture. An expanded gallery includes a large variety of paintings, limited-edition prints, and occasionally sculpture.

Kate's Kitchen
24 Market St., Sligo. ☎ **071/43022.**

Step into Kate's to savor the aromas of potpourri, soaps, and natural oils, as well as Crabtree & Evelyn products. The shop also has an outstanding delicatessen section, with gourmet meats, cheeses, salads, pâtés, and breads baked on the premises, all ideal makings for a picnic by Lough Gill. Don't miss the handmade Irish chocolates and preserves.

Keohane's Bookshop
Castle St., Sligo. ☎ **071/42597.**

Try this shop for works by William Butler Yeats and other Irish authors. There are also books and maps of Sligo and other Sligo-related publications.

Innisfree Crystal
The Bridge, Dublin road (N4), Collooney. ☎ **071/67340.**

Taking its name from the Lough Gill island immortalized in Yeats's poem "The Lake Isle of Innisfree," this crystal factory produces individually handcut glassware such as punch bowls, decanters, vases, and bowls. Each piece is hand-signed by one of the craftspeople. You can watch them work or browse in the showroom. The workshop is open Saturdays from 10am to 1pm in the summer months.

Michael Kennedy Ceramics
Church St., Sligo. ☎ **071/62586.**

One of Ireland's foremost ceramic artists, Michael Kennedy produces pottery and porcelain with layers of texture markings and drawings that form a maze of intricate patterns. He then applies glazes that reflect the strong tones and shades of the Irish countryside. The result is one-of-a-kind vases, jars, dishes, figurines, buttons, jewelry, and other pieces.

Music Room
Harmony Hill, Sligo. ☎ **071/44765.**

Located just off O'Connell Street, this small cottagelike store will draw you to it with the sounds of Irish music. This is a great spot to purchase Irish musical instruments and accessories. A sister shop, the **Record Room,** a half-block away on Grattan Street (☎ **071/43748**), offers cassettes, CDs, videos, and records.

✪ My Lady Art Gallery
Castle St., Sligo. ☎ **071/42723.**

Established in 1932 and recently expanded, this shop specializes in original watercolors of Sligo in standard and miniature sizes. There are also oil paintings and prints of Sligo, as well as new and used books on local history.

✪ M. Quirke
Wine St., Sligo. ☎ **071/42624.**

Michael Quirke started out as a butcher, but a few years ago he traded his cleaver for wood-carving tools and transformed his butcher shop into a craft studio. Step inside and watch as he transforms chunks of native timbers into Ireland's heroes of mythology, from Sligo's Queen Maeve to Cu Chulainn, Oisin, and other folklore characters. He also carves chess sets and other Irish-theme wood items.

Sligo Crystal Glass

Ballyshannon road (N15), Grange, Co. Sligo. ☎ **071/63251.**

Located 6 miles north of Sligo, this workshop is noted for its personalized engraving of such items as family crests on mirrors or glassware. The craftspeople also produce handcut crystal candlesticks, glasses, and curio items like crystal bells and scent bottles. Crystal pieces may be cut to a pattern of your creation or choice. Weekdays, you'll see the craftspeople at work.

Wehrly Bros. Ltd

3 O'Connell St., Sligo. ☎ **071/42252.**

Established in 1875, this is one of Sligo's oldest shops, noted for a fine selection of jewelry and watches as well as cold-cast bronze sculptures of Irish figures, silverware, Claddagh rings, Waterford crystal, Belleek china, and Galway crystal.

ACCOMMODATIONS
EXPENSIVE

✪ Cromleach Lodge

Ballindoon, Castlebaldwin, Co. Sligo. ☎ **071/65155.** Fax 071/65455. 10 rms. TV TEL. £106–£160 ($169.60–$256) double. No service charge. Rates include full breakfast. AE, MC, V.

One of the best places to stay in Sligo is not in the town at all, but 20 miles south at this lovely modern country-house hotel, nestled in the quiet hills above Lough Arrow and run by Moira and Christy Tighe. You may never want to leave as you gaze out the windows of the skylit bar and restaurant or from your guest room to see the panorama of lakeland and mountain scenery. The rooms are extra large by Irish standards and have all the comforts of a top hotel, including oversized beds, designer fabrics, and original oil paintings. Each room is named after a different part of the Sligo countryside (from Ben Bulben and Knocknarea to Moytura and Carrowkeel) and is decorated with colors reflecting its namesake. Half the rooms are nonsmoking, and there are separate smoking and nonsmoking lounges, still a novelty in Ireland. But the pièce de résistance here is the dining room (see "Dining," below).

MODERATE

Ballincar House Hotel

Rosses Point Rd., Sligo. ☎ **800/447-7462** from the U.S., or 071/45361. Fax 071/44198. 25 rms. TV TEL. £85–£110 ($136–$176) double. Service charge 10%. Rates include full breakfast. AE, CB, DC, MC, V.

Nestled on six tree-shaded pastoral acres overlooking Sligo Bay, this two-story hotel was built as a private residence in 1848, then was extended and opened as a lodging in 1969. The public rooms preserve the house's old-Ireland charm, with open fireplaces, period furnishings, and original oil paintings of the area. The guest rooms are decorated in contemporary country style, and most look out onto the gardens or vistas of Sligo Bay. Amenities include a full-service restaurant, bar, hard tennis court, sauna, and snooker table. It's located 2 miles northwest of the Sligo Town center.

✪ Markree Castle

Collooney, Co. Sligo. ☎ **800/223-6510** or 800/44-UTELL from the U.S., or 071/67800. Fax 071/67840. 30 rms. TV TEL. £96–£106 ($153.60–$271.35) double. No service charge. Rates include full breakfast. AE, CB, DC, MC, V. Closed several days at Christmas.

Located 8 miles south of Sligo off the main Dublin road, this is Sligo's oldest inhabited castle, having been the home of the Cooper family since 1640. The castle's current owner, Charles Cooper, who purchased the building from his brother a few years ago, is the 10th generation of his family to live at Markree. The original house was altered and extended over the years, but the dramatic four-story turreted stone facade still remains. Even the approach to the castle is impressive, via a mile-long driveway, along pasturelands grazed by sheep and horses and past lovely gardens that stretch down to the Unsin River. Inside, the decor is equally regal, with a hand-carved oak staircase, ornate plasterwork, and a stained-glass window that traces the Cooper family tree back to the time of King John of England. The guest rooms, restored and equipped with modern facilities, have lovely views of the gardens, and the restaurant, known as Knockmuldowney (see "Dining," below), is a masterpiece of Louis Philippe–style plasterwork. Facilities at the castle include horseback riding, falconry, and salmon fishing on the Ballisodare River.

Sligo Park Hotel

Pearse Rd., Sligo, Co. Sligo. ☎ **800/44-UTELL** from the U.S., or 071/60291. Fax 071/69556. 89 rms. TV TEL. £70–£90 ($112–$144) double. Service charge 10%. AE, DC, MC, V.

With a glass-fronted facade and skylit atrium lobby, this is Sligo's most contemporary hotel, set back from the road on seven acres of parkland just over a mile south of Sligo on the Dublin road (N4). It is surrounded by lovely gardens, with distant views of Ben Bulben to the north. The public areas are equally modern, enhanced by Irish art. Guest rooms are furnished in art deco style, with light woods, pastel-toned floral fabrics, quilted headboards, and framed scenes of the Sligo area. Dining/entertainment options include the totally refurbished Hazelwood Restaurant overlooking the gardens, the Rathanna Piano Bar, and a coffee shop, while hotel facilities include an indoor swimming pool, whirlpool, sauna, steam room, gym, and tennis court.

Southern Hotel and Leisure Centre

Lord Edward St., Sligo, Co. Sligo. ☎ **071/62101.** Fax 071/60328. 77 rms. TV TEL. £60–£70 ($96–$112) double. No service charge. Rates include full breakfast. AE, DC, MC, V.

This lovely old five-story hostelry in the northwest of Ireland is called Southern because it started out as part of the Great Southern chain, and retained half its name when it became an independent property more than a dozen years ago. For visitors who travel around Ireland by train or bus, it's ideal, situated next to the train and bus station and close to the center of town. Recently refurbished, it's retained its old-world charm while rejuvenating its guest rooms with dark-wood furnishings, local art, and quilted print fabrics. Dining and entertainment choices include the Garden Room Restaurant, Orient Express Bar, and Squires nightclub, and for the exercise-inclined there's an indoor heated swimming pool, gym, Jacuzzi, squash court, sauna, and steam room.

Yeats Country Hotel

Rosses Point Rd., Rosses Point, Co. Sligo. ☎ **800/44-UTELL** from the U.S., or 071/77211. Fax 071/77203. 79 rms. TV TEL. £60–£110 ($96–$176) double. Includes full Irish breakfast and service charge. AE, DC, MC, V. Closed Dec 24–Jan.

Located 5 miles northwest of Sligo Town next to an 18-hole golf course, this modern hilltop property overlooks several miles of sandy beach and the waters of Sligo Bay. The interior is decorated in a bright contemporary style, with light woods, soft pastels, and wide windows looking out onto the neighboring attractions. Facilities include a full-service restaurant, a lounge bar, two tennis courts, and a pitch-and-putt area.

DINING
EXPENSIVE

✪ Cromleach Lodge

Ballindoon, Castlebaldwin, Co. Sligo. ☎ **071/65155.** Fax 071/65455. Reservations required. Fixed-price dinner £30 ($48). AE, DC, MC, V. Mon–Sat 7–9pm, Sun 6:30–8pm. MODERN IRISH.

It's worth the drive 20 miles south of Sligo Town to dine at this lovely country house overlooking Lough Arrow. The panoramic views are secondary, however, to chef Moira Tighe's culinary creations. The menu changes nightly, depending on what is freshest and best from the sea and garden, but may include such dishes as boned stuffed roast quail with a vintage port sauce, wild Atlantic salmon, and loin of lamb scented with garlic and Irish Mist. The pudding of white chocolate mousse can be counted on for perfect closure. As a bonus, the dining room itself is a delight, with old-style decorated plaster moldings and chair rails, curio cabinets with figurines and crystal, ruffled valances, palm tree plants, and place settings of Rosenthal china and fine Irish linens and silver.

✪ Knockmuldowney

Markree Castle, Collooney, Co. Sligo. ☎ **071/67800.** Reservations required. Fixed-price lunch £12.50 ($20); fixed-price dinner £19.50 and £24.90 ($31.20 and $39.85). AE, DC, MC, V. Daily 7–9:30pm, Sun 1–2:30pm. Closed several days at Christmas. INTERNATIONAL.

Long before Charles and Mary Cooper bought Markree Castle (see "Accommodations," above), they were winning culinary plaudits for Knockmuldowney restaurant, then situated in a small house at the base of Knocknarea Mountain on the shores of Ballisodare Bay. When they acquired the castle, they simply brought the restaurant's name with them. And even though it's now housed in a more regal and spacious 60-seat setting under 19th-century Louis Philippe–style plasterwork, the spotlight is still on the food, with such entrées as suprême of chicken with Cashel blue cheese, escallops of pork with Morvandelle cream sauce, and roast farmyard duckling with black-cherry-and-port sauce.

MODERATE

Austie's / The Elsinore

Rosses Point Rd., Rosses Point, Co. Sligo. ☎ **071/77111.** Reservations recommended for dinner. Bar food £1.50–£9 ($2.40–$14.40); dinner main courses £5.50–£15 ($8.80–$24). MC, V. Daily 12:30–10pm. SEAFOOD/INTERNATIONAL.

Set on a hill with lovely views of the waters of Sligo Bay, this pub/restaurant has a seafaring decor of nautical knickknacks and fishnets, periscopes and corks, and paintings of sailing ships. Substantial pub grub is available during the day—there's open-face "sandbank" sandwiches of crab, salmon, or smoked mackerel; crab claw, prawn, or mixed seafood salads; and hearty soups and chowders. The dinner menu offers such fresh seafood choices as panfried Dover sole, baked trout amandine, and crab au gratin, as well as steaks and chicken curry. Lobster is also available, at market prices. Outdoor seating on picnic tables is available in good weather. The restaurant is located 4 miles northwest of Sligo.

✪ Glebe House

Collooney, Co. Sligo. ☎ **071/67787.** Reservations recommended. Main courses £8.75–£16 ($14–$25.60). AE, MC, V. May–Oct daily 6:30–9:30pm; Nov–Apr, Thurs–Sat 6:30–9:30pm. Closed second two weeks of Jan. IRISH/FRENCH.

Set in a restored Georgian house near Collooney village and the Owenmore River, this homey restaurant is run by an Irish/French couple, Brid and Marc Torraden.

They espouse a sort of *cuisine bourgeoise* and rely heavily on fresh herbs and vegetables picked from the gardens that surround the house. The menu changes daily but often includes symphony of the sea (the day's best catch), noisettes of lamb with garlic, chicken breast filled with basil and mustard seed, panfried wild salmon with sorrel, roast beef and Yorkshire pudding, and pancake of vegetables in a light mustard sauce. It is south of Sligo, off the main N4 road.

MODERATE/INEXPENSIVE

✪ Truffles
11 The Mall, Sligo. ☎ **071/44226.** Reservations recommended. Main courses £5.50–£10 ($8.80–$16). No credit cards. Tues–Sat 5–10:30pm, Sun 5–10pm. IRISH/ITALIAN.

"New Age" pizzas are the specialty of this innovative restaurant on the edge of town. Chef Bernadette O'Shea is constantly experimenting to create new styles and types of pizza, including the Californian Classic, with sun-dried tomatoes and roasted garlic; the Mexicano, with hot chile peppers and sausage; and an intrinsically Irish pizza with an assortment of local cheeses including Cashel Blue, smoked Brie, goat's cheese, cream cheese, cottage cheese, and Irish mozzarella on a bed of tomato sauce, crowned by an assortment of fresh herbs. All dishes are prepared with local organic produce, including some great main-course salads and pastas.

INEXPENSIVE

The Cottage
4 Castle St., Sligo. ☎ **071/45319.** Reservations not necessary. All items £1.50–£5 ($2.40–$8). No credit cards. Mon–Fri 8:30am–9pm, Sat 8:30am–6pm. IRISH/VEGETARIAN.

For a light meal or snack, try this cottage-style vegetarian and whole food restaurant in the heart of town. It's known for quiche, chili, pizza, baked potatoes with different fillings, crab claws, seafood chowders, and hot open sandwiches on French bread topped with melted cheese. There is either self-service or table service.

EVENING ENTERTAINMENT
PUBS

The Blue Lagoon Tudor Room
Riverside, Sligo. ☎ **071/42530.**

Overlooking the Garavogue River, this pub is a five-minute walk from the town center. It offers sessions of traditional Irish music on Monday nights, ballads on Thursdays, and a nightclub every Saturday night. There is no cover charge.

Hargadon's
4 O'Connell St., Sligo. ☎ **071/70933.**

More than a century old, this is the most atmospheric bar in the center of the downtown area. Although it is strictly a pub now, it also used to be a grocery shop, as you'll see if you glance at the shelves on the right. The decor is a mélange of dark-wood walls, mahogany counters, stone floors, colored glass, old barrels and bottles, snugs (small private rooms), and alcoves lined with early prints of Sligo.

Stanford's Village Inn
Main St., Dromahair, Co. Leitrim. ☎ **071/64140.**

If you're driving around Lough Gill from Sligo, this 160-year-old pub is a great midway stop for a drink or a snack. The decor is a delightful blend of old stone walls, vintage pictures and posters, oil lamps, and tweed-covered furnishings.

✪ The Thatch

Dublin-Sligo road (N4), Ballisodare, Co. Sligo. ☎ **071/67288.**

Established in 1638 as a coaching inn, this pub is about 5 miles south of Sligo on the main road. As its name suggests, it has a fully thatched roof and a whitewashed exterior, with a country-cottage motif inside. Irish traditional music is usually scheduled from 9pm on Thursdays year-round and Tuesday through Friday in July and August.

Yeats's Tavern

Ballyshannon road (N15), Drumcliffe, Co. Sligo. ☎ **071/63117.**

Located 4 miles north of Sligo, across the road from the famous churchyard where William Butler Yeats is buried, this pub honors the poet's memory with quotations from his works, as well as photos, prints, and murals. A modern tavern and restaurant with a copper-and-wood decor, it is a convenient place to stop for a snack or a full meal when touring Yeats Country.

THE PERFORMING ARTS

The Factory

Lower Quay St., Sligo. ☎ **071/70431.** Tickets, £2.50–£5 ($4–$8) depending on show. July–Aug, Tues–Sat 1:10pm.

In summer the Blue Raincoat Theatre Company presents a lunchtime series of Yeats's plays and other one-act Sligo-related plays at this small theater.

Hawk's Well Theatre

Temple St., Sligo. ☎ **071/61518.** Tickets, £6 ($9.60). Mon–Sat box office 10am–6pm; most shows at 8pm.

The premier stage of Ireland's northwest region, this modern 350-seat theater presents a varied program of drama, comedy, ballet, opera, and concerts of modern and traditional music. It derives its name from *At the Hawk's Well,* a one-act play by Yeats. The theater occasionally produces shows, but mostly hosts visiting professional and local companies.

2 Donegal Town

138 miles NW of Dublin, 176 miles NE of Shannon Airport, 41 miles NE of Sligo, 43 miles SW of Derry, 112 miles W of Belfast, 127 NE of Galway, 250 miles N of Cork, and 253 miles NE of Killarney.

GETTING THERE   Loganair operates regularly scheduled flights from Glasgow to **Donegal Airport,** Carrickfinn, Kincasslagh, Co. Donegal (☎ **075/48284**), about 40 miles northwest of Donegal Town on the Atlantic coast.

Bus Eireann (☎ **074/21309**) operates daily bus service to Donegal Town to and from Dublin, Derry, Sligo, Galway, and other points. All tickets are issued on the bus. Pickup and boarding point is in front of the Abbey Hotel on The Diamond.

If you're driving from the south, Donegal is reached via N15 from Sligo or A46 or A47 from Northern Ireland; from the east and north, it's N15 and N56; from the west, N56 leads to Donegal Town.

VISITOR INFORMATION   The Donegal Tourist Office, Quay Street, Donegal (☎ **073/21148**), is open from May through September, Monday through Saturday from 9am to 6pm, with extended hours in July and August according to demand.

TOWN LAYOUT   Donegal Town, which sits to the east of the River Eske, is laid out around a triangular central mall or market area called The Diamond. **Main Street**

Donegal Town

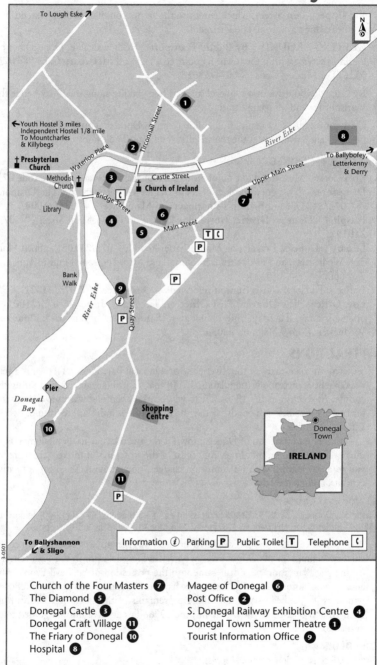

To Lough Eske

To Ballybofey, Letterkenny & Derry

River Eske

Ticonnaill Street

Youth Hostel 3 miles
Independent Hostel 1/8 mile
To Mountcharles
& Killybegs

Waterloo Place

Presbyterian Church

Methodist Church

Library

Castle Street

Church of Ireland

Upper Main Street

Bridge Street

Main Street

Bank Walk

River Eske

Quay Street

Pier

Donegal Bay

Shopping Centre

To Ballyshannon & Sligo

Donegal Town

IRELAND

3-0501

Information *i* Parking **P** Public Toilet **T** Telephone **C**

Church of the Four Masters **7**   Magee of Donegal **6**
The Diamond **5**   Post Office **2**
Donegal Castle **3**   S. Donegal Railway Exhibition Centre **4**
Donegal Craft Village **11**   Donegal Town Summer Theatre **1**
The Friary of Donegal **10**   Tourist Information Office **9**
Hospital **8**

and **Upper Main Street,** which comprise the prime commercial strip, extend in a northeast direction from The Diamond.

GETTING AROUND　By Public Transport　Easily walkable, Donegal has no local bus service within the town. If you need a taxi, call **McGroary Cabs** (☎ 073/35162) or **Marley Taxis** (☎ 074/33013).

By Car　If you drive into Donegal, there is free parking along the Quay beside the tourist office and off Main Street.

On Foot　Follow the signposted walking tour of Donegal Town; a booklet outlining the walk is available at the tourist office and most bookshops.

FAST FACTS: DONEGAL

Area Code　Most telephone numbers in the Donegal Town area use the code **073.**

Drugstores　Two good local choices are **Begley's Pharmacy,** on The Diamond (☎ 073/21232), and **Britton's Pharmacy,** on Main Street (☎ 073/21008).

Hospital　**Donegal District Hospital** is located on Upper Main Street (☎ 073/21019).

Library　**Donegal Library,** on Mountcharles Road (☎ 073/21105), is open Monday, Wednesday, and Friday from 3 to 6pm and Saturday from 11am to 1pm and 2 to 6pm.

Police　The local **Garda Station** is located on Quay Street (☎ 073/21021).

Post Office　The **Donegal Post Office** on Tirconnail Street (☎ 073/21001) is open Monday, Tuesday, and Thursday to Saturday from 9am to 5:30pm and Wednesday from 9:30am to 5:30pm.

ATTRACTIONS

Situated on the estuary of the River Eske on Donegal Bay, Donegal Town is a very walkable little metropolis (population 2,000) that's a pivotal gateway for touring the county. As recently as the 1940s, the town's central Diamond was used as a market for trading livestock and goods. Today the marketing is more in the form of tweeds and tourist goods.

The greatest attraction of Donegal town is the town layout itself, a happy mix of medieval and modern buildings. And most of the structures of interest are there for you to enjoy at will, with no admission charges, no audiovisuals, no interpretative exhibits, and no crowds.

✪ Donegal Castle

Castle St., Donegal. ☎ **073/22405.** Admission £2 ($3.20) adults, £1.50 ($2.40) seniors, £1 ($1.60) students and children, £5 ($8) family. Mid-June to Sept, daily 9:30am–6pm.

Built in the 15th century beside the River Eske, this magnificent castle was once the chief stronghold for the O'Donnell's, a powerful Donegal clan. In the 17th century, during the Plantation period, it came into the possession of Sir Basil Brook, who added an extension with 10 gables, a large bay window, and other, smaller mullioned windows in Jacobean style. The standing remains of the castle were beautifully restored and opened to the public in June 1996. Twenty-five-minute guided tours available.

The Diamond

Donegal. Free admission; continual access.

The Diamond is the triangular market area of town. It's dominated by a 25-foot-high obelisk erected as a memorial to the four early 17th-century Irish clerics from the local abbey who wrote *The Annals of Ireland,* the first recorded history of Gaelic Ireland.

Memorial Church of the Four Masters

Upper Main St., Donegal. ☎ **21026.** Free admission; donations welcome. Mon–Fri 8am–6pm, Sat–Sun 7:30am–7:30pm.

Perched on a small hill overlooking the town, this Catholic church is officially known as St. Patrick's Church of the Four Masters. It is of fairly recent vintage, built in 1935 in an Irish Romanesque style of red granite from nearby Barnesmore. It is dedicated to the four men who produced *The Annals of Ireland.* The church grounds are private.

South Donegal Railway Exhibition Centre

Anderson's Yard, off The Diamond, Donegal. Free admission. June–Sept, Mon–Sat 10am–5pm.

This center houses displays dealing with Donegal Co.'s narrow-gauge railway, which originally extended for 125 miles throughout all of Co. Donegal but ceased to operate by 1960. It's currently in the process of restoration; it is hoped to restore a section of the railway that runs through the scenic Barnesmore Gap. The current displays include photographs, artifacts, posters, tickets, and equipment.

✪ The Friary of Donegal

The Quay, Donegal. Free admission; continual access.

Often mistakenly referred to as The Abbey, this Franciscan house was founded in 1474 by the first Red Hugh O'Donnell and his wife, Nuala O'Brien of Munster. Sitting in a peaceful spot where the River Eske meets Donegal Bay, it was generously endowed by the O'Donnell family and became an important center of religion and learning. Great gatherings of clergy and lay leaders assembled here in 1539. It was from this friary that some of the scholars undertook to salvage old Gaelic manuscripts and compile *The Annals of the Four Masters* (1632–36). Unfortunately, little remains now of its glory days, except some impressive ruins of a church and a cloister.

Lough Derg

R232 to Pettigo, then R233 for 5 miles.

This lake, filled with many islands, lies about 10 miles east of Donegal. Legend has it that St. Patrick spent 40 days and 40 nights fasting in a cavern at this secluded spot, and since then it has been revered as a place of penance and pilgrimage. From June 1 to August 15, thousands of Irish people take turns coming to Lough Derg to do penance for three days at a time, remaining awake and eating nothing but tea and toast. It's considered one of the most rigorous pilgrimages in all of Christendom. No admission is charged; continual access.

SPORTS & OUTDOOR PURSUITS

BICYCLING   Rent a bike from **Doherty's,** Main Street (☎ **073/21119**). A day's rental costs £6 ($9.60) and £25 ($40) for a week. Open year-round Monday through Saturday from 9am to 6pm.

The north side of Donegal Bay offers great cycling roads—tremendously scenic and very hilly. One good but arduous route from Donegal Town follows the coast roads west to Glencolumbkille (day one), continuing north to Ardara and Dawros Head (day two), then back to Donegal (day three), taking in some of the most spectacular coastal scenery in Ireland along the way.

FISHING   For advice and equipment for fishing in Lough Eske and other local waters, contact **Doherty's Fishing Tackle,** Main Street (☎ **073/21119**). This shop stocks a wide selection of flies, reels, bait, and fishing poles. It's open year-round Monday through Saturday from 9am to 6pm.

SHOPPING

Most Donegal shops are open from Monday through Saturday from 9am to 6pm, with extended hours in summer and slightly reduced hours in winter.

✪ Donegal Craft Village
Ballyshannon Rd., Donegal. ☎ 073/22015.

You'll find this cluster of individual craft-workers' shops in a rural setting about a mile south of town. This project provides a creative environment for an ever-changing group of artisans to practice a range of ancient and modern craft: porcelain, ceramics, hand-weaving, batik, crystal, jewelry, metalwork, visual art, and Irish musical instrument making. You can buy some one-of-a-kind treasures or just browse from shop to shop and watch the craftspeople at work.

Forget-Me-Not/The Gift Shop
The Diamond, Donegal. ☎ 073/21168.

This shop features a wide selection of gifts both usual and unusual, from items such as handmade jewelry, Celtic art cards, and Donegal Co. banners and hangings to woolly sheep mobiles, Irish traditional music figures, tweed paintings, bog oak sculptures, and beaten-copper art.

The Four Masters Bookshop
The Diamond, Donegal. ☎ 073/21526.

Facing the monument commemorating the Four Masters, this shop specializes in books of Irish and Donegal interest, plus Waterford crystal, Celtic-design watches, Masons Ironstone figures, and souvenir jewelry.

✪ Magee of Donegal Ltd.
The Diamond, Donegal. ☎ 073/22660.

Established in 1866, this shop is synonymous with fine Donegal hand-woven tweeds. Weaving demonstrations are given throughout the day. Products on sale include tweed jackets, overcoats, hats, ties, and batches of material.

Melody Maker Music Shop
Castle St., Donegal. ☎ 073/22326.

If you're enchanted by the traditional and folk music of Donegal, stop in here for tapes and recordings and posters. This is also the main ticket agency for southwest Co. Donegal, handling tickets for most all concerts nationwide.

Wards Music Shop
Castle St., Donegal. ☎ 073/21313.

If you'd like to take home a harp, bodhran, bagpipe, flute, or tin whistle, this is the shop for you. It specializes in the sale of Irish musical instruments and instructional books. The stock also includes violins, mandolins, and accordions.

William Britton & Sons
Main St., Donegal. ☎ 071/21131.

Established in 1874, this shop stocks antique jewelry, silver, crystal, and clocks, as well as sports-related sculptures, pens, and watches. W. J. Britton is a registered valuer and a fellow of the National Association of Goldsmiths of Great Britain and Ireland.

ACCOMMODATIONS & DINING
EXPENSIVE

✪ St. Ernan's House

St. Ernan's Island, Donegal, Co. Donegal. ☎ **800/223-6510** from the U.S., or 073/21065. Fax 073/22098. 12 rms. TV TEL. £130–£150 ($208–$240) single or double. No service charge. Rates include full breakfast. MC, V. Closed mid-Nov to Apr.

This is one of the area's most unusual lodgings—an 1826 country house that occupies an entire small island in Donegal Bay and is connected to the mainland by its own causeway. The island, named for a 7th-century Irish monk, is planted with hawthorn and holly bushes that have been blooming for almost three centuries. The public areas and the Georgian-theme dining room, which is acclaimed for its cuisine, have all been magnificently restored, with delicate plasterwork, high ceilings, crystal chandeliers, gilt-framed oil paintings, heirloom silver, antiques, and open log fireplaces. The guest rooms, all individually decorated by proprietors Brian and Carmel O'Dowd, have traditional furnishings, with dark woods, designer fabrics, floral art, and period pieces; most have views of the water. It's a delightful spot, almost like a kingdom unto itself, yet less than 2 miles south of Donegal Town.

MODERATE

Harvey's Point Country Hotel

Lough Eske, Donegal, Co. Donegal. ☎ **073/22208.** Fax 073/22352. 20 rms. MINIBAR TV TEL. £80–£90 ($128–$144) double. Service charge 10%. Rates include full breakfast. AE, DC, MC, V. Closed weekdays Nov–Mar.

Situated 4 miles northwest of town, this modern, rambling, Swiss-style lodge is nestled amid a 13-acre woodland setting on the shores of Lough Eske at the foot of the Blue Stack Mountains. The guest rooms, most of which feature views of Lough Eske and the hills of Donegal, have traditional furnishings, some with four-poster beds; a hair dryer and tea/coffeemaker are standard equipment in each room. Public areas include a restaurant specializing in French cuisine and a piano bar / lounge. Facilities available for extra fees include two tennis courts, bicycle and boat hire, and trips on Harvey's Jarvey, a Clydesdale horse wagon.

Hyland Central

The Diamond, Donegal, Co. Donegal. ☎ **800/528-1234** from the U.S., or 073/21027. Fax 073/22295. 91 rms. TV TEL. £70–£90 ($112–$144) double. Service charge 10%. Rates include full breakfast. AE, DC, MC, V. Closed Dec 24–27.

Owned and operated by the Hyland family since 1941, this four-story hotel faces Donegal's main thoroughfare in front, while in back it has a modern extension that overlooks Lough Eske. Guest rooms are outfitted with traditional furnishings of dark woods and light floral and quilted fabrics; many rooms have views of the water. In-room extras include a tea/coffeemaker and garment press. The public areas include a new bistro/carvery overlooking Lough Eske and an old-world pub lounge. Among the facilities are an indoor heated swimming pool, Jacuzzi, steam room, sun bed, and gym.

MODERATE/INEXPENSIVE

The Abbey

The Diamond, Donegal, Co. Donegal. ☎ **800/4-CHOICE** from the U.S., or 073/21014. Fax 073/21014. 49 rms. TV TEL. £55–£75 ($88–$120) double. Rates include full breakfast and service charge. AE, DC, MC, V.

Set right in the heart of town, with The Diamond at its front door and the River Eske at its back, this vintage three-story hotel has been updated and refurbished in recent years. The guest rooms, about half of which are located in a new wing overlooking the river, have standard furnishings and bright floral fabrics; in-room amenities include a hair dryer and garment press. Dining and entertainment choices include the Eske restaurant overlooking the back gardens, the modern bilevel Eas Dun Bar and Corabber Lounge with views of the River Eske, and an outdoor beer garden / patio with great waterside views.

DINING

In addition to the hotel dining rooms listed above, try these two restaurants for a snack or light meal.

Belshade Restaurant

Above Magee Tweed, The Diamond. ☎ **073/222660.** Reservations not necessary. £1–£4.50 ($1.60–$7.20). AE, DC, MC, V. Mon–Tues and Thurs–Fri 10am–5pm, Sat 10am–5:30pm. Closed Nov–Mar. IRISH/SELF-SERVICE.

Located upstairs from Magee's Tweed shop, this 60-seat restaurant with its huge mural of Donegal on the wall conveys an aura of times past. The menu changes daily but usually includes prawn, cheese, and fruit salads, as well as sandwiches, soups, cakes, and tarts.

Errigal Restaurant

Upper Main St., Donegal. ☎ **073/21428.** Reservations not necessary. All items £1.50–£7.50 ($2.40–$12). No credit cards. Mon–Sat 9am–3pm and 5:30–11pm, Sun 3:30–11pm. IRISH.

Opposite the Church of the Four Masters, this family run restaurant is known for its fish and chips. It also serves fresh salmon and trout, chicken curry, steaks, chops, mixed grills, sandwiches, burgers, salads, and favorite traditional Irish dishes such as chicken Maryland.

DONEGAL AFTER DARK

If you're in Donegal during July and August, try to take in a performance of the Donegal Drama Circle at the **Donegal Town Summer Theatre,** O'Cleary Hall, Tirconnaill Street, Donegal (no phone). Performances are held on Tuesday, Wednesday, and Thursday at 9pm, and feature works by Donegal-based playwrights. No reservations are necessary; admission is £4 ($6.40) for adults and £2 ($3.20) for students.

PUBS

Biddy O'Barnes

Donegal-Lifford road (N15), Barnesmore, Co. Donegal. ☎ **073/21402.**

It's worth a detour into the Blue Stack Mountains and the scenic Barnesmore Gap, 7 miles northeast of Donegal Town, to visit this pub, which has been in the same family for four generations. Stepping inside is like entering a country cottage, with blazing turf fires, stone floors, wooden stools and benches, and old hutches full of plates and bric-a-brac. A picture of Biddy, who once owned this house, hangs over the main fireplace. On most evenings there's a session of spontaneous music in progress.

Charlie's Star Bar

Main St., Donegal. ☎ **073/21158.**

The wins and losses of Donegal's hurling and Gaelic football teams are the topics of conversation at this bar, where sports fans gather amid a decor of teams' jerseys, pictures, and equipment. On some nights, there is spontaneous fiddle music.

The Olde Castle Bar
Castle St., Donegal. ☎ **073/21062.**

There is an old-Donegal aura at this little pub, which has a welcoming open fireplace and a decor of etched glass, whitewashed walls, and old jars and crocks. In July and August, there is usually a cabaret on Monday from 9pm to midnight, with songs, dances, and stories. Cover charge is £2 ($3.20).

The Schooner Inn
Upper Main St., Donegal. ☎ **073/21671.**

A nautical decor of model ships and seafaring memorabilia prevails at this pub. There is music on most evenings, with traditional Irish music on Monday and Saturday, folk on Wednesday, and various singing acts on Thursday, Friday, and Sunday.

3 The Donegal Bay Coast

The Donegal Bay Coast extends for 50 miles: from Bundoran, 20 miles S of Donegal Town, to Glencolumbkille, 30 miles W of Donegal Town.

The Donegal Bay coast is comprised of two almost equal parts: the area from Ballyshannon north to Donegal Town (Southern Donegal Bay) and the area west of Donegal Town stretching to Glencolumbkille (Northern Donegal Bay). Looked at on a map, the Bay coast looks like a lobster claw reaching out from Donegal Town to grasp the bay's beautiful waters. Beaches, watersports, and coastal scenery are definitely the main drawing cards of this area, but you'll find that the Donegal Bay coast holds many other attractions, from bustling seaport towns to folk museums and craft centers.

GETTING TO & AROUND DONEGAL BAY   **Loganair** operates regularly scheduled flights from Glasgow to **Donegal Airport,** Carrickfinn, Kincasslagh, Co. Donegal (☎ 075/48284), about 40 miles north of Killybegs.

Bus Eireann (☎ 074/21309) operates daily bus service to Killybegs and Glencolumbkille on the northern half of the bay and to Ballyshannon and Bundoran on the southern half of the bay.

The best way to get to and around Donegal Bay is by car, following the main N15 route on the southern half of the bay and the main N56 route on the northern half of the bay.

VISITOR INFORMATION   Contact the **North West Tourism Office,** Aras Reddan, Temple Street, Sligo (☎ 071/61201); the **Letterkenny Tourist Office,** Derry Road, Letterkenny (☎ 074/21173); or **Bundoran Tourist Office,** Main Street, Bundoran, Co. Donegal (☎ 072/41350). The first two are open year-round; the third is open from June through August.

AREA CODES   The area codes for telephone numbers in this area are **072** and **073.**

SOUTHERN DONEGAL BAY
ATTRACTIONS

To reach the southern section of Donegal Bay, take the N15 road up the Atlantic coast, and at about 20 miles north of Sligo you'll come to **Bundoran,** the southern tip of Co. Donegal and a major beach resort. A favorite with Irish from both the Republic and the North, Bundoran takes on a carnival-like atmosphere in the middle of summer. In addition to its busy beaches and amusement arcades, there's an 18-hole golf course on the north side of the town overlooking Donegal Bay.

Noah's Bridge

During the great meltdown at the end of the last ice age—10,000 years ago, give or take a month or two—Europe's fauna and flora began to make their way north as the glaciers receded. Two by two, or whatever, they crossed the land bridge from France to Britain, then on to Ireland from what are now Wales and Scotland. It was a race of the species, a race against time. As ice became water, land became sea, the bridge from the Continent to Britain began to look more and more like the English Channel. Meanwhile, the Irish Sea rose to the occasion as well, leaving the poor snake stuck on British shores, presumably waving with a handkerchief.

In this particular race the first were first and the last were last, and many never made it at all. Two thousand years later, Ireland, now an island, had only a fraction of continental Europe's plants and wildlife, with England finishing somewhere between the two in species count.

Continuing up the coast, you'll pass **Ballyshannon,** dating from the 15th century and one of the oldest inhabited towns in Ireland; it's another favorite with beachgoers. At this point, leave the main road and head for the coastal resort of **Rossnowlagh,** one of the loveliest beaches in all of Ireland. At over 2 miles long and as wide as the tides allow, it's a flat sandy stretch, shielded by flower-filled hills, and ideal for walking. You'll see horses racing on it occasionally. This spot is a splendid vantage point for watching sunsets over the churning foam-rimmed waters of the Atlantic.

Overlooking the beach from a hilltop is the **Franciscan Friary,** Rossnowlagh (☎ 072/51342), which houses a small museum of local Donegal history. The complex also contains beautiful gardens and walks overlooking the sea, a tearoom with outdoor seating, and a craft shop. Open daily from 10am to 6pm. There is no admission charge, but donations are welcome.

From Rossnowlagh, return to the main road via the **Donegal Golf Club** at Murvagh, a spectacular setting nestled on a rugged sandy peninsula of primeval duneland, surrounded by a wall of dense woodlands. From here, the road curves inland and it's less than 10 miles to Donegal Town.

SPORTS & OUTDOOR PURSUITS

BEACHES   Donegal Bay's beaches are wide, sandy, clean, and flat—ideal for walking. The best are **Rossnowlagh** and **Bundoran.** At Rossnowlagh, surfing is a favorite pastime. When the surf is up, you can rent boards and wetsuits at £2.50 ($4) per hour per item; lessons are £5.50 ($8.80) per hour. For more information, phone ☎ 073/21053.

GOLF   The Donegal Bay coast is home to two outstanding 18-hole championship seaside golf courses. **Donegal Golf Club,** Murvagh, Ballintra, Co. Donegal (☎ 073/34054), is 3 miles north of Rossnowlagh and 7 miles south of Donegal Town. It's a par-73 course with greens fees of £18 ($28.80) on weekdays and £22.50 ($36) on weekends.

The Bundoran Golf Club, off the Sligo-Ballyshannon road (N15), Bundoran, Co. Donegal (☎ 072/41302), is a par-69 course designed by the great Harry Vardon. The greens fees are £16 ($25.60) on weekdays and £18 ($28.80) on weekends.

HORSEBACK RIDING   Stracomer Riding School Ltd., off the Sligo-Ballyshannon road (N15), Bundoran, Co. Donegal (☎ 072/41787), specializes in

County Donegal

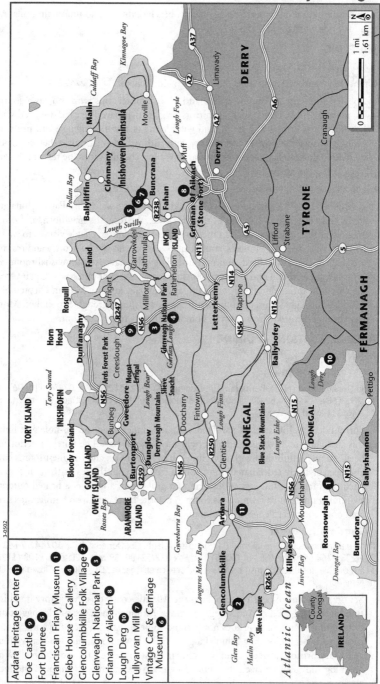

Ardara Heritage Center 🔟
Doe Castle 🟢
Fort Dunree 🟢
Franciscan Friary Museum 🟢
Glebe House & Gallery 🟢
Glencolumbkille Folk Village 🟢
Glenveagh National Park 🟢
Grianan of Aileach 🟢
Lough Derg 🔟
Tullyarvan Mill 🟢
Vintage Car & Carriage Museum 🟢

trail riding on the surrounding farmlands, beaches, dunes, and mountain trails. An hour's ride averages £10 ($16).

SHOPPING

Barry Britton Design

Off the Ballyshannon-Donegal road, Rossnowlagh, Co. Donegal. ☎ 072/52220.

Located in a cottage opposite the Sand House Hotel, this workshop is a source of unusual artistic crafts, such as mirrors or glass that have been hand-etched with heraldic crests or nautical, floral, and wildlife designs; wall hangings; and prints of Donegal, as well as posters and pottery with surfing and Irish music themes. Open daily June through September from 10am to 6pm; schedule varies the rest of the year.

Donegal Parian China

Bundoran road (N15), Ballyshannon, Co. Donegal. ☎ 072/51826.

Established in 1985, this pottery works produces delicate wafer-thin Parian china gift items and tableware in patterns of the shamrock, the rose, the hawthorn, and other Irish flora. Free guided tours, commencing every 20 minutes, enable visitors to watch as vases, bells, spoons, thimbles, wall plaques, lamps, and eggshell coffee and tea sets are shaped, decorated, fired, and polished. They also have an audiovisual room, an art gallery, a tearoom, and a showroom/shop for on-the-spot purchases. Open October through April, Monday through Friday from 9am to 6pm; May and September, Monday through Saturday from 9am to 6pm; and June through September, Monday through Saturday from 9am to 6pm and Sunday from 1 to 6pm.

ACCOMMODATIONS & DINING

Moderate

Great Northern Hotel

Sligo-Donegal road (N15), Bundoran, Co. Donegal. ☎ 072/41204. Fax 072/41114. 96 rms. TV TEL. £88–£96 ($140.80–$135.60) double. Includes full Irish breakfast and service charge. AE, MC, V. Closed Jan–Apr.

Surrounded by 130 acres of parkland and sand dunes beside an 18-hole golf links, this sprawling multiwinged hotel is right on Donegal Bay. The hotel's interior has been recently refurbished with a bright modern Irish motif, and the guest rooms have also been stylishly redecorated; most rooms have views of the sea or the golf course. Facilities include a full-service restaurant, a grill room, a lounge, a heated outdoor swimming pool, and a lawn tennis court. A favorite hotel with Irish families, it's situated on the northern edge of Bundoran.

✪ Sand House Hotel

Off the Ballyshannon-Donegal road (N15), Rossnowlagh, Co. Donegal. ☎ 800/447-7462 or 800/223-6764 from the U.S., or 072/51777. Fax 072/52100. 39 rms. TEL. £80–£100 ($128–$160) double. Includes full Irish breakfast and service charge. AE, DC, MC, V. Closed late Oct to early Apr.

Set on a crescent of beach overlooking the Atlantic coast, this three-story hotel is a standout among all the Co. Donegal lodgings. Although there are subtle suggestions of turreting on the roof, it does not pretend to be a castle. In fact, the Sand House had its early beginnings as a fishing lodge in 1886. It was not until 1949 that Vincent and Mary Britton moved in and began their quest to create a top-notch hotel. With open log and turf fireplaces, the public rooms are decorated with antiques and local artwork, and a sunlit, plant-filled conservatory offers great views of the sea. Guest rooms are decorated with traditional dark-wood furnishings, designer fabrics, antiques, and such period pieces as hand-carved armoires and vanities; some have canopied or four-poster beds. Of course, the wide picture windows with their vistas of the Atlantic add the crowning touch.

The dining room—which, surprisingly, does not overlook the sea—is presided over by a creative chef who specializes in locally harvested Donegal Bay lobster, oysters, scallops, mussels, and other seafoods. The resident's lounge, cozy with an open fireplace, is a relaxing old-fashioned setting, while the Surfers Bar is a larger gathering spot with a nautical decor.

Hotel facilities include a 2-mile beach for walking, swimming, surfing, and other watersports; a tennis court; and croquet.

Moderate/Inexpensive

✪ Bruckless House

Bruckless, Co. Donegal (signposted on N56, 12 miles west of Donegal Town). ☎ **073/37071.** Fax 073/37070. 4 rooms. £60 ($96) double with bath; £50 ($80) double with shared bath. Includes full Irish breakfast. No service charge. AE, MC, V. Apr–Sept.

Clive and Joan Evans have restored their mid–18th-century farmhouse with such care and taste that every room is a pleasure to enter and enjoy. Furniture and art brought back by the Evans's from their years in China adds a special elegance. All of the bedrooms are smoke-free, spacious, and bright; the sitting and dining rooms are gracious and comfortable; and Joan's gardens have twice in recent years taken first prize in Co. Donegal's country garden competition. Inside and out, Bruckless House is a gem. Be sure to ask Clive to introduce you to his fine Connemara ponies, which he raises and treasures.

DINING

✪ Smugglers Creek

Rossnowlagh, Co. Donegal. ☎ **072/52366.** Reservations required for dinner. Bar food £2–£7 ($3.20–$11.20) all items; dinner main courses £8–£12.50 ($12.80–$20), lobster £19 ($30.40). AE, DC, MC, V. Daily 12:30–9:30pm. Closed Mon–Tues Oct–Easter. SEAFOOD/IRISH.

For great food with grand sunset views, don't miss this little gem perched on a cliff overlooking Donegal Bay. It's housed in an 1845 stone building that has been restored and enlarged to include a conservatory-style dining area with open fireplaces, beamed ceilings, stone walls, wooden stools, porthole windows, crab traps, and lobster pots. Besides the views and homey/nautical decor, seafood is the star attraction here, and proprietor Conor Britton even pulls his own oysters and mussels from local beds. The bar menu ranges from soups, salads, and sandwiches to buttered garlic mussels or fresh pâté. Dinner entrées include Smugglers sea casserole (scallops, salmon, and prawns with Mornay sauce), deep-fried squid with Provençale sauce, tiger prawns in garlic butter, wild Irish salmon hollandaise, steaks with whiskey sauce, and vegetarian pasta or stir-fry dishes.

EVENING ENTERTAINMENT

In summer, Rossnowlagh is a hub of social activity. Many people flock to the **Sand House Hotel,** Rossnowlagh, Co. Donegal (☎ 072/51777), to enjoy the nautical atmosphere of the Surfers Bar and to see the Slice of Ireland Cabaret. It's a two-hour show of Donegal-theme music, song, dance, poetry, comedy, and drama, presented June through September on Wednesdays at 9pm. Admission is £3 ($4.80).

Nearby at the **Summer Theatre,** staged at the Franciscan Friary Hall, Rossnowlagh (☎ 072/51342), the Coolmore Players present classic dramas by Irish playwrights. Performances are Thursdays in August at 8:30pm; admission is £3 ($4.80) for adults and £1.50 ($2.40) for children and seniors.

Farther south, **Dorrian's Thatch Bar,** Main Street, Ballyshannon, Co. Donegal (☎ 072/51147), holds nightly sessions of Irish traditional music in summer.

NORTHERN DONEGAL BAY
ATTRACTIONS
From Donegal Town follow the main road (N56) for a slow, scenic drive along the northern coast of Donegal Bay. You'll encounter narrow roads, sheer cliffs, craggy rocks, boglands, and panoramic mountain and sea views. You'll also see the thatched-roof cottages that are distinctively typical of this area—with rounded roofs, because the thatch is tied down by a network of ropes (sugans) and fastened to pins beneath the eaves, to protect it from the prevailing winds off the sea. It's only 30 miles out to Glencolumbkille, but plan on at least several hours' drive.

Your first stop could be at Killybegs—where, if your timing is right, you can watch the fishing boats unloading the day's catch—or at Studio Donegal in Kilcar, if you're casting for tweed. A must-stop is **Slieve League,** the highest sea cliffs in Europe. The turn-off for the Bunglas viewing point is at Carrick. Once at the cliffs, you must decide whether you want to merely gaze at their 1,000-foot splendor or to experience them up-up-up close and personal on the wind-buffeted walk along their ridge. This walk is for the fearless and fit.

Just before you come to Killybegs, the N56 road swings inland and northward. Continue on the coastal road westward to **Glencolumbkille,** an Atlantic outpost dating back 5,000 years. It is said that St. Columba established a monastery here in the 6th century and gave his name permanently to the glen. In the 1950s, this area was endangered by a 75% emigration rate, until the parish priest, James McDyer, focused the energies of the town not only on assuring the community's future but also on preserving its past. He helped accomplish both by founding the **Glencolumbkille Folk Museum** (☎ 073/30017). Built by the people of Glencolumbkille in the form of a tiny village, or *clachan,* this modest theme park of thatched cottages—each outfitted with period furniture and artifacts—reflects with simple clarity life in this remote corner of Ireland over the past several centuries. Two miniature playhouses are on hand for children. Current plans call for an extended tearoom and reception hall to accommodate the ever-increasing number of visitors. The tearoom, whose current specialty, Guinness cake, is to die for, will soon be serving a simple menu of traditional Irish dishes, such as stews and *brútin,* comprised mainly of hot milk and potatoes. In the *sheebeen,* a shop of traditional products, don't dismiss the admittedly bizarre-sounding local wines—fuchsia, heather, seaweed, and tea and raisin—until you've tried them all. They're surprisingly good. The medium-dry heather wine finishes first on my list. Admission and tour is £2.50 ($4) for adults and £1.50 ($2.40) for seniors and children. It's open from Easter through September, Monday through Saturday from 10am to 6pm and Sunday from noon to 6pm; hours extend to 6:30pm in high season.

To continue touring onward from Glencolumbkille, follow the signs for Ardara over a mountainous inland road. Soon you'll come to **Glengesh Pass,** a narrow, scenic roadway that rises to a height of 900 feet before plunging into the valley below. The road leads eventually to **Ardara,** known for its tweed and woollen craft centers (see "Atlantic Highlands," below).

SPORTS & OUTDOOR PURSUITS
BICYCLING   The north side of Donegal Bay offers great cycling roads—tremendously scenic, and very hilly. One good but arduous route from Donegal Town follows the coast roads west to Glencolumbkille (day one), continuing

north to Ardara and Dawros Head via Glengesh Pass (day two), then back to Donegal (day three), taking in some of the most spectacular coastal scenery in Ireland along the way.

FISHING   Surrounded by waters that hold shark, skate, pollock, conger, cod, and mackerel, **Killybegs** is one of the most active centers on the northwest coast for both commercial and sport sea-fishing. Brian McGilloway of Killybegs (☎ **073/31144**) operates full-day fishing expeditions for visitors on board the 34-foot M.V. *Susanne* from Blackrock Pier. Prices average £20 ($32) per person per day, plus £5 ($8) for rods and tackle. The daily schedule and departure times vary according to demand; reservations are required.

At **Mountcharles,** a coastal town midway between Donegal Town and Killybegs, deep-sea fishing trips are organized by Michael O'Boyle, Old Road (☎ **073/35257**). Outings are slated daily from 11am to 5pm and cost £15 ($24) per person. This company also offers guided boat trips and wildlife cruises on demand, priced from £15 ($24) per person with a two-hour minimum booking.

WALKING   The peninsula that extends westward from Killybegs possesses some of the most spectacular coastal scenery in Ireland, and much of it is only accessible from the sea or on foot. The grandeur of the Slieve League cliffs is not to be missed, and the best way to visit this natural monument is to hike from the Bunglass lookout point to Tramane Strand in Malin Beg, a few miles southwest of Glencolumbkille. This walk involves a crossing of the renowned "One Man's Pass," a narrow ridge with steep drops on both sides that should not be attempted by the acrophobic or by anyone wearing high heels. The distance from Bunglass to Trabane Strand is 9 miles, and you will have to arrange a pickup at the end. The summits of the Slieve League, rising almost 2,000 feet above the sea, are often capped in cloud, and you should think twice about undertaking the walk if there is danger of losing visibility along the way.

Another walk that's less well known than the Slieve League but just as spectacular is the coastal walk between Glencolumbkille and the town of Maghera (which is not so much a town as a small cluster of houses, actually). Glencolumbkille is dominated to the north by Glen Head, topped by a stone tower; this walk begins with a climb to the tower and then continues along the cliff face for 15 miles, passing only one remote outpost of human habitation along the way, the tiny town of Port. For isolated sea splendor, this is one of the finest walks in Ireland, but should only be undertaken in fine weather by experienced walkers with adequate provisions.

SHOPPING

Studio Donegal
The Glebe Mill, Kilcar, Co. Donegal. ☎ **073/38194.**

Started in 1979, this hand-weaving enterprise is distinguished by its knobby tweed, subtly colored in tones of beige, oat, and ash. You can walk around both the craft shop and the mill and see the chunky-weave stoles, caps, jackets, and cloaks in the making. Other products fashioned of this unique tweed include tote bags, cushion covers, table mats, tapestries, and wall hangings. It's located between Killybegs and Glencolumbkille, about 20 miles west of Donegal Town. Open Monday through Saturday from 10am to 6pm, with extended hours in summer.

Teresa's Cottage Industries, Ltd.
Donegal-Killybegs road (N56), Bruckless. ☎ **073/37080.**

For more than 20 years, Teresa Gillespie and her team of local folk have been producing delicately embroidered linens and lace, crochet work, and knitwear. If you stop at this busy shop, you not only can buy at the source but also see the craftspeople at work. Open Monday through Saturday from 10am to 6pm, with extended hours in summer.

ACCOMMODATIONS & DINING
Moderate
✪ Bay View Hotel

1–2 Main St., Killybegs, Co. Donegal. ☎ **073/31950.** Fax 073/31856. 38 rms. TV TEL. £72–£80 ($115.20–$128) double. No service charge. Rates include full breakfast. MC, V.

Situated on the harbor in the middle of town, this four-story hotel was completely renovated and refurbished in 1992. Guest rooms are decorated in contemporary style with light pine furnishings, bright quilted fabrics, and brass accessories, all enhanced by wide-windowed views of the marina and fishing boats.

Dining/Entertainment: Choices include the ground-floor Bay View Brasserie for light meals all day; the traditional first-floor dining room with lovely bay views and contemporary art; and two bars: the ground-floor Fisherman's Wharf and the first-floor Upper Deck cocktail lounge.

Facilities: Indoor heated swimming pool, sauna, steam room, Jacuzzi, gym.

Moderate/Inexpensive
The Glencolumbkille Hotel

Glencolumbkille, Co. Donegal. ☎ **073/30222.** 30 rms. TV TEL. £35–£80 ($56–$128) double. No service charge. Rates include full breakfast. DC, MC, V.

If you want to get away from it all, this hotel is the most westerly outpost you can get in Donegal. Edged by Malin Bay and the Atlantic Ocean, encircled by craggy mountains that are populated mostly by meandering woolly sheep, it's a lovely spot, with turf fireplaces to warm you and a cottage atmosphere to cheer you. There's a good dining room, with panoramic views of the countryside, and the guest rooms have standard furnishings and views of the sea or the valley. Staying here for a few days will put color in your cheeks and recharge your inner batteries.

DINING
✪ The Blue Haven

Largymore, Kilcar, Co. Donegal. ☎ **073/38090.** Reservations recommended for dinner. Bar food all items £1.50–£6 ($2.40–$9.60); dinner main courses £5–£10 ($8–$16). MC, V. May–Sept, daily 11am–11pm. IRISH.

Set on a broad open sweep of Donegal Bay between Killybegs and Kilcar, this modern skylit restaurant offers 180° views of the bay from a semicircular bank of windows. It's an ideal stop for a meal or light refreshment while touring. The bar food menu, available throughout the day, offers soups, sandwiches, and omelets with unusual fillings. The dinner menu includes fillet of rainbow trout, lemon sole bonne femme, T-bone and sirloin steaks, and savory mushroom pancakes.

PUBS

The don't-miss pub in Ardara is **Nancy's** on Front Street (no phone), which has to be one of the smallest pubs in Ireland, yet what it lacks in size it makes up for in character and charm. The **Harbour Bar,** Main Street, Killybegs, Co. Donegal (☎ 073/31049), holds an Irish music night on Tuesdays during July and August.

For good conversation and atmosphere at any time, step through the half-door at the **Piper's Rest,** Kilcar, Co. Donegal (☎ 073/38205), a thatched-roof pub with original stone walls, arches, flagged floors, an open turf fire, and a unique stained-glass window depicting a piper. As its name implies, music may erupt at any time, and usually does on summer nights.

4 The Atlantic Highlands

The Atlantic Highlands start at Ardara, 25 miles NW of Donegal Town, 10 miles N of Killybegs.

GETTING TO & AROUND THE ATLANTIC HIGHLANDS   **Loganair** operates regularly scheduled flights from Glasgow to **Donegal Airport,** Carrickfinn, Kincasslagh, Co. Donegal (☎ **075/48284**), in the heart of the Atlantic coast.

Bus Eireann (☎ **074/21309**) operates daily bus service to Ardara and Glenties.

The best way to get to and around Donegal's Atlantic Highlands is by car, following the main N56 route.

VISITOR INFORMATION   Contact the **North West Tourism Office,** Aras Reddan, Temple Street, Sligo (☎ **071/61201**); the **Letterkenny Tourist Office,** Derry Road, Letterkenny (☎ **074/21173**); or the **Donegal Tourist Office,** Quay Street, Donegal (☎ **073/21148**). The first two are open year-round; the third office is open from May through September.

AREA CODES   The area codes for telephone numbers in this region are **074** and **075.**

THE LOWDOWN ON THE HIGHLANDS

Scenery is the keynote to the Atlantic Highlands of Donegal—vast stretches of coastal and mountain scenery, beaches and bays, rocks and ruins. It's sometimes lonely but always breathtaking. Set far off the beaten track and deep amid the coastal scenery is Mount Errigal, the highest mountain in Donegal (2,466 feet), which gently slopes down to one of Ireland's greatest visitor attractions, the Glenveagh National Park.

The best place to start a tour of Donegal's Atlantic Highlands is at Ardara, a small town on the coast about 25 miles northwest of Donegal Town. From here, it's easy to weave your way up the rest of the Donegal coast. This drive can take four hours or four days, depending on your own particular time schedule and interests.

The deeper you get into this countryside, the more you'll be immersed into a section known as the Gaeltacht, or Irish-speaking area. This really should present no problems, except that most of the road signs will be only in Irish. Now, if you keep to the main road (N56), you should have no difficulties, but if you follow little roads off to the seashore or down country paths, you may have a problem figuring out where you're going (unless you can read Irish). In many cases, the Irish word for a place bears no resemblance to the English equivalent (An Clochan Liath in Irish is *Dungloe* in English), so our best advice is to buy a map with place names in both languages or to stick to the main road.

ATTRACTIONS

Ardara, known for its local tweed and sweater industries, is worth a stop for shoppers. North of Ardara, the route travels inland near Gweebarra Bay and passes via Dungloe to an area known as **The Rosses,** extending from Gweebarra Bridge as far north as Crolly. This stretch presents a wealth of rock-strewn land, with frequent mountains, rivers, lakes, and beaches. Here you can visit **Burtonport** (otherwise known as Ailt an Chorrain), one of the premier fishing ports of Ireland; it's said that more salmon and lobster are landed there than at any other port in Ireland or Britain.

North of the Rosses between Derrybeg and Gortahork is an area known as the **Bloody Foreland,** a stretch of land that derives its name from the fact that its rocks take on a warm ruddy color when lit by the setting sun. This is something that should not be missed.

By now, you'll be approaching the top rim of Donegal, which is dominated by a series of small peninsulas or fingers of land jutting out into the sea. Chief among these scenic areas are **Horn Head** and **Ards.** The latter contains a forest park with a wide diversity of terrain: woodlands, a salt marsh, sand dunes, seashore, freshwater lakes, and fenland.

In Tory Sound, 9 miles north of the mainland, lies Tory Island, treelessly desolate and seemingly uninhabitable. The truth is that Tory Island, all of 2^1/$_2$ miles long and less than a mile wide, has been settled for thousands of years and currently boasts nearly 200 year-round inhabitants. Known for its painters and pirates, ruins and bird cliffs, Tory makes a great adventure, as does the crossing, which can be made daily, weather permitting, from either Bunbeg or Magheraroarty with **Donegal Coastal Cruises,** Strand Road, Middletown, Derrybeg, Co. Donegal (☎ **075/31320** or 075/ 31340; fax 075/31665).

After Horn Head, the next spit of land to the east is **Rosguill.** The 10-mile route around this peninsula is called the Atlantic Drive. This leads you to yet another peninsula, the **Fanad,** with a 45-mile circuit between Mulroy Bay and Lough Swilly. The resort of **Rathmullan** is a favorite stopping point here.

After driving to all these scenic peninsulas, it may come as a surprise that many of the greatest visitor attractions of the Atlantic Highlands are not along the coast at all, but inland, a few miles off the main N56 road near Kilmacrennan.

✪ Glenveagh National Park

Church Hill, Co. Donegal. ☎ **074/37088.** Admission £2 ($3.20) adults, £1.50 ($2.40) seniors, £1 ($1.60) students and children; castle tour £2 ($3.20) adults, £1.50 ($2.40) seniors, £1 ($1.60) students and children. No credit cards. Easter until first Sun in Nov daily 10am–6:30pm; 10am– 7:30 on Sun in July and Aug. Closed Fridays Oct–Nov. Main entrance on R251.

Deep in the heart of Co. Donegal, far off the coastal path, this 35,000-acre estate is considered by many to be Ireland's finest national park. The core of the park is the Glenveagh Estate, originally the home of the notorious landlord John George Adair, much-despised for his eviction of Irish tenant farmers in 1861, who built the castle in the 1870s. From 1937 to 1983 the estate prospered under the stewardship of Henry McIlhenny, a distinguished Philadelphia art historian (of the Tabasco Sauce family) who restored the baronial castle and planted gardens full of exotic species of flowers and shrubs. McIlhenny subsequently gave Glenveagh to the Irish nation for use as a public park, and today this fairy-tale setting includes extensive woodlands, herds of red deer, alpine gardens, a sylvan lake, and the highest mountain in Donegal, Mount Errigal. Visitors can tour the castle and gardens and explore the parklands on foot. In addition, the complex includes a visitor center with a continual audiovisual show; displays on the history, flora, and fauna of the area; and signposted nature trails. There's a self-service restaurant in the visitor center and a tearoom in the castle.

Doe Castle

3^1/$_2$ miles off N56 on a signposted turnoff just south of Creeslough. Free admission.

This tower house is surrounded on three sides by the waters of Sheep Haven Bay and on the fourth by a moat carved into the bedrock that forms its foundation. The central tower is enclosed by a battlemented wall with round towers at the corners; the view from the battlements across the bay is superb. Built in the early 16th century, the castle was extensively restored in the 18th century and was inhabited until 1843. If the entrance is locked, the key can be obtained from the house nearest the castle; there is no entrance fee. With its remote seaside location and sweeping views of the nearby hills, this is one of the most beautifully situated castles in Ireland.

✪ The Glebe House and Gallery

Church Hill. ☎ **074/37071.** Admission £2 ($3.20) adults, £1.50 ($2.40) seniors, £1 ($1.60) students and children. May–Oct Mon–Thurs and Sat 11am–6:30pm, Sun 11am–6:30pm. 11 miles NW of Letterkenny on the Churchill road (R251).

Sitting in woodland gardens on the shores of Lough Gartan about 4 miles southwest of Glenveagh, this Regency-style house was built as a rectory in the 1820s. It was owned until recently by English artist Derek Hill, who donated the house and his own art collection to the Irish government for public use and as an enhancement to the area he loves. The house is decorated with Donegal folk art, Japanese and Islamic art, Victoriana, and William Morris papers and textiles. The adjacent stables have been converted into an art gallery housing the 300-item Hill Collection of works by Picasso, Bonnard, Kokoschka, Yeats, Annigoni, Pasmore, and Hill himself. It's more than surprising to find this first-rate 20th-century art collection in this remote part of Donegal, but then, this is a surprising place.

Ardara Heritage Center

Ardara, Co. Donegal. ☎ **075/41262.** Admission £2 ($3.20) adults, £1 ($1.60) students, 50p (80¢) children. Easter–Oct Mon–Sat 10am–6pm, Sun 2–6pm. On N56 in the center of town.

Ardara has long been a center for weaving, and varied displays represent the history of tweed production in the region. There is a weaver in residence who is sometimes present to demonstrate techniques. A video provides an outline of nearby places of interest. The center opened in 1995, and the offerings are still somewhat sparse, not justifying the entry fee unless you have a particular interest in tweeds and their production. A cafe serves inexpensive teas, soups, and simple meals.

SPORTS & OUTDOOR PURSUITS

BEACHES   Some of the most pristine and secluded beaches in Ireland are to be found along the northern and western coasts of Donegal. There are few such places anywhere else where you can be so alone on such magnificent expanses of sea-sand. The only problem here is finding a sunny day. There are several popular beaches on Dawros Head, including **Traighmore Strand** in Rossbeg and extensive beaches in Portnoo and Navan. **Magheroarty** near Falcarragh on the northern coast has a breathtaking beach, unspoiled by crowds or commercial development. The same goes for **Tramore** beach on the west side of Horn Head near Dunfanaghy; you have to hike a short distance to get there and will be rewarded by miles of white sand and seclusion. Other secluded and sandy beaches ideal for walking and jogging include Carrigart, Downings, Marble Hill, and Port na Blagh.

BICYCLING   Raleigh mountain bikes can be rented with panniers and accessories from **Church Street Cycles,** Letterkenny, Co. Donegal (☎ **074/26204**) for £7 ($11.20) per day and £30 ($48) per week, with a £40 ($64) deposit (no credit cards accepted). Letterkenny is a good starting point for exploring the coast of northern Donegal—Horn Head, Inishowen Peninsula, Tory Island, and Bloody Foreland Head are all within an easy day's ride.

BIRD-WATCHING   **Horn Head** is a nesting site for many species of sea birds and has the largest nesting population of Razorbills in Ireland. **Malin Head,** at the end of the Inishowen Peninsula, is the northernmost point on the Irish mainland, and once was the site of a bird observatory; it's a good site for watching migrants in late autumn.

FISHING   The rivers and lakes in this area produce good catches of salmon, sea trout, and brown trout, and the coastal waters yield flounder, pollock, and cod. Fishing expeditions are offered by charter boats, fishing boats, and trawlers. For details, contact the **Dunfanaghy Angling Association** (☎ 074/36208), **Creeslough Angling Association** (☎ 074/38004), or the **Downings Bay Sea Angling Club** (☎ 074/55161).

GOLF   One of Ireland's most challenging golf courses is the **Rosapenna Golf Club,** Atlantic Drive, Downings, Co. Donegal (☎ 074/55301), an 18-hole championship seaside par-70 links course. It was laid out in 1983 by Tom Morris of St. Andrews. Greens fees are £12 ($19.20) on weekdays and £15 ($24) on weekends.

Other 18-hole courses in this part of Donegal are **Dunfanaghy Golf Club,** Dunfanaghy, Co. Donegal (☎ 074/36335), a seaside par-68 course with greens fees of £10 ($16) on weekdays and £12 ($19.20) on weekends; **Narin & Portnoo Golf Club,** Narin-Portnoo, Co. Donegal (☎ 075/45107), a par-69 seaside course with greens fees of £12 ($19.20) on weekdays and £15 ($24) on weekends; and **Portsalon Golf Club,** Portsalon, Co. Donegal (☎ 074/59459), a seaside par-69 course with greens fees of £10 ($16).

WALKING   A section of **the Ulster Way** passes through Donegal between the towns of Falcarragh to the north and Pettigo to the south, on the border with Fermanagh. This trail traverses some remote and wild terrain, passing Errigal Mountain and Glenveagh Park before heading south into the Blue Stack Mountains.

There are some incredible walks on **Hook Head,** signposted off N56 just west of Dunfanaghy. Follow the Hook Head Drive to the concrete lookout point; from here you can walk out to a ruined castle on the headland and continue south along a line of impressive quartzite sea cliffs that glitter in the sun as though covered with a sheet of ice. This is a moderately difficult walk.

The **Ards Forest Park** is located on a peninsula jutting out into Sheep Haven Bay, about 3¹/₂ miles south of Dunfanaghy on N56. The park is mostly forested and also includes an area of dunes along the water. There are signposted nature trails and a guidebook that can be purchased as you enter the park.

SHOPPING

Ardara is a hub of tweed and woollen production. Most shops are open Monday through Saturday from 9am to 5:30pm, with extended hours in summer. These shops are all on the main street of the town (N56).

C. Bonner & Son
Ardara, Co. Donegal. ☎ 075/41303.

This firm produces its own hand-knit and hand-loomed knitwear, including linen-cotton and colorful sheep-patterned lambswool sweaters. The shop also sells sheepskins, pottery, wildlife watercolors, wool hangings, linens, crystal, and china.

John Molloy
Ardara, Co. Donegal. ☎ 075/41243.

In the heart of wool and weaving country, this factory shop is well stocked with hand knits, homespun fashions, sports jackets, tweed scarves and rugs, and all types of caps, from kingfisher to ghillie styles. There's even a bargain bin.

Kennedy of Ardara
Ardara, Co. Donegal. ☎ 075/41106.

Established in 1904, this family owned knitwear company employs about 500 home workers who hand-knit or hand-loom bainin sweaters, hats, scarves, and jackets in native Donegal patterns and colors. The shop also sells turf crafts, pottery, and dolls.

ACCOMMODATIONS
MODERATE

Arnolds Hotel

Dunfanaghy, Co. Donegal. ☎ **074/36208.** Fax 074/36352. 34 rms. TV TEL. £56–£76 ($89.60–$121.60) double. No service charge. Rates include full breakfast. AE, DC, MC, V. Closed Nov 10–Mar 15.

In the Arnold family for three generations, this is a truly family run business, with brothers Derek and William acting as desk clerks, porters, waiters, and whatever else needs doing. The Arnolds Hotel is an ideal base for touring northwest Donegal and for exploring Glenveagh National Park. If you have in mind a round of golf or fishing or pony-trekking, these can all be arranged at the front desk. Or you may want to stay put, as the hotel enjoys views of Sheephaven Bay and Horn Head, and serves great food.

Fort Royal Hotel

Rathmullan, Co. Donegal. ☎ **800/447-7462** from the U.S., or 074/58100. Fax 074/58103. 15 rms. TV TEL. £70–£100 ($112–$160) double. No service charge. Rates include full breakfast. AE, DC, MC, V. Closed Nov–Mar.

Built in 1819, this rambling, three-story country house has been a hotel since 1948, owned by the Fletcher family. It is situated on 18 acres of gardens and woodlands with a small sandy beach overlooking the water on the western shore of Lough Swilly, 1 mile north of the village. Both the public areas and the guest rooms are decorated with traditional furnishings, period pieces, and oil paintings showing scenes of Donegal. Facilities include a restaurant, lounge, tennis court, squash court, and golf course.

○ Rathmullan House

Lough Swilly, Rathmullan, Co. Donegal. ☎ **800/223-6510** or 800/44-UTELL from the U.S., or 074/58188. Fax 074/58200. 23 rms (21 with bath). TEL. £75–£82.50 ($120–$132) double. Includes full Irish breakfast and service charge. AE, DC, MC, V. Closed Nov to mid-Mar.

Located on the western shores of Lough Swilly about a half mile north of town, this secluded country mansion is surrounded by colorful rose gardens and mature trees. The mostly Georgian interior features intricate ceilings, crystal chandeliers, oil paintings, white marble log-burning fireplaces, and an assortment of antiques and heirlooms collected over the years by owners Bob and Robin Wheeler. The guest rooms vary in size and style of furnishings, but most have a comfortable Irish motif and overlook the lake and gardens. The restaurant, housed in a glass-enclosed pavilion crowned by a flowing silk Arabian-tent design, specializes in seafood. Light snacks and refreshment can be found in an atmospheric cellar bar. House facilities include an indoor heated saltwater swimming pool, sauna, steam room, drawing room, well-stocked library, private beach, and equipment for boating and sea-trout fishing.

Rosapenna Golf Hotel

Atlantic Dr., Downings, Co. Donegal. ☎ **800/528-1234** from the U.S., or 074/55301. Fax 074/55128. 46 rms. TV TEL. £85–£95 ($136–$152) standard double. Deluxe rooms £15 ($24) extra. Service charge 12.5%. Rates include full breakfast. AE, DC, MC, V. Closed Nov to late Mar.

Surrounded by Sheephaven Bay and the hills of Donegal, this contemporary two-story hotel is a favorite with golfers, who flock here to enjoy the hotel's 18-hole seaside course. Nongolfers come just for the scenery and seclusion, as well as for the hotel's proximity to northern Donegal attractions. Other amenities include two all-weather tennis courts and windsurfing. The bedrooms, dining area, and lounges are all modern, with an emphasis on panoramic views of land and sea.

INEXPENSIVE

Ostan Na Rosann/Hotel of the Rosses

Dungloe, Co. Donegal ☎ **075/21088.** Fax 075/21365. 48 rms. TV TEL. £40–£50 ($65–$77.50) double. Service charge 10%. Rates include full breakfast. AE, DC, MC, V. Closed Jan–Mar.

On a hill overlooking the waters of the Atlantic, this modern ranch-style hotel sits in the heart of the Rosses, a scenic Gaelic-speaking area. The guest rooms have standard furnishings with light floral fabrics and wide-windowed views of the sea. A popular hotel with Irish families, it offers a dining room, lounge, nightclub with disco dancing, indoor heated swimming pool, Jacuzzi, steam room, sauna, and gym.

DINING
MODERATE

✪ Water's Edge

The Ballyboe, Rathmullan, Co. Donegal. ☎ **074/58182.** Reservations recommended for dinner. Bar menu, all items, £1.20–£5.25 ($1.90–$8.40); main courses £6–£12.50 ($9.60–$20). MC, V. Easter–Sept daily noon–9:30pm, mid-Oct to mid-Mar Tues–Sun 6–9pm. IRISH/INTERNATIONAL.

As its name implies, this restaurant is situated right on the edge of picturesque Lough Swilly, on the south end of town. Although the glassy facade on three sides gives the 70-seat dining area a modern look, the interior is actually quite traditional, with beamed ceilings, an open fireplace, nautical bric-a-brac, and watercolors of Donegal landscapes. The menu blends Irish dishes with such international favorites as wild salmon in brandy-bisque sauce, chicken Kiev, prawns Provençale, and steaks. Bar food, served all day, ranges from soups and sandwiches to pâtés, scampi, and fish and chips.

EVENING ENTERTAINMENT

Almost all the pubs in this Irish-speaking area provide spontaneous sessions of Irish traditional music in summer. Two places known for music are the **Lakeside Centre,** Dunlewey (☎ **075/31699**), and **Leo's Tavern,** Meenaleck, Crolly (☎ **075/48143**). The highly successful Irish group Clannad and singer Enya got their start at Leo's.

5 Inishowen Peninsula

Buncrana, the Inishowen's chief town, is 70 miles NE of Donegal Airport, 52 miles NE of Donegal Town, 12 miles NW of Derry, 90 miles NE of Sligo, 223 miles NE of Shannon, and 161 miles NW of Dublin.

GETTING TO & AROUND THE INISHOWEN PENINSULA The **Lough Swilly Bus Company** (☎ 074/22853) operates a regular service from Buncrana to Cardonagh and Moville, with connections to other points.

The best way to get to and around the Inishowen Peninsula is by car, following the signposted 100-mile Inishowen 100 route.

VISITOR INFORMATION Contact the **North West Tourism Office,** Aras Reddan, Temple Street, Sligo (☎ 071/61201); the **Letterkenny Tourist Office,** Derry Road, Letterkenny (☎ 074/21173); or the **Inishowen Tourism Office,** Chapel Street, Cardonagh, Co. Donegal (☎ 077/74933). The first two are open year-round; the third office is open from May through September.

AREA CODES   The area codes for telephone numbers in this region are **074** and **077.**

ATTRACTIONS

Bounded by Lough Swilly on the left and Lough Foyle on the right, the Inishowen is a triangular peninsula stretching from Bridgend to Ireland's most northerly point, Malin Head on the Atlantic Ocean.

The Inishowen gets its name from Eoghain, a son of King Niall of the Nine Hostages, who lived at the time of St. Patrick in the 5th century ("Inis Eoghain" means "the island of Owen"). The king named this amazing finger of land for his son.

To drive around the Inishowen is to traverse a ring of seascapes, mountains, valleys, and woodlands. It's been said that Donegal is a miniature Ireland; just so, it's claimed by Donegal folk that Inishowen is a miniature Donegal.

In spite of its remote location, the Inishowen Peninsula circuit is one the best-marked roads in Ireland, with all directionals clearly printed in English and Irish, as well as in miles and kilometers. Among the many features of this 100-mile route is a string of beach resorts like Ballyliffin, Buncrana, Greencastle, and Moville. It's natural wonders include the **Gap of Mamore,** five miles north of Buncrana, a pass rising to 800 feet and then slowly descending on a corkscrew path to sea level, and **Slieve Snacht,** a 2,019-foot mountain.

The peninsula's most impressive historic monument is the hilltop fort known as ✪ **Grianan of Aileach,** 10 miles south of Buncrana. One of the best examples of a ring fort in all Ireland, it was built as a temple of the sun around 1700 B.C. From the mid–5th century to the early 12th it was the royal residence of the O'Neills, the kings of this area.

After you've toured the Inishowen, or perhaps stayed a few days, head back south, driving through Letterkenny, the largest town in the county (population 5,000), located on a hillside overlooking the River Swilly. There, you can link up with N56, the main road, and drive to the junction of the twin towns of Ballybofey and Stranorlar, changing here to N15. This will take you to yet another scenic Donegal drive, the **Barnesmore Gap,** a vast open stretch through the Blue Stack Mountains, which, in turn, will lead you into Donegal Town and points south.

Fort Dunree

Buncrana, Co. Donegal. ☎ **077/61817.** Admission £1.50 ($2.40) adults, 75p ($1.20) seniors and children. June–Sept Tues–Sat 10am–6pm, Sun 12:30–6pm. Signposted on the coast road N of Buncrana.

Perched on a cliff overlooking Lough Swilly, this is a military/naval museum incorporating a Napoleonic martello tower at the site of World War I defenses on the north Irish coast. It features a wide range of exhibitions, an audiovisual center, and a cafeteria housed in a restored forge. Even if you have no interest in military history, it's worth a trip here for the view. Dunree has one of the best vantage points in Donegal for unencumbered seascapes and broad mountain vistas.

Tullyarvan Mill

Off Main St., Buncrana, Co. Donegal. ☎ **077/61613.** Admission to museum £1.50 ($2.40) adults, 75p ($1.20) seniors, students, and children over age 6; music evenings £3 ($4.50). Easter–Sept Mon–Sat 10am–6pm, Sun 2–6pm; music, Thurs evenings in Aug at 9pm.

Housed in an old mill on the northern edge of town, this is the cultural and exhibition center of the Inishowen Peninsula. The building includes a textile museum and other interpretive displays on the crafts and the wildlife of the region. On summer evenings, a program of traditional music and dancing is presented. There's a coffee shop and a craft shop with items made in the area.

Vintage Car & Carriage Museum

Buncrana, Co. Donegal. ☎ **077/61130.** Admission £1.50 ($2.40) adults, 50p (80¢) children. May–Sept daily 10am–8pm; Oct–Apr Sun noon–5pm.

Transportation of yesteryear is the theme of this museum, which houses a large collection of classic cars, horse-drawn carriages, Victorian bicycles, and vintage motorcycles, as well as model-car and railway exhibits.

SPORTS & OUTDOOR PURSUITS

BEACHES Ballyliffin, Buncrana, Greencastle, and Moville have safe and sandy beaches that are ideal for swimming or walking.

GOLF Donegal's northern coast is believed to be one of the first places where golf was ever played in Ireland, and it's been played on the Inishowen for more than 100 years.

The Inishowen has three 18-hole golf courses. The **Ballyliffin Golf Club,** Ballyliffin, Co. Donegal (☎ 077/76119), the most northerly golf course in Ireland, is a par-71 links course with greens fees of £8 ($12.80) on weekdays and £12 ($19.20) on weekends. The **North West Golf Club,** Fahan, Buncrana, Co. Donegal (☎ 077/61027), founded in 1890, is a par-69 seaside course with greens fees of £10 ($16) on weekdays and £15 ($24) on weekends. **Greencastle Golf Course,** Greencastle, Co. Donegal (☎ 077/81013), is a par-69 parkland course with greens fees of £9 ($14.40) on weekdays and £13 ($20.80) on weekends.

WATERSPORTS The Inishowen's long coastline, sandy beaches, and combination of open ocean and sheltered coves offer great opportunities for watersports. Additionally, the northwest coast presents some of the most challenging surfing conditions in the world. For advice and specific information, contact the local **Irish Surfing Association** (☎ 072/51261).

ACCOMMODATIONS
MODERATE

Mount Errigal

Derry Rd., Ballyraine, Letterkenny, Co. Donegal. ☎ **074/22700.** Fax 077/25085. 82 rms. TV TEL. £66–£84 ($105.60–$134.40) double. No service charge. Rates include full breakfast. AE, DC, MC, V.

Located south of Lough Swilly and less than a mile east of town, this contemporary two-story hotel is a handy place to stay midway between the Inishowen Peninsula and Donegal Town, within 20 miles of Glenveagh National Park. Although the exterior has a rather ordinary gray facade, the inside is bright and airy, with skylights, light woods, hanging plants, colored and etched glass, and brass fixtures. The bedrooms are outfitted in contemporary style, with cheerful colors and modern art, as well as good reading lights over the beds, hair dryers, garment presses, and teamakers. Dining and entertainment choices include the full-service Glengesh Restaurant and the Buffet Counter coffee shop. The old-world lounge, Blue Stack Bar, offers piano music Monday through Thursday and live bands on the weekends. Hotel facilities include an indoor heated swimming pool, sauna, steam room, and gym.

Redcastle Hotel

Redcastle, Moville, Co. Donegal. ☎ **077/82073.** Fax 077/82214. 31 rms (26 with bath). TV TEL. £50–£70 ($80–$112) double. No service charge. Rates include full breakfast. AE, DC, MC, V.

Set on the shores of Lough Foyle on the Inishowen's eastern coast, this country inn–style hotel offers a combination of old-world charms and modern comforts. The guest rooms are furnished with designer fabrics, and each has a view of the lake or the adjacent golf course. In-room hair dryers and tea/coffeemakers are also supplied. The public areas include a coffee shop, a lounge, and the Art Gallery Restaurant, offering views and contemporary art. Facilities include a nine-hole golf course, two swimming pools, Jacuzzi, sauna, steam room, gym, and tennis court.

INEXPENSIVE

Hotel Clanree

Derry Rd., Ballaghderg, Letterkenny, Co. Donegal. ☎ **074/24369.** Fax 074/25389. 21 rms. TV TEL. £50–£60 ($80–$96) double. No service charge. Rates include full breakfast. AE, MC, V.

Opened in 1992, this contemporary red-brick two-story hotel sits on the main road near the tourist office at the eastern edge of town. It's a good central location midway between the Inishowen Peninsula and Donegal Town, within 20 miles of Glenveagh National Park. The public rooms have been designed in Irish traditional style, with dark woods and rich colors, while the guest rooms have standard furnishings with scenes of Donegal and multitoned fabrics. In-room amenities include a hospitality tray, hair dryer, and garment press. Dining facilities include the Aileach Room Restaurant and Tara Lounge Bar.

✪ Strand

Ballyliffin, Clonmany, Co. Donegal. ☎ **077/76107.** Fax 077/76486. 12 rms. TV TEL. £50 ($80) double. No service charge. Rates include full breakfast. MC, V. Closed Dec.

Set on a hillside overlooking Pollan Strand, with views of nearby Malin Head, this small family run hotel is located on the edge of town, set apart amid its own palm tree–lined rose gardens. The decor is modern Irish, with wide windows and traditional touches. Guest rooms have standard furnishings with such extras as tea/coffeemakers and hair dryers. Amenities include a good restaurant and a lounge bar known for its local entertainment.

DINING
EXPENSIVE/MODERATE

Restaurant St. Johns

Fahan, Co. Donegal. ☎ **077/60289.** Reservations required. Fixed-price dinner £20–£24 ($32–$38.40). AE, DC, MC, V. Tues–Sat 6–10pm. IRISH.

Set on its own grounds overlooking Lough Swilly, this lovely Georgian house has two dining rooms, each with a cozy elegance. Open turf fireplaces, Waterford crystal, embroidered linens, and richly textured wallpaper add to the ambience. Best of all, the food is dependably good—baked Swilly salmon with lemon sauce, roast duck with port-and-orange sauce, spiced lamb en croûte with gooseberry-and-mint sauce, and John Dory with fennel.

INEXPENSIVE

Kealy's Seafood Bar

Greencastle, Co. Donegal. ☎ **077/81010.** Reservations not necessary. Bar food, all items £1–£5 ($1.60–$8). MC, V. Tues–Sun 12:30–5pm. SEAFOOD.

For a light meal or snack overlooking Lough Foyle and the fishing boats belonging to the Foyle Fishermen's Co-op, try this little harbor-front eatery. Menu items include Greencastle seafood chowder, local oysters, smoked-salmon salad, deep-fried plaice, southern-fried chicken, sandwiches, lasagna, and burgers.

15 Along the River Shannon's Shores

No matter where you find yourself in Ireland's midlands, you're never far from the Shannon. It is Ireland's fluid, winding spine, dividing east from west, flowing through lowland fields and bogs, and communing with countless lakes and lesser rivers. Although constantly moving, the Shannon is the immovable constant by which we take our bearings in Ireland's heartland.

At 230 miles in length, the Shannon is the longest river in Ireland or Great Britain. It influences and defines more of the Irish landscape than any other body of water. Rising in Co. Cavan, it flows south through the heartland of Ireland, touching nine other counties—Leitrim, Roscommon, Longford, Westmeath, Offaly, Galway, Tipperary, Clare, and Limerick—before reaching its mouth and separating Counties Kerry and Clare as the Shannon estuary waters meet the Atlantic.

The Shannon takes many shapes and forms as it flows through the Irish landscape. At some points it's almost 10 miles across; at others it narrows to a few hundred yards. For centuries the river was primarily a means of transportation and commerce, Ireland's most ancient highway; more recently it's chiefly been a source of enjoyment and recreation.

The river can be divided into three segments: the Lower Shannon and Lough Derg, stretching from Killaloe to Portumna; the Middle Shannon, a narrow passage from the Birr/Banagher area to Athlone; and the Upper Shannon, from Lough Ree to Lough Allen and the river's source in Co. Cavan. In this chapter we explore the river from the south end, working our way northward. This is not to imply the river flows in that direction; rather, it's to help you start off touring in the area where there's the greatest number of things to do and see.

While it's unlikely that you will follow the Shannon for all of its 214 navigable miles, you'll encounter it in almost every cross-country route you take. So, whether you trace or cross its path, it makes sense here to point out some of the many delights to be found along and nearby the Shannon's shores.

1 Lower Shannon: The Lough Derg Drive

Killaloe is 16 miles NE of Limerick and 25 miles E of Ennis; Portumna is 40 miles SE of Galway and 27 miles E of Gort.

The River Shannon's Shores

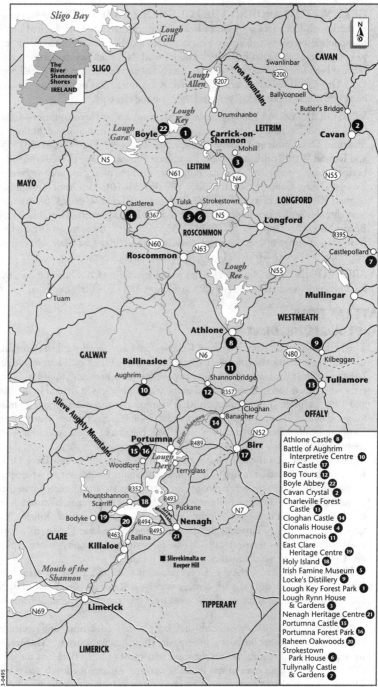

Athlone Castle ⑧
Battle of Aughrim
   Interpretive Centre ⑩
Birr Castle ⑰
Bog Tours ⑫
Boyle Abbey ㉒
Cavan Crystal ②
Charleville Forest
   Castle ⑬
Cloghan Castle ⑭
Clonalis House ④
Clonmacnois ⑪
East Clare
   Heritage Centre ⑲
Holy Island ⑱
Irish Famine Museum ⑤
Locke's Distillery ⑨
Lough Key Forest Park ①
Lough Rynn House
   & Gardens ③
Nenagh Heritage Centre ㉑
Portumna Castle ⑮
Portumna Forest Park ⑯
Raheen Oakwoods ⑳
Strokestown
   Park House ⑥
Tullynally Castle
   & Gardens ⑦

3-0495

447

GETTING TO & AROUND THE LOUGH DERG AREA   The best way to get to the Lough Derg area is by car or boat. Although there are some limited public transportation services, you'll need a car to get around the lake. Major roads that lead to Lough Derg are the main Limerick-Dublin road (N7) from points east and south, N6 and N65 from Galway and the west, and N52 from northerly points. The Lough Derg Drive itself, which is well signposted, is a combination of R352 on the west bank of the lake and R493, R494, and R495 on the east bank.

VISITOR INFORMATION   Since Lough Derg unites three counties—Clare, Galway, and Tipperary—there are several sources of information, including the **Shannon Development Tourism Group,** Shannon, Co. Clare (☎ **061/361555**), and **Ireland West Tourism,** Victoria Place, Eyre Square, Galway (☎ **091/563081**), both of which are open year-round. Seasonal information offices include the **Nenagh Tourist Office,** Connolly Street, Nenagh (☎ **067/31610**), open April through September; **Killaloe Tourist Office,** The Bridge, Co. Clare (☎ **061/376866**), open May through September; **Tipperary Lake Side & Development,** The Old Church, Borrisokane, Co. Tipperary (☎ **067/27155**); open May through August; and the **East Clare Tourist & Development Association,** Holiday East Clare, Drewsboro, Scarriff, Co. Clare (☎ **061/921433**), open May through September.

AREA CODES   The area codes for this region are **061** for Co. Clare numbers, **067** for Tipperary numbers, and **0509** for Co. Galway and Co. Offaly numbers.

ATTRACTIONS
THE LOUGH DERG DRIVE

The Lower Shannon, stretching from Killaloe, Co. Clare, northward to Portumna, Co. Galway, encompasses one huge lake, **Lough Derg.** Often called an inland sea, Lough Derg was the main inland waterway trading route between Dublin and Limerick when canal and river commercial traffic was at its height in Ireland in the 18th and 19th centuries. It is the Shannon River's largest lake and widest point: 25 miles long and almost 10 miles wide, with more than 25,000 acres of water. Today Lough Derg can be described as Ireland's pleasure lake, because of all the recreational and sporting opportunities it provides.

The road that rims the lake for a perimeter of 95 miles, the **Lough Derg Drive,** is one of the most scenic routes in Ireland, a continuous natural setting where panoramas of hilly farmlands, gentle mountains, bucolic forests, and glistening waters are unspoiled by condominiums, billboards, and other signs of commercialization. Most of all, the drive is a collage of colorful shoreline towns, starting with Killaloe, Co. Clare, and Ballina, Co. Tipperary, on the south banks of the lake. They're called twin towns because they're usually treated as one intertwined community—only a splendid 13-arch bridge over the Shannon separates them.

Killaloe is home to Ireland's largest inland marina and a host of watersport centers. Of historical note is a 9th-century oratory, said to have been founded by St. Lua—hence the name Killaloe, which comes from the Irish: *Cill* (meaning "church") of Lua.

Nearby is another oratory and cathedral, built in the 12th century and named for 6th-century St. Flannan; it boasts an exquisite Romanesque doorway. **Kincora,** on the highest ground at Killaloe, was the royal settlement of Brian Boru and the other O'Brien kings, but no trace of any building remains. Killaloe is a lovely town with lakeside views at almost every turn and many fine restaurants/pubs offering outdoor seating on the shoreline.

Five miles inland from Lough Derg's lower southeast shores is **Nenagh,** the chief town of north Tipperary, lying in a fertile valley between the Silvermine and Arra Mountains.

On the north shore of the lake is **Portumna,** which means "the landing place of the oak tree." A major point of traffic across the Shannon, Portumna has a lovely forest park and a remarkable castle that's currently being restored.

The rest of the Lough Derg Drive is scattered with memorable little towns and harborside villages like **Mountshannon** and **Dromineer.** Some, like **Terryglass** and **Woodford,** are known for atmospheric old pubs wherein spontaneous sessions of traditional Irish music are likely to occur. Others, like **Puckane** or **Ballinderry,** offer unique crafts or locally made products.

The Lough Derg Drive is the Shannon River at its best.

Portumna Castle

Off N65, Portumna, Co. Galway. No phone. Free admission to gardens. Daily 8am–4pm.

Built in 1609 by Earl Richard Burke, this castle on the northern shores of Lough Derg is said to have been one of the finest 17th-century manor houses ever built in Ireland. It was accidentally gutted by fire in 1826, but its Dutch-style decorative gables and rows of stone mullioned windows were spared. Although the castle is currently being restored and is not accessible to the public, the surrounding gardens and lawns are open to visitors.

Portumna Forest Park

Off N65, Portumna, Co. Galway. No phone. Admission £1 ($1.60) adults. Daily dawn–dusk.

On the shores of Lough Derg, this 1,400-acre park is east of the town, off the main road. It offers miles of nature trails and signposted walks, plus viewing points and picnic areas.

East Clare Heritage Centre / Holy Island Tours

Tuamgraney, Co. Clare. ☎ **061/921351.** Admission to Centre £1 ($1.60) adults, 50p (80¢) children; Holy Island Tours £5 ($8) adults, £3 ($4.80) children. Centre, May–Sept Mon–Sat 9am–5pm, Sun 1–5pm; Holy Island Tours, May–Sept 11am–3pm, weather permitting. Off the Portumna-Ennis road (R352).

Housed in the restored 10th-century church of St. Cronan, this center explains the heritage and history of the East Clare area through a series of exhibits and an audiovisual presentation. In addition, a pier across the road from the center is the starting point for a 15-minute boating excursion to nearby Inishcealtra (Holy Island), in Lough Derg. The trip includes a 45-minute guided tour of the island.

Nenagh Heritage Centre

Off Kickham St., Nenagh, Co. Tipperary. ☎ **067/32633.** Admission £2.50 ($4) adult, £1 ($1.60) seniors, students and children, £4 ($6.40) family. Mid-May through Sept Mon–Fri 10am–5pm, Sun 2:30–5pm.

Models of the whole Lough Derg area, with its main port villages, are on display at this center, 5 miles east of the lakeshore. Located in two stone buildings dating from about 1840, this site was once a jail, then a convent and a school. Now, as a museum, it showcases collections of local arts, crafts, photography, and memorabilia. It's also the family history research center for northern Tipperary.

SIGHTSEEING CRUISES

R&B Marine Services Ltd.

Derg Marina, Killaloe, Co. Clare. ☎ **061/376364.** £5 ($7.50) adults, £3 ($4.50) children, £14 ($7.50) family. May–Sept daily at 3pm.

Enjoy a cruise of Lough Derg on board the 48-seat *Derg Princess*, a covered river bus. Departing from Killaloe marina, the cruise takes one hour, traveling past the fort of Brian Boru and into Lough Derg.

Shannon Sailing Ltd.

New Harbour, Dromineer, Nenagh, Co. Tipperary. ☎ **067/24499**. £5 ($8) adults, £3 ($4.80) children. May–Sept daily; schedule varies.

This company operates a covered 53-seat water bus, the *Ku-ee-tu*, sailing from the southeastern shore of Lough Derg at Dromineer on a 1¹/₂-hour cruise with full commentary on local sights.

SPORTS & OUTDOOR PURSUITS

CRUISING   The following companies rent cabin cruisers along this section of the Shannon: **R&B Marine Services Ltd.,** Derg Marina, Killaloe, Co. Clare (☎ **061/376364**); **Emerald Star Line,** The Marina, Portumna, Co. Galway (☎ **0509/41120**); **Shannon Castle Line,** The Marina, Williamstown, Co. Clare (☎ **061/927042**); and **Shannon Sailing,** The Marina, Dromineer, Co. Tipperary (☎ **067/24295**). The craft range from two to eight berths; rates average £60 to £100 ($96 to $160) per person per week.

FISHING   Often called an angler's paradise, Lough Derg has good stocks of brown trout, pike, bream, and perch. Fish ranging in weight from 36 to 90 pounds have been caught in this lake. Brown trout average one to six pounds. For tackle and guidance on local fishing, visit one of these shops: **Eddie Fahey,** Ballyminogue, Scariff, Co. Clare (☎ **061/921019**); **Norrie Guerin,** Ivy House, Mountshannon, Co. Clare (☎ **061/927184**); **Whelan's,** Summerhill, Nenagh, Co. Tipperary (☎ **067/31301**); **D&H Clarke Ltd.,** Portumna, Co. Galway (☎ **0509/41049**); and the **Open Season Shop,** Friar Street, Nenagh, Co. Tipperary (☎ **0509/41071**).

GOLF   Lovely parkland and woodland golfing in the Lough Derg area is offered at 18-hole clubs such as **Portumna Golf Club,** Portumna, Co. Galway (☎ **0509/41059**), with greens fees of £10 ($16), and **Nenagh Golf Club,** Beechwood, Nenagh (☎ **067/31476**), with greens fees of £12 ($19.20) on weekdays and £15 ($24) on weekends. In addition, the **East Clare Golf Club,** Scariff/Killaloe Road, Bodyke, Co. Clare (☎ **061/921322**), is expanding from nine holes to an 18-hole championship course.

SWIMMING   Lough Derg is known for clear and unpolluted water that's ideal for swimming, particularly at Castle Lough, Dromineer, and Portumna Bay. Portumna Bay has changing rooms and showers.

WALKING   There are some excellent walks in Portumna Forest Park, Raheen Woods, and along the shoreline of Lough Derg. Also, for a touch of scenic wilderness, walk a portion of the Slieve Bloom Way, a circular 21-mile signposted trail that begins and ends in Glenbarrow, Co. Laois.

WATERSPORTS   Watersports are the pièce de résistance of a visit to Lough Derg. If you enjoy boating, tubing, waterskiing, windsurfing, canoeing, or other water-based sports, this is the place for you. Here are a few of the businesses that specialize in these activities.

Lough Derg Sailing

Mountshannon Harbour, Mountshannon, Co. Clare. ☎ **061/927131**. £10 ($16) for two hours, £35 ($56) per day. May–Sept daily; times of departure by appointment.

With its nontidal waters and numerous bays, islands, and harbors, Lough Derg is ideal for sailing. This company offers daily sailing trips on the 29-foot yacht

Sangazure, with instruction and training on board. The activities are especially geared toward beginners who want to learn the basics of sailing.

Haskett's Boat Hire
At the bridge, Killaloe, Co. Clare. ☎ **061/376693.** £7 ($11.20) per hour or £30 ($48) per day. June–Sept daily 10am–6pm or later.

Located opposite the tourist office, this firm rents 19-foot lake boats with outboard motors for fishing or pleasure cruising. If you hire a boat for a minimum of two hours, you get two complimentary Irish coffees at a nearby pub.

Whelan's Boat Hire
At the bridge, Killaloe, Co. Clare. ☎ **061/376159.** £6 ($9.60) per hour or £25 ($40) per day. June–Aug daily 9am–9pm.

Whelan's rents 19-foot lake boats with outboard engines for sightseeing or fishing in the waters of Lough Derg. Prices include fuel, fishing gear, and rainwear.

Watersports Lough Derg
Two Mile Gate, Killaloe, Co. Clare. ☎ **088/588430** (mobile phone). Waterskiing from £12 ($19.20), speedboat rides from £3 ($4.80) per person, tubing from £6 ($9.60), Jet Skis from £12 ($19.20). May–Oct daily 11am–dusk.

This outdoor center offers waterskiing, speed boat rides, tubing, and Jet Skiing.

SHOPPING

Eugene & Anke McKernan
Handweavers, Main St., Tuamgraney, Co. Clare. ☎ **061/921527.**

A husband-and-wife team, Eugene and Anke offer a colorful array of distinctive tweed scarves, jackets, vests, and blankets. The couple hand-weaves all items on the premises, which were formerly police barracks. Visitors are welcomed to the workshop to see the weaving process. Open daily May through September; hours vary October through April.

Lakeshore Foods Factory Shop
Coolbawn, Ballinderry Village, Nenagh, Co. Tipperary. ☎ **067/22094.**

Originally the village forge, this old building was restored and converted into a small factory and shop for fine mustards, sauces, and dressings. It's on the Lough Derg Drive, between the villages of Puckane and Terryglass.

Old Church Craft Shop & Gallery
The Old Church, R493, Terryglass, Co. Tipperary. ☎ **067/22209.**

Built on the site of the original abbey of St. Columba (A.D. 549), this current stone-faced building dates from 1838. Transformed into a craft shop in 1984, it is a treasure trove of locally produced crafts and products, such as Terryglass pottery, Rathbone traditional beeswax candles, Irish bonsai plants, bog oak pendants, wildlife mobiles, boxwood products from Birr castle, Jerpoint glass, decorated horseshoes, miniature watercolors of Shannon River scenes, and books about the Shannon. The gallery has watercolors by artist/owner Jenny Boelens on permanent display. Open Tuesday to Saturday from 10am to 6pm and Sunday from noon to 6pm.

Walsh Crafts
R493, Puckane, Nenagh, Co. Tipperary. ☎ **067/24229.**

A rustic thatched-roof cottage, complete with traditional half-door, serves as the workshop for Paddy Walsh, a craftsman who carves and paints on natural wood. His works depict Ireland past and present, with Celtic and rural scenes and pieces with heraldic and religious themes. The pieces range from pendant-size figurines and symbols—such as St. Patrick, the harp, or a dove—to portrait-size scenes of Irish music sessions, pub facades and interiors, farmyards, cottages, castles, sporting events, and Christmas tableaux. The craft is ingenious and truly Irish, a great souvenir. Visitors are welcome to watch Paddy and his staff as they carve the wood and then paint the colorful motifs. Open daily from 9:30am to 6pm or later.

ACCOMMODATIONS
MODERATE
Dromineer Bay Hotel

Dromineer Bay, Nenagh, Co. Tipperary. ☎ **067/24114.** Fax 067/24288. 24 rms. £58–£70 ($92.80–$112) double. No service charge. Rates include full breakfast. AE, DC, MC, V.

Tucked along the shores of Lough Derg beside the Dromineer Yacht Club, this two-story hotel has long been a favorite with fishermen and now also appeals to tourists seeking an informal riverside retreat. More than 100 years old, it was originally a coast guard inn. Recently expanded and renovated by innkeepers Denis and Lily Collison, the rooms are small and simply furnished, although some have four-poster beds and antiques. Facilities include the Moorings restaurant, open for dinner; the Boat House bar / coffee shop / delicatessen for snacks and lunch; and the Captain's Deck Bar, with an open-air deck upstairs offering fine views of the water. For a little local color, browse the bar walls; they're decorated with photographs telling the history of the hotel and the village.

Gurthalougha House

Ballinderry, Terryglass, Nenagh, Co. Tipperary. ☎ **800/223-6510** from the U.S., or 067/22080. Fax 067/22154. 8 rms. TV TEL. £64–£76 ($102.40–$121.60) double. No service charge. Rates include full breakfast. AE, MC, V. Fully open Mar–Oct; open weekends Nov–Jan.

A mile-long winding driveway leads through 150 acres of forest to this two-story early 19th-century Georgian house, set on the northwest edge of Lough Derg. Originally a hunting lodge, it's built around a cobbled courtyard bursting with flowers. The public areas include an antique-filled drawing room, a library, and a dining room, all of which have views of the lake across to the mountains of Clare and Galway. Guest rooms are individually decorated with period pieces and antiques. Innkeeper/chef Michael Wilkinson is known for his innovative country-house cooking; sumptuous breakfasts are brought to the guest rooms or served beside the peat fire in the dining room. Facilities include two hard tennis courts, signposted woodland walks, use of boats and Windsurfers, swimming from the jetty, and croquet; fishing can be arranged for an extra fee. Children and dogs are accepted by prior arrangement.

Lakeside Hotel

Killaloe, Co. Clare. ☎ **800/447-7462** from the U.S., or 061/376122. Fax 061/376431. 45 rms. TV TEL. £55–£85 ($88–$136) double. No service charge. Rates include full breakfast. AE, DC, MC, V.

Perched on the southern banks of Lough Derg and shaded by ancient trees, this two-story country house–style hotel has one of the loveliest settings of any property in the area. It was completely refurbished in 1994 in a bright contemporary style. The guest rooms have standard furnishings but are greatly enhanced by wide-windowed views of the lake or gardens. Nine superior family suites are available. The facilities include a restaurant and bar lounge overlooking the Shannon, an indoor heated swimming pool with water slide, Jacuzzi, sauna, gym, steam room, and tennis court. The hotel is on the Ballina side of the bridge, on the edge of town next to the marina.

INEXPENSIVE

Lantern House

Ogonnelloe, Tuamgraney, Co. Clare. ☎ **061/923034.** Fax 061/923139. 9 rms. TV TEL. £38–£40 ($60.80–$64) double. Rates include full breakfast. AE, DC, MC, V. Mid-Feb to Nov.

This modern guest house, where guests receive a warm welcome from proprietors Liz and Phil Hogan, overlooks wide vistas on Lough Derg. Palm trees grow on the well-tended high grounds. All the public rooms overlook the Shannon, as do some of the bedrooms. Furnishings are comfortable and "home-style." The cozy lounge has a fireplace, and residents can enjoy a drink at a small bar. The accompanying restaurant is widely acclaimed (see "Dining," below). Lantern House is 6 miles north of Killaloe on the main road.

Portumna Park Hotel

Portumna, Co. Galway. ☎ **0509/41121.** Fax 0509/41357. 29 rms. TV TEL. £50 ($80) double. No service charge. Rates include full breakfast. DC, MC, V.

Set back from the main road in a garden setting on the western edge of Portumna, this contemporary, rambling, ranch-style inn is the prime hotel on Lough Derg's north shore. Under new ownership and totally refurbished in 1994, it offers standard guest rooms with light woods, floral fabrics, and floor-to-ceiling windows. Most rooms look out on the surrounding gardens and forest. A patio has outdoor seating. The public areas include a chalet-style restaurant with a knotty-pine decor and an old-world pub with paneled walls, lantern lights, and dark-wood trim.

RENT-A-COTTAGE

For an area of such amazing beauty and wide-open spaces, the Lough Derg region has surprisingly few hotels. In many ways, that's part of its alluring attraction— natural lakelands and forests unspoiled by condos, hotels, motels, and fast-food eateries. This area, perhaps more than most other parts of Ireland, calls out for visitors to settle in and become part of the way of life. And that is why the "Rent an Irish Cottage" program was pioneered here almost 30 years ago.

The Shannon Development Company came up with the idea of building small rental cottages in these rural areas where other types of satisfactory accommodations were scarce. The cottages were designed in traditional style, with exteriors of white stucco, thatched roofs, and half-doors, but aside from the turf fireplaces, all of the furnishings, plumbing, heating, and kitchen appliances inside were totally up-to-date. The cottage rental idea was an instant success with Irish people from Dublin and other large cities wanting to get away from it all, and it is becoming equally popular with visitors from abroad who want to live like the locals.

The cottages, built in groups of 8 to 12, are set on picturesque sites in remote villages such as Puckane, Terryglass, and Whitegate, either overlooking or close to Lough Derg's shores. There are no restaurants or bars on site, and guests are encouraged to shop in the local grocery stores and cook their own meals and to congregate in the local pubs each evening. In other words, after a day or two the visitors become part of the community. Rates range from £150 to £450 ($240 to $720) per cottage per week, depending on the size of the cottage (one to four bedrooms) and time of year. Rental rates include bed linen and color TV; metered electricity is extra. For more information, contact **Rent an Irish Cottage plc.,** 85 O'Connell St., Limerick, Co. Limerick (☎ **061/411109;** fax 061/314821).

In recent years, cottages with slate or tile roofs and modern designs have been built by individual owners. One of the loveliest cottage settings belongs to the **Mountshannon Village Cottages,** Mountshannon, Co. Clare, a cluster of nine pastel-toned one- and two-story cottages perched on a hill overlooking Lough Derg at Mountshannon Harbour. Grouped like a private village around a garden court-yard, these cottages cost £130 to £430 ($208 to $688) per week depending on the time of year and number of bedrooms required. Some weekend rentals are also available, from £80 to £220 ($128 to $352) per cottage. For more informa-tion, contact Bridie Cooke, Gortatleva, Bushypark, Galway, Co. Galway (☎ and fax **091/525295).**

DINING
EXPENSIVE/MODERATE

✪ Brocka-on-the-Water
Kilgarvan Quay, Nenagh, Co. Tipperary. ☎ **067/22038.** Reservations required. Fixed-price din-ner £24 ($38.40). No credit cards. May–Oct Mon–Sat 7–9:30pm. INTERNATIONAL.

A small country lane, signposted off the Lough Derg Drive, leads to this country-house restaurant in a garden setting near the shores of Lough Derg. Rather than seek-ing waterside views, people flock here for the Byrne family's innovative cuisine and warm hospitality. You'll also delight in the antique furnishings. Each table is set with Waterford crystal lamps, Newbridge silver, hand-embroidered linens, and fresh flow-ers. The menu changes nightly, but specialties often include baked stuffed sole with a sauce of dill and lemon cream, panfried sirloin steak Gaelic-style (flamed in whis-key), ribbons of chicken breast with root ginger and honey, and pork medaillons with herb bread crumbs and plum sauce. Many of the dishes are decorated with or use fresh edible flowers from the garden as part of the recipe. To finish off the meal, don't miss the carragin mousse or farmhouse cheeses from local farms.

MODERATE

Goosers
Killaloe/Ballina, Co. Clare. ☎ **061/376791.** Reservations recommended for dinner. Bar food, all items £2–£9.50 ($3.20–$15.20); fixed-price lunch £14.50 ($23.20); dinner main courses £12.50–£21 ($20–$33.60). MC, V. Daily 11am–11pm. IRISH.

With a thatched roof and bright mustard-colored exterior, this popular pub/restau-rant sits on the Ballina side of the Shannon, looking out at the river and the broad vista of Killaloe. Its informal two rooms have open fireplaces, stone walls and floors, and beamed ceilings, and its pub area contains window seats, sugan chairs, and lots of nautical and fishing memorabilia. The restaurant has booth seating and windows that overlook an adjacent garden, and there's picnic-table seating outside in good weather. The bar food menu lists the usual standards, including such traditional dishes as bacon and cabbage and Irish stew. The restaurant menu focuses on seafood, lobster, salmon, sole, and monkfish.

Lantern House
Ogonnelloe, Co. Clare. ☎ **061/923034.** Reservations recommended. Main courses £9.50–£14.50 ($15.20–$23.20). AE, MC, V. Mid-Feb to Oct Mon–Sat 6–9:30pm and Sun 6–8:30pm. Closed Mon off-season. IRISH.

Perched high on a hillside amid palm tree–lined gardens just north of Killaloe, this country-house restaurant enjoys panoramic views of Lough Derg and the verdant hills of the surrounding countryside. Host Phil Hogan extends a warm welcome to all comers, and the candlelit dining room exudes old-world charm, with a beamed ceiling, wall lanterns, and lace tablecloths. Menu choices might be poached fresh local salmon, panfried sole, scallops Mornay, or sirloin steaks.

Peter's Restaurant

Killaloe/Ballina, Co. Clare. ☎ **061/376162.** Reservations recommended. Fixed-price lunch £9.50 ($15.20); main courses £8.50–£15 ($13.60–$24). AE, MC, V. Sun 1–3pm, daily 7–10pm. CONTINENTAL.

Set in a restored old railway station, this restaurant sits beside Lough Derg, overlooking the water, on the Ballina side of the Killaloe bridge. The plant-filled conservatory-style room has a patio/terrace for fair-weather dining. The menu offers a variety of steaks as well as such dishes as beef Stroganoff, duck à l'orange, noisettes of lamb, brochette of monkfish, and fillet of trout amandine.

INEXPENSIVE

Irish Molly's

Killaloe/Ballina, Co. Clare. ☎ **061/76632.** Reservations recommended for dinner. All items £1.60–£12.50 ($2.56–$20). AE, MC, V. Daily 12:30–11:30pm. IRISH.

Next to the Killaloe bridge, this brightly colored pub/restaurant offers views of Killaloe Harbour from most of its windows. The informal interior is like that of a comfortable cottage, with beamed ceilings, wall shelves lined with old plates, vintage clocks, pine and mahogany furnishings, period pictures and prints of the Shannon area, and a stove fireplace. The menu offers both light fare and full dinner selections, such as baked Limerick ham, grilled trout amandine, and charcoal-grilled steaks. The open-face fresh crab sandwich on brown bread is especially worth a stop. Outdoor seating is available on picnic-style tables.

PUBS

Although there are public houses in every town around the Lough Derg route, the pubs of Terryglass, Co. Tipperary, on the east shore, and the pubs of Woodford, Co. Galway, on the west shore, are particularly well known for their lively sessions of Irish traditional music.

✪ **The Derg Inn,** Terryglass, Co. Tipperary (☎ 067/22037), with three cozy rooms inside, has a beer garden courtyard. It's worth a visit just to see this pub's decor of Tipperary horse pictures, old plates, books, beer posters, vintage bottles, hanging tankards, and lanterns. However, most people come for the free traditional music on Wednesdays and Sundays.

Paddy's Bar, Terryglass, Co. Tipperary (☎ 067/22147), is known for its fine display of antiques as well as traditional music seven nights a week in summer.

On Lough Derg's western shores, the town of Woodford, Co. Galway, is particularly celebrated as a mecca for Irish traditional music of the old style. Fiddler and tin-whistle player Anthony Coen, born in Woodford of a musical family that includes six traditional musicians out of nine children, is one of the best at his instruments, and is often accompanied by his own talented daughters Dearbhla on the flute and tin whistle and Eimer on the concertina and bodhran. They can often be heard at **J. Walsh's Forest Bar,** Woodford (☎ 0509/49012), or at **Moran's,** Woodford (☎ 0509/49063), overlooking the Woodford River. The latter establishment is a curiosity in itself, since it's probably the only pub in Ireland where you'll find two clerics serving drinks at the bar during summer. Both Carmelite Order priests, they are the sons of the owner and spend their vacation time helping out in the family business. Only in Ireland!

2 Middle Shannon: From Birr to Athlone

Birr is 15 miles E of Portumna; Athlone is 60 miles E of Galway.

GETTING TO & AROUND THE MIDDLE SHANNON   The best way to get to the Middle Shannon area is by car or boat. Although there's public transportation, you'll need a car to get around the river banks. Major roads that lead to this area are the main Galway-Dublin road (N6) from points east and west, N62 from the south, and N55 and N61 from the north.

VISITOR INFORMATION   Information on this area can be obtained year-round from the **Ireland West Tourism Office,** Victoria Place, Eyre Square, Galway (☎ **091/63081**), and the **Midlands Tourism Office,** Clonard House, Dublin Road, Mullingar, Co. Westmeath (☎ **044/48761**). Both are open Monday through Friday from 9am to 6pm and on Saturday during peak season.

Seasonal Tourist Information points are also operated from May or June to September at signposted sites in the following locations: **Athlone** (☎ **0902/94630**); **Aughrim** (☎ **0905/73939**); **Ballinsloe** (☎ **0905/42131**); **Birr** (☎ **0509/20110**); and **Clonmacnois** (☎ **0905/74134**).

AREA CODES   Telephone area codes for this region of the Shannon include **044, 091, 0506, 0509, 0902,** and **0905.**

ATTRACTIONS

The middle section of the Shannon River is the home of one of Ireland's greatest historic sites: the early Christian settlement of **Clonmacnois,** a spot that has been drawing visitors since the 6th century.

This region also includes vast stretches of boglands, as well as the inland town of **Birr,** known for its magnificent and historic gardens, and **Banagher,** a river town with a picturesque harbor.

In addition, this stretch of the river curves into **Athlone,** the largest town on the Shannon and a leading inland marina for mooring and hiring boats. Athlone's other claim to fame is that it produced Ireland's most famous operatic tenor, the great John McCormack.

Birr Castle

Rosse Row, Birr, Co. Offaly. ☎ **0509/20056.** Admission Jan–Mar and Nov–Dec £2.60 ($4.16) adults, £1.30 ($2.10) children over 5; Apr–Oct £3.20 ($5.12) adults, £1.60 ($2.56) children over 5. Jan–Apr and Oct–Dec daily 9am–1pm and 2–5pm; May–Sept daily 9am–6pm. 23 miles SW of Tullamore, via N52.

The main attraction of this inland estate 12 miles east of the river is its 100-acre garden. The demesne of the Parsons family, now the earls of Rosse, the estate is laid out around a lake and along the banks of the two adjacent rivers and contains more than 1,000 species of trees and shrubs, including magnolias, cherry trees, chestnut, and weeping beech. The box hedges are featured in the *Guinness Book of Records* as the tallest in the world, and the hornbeam cloisters are a unique feature. Farther along the path you may combine a bit of star-gazing with the garden stroll, as the grounds also contain an astronomical exhibit, including an 1845 six-foot reflecting telescope, then the largest in the world, built by the third earl of Rosse and currently being restored to form a part of the new Historic Science Centre. As a bonus during summer, you can usually find additional rotating exhibits dealing with the history of Birr Castle and its residents. The 17th-century castle/residence itself is not open to the public.

Cloghan Castle

Lusmagh, Banagher, Co. Offaly. ☎ **0509/51650.** Admission £3.50 ($5.60) adults, £3 ($4.80) seniors, £7.50 ($12) family. June–Sept Wed–Sun 2–6pm.

Located 3 miles south of Banagher, this fortress is said to date from the 13th century and has been inhabited for 800 years. It is currently the home of Brian and Elyse Thompson. The castle structure consists of a large stone keep with walls 10 feet thick in places. A Georgian addition was built around 1800 and other additions accrued over the last 300 years. The keep stands within four stone towers that originally were joined by a huge fortified earthen wall. Guided tours of the interior include a look at the stark medieval stone walls, enhanced by hand-carved oak furniture, and at paintings and accessories from the colorful Georgian period. The great hall is 50 feet long and 40 feet high, with a fine plaster ceiling and galleries at either end. The castle sits in a lovely 60-acre parkland setting that's grazed by a flock of Jacob sheep.

✪ Bog Tours

Bord na Mona / The Irish Peat Board, Blackwater Works, Shannonbridge, Co. Offaly. ☎ **0905/ 74114.** Tours £3 ($4.80) adults, £2.50 ($4) seniors and students, £2 ($3.20) children. Daily 10am–5pm; tours on the hour. Signposted from Shannonbridge.

Bog land discoveries are the focus of this tour in the heart of the Irish midlands on the east bank of the Shannon. Visitors are invited to board the narrow-gauge Clonmacnois and West Offaly Railway for a 5-mile circular ride around the Blackwater bog. The commentary explains how the bog land was formed and became a vital source of fuel for Ireland. The route includes a firsthand look at turf cutting, stacking, and drying, and close-up views of bog plants and wildlife. Participants can even take a turn at digging the turf or pick some bog cotton en route. The ride lasts approximately 45 minutes. The visitor center also offers an audiovisual story about the bog.

Battle of Aughrim Interpretative Centre

Galway-Dublin road (N6), Aughrim, near Ballinasloe, Co. Galway. ☎ **0905/73939.** Admission £3 ($4.80) adults, £2 ($3.20) seniors and students, £1 ($1.60) children, £6 ($8) family. MC, V. Easter to early Oct daily 10am–6pm.

Using a high-tech three-dimensional audiovisual presentation, this center invites visitors to relive July 12, 1691: the Battle of Aughrim. On that day the army of James II of England confronted the forces of his son-in-law, William of Orange, and staged the bloodiest battle in Irish history. The confrontation involved 45,000 soldiers from eight European countries and cost 9,000 lives, changing the course of Irish and European history. The center, which also houses a bookshop, craft shop, and cafe, is in Aughrim village and adjacent to the actual Aughrim battlefield, which is now signposted for visitors. Aughrim is situated on the main Dublin-Galway road, about 12 miles west of the Shannonbridge/Clonmacnois area.

✪ Clonmacnois

Shannonbridge, Co. Offaly. ☎ **0905/74195.** Admission £2.50 ($4) adults, £1.75 ($2.80) seniors, £1 ($1.60) students and children, £6 ($9.60) family. Mid-Mar to mid-May and Sept–Oct daily 10am–6pm; mid-May to early Sept daily 9am–7pm; Nov to mid-Mar daily 10am–5:30pm. On R357, 4 miles N of Shannonbridge.

Resting silently on the east bank of the Shannon, this is one of Ireland's most profound ancient sites. The monastic community of Clonmacnois was founded in 548 by St. Ciaran at the crucial intersection of the Shannon and the Dublin-Galway land route and soon became one of Europe's great centers of learning and culture. For nearly 1,000 years Clonmacnois flourished under the patronage of numerous Irish kings. The last high king, Rory O'Conor, was buried here in 1198. In the course of time, Clonmacnois was raided repeatedly by native chiefs, Danes, and Anglo-Normans, until it was finally abandoned in 1552. Today's visitor can see the remains of a cathedral, a castle, eight churches, two round towers, three sculpted high crosses, and more than 200 monumental slabs. The site includes an exemplary visitors center with a beautifully designed exhibition, a first-rate audiovisual program, and pleasant tearooms.

Athlone Castle

Athlone, Co. Westmeath. ☎ **0902/92912.** Admission £2.20 ($3.50) adults, £1.60 ($2.55) students, 80p ($1.30) children to age 12. May–Sept Mon–Sat 10am–5pm, Sun noon–5pm.

Built in 1210 for King John of England, this mighty stone fortress sits on the edge of the Shannon. It played an important part in Athlone's history, first as the seat of the presidents of Connaught and later as the headquarters of the governor of Athlone during the first Siege of Athlone in 1690 and the second in 1691. Declared a national monument in 1970, it was recently restored and adapted for use as a visitor center, museum, gallery, and tearoom. The exhibition area offers an audiovisual presentation on the Siege of Athlone, plus displays on the castle itself, the town of Athlone, the flora and fauna of the Shannon region, and John McCormack, the great Irish tenor and Athlone's most honored son. The castle's original medieval walls have been preserved, as have two large cannons dating from the reign of George II and a pair of 10-inch mortars that were cast in 1856. Located on the riverbank, it's signposted from all directions.

Locke's Distillery

Kilbeggan, Co. Westmeath. ☎ **0506/32134.** Admission £3 ($4.80) adults, £2 ($3.20) seniors and students, £8 ($12.80) family. Apr–Oct daily 9am–6pm; Nov–Mar daily 10am–4pm. On N6, E of Athlone.

Established in 1757, this 18th- and 19th-century enterprise was one of the oldest licensed pot-still whiskey distilleries in the world. After producing whiskey for almost 200 years, it closed in 1953, but in the past 15 years a local group has succeeded in restoring it as a museum. A 35-minute tour will not only tell you how whiskey was distilled using old techniques and machinery, but also inform you about the area's social history. It's located east of Athlone on the main road (N6), almost midway between Dublin and Galway, making it a good stop off point while you're on a cross-country journey or touring in the area. On the premises are a restaurant, coffee shop, and craft shop.

Charleville Forest Castle

Off N52/Birr road, Tullamore, Co. Offaly. ☎ **0506/21279.** Admission £2.50 ($4) adults, $2 ($3.20) seniors and students, £1.50 ($2.40) children. April–May Sat–Sun 2–5pm; June–Sept Wed–Sun 11am–5pm.

Designed in 1798 by Francis Johnston, one of Ireland's foremost architects, this castle took 12 years to build and was the first of the great Gothic houses. Today it's considered one of the best of the early 19th-century castles remaining in Ireland. The castle has a fine limestone exterior, with fanciful towers, turrets, and battlements. The rooms inside have spectacular ceilings and plasterwork and great hand-carved stairways, as well as secret passageways and dungeons. Admission includes a guided tour.

SIGHTSEEING CRUISES

Rosanna Cruises
Cranagh, St. Enda's House, The Strand, Athlone, Co. Westmeath. ☎ **0902/73383.** Fax 0902/ 73392. Lough Ree trip £4.50 ($7.20) adults, £3.50 ($5.60) children; Clonmacnois trip £9 ($14.40) adults, £4 ($6.40) children. July–Sept Lough Ree trip (1¹/₂ hrs) daily 2:30 and 4:30pm; Clonmacnois trip (4 hrs) Wed and Thurs 10am.

Cruises of the inner lakes of Lough Ree or to Clonmacnois are offered by this company on board the 71-passenger *Viking I,* providing a live commentary on the 300-year Viking history on the Shannon and Lough Ree and refreshments. Departures are from The Strand.

Shannon Holidays
Jolly Mariner Marina, Athlone, Co. Westmeath. ☎ **0902/72892.** £4.50 ($7.20) adults, £2.50 ($4) children. May–Sept, times vary.

This company operates cruises around Lough Ree on board the 60-passenger MV *Ross.* Average cruising time is 90 minutes, and the boat has a sundeck and a covered deck with a bar and coffee shop.

Silverline Cruisers Ltd.
The Marina, Banagher, Co. Offaly. ☎ **0509/51112.** £4.50 ($7.20) adults, £3 ($4.80) children. May–Sept, times vary.

This company operates 90-minute cruises via the *River Queen,* a 54-seat enclosed river bus. The trip starts out by passing under the seven-arched Banagher Stone Bridge, then passes Martello towers and fortresses on its way downstream to Victoria Lock, the largest lock on the entire Shannon system. The taped commentary covers all the historical aspects of the route. There's a bar on board.

SPECTATOR SPORTS & OUTDOOR PURSUITS

CRUISING   The following companies rent cabin cruisers, usually for a minimum of one week, along this section of the Shannon: **Athlone Cruisers,** Jolly Mariner Marina, Athlone, Co. Westmeath (☎ **0902/72892;** fax 0902/74386); **Ballykeeran Cruisers, Ltd.,** Ballykeeran, Athlone, Co. Westmeath (☎ **0902/85163;** fax 0902/ 85431); **Carrick Craft Cruisers,** The Marina, Carrick-on-Shannon, Co. Leitrim (☎ **078/20236;** fax 078/21336); **Silver Line,** The Marina, Banagher, Co. Offaly (☎ **0509/51112;** fax 0509/51632); and **Tara Cruisers, Ltd.,** Carrick-on-Shannon, Co. Leitrim (☎ **078/20736;** fax 078/21284). Craft range from 2- to 10-berths; rates average £438 to £1,870 ($700.80 to $2,992) per week in high season.

A new cruising company operating at the quay, Carrick-on-Shannon, offers one-hour and 45-minute cruises aboard the **Moon River** cruiser for £5 ($8) adults, £2.50 ($4) children under 16, daily in high season at 2:30 and 4:30pm. On Saturday nights, the Moon River becomes a floating pub, with live local music presented from midnight to 3am. Reservations recommended (☎ **088/21777**).

GOLF   **Birr Golf Club,** Birr, Co. Offaly (☎ **0509/20082**), is an 18-hole course set amid 112 acres of parkland countryside; the greens fees are £10 ($16) on weekdays and £12 ($19.20) on weekends.

In the Athlone area are the 18-hole **Athlone Golf Club,** Hodson Bay, Athlone, Co. Roscommon (☎ **0902/92073**), with greens fees of £12 ($19.20) on weekdays and £15 ($24) on weekends; and the new 18-hole championship **Mount Temple**

Golf Club, Moate, Co. Westmeath (☎ **0902/81545**), 5 miles east of Athlone, charging greens fees of £7 ($11.20) on weekdays and £10 ($16) on weekends.

HORSE RACING   Horse racing is held in July, August, and September at the **Kilbeggan Racecourse,** Loughnagore, Kilbeggan, Co. Westmeath, located off the main Mullingar road (N52), a mile from town, on Mullingar Road. Admission is £5 ($8) for adults and £2.50 ($4) for students.

ACCOMMODATIONS & DINING
MODERATE

✪ Brosna Lodge Hotel
Main St., Banagher, Co. Offaly. ☎ **0509/51350.** Fax 0509/51521. 14 rms. TEL. £35–£50 ($56–$80) double. No service charge. Rates include full breakfast. DC, MC, V. Closed Dec 24–Jan.

Although it sits along the main thoroughfare in a busy river town near Clonmacnois, this two-story hotel has a warm country atmosphere, thanks to a beautiful flower-filled front garden and the enthusiastic innkeeping of owners Geraldine and Aidan Hoare. The public areas, which include Snipes Restaurant, a cozy old-world bar, and a TV lounge, are furnished with traditional period pieces and local antiques. The guest rooms are bright and airy and overlook the gardens or the town. Best of all, it's just a short walk to the riverfront.

Dooly's Hotel
Emmet Sq., Birr, Co. Offaly. ☎ **0509/20032.** Fax 0509/21332. 18 rms. TV TEL. £65 ($104) double. No service charge. Rates include full breakfast. AE, DC, MC, V.

Dating from 1747, this three-story Georgian hotel is located in the center of town. Although one of Ireland's oldest former coaching inns, it's been thoroughly restored and refurbished in recent years. The public areas retain their Georgian charm, while the guest rooms offer all the modern conveniences, such as tea/coffeemakers; rooms have views of the town or back garden. Facilities include the Emmet Restaurant for international fare; the old-world Coach House Bar; and a coffee shop that's open 10am to 10pm, handy for travelers in search of a meal at odd hours.

✪ Hodson Bay Hotel
Roscommon Rd., Athlone, Co. Westmeath. ☎ **0902/92444.** Fax 0902/92688. 93 rms. TV TEL. £70–£110 ($112–$176) double. No service charge. Rates include full breakfast. AE, DC, MC, V.

On the shores of Lough Ree, this four-story hotel stands out on the harbor front with a pale lemon–colored facade. Totally renovated and extended in 1992, the guest rooms have a contemporary decor of light-wood furnishings and pastel-toned quilted fabrics. The public areas and most of the bedrooms overlook the marina and Hodson's Pillar, a stone monument located on an island offshore and reputed to mark the center of Ireland. Dining and entertainment facilities include L'Escale Restaurant for formal dining and the Waterfront Bar & Buttery for light fare. Recreational facilities include an indoor heated swimming pool, sauna, steam room, gym, solarium; adjacent to 18-hole golf course.

Prince of Wales
Church St., Athlone, Co. Westmeath. ☎ **0902/72626.** Fax 0902/75658. 72 rms. TV TEL. £60–£80 ($96–$128) double. No service charge. Rates include full breakfast. AE, DC, MC, V.

Dating from the 1780s and originally known as Rourke's Hotel, this three-story property is in the center of Athlone on a busy street. In spite of its age, it has a modern interior with tasteful brass touches and paneled walls. The guest rooms offer contemporary Irish furnishings with light woods and multitoned fabrics, plus all modern conveniences, including tea/coffeemakers and garment presses. A historical note: The hotel took its present name in 1863 to mark the marriage of the heir to the British throne. Dining and entertainment choices include the Beech Tree restaurant, the Cherry Tree coffee shop, and the old-world Hunters bar.

PUBS

Of all the river towns in this section of the Shannon, Banagher is particularly well known for lively Irish traditional music sessions at two of its pubs: **J. J. Hough's,** Main Street (☎ 0509/51499), with music every night during summer and Friday to Sunday during the rest of the year; and the **Vine House,** West End (☎ 0902/51463), with music every night during summer.

3 Upper Shannon: From Lough Ree to Lough Allen

Roscommon is 51 miles NE of Galway, 91 miles NW of Dublin; Longford is 80 miles NW of Dublin, 27 miles NE of Athlone; Carrick-on-Shannon is 35 miles SE of Sligo; Cavan is 65 miles NW of Dublin.

GETTING TO & AROUND THE UPPER SHANNON   The best way to get to the Upper Shannon area is by car or boat. Although there's public transportation, you'll need a car to get around the riverbanks and to the various attractions. Among major roads that lead to this area are the main Dublin-Sligo road (N4), the main Dublin-Cavan road (N3), N5 and N63 from Castlebar and the west, N61 and N55 from the south.

VISITOR INFORMATION   Year-round information on **Co. Roscommon** is available from the **Ireland West Tourism Office,** Victoria Place, Eyre Square, Galway (☎ 091/63081); on **Co. Longford** from the Midlands East Tourism Office, Clonard House, Dublin Road, Mullingar, Co. Westmeath (☎ 044/48761); on **Co. Cavan** from the Cavan Tourist Office, Farnham Street, Cavan, Co. Cavan (☎ 049/31942); and on **Co. Leitrim** from the North-West Tourism Office, Aras Reddan, Temple Street, Sligo (☎ 071/61201).

   Seasonal information points, operating from June through August, are signposted in the following towns: Boyle (☎ 079/62145), Carrick-on-Shannon (☎ 078/20170), Longford (☎ 043/46566), and Roscommon (☎ 0903/26342).

AREA CODES   Telephone area codes in the Upper Shannon region include **043, 044, 049, 071, 078, 091,** and **0903.**

ATTRACTIONS

The Upper Shannon River region is home to a remarkable assortment of castles, great houses, and museums, including one of Ireland's newest and most significant collections, the **Irish Famine Museum,** at Strokestown, Co. Roscommon, which is of special importance as Ireland commemorates the 150th anniversary of the Great Hunger. This museum chronicles the great tragedy that changed the course of history in Ireland and the world, sending forth the Irish diaspora to England, the United States, Canada, and Australia.

In addition, the shores of the Upper Shannon encompass **Lough Ree,** the second-largest of Shannon's lakes. Considered almost an inland sea, it's distinguished by long, flat vistas across the farming countryside of Counties Roscommon, Westmeath, and Longford.

Of these, Longford gives the river its literary associations. This eastern bank of the Shannon is often referred to as Goldsmith country because 18th-century dramatist, novelist, and poet Oliver Goldsmith was born here at Pallas, near Ballymahon. Although Goldsmith did much of his writing in London, it's said that he drew on many of his Irish experiences for his works, including *She Stoops to Conquer.*

Above Lough Ree the river is relatively narrow until it reaches the town of **Carrick-on-Shannon,** in Co. Leitrim, which is situated on one of the great ancient crossing places of the Shannon. The town is particularly known as a center for boating, with a vast marina in the middle of the town where many local companies rent cabin cruisers.

The whole county of **Leitrim** is uniquely affected by the Shannon's waters. It's divided into two parts, almost wholly separated from one another by Lough Allen. A storage reservoir for a nearby hydroelectric plant, Lough Allen is the Shannon's third-largest lake, 7 miles long and 3 miles wide. North of Lough Allen, in Co. Cavan, is the source of the Shannon River: the **Shannon Pot** on the southern slopes of the Cuilcagh Mountain.

The scope of the Shannon has been broadened in recent years so it's now possible to travel from the Shannon River to Lough Erne, using a stretch of water known as the Ballinamore-Ballyconnell Canal. Following a painstaking restoration, it was reopened in the spring of 1994, after a lapse of 125 years. Because it provides a clear path from the Shannon in the Republic of Ireland to Lough Erne in Northern Ireland, the new passage is officially designated the Shannon-Erne Waterway. It's a symbol of cross-border cooperation and a touchstone in a new golden age of Irish waterways travel.

Boyle Abbey

Boyle, Co. Roscommon. ☎ **079/62604.** Admission £1 ($1.60) adults, 70p ($1.15) seniors, 40p (65¢) children and students, £5 ($4.80) family. Mid-June to mid-September daily 9:30am–6:30pm. On the N4.

Boyle Abbey was founded in 1161 as a daughter-house of the Cistercian Abbey at Mellifont. Today it is the most impressive survivor of the early Irish Cistercian settlements of the late 12th and early 13th centuries. The Cistercian Order was founded in 11th-century France as a return to the uncompromised simplicity and tranquil austerity of the monastic calling. The abbey was to be a haven of otherworldliness, and yet the world's savagery more than once descended on Boyle. Its walls were torn down and its monks murdered. What remains is a complex fossil clearly imprinted with both the serene and violent aspects of the abbey's history. The ruins of Boyle Abbey evoke in visitors a sense of what this place has seen and suffered and enjoyed. The interpretive center, housed in the restored gatehouse, is informative and thoughtfully designed.

Lough Key Forest Park

Boyle, Co. Roscommon. ☎ **079/62363.** Admission to park £1.50 ($2.40) adults, £1 ($1.60) children, £3 ($4.80) family. Open year-round daily dawn–dusk. Park entrance located on the main Dublin-Sligo road (N4), 2 miles E of the town of Boyle.

If you're driving cross-country and want to stop for a picnic and a walk, or if you're traveling with children and are in search of a perfect place to let them loose, look no further.

Spanning 840 acres along the shores of Lough Key and comprised of mixed woodlands, a lake, and more than a dozen islands, this is one of Ireland's foremost lakeside parks. The grounds include nature walks, ancient monuments, ring forts, a central viewing tower, picnic grounds, a cafe, and a shop. In addition to cypress groves and other diverse foliage, you'll find a unique display of bog gardens, where a wide selection of peat-loving plants and shrubs flourishes. Deer, otters, hedgehogs, birds, pheasants, and many other forms of wildlife roam the park. The lake is navigable from the Shannon via the Boyle River. Power boats and rowboats are available to rent, and there are pony and cart rides through the park.

Lough Rynn House & Gardens

Mohill, Co. Leitrim. ☎ **078/31427.** Admission £1.50 ($2.40) adults, 70p ($1.15) seniors and students, or maximum of £3.50 ($5.60) per car; additional £1 ($1.50) adults, 50p (80¢) seniors and students for guided tour. May–Aug 10am–7pm. Located S of Carrick-on-Shannon, on the outskirts of Mohill, 3¹/₂ miles from the main Dublin-Sligo road (N4).

Seat of the Clements, the earls of Leitrim, this estate comprises 100 acres of woodland, ornamental gardens, open pastures, and lakes. Of particular interest is the three-acre terraced walled garden dating from 1859. It's one of the largest of its kind in the country, laid out in the manner of a Victorian pleasure garden. The arboretum contains specimens of the tulip tree, California redwood, and other exotic species, including the oldest monkey puzzle tree in Ireland. Four thousand years of history can be seen in one 180° sweep of the eye at the rear of the house. The Neolithic burial tomb atop Druids Hill was constructed about 2000 B.C.; Reynolds Castle, a lonely sentinel by the lakeshore, dates from the 16th century; and Lough Rynn House itself was built in 1832.

✪ Clonalis House

Castlerea, Co. Roscommon. ☎ **0907/20014.** Admission £2.50 ($4) adults, £1.75 ($2.80) seniors and students, £1 ($1.60) children over 7. June to mid-Sept Tues–Sun noon–5pm. Located 10 miles off the main Dublin-Longford-Castlebar road (N5).

Standing on land that has belonged to the O'Conors for more than 1,500 years, this is one of Ireland's great houses. It's the ancestral home of the O'Conors, kings of Connaught, and the home of the O'Conor Don, the direct descendant of the last high king of Ireland.

The house itself, built in 1880, is a combination of Victorian, Italianate, and Queen Anne architecture, with mostly Louis XV–style furnishings, plus antique lace, horse-drawn farm machinery, and other memorabilia. It's primarily a museum of the O'Conor (O'Connor) family, with portraits, documents, and genealogical tracts dating back 2,000 years. Displays also include a rare ancient harp that's said to have belonged to Turlough O'Carolan (1670–1738), the blind Irish bard who composed songs still sung today. The grounds, with terraced and woodland gardens, also hold the O'Conor inauguration stone, similar to the Stone of Scone at Westminster Abbey.

✪ The Irish Famine Museum

Strokestown Park, Strokestown, Co. Roscommon. ☎ **078/33013.** Admission £3 ($4.80) adults, £2.50 ($3) seniors and students, £1.50 ($1.50) children. Easter–Oct Tues–Sun 11am–5:30pm. On the main Dublin-Castlebar road (N5).

One of the most defining events of Ireland's history, the Great Potato Famine of the 1840s, is the focus of this museum opened in 1994. Housed in the stable yards of Strokestown Park House (see below), this museum illustrates how and why the famine started, how English colonial officials failed to prevent its spread, and how it reduced the Irish population of 8.1 million by nearly 3 million through death and mass emigration. The exhibits range from photographs, letters, documents, and satirical cartoons to farm implements and a huge cauldron that was used for soup to feed the people in a famine-relief program. This museum is particularly interesting for Irish Americans, tens of millions of whom trace their ancestry to those who left the country during and after the famine. The museum also seeks to relate the events of the Irish famine to contemporary world hunger and poverty. A four-acre pleasure garden has been recently restored and is open to the public for an additional fee.

Strokestown Park House

Strokestown, Co. Roscommon. ☎ **078/33013.** Admission £3 ($4.80) adults, £2.50 ($4) students and seniors, £1 ($1.60) children. June to mid-Sept Tues–Sun noon–5pm. On the main Dublin-Castlebar road (N5).

A Georgian Gothic arch at the end of Ireland's widest main street leads into this estate, the seat of the Pakenham-Mahon family from 1600 to 1979. The present 45-room Palladian house, designed for Thomas Mahon by German architect Richard Castle in the 1730s, incorporates parts of an earlier tower house. The center block is fully furnished as it was in earlier days, surrounded by two wings. The north wing houses Ireland's last galleried kitchen (a kitchen gallery allowed the lady of the house to observe the culinary activity without being part of it), while the south wing is an elaborate vaulted stable, often described as an equine cathedral.

Tullynally Castle and Gardens

Castlepollard, Co. Westmeath. ☎ **044/61159.** Castle, £2 ($3.20) adults, 50p (80¢) children; castle and gardens, £3.50 ($5.60) adults, £2 ($3.20) children. Castle open mid-Jun to mid-Aug 2–6pm; gardens open May–Sept 10am–6pm. About 20 miles E of Longford and 13 miles N of Mullingar, off the main Dublin-Sligo road (N4).

A turreted and towered Gothic-Revival manor, this house has been the home of the Pakenham family, the earls of Longford, since 1655. The highlights include a great hall that rises through two stories, with a ceiling of plaster Gothic vaulting, and a collection of family portraits, china, and furniture. There's also a collection of 19th-century gadgets. The 30-acre grounds are an attraction in themselves, with various woodland walks, a linear water garden, a Victorian grotto, and an avenue of 200-year-old Irish yew trees. Tullynally is near Lough Derravaragh, an idyllic spot featured in the legendary Irish tale *The Children of Lir.*

Cavan Crystal

Dublin road (N3), Cavan, Co. Cavan. ☎ **049/31800.** Free admission. Factory shop, Mon–Fri 9am–5:30pm, Sat 10am–5pm, Sun 2–5pm; factory tours, Mon–Fri 10:30am–3:30pm at regular intervals.

One of the top three crystal companies of Ireland, this establishment is known for its delicate glassware, mouth-blown and hand-cut by skilled craftspeople. Visitors are invited to watch as skilled master blowers fashion the molten crystal into intricate shapes and designs, followed by the precision work of the master cutters. The glassware is for sale in the factory shop. A new visitor's center is scheduled for completion by 1997 and will likely charge an admission fee of £1.50 ($2.40).

SPORTS & OUTDOOR PURSUITS

CRUISING   The following companies rent cabin cruisers along this part of the Shannon: **Athlone Cruisers,** Jolly Mariner Marina, Athlone, Co. Westmeath (☎ 0902/72892); **Carrick Craft,** The Marina, Carrick-on-Shannon, Co. Leitrim (☎ 078/21248); and **Emerald Star Line,** The Marina, Carrick-on-Shannon, Co. Leitrim(☎ **078/20234**).

GOLF   There are two 18-hole championship golf courses in the area that should not be missed. Opened in 1993, the **Glasson Golf and Country Club,** Glasson, Co. Westmeath (☎ **0902/85120**), is situated on the shores of Lough Ree, 6 miles north of Athlone. Greens fees are £25 ($40) on weekdays and £30 ($48) on weekends. Equally new is the **Slieve Russell Hotel Golf Club,** Cranaghan, Ballyconnell, Co. Cavan (☎ **049/26444**). Greens fees for those not staying at the hotel are £20 ($32) on weekdays and £30 ($48) on weekends.

Two other 18-hole courses in the area are **County Cavan Golf Club,** Arnmore House, Drumellis, Co. Cavan (☎ **049/31283**), and **County Longford Golf Club,** Dublin Road, Longford (☎ **043/46310**). Both charge greens fees of £10 ($15) on weekdays and £12 ($18) on weekends.

HORSEBACK RIDING   Moorlands Equestrian Center, Drumshanbo, Co. Leitrim (☎ **078/41500**; fax 078/41095), offers lessons, as well as trail rides along Lough Allen and the nearby hills. Children are welcome. During the off season thoroughbreds are trained for racing, and B.H.S. certification courses in equestrian science are offered. Book lessons or trail rides at least one day in advance; ask for Karen or Neil McManus.

ACCOMMODATIONS & DINING
EXPENSIVE

✪ **Slieve Russell Hotel**

Ballyconnell, Co. Cavan. ☎ **049/26444.** Fax 049/26474. 151 rms. TV TEL. £120–£150 ($192–$240) double. No service charge. Rates include full breakfast. AE, DC, MC, V.

Set on 400 acres of parklands and gardens, including 50 acres of lakes and ponds, this impressive four-story hotel is named after a nearby mountain that's known in Irish as Slieve Rushen. Although relatively new, the hotel captures the opulence and charm of a bygone era, with public areas that boast marbled colonnades, huge open fireplaces, plush carpets, marble staircases, and wrought-iron trim. The conservatory-style Fountain Room exudes a country garden atmosphere, with its skylit glass dome and array of leafy plants. Guest rooms are modern and large, with light-wood furnishings, pastel-toned fabrics, and brass accessories. Each room has a garment press, tea/coffeemaker, and hair dryer. Situated near the Shannon-Erne Waterway, this hotel is a good base for touring not only the upper Shannon area but also the attractions of Enniskillen and Northern Ireland.

Dining/Entertainment: Choices include the Conall Cearnach Restaurant for gourmet cuisine, the brasserie-style Brackly Restaurant for light fare, The Kells Bar with a stunning decor of illustrations from the Book of Kells, and the intimate Pike Bar for residents.

Services: Concierge, room service, baby-sitting, laundry and dry-cleaning service.

Facilities: 18-hole championship golf course, heated indoor swimming pool, sauna, steam room, Jacuzzi, exercise room, two squash courts, four all-weather tennis courts, hairdressing salon, gift shop, walking trails.

INEXPENSIVE

✪ **Glencarne House**

Ardcarne, Carrick-on-Shannon, Co. Leitrim (signposted on N4, between Carrick-on-Shannon and Boyle). ☎ **079/67013.** 5 rooms. £40 ($64) double. Closed Nov–Feb. Includes full Irish breakfast. No service charge. No credit cards.

Situated on a hundred-acre working farm, Glencarne is a beautifully restored late Georgian house with great charm and warmth. The two front rooms (nos. 1 and 2) enjoy a sweeping view of the valley below, and an especially spacious double with adjoining twin combine to make an elegant family suite. Rooms feature brass poster beds, antique furnishings, and fresh flowers in abundance. Dinner is the high point of life at Glencarne, when the Harringtons draw from their own produce and meats and present a fresh, sumptuous fixed-price feast at £15 ($24). Then, when there's nothing left to do but collapse, orthopedic beds are there to catch you.

Hotel Kilmore

Dublin road (N3), Cavan, Co. Cavan. ☎ **049/32288.** Fax 049/32458. 39 rms. TV TEL. £68–£80 ($108.80–$128) double. No service charge. Rates include full breakfast. AE, DC, MC, V.

Located 2 miles south of Cavan Town, this modern hotel was built in the early 1980s and has recently been totally refurbished. The public areas are airy and bright, overlooking the garden with its trio of fountains. Guest rooms have standard furnishings. Facilities include the Annalee Restaurant, which specializes in fish and game dishes.

Park Hotel

Deer Park Lodge, Cavan-Dublin road (N3), Virginia, Co. Cavan. ☎ **049/47235.** Fax 049/47203. 19 rms (16 with bath). TV TEL. £100 ($160) double. No service charge. Rates include full breakfast. AE, DC, MC, V. Closed Nov to mid-Mar.

Set on 100 acres of woodlands and gardens beside Lough Ramor, this hotel dates from 1751. It was originally known as Deer Park Lodge, a sporting and summer residence of the marquis of Headfort, and was converted into a hotel in the 1930s. It has since had a number of renovations and extensions, making for lots of connecting corridors and varying standards of bedrooms. The public areas retain a definite 18th-century charm, with high ceilings, elaborate chandeliers, period furnishings, and original oil paintings. The amenities include a restaurant, a lounge bar, a nine-hole golf course, a hard tennis court, fishing privileges, boating equipment, and forest walking trails. As a point of interest, this hotel and its kitchen are used as the Irish campus for the Baltimore International Culinary College in the off-season.

Ross Castle and House

Mount Nugent, Co. Cavan (signposted from Mount Nugent). ☎/ fax **049/40218** Ross House; 049/40237 Ross Castle. 11 rms (9 with bath; some with shower only), 2 apartments, one 3-bedroom self-catering cottage. TEL. TV in house rooms. £40 ($64) double. No service charge. MC, V. Castle and cottage open year-round. House open Mar–Nov.

This 400-acre, family run horse, cattle, and sheep farm on Lough Sheelin offers appealing options in accommodations and activities. It's simply one of the most unique and affordable hideaways I have discovered in Ireland.

Ross Castle is a 16th-century fortified tower that's said to be haunted by a lovesick bride-to-be named Sabrina, whose lover, Orwin, was drowned in Lough Sheelin en route to their elopement. They're buried together in a nearby field. Today, the place is restored, with central heating throughout (even in the tower rooms), and is managed by Viola Harkort.

Nearby Ross House, where your hosts will be Peter and Ulla Harkort, is a spacious and comfortable manor house, the oldest portions of which date from the mid–17th century. Horseback riding, tennis courts, fishing boats with or without motors (the place is noted for its brown trout and is stocked with pike and perch), sauna, and Jacuzzi are all on hand. One of the Harkorts' daughters, a physiotherapist at the regional hospital, offers guests massages in the evening, by prior appointment. On request, three-course dinners are served for £13 ($20.80), with an excellent small selection of wines, modestly priced.

Whether you fish or not, for trout or ghosts, this is a most congenial spot.

A PUB

Although there are many good pubs in the area, don't miss the **Derragarra Inn,** Butlersbridge, Co. Cavan (☎ **049/31003**), for a drink or a meal. More than 200 years old, it's full of local farm implements and crafts, as well as exotic souvenirs collected by former owner John Clancy during his travels around the world. Relax by the old turf fireplace or on the garden patio. It's located 4 miles north of Cavan Town.

16 Northern Ireland

The title of this chapter, "Northern Ireland," designates a political rather than a geographical destination. It is not simply a matter of longitude and latitude. Parts of the Republic, or "the South," lie farther north than "the North," whose boundaries follow historical, not topographical, contours and divisions. Think of the sinuous Mason-Dixon Line that once divided the American North and South, and then imagine that the Civil War had ended differently, with two Americas. Imagine that traveling from Philadelphia to Baltimore entailed showing your passport and changing currency.

There is no avoiding the fact, even in a guidebook for vacationers, that Ireland is a land divided by a line drawn in hatred and violence. Two years of peace—1994 to 1996, the first in several decades in the North—served to highlight the absurdity and waste of "the Troubles" that have haunted Northern Ireland for as long as most living Irish can remember. To outsiders the Troubles are incomprehensible. Other peoples' prejudices and quarrels usually are.

Introducing Northern Ireland is like introducing a wonderfully gifted and accomplished individual who all the same has "a problem," sometimes under control and sometimes not. Northern Ireland has everything going for it except that it lies over a fault line, so to speak, which occasionally threatens to shift and shake the pictures off the wall.

From a visitor's perspective, the violence is remarkably contained, and, like diplomats, foreigners enjoy a certain immunity. Derry and Belfast at their worst are as safe for visitors as most any comparable American city, and the Ulster countryside is as idyllic and serene as Vermont. Unless the situation worsens, driving through Northern Ireland is no more cause for fear than driving to work.

The truth is that Northern Ireland is as welcoming and gracious as the South, and as beautiful. It is, after all, Ireland. Long the industrial center of the island, the North has traditionally been noticeably more prosperous than the South; but that difference is less and less perceptible. The Republic's economic successes in the past two decades, as well as the leveling effects of participation in the European Community (EC), continues to blur the economic and social differences between the North and the South. One day, maybe even soon, a united Europe may render obsolete and irrelevant the very idea of a divided Ireland.

GETTING TO THE NORTH   By Air   From New York, American Transair operates scheduled service into **Belfast International Airport** (☎ 01849/422888). Flights from Britain land at **Belfast City Airport** (☎ 01232/457745) and **Eglinton Airport,** Derry (☎ 01504/810784).

By Ferry   The quickest crossing from Britain to Northern Ireland is the 90-minute **SeaCat** (☎ 0345/523523), a catamaran service from Stranraer, Scotland. Other ferry services into Belfast include **Norse Irish Ferries** (☎ 01232/779090) from Liverpool and the **Isle of Man Steam Packet Co.** (☎ 01624/661661) from the Isle of Man. In addition, there is **Stena Sealink** (☎ 01776/802102) from Stranraer, Scotland, to Larne, and **P & O European Ferries** (☎ 01581/200276) from Cairnyan, Scotland, to Larne.

By Train   Trains from the Irish Rail and Northern Ireland Railways systems travel from Dublin daily into Northern Ireland, arriving at **Belfast Central Station,** East Bridge Street (☎ 01232/899411). The boat train service from Stranraer, Scotland, terminates at **Yorkgate Station,** York Street, Belfast (☎ 01232/235282).

By Bus   Ulsterbus operates buses between Belfast and all parts of Northern Ireland and the Republic. For schedules and prices, phone the **Ulsterbus Enquiries Hotline** (☎ 01232/333000).

By Car   Northern Ireland is directly accessible from the Republic of Ireland via many main roads and secondary roads. At some points, there are border crossing checkpoints. Main roads leading to Northern Ireland from the Republic include N1 from Dublin, N16 from Sligo, N15 from Donegal, and N3 from Cavan.

GETTING AROUND IN THE NORTH   By Bus   Ulsterbus (☎ 01232/333000) runs daily scheduled services from Belfast to major cities and towns throughout Northern Ireland. From the **Europa Bus Centre,** Glengall Street, Belfast (☎ 01232/320011), there are buses leaving for destinations in Counties Armagh, Tyrone, Derry (west), Fermanagh, and Down (west); and from the **Oxford Street Bus Station,** Oxford Street, Belfast (☎ 01232/232356), for destinations in Counties Antrim, Down (east), Derry (east) and Cookstown.

To save money, ask about the **Freedom of Northern Ireland bus passes,** valid for unlimited travel on all Ulsterbus and Citibus services operating within Northern Ireland. A one-day pass costs £9 ($13.95) adult, £4.50 ($6.98) child, and a seven-day pass costs £28 ($43.40) adult, £14 ($21.70) child. Tickets can be bought at all Ulsterbus depots, but not from bus drivers.

By Sightseeing Tour   From June through August, **Ulsterbus** (☎ 01232/333000) operates a wide variety of full-day and half-day coach tours from the Europa Bus Centre, Glengall Street, Belfast, to places such as the Glens of Antrim, Causeway Coast, Fermanagh Lakelands, Sperrin Mountains, the Mountains of Mourne, and Armagh. There are also tours designed to take you to specific attractions such as the Giant's Causeway, Old Bushmills Distillery in Bushmills, Navan Centre in Armagh, Ulster-American Folk Park in Omagh, and Tyrone Crystal Factory in Dungannon. Tour prices range from £2 to £7 ($3.10 to $10.85) for a half-day tour and £6 to £12 ($9.30 to $18.60) for full-day trips.

During July and August, Ulsterbus also operates a daily open-top bus service from Coleraine to the Giant's Causeway and back. The journey lasts 50 minutes and may be broken at Portstewart, Portrush, Portballintrae, or Bushmills. Price is £2.60 ($4.05) adult round-trip, £1.90 ($2.95) children round-trip, and £1.90 ($2.95) one way. For schedule, call ☎ 01265/43334.

The North

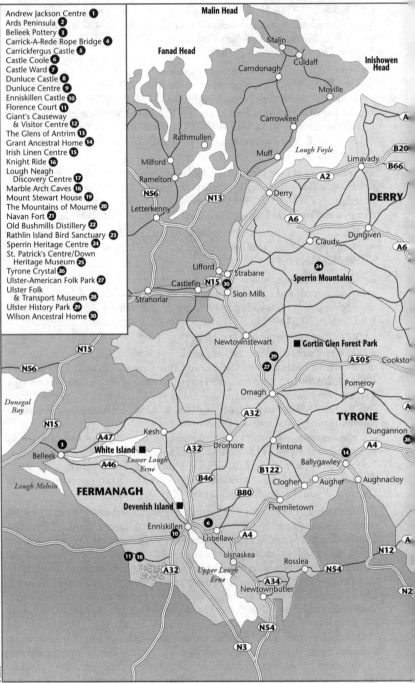

Malin Head

Fanad Head

Malin

Culdaff

Inishowen
Head

Carndonagh

Moville

Carrowkeel

Rathmullen

Lough Foyle

Muff

Milford

Ramelton

Limavady

B20

B66

N56

Derry

A2

DERRY

Letterkenny

N13

A6

Dungiven

Claudy

A6

Lifford

Strabane

Sperrin Heritage Centre ㉔

Castlefin

N15 ㉚

Sion Mills

Stranorlar

Sperrin Mountains

N15

N56

Newtownstewart

Gortin Glen Forest Park

Donegal
Bay

N15

Omagh

㉙
㉗

A505

Cooksto

Pomeroy

TYRONE

A

Kesh

A47

A32

Dromore

Fintona

Dungannon

㉖

A4

White Island

A32

B46

㉖

B122

Ballygawley

㉔

Aughnacloy

Belleek

A46

Lower Lough
Erne

Clogher

Augher

Lough Melvin

FERMANAGH

B80

Fivemiletown

Devenish Island

A4

N12

Enniskillen

❿

Lisbellaw

❻

Lisnaskea

A

Upper Lough
Erne

Rosslea

N54

❶❶ ⓲

A32

A34

Newtownbutler

N54

N2

N3

3-0506

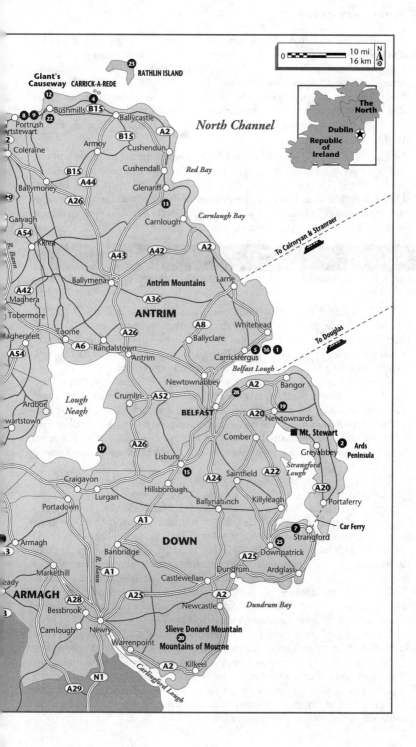

By Rail   **Northern Ireland Railways,** 28 Wellington Place, Belfast (☎ 01232/ 230310), operates trains throughout Northern Ireland from two stations in Belfast: Central Station, East Bridge Street, Belfast (☎ 01232/899411), for all destinations except Larne; and Yorkgate Station, York Street, Belfast (☎ 0232/235282), for the Larne boat train. If you're going to be spending a week in the North, ask about the Rail Runabout, providing seven consecutive days of travel on all scheduled rail routes in Northern Ireland and to Dundalk in the South for £25 ($38.75) adult, £12.50 ($19.40) child.

By Car   The best way to travel around the Northern Ireland countryside is by car. The roads are in extremely good condition and are very well signposted. Distances between major cities and towns are short. If you wish to rent a car, **Avis, Budget, Dollar, Europacar,** and **Hertz** all have depots in Belfast city and in at least one of the Belfast airports. Alternatively, if you rent a car in the Republic, you can drive it in the North as long as you arrange the proper insurance.

1 Belfast

Belfast is 103 miles N of Dublin, 211 miles NE of Shannon, 125 miles E of Sligo, and 262 miles NE of Cork.

GETTING AROUND   **Citybus,** Donegall Square West, Belfast (☎ 01232/ 246485), provides local bus services within the city. Departures are from Donegall Square East, West, and North, plus Upper Queen Street, Wellington Place, Chichester Street, and Castle Street. There is an information kiosk on Donegall Square West for guidance on where to get a bus to a certain locale.

If you've brought a car into Belfast, it's best to leave it parked at your hotel and take local transport or walk around the city. If you must drive and want to park your car downtown, look for a blue "P" sign that shows a parking lot or a parking area. In Belfast, there are a number of control zones, indicated by a pink and yellow sign, where no parking is permitted. In general, on-street parking is limited to an area behind City Hall (south side), St. Anne's Cathedral (north side), and around Queen's University and Ulster Museum.

Taxis are available at all main rail stations, ports, and airports. Most metered taxis are the London-type black cabs with a yellow disk on the window.

For an overview of the city, **Citybus Tours** (☎ 01232/458484), offers a three-hour Belfast City Tour, departing daily at 1pm from late June to September on Tuesday, Wednesday, and Thursday. It's priced at £7 ($10.85) for adults, £4.50 ($6.95) for seniors and children, £15 ($23.25) family. In addition, there is an **evening tour** spotlighting Belfast's landmark buildings, with a commentary by a member of Belfast's Civic Trust; departures are on Wednesdays at 7pm from the end of June to September. Reservations are required for the latter tour. All tours depart from Castle Place, two blocks north of Donegall Square. Tickets can be purchased in advance from the Citybus Ticket Kiosk on Donegall Square West.

Belfast is a good city for walking. To guide visitors on the best and safest areas for a stroll, the Belfast City Council has produced five different self-guided walking tour leaflets: city center southward to Shaftesbury Square; city center northward to the *Irish News* office; Shaftesbury Square southward to the university area; city center northeast to the port area; and Donegall Square south to Donegall Pass. Each walk is about a mile in length and an hour in duration. Ask for a leaflet for the walk or walks that interest you at the Northern Ireland Tourist Office.

Belfast

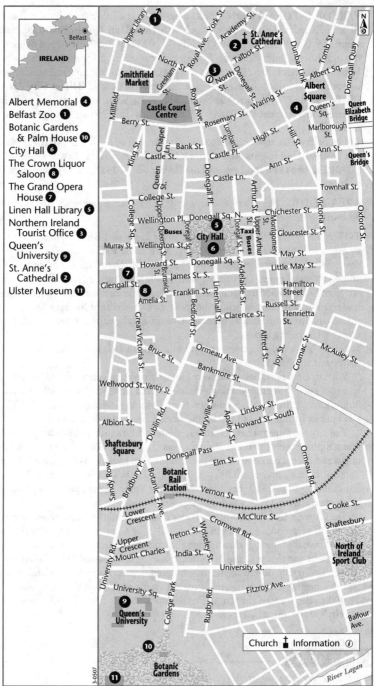

IRELAND

Belfast

Albert Memorial 4
Belfast Zoo 1
Botanic Gardens
  & Palm House 10
City Hall 6
The Crown Liquor
  Saloon 8
The Grand Opera
  House 7
Linen Hall Library 5
Northern Ireland
  Tourist Office 3
Queen's
  University 9
St. Anne's
  Cathedral 2
Ulster Museum 11

Upper Library St.
Belfast Zoo 1
Academy St.
St. Anne's Cathedral 2
York St.
North St.
Royal Ave.
Talbot St.
Gresham St.
Smithfield Market
3
North St.
Donegall St.
Dunbar Link
Tomb St.
Albert Sq.
Donegall Quay
Waring St.
Albert Square
Castle Court Centre
Royal Ave.
Rosemary St.
Queen's Sq.
4
Queen Elizabeth Bridge
Millfield
Berry St.
Chapel Ln.
Bank St.
Lombard St.
High St.
Hill St.
Marlborough St.
Ann St.
Queen's Bridge
King St.
Castle St.
Castle Pl.
Ann St.
Townhall St.
Queen St.
Castle Ln.
Arthur St.
Chichester St.
Victoria St.
Oxford St.
College Sq.
College St.
Wellington Pl.
Donegall Pl.
Donegall Sq. N.
Upper Arthur St.
Montgomery St.
Gloucester St.
Linen Hall Library 5
Buses
City Hall 6
Donegall Sq. E.
Taxi Buses
May St.
Murray St.
Wellington St.
Donegall Sq. W.
Donegall Sq. S.
Adelaide St.
Little May St.
Howard St.
Donegall Sq.
Hamilton Street
The Grand Opera House 7
Brunswick St.
James St. S.
Linenhall St.
Russell St.
Henrietta St.
Glengall St.
The Crown Liquor Saloon 8
Franklin St.
Clarence St.
Amelia St.
Bedford St.
Alfred St.
Joy St.
Cromac St.
McAuley St.
Great Victoria St.
Bruce St.
Ormeau Ave.
Bankmore St.
Wellwood St.
Ventry St.
Maryville St.
Lindsay St.
Apsley St.
Howard St. South
Albion St.
Dublin Rd.
Ormeau Rd.
Shaftesbury Square
Donegall Pass
Elm St.
Sandy Row
Bradbury Pl.
Botanic Ave.
Botanic Rail Station
Vernon St.
Cooke St.
Shaftesbury
Lower Crescent
McClure St.
Upper Crescent
Ireton St.
Cromwell Rd.
Mount Charles
Wolseley St.
India St.
North of Ireland Sport Club
University Rd.
University St.
University Sq.
College Park
Fitzroy Ave.
Queen's University 9
Rugby Rd.
Balfour Ave.
Botanic Gardens 10
Church ✝ Information ⓘ
11
River Lagan

3-0507

473

VISITOR INFORMATION   Brochures, maps, and other data about Belfast and all of the North are available from the **Northern Ireland Tourist Board,** St. Anne's Court, 59 North St., Belfast BT1 1NB (☎ **0232/246609**). It's open September through June, Monday through Saturday, from 9am to 5:15pm; July and August, Monday through Friday, 9am to 7pm, Saturday 9am to 5:15pm, and Sunday noon to 4pm. In addition, there is a tourist information desk at **Belfast City Airport** (☎ **01232/457745**), open year-round daily from 5:30am to 1pm; and at **Belfast International Airport** (☎ **01849/422888**), open daily 24 hours except on Christmas day.

The Belfast Gay and Lesbian Resource centers can be reached at **NIGRA / Northern Ireland Gay Rights Association,** Cathedral Buildings, Lower Donegall St. (☎ **01232/664111**); and **Lesbian Line Belfast** (☎ **01232/238688**) Thursdays 7:30 to 10pm.

AREA CODE   The telephone area code for Belfast numbers is **01232,** unless otherwise indicated.

TOWN LAYOUT   Nestled beside the River Lagan and Belfast Lough and ringed by gentle hills, Belfast has a lovely setting, often called a Hibernian Rio. The core of downtown Belfast sits beside the west bank of the River Lagan. The city revolves around a central point, Donegall Square, which holds the city hall; all roads radiate out from Donegall Square. Donegall Place, which extends northward from the square, leads to Royal Avenue, a prime shopping district. Bedford Street, which extends southward from the square, becomes Dublin Road, which, in turn, leads to the Queen's University area.

Nearly half a million people, a third of Northern Ireland's population, reside in the Belfast city limits.

With its large port, Belfast is a very industrialized city, often referred to as the engine room that drove the whirring wheels of the industrial revolution in Ulster. Major industries range from linen production to rope-making and shipbuilding. The *Titanic* was built in Belfast port, and today the world's largest dry dock is here.

The city's architecture is rich in Victorian and Edwardian buildings with elaborate sculptures over the doors and windows. Stone heads of gods, poets, scientists, kings, and queens peer down from the high ledges of banks and old linen warehouses. Some of Belfast's grandest buildings are on the banks of Waring Street. The Ulster Bank, dating from 1860, has an interior like a Venetian palace, and the Northern Bank, dating from 1769, was originally a market house.

The Queen's University, with its Tudor cloister, dominates the southern sector of the city. The original edifice was built in 1849 by Charles Lanyon, who designed more of Belfast's buildings than anyone else, and was named for Queen Victoria, who visited Belfast in that year and had just about everything named in her honor for the occasion—literally dozens of streets, a hospital, a park, a manmade island, and the harbor's deepwater channel are all named after her. Today, the university serves 12,000 students and is the setting for the annual Belfast Festival at Queen's, one of the city's major annual arts events.

Impressions

Ulster: where every hill has its hero and every bog its bones.
                                    —Sam Hanna Bell (b. 1909), "In Praise of Ulster"

Northwest of downtown is Cave Hill, 1,182 feet above sea level and the home of the Belfast Castle estate. This 200-acre estate is a public park, ideal for walking, jogging, picnicking, and enjoying the fine views of the city.

ATTRACTIONS

✪ City Hall

Donegall Sq. ☎ **01232/320202,** ext. 2227. Free admission. Guided tours available in July–Aug Mon–Fri at 2:30pm and Sept–June Wed at 10:30am or by appointment. Reservations required.

Opened in 1906, this magnificent public building is the core of Belfast, the axis around which the whole city radiates. It was built of Portland stone after Belfast was granted the status of a city by Queen Victoria in 1888. Similar to an American state capitol building except for the big statue of Queen Victoria at the front, it dominates the main shopping area.

✪ Linen Hall Library

17 Donegall Sq. N. ☎ **01232/321707.** Free admission. Mon–Wed and Fri 9:30am–5:30pm, Thurs 9:30am–8:30pm, Sat 9:30am–4pm.

Established in 1788 as an independent charitable institution, this is Belfast's oldest library. It is known for its collections of Irish books, local historical documents, Robert Burns's books, and books on heraldry.

✪ Ulster Museum

Stranmillis Rd. ☎ **01232/3812251.** Free admission. Mon–Fri 10am–5pm, Sat 1–5pm, Sun 2–5pm.

Built in the grand Classical Renaissance style, with an Italian marble interior, this museum summarizes 9,000 years of Irish history with exhibits on Irish art, furniture, glass, ceramics, costume, industrial heritage, and a permanent display of products "Made in Belfast." One of the best-known exhibits is the collection of gold and silver jewelry recovered by divers in 1968 off the Antrim coast from the 1588 wreckage of the Armada treasure ship *Girona*. Other permanent collections focus on waterwheels and steam engines, Irish linen-making, the post office in Ireland, coins and medals, early Ireland, Irish flora and fauna, and the living sea.

✪ Belfast Botanic Gardens & Palm House

Stranmillis Rd. ☎ **01232/324902.** Free admission. Palm House and Tropical Ravine open Apr–Sept Mon–Fri 10am–noon, Sat–Sun 1–5pm; Oct–Mar Mon–Fri 10am–noon and 1–4pm, Sat–Sun 1–4pm; gardens open 8am–sunset.

Dating from 1828, these gardens were established by the Belfast Botanic and Horticultural Society. Ten years later a glass house, or conservatory, was added, designed by noted Belfast architect Charles Lanyon. Now known as the Palm House, this unique building is one of the earliest examples of curvilinear cast-iron glass-house construction. It contains many rare plant specimens, including such tropical plants as sugar cane, coffee, cinnamon, banana, aloe, ivory nut, rubber, bamboo, guava, and the striking bird of paradise flower. The Tropical Ravine, also known as the fernery, provides a setting for plants to grow in a sunken glen. Take time also to stroll in the surrounding outdoor gardens of roses and herbaceous borders, established in 1927.

Belfast Zoo

Antrim Rd. ☎ **01232/776277.** Admission £4.40 ($6.80) adults, £2.20 ($3.40) children ages 4–16. Apr–Sept daily 10am–5pm; Oct–Mar 10am–3:30pm.

Set in a picturesque mountain park on the slopes of Cave Hill overlooking the city, this zoo was founded in 1920 as Bellvue Gardens. A completely new and modern zoo was designed in recent years, with emphasis on conservation, education, and on breeding rare species including Hawaiian geese, Indian lions, red lechwe, and golden lion marmosets.

SHOPPING

Shops in Belfast city center are open on Monday through Saturday from 9am to 5:30pm, with many shops remaining open until 8 or 9pm on Thursday.

Before you start to shop, take time to stop into the **Craftworks Gallery,** Bedford House, Bedford St. (☎ **01232/244465**), a display center and shop for the work of individual craftspeople from all over Northern Ireland. This gallery will also supply you with a free copy of the brochure "Crafts in Northern Ireland," detailing local crafts and where to find them. It is just behind Belfast City Hall. The Castle Court Shopping Centre on Royal Avenue is the main downtown multistory shopping mall, with dozens of boutiques and shops.

Belfast's leading department stores are Anderson & McAuley, and Marks & Spencer, both on Donegall Place, and Debenham's in the Castle Court Shopping Centre on Royal Avenue. Some other shops to look for include:

Prospect House Books
93 Dublin Rd. ☎ **01232/245787.**

This shop features rare, old, and out-of-print volumes. Books are bought and sold here.

Smyth's Irish Linens
65 Royal Ave. ☎ **01232/322983.**

If you want to stock up on fine Irish linen damask tablecloths, napkins, and handkerchiefs, head for this shop in the heart of the city's prime shopping thoroughfare. It also stocks other traditional gift items and souvenirs.

Tom Caldwell Gallery
40 Bradbury Place. ☎ **01232/323226.**

Come here for a selection of paintings, sculptures, and ceramics by living artists, as well as handcrafted furnishings, rugs, and cast-iron candelabras. Open Monday to Friday 9:15am to 5pm and Saturday 10am to 1pm.

ACCOMMODATIONS
VERY EXPENSIVE / EXPENSIVE

✪ **Culloden Hotel**
142 Bangor Rd., Craigavad, Holywood, Co. Down BT18 OEX. ☎ **01232/425223.** Fax 0232/426777. 79 rms, 7 suites. TV TEL. £150 ($232.50) double, £200–£350 ($310–$542.50) suite. AE, DC, MC, V.

The Belfast area's finest hotel, recently awarded five-star status, is not in Belfast at all, but 5 miles to the east on the southern shore of Belfast Lough, technically in Co. Down. Set on 12 acres of secluded gardens and woodlands, this hotel incorporates a Gothic mansion built in 1876 of Scottish stone by William Auchinleck Robinson, a government official who named it Culloden House in honor of his wife, the former Elizabeth Jane Culloden. On his death, the house passed to the Church of Ireland and was used as a residence by a succession of bishops, then was sold into private ownership and remained a residence until it was opened as a hotel in 1963. It was purchased in 1967 by the Hastings Hotel Group, which has extended and refurbished it in luxurious style, outfitting it with many fine antiques and paintings, plasterwork ceilings, and Louis XV chandeliers. Guest rooms offer contemporary furnishings with a Victorian flair.

Dining/Entertainment: Choices include the elegant Mitre Restaurant overlooking the gardens; the Gothic Bar; and the Cultra Inn (☎ **01232/425840**), a casual pub/restaurant on the grounds of the hotel.

Facilities: Octagonal-shaped swimming pool, gym, Jacuzzi, steam room, all-weather tennis court, squash court, putting green, croquet lawn, hairdressing salon.

EXPENSIVE

Europa Hotel

Great Victoria St., Belfast, Co. Antrim BT2 7AP. ☎ **01232/327000.** Fax 01232/327800. 184 rms. TV TEL. £145 ($224.75) double. Luxury suites available. AE, DC, MC, V.

Situated in the heart of the city beside the Grand Opera House, this is Belfast's largest and most modern hotel. Total renovation was completed in 1995, after damage from a 1993 bombing, and the rooms are gleaming and comfortable with such in-room amenities as tea/coffeemakers and hair dryers. Facilities include a restaurant, bistro, bar, nightclub, and secure, patrolled parking.

MODERATE

✪ Dukes Hotel

65–67 University St., Belfast, Co. Antrim BT7 1HL. ☎ **01232/236666.** Fax 01232/237177. 21 rms. TV TEL. £105 ($162.75) double. Rates include full breakfast. AE, MC, V.

Located in a tree-lined residential area near the university, this hotel is housed in a former Victorian residence. The interior decor is bright and modern with art deco furnishings, waterfalls, and plants. Guest rooms are contemporary, with double-glazed windows, light wood furnishings, floral fabrics, modern art, and such amenities as a bathroom phone, mirrored closets, hair dryer, tea/coffeemaker, and a complimentary basket of fruit. Refurbishment of all bedrooms and public areas was completed in June 1996. Facilities include Dukes Restaurant, Duke's Bar, 24-hour room service, and a health club with gym and sauna. It's located off Botanic Avenue, within a half-mile walk of the center of the city.

Plaza Hotel

15 Brunswick St., Belfast, Co. Antrim BT2 7GE. ☎ **800/221-2222** from the U.S., or 01232/333555. Fax 01232/232999. 75 rms. TV TEL. £90 ($139.50) double. Rates include breakfast. AE, DC, MC, V.

Located in the heart of the city, less than two blocks from City Hall, this modern, nine-story hotel was opened in 1990. It's within walking distance to all major city sights. The guest rooms are contemporary in style, with light woods, floral fabrics, and amenities such as hair dryers and garment presses. Dining and entertainment choices include the Amelia Garden, an upstairs conservatory-style restaurant, and George C. McClatchy's Public Bar on the ground floor.

INEXPENSIVE

Ash-Rowan Guest House

12 Windsor Ave., Belfast, Co. Antrim BT9 6EE. ☎ **01232/661758.** Fax 01232/663227. 4 rms. TV TEL. £60 ($93) double. Rates include full breakfast. MC, V.

Situated on a quiet, tree-lined street in a residential neighborhood, this four-story Victorian house sits between Lisburn and Malone Roads near Queen's University. Proprietors Evelyn and Hazlett have outfitted it with country-style furnishings, family heirlooms, and antiques, along with bouquets of fresh flowers from their garden. The rates include a choice of eight different traditional breakfasts including the Ulster fry or scrambled eggs with kippers or smoked salmon. There is a private parking lot outside.

DINING
EXPENSIVE

Restaurant 44

44 Bedford St. ☎ **01232/244844.** Reservations recommended. Main courses £7.95–£13.95 ($12.30–$21.60); fixed-price lunch £8.95–£13.95 ($13.85–$21.60); fixed-price dinner £10.95–£15.95 ($16.95–$24.70). AE, DC, MC, V. Daily noon–3pm, Mon–Sat 6–11:30pm. CONTINENTAL.

Defining itself as a Colonial-style brasserie, this midcity restaurant sits between City Hall and the BBC studios. The menu lists such creative dishes as chicken with basil mousse, charcoal-grilled fillet of beef with prawns and butter sauce, fillet of salmon with green vegetable caviar and saffron sauce, and Mediterranean vegetable strudel with eggplant, artichokes, tomatoes, garlic, and herbs, wrapped in zucchini. To bring perfect closure, try the garden berry pudding.

✪ Roscoff

7 Lesley House, Shaftesbury Sq. ☎ **01232/331532.** Reservations required. Main courses £16.50 ($25.55); fixed-price lunch £16.50 ($25.55); fixed-price dinner £28.95 ($44.85). AE, DC, MC, V. Mon–Fri 12:15–2:15pm, Mon–Sat 6:30–10:15pm. INTERNATIONAL.

Although the decor at this Michelin-starred restaurant is simple, with frosted windows, black-and-white furnishings, and white walls adorned by modern art, the menu is definitely artistic, thanks to chef/owner Paul Rankin's penchant for using the best of Ulster produce in creative combinations of taste and color. The menu offers dishes such as rack of lamb, charcoal-grilled beef fillet with bacon and Roquefort sauce, fillet of Irish salmon with asparagus and chervil, and steamed symphony of seafood with salmon, mako, monkfish, brill, sole, prawns, and lobster.

MODERATE

Ⓢ La Belle Epoque

61/63 Dublin Rd. ☎ **01232/323244.** Reservations suggested. Lunch main courses £5.95–£10.95 ($9.20–$16.95); dinner main courses £6.95–£10.50 ($10.75–$16.25). AE, DC, MC, V. Mon–Fri noon–11pm, Sat 6–11pm. FRENCH.

Housed in a double shop-front brick building, this brasserie-style restaurant sits at the corner of Ventry Lane. The menu offers a creative mixture of fruit- and vegetable-based sauces with dishes such as chicken with almond crust and mushroom sauce, veal in creamy artichoke sauce, fillet of turbot with salmon trout mousse, and panfried salmon with broccoli and ginger sauce. All unusual and delicious.

✪ Nick's Warehouse

35 Hill St. ☎ **01232/439690.** Reservations suggested. Lunch or dinner main courses £5.95–£18.95 ($9.20–$29.35). AE, DC, MC, V. Mon–Fri noon–3pm, Tues–Sat 6–9pm (drinks up to 11pm). INTERNATIONAL.

Set in an old warehouse between St. Anne's Cathedral and the tourist office, this restaurant offers a wine bar setting downstairs and a classy dining room upstairs, with brick walls and an open kitchen. They offer a variety of international appetizers, from gazpacho to curly kale soup to a platter of Italian salami or gravlax (cured Norwegian salmon). Main courses include sirloin steaks, hot-and-sour beef with water chestnuts, lamb chops with honey and ginger sauce, and fillet of salmon with a fennel hollandaise. There is always an interesting vegetarian offering as well.

MODERATE/INEXPENSIVE

Bananas

4 Clarence St. ☎ **01232/244844.** Reservations suggested for dinner. Main courses £4.95–£11.95 ($7.65–$18.50). MC, V. Mon–Fri noon–3pm, Mon–Sat 5–11:30pm. INTERNATIONAL.

Situated around the corner from Ulster Hall, this informal little restaurant blends culinary influences from Thailand, Mexico, California, and the Continent. The menu offers a variety of tapas, Cajun chicken or chicken Kiev, salads, steaks, sandwiches, pastas, and vegetable goulash. As might be expected, the featured dessert is roast bananas in puff pastry.

❸ Saints & Scholars

3 University St. ☎ **01232/325137.** Reservations not accepted. Fixed-price lunch £4.95–£8.95 ($7.65–$13.85); dinner main courses £4.95–£9.95 ($7.65–$21.50). AE, MC, V. Mon–Sat 12:30–2:30pm and 5:30–10:30pm. INTERNATIONAL.

Situated two blocks from the Botanic Gardens and the Queen's university, this restaurant has a collegiate atmosphere, with a variety of book-filled dining rooms, eclectically decorated with rattan furnishings, ceiling fans, plants, and wall coverings of Celtic design. The blackboard-style menu offers dishes such as wok-roasted monkfish; salmon en croûte with spinach; trout in pastry with oranges, bananas, and honey; pink duck breast with green peppercorn and brandy sauce; rack of lamb; steaks; salads; and pastas.

Skandia

50 Howard St. ☎ ☎ **01232/240239.** Reservations suggested for dinner. Dinner main courses £4–£11 ($6.20–$17.05). AE, MC, V. Mon–Sat 9:30am–11pm. IRISH.

Located in the heart of the city a block west of Donegall Square, this restaurant is a convenient and dependable place to dine at any time of day. It has a homey atmosphere with banquette seating and a salad bar in the middle of the room, and offers dishes such as grilled salmon, scampi, or turbot steamed with celery, mushrooms, and nuts, as well as salads, pastas, vegetarian dishes, burgers, steaks, ribs, and omelets. This restaurant is a favorite with families.

INEXPENSIVE

Harveys

95 Great Victoria St. ☎ **01232/233433.** Reservations not required. Main courses £4.95–£7.95 ($7.65–$12.30). MC, V. Mon–Thurs and Sun 5–11:30pm, Fri–Sat 5pm–midnight. INTERNATIONAL.

An American atmosphere prevails here with a decor of U.S. flags and a menu that offers choices such as steaks, burgers, salads, pizza, tacos, pastas, and a signature Frisco Bay platter (prawns, crab claws, scampi, mussels, and langoustines), as well as beef Stroganoff, chicken Kiev, and smoky pork fillet stuffed with cheese and smoked bacon.

BELFAST AFTER DARK
PUBS

❂ Crown Liquor Saloon

Great Victoria St. ☎ **01232/249476.**

Dating from 1826 and situated opposite the Grand Opera House, this gaslit pub, a feast of Victoriana, is a member of the National Trust. Step inside and see the marvelous array of 10 snugs (small private rooms) on the right, each with its own door and call bell, as well as the tin ceiling, tile floor, etched and smoked glass, beveled mirror with floral and wildlife decorations, scalloped lamps, and long bar with inlaid colored glass and marble trim.

Kelly's Cellars

Bank St., Belfast. ☎ **01232/324835.**

Recognized as Belfast's oldest tavern in continuous use, this pub dates back to 1720 and has had a storied history, including being a headquarters for leaders in the 1798 Insurrection. Situated just off Royal Avenue, it's also been a favorite haunt for actors and novelists. The decor is rich in vaulted ceilings, paned windows, old barrels, white-washed arches, and wooden snugs, and is festooned with such memorabilia as old ledgers, coins, china, prints, maps, and international soccer caps. There is often traditional music on tap in the evenings.

Pat's Bar

Prince's Dock St. ☎ **01232/744524.**

For a taste of Belfast's harbor atmosphere, join the sailors, dockers, and local businesspeople at this pub at the gates of Prince's Dock. The decor includes an antique hand-carved beech bar, pine-wood furnishings, red-tile floor, black-and-white photos of the pub's earliest days, and an interesting collection of memorabilia given to the bar's owner by sailors passing through the port—clogs, swords, tom-toms and maracas, a telescope, and a bayonet. There is traditional Irish music on Friday and Saturday nights from 9pm.

White's Tavern

Winecellar Entry, off High St. ☎ **01232/243080.**

Tucked in a historic cobblestoned trading lane between High and Rosemary streets, this old tavern was established in 1630 as a wine and spirit shop. It's full of old barrels and hoists, ornate snugs, brick arches, large copper measures, framed newspaper clippings of the 200-year-old vintage, quill pens, and other memorabilia. A good pub for conversation and browsing.

ARTS IN THE EVENING

The leading concert and performance halls in Belfast are the **Grand Opera House,** Great Victoria Street (☎ **01232/241919**), which presents a wide variety of entertainment; **Ulster Hall,** Bedford Street (☎ **01232/323900**), which stages major concerts from rock to large-scale choral and symphonic works by the Ulster Orchestra and Northern Ireland Symphony Orchestra; and **Kings Hall,** Lisburn Road (☎ **01232/665225**), for superstar concerts and other musical events.

Theaters include the **Arts Theatre,** Botanic Avenue (☎ **01232/316900**), for popular theatrical productions; **Lyric Theatre,** Ridgeway Street (☎ **01232/381081**), for new plays by Irish and international playwrights; and the **Belfast Civic Arts Theatre,** 41 Botanic Ave. (☎ **01232/316900**), for popular shows, musicals, and comedies.

Tickets, priced from £7 to £30 ($10.85 to $45.50) for most events, can be purchased in advance from the **Virgin Ticket Shop,** Castle Court, Belfast (☎ **01232/323744**).

2 Excursions from Belfast

ARDS PENINSULA

10 miles E of Belfast.

The Ards Peninsula curls around the western shore of Strangford Lough, and at 18 miles long is one of the largest inland sea inlets in the British Isles. A place of great natural beauty, the peninsula boasts a wonderful bird sanctuary and wildlife reserve, and its shores are home to multifarious species of marine life. Two roads traverse the peninsula: A20 (the Lough road) and A2 (the coast road). Of the two, the Lough road is the more scenic.

At the southern tip of the Lough, there is a continuous car ferry service connecting Portaferry with Strangford on the mainland side. It runs from 7:30am to 10:30 or 11pm each day. No reservations are needed. The one-way fare is £2.40 ($3.70) for a car and driver and 60p (93¢) for each passenger.

Sea-fishing trips from Portaferry into the waters of Strangford Lough and along the Co. Down coast are organized by Peter Wright, **Norsemaid Sea Enterprises,** 152 Portaferry Rd., Newtownards, Co. Down (☎ **01247/812081**). Reservations are required. This company also offers diving charters, day cruises, and wildlife cruises.

There are two National Trust properties in this area, one on the Ards Peninsula and the other just across the lough at Portaferry:

✪ Castle Ward

Strangford, Co. Down. ☎ **01396/881204.** House, £2.60 ($4.05) adults, £1.30 ($2) children, £6.50 ($10.10) family; estate, £1.75 ($2.70) per car in off season, £3.50 ($5.45) per car in high season. House Apr, Sept, and Oct Sat–Sun 1–6pm; May–Aug Mon–Wed and Fri–Sun 1–6pm; estate year-round dawn to dusk.

Situated 1 1/2 miles west of Strangford village, this National Trust house dates from 1760 and is half classical and half Gothic in architectural style. It sits amid a 700-acre country estate of formal gardens, woodlands, lakelands, and seashore. A restored 1830s cornmill and a Victorian-style laundry are on the grounds, and there's a theater in the stable yard that's a venue for operatic performances in summer.

✪ Mount Stewart House

Newtownards (on the A20 road), Co. Down. ☎ **012477/88387.** House, garden, and temple £3 ($13.95) adults, £1.50 ($2.30) children; garden and temple £2.70 ($4.20) adults, £1.35 ($2.10) children; temple only £1 ($1.55) per person. House, Apr and Oct Sat–Sun 1–6pm, May–Sept Mon and Wed–Sun 1–6pm; garden, Apr–Sept daily 10:30am–6pm, Oct Sat–Sun 10:30am–6pm; temple same as house except hours are 2–5pm.

Once the home of Lord Castlereagh, this 18th-century house sits on the eastern shore of Strangford Lough, about 15 miles east of Belfast. It has one of the greatest gardens in the care of the National Trust, with an unrivaled collection of rare and unusual plants. The interior of the house is noteworthy for its art works, including *Hambletonian* by George Stubbs, one of the finest paintings in Ireland, and family portraits by Batoni, Mengs, and Lazlo. The Temple of the Winds, a banqueting house built in 1785, is also on the estate.

ARMAGH

40 miles SW of Belfast.

VISITOR INFORMATION   Stop into the **Armagh Tourist Information Office,** 40 English St., Armagh (☎ **01861/527808**). It's open from April through September, Monday through Saturday from 10am to 7pm and on Sunday from noon to 7pm; from October through March, Monday through Saturday from 10am to 5pm and on Sunday from 2 to 5pm.

One of Ireland's most historic cities, Armagh takes its name from the Irish *Ard Macha* or Macha's Height, after the legendary pagan queen Macha, who is said to have built a fortress here in the middle of the first millennium B.C.

This fort, known originally as Eamain Macha, still exists today, known simply today as ✪ **Navan Fort,** Killylea Road, Armagh (☎ **01861/525550**). Situated 2 miles west of Armagh, it reflects more than 7,500 years of Irish history, from Mesolithic hunters, Neolithic farmers, and Bronze Age peoples to the Celts and eventually into the Christian era.

Navan was the earliest capital of Ulster and seat of the province's kings for over 700 years. Today it's a system of earthenworks, settlement sites, and grassy mounds. The story of the fort is told at a new visitors center, specially designed to be an integral part of the landscape, using a series of audiovisual presentations including the 10-minute *The Dawning,* an introduction to the history of the area; the 35-minute *Real World,* an explanation of the archaeology of the region; and the 30-minute *The Other World,* a dazzling review of all the legends of Navan. Admission is £3.95 ($5.35) adults, £2.25 ($3.05) children, £7 to £10 ($10.85 to $15.50) family. It's open April to June and September, Monday through Friday 10am to 6pm, Saturday 11am to 6pm, Sunday noon to 6pm; July and August, Monday through Saturday 10am to 7pm, Sunday 11am to 7pm; October through March, Monday through Friday 10am to 5pm, Saturday 11am to 5pm, Sunday noon to 5pm.

Most of Armagh's history, however, focuses on the 5th century, when St. Patrick chose this place as a base from which to spread Christianity; he called it "my sweet hill" and built a stone church here. Ever since then, Armagh has been considered the ecclesiastical capital of Ireland, and today there are two St. Patrick's cathedrals, Catholic and Anglican, seats of the primates of both sects.

Many of the public buildings and the Georgian town houses along the Mall are the work of Francis Johnston, a native of Armagh, who also left his mark on Georgian Dublin. Buildings, as well as doorsteps and pavements, are made of warm-colored pink, yellow, and red local limestone that make the city glow even on a dull day.

In addition to being Ireland's spiritual capital, this area is known for its apple trees, earning Armagh the title "the Orchard of Ireland."

CARRICKFERGUS

12 miles NE of Belfast.

VISITOR INFORMATION   Stop into the **Carrickfergus Tourist Information Office,** Heritage Plaza, Antrim Street, Carrickfergus, Co. Antrim (☎ **01960/ 366455**). It's open Monday through Friday from 9am to 5pm, Saturday 10am to 6pm and Sunday 2 to 6pm with limited hours September through April.

ATTRACTIONS

It's said that Carrickfergus, Co. Antrim, was a thriving town when Belfast was a sandbank. In 1180, John de Courcy, a Norman, built a massive keep at Carrickfergus, the first real Irish castle, to guard the approach to Belfast Lough. Today visitors can tour the well-preserved ✪ **Carrickfergus Castle,** Antrim Street, Carrickfergus (☎ **01960/365190**), and enjoy an audiovisual presentation on the castle's history. In the summer months, medieval banquets, a medieval fair, and a crafts market are held here. Gifts and refreshments are also available. It's open from April through September, Monday through Saturday from 10am to 6pm and on Sunday from 2 to 6pm; from October through March, Monday through Saturday from 10am to 4pm and on Sunday from 2 to 4pm. Admission is £2.70 ($4.20) adults, £1.35 ($2.10) seniors and children.

In addition, **Knight Ride,** Antrim Street, Carrickfergus (☎ **01960/366455**), is an action-packed monorail that takes passengers on a reenactment of the history of the town from A.D. 531. Admission to the ride is £2.70 ($4.20) adults, £1.35 ($2.10) seniors and children, £7.30 ($11.30). It's open from April through September,

Monday through Saturday from 10am to 6pm, Sunday noon to 6pm; from October through March, Monday through Saturday from 10am to 5pm and Sunday noon to 5pm. Reduced rate tickets for admission to both the castle and the ride are £4.85 ($7.50) adults, £2.40 ($3.70) seniors and children, £13.50 ($20.90) family.

This area is also the setting of the **Andrew Jackson Centre,** Boneybefore, Carrickfergus (☎ **01960/366455**), a simple one-story cottage with earthen floor and open fireplace that was the home of the parents of Andrew Jackson, seventh president of the United States. His parents left here and emigrated to the United States in 1765. The house now contains a display on the life and career of Andrew Jackson and Ulster's connections with America. On weekends in July and August there are craft demonstrations reflecting rural folklife, such as sampler-making, basket-weaving, griddle-making, patchwork-quilting, and lace-making. Admission is £1.20 ($1.85) adults, 60p (95¢) seniors and children. It's open from May through October, Monday through Friday, 10am to 1pm and 2 to 6pm, Saturday and Sunday from 2 to 6pm.

CULTRA
7 miles E of Belfast.

One of the most popular attractions in the Belfast area is actually in Co. Down, the ✪ **Ulster Folk & Transport Museum** at Cultra, Holywood (☎ **01232/428428,** or 01232/421444 for 24-hour information). It encompasses many parts of Ulster's past, all brought together onto one 176-acre site.

Sixty acres are devoted to a unique outdoor museum that contains a series of 19th-century buildings, all saved from the bulldozer's path and moved intact from their original sites in various parts of Northern Ireland. You can walk among 19th-century farmhouses, mills, and churches; climb to the terraces of houses; and peruse rural schools, a forge, bank, print shop, and a small conical hut where a watchman would sit with his musket guarding the linen laid out on the green to bleach in the sun. There are demonstrations of people cooking over an open hearth, plowing the fields with horses, thatching roofs, and practicing traditional Ulster crafts such as textile-making, spinning, quilting, lace-making, printing, spade-making, and shoe-making.

In addition, there is an exhibit on Irish railways, considered one of the top 10 of its kind in Europe. In 1996, a new "Car in Society" exhibit with a wonderful collection of automobiles opened at the museum, enhancing an already impressive center. Admission is £3 ($4.65) for adults, £2 ($3.10) for children. It's open during July and August, Monday through Saturday, 10:30am to 6pm, and on Sunday, noon to 6pm; April through June and in September, Monday through Friday, 9:30am to 5pm, Saturday from 10:30am to 6pm, Sunday from noon to 6pm; and October through March, Monday through Friday from 9:30am to 4pm, and on Saturday and Sunday from 12:30 to 4:30pm.

LISBURN
10 miles SE of Belfast.

The linen industry, long synonymous with Northern Ireland, is the focus of the new **Irish Linen Centre,** Lisburn Museum, Market Square, Lisburn, Co. Antrim (☎ **01846/663377**). This museum invites visitors to trace the production of linen, from its earliest days in the 17th century to the high-tech industry of today. There are opportunities to see linen in all stages of production, both up close and personal in a weaving workshop with hand looms and via audio-visual presentations.

Admission is £2.75 ($4.25) for adults, £1.75 ($2.70) for seniors and children. Hours are April through September, Monday through Saturday from 9:30am to 5:30pm; fromOctober through March the center closes at 5pm daily and is closed Sundays.

LOUGH NEAGH

10 miles W of Belfast.

Lough Neagh, at 153 square miles, is the largest lake in the British Isles. Often called an inland sea, the lough is 20 miles long and 10 miles wide, with a 65-mile shore. It is famous for its eels, an Ulster delicacy. Hundreds of tons of eels from Lough Neagh are exported each year.

Lough Neagh is also a playground for Belfast residents. To sample the outdoor activity, head for the **Lough Neagh Discovery Centre,** Oxford Island, Craigavon, Co. Armagh (☎ **01762/322205**). Situated midway between Belfast and Armagh city, this center is on the southern shore of Lough Neagh at Oxford Island, a nature reserve with a range of habitats such as reed beds, woodlands, and wildflower meadows. It serves as an introduction to all that the lough has to offer, with historical and geographic exhibits, an interactive ecolab explaining the ecosystems of the lough, walking trails, bird-watching observation points, and picnic areas. **Boat trips** on Lough Neagh, lasting about 45 minutes, depart regularly from the discovery center jetty. Admission to the center is £2.50 ($3.90) adults, £1.50 ($2.35) children; boat trips cost £3 ($4.65) for adults, £1.50 ($2.35) for children. It's open in September and April, Monday through Friday 10am to 7pm, on Saturday from 10am to 8pm, and on Sunday from noon to 8pm; from May through August, daily from 10am to 9pm; and October through March, on Monday through Friday 10am to 5pm, on Saturday and Sunday from noon to 5pm.

THE MOUNTAINS OF MOURNE

20 miles SW of Belfast.

VISITOR INFORMATION   Stop into the **Downpatrick Tourist Information Centre,** 74 Market St., Downpatrick, Co. Down (☎ **01396/612233**), or the **Newcastle Centre,** 10–14 Central Promenade, Newcastle, Co. Down (☎ **013967/22222**). Both offices are open year-round, with varying days and hours according to the season.

ATTRACTIONS

Sweeping down to the Irish Sea in the southeast corner of Northern Ireland, ✪ **the Mountains of Mourne** consist of 12 shapely summits rising above 2,000 feet, dominated by the barren peak of Slieve Donard, at 2,796 feet the highest mountain in Northern Ireland.

It's worth the drive from Belfast to see this beautiful coastal panorama. Alternately, if you're coming from the Republic of Ireland, the A2 drive along the coast is particularly scenic, with the mountains in the background.

The Mountains of Mourne also lead to Downpatrick, one of the north's oldest cities and a place closely identified with St. Patrick. History tells us that when Patrick came to Ireland in 432 to begin his missionary work, strong winds blew his boat into this area. He had meant to sail up the coast to Co. Antrim, where as a young slave he had tended flocks on Slemish Mountain. Instead, he settled here and converted the local chieftain Dichu and his followers to Christianity. Over the next 30 years Patrick roamed to many other places in Ireland carrying out his work, but he wound up here to die and is said to be buried in the graveyard of Downpatrick Cathedral. A large stone marks the spot.

For an overview on St. Patrick's association with this area, stop into the **St. Patrick's Centre / Down Heritage Museum,** The Mall, Downpatrick, Co. Down (☎ **01396/615218**). It's open from Tuesday through Friday, 11am to 5pm, and on Saturday from 2 to 5pm; from July to mid-September it's also open on Sunday 2 to 5pm.

This area is also home of Newcastle, a favorite seaside resort of the Irish, and site of one of the world's great golf courses, ✪ **Royal County Down,** Newcastle, Co. Down (☎ **013967/23314**). Nestled in huge sand dunes with the Mountains of Mourne in the background, this 18-hole, par-71 championship course was created in 1889. Greens fees are £35 ($54.25) on weekdays and £40 ($62) on weekends.

3 The Antrim Coast

VISITOR INFORMATION   There are **tourist information centers** at the following locations: 7 Mary St., Ballycastle, Co. Antrim (☎ **012657/62024**); 44 Causeway Rd., Bushmills, Co. Antrim (☎ **012657/31855**); and Dunluce Centre, Sandhill Drive, Portrush, Co. Antrim (☎ **01265/823333**). All are open year-round, with hours varying according to the seasons.

THE GLENS OF ANTRIM

Heralded in story and song, the Glens of Antrim consist of nine green valleys, sitting north of Belfast and stretching from south to north. All of these glens have individual names, each based on a local tale or legend. Although the meanings are not known for certain, the popular translations are as follows: Glenarm (glen of the army), Glencloy (glen of the hedges), Glenariff (ploughman's glen), Glenballyeamon (Edwardstown glen), Glenaan (glen of the rush lights), Glencorp (glen of the slaughter), Glendun (brown glen), Glenshesk (sedgy glen), and Glentaisie (Taisie's glen).

The people who live in the Glens of Antrim are descendants of both the ancient Irish and their cousins, the Hebridean Scots, so this area is one of the last places in Northern Ireland where Gaelic was spoken. To this day, the glen people are known to be great storytellers.

In all, the area identified as the Antrim coast is 60 miles long, stretching north of Larne and then west after passing Bushmills and the Giant's Causeway to Portrush. The route takes in marine seascapes and chalky cliffs and includes the National Trust village of Cushendun with pretty Cornish-style cottages as well as a string of beach resorts that are favored by Irish and English vacationers, such as Portrush, Portstewart, and Portballintrae. This coastal drive also meanders under bridges and arches, passing bays, sandy beaches, harbors, and huge rock formations. Two of Ireland's foremost attractions are also here: the Giant's Causeway and Old Bushmills Distillery. Each August, the seaside town of Ballycastle plays host to one of Ireland's oldest traditional gatherings, the Oul' Lammas Fair.

ATTRACTIONS

✪ Giant's Causeway Centre

44 Causeway Rd., Bushmills, Co. Antrim. ☎ **02657/31855.** Causeway free; audiovisual and exhibition, £1 ($1.55) adults, 80p ($1.25) seniors, 50p (80¢) children, £2.50 ($3.90) family. Parking £2 ($3.10). Mid-Mar through May, daily 11am–5pm; June, daily 11am–5:30pm; July–Aug, daily 10am–7pm; Sept–Oct, Mon–Fri 11am–5pm, Sat–Sun 10:30am–5:30pm.

Declared a World Heritage Site, this natural rock formation is often called the eighth wonder of the world. It consists of roughly 40,000 tightly packed basalt columns that extend for 3 miles along the coast. The tops of the columns form stepping stones that lead from the cliff foot and disappear under the sea. They're mostly hexagonal in shape, and some are as tall as 40 feet. Scientists estimate that they were formed 60 or 70 million years ago by volcanic eruptions and cooling lava. The ancients, on the other hand, believed the rock formation to be the work of giants. Another legend has it that Finn MacCool, the Ulster warrior and commander of the king of Ulster's armies, built the causeway as a highway over the sea to bring his girlfriend from the Isle of Hebrides. (And you thought sending a limo was cool.) Start a visit to the causeway at the Visitor Centre, where there is a continuous 25-minute audiovisual show that illustrates the formation and history of the site. To reach the causeway itself, you have a choice of taking a shuttle bus (80p; $1.24 round-trip) or following a circular walk. The walk goes past amphitheaters of stone columns and formations with fanciful names like Honeycomb, Wishing Well, Giant's Granny, King and his Nobles, and Lover's Leap, and up a wooden staircase to Benbane Head and back along the cliff top.

✪ Old Bushmills Distillery

Main St., Bushmills, Co. Antrim. ☎ **012657/31521.** Admission £2.50 ($3.90) adults, £2 ($3.10) seniors and students, £1 ($1.55) children. Jan–May and Sept–Dec Mon–Thurs 9am–noon and 1:30–3:30pm, Fri 9am–noon; June–Aug, Mon–Thurs 9am–4pm.

Licensed to distill spirits in 1608 but with historical references dating from 1276, this is not only the oldest distillery in Ireland, but the oldest in the world. Visitors are welcome to tour the facility and watch the whole whiskey-making process, starting with fresh water from the adjacent River Bush and continuing through distilling, fermenting, and bottling. At the end of the tour, you can sample the wares in the Poststill Bar, where there are also some fascinating exhibits on the long history of the distillery. Tours depart regularly and last about 25 minutes.

Carrick-A-Rede Rope Bridge

Larrybane, Co. Antrim. ☎ **012657/31159** or 012657/32143. Free admission. Bridge up spring to mid-Sept; center early April to May, Sat–Sun 1–5pm; June–Aug, daily 2–6pm. Parking £2 ($3.10).

Located 5 miles west of Ballycastle off the A2 road, this open rope bridge spans a chasm 60 feet wide and 80 feet above the sea between the mainland and a small island. The bridge is put up each spring by local fishermen to give access to a salmon fishery on the island, but it can be used by visitors for a thrilling walk and the chance to call out to each other, "Don't look down!"

Dunluce Castle

Bushmills-Portrush road, Dunluce, Co. Antrim. ☎ **012657/31938.** Admission £1.50 ($2.30) adults, 75p ($1.15) seniors and children under 10. April–Sept, Mon–Sat 10am–7pm, Sun 2–7; Oct–Mar, Tues–Sat 10am–4pm, Sun 2–4pm.

Situated 3 miles east of Portrush off the A2 road, this site was once the main fort of the Irish MacDonnells, chiefs of Antrim. It's the largest and most sophisticated castle

▮ Impressions

There is something inexpressibly weird about those millions of mathematically formed pillars which thrust themselves upward at the edge of the sea. And the whole scene is a shade of metallic grey. I have never seen stones that so closely resemble iron or steel. The [Giant's] Causeway has a queerly modern look! It is Cubist.

—H. V. Morton, *In Search of Ireland,* 1930

in the North, consisting of a series of fortifications built on rocky outcrops extending into the sea. The present castle incorporates two of the original Norman towers dating from 1305 and was the power base of the north coast for 400 years. The visitor center shows an audiovisual presentation with background on the site.

Dunluce Centre

Dunluce Ave., Portrush. ☎ **01265/834444.** Turbo Tours £2.20 ($3.40), Earthquest £1.50 ($2.30); Myths & Legends £2.20 ($3.40); Tower 50p (75¢); all four attractions £4 ($6.20), £15 ($23.25) family. Apr–June, Mon–Fri noon–5pm, Sat and Sun noon–7pm; July–Aug, daily 10am–8pm; Sept–Mar, weekends noon–5pm.

Opened in June 1993, this family oriented entertainment complex provides a variety of indoor activity. It offers a multimedia show, *Myths & Legends,* that illustrates the folklore of the Antrim coast, as well as "Turbo Tours," a thrill ride that simulates a modern-day space ride, and "Earthquest," an interactive display on the wonders of nature. There is also a viewing tower with panoramic views of the coast, a Victorian-style arcade of shops, and a restaurant with a children's play area.

Rathlin Island Bird Sanctuary

Off the coast of Ballycastle, Co. Antrim. ☎ **012657/63935.** Round-trip £5.60 ($8.70) adults, £4.45 ($6.90) seniors, £2.80 ($4.35) children under 14. Daily year-round at 10:30am and 5pm (4pm in winter) from Ballycastle; at 9am and 4pm (3pm in winter) from Rathlin.

For peace and solitude, plan a trip to this boomerang-shaped island, lying 6 miles off the coast north of Ballycastle and 14 miles south of Scotland. It is almost 4 miles long, yet less than a mile wide at any point, and is almost completely treeless, with a rugged coast of 200-foot-high cliffs, a small beach, and a native population of 100. It's a great bird-watching center. Boat trips are operated daily from Ballycastle pier; crossing time is 50 minutes.

ACCOMMODATIONS
MODERATE

✪ Bushmills Inn

25 Main St., Bushmills, Co. Antrim BT57 8QA. ☎ ☎ **012657/32339.** Fax 012657/32048. 11 rms (4 with bath). TV TEL. £88 ($136.40) double. Rates include full breakfast. MC, V.

Situated in the center of the famous whiskey-making village of the same name, this inn dates from the 17th century. It was totally restored and refurbished in 1987. The interior has a definite old-world charm, with open turf fireplaces, gas lamps, and antique furnishings. Guest rooms are comfortable and contemporary in design, with country pine and caned furniture, floral wallpaper, brass fixtures, and vintage prints. Facilities include a lounge bar, a gallery / drawing room, and the Barony restaurant, which features recipes using Bushmills whiskey.

Causeway Coast Hotel

36 Ballyreagh Rd., Portrush, Co. Antrim BT56 8LR. ☎ **01265/822435.** Fax 0265/824495. 21 rms. TV TEL. £75 ($116.25) double. Rates include full breakfast. AE, MC, V.

Opposite the nine-hole Ballyreagh Golf Course and overlooking the Atlantic coastline, this rambling resort is located between Portstewart and Portrush, but away from the bustle of both towns. Guest rooms have modern furnishings with pastel tones and added amenities such as garment presses, hair dryers, and tea/coffeemakers. Some rooms have sea views and private balconies. The property also includes self-catering apartments with kitchens. Dining options are the Dunluce restaurant, Tramways Steak Bar, and the Wine Bar.

Londonderry Arms

20 Harbour Rd., Carnlough, Co. Antrim BT44 OEU. ☎ **800/44-PRIMA** from the U.S., or 01574/885255. Fax 0574/885263. 22 rms. TV TEL. £75 ($116.25) double. Rates include full breakfast. AE, DC, MC, V.

Located at the foot of Glencloy, one of the nine Antrim glens, this ivy-covered former coaching inn was built in 1848 and was at one point owned by Sir Winston Churchill through a family inheritance. It has been a hotel in the hands of the O'Neill family since 1947. It sits in the heart of a delightful coastal town with views of the harbor across the street. The hotel was renovated and upgraded this year. Guest rooms have traditional furnishings with dark woods and floral fabrics. A restaurant and lounge are also on the premises.

Magherabuoy House Hotel

41 Magheraboy Rd., Portrush, Co. Antrim BT56 8NX. ☎ **01265/823507.** Fax 0265/824687. 38 rms. TV TEL. £80 ($124) double. Rates include full breakfast. AE, DC, MC, V.

Nestled amid gardens on high grounds on the edge of town, this country manor–style hotel enjoys panoramic views of the town and seacoast, yet is away from all of the resort hubbub. The interior's traditional ambience—dark woods, gilded mirrors, and open fireplaces—contrasts with the guest rooms, which are contemporary and smart with pastel-toned frilly fabrics, brass fittings, and floral wallpapers. Public facilities include a restaurant, lounge, snack bar, nightclub, and a leisure complex with Jacuzzi and gym.

Marine Hotel

1 North St., Ballycastle, Co. Antrim BT64 6BN. ☎ **012657/62222.** Fax 02657/69507. 32 rms. TV TEL. £70 ($108.50) double. Rates include full breakfast. AE, DC, MC, V.

Sitting right on the harbor at Ballycastle, this newly refurbished three-story contemporary-style hotel is a favorite with Irish vacationers. The guest rooms offer lovely views of the sea and bright modern furnishings. Facilities include the Glass Island restaurant; Marconi lounge bar; and Legends; a nightclub featuring a variety of music from disco to cabaret, country western, jazz, and popular tunes. A country club is also run by the hotel and offers pool, sauna, and fitness room.

DINING

MODERATE

✪ Hillcrest Country House

306 Whitepark Rd., Giant's Causeway, Co. Antrim. ☎ **012657/31577.** Reservations required. Main courses £7.25–£9.95 ($11.25–$15.40). MC, V. April–Sept, Mon–Sat noon–6:45pm; Tues–Sat, 6:45–9:30pm. IRISH.

Surrounded by lovely gardens and situated opposite the entrance to the Giant's Causeway, this restaurant offers lovely wide-windowed views of the coast, which are particularly beautiful at sunset. The menu emphasizes local ingredients and creative sauces: salmon baked with cucumbers, mushrooms, and fennel sauce; grilled venison with game mousse laced with Black Bush Irish whiskey; roast North Antrim duck with sage and onion stuffing and peach brandy; and noisettes of lamb with rosemary and garlic sauce.

✪ Ramore

Ramore St., The Harbour, Portrush, Co. Antrim. ☎ **0265/824313.** Reservations required. Main courses £6.95–£10.95 ($10.75–$16.95). MC, V. Tues–Sat 6:30–10:30pm. INTERNATIONAL.

Situated on the east end of the harbor overlooking boats and the sea, this restaurant is known for its international menu choices, such as chicken breast with fresh asparagus and vinaigrette of pine nuts, sun-dried tomatoes, Parmesan, and truffle oil; duck on a bed of shredded cabbage; and pork filled with Parma ham and Emmenthal cheese; as well as paella, Thai chicken, tempura prawns, fish of the day, rack of lamb, and steaks.

INEXPENSIVE

Ⓢ Sweeney's Wine Bar

6b Seaport Ave., Portballintrae, Co. Antrim. ☎ **012657/31279.** Reservations recommended for dinner. Main courses £4–£6 ($6.20–$9.30). No credit cards. Mon–Sat 12:30–10pm; Sun 12:30–2:30pm and 7–9pm. IRISH.

Situated on the coast, this is a pubby and informal spot with a conservatory-style extension and outdoor seating in good weather. The menu features pub grub—burgers, pastas, seafood plates (prawns, scampi, cod, and white fish), seafood pie, steak and kidney pie, and stir-fry vegetables.

Victorianna Restaurant

Dunluce Ave., Portrush, Co. Antrim. ☎ **01265/824400.** Reservations not accepted. Main courses £1.90–£4 ($2.90–$6.10). No credit cards. May–Aug, Mon–Sun 10am–10pm; Sept, Mon–Thurs 11am–6pm and Fri–Sun 11am–10pm; Oct–Apr, Fri–Sun 2–9pm. SELF-SERVICE.

Located in the new Dunluce Center, this Victorian-theme bilevel restaurant is a great place to stop for refreshment when touring the Antrim coast. The menu includes sandwiches, omelets, salads, pastas, and steaks, as well as sausage, beans, and chips and "Ulster fry," a cheese and onion pie.

4 Derry & the Northwest Passage

Derry is 73 miles NW of Belfast, 39 miles SW of Portrush, 70 miles NW of Armagh, 61 miles NE of Enniskillen, 144 miles NW of Dublin, and 220 miles NE of Shannon.

GETTING AROUND   Local bus service to suburban areas outside the city is operated by **Ulsterbus,** Foyle Street Depot, Derry (**01504/262261**). There is no bus service within the city walls since it's small and easily walkable.

There are **taxi stands** at the Ulsterbus, Foyle Street Depot (☎ **01504/262262**), and at the **Northern Ireland Railways Station,** Duke Street, Waterside, Derry (☎ **01504/42228**). To call a cab, contact **Central Taxis** (☎ **01504/261911**), **City Radio Cabs** (☎ **01504/264466**), **Foyle Taxis** (☎ **01504/263905**), or **Tower Taxis** (☎ **01504/371944**).

From June through September, Ulsterbus operates **Civic Bus Tours** of the Derry sights, in cooperation with the **Foyle Civic Trust** (☎ **01504/262211**). Tours are scheduled for Tuesday and Thursday (hours vary) and the cost is £2.50 ($3.90) adults, £2 ($3.10) seniors, and £1.50 ($2.35) children.

In July and August, the Derry City Council (☎ **01504/365151,** ext. 307) sponsors **Inner City Walking Tours,** departing from the Tourist Information Centre, 8 Bishop St., Derry (☎ **01504/267284**). Tours are conducted Monday through Saturday at 10:30am and 2:30pm; price is £1.50 ($2.35) per person.

VISITOR INFORMATION   The **Derry Tourist Information Centre** is at 8 Bishop St., Derry (☎ **01504/267284**). It's open from October through June, Monday through Friday from 9am to 5pm; and July through September, Monday through Saturday from 9am to 8pm and Sunday from 10am to 6pm.

AREA CODE   The telephone area code for numbers in the Derry area is **01504,** unless otherwise indicated.

CITY LAYOUT   The focal point of Derry is the Diamond, a square in the center of the city, sitting just west of the banks of the Foyle River. From the Diamond, four streets radiate: Bishop, Ferryquay, Shipquay, and Butcher. Each street extends for several blocks and ends at a walled gateway of the same name (Bishop's Gate, Ferryquay Gate, Shipquay Gate, and Butcher's Gate). The gates are all connected by a massive wall that rings the inner city.

Two bridges connect the east and west banks of the River Foyle: the Craigavon Bridge, built in 1933 and one of the few examples of a double-decker bridge in the British Isles; and the Foyle Bridge, Ireland's longest bridge, which was opened in 1984 and provides a dual-lane carriageway about 2 miles north of the Craigavon Bridge. West of the river is Derry's walled inner city and an area west of the walls called Bogside. East of the Foyle are the prime residential districts, in an area usually referred to as Waterside. All of the fine hotels and restaurants are in the Waterside area.

REGARDING DERRY

Derry, also known as Londonderry, is the second largest city of Northern Ireland (population: 90,000) and the unofficial capital of the northwestern region of the province.

The city derives its name from the Irish words *Doire Calgach,* meaning "the oak grove of Calgach." Calgach was a pagan warrior who set up a camp here in pre-Christian times. The name survived until the 10th century, when it became known as *Doire Colmcille* in honor of St. Columb, who founded his first monastery in Derry in A.D. 546. He is supposed to have written, "The angels of God sang in the glades of Derry and every leaf held its angel." Over the years the name was anglicized to Derrie or simply Derry.

Set on a hill on the banks of the Foyle estuary, Derry has often come under siege since it is strategically close to the open sea. At the time of the Plantation of Ulster in the 17th century, the City of London sent master builders and money to rebuild the ruined medieval town, and hence the name became Londonderry.

A legacy from that era is the city's great 17th-century walls, about a mile in circumference and 18 feet thick. Although they were the focus of sieges in 1641, 1649, and 1689, the walls have withstood the test of time and are unbroken and complete. They make Derry one of the finest examples of a walled city in Europe.

The rest of the city's architecture is largely Georgian, with brick-fronted town houses and imposing public buildings. Basement-level pubs and shops are common.

About 12 miles east of the city is another Georgian enclave, the town of Limavady in the Roe Valley. It was here that Jane Ross wrote down the tune of a lovely air that she heard, played by a fiddler as he passed through town. It was to become the famous "Londonderry Air," otherwise known as "Danny Boy."

Moving about 15 miles south of Derry is Strabane in Co. Tyrone. It begins an area known as the Northwest Passage, stretching inland from Strabane to Armagh. This is a part of Northern Ireland that has a number of unique attractions, such as the Sperrin Mountains, the Ulster-American Folk Park, Tyrone Crystal, and the ancestral homes of two U.S. presidents, all well worth a detour from Derry or when en route between the eastern and western halves of Northern Ireland.

ATTRACTIONS

✪ Cathedral of St. Columb

London St. ☎ **01504/262746.** Cathedral free; Chapter house 50p (80¢). Mon–Sat 9am–1pm and 2–4:30pm.

Located within the city walls near the Bishop's Gate, this cathedral, built as a Church of Ireland edifice between 1628 and 1633, is a fine example of the Planters Gothic style of architecture. It was the first cathedral in the British Isles to be built after the Reformation. Several sections were added afterward, including the impressive spire and stained-glass windows that depict scenes from the great siege of 1688–89. In the chapter house, there is a display of city relics, including the four original keys to the city gates, and an audiovisual presentation that provides background on the history of the building and the city.

✪ St. Eugene's Cathedral

Great James St. Free admission. June–Sept, daily 9am–9pm; Oct–May, 9am–8:30pm.

Designed in the Gothic Revival style, this is Derry's Catholic cathedral, nestled in the heart of the Bogside district just beyond the city walls. The foundation stone was laid in 1851, but it took until 1873 for the work to be completed. The spire was added in 1902. It's built of local sandstone and is known for its stained-glass windows depicting the Crucifixion, by Meyer of Munich.

Tower Museum

Union Hall Place. ☎ **01504/372411.** Admission £3 ($4.65) adults, £1 ($1.55) children, £6 ($9.30) family. July and Aug, Mon–Sat 10am–5pm and 2–5pm on Sun; closed Mon and Sun the rest of the year.

Occupying the ground floor of the O'Doherty Tower, a medieval-style fort, this museum presents the history of the city in walk-through format from prehistoric times to the present. In the O'Doherty Tower above the museum are artifacts from the Spanish Armada ships wrecked off the Irish coast in 1588. New audiovisual programs add to the exhibit. It's just inside the city walls next to Shipquay Gate.

Heritage Library

14 Bishop St. ☎ **01504/269792.** Free admission; varying charges for research. Mon–Fri 9am–5pm.

Did your ancestors come from Derry or nearby? If you're of Irish ancestry, it's possible, maybe even likely, since Derry served as the principal port for thousands of emigrants who left Ulster for the New World in the 18th and 19th centuries, and records show that Ulster men and women became the second most numerous group in the colonial population and played an important role in the American Revolution and the settlement of the west. This genealogy center, located a block from the Cathedral of St. Columb, will help you research your roots.

Guildhall

Shipquay Place, Derry. ☎ **01504/377335.** Free admission. Mon–Fri 9am–5pm. Weekends by appointment.

Situated just outside the city walls between Shipquay Gate and the River Foyle, this Tudor Gothic–style building looks much like its counterpart in London. The original structure on this site was built in 1890, but it was rebuilt after a fire in 1908 and after a series of bombs in 1972. The hall is distinguished by its huge four-faced clock and by its stained-glass windows, made by Ulster craftsmen, that illustrate almost every episode of note in the city's history. The hall is used as a civic and cultural center for concerts, plays, and exhibitions.

Amelia Earhart Centre

Ballyarnett, Co. Derry. ☎ **01504/354040.** Free admission. Cottage, Mon–Thurs 9am–4:30pm, Fri 9am–1pm; farm and sanctuary, Mon–Fri 10am–dusk, Sat–Sun 10am–dusk.

Located 3 miles north of Derry off the A2 road, this cottage commemorates the landing of Amelia Earhart here in 1932, as the first woman to fly the Atlantic solo. The grounds encompass the Ballyarnett Community Farm and Wildlife Centre, with a range of farmyard animals and wildlife.

SHOPPING

The inner city of Derry offers some fine shopping, including a modern multistory mall, the Richmond Centre, facing the Diamond at the corner of Shipquay and Ferryquay streets. It houses more than 30 specialty shops and boutiques. In general, shops are open Monday through Thursday and on Saturday from 9am to 5:30pm and on Friday from 9am to 9pm.

Austins
The Diamond. ☎ **01504/261817.**

This is the city's landmark three-story Victorian-style department store, specializing in fashions, perfumes, china, crystal, and linens. The coffee shop on the third floor looks out on a panorama of the city.

Bookworm Community Bookshop
18 Bishop St. ☎ **01504/261616.**

This shop specializes in books on Irish history, politics, poetry, art, and fiction, as well as maps, guides, and postcards. It's situated at the corner of London Street.

✪ Derry Craft Village
Shipquay St. ☎ **01504/260329.**

Located in the heart of the inner city near the Tower, with entrances on Shipquay and Magazine streets, this unique shopping complex reflects Old Derry, with architecture of the 16th to 19th centuries housing retail shops, workshops, residential units, and a thatched-cottage pub.

ACCOMMODATIONS & DINING
MODERATE

Beech Hill Country House Hotel
32 Ardmore Rd., Derry, Co. Derry BT47 3QP, Co. Derry. ☎ **800/44-PRIMA** from the U.S., or 01504/49279. Fax 01504/45366. 17 rms. TV TEL. £85 ($131.75) double. Rates include full breakfast. AE, MC, V.

In a residential area southeast of the city, this country-house hotel dates from 1729. Antiques and marble fireplaces decorate the public areas, and some of the pleasant guest rooms have four-poster beds with frilly floral covers. The hotel's Ardmore restaurant is, amazingly, all nonsmoking, and there's a lounge for relaxing. The wooded grounds are lovely, and there's an arbor of beech trees for which the hotel is named.

Broomhill House Hotel
Limavady Rd., Derry, Co. Derry BT47 1LT. ☎ **01504/47995.** Fax 01504/49304. 42 rms. TV TEL. £60 ($93) double. Rates include full breakfast. MC, V.

Lovely views of Lough Foyle are a feature of this modern hotel, set on its own grounds in a residential area 1¹/₂ miles east of the city on the main road near the Foyle Bridge. Guest rooms are modern, with standard furnishings, welcome tray, and garment press. Among facilities are the Garden Restaurant, with lovely views of the river and the city.

✪ Everglades Hotel
Prehen Rd., Derry, Co. Derry BT47 2PA. ☎ **01504/46722.** Fax 0504/49200. 52 rms. TV TEL. £84 ($130.20) double. Rates include full breakfast. AE, DC, MC, V.

Set on a hill overlooking the east bank of Lough Foyle in the prosperous Waterside district, this three-story contemporary hotel takes its name from Florida's Everglades and bears the great seal of Florida as its hotel crest. Like much of Florida, the hotel is built on reclaimed waterfront land. Guest rooms have modern furnishings with light woods, floral designer fabrics, and rattan touches; extras include a garment press, hair dryer, and tea/coffeemaker. Public facilities include the Seminole Restaurant and Cibola Bar.

DINING

ⓢ Schooner's

59 Victoria Rd., Derry. ☎ **01504/311500.** Reservations only for parties over 7 people or for Sun lunch. Lunch main courses £3.95–£6.45 ($6.10–$10); dinner main courses £4.95–£8.95 ($7.65–$13.85). AE, MC, V. Mon–Sat noon–10pm, Sun 5–9pm. INTERNATIONAL.

A seaworthy atmosphere prevails at this classy restaurant, with a 30-foot schooner as part of the decor and a glass-front wall that overlooks the water along the east bank of the River Foyle. The menu, similar at lunch and dinner, offers innovative entrées such as paupiettes of plaice filled with smoked salmon and prawns, coated in a smoked-salmon sauce; baked fillet of trout with hazelnut butter; suprême of chicken coated in a crab and bacon sauce; sweet and tangy pork with honey and apple dip; mushroom stroganoff; fillet, T-bone, or minute steaks served with a choice of peppercorn, Diane, or barbecue sauce; and Schooner's Specialty, a breast of chicken stuffed with broccoli and cheddar cheese and wrapped in puff pastry.

PUBS

Derry pubs are known for their music and quiz evenings. Three of the best are right along the same street: **Dungloe Bar,** 41/43 Waterloo St. (☎ **01504/267716**); **Gweedore Bar,** 61 Waterloo St. (☎ **01504/263513**); and **Castle Bar,** 26 Waterloo St. (☎ **01504/263118**).

ALONG THE NORTHWEST PASSAGE

The many attractions along this inland corridor start at Strabane and continue through the Sperrin Mountains of Co. Tyrone to Armagh.

Gray's Printing Press

49 Main St., Strabane, Co. Tyrone. ☎ **01504/884094.** Admission £1.50 ($2.35) adult, 75p ($1.15) children, £3.75 ($5.80) family. Apr–Sept, Mon–Wed and Fri–Sat 2–5:30pm.

This print shop, with its attractive bow-front window, dates from 1760. Behind the shop there's an exhibit of 19th-century hand-operated printing presses. John Dunlop, founder of the first daily newspaper in the United States and printer of the American Declaration of Independence, learned his trade here. An audiovisual show provides insight into how the original presses operated and the part played by Dunlop in America's early printing days.

Sperrin Heritage Centre

274 Glenelly Rd., Cranagh, Co. Tyrone. ☎ **016626/48142.** Centre £1.80 ($2.80) adult, 80p ($1.25) seniors and children; panning for gold 65p ($1.00) adults, 35p (55¢) children. Apr–Sept, Mon–Fri 11am–6pm, Sat 11:30am–6pm and Sunday from 2–7pm. East of Plumbridge off B47.

Southeast of Derry, the Sperrin Mountains rise up out of Co. Tyrone. From the 2,240-foot peak of Sawel, the tallest of these mountains, you can see as far as the Foyle Estuary and across the Northern Ireland countryside to Lough Neagh and the Mournes. This is splendid walking country in open lands frequented by golden plover, red grouse, and thousands upon thousands of sheep. In the midst of this mountain setting is the Sperrin Heritage Centre, with exhibits on natural history and gold-mining in the area. Visitors can even try a hand at panning for gold. There is a cafe and craft shop on the grounds.

✪ Ulster-American Folk Park

Mellon Rd., Castletown, Camphill, Omagh, Co. Tyrone. ☎ **01662/243292.** Admission £3.50 ($5.40) adults, £1.70 ($2.65) seniors and children under 16, £10 ($15.50) family. Oct–Mar, Mon–Fri 10:30am–5pm; Apr–Sept, Mon–Sat 11am–6:30pm, Sun 11:30am–7pm.

Situated 3 miles north of Omagh on the A5 road, this outdoor museum seeks to present the story of emigration from this part of rural Ireland to America in the 18th and 19th centuries. There are reconstructions of the thatched cottages that the emigrants left behind, and prototypes of the log cabins that became their new homes in the frontiers of America. The park developed around the homestead where Thomas Mellon was born in 1813. He went to Pittsburgh and prospered to the point where his son Andrew became one of the world's richest men. Funding to build this excellent park was donated in part by the Mellon family. Walk-through exhibits include a forge, weaver's cottage, smokehouse, schoolhouse, post office, and a full-scale replica of an emigrant ship set in a dockside area that features original buildings from the ports of Derry, Belfast, and Newry. It takes about two hours to do a self-guided tour of all the exhibits, which are staffed by interpreters in period costume. Various musical events that tie in with the Ulster-American theme, such as a bluegrass music festival in September, are hosted on the site each year.

✪ Grant Ancestral Home

Dergina, Ballygawley, Co. Tyrone. ☎ **0166255/7133.** Admission £1 ($1.55) adults, 50p (75¢) children. Apr–Sept, Mon–Sat 12–5pm, Sun 2–6pm.

Located 20 miles southeast of Omagh off the A4 road, this farm cottage was the home of the ancestors of Ulysses S. Grant, 18th president of the United States. Grant's maternal great-grandfather, John Simpson, was born here and emigrated to Pennsylvania in 1738 at the age of 22. The cottage has two rooms with mud floors and has been restored and furnished with period pieces, including a settle-bed and dresser. The site includes a visitor center with audiovisual presentation, various exhibits including a collection of typical 18th-century agricultural implements, and a tearoom.

Wilson Ancestral Home

Off Plumbridge Rd., Dergalt, Strabane, Co. Tyrone. ☎ **01662/243292.** Admission 50p (80¢) adults, 25p (40¢) children. Apr–Sept, daily 2–6pm.

Situated on the slopes of the Sperrin Mountains, this small, thatched, whitewashed cottage was the home of Judge James Wilson, grandfather of Woodrow Wilson, 28th president of the United States. James Wilson left the house in 1807 at the age of 20. It contains some of the original furniture of the Wilson family, including a tiny outshot bed (sleeping nook) in the kitchen close to the fire, larger curtained beds, and a portrait of the president's grandfather over the fireplace. The modern farmhouse next door is still occupied by Wilsons.

Ulster History Park

Cullion, Omagh, Co. Tyrone. ☎ **016626/48188.** Admission £3.25 ($5.05) adults, £1.95 ($3) seniors, students, and children, £10 ($15.50) family. Apr–Sept, Mon–Sat 10:30am–6:30pm, Sun 11:30am–7pm; Oct–Mar, Mon–Fri 10:30am–5pm.

Ireland's history from the Stone Age through the 17th-century Plantation period is the focus of this outdoor theme park, located 7 miles north of Omagh. There are full-scale models of homes, castles, and monuments through the ages, including

a Mesolithic encampment, Neolithic dwelling, crannog lake dwelling, church settlement with round tower, and motte-and-bailery type of castle common.

✪ Tyrone Crystal

Oaks Rd., Killybrackey, Dungannon, Co. Tyrone. ☎ **01868/725335.** Free admission.
Mon–Sat 9am–5pm; 40-min tours Mon–Thurs at 9:30am and 3:30pm, Fri 9:30am–noon,
Sat (Apr–Oct) 9:30am–3:30pm.

With a 200-year-old tradition, this crystal factory is one of Ireland's oldest and best
known. Visitors are welcome to tour the operation and see glass being blown and
crafted, carved, and engraved by hand. A 25-minute audiovisual presentation tells the
story of the development of Tyrone Crystal through the years, a showroom displays
the finished products, and a very good cafe adds sustenance. It is located just under
2 miles east of the town.

DINING

✪ Mellon Country Inn

134 Beltany Rd., Omagh, Co. Tyrone. ☎ **016626/61224.** Reservations not required.
Lunch main courses £2.95–£10.95 ($4.55–$16.95); main courses £7.95–£18.95 ($12.30–
$29.35). AE, DC, MC, V. Mon–Sat 10:30am–9:30pm, Sun 12:30–5pm and 6:30–8:30pm.
INTERNATIONAL.

Located 1 mile north of the Ulster-American Folk Park, this old-world country inn
combines an Irish theme with a connection to the Mellons of Pennsylvania. One of
the dining rooms, the Pennsylvania room, has log cabin–style decor. Simple fare is
served—burgers, soup, salads, and ploughman's platters—as well as elegant dishes
such as lobster Newburg, beef Stroganoff, coquilles St-Jacques, and sole bonne
femme. The house specialty is Tyrone black steak, a locally bred hormone-free beef.
Food is available all day, including late breakfast and afternoon tea.

5 Enniskillen & the Fermanagh Lakelands

Enniskillen is 83 miles SW of Belfast, 61 miles SW of Derry, 52 miles W of Armagh, 27 miles SW
of Omagh, 108 miles NW of Dublin, and 168 miles NE of Shannon.

GETTING AROUND   The best way to get around Enniskillen and the surrounding lakelands of Lough Erne is by car. Enniskillen itself sits in the middle of Lough
Erne, wedged between the upper and lower shores. The total signposted driving circuit around the lake is 65 miles.

VISITOR INFORMATION   Contact the **Fermanagh Tourist Information Centre,** Wellington Road, Enniskillen, Co. Fermanagh (☎ **01365/323110**). It's open
in July and August, Monday through Friday from 9am to 6:30pm, Saturday from
10am to 5pm, and Sunday from 10am to 3pm; Easter to June and in September,
Monday through Friday from 9am to 1pm and 2 to 5pm, and Saturday from 10am
to 5pm; October to Easter, Monday through Friday from 9am to 1pm and
2 to 5pm.

AREA CODE   The telephone area code for the Enniskillen area is **01365,** unless
otherwise indicated.

THE FACTS ON FERMANAGH & ENNISKILLEN

Tucked in the extreme southwest corner of Northern Ireland, Co. Fermanagh is
resort country, dominated by the waters of Lough Erne, a long lake dotted with
154 islands and rimmed by countless alcoves and inlets. It has 50 miles of cruising
waters, ranging from a shallow channel in some places to a 5-mile width in others.

The largest island in this lakeland paradise, situated right between the lower and upper branches of Lough Erne, is Enniskillen, a delightful resort town that was the medieval seat of the Maguire clan and a major crossroads between Ulster and Connaught. At the northern tip of the lake is Belleek, sitting right on the border with the Republic of Ireland, and known the world over for delicate bone chinaware. At the southern end of the lake is Co. Cavan and another slice of border with the Irish Republic. In the surrounding countryside there are diverse attractions, from stately homes at Florence Court and Castle Coole to the unique Marble Arch Caves.

ATTRACTIONS

✪ Enniskillen Castle

Castle Barracks, Enniskillen. ☎ **01365/325000.** Admission £2 ($3.10) adults, £1.50 ($2.35) seniors and students, £1 ($1.55) children. May–June and in Sept, Mon 2–5pm, Tues–Fri 10am–5pm, Sat 2–5pm; July–Aug, Tues–Fri 10am–5pm, Sat–Sun 2–5pm.

Dating from the 15th century, this magnificent stone fortress sits overlooking Lough Erne on the western edge of town. It incorporates three museums in one—the medieval castle itself with its unique twin-turreted Watergate tower, once the seat of the Maguires, chieftains of Fermanagh; the county museum, with exhibits on the area's history, wildlife, and landscape; and the museum of the famous Royal Inniskilling Fusiliers, with a collection of uniforms, weapons, regimental memorabilia, and medals dating from the 17th century. New exhibits include life-size figurines and 3-D models of old-time castle life.

✪ Belleek Pottery

Belleek, Co. Fermanagh. ☎ **013656/58501.** Free admission; tours £1 ($1.55) adults and children over 12. Mar–Sept, Mon–Fri 9am–6pm, Sat 10am–6pm, Sun 2–6pm; July–Aug, Mon–Fri 9am–8pm, Sat 10am–6pm, Sun 2–6pm; Oct–Feb, Mon–Fri 9am–5pm.

With the possible exception of Waterford crystal, Belleek china is the name most readily identified throughout the world as a symbol of the finest Irish craftsmanship. Established in 1857, this pottery enterprise produces distinctive and delicate porcelain china, made into tableware, vases, ornaments, and other pieces. The visitor center has a museum showing the product from earliest days to the present. Tours are conducted weekdays every 20 minutes, with the last tour at 3:30pm.

✪ Florence Court

Florence Court, Co. Fermanagh. ☎ **01365/348249.** Admission £2.70 ($4.20) adults, £1.35 ($2.10) children. Apr and Sept, Sat–Sun 1–6pm; May–Aug, 1–6pm; closed Tues. Located off the A32 road.

One of the most beautifully situated houses in Northern Ireland, this 18th-century manor is set among dramatic hills, 8 miles southwest of Upper Lough Erne and Enniskillen. Originally the seat of the earls of Enniskillen, its interior is rich in Rococo plasterwork and antique Irish furniture, while its exterior has a fine walled garden, ice house, and water wheel–driven sawmill.

✪ Castle Coole

Belfast-Enniskillen road (A4), Enniskillen, Co. Fermanagh. ☎ **01365/322690.** House £2.60 ($4.05) adults, £1.30 ($2) children, £6.50 ($10.10) family; grounds £1.50 ($2.35) car. Apr and Sept, Mon–Fri 1–6pm (also Apr, Sat–Sun 5–9pm); May–Aug, daily (except Thurs) 1–6pm.

Located on the east bank of Lower Lough Erne, about 1 1/2 miles southeast of Enniskillen, this neoclassical mansion was designed by James Wyatt for the earl of Belmore and was completed in 1796. Its rooms include a lavish state bedroom hung with crimson silk, said to have been prepared for George IV. Other features include a Chinese-style sitting room, as well as magnificent woodwork, fireplaces, and furniture dating back to the 1830s. The house is surrounded by a fine woodland estate.

✪ Marble Arch Caves

Marlbank, Florence Court, Co. Fermanagh. ☎ **01365/348855.** Admission £5 ($7.75) adults, £2 ($3.10) children under 18, £3 ($4.65) seniors and students. Reservations recommended. Mid-Mar to end of Sept, daily 10am–4:30pm.

Located off A32, west of Upper Lough Erne and 12 miles from Enniskillen near the Florence Court estate, these caves are considered among the finest in Europe for exploring underground rivers, waterfalls, winding passages, and hidden chambers. Visitors are taken underground on electrically powered boat tours led by knowledgeable guides who explain the origins of the amazing stalactites and stalagmites.

SIGHTSEEING CRUISES

Erne Tours Ltd., Enniskillen, Co. Fermanagh. (☎ **01365/322882**), operates **cruises on Lower Lough Erne** on board the MV *Kestrel,* a 63-seat cruiser, departing from the Round O Jetty, Brook Park, Enniskillen. Trips last for just under two hours; they operate daily in July and August at 10:30am, 2:15pm, and 4:15pm; in May and June on Sunday at 2:30pm; and in September on Tuesday, Saturday, and Sunday at 2:30pm. The fare is £3 ($4.65) for adults and £1.50 ($2.35) for children under 14.

Cruises on Upper Lough Erne are operated by the **Share Centre,** Smith's Strand, Lisnaskea (☎ **01365/722122**). These 1¹/₂-hour trips are conducted on board the *Viking,* a 30-passenger canopied long ship. Sailings are scheduled in April through June and in September, on Saturday and Sunday at 3pm; in July and August, daily (except Tuesday) at 3pm and sometimes at 11am, according to demand. The fare is £4 ($6.20) for adults, and £3 ($4.65) for seniors and children under 16. Share Centre also offers other watersports activities and self-catering chalets.

Ferry crossings to some of the many islands in Lough Erne are also offered by independent boatmen. From April through September a ferry runs from Devenish Island from Trory Point, 4 miles from Enniskillen on A32; and from June through September a ferry runs to White Island, departing from Castle Archdale Marina, 10 miles from Enniskillen on the Kesh road. Departures on both services are Tuesday through Saturday from 10am to 7pm and on Sunday from 2 to 7pm. Fare is £1 ($1.55) for adults and 50p (80¢) for children.

SPORTS ON THE LOUGH

The Lakeland Canoe Center, Castle Island, Enniskillen (☎ **01365/324250**), is a watersports center based on an island west of downtown. It offers a full day of canoeing and other sports, including archery, cycling, dinghy sailing, and windsurfing, from £11 ($17.05) per day. Camping is also available for a fee of £4 ($6.20) per night, and simple accommodations are available for £9 ($13.95) per night.

On Lower Lough Erne, north of town, **motorboats** can be hired from **The Beeches,** Killadeas (☎ **01365/621557**), or **Manor House Marine,** Killadeas (☎ **01365/628100**). Charges average £25 to £30 ($38.75 to $46.50) for a half day to £40 to £45 ($62 to $69.75) for a full day.

SHOPPING

Enniskillen has fine shops along its main street, which changes its name six times (from East Bridge to Townhall, High, Church, and Darling, to Ann) as it runs the length of the town. Most shops are open Monday through Saturday from 9:30am to 5:30pm.

The largest shopping complex is Erneside Shopping Center, a modern bilevel skylit mall on Shore Road, just off Wellington Road. This center stays open until 9pm on Thursday and Friday.

The town's former Butter Market offers a nifty shopping experience. Dating from 1835 and now restored and transformed into the **Enniskillen Craft and Design Centre,** Down Street (☎ **01365/324499**), it offers craft workshops and retail outlets, with occasional traditional music, craft fairs, and street theater to enliven the atmosphere.

ACCOMMODATIONS
MODERATE

✪ Manor House Country Hotel
Killadeas, Irvinestown, Enniskillen, Co. Fermanagh BT94 1NY. ☎ **01365/21561.** Fax 01365/ 21545. 46 rms. TV TEL. £80 ($124) double. Rates include full breakfast. AE, MC, V.

Dating from 1860, this splendid three-story Victorian mansion has had a varied history that's included its use by American forces as a base during World War II. The public areas are full of antiques and ornate plasterwork, and the windows look out to Lough Erne. Guest rooms are furnished in traditional style with dark woods, frilly fabrics, and decorative wallpaper; some rooms have four-posters or half-canopy beds, and each has a garment press and tea/coffeemaker. Facilities include an indoor heated swimming pool, gym, steam room, sauna, tennis court, marina, and beauty salon. It sits on the shores of Lower Lough Erne, 5¹/₂ miles north of Enniskillen.

INEXPENSIVE

⦵ Belmore Court Motel
Tempo Rd., Enniskillen, Co. Fermanagh BT74 6HR. ☎ **01365/326633.** Fax 01365/326362. 30 units. TV TEL. £38–£45 ($58.90–$69.75) double or single. Rates include continental breakfast. AE, MC, V.

One of the newest lodgings in the area, this three-story motel offers a variety of accommodations; most have kitchenettes and about a third of the rooms have two bedrooms or a bedroom and sitting room. All units have contemporary furnishings with light woods, floral fabrics, down comforters, and vanity area/desks, plus tea/ coffeemakers. It is on the east edge of town, within walking distance to all the major sights and shops.

DINING
MODERATE

✪ Franco's
Queen Elizabeth Rd., Enniskillen. ☎ **01365/324424.** Reservations not accepted. Lunch main courses £3.50–£10.50 ($5.45–$16.30); dinner main courses £6.95–£18.95 ($10.75–$29.35). AE, DC, MC. Mon–Sat noon–11:30pm, Sun 5–10pm. IRISH/ITALIAN.

Situated next to the Butter Market in three converted and restored buildings that were once part of Enniskillen's working waterfront, this restaurant blends old-world ambience and the legacy of the sea with contemporary recipes and fresh local ingredients. Choices might be fillet of beef en croûte, black sole and salmon with sorrel sauce, lobster thermidor, Lough Melvin salmon on a bed of spinach in pastry and saffron sauce, and duck breast in plum sauce, as well as a wide variety of specialty pastas and pizzas. From Wednesday through Sunday, there is traditional music starting at 9pm.

MODERATE/INEXPENSIVE

Saddlers

66 Belmore St., Enniskillen. ☎ **01365/326223.** Reservations not necessary. Lunch main courses £2.95–£4.95 ($4.55–$7.65); dinner main courses £5.95–£10.95 ($9.20–$16.95). MC, V. Mon–Sun noon–2:30pm and 4–10:45pm. INTERNATIONAL.

An equestrian atmosphere prevails at this restaurant over the Horse Show Bar. Barbecued pork ribs, steaks, surf-and-turf, burgers, and mixed grills are the hearty choices, along with local seafoods, salads, pizzas, pastas, and a house special of sirloin Sandeman with bacon, shallots, peppercorns, and port wine sauce.

ENNISKILLEN AFTER DARK

The outstanding public house of the area is ✪ **Blakes of the Hollow,** 6 Church St., Enniskillen (☎ **01365/322143**). Opened in 1887, this pub has been in the Blake family ever since, retaining its original Victorian decor and ambience, with a long marble-topped mahogany bar and pine-wood alcoves.

Plan an evening at the **Ardhowen Theatre,** Dublin Road, Enniskillen (☎ **01365/ 325440**). Also known as the Theatre by the Lakes because of its enviable position overlooking Upper Lough Erne, it presents a varied program of concerts, drama, cabarets, jazz, gospel, blues and other types of modern music. Tickets run from £3 to £6 ($4.65 to $9.30) for most performances; curtain time is usually 8:30pm.

Appendix: A Few Irish Words to Know

Whatever you do, don't try to pronounce anything. The Irish language is more confounding and complex than the minotaur's maze, and as difficult to get your tongue around as the language of the Kalahari bushmen. We must count ourselves blessed that even the proudest Irish-speaker will take pity on the Irish-challenged and switch to English when necessary.

Here's a few words that you'll likely encounter, both on the road and in the pages of this book. Good luck.

Words & Prefixes in Place Names

anna, canna   a marsh
ard   a height; hill
aw, ow   a river
áth   a river ford
bal, baile, bally   a town or settlement
barn, bearna   a gap
bawn, bán   white
beg, beag   small
boirreann   a rocky place
boy, buidhe   yellow
cahir, caher, carrick, carraig   a rocky hill
cashel, caiseal   a castle
cloch, clogh, cloich   a stone
cluain, clon, clun   a meadow
derg, dearg   red
doo, du, dubh, duv   black
drom, drum   a ridge
dun   a fort
glas, glen, gleann   a valley
inch, innis, inish, ennis   island

ken, kin, ceann   a headland
kil   church or monastic cell
knock   hill
lis, liss, lios   a fort
lough   lake
ma, magh, may, moy   a plain
mone, mona   a bog; turf
mor   large, great
owen, avon   a river
rath   earthen fort
rinn, reen   a point
roe, ruadh   red
ros, ross   a peninsula; *also* a wood
shan, shane, sean   old
slieve   mountain
tir, tír, tyr   country
tra, traw, tráigh   a beach or strand
tubber, tobar   a well
turlough   "a dry lake"; geographical feature typical to the Burren

Words You're Bound to Come Up Against

aerphort   airport
An Lar   city center
bawn   a castle enclosure
bodhrán   a large frame drum
Bord Fáilte   the Irish Tourist Board
boxty   a potato pancake filled with meats, vegetables, or fish
ceili   Irish dance
coddle   boiled bacon, sausages, onions, and potatoes
colcannon   potatoes mashed with scallions and cabbage
crack, the   good conversation, a good time
crubeens   pig's feet
currach, curragh   traditional west coast fishing boat
Dáil   "meeting"; the Irish house of representatives
fáilte   welcome
feis   festival
fir   men

fleadh   music festival
gaeltacht   Irish-speaking area
Garda Siochana   "guardians of the peace"; the police
lei thras   toilets
mna   women
ogham   4th–7th century Irish script
oifig an phoist   post office
óstlann   hotel
poitin   Irish moonshine
seanachie   storyteller
Seanad   the Irish senate
sheebeen   a shop
sliotar   hard leather ball used in hurling
taoiseach   Ireland's prime minister
teach ósta   hotel
telefón   telephone
uilleann pipes   Irish bagpipes
uisce beatha   "the water of life"; the original Irish word for whiskey

Some Moderately Useful Phrases

Dia duit *(Eea ditch)*   Good-day; hello.
Slán agat *(Slawn ugut)*   Good-bye (used if you're the person leaving).
Slán leat *(Slawn lyat)*   Good-bye (used if you're the person staying).
Cá mhéad sin? *(Ka vayd shin?)*   How much is it?
Cad é mar atá an iascaireacht anseo? *(Kajay mar ataw in eeaskarakht unshaw?)*   How is the fishing here?
An bhfuil rud ar bith le feiceáil thart anseo? *(Un will rud er bih le fekoil hart unshaw?)*   Is there anything to see around here?
Tá an bradán an-bhlasta *(Taw un braddan ann-blasta)*   The salmon is tasty.
An bhfuil seomra folchtha or an úrlar seo? *(Un will shumra fulka air in urlar shaw?)*   Is there a bathroom on this floor?
Tabhair dom dhá phionta leanna le do thoil *(Tawar dum gau finnta lann le du hul)*   Give me two pints of beer, please.
Sláinte! *(Slauntcha!)*   Cheers!
Dul chun drabhláis *(Dul hun drowlish)*   To go on a spree of revelry and debauchery.
Glac an traein dheireanach go Clarkesville *(Glag in treyn yeranakh gu Clarkesville)*   Take the last train to Clarkesville.

Index

FROMMER'S COMPLETE TRAVEL GUIDES

(Comprehensive guides to destinations around the world, with selections in all price ranges—from deluxe to budget)

Acapulco/Ixtapa/Zihuatenjo
Alaska
Amsterdam
Arizona
Atlanta
Australia
Austria
Bahamas
Bangkok
Barcelona, Madrid &
　Seville
Belgium, Holland &
　Luxembourg
Berlin
Bermuda
Boston
Budapest & the Best of
　Hungary
California
Canada
Cancún, Cozumel & the
　Yucatán
Caribbean
Caribbean Cruises & Ports
　of Call
Caribbean Ports of Call
Carolinas & Georgia
Chicago
Colorado
Costa Rica
Denver, Boulder &
　Colorado Springs
Dublin
England

Florida
France
Germany
Greece
Hawaii
Hong Kong
Honolulu/Waikiki/Oahu
Ireland
Italy
Jamaica & Barbados
Japan
Las Vegas
London
Los Angeles
Maryland & Delaware
Maui
Mexico
Mexico City
Miami & the Keys
Montana & Wyoming
Montréal & Québec
　City
Munich & the Bavarian
　Alps
Nashville & Memphis
Nepal
New England
New Mexico
New Orleans
New York City
Northern New England
Nova Scotia, New
　Brunswick & Prince
　Edward Island

Paris
Philadelphia & the Amish
　Country
Portugal
Prague & the Best of the
　Czech Republic
Puerto Rico
Puerto Vallarta, Manzanillo
　& Guadalajara
Rome
San Antonio & Austin
San Diego
San Francisco
Santa Fe, Taos &
　Albuquerque
Scandinavia
Scotland
Seattle & Portland
South Pacific
Spain
Switzerland
Thailand
Tokyo
Toronto
U.S.A.
Utah
Vancouver & Victoria
Vienna
Virgin Islands
Virginia
Walt Disney World &
　Orlando
Washington, D.C.
Washington & Oregon

FROMMER'S FRUGAL TRAVELER'S GUIDES

(The grown-up guides to budget travel, offering dream vacations at down-to-earth prices)

Australia from $45 a Day
Berlin from $50 a Day
California from $60 a Day
Caribbean from $60 a Day
Costa Rica & Belize from
　$35 a Day
Eastern Europe from
　$30 a Day

England from $50 a Day
Europe from $50 a Day
Florida from $50 a Day
Greece from $45 a Day
Hawaii from $60 a Day
India from $40 a Day
Ireland from $45 a Day
Italy from $50 a Day

Israel from $45 a Day
London from $60 a Day
Mexico from $35 a Day
New York from $70 a Day
New Zealand from $45 a Day
Paris from $60 a Day
Washington, D.C. from
　$50 a Day

FROMMER'S PORTABLE GUIDES

(Pocket-size guides for travelers who want everything in a nutshell)

Charleston & Savannah   Las Vegas   Washington, D.C.   New Orleans   San Francisco

FROMMER'S FAMILY GUIDES

(The complete guides for successful family vacations)

California with Kids	New England with Kids	San Francisco with Kids
Los Angeles with Kids	New York City with Kids	Washington, D.C. with Kids

FROMMER'S AMERICA ON WHEELS

(Everything you need for a successful road trip, including full-color road maps and ratings for every hotel)

California & Nevada	Midwest & the Great	Northwest & the	Southwest
Florida	Lake States	Great Plains States	Texas & the South-
Mid-Atlantic	New York & the New	Southeast	Central States
	England States		

FROMMER'S WALKING TOURS

(Memorable neighborhood strolls through the world's great cities)

Berlin	Montréal & Québec City	Spain's Favorite Cities
Chicago	New York	Tokyo
England's Favorite Cities	Paris	Venice
London	San Francisco	Washington, D.C.

SPECIAL-INTEREST TITLES

Arthur Frommer's Branson!

Arthur Frommer's New World of Travel

The Civil War Trust's Official Guide to the Civil War Discovery Trail

Frommer's America's 100 Best-Loved State Parks

Frommer's Caribbean Hideaways

Frommer's Complete Hostel Vacation Guide to England, Scotland & Wales

Frommer's Food Lover's Companion to France

Frommer's Food Lover's Companion to Italy

Frommer's Great European Driving Tours

Frommer's National Park Guide

Outside Magazine's Adventure Guide to New England

Outside Magazine's Adventure Guide to Northern California

Places Rated Almanac

Retirement Places Rated

USA Sports Traveler's and TV Viewer's Golf Tournament Guide

USA Sports Minor League Baseball Book

USA Today Golf Atlas

Wonderful Weekends from NYC

FROMMER'S IRREVERENT GUIDES

(Wickedly honest guides for sophisticated travelers)

Amsterdam	Manhattan	Paris	U.S. Virgin Islands
Chicago	Miami	San Francisco	Walt Disney World
London	New Orleans	Santa Fe	Washington, D.C.

UNOFFICIAL GUIDES

(Get the unbiased truth from these candid, value-conscious guides)

Atlanta	Euro Disneyland	Mini-Mickey
Branson, Missouri	The Great Smoky & Blue	Skiing in the West
Chicago	Ridge Mountains	Walt Disney World
Cruises	Las Vegas	Walt Disney World Companion
Disneyland	Miami & the Keys	Washington, D.C.

BAEDEKER
(With four-color photographs and a free pull-out map)

Amsterdam	Florence	London	Scotland
Athens	Florida	Mexico	Singapore
Austria	Germany	New York	South Africa
Bali	Great Britain	Paris	Spain
Belgium	Greece	Portugal	Switzerland
Budapest	Greek Islands	Prague	Thailand
California	Hawaii	Provence	Tokyo
Canada	Hong Kong	Rome	Turkish Coast
Caribbean	Ireland	San Francisco	Tuscany
China	Israel	St. Petersburg	Venice
Copenhagen	Italy	Scandinavia	Vienna
Crete	Lisbon		

FROMMER'S BY NIGHT GUIDES
(The series for those who know that life begins after dark)

Amsterdam	London	Miami	Paris
Chicago	Los Angeles	New Orleans	San Francisco
Las Vegas	Manhattan		

FROMMER'S BEST BEACH VACATIONS
(The top places to sun, stroll, shop, stay, play, party, and swim, with ratings for each beach)

California	Hawaii	New England
Carolinas & Georgia	Mid-Atlantic (from New	
Florida	York to Washington, D.C.)	

FROMMER'S BED & BREAKFAST GUIDES
(Selective guides with four-color photos and full descriptions of the best inns in each region)

California	Great American Cities	New England	The Rockies
Caribbean	Hawaii	Pacific Northwest	Southwest

FROMMER'S DRIVING TOURS
(Four-color photos and detailed maps outlining spectacular scenic driving routes)

Australia	France	Italy	Spain
Austria	Germany	Scandinavia	Switzerland
Britain	Ireland	Scotland	U.S.A.
Florida			

FROMMER'S BORN TO SHOP
(The ultimate guides for travelers who love to shop)

France	Hong Kong	Mexico
Great Britain	London	New York

TRAVEL & LEISURE GUIDES
(Sophisticated pocket-size guides for discriminating travelers)

Amsterdam	Hong Kong	New York	San Francisco
Boston	London	Paris	Washington, D.C.

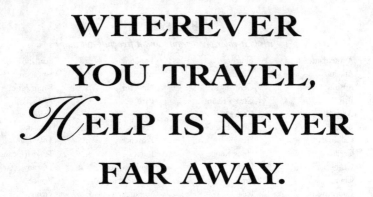

WHEREVER YOU TRAVEL, *H*ELP IS NEVER FAR AWAY.

From planning your trip to providing travel assistance along the way, American Express® Travel Service Offices are always there to help.

Ireland

American Express Travel Service
116 Grafton Street
Dublin
1/677-2874

Travel

http://www.americanexpress.com/travel